A Guide for Developing
Client/Server Applications

J. Ranade Workstation Series

PowerBuilder

**A Guide for Developing
Client/Server Applications**

Joseph J. Bambara

Paul R. Allen

McGraw-Hill, Inc.

New York San Francisco Washington, D.C. Auckland Bogotá
Caracas Lisbon London Madrid Mexico City Milan
Montreal New Delhi San Juan Singapore
Sydney Tokyo Toronto

Library of Congress Cataloging-in-Publication Data

Bambara, Joseph J.
    PowerBuilder : a guide for developing client/server applications /
by Joseph J. Bambara & Paul R. Allen.
        p.   cm.
    Includes index.
    ISBN 0-07-005413-4
    1. Client/server computing.   2. PowerBuilder.   I. Allen, Paul R.
    II. Title.
QA76.9.C55B35   1995
005.2—dc20   95-8323
                                                             CIP

pbk 1 2 3 4 5 6 7 8 9 FGR/FGR 9 9 8 7 6 5

ISBN 0-07-005413-4

The sponsoring editor for this book was Gerald Papke. John Baker was the manuscript editor, and the director of production was Katherine G. Brown. This book was set in ITC Century Light. It was composed in Blue Ridge Summit, Pa.

Printed and bound by Quebecor Printing, Fairfield.

To Roseanne, Vanessa, and Michael
— Joseph J. Bambara

To Martha, Winnie, and Charlie
— Paul R. Allen

Contents

Part 2 Development

Acknowledgments

I would like to thank Jay Ranade and Jerry Papke for first presenting the opportunity to write this book. I also would thank John Baker and Dawn Bowling and all of the folks at McGraw-Hill, Inc. for their hard work and dedication in producing the book. Thanks to Mark Ashnault, Rod Erb, Peggy Newfield, and Colleen Molter of QED for reviewing the text and assisting in the preparation of figures and artwork included in the book.

I would like to thank my friends and colleagues from Merrill Lynch, Kraft General Foods (Shelley Raidbard and Ren Liu), Pepsi (Mariuz Kossarski), Philip Morris, Viacom, First Boston, Goldman Sachs, IBM, AIG, Powersoft (Cathy Lanigan, Sue Donahue, Rachel Stockton, Richard Dill, and Bill Rabkin), and Sybase for providing encouragement as well as challenging environments in which development computing is done with style and verve.

I also want to thank Gerald Feldman, Silvia Farkas, Paul Baneky, Joseph Licata, Robert Hussey, James Ell, Rocco La Rocco, Mukesh Seghal, Allan Eklund, Paul Morris, Tom Torregrosso, and Timothy Parcell, also John Strampfer, Robert Dieckmann, and Professors Lawrence Wein and Brian Comerford for facilitating key career opportunities that helped me develop the skills required to write the book.

Thanks to Fred Neilson, Lenny, the Cozzis, and all the hockey people and players (Stu, Brian, Sheps, et. al.) at the Port Washington Skating Academy for providing an environment in which I could get up a good sweat and relieve any latent stress built up during the eleven months it took to complete the text.

Thanks to George Anderson, Herb Karlitz, and Helen Chin for their friendship and encouragement.

Thanks to my coauthor Paul R. Allen for his friendship, consistent hard work, energy, excellent team play, and encouragement.

Thanks to my dad Joseph, my mom Millie, my brothers Vincent and Richard, my sister Patricia, my father-in-law Joseph, and the rest of my family who are always there when I need them.

Foremost, I thank my wife Roseanne and my children Vanessa and Michael who are and have always been patient, loving, helpful, and encouraging no matter what new career challenge I attempt to pursue. Roseanne, thanks for simultaneously reviewing and keying a good deal of the text while preparing the world's best food. I could not have done it without you.

Joseph J. Bambara
Greenvale, New York
April, 1995

First and foremost I must give praise and thanks to my wife, Martha, for tolerating [the lack of] me while writing this book. Martha, I could not have done any of this without your patience and understanding, you are the one!

My very special thanks to my coauthor, Joseph J. Bambara, for first suggesting that we write this book together, then for his continuous encouragement, strength, perseverance, but, above all, his great friendship.

I want to thank Jerry Papke and Jay Ranade for giving us this opportunity of a lifetime. I would like to thank everybody else at McGraw-Hill, Inc., especially John Baker and Dawn Bowling, for their patience and hard work in producing the book.

I would like to thank my friends and colleagues at Merrill Lynch, Chemical Bank, Bain Securities, Wilco, and MK Electric for giving me the opportunities to learn and work in such dynamic and challenging environments. Specifically, I would like to thank Sheila Saye, Gerardo Raimato, John Cantrell, John Strampfer, Jim McAna, Dave Pavero, Ed Keenan, Paul Potwardski, Don Trojan, John Pezzullo, Martin Lehrman, Everett Young, Marty Eisen, Holly Bowers, Christine Reagan, John Tuten, Christine Colbert, Bob Friedman, Roy Staines, Terry Kirby, Bob Elliott, and Jon Loom.

I would like to acknowledge and thank Powersoft and the countless CODE partners for making PowerBuilder the hugely successful product that it is and for all of your assistance in writing this book. Specifically, I would like to thank Cathy Lanigan, Sue Donahue, and Rachel Stockton.

I also would like to thank Lawrence Byron-Sinclair, Steve Adamson, Peter Naughton, Jim Burns, and Ian Stokes for their helpful advice and direction at key stages of my career.

Very special thanks to Rod Erb at RKE Consulting and Mark Ashnault for the invaluable comments that they provided while reviewing the manuscript.

Special thanks to George Anderson at Enterprise Engineering and Alex Berson for their timely advice and friendship during this endeavor.

It also is my pleasure to thank Carmen, Luz-Mery, Hernan, Rodrigo, Jaime, Edwin, Juan-Carlos, Andy, Carolina, and Jerry for welcoming me into their family and always being there whenever I need them.

Finally, I thank my parents, Carole and Terence, my sisters, Lorisa and Hayley, and the rest of my family for their never-ending love, optimism and unconditional support.

Paul R. Allen
New York, New York
April, 1995

Preface

In recent years the information technology industry has undergone a renaissance of development. Large firms are downsizing or rightsizing from mainframe host-based to multiplatform applications that incorporate networks of cooperative processing. Smaller firms are outgrowing their standalone PC applications and migrating them to Local Area Networks (LAN), which include file and database servers. There is a tremendous number of new development efforts underway in the computing industry. Thankfully, there is a common denominator that can facilitate this wealth of new development. Graphical user interface (GUI) front-end development tools, like PowerBuilder, exist a plenty, with each providing some showcased feature. They are all good, but none to date provides as comprehensive an environment as Power-Builder. It is a tool that provides crossplatform, full-function GUI features coupled with the ability to easily connect to a wide variety to database servers. For this reason, it is the choice of many development efforts that have emerged from this down-sizing, rightsizing, and upsizing process.

The book is intended to introduce the reader to the best approach to learning PowerBuilder, educate those new to the client/server world with an understanding of the concepts and theories behind this paradigm, and present an understanding of event-driven programming, the graphical user interface, object-oriented programming (OOP) techniques, and relational database access. The book also will help experienced developers migrate their skills from large mainframe environments or standalone PC environments to the client/server paradigm. The book encourages experienced developers to leverage their old skills with new skills to develop applications that involve multiple tiers of platform architecture and weave these components together to deliver applications in tune with current presentation possibilities.

Introduction

A roadmap for navigating the book follows. Part 1, "An Introduction," is comprised of chapters 1 through 5. It will introduce the reader to PowerBuilder. Chapter 1, "Getting Started," embellishes on the history of Powersoft and its flagship product that development managers are choosing above all else. In addition, everything one needs to know about the complete Powersoft product line is presented. This will assist new development efforts at the planning of software and hardware procurement stages.

In chapter 2, "The PowerBuilder Environment," the comprehensive PowerBuilder development environment is defined as itemized in the following sentences. In an introductory fashion, object-oriented development techniques are reviewed. The PowerBuilder libraries used to capture the PowerBuilder source code are explained. The PowerBuilder painters used to develop the PowerBuilder objects and source code are identified. Finally, the steps required to build a PowerBuilder application are described.

In chapter 3, "Planning Client/Server Development," an overview of client/server computing including the architecture, strategies, and theories is described. The phases of a development effort, which include many that will be familiar to an experienced developer, are presented. The book goes further and includes the additional steps required in most client/server application development efforts. Distinctions between mainframe development and client/server development will be drawn by examining the traditional techniques and contrasting them with contemporary variations on the same themes.

In chapter 4, "Setup Development Environment," you will learn how to set up your PowerBuilder development environment. This chapter will help you plan the environment, including standards, guidelines, and good practices. Detailed help is provided to install PowerBuilder correctly on development platforms existing at the time of this writing. The book also will review techniques and protocol settings required to connect to the various database platforms. With respect to network-based development, the book points out approaches that might be employed to facilitate sharing in a workgroup development environment. Also discussed is the proper planning required to use PowerBuilder and the "how to" of sketching out the application flow to produce consistent, stable, and reliable application delivery.

Chapter 5, "Developing the Application," provides a detailed overview of how to develop an application. The prerequisites to the development environment are outlined. The importance of database design and the need to virtually complete the database design before full scale development begins is emphasized. How to choose a window menu interface architecture also is considered here. The "how" and "when" to build basic PowerBuilder objects—windows, menus, and DataWindows—is introduced. Customizing objects to extend the application events with scripts also is considered.

Part 2, "Development," which is comprised of chapters 6 through 16, will expand and extend the concepts introduced in Part 1, especially those presented in chapter 5. Chapter 6, "Defining an Application," covers the definition of an application. This is done by covering the four PowerBuilder painters that affect the application definition. The Application painter allows you to create the application object and specify general application properties. The Library painter is used to maintain PowerBuilder libraries and their contents. It also is used as an initial location for the developer to launch the required painter to edit existing objects. The Project painter, although it is a deployment tool, is covered so as to reinforce the need for a template for the production executable and any related files. The Preferences painter is used to specify the development environment defaults and preferences for the application, database, windows, menu, and DataWindow objects.

Chapter 7, "Creating a Window/Menu Interface," chapter 8, "Building Windows," and chapter 9, "Building Menus," cover the painters used to create the window and menu interface. They provide an overview of the Multiple Document Interface (MDI), which is common in many of today's Windows products. The steps necessary to construct the interface by building the components (the MDI frame, menus, tool-bars, and sheets) and the techniques that can be used to manipulate these components in an application are presented. They show you how to associate menus with particular sheets and their embedded functionality, including the use of scripts to define events, functions, and structures to house the variables used in these scripts.

Chapter 10, "Building DataWindows," and chapter 11, "The Database Transaction," introduce and expand upon the development and use of the DataWindow. The DataWindow really is what separates PowerBuilder from a lot of the other GUI tools. The DataWindow will allow the developer to access and update relational database objects without the need to know extensive SQL data manipulation language (DML). How to select a data source and format the result presentation is covered in detail. After the DataWindow creation basics are mastered, the text continues to drill down to the essence of the database transaction: the various options for connecting to the database. DataWindow control behavior is presented with a developer's perspective. The reader goes behind the scenes to discover how the actual database update takes place and how to control the cost of the database access. Moreover, you will learn how to dynamically construct and manipulate the DataWindow to provide specialized features such as *ad hoc* database query tools that users need to perform dynamic business functions.

Chapter 12, "Adding Scripts," reviews PowerScript, PowerBuilder's soon to be fully compilable programming language. PowerScript becomes the glue that ties all of the objects that are defined in the libraries together. While PowerScript contains the eight basic constructs found in most other languages, it also provides over 500 functions (even more if you include the FUNCky extension library) that can be used to facilitate the application requirements.

In chapter 13, "Testing and Verifying Applications," the PowerBuilder debugger is presented. Additional validation and performance benchmarking techniques also are discussed.

In chapter 14, "Refining Your Code," chapter 15, "User-Defined Functions and Structures," and chapter 16, "Building a User Object," PowerBuilder refinement techniques are introduced. At some point during PowerBuilder development, you begin to realize that you repeat (over and over again) a particular piece of functionality. With a little work, you can make this functionality generic so that it can be written in a fashion that is extendible, and above all, reusable by other developers and probably other applications. The functionality can range from a simple business date calculation routine to a standard for an application framework that provides the links to attach generic database update routines. It takes time for an organization's developers to gain the proper experience. With experience, creative and open ways to construct generic functionality will make developers even more productive. Hopefully these chapters will provide some ideas necessary to catalyze and show you this development direction.

Part 3, "Deployment," is comprised of chapters 17 through 21. Chapter 17, "Preparing the Application for Production," and chapter 18, "Distributing the Application," provide real-world experience and help to create and distribute the production executable. Chapter 19, "Managing the Database," and chapter 20, "Related Tools, Libraries, and Publications," delve deeper into the database and related options available for PowerBuilder. While chapters 19 and 20 are not advanced, they do present features and options that typically are deployed in larger scale development. Chapter 21, "Standards and Guidelines," provides an example of the areas that should be standardized, especially when implementing large-scale enterprise-wide solutions. Note that chapters 19 through 21 can and should be browsed or read early in the reader's use of the book. Their content is referenced in many places throughout the book. The reader is encouraged to jump around per his or her interest from chapter to chapter. An attempt was made to follow the development lifecycle as a form of stepwise material presentation, especially in chapters 6 through 21.

In conclusion, the book will not only provide an introductory treatment of PowerBuilder development, but, it also will be useful later on as your reach each milestone in the development lifecycle as a checklist to ensure that you have considered your options. No book can satisfy all needs, but this guide was written by two developers who have been implementing computer-based solutions for a period fast approaching 40 years. In any event, we hope you enjoy reading the book and that it improves your PowerBuilder development capabilities.

An Introduction

1

Getting Started

This chapter introduces you to the company that developed PowerBuilder, Powersoft. The chapter presents some of the history behind Powersoft, its product line, and more specifically PowerBuilder Enterprise, the flagship product. (See Figure 1.1.) Although this book is intended for both new and experienced developers, some of the topics discussed in this chapter will be better understood with some PowerBuilder product exposure. Readers that are completely new to PowerBuilder might want to browse through this chapter and return later after reading the remainder of the book.

Why PowerBuilder?

PowerBuilder is one of the leading application development tools used to migrate applications to, or develop new applications using, the client/server paradigm. End-users have become tired of dreary looking products that use a nonintuitive interface to a proprietary file system. They want applications to be delivered with a Graphical User Interface (GUI) and a database engine that supports Structured Query Language (SQL), and they are demanding short development cycles. They want to get their hands on something, anything, now! The demand for Rapid Application Development (RAD) has made PowerBuilder one of the premiere choices for the delivery of client/server technology today. Let's see how it all began . . ..

The past

To see how PowerBuilder has evolved to what it is today, you have to go back to the early 1980s to a small group of people, headed by Dave Dewan and Mitchell Kertzman. This team built development tools for the IDMS database running in the IBM mainframe environment.

In 1983, two years after the IBM Personal Computer was introduced, this group started a project to build a development tool for the PC. The applications developed

Figure 1.1 PowerBuilder Enterprise.

using this tool were to run partially on the PC, with a graphical user interface, and partially on the mainframe, with a relational database. This was an ambitious project, considering that the group had to build their own GUI platform, relational database, and the communications interface.

Despite this challenge, the project proceeded, but so did the rest of the computer industry. Microsoft was about to switch its development direction from OS/2 to Windows (and now Windows NT), and several relational database management systems (Oracle and Sybase) were establishing significant market share. It was now 1988, roughly about the same time that David Litwack joined the company. At this point, the group decided they had a product that was not worth rewriting to fit into these newly established, or nearly established, architectures. So instead, leveraging the experience they had gained together, the group set about developing yet another tool, this time an add-in for Microsoft Excel.

This tool, named PowerStation, gave the user of Excel the ability to issue SQL calls to, and receive data back from, the database. At the conclusion of this project came the impetus for a much more complete product. It took the next two and a half years of intense development before finally shipping PowerBuilder Version 1.0 to the IBM PC-compatible platform in June 1991. However, it was not until the release of Version 2.0 in June 1992 that PowerBuilder had the industry turned on with several corporations considering it for developing client/server applications.

With the rapidly increasing license base, it came time for the principal members of Powersoft to complete the legitimization of the company by floating it on one of the stock exchanges. The Powersoft Corporation was very successfully floated on the NASDAQ Exchange (NASDAQ: PWRS) sometime in 1993.

The flotation served two purposes: rewarding the principals for their time investment in making the product to begin with and, more importantly, a large injection of cash into the company for research and development and mergers and acquisitions.

When the company became publicly owned, its tactic was to expand and diversify the product line. When it comes to products, you either develop them or you buy from somebody that already has developed them. In 1993, Powersoft did both. Powersoft announced the release of two new products that would coincide with the next release of PowerBuilder, Version 3.0, on July 7, 1993. The products were called PowerViewer, an end-user ad hoc query tool, and PowerMaker, a simplified end-user database maintenance and ad hoc reporting tool. These new products essentially were implementations of the DataWindows technology present in the flagship product PowerBuilder.

The next major announcement came in November 1993. Powersoft announced the acquisition of Watcom International Corporation, a Canadian company that is based in Waterloo, Ontario. Watcom specializes in providing high-performance development tools. Watcom had established itself as an industry leader of C/C++ compiler technology and recently had introduced Watcom SQL, a family of client/server SQL database products.

The merger was proposed as a result of the two companies working very closely with each other to bundle the single-user version of the Watcom SQL database with Version 3.0 of PowerBuilder. The merger with Watcom has greatly improved the area of performance in the release of Version 4.0 of PowerBuilder. Simply recompiling Version 3.0a runtime DLL's with the Watcom C/C++ compiler resulted in an immediate improvement in performance.

However, despite the introduction of these lower-cost siblings, the PowerBuilder product itself still was considered a "high-end" or "Enterprise" solution with the associated price tag, around $3395 U.S. This changed with an announcement in early 1994 and with the release, in May, of PowerBuilder Desktop at an introductory price tag of $249 U.S. (now $649 U.S.).

The Desktop version uses the same code as the Enterprise version but ships with reduced database connectivity and no version control options. The Desktop product is designed for the market of individual developers that build standalone Windows applications with "desktop" databases (for example, Watcom SQL, Microsoft Access, dBase, Paradox, ODBC, etc.)

During that same month, at the International User Conference, David Litwack, the President of Powersoft, presented the future goals of Powersoft. This was the shopping list of enhancements to PowerBuilder that came with the release of version 4.0 and will continue with the next versions:

- Expand to multiple platforms (Windows NT/Macintosh/UNIX)
- Improve quality-control procedures
- Make the products faster by incorporating Watcom compiler technology
- Enhanced DataWindow reporting: embedded DWs, combination DWs
- Make development interface easier: cut and paste, undo, etc.
- Enhancing the database support by taking advantage of DBMS features
- Expand the CODE relationships. (For more on CODE, see chapter 20, "Related tools, libraries, and publications.")
- Assimilate new and evolving technologies into the product line

Sometime in November 1994, during the beta testing phase of Version 4.0, an announcement of a merger between Sybase and Powersoft stunned the industry. Sybase, Inc. (NASDAQ:SYBS) is one of the leading worldwide suppliers of client/server-based products and services. Sybase, at the time, was the second largest RDBMS vendor and provider of database connectivity/interoperability software.

After the initial shock, there were questions as to whether the new ownership would adversely affect the relationships that it had with the other RDBMS vendors, especially Oracle. The merged company soon followed up with several press releases announcing that Powersoft would continue to operate as an independent subsidiary with the charter of expanding its position as a leading provider of database independent development tools. It also emphasized its commitment to open systems, identifying that a key competitive advantage of PowerBuilder is the native database drivers that capitalize on the particular qualities of the database management systems.

Powersoft will continue to participate in the early release programs of each of the databases that it supports while maintaining the appropriate confidentiality. It really wouldn't be good for business if Sybase and Powersoft were seen to be biased toward the Sybase RDBMS to the detriment of the other databases. However, time will tell if the best laid plans and intentions pan out and if the widespread market acceptance of PowerBuilder continues. Obviously, we think it will!

The present

The multiplatform approach will allow PowerBuilder to be scalable by employing an API layer between PowerBuilder and the particular operating system. That is to say that the API converts the PowerBuilder request into the particular set of platform operating system commands to effect the desired result. In any event, PowerBuilder insulates the developer from most of the problems of porting an application from one platform to another. It also facilitates the migration from one back-end DBMS to another. A simple SELECT statement should create the same result using any ANSI SQL-compliant DBMS.

There are some challenges for developers. They must be wary of unique platform features and choose the least common denominator if they want the application to be truly cross platform capable.

By the time you read this book, Powersoft will have completed the staged release of Version 4.0 that is depicted in Table 1.1.

Also, Powersoft should have announced and possibly released PowerBuilder for Windows 95, the long awaited 32-bit replacement for 16-bit Windows. Powersoft continues to state that a native version of PowerBuilder for OS/2 is in the works, but,

TABLE 1.1 The Staged Release of PowerBuilder Version 4.0

Operating system (processor)	Release date
Windows and Windows NT (Intel)	December of 1994
System 7 (Apple Macintosh—Motorola)	Fourth quarter of 1995
Motif for Solaris (SunSPARC), Motif for UX (HP), and Motif for AIX (IBM RS/6000)	Third quarter of 1995

this might take some time due to the fact that Powersoft chose the Windows API as the porting layer to other platforms, and porting technology to OS/2's Presentation Manager is not available yet. Once again, time will tell if things get worked out on this front. However, Powersoft will continue to support the Windows version that will run in a Windows session under OS/2.

When the staged release of Version 4.0 to each of the new platforms is complete, Powersoft has stated that it will release future upgrades to each platform at the same time. This can be achieved because of the way it has organized the development teams. Powersoft development is comprised of the following teams: a development team and a porting team.

The development team develops, maintains, and enhances the "core" PowerBuilder source code. Each porting team's responsibility is to develop the porting layer, which is based on Microsoft's Windows API, for each of the platforms. Powersoft has chosen Windows API because it is a robust and substantially widespread API that more and more operating systems are catering for.

With this approach Powersoft has achieved cross-platform application compatibility. Consequently, an application now can be developed and saved in a PowerBuilder Library on one platform, copied to another platform, loaded, and run without any changes. However, as expected, if you create and use any specific code for a particular platform, then the application will not work as expected when copied to any of the other platforms. (The nature of the remainder of this section covers some of the specifics of PowerBuilder. If you are new to PowerBuilder, you might want to skip to the section "The product line" and come back later.)

If you set up your application to execute a low-level Windows SDK function, you will find that the same code will not work on the Macintosh. This might seem a little limiting, so Powersoft has given you an extension to the PowerBuilder scripting language that will allow you to determine on which platform you are running so that you can make the appropriate platform specific calls. For example:

```
ENVIRONMENT  L_eEnv
IF GetEnvironment(L_eEnv) <> 1 THEN RETURN
CHOOSE CASE L_eEnv.OSType
CASE Macintosh!
    CALL wf_Macintosh_function
CASE Windows!
    CALL wf_Windows_function
CASE WindowsNT!
    CALL wf_WindowsNT_function
CASE ELSE
    MessageBox ("WARNING",
                "Application is not fully supported on this platform!")
END CHOOSE
```

This feature will give you the ability to maintain a single copy of the source for the application that you develop and distribute to multiple platforms.

The following is a list of the major new features of PowerBuilder Enterprise Version 4.0:

- Multiple platforms: Windows, Windows NT, Apple Macintosh, and UNIX
- Faster and uses high-performance code that was created using the Watcom C/C++ compiler

- The ability to embed and link DataWindows within a DataWindow
- Improved object management with faster loading of inherited objects
- Support for stored procedures and triggers in Watcom SQL 4.0
- Data Pipeline object, a database transfer and replication tool
- Support for OLE 2.0 Containers and Automation
- Ease of use enhancements, Undo/Redo, Cut and paste objects in painters
- Integrated Watcom C/C++ environment for creating fast code in DLLs
- PowerTips or Timed MicroHelp for toolbars like MS-Office
- Multimedia and pen support
- Greatly improved source control

With the release of 4.0 and the merger with Sybase, Powersoft can say to the industry, with conviction, that they are going to be around for the next decade, leading us through the ever changing world of client/server computing.

The future

Since its introduction, PowerBuilder has proven to be a winner, year after year collecting accolades from leading magazines and publications in the Information Systems industry.

Powersoft, since its beginning, has identified the following requirements for its market:

- Strong graphical user interface
- Widespread database connectivity
- Flexible data access
- Source management

Through the implementation of these requirements in successive versions of PowerBuilder, Powersoft has evolved to a point where they identify with the following technological strategies:

- Cross-platform development
- Improved compiler technology
- Distributed applications: two- and three-tier transaction objects and application partitioning (Connection and service objects are coming soon)
- Work group development

The acquisition of Watcom International with its compiler technology and experience has lead to significant improvements with the performance and features of the product. For example, a benchmark for a section of PowerScript code that contained a simple loop took 19 seconds to process in Version 3.0a, took 7 seconds in Version

4.0, and will take less than 1 second in the next release. The Watcom compiler technology will continue to be a significant impact as it is more tightly integrated in the future. All of this has made, and will continue to make, PowerBuilder the most popular scalable multiplatform development tool. So, if you know how to deliver client/server applications using PowerBuilder, you will be very much in demand. This is the perfect opportunity to invest some time in learning how to develop and deliver industrial strength applications using PowerBuilder in the real world of client/server computing. Good luck!

The Product Line

PowerBuilder Enterprise remains the flagship product for Powersoft. However, with the release of Version 4.0, the product line for Powersoft has changed. The PowerBuilder Enterprise now is a multiplatform release (Windows, Windows NT, Macintosh, and UNIX) with PowerBuilder Team/ODBC and Desktop continuing on the Windows platform only. PowerViewer and PowerMaker have been consolidated into one product and renamed as InfoMaker. This section provides the details for the new Powersoft product lineup.

PowerBuilder Enterprise for Windows

Released in December 1994, PowerBuilder for Windows/Windows NT has the following software integrated and packaged with the release. The Watcom/PB DLL Toolkit allows you to easily code and call C/C++ DLLs from PowerBuilder, including integrated debugging and automatic generation of C/C++ DLL definitions for PowerBuilder. It also includes a data migration tool: the Data PipeLine. Also packaged with the product is a copy of InfoMaker, which becomes an OLE 2.0 server when you embed DataWindows into other objects such as Word documents or Excel spreadsheets. The Enterprise version also comes with an add-on product, the Advanced Developer Toolkit, that includes a class library of reusable objects, a suite of advanced utilities, and numerous ready-made applications that include support for accessing VIM-compliant electronic mail systems via Lotus Notes, NetWare services and pen computing. (Price $3295 U.S.)

PowerBuilder Enterprise for Macintosh

Expected to be released during the first quarter of 1995, PowerBuilder for Macintosh (680x0 processor) includes a standalone version of Watcom SQL 4.0 database for the Macintosh. A version of PowerBuilder Enterprise for the PowerMacintosh also is planned. More specific details were unavailable at the time of writing this book. (Price not available.)

PowerBuilder Enterprise for Motif

PowerBuilder Enterprise for Motif (Sun SPARC-Solaris, HP-UX, IBM RS/6000-AIX) is expected to be released during the second quarter of 1995. Specific details were unavailable at the time of writing this book. (Price not available.)

PowerBuilder Team/ODBC for Windows

Released in December of 1994, PowerBuilder Team/ODBC for Windows (Intel and compatibles) is a version of PowerBuilder that provides team development capabilities and server database connectivity through ODBC. (Price $2295 U.S.)

PowerBuilder Desktop for Windows

Released in December of 1994, PowerBuilder Desktop for Windows (Intel and compatibles) is designed to meet the needs of individual developers that need to build single-user applications for Windows with the Watcom SQL and other supported desktop class ODBC databases (MS Access, Paradox, dBase, Btrieve, etc.). (Price $695 U.S.)

InfoMaker for Windows

Released in December of 1994, InfoMaker for Windows (Intel and compatibles) is the second generation end-user data access and reporting tool that replaces the PowerViewer and PowerMaker products from the prior release. (See Figure 1.2.)

InfoMaker contains the capability for developing queries and presenting high-quality reports with its implementation of PowerBuilder's DataWindow technology, enabling end-users to create and maintain applications without programming. InfoMaker includes a standalone version of Watcom SQL 4.0 database. (Price $249 U.S.)

The sample application

The PowerBuilder sample application (see Figure 1.3) is a Watcom SQL-based application that demonstrates most of the functions available in PowerBuilder. The source is included. After you learn how to use the painters in PowerBuilder, it is

Figure 1.2 InfoMaker.

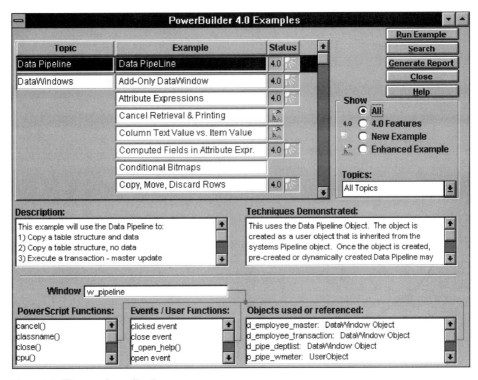

Figure 1.3 The sample application.

worth spending a significant amount of time running and testing the sample and looking at the source to see how things are done.

When you run the sample, the box that is labeled Window Name provides you with a starting point in the Library painter for investigating the code for a particular feature that you might be interested in.

Advanced Developer Toolkit

The Advanced Developer Toolkit is included with the Enterprise and Team/ODBC and is an optional purchase for the Desktop version. The Toolkit comes with a class library of reusable objects and an example MDI application that shows you how to effectively use the class library. It is worthwhile to study in detail and use the example if you have not developed or purchased a class library.

The Application Library. The Application Library is an example implementation of a reusable object class library. It comes with the Enterprise edition. If you have purchased PowerBuilder Desktop, call the Powersoft to purchase it. The library is a collection of reusable windows, menus, functions, and user-defined objects that could be used by a developer to accelerate the process of building and delivering an application in PowerBuilder.

Components. The PowerBuilder Application Library actually is three libraries:

- Application Framework (SYS.PBL) contains the base class MDI frame and MDI sheets that should be inherited from.
- Windows Object Library (UTLWIN.PBL) contains reusable windows and window-related functions.
- Function Object Library (UTLFUNC.PBL) contains reusable utility functions.

Sample application. The Application Library sample application is constructed using the Application Library objects. Like the standard sample application, you should spend some time running this application and, when necessary, inspecting the code to see how the Application Library objects are being used.

Example application. Also included in the Application Library is an example application that demonstrates the usage of the Application Library objects that are not used in the sample application. The example application allows you to execute a series of windows that show working examples of the functions and objects that are included in the Application Library.

PB Toolkit Utilities. With the Advanced Developer Toolkit is a set of utilities (see Figure 1.4) that will help during the development and deployment of a medium to large scale PowerBuilder application. (Price $595 U.S.)

- DWEAS: After you change the extended attributes of any columns in a table with this utility, you can synchronize the DataWindows that might use these columns instead of manually wading through your libraries.
- DWCHECK: DataWindow SQL Verifier.
- PEAR: Extended Attribute Reporter that shows the contents of the PowerBuilder data dictionary and repository.
- XREF: Builds an object, variable, event, and function cross reference for an application.
- SPUD: Allows you to convert DataWindow retrieval and update to use stored procedures.
- PBSETUP: Install disk builder for professional-looking application deployment.
- ImageEdit: A drawing tool for visual resources (e.g., bitmaps, icons, and cursors).

In addition to the utility programs included with the toolkit, there is a collection of ready-made applications that you can use, examine to learn new techniques, and take components from to use in your applications. (See Table 1.2.)

Figure 1.4 The Developers Toolkit.

TABLE 1.2 Ready-Made Applications

Application	Description
Areacode	Telephone areas code look-up window
Asset	Multimedia resource catalog manager
Bookkeep	Visual representation of book storage
Bugtrak	Bug tracking and reporting
Cashtrak	Personal account manager
Cisdemo	CompuServe communications front-end
Contact	Personal contact manager
Dbpipe	Data Pipeline demonstration
Diet	Food diet tracking
Expense	Corporate expense tracking and reporting
Maketabs	Simulated tab folder object demonstration
Olesamp	OLE 1.0 demonstration
Org	Organization chart drawing tool
Pim	Personal information manager
Pubs	Example MDI application for the pubs database
Skills	Skills/training inventory manager
Timemgmt	Project management tool, implemented with application library
Workflow	MS Mail document routing using OLE 2.0

FUNCky Library for PowerBuilder

The FUNCky Library for PowerBuilder (see Figure 1.5) is an add-on library that provides additional useful functions (e.g., bit manipulation and file, date, and string management) for your PowerBuilder applications. (Price $99 U.S.)

Getting Help

If you need assistance when using PowerBuilder, in addition to this book and the manuals that came with PowerBuilder, you have the following sources of information available:

- PowerBuilder help
- InfoBase and Online Books
- Powersoft FaxLine Service

Figure 1.5 The FUNCky Library for PowerBuilder.

- Powersoft Bulletin Board Service
- World Wide Web (WWW), Usenet newgroups, and FTP sites
- CompuServe
- Sales and Marketing
- Customer hotline and installation support
- Education/training and consulting services
- Local user groups
- Annual User Meeting & Training Conference
- PowerBuilder certification (CPD)

Online PowerBuilder help

Included with the development environment, there are several help files that are formatted for the Microsoft Help engine (WINHELP.EXE). The help files are designed to provide step-by-step instruction for using the painters and PowerBuilder features.

The help files have been built for contextual style of interaction. If you are in a particular dialog and press the Help key or button, you will be presented with the help that relates to that dialog. Once you are in PowerBuilder Help, you can move to various other topics.

InfoBase and Online Books

Included with each copy of PowerBuilder is the Powersoft InfoBase CD-ROM, which provides question and answer technical tips, FaxLine documents, how-to videos, information on the FUNCky add-in, an archive of the technical questions that appear on the CompuServe forum, and an installable copy of the WinCIM software to get you started.

Powersoft, like many other software vendors, no longer provides the complete printed documentation with the product. Instead it provides you with a similar product to the InfoBase CD, called Online Books (see Figure 1.6).

Online Books, as its name implies, is a complete set of documentation in electronic form. This will enable you to scan for combinations of words and print excerpts of the documentation. If you still want a copy of the printed documentation, you can order it from Powersoft.

Powersoft FaxLine Service

The Powersoft FaxLine Service is an automated system, much like todays voice-mail systems, where you can request up to five documents to be sent to a fax machine. The documents available on FaxLine cover the following six categories:

- Technical services
- Education services

Figure 1.6 Powersoft's Online Books.

- Marketing information
- General information
- Partnership program information
- Watcom marketing information

Through the FaxLine, you can obtain a directory listing of the FaxLine documents in each of the categories. Over time, this information also is made available on the seasonally released InfoBase CD; however, to get the newest documents, use the FaxLine system. To order fax documents, call FaxLine North America, 508-287-1600, or FaxLine Europe, 44-1628-416500 or 44-1494-555522. The FaxLine service is available 24 hours a day.

Powersoft Bulletin Board Service

The Powersoft Bulletin Board Service (BBS) enables you to download fixes, sample code, and technical write-ups. You also can upload files for review by the technical support team. To use the bulletin board service, call BBS North America, 508-287-1850, or BBS Europe, 44-1628-24402. The Powersoft BBS is available 24 hours a day.

World Wide Web (WWW), Usenet, and file transfer protocol (FTP)

With an ever-increasing list of vendors providing access to information via a combination of World Wide Web (WWW) pages, Usenet newsgroups, and file transfer protocol (FTP) sites, it was only a matter of time before this happened with the PowerBuilder product.

To join the Usenet newsgroup, you need to subscribe to *comp.soft-sys.power-builder*. This newsgroup provides a forum to post questions and allow other subscribers to respond either directly to your e-mail account or, more usefully, back to the newsgroup.

Powersoft has an FTP site: *ftp.powersoft.com*. There are several other FTP sites that are maintained independently of Powersoft:

- *ftp.netcom.com* [directory/pub/jjabt]

- *ftp.oar.net* [directory/pub/psoft]

In addition, there is a WWW page set up at *http://web.syr/~estephe/pb.html*.

CompuServe forum

If you are a CompuServe subscriber, you can use the Powersoft forum, which was created to answer questions about Powersoft products and services. To access the Powersoft forum, log onto CompuServe and type: GO Powersoft.

Figure 1.7 contains a list of topics available for discussion in the forums and downloading from the libraries.

Sales and marketing

To enquire about a product or to speak to a sales or marketing representative, call Sales and Marketing, 800-395-3525.

Title	Topics	Msgs
General Information	195	478
PowerBuilder	422	1135
PowerMaker/Viewer	13	20
Product Marketing	14	36
PB Desktop	59	129
DBMS Connections	84	184
DataWindows	122	263
User Groups	4	4
3rd Party Vendors	36	85
Powersoft Services	9	25
Classified Ads	52	102
Hot Topics	5	14
WATCOM SQL	144	299
WATCOM C/C++	133	217
WATCOM VX-REXX	61	130
WATCOM FORTRAN 77	10	18

| Select | Mark | All | Close |

Figure 1.7 PowerSoft/Watcom forums on CompuServe.

Customer hotline and installation support

For details on how you can obtain customer support, call Annual Product Support Plans, 800-YES-POWER (937-7693). Other customer support numbers are:

- Pay Per Issue Support: 508-287-1950
- Customer Service Fax Number: 508-369-4992
- Customer Relations: 508-287-1900

The international support numbers are:

- Powersoft UK: 44-628-34500
- Powersoft Belgium: 32-235-23333
- Japan (Nichimen Data Systems): 81-3-3864-7429
- Powersoft Latin America: 713-977-0752
- Powersoft Singapore: 65-378-0140
- Powersoft Spain: 34-1-593-2636
- Powersoft France: 33-1-473-17172

For help during installation of a product, call Installation Support North America, 508-287-1750. For bug reporting, download the file PBBUG.TXT from the Powersoft Bulletin Board System or CompuServe or call FaxLine and request document #1010. For enhancement requests, download the file PBNHANCE.TXT from the Powersoft Bulletin Board System or CompuServe or call FaxLine and request document #1009.

Education, training, and consulting services

Powersoft maintains a list of training classes available for the following topics. The classes are given by Powersoft or approved Powersoft education centers.

- PowerBuilder: The Basics (1 day)
- PowerBuilder: Starting from a Framework (2 days)
- Transition to Client/Server Environment (1 day)
- Effective Graphical User Interface Design (1 day)
- Introduction to PowerBuilder (4 days)
- Mastering DataWindows (2 days)
- PowerBuilder Performance, Tuning, and Techniques (2 days)
- Object-Oriented Analysis and Design Using PowerBuilder (3 days)
- Introduction to InfoMaker (3 days)
- Managing the Watcom SQL Environment (1 day)

Powersoft also provides Computer-Based Training (CBT) with the following titles:

- Moving from PowerBuilder Version 3.0a to Version 4.0
- PowerBuilder: The Basics
- Developing PowerBuilder Applications, Part 1
- Developing PowerBuilder Applications, Part 2
- DataWindow Concepts

For details on training class schedules, approved education centers, and the Computer-Based Training, call:

- Training & Education, North America: 508-287-1700, Option 2.
- Training & Education, Europe: 44-1908-216016
- Consulting Services: 508-287-1638

Local user groups

There are countless user groups being run across the United States. As the popularity of the product rises, these undoubtedly will spring up across the globe. They provide developers and users of the products in the local communities with a forum for exchanging information and provide the Powersoft CODE partners a place to demonstrate, and obviously sell, their wares. For a list of user groups in your area, call Powersoft.

Annual User Meeting and Training Conferences

There are two events that usually are held in June each year. The International User Meeting and Training Conference took place at a location in the United States in 1995 at the Walt Disney World Dolphin, Lake Buena Vista, Florida. In 1995, The European User Meeting and Training Conference was held at the Intercontinental Hotel in Berlin, Germany.

These conferences provide an environment for discussion, demonstration, and training sessions for the Powersoft product line and the CODE partner add-on products. They also provide a relaxed forum for people to swap the invaluable "war-story" experiences that they gained by actually using and implementing the product features.

PowerBuilder certification (CPD)

The CPD is a Certified PowerBuilder Developer who is recognized by Powersoft as a person who has demonstrated a proficiency in PowerBuilder skills. The program is divided into two levels:

- *Associate* is designed to show proficiency in the fundamental, and some advanced, concepts. The test is comprised of two multiple choice examinations (1 hour each) that are taken using a interactive session on a computer. The first covers the fundamentals; the second covers the advanced features.

- *Professional* is designed to show an indepth understanding of PowerBuilder and its advanced techniques. To take this test, you first must pass the Associate tests. You then take a test that requires you to build pieces of an application to solve given requirements using nontrivial methods.

For more information on certification, call 1-800-407-EXAM or the FaxLine service (508-287-1600) and request document #1616.

2

The PowerBuilder Environment

PowerBuilder is a tool that provides an integrated development environment packaged into one piece of software. It can run on most of the existing client/server platforms that are available. The environment has expanded in other ways. Many third-party vendors have added PowerBuilder interfaces to their products. Others have developed class and function libraries that can be installed as instant development standards. This combination makes PowerBuilder one of the most comprehensive environments available for today's client/server development. This chapter will present definitions and terminology that will be expanded upon later. If you are familar with these ideas, then just quickly browse through them and move on to the next chapter.

Definition

PowerBuilder is a graphical PC-based client/server application development environment. Using PowerBuilder, you can develop powerful applications executable on a multitude of platforms (e.g., Microsoft Windows) that can access your server databases on various DBMs platforms, including but not limited to Sybase, DB2/ MVS, Oracle, DB2/6000, and DB2/2. PowerBuilder applications are intended to fit the workstation environment upon which they are developed. PowerBuilder applications can be developed to work in a fashion similar to other Windows applications that you might be familiar and comfortable with. Microsoft's Word and Excel are examples of the multiple document interface (MDI) application style. MDI-based PowerBuilder applications consist of windows sheets that are contained in a window frame with a menu and a toolbar and other controls that users interact with. You can use all of the standard Windows controls—such as command buttons, checkboxes, dropdown listboxes, and edit boxes—as well as special PowerBuilder controls that facilitate applications development and are easy to use.

PowerBuilder provides all of the tools that you need: object painters, utilities, editor, and compiler to build enterprise capable applications for the financial, entertainment, and sports industries, just to name a few.

If you are new to PowerBuilder, you should finish this chapter, then spend the two hours of semi-uninterrupted time that it takes to do the PowerBuilder tutorial that appears in the "Getting Started" manual. The tutorial guides you through the process of building a basic PowerBuilder application.

It is not exciting, but it will be a good first step in the iterative learning process that will lead most experienced developers to become PowerBuilder productive in the short term.

Objects and classes

PowerBuilder builds upon newer development techniques that were introduced at the commercial advent of the graphic user interface. As we describe these techniques, you will start to hear some new terms. We will review them quickly so that you can begin the process of improving your client/server and object-oriented vocabulary. The terms that are basic to object orientation—terms like object, class, and instance—are used in PowerBuilder.

An *object* is a software packet that contains related procedures and data.

A *class* is a set of objects that share a common structure and a common behavior. It contains the attributes, functions, and events that make up the formal definition of an object. In PowerBuilder, each window, such as w_schedule_sheet, is a class. The class w_schedule_sheet is created when the window is defined in the Window painter and stored in a PowerBuilder library.

An *instance* is one case (copy) of a class. For example, the user might want to open more than one schedule (i.e., more than one copy of w_schedule_sheet) at a time. Each would be an instance of the class with its own instance variables.

Instances

In PowerBuilder, you can have several copies of one window on the screen at the same time. Figure 2.1 is an illustration of how you create/inherit and use window object w_schedule_sheet. Each of these is an instance of the class w_schedule_sheet. An instance of w_schedule_sheet is created at execution when an Open (or Open-Sheet) function is executed. An instance can have its own set of variables, each with a separate block of storage. Conversely, shared variables are class variables, which are shared by all instances of a class that exist at the same time (i.e., one block of storage), while instance variables are available separately to each instance (i.e., one block of storage for each instance).

Should you use two instances of the same window or two similar windows in your application? Multiple instances of the same window share a class definition in memory and take up less room.

If you create two different windows and instantiate (load) each one, you have two class definitions and two instances (copies) loaded into memory at runtime. If you create one window and instantiate it twice, there is one class definition and two in-

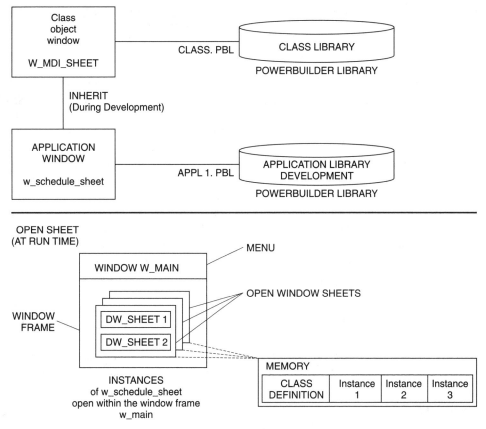

Figure 2.1 Inheritance and instances.

stances loaded into memory. The storage that is required is reduced because the class definition is not repeated (i.e., loaded twice).

Encapsulation

Encapsulation incorporates into an object definition the object's data attributes and its processing methods (functions and event scripts). An encapsulated object presents a well-defined interface to other objects that want to interact with it and hides within itself its definition and processing details.

When you build an application, window, menu, or user object, you are building an encapsulated object. Each of these objects can have its own set of functions that defines the interface to that object. For windows and user objects, that interface also can include user-defined events.

Each of these objects can contain its own set of attributes, at either the shared or instance variable scope. For example, if your application uses a vendor or inhouse class library, you can incorporate a user object data window control that has included a set of special user events (e.g., ue_filesave with specialized database processing; for example, insert, update a table based upon the setting of the objects instance variables).

Inheritance

Inheritance is the method whereby a class can derive data and procedures from previously defined classes. For readers who are or were mainframe developers, it is a fancy version of the mainframe COBOL COPY function that is used to basically inherit project base subroutines as they were called from a common mainframe LOADLIB. Inheritance in PowerBuilder is refined and can be very useful. PowerBuilder supports inheritance for windows, menus, and user objects. Once you have defined and saved one of these objects in a library, you can create a new object that inherits the original definition.

An inheritance relationship establishes a two-level hierarchy in which the original object (from which the new object is inherited) is called the *ancestor* and the new object that does the inheriting is called the *descendant*. The descendant can add new components to the original as well as augment or override the ancestor's behavior.

Inheritance ensures consistency in the processing and look of the object. When you make a change in an ancestor object, the change is reflected in all descendants automatically at execution time without recompiling the descendant.

The descendant inherits the ancestor's scripts so that you do not have to recode them. This is similar to the old mainframe COPY code methodology but is an improvement as additions to the base ancestor code are inherited automatically. Be aware that this is not always the case; database extended attributes, like edit styles, are not inherited if the object containing the column already has been built.

Polymorphism

With polymorphism, the same set of operations (functions or event scripts) can work on different objects, although sometimes in a different way. (See Figure 2.2.) For example, you can define a Save function for a wide range of objects. Each has its own definition of what Save does, but any user of that object will have an idea of what will happen when they call it. A menu item called "Save" might have a script behind it that triggers an event (e.g., ue_filesave). The script behind the event might be different depending upon the object that is active. For example, the window w_daily_tv_schedule might cause 48 rows that represent each half hour of the day to be inserted or updated to the database table that contains scheduling data.

Each generic object type (menus, CommandButtons, windows, ListBoxes, etc.) has a set of standard functions defined for it. When a particular function is defined for a set of objects, but acts appropriately for the referenced object type, this is polymorphism.

For example, the SetFocus function operates on both CommandButtons and ListBoxes (as well as many other object types). For the CommandButton, SetFocus() sets the input focus to the CommandButton and draws a focus rectangle around the displayed text. For the ListBox, SetFocus() sets the input focus and draws a focus rectangle around the currently selected item if an item has been selected or, if an item has not been selected, draws the focus rectangle around the first entry in the ListBox.

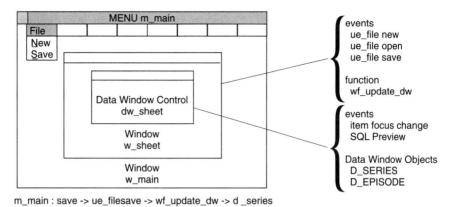

m_main : save -> ue_filesave -> wf_update_dw -> d _series

Clicked menu item triggers user event in current Window sheet which calls
Window function to execute PB UPDATE of current Data Window Object

Figure 2.2 Polymorphism and encapsulation.

When you define a set of objects, whether windows user objects or menus, you
also can define common functions among those objects that act according to the object type that was specified. For example, several objects might have an Initialize
function:

- In one object, this function reads some values from an .INI file.

- In another object, the Initialize function opens and displays a logon window.

- In a third object, the Initialize function retrieves values from a database.

Assume an application has a Multiple Document Interface (MDI) frame with several sheets in it. Each sheet is unique, containing different information. For example,
one sheet contains information on the TV series, another sheet contains information
on TV episodes, and so on.

For simplicity, a global array of windows keeps track of each opened sheet. You
can use this array to loop through and perform operations on each of the windows.

A menu item from the frame provides the option to Save Changes. This requires
going to each sheet and updating its data in the database. Because each sheet is different, each sheet needs its own unique function to perform the save.

Using the nonpolymorphic approach, you could solve the problem using the following PowerScript, which is the basic PowerBuilder programming language:

```
// Assume global array GC_Window_Array{} is of type
// Window (global variables should be kept to a minimum)
choose case classname (GC_Window_Array{I})
case "series"
w_series.wf_update_series()
case "episode"
w_episode.wf_update_episode()
case "AndSoOn"
....
end choose
next
```

In this example, you have encapsulated the update logic into functions that are associated with each of the sheets. Each of these functions has a different name (wf_update_*tablename*). Using polymorphism to solve the same problem, you set things up differently. In particular, the update functions are given a common interface function. Using a polymorphic approach you would perform the following steps:

Step 1 Create a common ancestor base sheet for each of the sheets to use as an ancestor. Call it w_sheet_base.

Step 2 Add a default wf_update( ) function to BaseSheet. This function will determine which object is to be updated and perform the appropriate update functionality. This functionality might be the same for most of the objects.

Step 3 Inherit each of the individual sheets from the ancestor BaseSheet w_sheet_base.

Step 4 Create each of the update functions that was described previously as wf_update. (Note that the function type and number and type of arguments for each of these wf_update functions must match exactly.)

Step 5 Change the global array Window_Array{} to be of type Base Sheet.

Now, this is the same loop using polymorphism:

```
For I = 1 upperbound (Window_Array)
      GC_Window_Array{I}.wf_update()
Next
```

By renaming each of the different sheets' database update functions to wf_update( ), you create different functions with the same interface (i.e., different sheets can be associated with different data window objects). This is the concept that polymorphism is based on.

By placing the default wf_update function in the BaseSheet ancestor window, the compiler allows the, `GC_Window_Array{I}.wf_update()` to pass the syntax check. This would not work if Window_Array still were of type Window or if wf_update( ) were not defined in BaseSheet.

The wf_update will execute the dynamically associated datawindow objects, thereby updating a different relational table. When GC_Window_Array{I}.wf_update is called, the system looks at the type of the object instance that is stored in Window_Array{I} and calls the UpdateDB( ) function that is associated with that type. This is called *runtime binding*.

You might expect `GC_Window_Array{I}.wf_update()` to call the default function that is defined in BaseSheet. The compiler checks to see that wf_update( ) is a function associated with BaseSheet; however, at runtime, the declared type of Window_Array is ignored. Instead, the object instance that is contained within the Window_Array is examined, and the wf_update( ) function that is associated with that instance is bound.

When you analyze a system as a set of objects, you generally find polymorphic behavior quite common. Programming polymorphically has several benefits. It makes objects independent of each other. Look at the previous before and after examples. The first one refers to each sheet type by name and accesses their variables and functions. The second example has no references to the individual sheets at all. It allows you to add new objects with minimal changes. In the first example, adding a new sheet type would require a new case in the choose statement. In the second, no code changes are necessary.

All of this leads to simpler, more flexible systems. Polymorphism is one of the most effective reusability tools available.

PowerBuilder can help to convert online application systems based upon the older modal pseudo-conversational transaction to open multiple transaction processing based upon object-oriented development technique. Object-oriented development techniques are useful tools that:

- Speed up the development process
- Improve code quality and efficiency

However, object-oriented development techniques won't write the application for you. They won't prevent you from writing bogus code. They won't prevent you from building latent bugs into your application. However, they will make it easier to find and correct them. Remember that using object orientation in your application is always a design decision. These concepts will be explained later. Now, we will discuss the tools that will lead an experienced, as well as a new, developer to a working knowledge of the PowerBuilder.

The Development Tools

You build the components of your application using the PowerBuilder painters, which provide an assortment of tools for building and/or testing objects. Those of us old enough to remember will recall the character-based mainframe "test" environment. This environment, in most development shops, would consist of a hodgepodge of IBM/MVS/TSO menu options that would provide the capability to edit and maintain your source code, compile and create executable load modules, and submit job control language to execute the programs in batch or under the aegis of an online teleprocessing monitor, such as IBM's CICS. PowerBuilder is not unlike that old environment in that it combines all of these tools needed to build an enterprise capable application into a single integrated window frame. You create and maintain a window in the Window painter. There you define the properties of the window and add controls, such as buttons and edit boxes. PowerBuilder provides painters for each type of object that you build during the course of your application development. These objects include the following:

- Application object
- Window object
- Menu object
- DataWindow object

These objects are stored in a special library (a file in the platform operating system known as a PowerBuilder library).

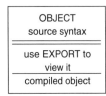

Figure 2.3 The parts of an object.

The contents of PowerBuilder Libraries (.PBL)

A PowerBuilder Library (.PBL file) contains only PowerBuilder objects, such as Application, Window, Menu, DataWindow, Function, Structure, and User Object. Each of the objects has two parts: the source object and the compiled object. (See Figure 2.3.)

The *source* is a syntactic representation of the object that includes the script code. You create and modify it with the painters. The *compiled object* is a binary representation of the object, similar to an .OBJ file in the C language. PowerBuilder creates the compiled object automatically each time you close the painter or issue the Save or Save As command from the File menu. Try to keep your PowerBuilder Libraries (.PBL files) smaller than 800K and with fewer than 50 to 60 objects. Break them into libraries that contain different objects or perhaps different parts of the application. This will make them easier to search as well as maintain. The setup and maintenance of PBLs is discussed in more detail in chapters 3 and 4.

Events and scripts

Like most online applications, PowerBuilder applications are event-driven: users control the flow of the application by triggering events; developers "script" the response to the event. For example, when a user clicks a button, chooses an item from a menu, or enters data into an edit box, an event is triggered. In PowerBuilder, you write scripts that specify the processing that should happen when the event is triggered. These events provide the developer with opportunities to customize processes.

For example, buttons have a Clicked event. You might write a script for an add button whose Clicked event specifies that the data window's current content is validated and used to update the database rows whenever the user clicks the button. Similarly, edit boxes have a Modified event, which is triggered each time the user changes a value in the box.

You write scripts using PowerScript, the PowerBuilder language. Scripts consist of PowerScript commands, functions, and statements that perform processing in response to an event. This script language is easy to learn and its construct to experienced developers will be familiar. The Script development window appears at various points within the object painters. For example, it appears, in the application, window menu function, and user object painters, that clicking the right mouse bottom usually is all that is required. For example, the script for a window button's Clicked event might retrieve and display information from the database; the script for an edit box's Modified event might evaluate the data and perform processing based on the data.

Scripts also can trigger events. For example, the script for a Clicked event in a button might open another window, which triggers the Open event in that window.

Scripting is fairly easy to learn. The constructs are familiar and there are lots of built-in functions that can perform common tasks. PowerScript provides a rich assortment of built-in functions that you can use to act upon the objects and controls in your application. For example, there is a function to open a window, a function to close a window, a function to enable a button, a function to retrieve data, a function to update the database, and so on. In addition, you can build your own functions and user objects to define processing that is repeated during your application to define processing unique to your application.

PowerBuilder applications consist of an assortment of objects—starting with the application object—that responds to user-initiated events. These objects are developed and linked together to provide the developed application functionality. Developers maintain their objects, such as windows and menus, in PowerBuilder libraries (PBL files). When you run your application, PowerBuilder retrieves the object from the library. PowerBuilder provides a Library painter for you to manage your libraries.

When you have completed your application or think you have completed your application, you will create an executable version to post to other users. PowerBuilder provides various ways to package your application for distribution. This will be standardized within larger development projects that require quality assurance.

The Environment

When you start PowerBuilder, it opens in a window that contains a menu bar and the PowerBar. The menu bar can be used to start or delay the current application. The toolbar or PowerPanel (a window sheet contains all of the toolbar items with text) provides access to all of the painters. (See Figure 2.4.) You can open painters and perform other tasks by clicking an icon in the PowerBar.

The PowerBar displays when you begin a PowerBuilder session. The PowerBar is the focal point for developing PowerBuilder applications. From the PowerBar, you can open any of the PowerBuilder painters as well as debug or run the current application, request help, or customize PowerBuilder to meet your needs. The Power-Bar captures in one frame all of the tools required for development. You also can customize the PowerBar. You can add icons for operations you perform frequently. You choose File|Toolbar|Customize to add additional icons.

Figure 2.4 The PowerPanel.

You can switch between the PowerBar, which is a toolbar that you can customize and move around, and the PowerPanel, which is a window that displays a fixed set of icons. The PowerPanel will probably be used in the beginning until a developer becomes familiar with all the pointer icons.

To use the PowerPanel, select `PowerPanel` from the File menu. The PowerPanel displays. You can launch any icon from here. Its description is in the text box and displays if the left mouse button is depressed.

The painters

The icons in the PowerBar (and in the PowerPanel) represent each of the main painters and tools that frequently are used in PowerBuilder. When you are ready to begin development, you should review your object naming convention and standards and proceed to create the application objects. The first object that you create requires the Application painter, in which you specify information about your application, such as its name and the PowerBuilder libraries in which the application's objects will be saved. Additionally any standards for naming and its size can be specified. Basically, a little planning can save a lot of repetitive extra work if the proper standard is used at the beginning of the project. How many PowerBuilder libraries you will need, the use of class libraries, and development standards should be in place early in the project life cycle.

Next you probably would use the Window painter, in which you build the windows used in the application. Here if you were developing a Multiple Document Interface (MDI) application, you might begin by inheriting a class library "window frame" and "window sheet" to build your application frame and sheets. Once the frame is set up, you would use the Menu painter to build the menus (as few as possible; they are expensive) that the windows will use to trigger events, scripts and object functions. In a well-conceived MDI application using the polymorphism, you might have only one menu associated with the application frame.

Having set up the basic start and end of the application using the menu window frame and sheets, you next might use the data DataWindow painter, in which you create objects called DataWindows that access information from the database. The DataWindow painter is the most powerful and comprehensive painter. You develop the SQL to access the data and the style (eight varieties) in which the data is presented to the user for most, if not all, database interaction.

The Structure painter provides you with the ability to define structures (groups of variables) for use in your application. Structures are stencils that can be used to reference a block of storage that contains related data. The columns in a particular database table row could be defined as a structure.

The Preferences painter allows you to set defaults for PowerBuilder properties. This also can be accomplished by editing the PB.INI file. As you become familiar with PowerBuilder and its features, you can ascertain almost everything about the development environment by reviewing the PB.INI file. The Preference painter is a fancy editor used to update PB.INI.

The Help window (the big question mark), which invokes the PowerBuilder online Help system, should be used throughout the development process to provide answers to syntax or semantic questions. The semantics also can be determined by using the Faxback or BBS PowerBuilder information sources. More on this later.

For small development projects using Watcom, XDB, or perhaps OS/2's DB2, the Database painter provides you with a good environment in which you can maintain databases, control user access to databases, and manipulate data in databases. For large development projects where a central DBA is responsible for a database maintenance, the Database painter is a good place to review database definition and other database attributes.

To test your SQL brainstorms, the Query painter lets you graphically define and save SQL SELECT statements for reuse with DataWindow objects.

As you become a mature developer, you will use the Function painter to create functions to perform processing specific to your application. Repetitive processing, done in a number of places within an application, lends itself a candidate to being coded as a function. There are various kinds of functions, ranging from global (for use throughout the application or development environment) to functions that are embedded within the object and can be inherited. Providing the securities settlement date for a particular trade date might be a good candidate for a securities trading application.

The Library painter in which you create and maintain libraries of PowerBuilder objects (PBLs) is similar to the File Manager in Windows. (See Figure 2.5.) It is a

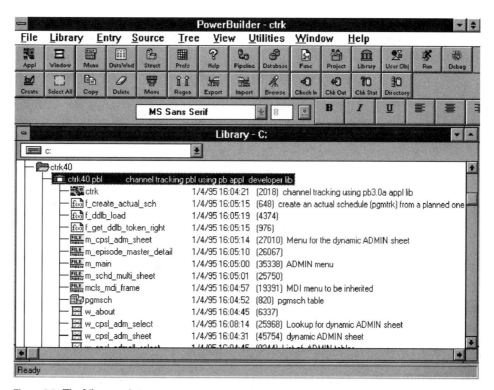

Figure 2.5 The Library painter.

nice place to work from after you have created the majority of application objects and you are refining and testing. You need only double-click to launch or open the object in the painter in which it can be amended (e.g., if you double-click a window object, it is opened in the Window painter).

The User Object painter is used to build custom objects that you can save and use repeatedly. For example, you can create a user object data window control that contains user events and script processing to handle the typical file/database functions such as Insert, Save, Delete, and Query.

To test your application using the development PBLs, use the application Run painter to run your current PowerBuilder application as if it were in a user environment.

The Debug painter allows you to set breakpoints (i.e., points in the application to pause) and run your application a statement at a time. It is similar to IBM's CICS interactive debugging tools, such as InterTest, Expediter, or MicroFocus COBOL/Animator environments. This is an excellent way to become familiar with an application's execution path.

As you will see, the PowerBuilder painters provide a comprehensive development environment. Virtual one-stop shopping for the well-formulated development team can be achieved without procuring a multitude of other products required by competitor development tools.

Using the painters

Most features are common to all painters (for example, opening a PowerBuilder painter or tool). To open a painter or use a tool from the PowerBar or PowerPanel, click the icon in the PowerBar that represents the painter or tool or double-click the icon in the PowerPanel or press Tab to highlight the icon and press Enter.

The PowerBuilder painters behave like other MDI tools like Word or Excel. You can quickly open any of the last four objects that you worked on; PowerBuilder lists them at the bottom of the File menu. To open one of them, open the File menu and select the object.

The PowerBuilder control menu is in the upper-left corner of the PowerBuilder window. The PainterBar control menu is in the upper-left corner of the painter window. Both menus allow you to use the keyboard instead of the mouse to manipulate windows.

The menu bar (under the title bar) lists the top-level menu items for the active painter. Each item on the menu bar has a dropdown menu that lists available items that are related to the top-level item. The items in the menu bar and the items on the dropdown menus vary for each painter. Table 2.1 lists the menu items that display in most painters and summarizes their use. They again function as any other MDI application.

At the bottom of the PowerBuilder window is a MicroHelp line, which PowerBuilder uses to display status information throughout a session. For example, if you want to see what a particular menu item does, select it and read its description in MicroHelp. PowerBuilder 4.0 also includes shadow text, which gives you a smaller function description.

TABLE 2.1 The Menu Items that Display in Most Painters

Menu	Option	Description
File	New	Clear the painter workspace so that you can build a new object (for example, a new window or menu). If there is an unsaved object in the workspace,one in which modifications have been made, PowerBuilder prompts you to save the object before proceeding to open the new object.
	Open	Open an object that was created in the painter (for example, a window in the Window painter). If there is an unsaved object in the workspace, PowerBuilder prompts you to save it before it opens the object.
	Close	Close the painter. PowerBuilder prompts you to save your work, then closes the painter.
	Save	Save the current object under its current name and in the same PowerBuilder library.
	Save As	Save the current object under a new name in the same library or a different library.
	Run	Run the current application. Begin the default application execution just as the user would see it.
	Debug	Debug the current application. Here you can choose stops or breakpoints within the application script processing.
	PowerPanel	Display the PowerPanel
	Print	Print the definition of the current object.
	Printer	Open the standard Windows
	Setup	Printer Setup dialog box.
	Exit	End your PowerBuilder session. PowerBuilder prompts you to save your work, then closes all painters and terminates your PowerBuilder session.
1, 2, 3, 4		Open a recently used object (i.e., the last four that you have worked on).
Edit		Display editing options provided by the particular painter. Arrange the open windows and icons.
Window		Manipulate the toolbars, or activate another open window.
Help		Access online Help.

The workspace within the painter

The painters provide a workspace in which you work with the object that you are building. For example, in the Window painter workspace, you build the window by placing controls. In the Database painter workspace, you work with database tables, indexes, and keys. PowerBuilder provides several toolbars that make working quick and easy. When you open a painter, the Select window for the painter displays, prompting you to specify the object that you want to work on.

Sometimes you want to find something you worked on but forgot where you put it. PowerBuilder provides a browser that you can use to list all objects that contain a specified text string. To use the browser, perform the following steps:

Step 1 Click the Browse button in the Select window. The Browse window displays, as shown in Figure 2.6.

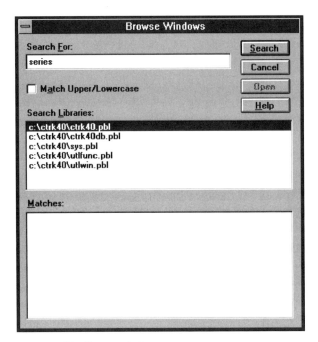

Figure 2.6 The Browse window.

Step 2 To search for an object, enter all or part of the text that you want to locate (the search string) in the top box. Wildcards are not allowed.

Step 3 Specify the libraries that you want searched (all of the libraries in the application's library search path are listed).

Step 4 Click the Search button.

PowerBuilder begins searching for the text. If you are in the Window painter, Power-Builder searches through all of the windows; if you are in the Menu painter, Power-Builder searches through all of the menus; and so on. PowerBuilder searches all of the attributes, scripts, variables, functions, and structures for the search string.

PowerBuilder considers a match to be any text that contains the search string. All of the matches are displayed in the Match box, just like the Windows File Manager. For each match, PowerBuilder displays the matching text and information about where the match was found (for example, the line of script or the attribute of an object or control that contains the search string).

Working with the object

After you locate the object, you can open it directly. To open the object, double-click the object that you want to open or select the object from the list in the Match listbox and click the Open button. You can change the fonts that PowerBuilder uses in some painters and in MicroHelp. In the PowerScript painter and the DOS file editor, this is helpful for setting up defaults for an application or the development environment.

Toolbars make working with PowerBuilder easier and faster. They contain icons that you can use to open painters and tools, manipulate controls, and execute commands. PowerBuilder uses four toolbars:

- PowerBar: The PowerBar has icons for opening painters and other tools.
- PainterBar: The PainterBar has the icons for manipulating components in the current painter.
- StyleBar: The StyleBar has icons for changing the attributes of text such as typeface, point size, and font.
- ColorBar: The ColorBar has icons for changing colors of components in the current painter and for defining custom colors.

You can control whether to display individual toolbars. If you display a toolbar, you can choose where to display it and whether to display text on the icons. Choosing to display text affects all of the toolbars: either all of the toolbars display text or all of them omit text.

You can use the mouse to move a toolbar. To move a toolbar with the mouse, perform the following steps:

Step 1 Position the pointer on empty space within the toolbar.

Step 2 Press and hold the left mouse button.

Step 3 Drag the toolbar and drop it where you want it.

As you move, an outlined box shows the current position and type of the toolbar. When you get close to an edge, the box is a narrow rectangle, which means that the toolbar is located at that edge (for example, the bottom). When you are in the middle area of the screen, the box is more square, which means the toolbar is floating.

After you use PowerBuilder for a while, you will find yourself doing certain operations frequently. You can customize the toolbars with PowerBuilder icons and with icons that invoke other Windows applications, such as the Calculator or Notepad.

To speed up the processing of getting to these operations, you can add, move, and delete icons in the PowerBar and in the PainterBars. You cannot access icons in the StyleBar or ColorBar.

To add an icon to a toolbar, perform the following steps:

Step 1 Position the pointer on the toolbar and click the right mouse button to display the pop-up menu.

Step 2 Select Customize. The Customize window displays. (See Figure 2.7.)

Step 3 Click the palette of icons that you want to use in the Select palette group.

Step 4 Choose an icon from the Selected palette area (you might need to scroll to see all available icons). If you choose an icon from the Custom palette, another dialog box displays so that you can define the icon.

PowerBuilder provides several handy icons that do not display by default on the PowerBar but which you can add. To see what is available, scroll the list of icons and

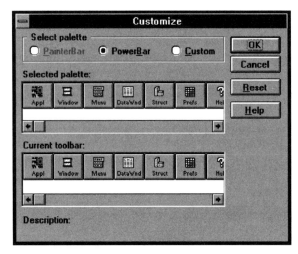

Figure 2.7 The customize PowerBar.

select one. PowerBuilder lists the description for the selected icon.

Position the pointer on your choice, press and hold the left mouse button, drag the icon to the position that you want in the Current toolbar box, and drop the icon. PowerBuilder adds the icon to the current toolbar.

You can add a custom icon to a toolbar. A custom icon can:

- Invoke a PowerBuilder menu item
- Run an executable outside of PowerBuilder
- Run a query or report
- Place a user object in a window or in a custom user object
- Assign a display format or create a computed field in a DataWindow object

PowerBuilder provides a context-sensitive pop-up menu that lists items appropriate to the currently selected object on the screen or the current position of the pointer. The pop-up menu is available everywhere in PowerBuilder. You will find that the pop-up menu makes it easy to work quickly.

For example, if the pointer is on a command button that you have placed in a window in the Window painter, the pop-up menu lists items that apply to a command button.

Perform the following steps to use a pop-up menu:

Step 1 Select one or more objects, or position the pointer on an object or in open space.

Step 2 To select one object, click it. To select multiple objects, press and hold Ctrl, and click each of the objects.

Step 3 Click the right mouse button. The appropriate pop-up menu displays.

Step 4 Click the item that you want. If other windows display, continue supplying information as appropriate.

The PowerBuilder painter windows

Each PowerBuilder painter displays in its own window. Because PowerBuilder itself is an MDI application, you can open several painters at once, and you can open several instances of a painter at once. For example, if you want to see several windows that you are building at once, you open the Window painter several times and specify a different window each time thereby opening multiple windows. Perform the following steps to open each window:

Step 1 Click one of the painter icons in the PowerBar. The Select window for the object (window, DataWindow object, and so on) displays.

Step 2 Select an existing object or begin working on a new object. The painter opens in a window.

Like other Windows applications, PowerBuilder lists open windows as items on the Window menu in the menu bar. The window with the checkmark is the active one. A window must be the active window for you to work in it.

To make a visible window the active window, click anywhere in the window. To make a window that is not currently displayed the active window, select Window from the menu bar, and choose the window from the list.

Tiling (see Figure 2.8) allows you to see the contents of more than one window at once. When you specify Tile, PowerBuilder displays the contents of all of the cur-

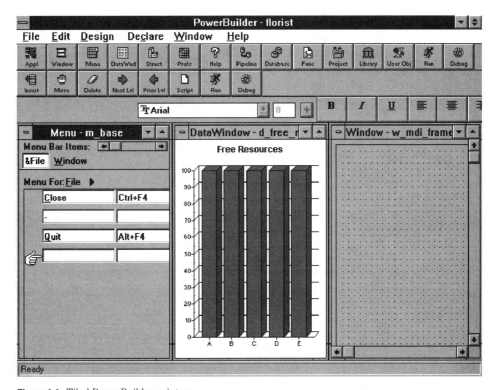

Figure 2.8 Tiled PowerBuilder painters.

rently open windows. For example, you can display the Database painter next to the DataWindow painter and switch between the two as you work on a DataWindow object. You also might want to display more than one DataWindow object at once so that you can see how you handled particular needs in other DataWindow objects.

When you work on a tiled screen, the PainterBar that you see goes with the currently active window. Scroll bars allow you to move to areas of the active window that are not currently displayed.

When you specify Cascade, PowerBuilder displays all of the currently open windows, one on top of another. The currently active window is on top, with its contents displayed. The other windows are behind with their title bars displayed. To make another window active, click in the window's title bar.

Using Help

PowerBuilder has extensive online Help, which is based on the Microsoft Windows 3.*x* Help system. (See Figure 2.9.) Online Help supplements the information in the PowerBuilder manuals and provides both reference and task-oriented information.

To access PowerBuilder online Help, use the Help menu on the menu bar, click the `Help` icon in the PowerBar, click the `Help` button in a window, or press F1.

When you use the Help menu, the `Help` icon, or F1, PowerBuilder displays the PowerBuilder Index. From there, you can move to other topics. When you click the

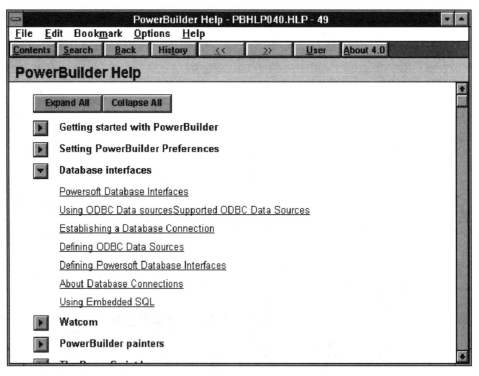

Figure 2.9 PowerBuilder Help.

Help button in a window, PowerBuilder displays information about the window. From there you can move to other topics.

To learn to use online Help, press F1 from anywhere within online Help, then go to the topic "How to use Help."

You can press Shift–F1 to get context-sensitive help in the PowerScript painter and Function painter. Click the About 4.0 button at the top of the PowerBuilder Help window to learn about features that are new in version 4.0.

Building an Application

The following list contains the basic steps that you follow when building a Power-Builder application. After you complete Step 1, you can work in any order. That is, you can define the objects that are used in your application in any order, as you need them.

Step 1 Create the application object, which is the entry point into the application. The application object names the application, specifies which libraries to use to save the objects, and specifies the application-level scripts.

Step 2 Create the windows. Place controls in the window and build scripts that specify the processing that will occur when events are triggered.

Step 3 Create the DataWindow objects. Use these objects to retrieve data from the database, to format and validate data, to analyze data through graphs and crosstabs, to create reports, and to update the database.

Step 4 Create the menus. Menus in your windows can include a menu bar, dropdown menus, and cascading menus. You also can create pop-up menus in an application. You define the menu items and write scripts that execute when the items are selected.

Step 5 Create the user objects. If you want to be able to reuse components that are placed in windows, define them as user objects and save them in a library. Later, when you build a window, you can simply place the user object instead of having to redefine the components.

Step 6 Create the functions and structures. To support your scripts, you probably want to define functions to perform processing unique to your application and structures to hold related pieces of data.

Step 7 Test and debug your application. You can run your application anytime. If you discover problems, you can debug your application by setting breakpoints, stepping through your code statement by statement, and looking at variable values during execution.

When your application is complete, you prepare a release candidate executable. Then you have a dress rehearsal system test, involving the user. If all goes well and the user approves and signs off, you prepare a final executable version to distribute to your users.

This is the PowerBuilder environment in a brief overview fashion. We will revisit the environment as well as the process in greater detail as we move through the next chapters. If you are unfamiliar with Windows-like environments, then this might seem new to you; otherwise, you will see that the PowerBuilder functions just like any other MDI application.

3

Planning Client/Server Development

The purpose of this chapter is to introduce you to the concepts of the client/server computing paradigm and how it affects the development of an application for this environment. We first will provide an overview of client/server, then continue with a explanation of phases of a project and how these phases can be implemented during a project.

Client/Server Computing Overview

In the past five years, the information systems industry has seen the catch phrases *client/server* and *object-oriented* become the most fashionable terms around. The bad news is that, to be considered "successful," you must know them, use them, or be able to implement them. The good news is that, beneath the sheets, the processes involved are not complicated or particularly new and innovative. However, the client/server paradigm will be around for some time; therefore, if you haven't had time to learn about it, now is the perfect opportunity. First, let's get some definitions out of the way, then describe the architecture and strategies involved.

Client/server definition

The *client* (see Figure 3.1) is a consumer of services. It is the process that begins a conversation by issuing a request to be serviced by another process, known as the server process.

The *server* (see Figure 3.1) is a provider of service. It is a process that waits for requests. When it receives a request, it carries out a service and returns a response (or result) to the calling client. A server process is capable of handling requests from several clients processes and is responsible for the management of responses. This relationship can be likened to a customer (client) placing an order (request for service) to a waiter/waitress (server) in a restaurant.

Figure 3.1 The client/server relationship.

The client/server model provides the developer with an opportunity to partition the application and distribute it in several distinct processes. The client/server paradigm has given corporate developers the ability to downsize or rightsize large mainframe host-based applications to relatively inexpensive hardware and software. It also has provided the platform in which to upsize standalone PC applications that have outgrown their single-processor constraints and become inadequate for sharing data across the enterprise.

Don't let anybody tell you that client/server is the "silver bullet" solution to application development, because there isn't one! The transition to client/server actually might take some time before you begin seeing any payback. It might take several years to train the staff needed to reengineer or migrate (basically rewrite) legacy mainframe applications to the client/server platform. You will find that the first application is the hardest, just like anything else that is new. However, if you stick to it, you will find that, by using client/server, you can get:

- *Scalability*—Moving to a more modular architecture enables you to add hardware power to match demand without rewriting software.

- *Usability*—Because client/server and graphical user interface (GUI) go practically hand-in-hand these days, applications have become more usable. The GUI is an excellent environment to handle sophisticated user interfaces (Windows, Mac, and Motif) as opposed to the character-based terminals attached to mainframe hosts.

Tiered architecture

Client/server applications can be architected using one or more tiers. The tiers are typically, but not always, synonymous to the number of nodes involved. These architectures are commonly known as:

- Single tier
- Two tier
- Three tier

Single tier. In a single-tier architecture (see Figure 3.2), the client and server processes are running on the same machine's processor. For example, when you purchase PowerBuilder, it comes with a standalone version of the Watcom SQL database. When you run the "client" example, it connects to the "server" database. The performance of a single-tier production application is linked not only to the design of the application but to the speed of the processor and workstation hardware. They are subject to decreased performance because the processor is being shared by the client and server processes. Some commercial software uses this architecture, such as Microsoft's OLE implementation. When you embed an Excel spreadsheet in a Word document, Excel becomes a server to the Word client.

This type of client/server implementation is suited to smallscale or "start-up" environments. The application can be implemented on a single processor. Then, when the need arises and the software supports it, they can be upgraded to a distributed environment.

Two tier. In a two-tier architectured solution (see Figure 3.3), the concept of the network is introduced. Both the client workstation and server are connected by a network (e.g., TCP/IP, IPX/SPX, or Vines).

The client process running on the client workstation issues its requests via the network to the server process running on a server.

Until quite recently, the two-tier architecture was the more common choice for client/server development, simply because it was straightforward. Typically, the client workstation handles the presentation of information while the server provides the container for and access to the data. The actual logic, or business rules, are handled by one or more of the following: the client (i.e., in PowerScript), the server (i.e., declared constraints such as unique indexes or primary and foreign key relationships), or procedural code such as stored procedures and triggers.

Three tier. A three-tier architectured solution (see Figure 3.4) is very similar to the two-tier solution. They both are implemented across a network with the client process running on a client workstation issuing a request to server process running on a server. However, how the service is carried out is where the third tier comes in. The server that receives the request, in turn, can become a client to another server process. For example, a client process sends a specific request, which is handled by

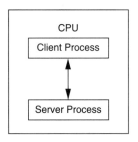

Figure 3.2 Single-tier architecture.

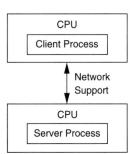

Figure 3.3 Two-tier architecture.

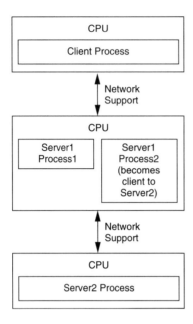

Figure 3.4 Three-tier architecture.

Process1 on Server1. The same client process also could send a different request to Server1, in which Server1 becomes a client process and requests a service from the Server2 process. The Server2 process responds with data to the Server1 Process2, which in turn returns the data to the originating client process.

There are many possible implementations of this type of architecture. In our example, the client process is a PowerBuilder application running on an IBM-compatible PC workstation, the Server1 Process1 is a Sybase SQL Server System 10 engine running on a UNIX machine, the Server1 Process2 is an MDI Gateway running on the same UNIX machine, and the Server2 Process is running on an IBM mainframe retrieving information from a DB/2 database.

A three-level architecture is better suited for enterprise-wide data contained on a (third-tier) host that needs to be accessed by local workgroups, which also store data on their (second-tier) server. The client does not need to know where the data is stored, just the name of the procedures that will interact with the servers that contain the data.

The distribution of data determines the architecture that you will need for your projects. Whatever approach you take, PowerBuilder is capable of addressing it. Now, let's see how the strategy affects the choice of tools, architecture, and development approach for client/server environments.

Processing layer strategy

Client/server implementations can range from slapping a graphical user interface onto an existing application to completely engineering or reengineering a distributed database application. The client/server strategy is the distribution of the process layers (see Figure 3.5) in an application. The process layers being: presentation, business rules or logic, and data access.

The strategies are defined in terms of distributing the layers for presentation, business rules, and data access logic across the client and the server. The *presentation layer* is responsible for all that is involved with the processing of the user interface, including the formatting of information for display. The *business rules layer* is responsible for implementing the rules defined for the data. The *data access layer* handles all processing related to retrieving and maintaining data. Client/server tools, like PowerBuilder, implement a layered architecture to provide maximum flexibility in distribution decisions. This section illustrates some of the more popular client/server strategies, indicating which situations prompt for the use of the strategy.

Distributed presentation strategy (DP).   The distributed presentation strategy (see Figure 3.6) is the simplest form of client/server implementation. The presentation layer is present on the client and the server, which typically is a character-based host mainframe application. This approach provides a quick way to get the much-in-demand GUI front end on an existing application that is too costly to rewrite or that might take too long to reengineer at this point in time.

Using this strategy, the majority of the processing takes place on the server, including a large percentage of the presentation component. The remainder of the presentation component runs on the client, typically using a graphical user interface (GUI). The client probably will need some additional logic that is aware of the navigation of the existing legacy host application. This sometimes is referred to as *screen scraping*, because the host-based screen information is scraped off and translated into the GUI running on the client. This implementation is suited for integrating multiple, existing applications on a workstation or front-ending mainframe applications with PC products (e.g., Microsoft Excel).

Figure 3.5 The client/server processing layers.

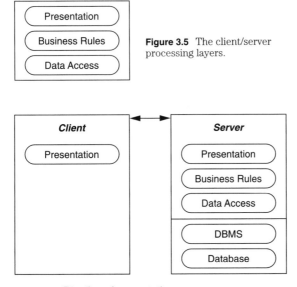

Figure 3.6 Distributed presentation.

Remote presentation strategy (RP). The remote presentation strategy (see Figure 3.7) places all of the presentation logic on the client but leaves the business rules and data access processing on the server. These also are known as *skinny applications*, because they do not take up much space or require substantial processing on the client machine.

This strategy most often is applied where there is a mix of client workstations (e.g., Windows, Mac, and Motif). Because of the similarities among the GUI components, products support a single-source presentation component running on all platforms. The business logic and data access layers remain on the server. This type of implementation is suitable for data-centric or simple transaction processing, with no database validation on the client or low-powered client workstations.

Distributed business logic strategy (DBL). The distributed business logic strategy (see Figure 3.8) can be complicated by the need to synchronize the business rules processes running on both client and server. The data remains server-based. This type of implementation is suitable for a mix of data- and presentation-level processing, complex processing demands, or downsizing an existing mainframe application.

Remote data management strategy (RDM). The remote data management strategy (see Figure 3.9) has all of the application running on the client, but the data remains on the server.

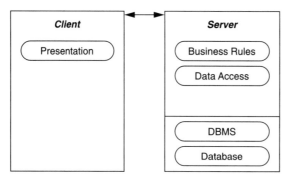

Figure 3.7 Remote presentation.

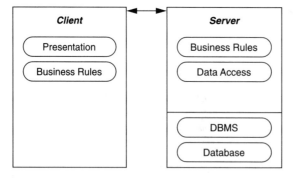

Figure 3.8 Distributed business rules.

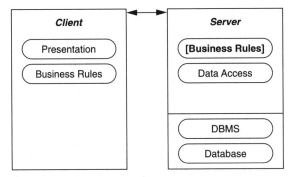

Figure 3.9 Remote data management.

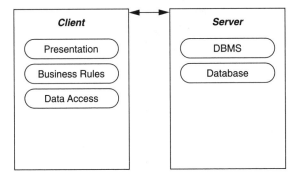

Figure 3.10 Distributed data management.

It is a common model for two-tiered client/server applications that are driven largely by the capabilities of common tools. Depending on the DBMS in use, there might be some business rules running on the server, as triggers and stored procedures.

This type of implementation is suitable for powerful workstations or presentation oriented processing.

Distributed data management strategy (DDM). In the distributed data management strategy model (see Figure 3.10), the data is stored on several servers and can be split across the client and the server. The distribution model used and the complexity of the transactions will determine how complex distributed database implementation will be.

This type of implementation is suitable for naturally segmented usage and storage of data or simple, single-location, single-table updates.

Technology highlights

The technology that has been made available in the last five years is largely responsible for attracting corporations, small businesses, and individuals and leading them all down the client/server pathway. Powersoft, and to a large extent David Litwack, recognized the picture early on and positioned the company for the new order. We now are going to review the technology highlights that are the major reasons for the success of client/server computing today.

The graphical user interface (GUI). A graphical user interface is an essential part of most client/server systems. The user interface is the external view of the system as it is presented to the user of the system. The appeal of the user interface is constrained by the presentation system (e.g., MS-Windows, OS/2 PM, and OSF Motif), the development tools (e.g., PowerBuilder, SQL Windows, and Visual Basic), and the visual painting skills of the developer. However, the development tool might not exploit the presentation system to its fullest. Similarly, an inexperienced designer will not get the best from the tool.

A good GUI is easy to learn, satisfying to use, effective for the task, and consistent in appearance and interaction, with the same look and feel as other popular GUIs (e.g., Word and Excel). Other design features should prevent the user from making errors, put the user in control, and above all be intuitive. Ugly GUIs make a product much harder to sell and less pleasurable to use.

Some additional considerations for GUI design are:

- Accommodate unskilled or infrequent user

- Give immediate feedback

- Permit reversible actions

- Display descriptive and helpful messages

- Use of symbols and visual metaphors (icons and toolbars)

- Aesthetics

- Proportion

- Typography

- Use of color

For further reading on graphical user interface design, see *Microsoft Application Design Guide* and *CUA91 Guide to User Interface Design*.

Distributed intelligent database. Data often has both localized and global use. Distributed database provides the opportunity to service both needs. Distributed database technology provides the ability for a single logical database to reside across a network on several computers. By putting data closer to where it is used, you will reduce network traffic and improve throughput.

The biggest issue is in the processing of transaction updates. There are currently two methods for distributed update:

- *Two-phase commit* is an approach where the distributed nodes all coordinate to either accept or reject the updates together. The overhead of ensuring that all databases are updated simultaneously usually has an adverse effect on the performance.

- *Replication* is an approach where the computer that initially accepts the transaction takes responsibility to replicate it on the other databases. There is a lag before all databases are consistent and a storage overhead. However, performance is considered better using this approach.

In addition, most of today's database management systems have some form of procedural intelligence in the database, in the form of triggers or stored procedures. This processing logic is separate and distinct from the programs that invoke it. A *trigger* is a piece of processing logic that is not explicitly called by a program. It is initiated by an action, such as an insert, update, or delete on a table within the database. It typically is used to enforce referential integrity so that you cannot delete a customer that has outstanding orders. A *stored procedure* is a function written in SQL that is explicitly called by a program to retrieve and/or maintain information in the database.

Networks. When several computers are involved in processing, the network is an essential component, providing the means to link them together. In a client/server architecture, a local area network often connects a workstation to file or data services running on local servers. The architecture also might include a wide area network linking local area networks together.

End-user tools. Utilizing the power of the desktop should include empowering the users to satisfy some of their own needs through end-user computing. This includes giving the user access to data on the server by means of tools like Forest & Trees or Microsoft's Excel (via MS query and ODBC), providing reporting against server data.

Desired characteristics

To be successful in client/server development, you also have to pay attention to areas that might or might not have been stressed to be that important. These can be summarized into the following: consistency, stability, quality, usability.

Consistency. The single greatest factor that contributes to user satisfaction is consistency. A consistent but weak interface design is preferable to an excellent but inconsistent one. Users expect that the same types of actions will occur in the same way each time they encounter them. That is not always true within a system. However, the challenge is to provide not only one consistent system, but also a consistent work environment. That means consistency across systems and the other tools that the user accesses.

Consistency is provided for in the method through the planning stage and by means of a new approach to user interface design. The planning stage provides a cross application view of client/server development. The design approach (i.e., visualize, abstract, and detail) ensures consistency within an application by maximizing reuse and inheritance.

Stability. Client/server technology still is relatively immature. This, combined with possible wide distribution, creates a fragile environment. The distribution also adds complexity in providing support and analyzing breakdowns. Therefore, it becomes the responsibility of the designer to build stability into the system.

Designing applications for a perfect world where the business always works as expected and the technology always performs as promised is easy but unreal. Creating stable applications means anticipating problems and expecting the unexpected. Throughout the methodology, you address integrity checking, risk analysis, and stability design. In analysis, you collect business rules and also examine the resilience of the business model to future change. In design, you implement the integrity rules (sometimes twice to cater for end-user access and front-end checks), you introduce design integrity constraints, such as referential integrity checks, and, in stability design, you specifically examine and correct for weaknesses of client/server implementations.

Quality. Quality is an essential attribute for all applications; however, it takes on a special meaning in a client/server implementation. This is due primarily to the complexities involved in distributing and upgrading the applications.

Changing a mainframe application is relatively simple. New code can be installed on the mainframe overnight, and everyone has access to it in the morning. Perhaps there is a need to reorganize the database, and that can be done over the weekend. Translate that into a distributed client/server environment, and the increase in complexity is dramatic. The code must find itself to 400 workstations at 20 sites nationwide; each site has a piece of the distributed database.

These demands require that you minimize the number of software releases and that each release is of high quality. Quality is achieved by applying a robust methodology and testing the quality at each point in the process.

Usability. In spite of the emphasis placed by product vendors on cost savings, the lead time to realize the benefit for most organizations is lengthy. Due to a combination of learning costs, the need to migrate from existing hosts, and the costs of installing new hardware and software, it can be up to three years before promised savings materialize. Short-term benefits are realized from the enhanced usability of the applications. A client/server application can improve user productivity and enjoyment by providing the user with:

- A graphical user interface (GUI), which provides for easier manipulation and access to information
- Integration of information and processing with familiar desktop tools (e.g., MS Word for Windows or MS Excel)
- Easier access to data resident locally to the user
- Consistency in the user interface across applications and tools
- Access to and analysis of data through end-user tools and executive information systems

Unfortunately, these benefits do not come automatically. A client/server tool does not guarantee good GUI design; an intelligent DBMS does not in itself imply data that the user can access. Usability must be a focus for the development team and of the development method.

If you roll out an application without paying special attention to these characteristics, you might find that what should have been a success can quickly become an embarrassment.

Other considerations

Distribute the process, not processes. There have been distributed systems before the emergence of the client/server architecture. Digital Equipment Corporation built its reputation on real-time and distributed applications. IBM's midrange System 38 and AS 400 were used regularly to implement distributed systems. In these previous generations of commercial applications, distribution usually indicated that separate processes were being executed on different processors. In other words, the application was distributed.

In a client/server architecture, it is a single business process itself that is distributed. A single process now can run on different machines. This brings some new design challenges and issues.

Objects and events. In the client/server methodology, you examine objects and events in both analysis and design. There are two primary reasons:

- Object and event analysis permits you to model real-world concepts in your analysis. This in turn allows you to base the user interface on real-world concepts. Most experts in the field agree that this is the best basis for a graphical user interface.
- Leading client/server development tools support class hierarchies and inheritance in design. Using an object and event approach maximizes the use of those tools.

Business rules. You use business rules as an analysis technique in the client/server methodology. This replaces the older and more traditional action diagram or structured English representation of business logic. Business rules have the advantage of being not only a more modular representation of business facts, but also simpler for businesspeople to review and refine.

The modularity of business rules provides a distinct advantage in a client/server methodology. It provides you with the flexibility to decide at the design stage where you will implement the rule (i.e., on the client, on the server, or on both). The classification of rules also guides you in deciding where the rule should be implemented.

Application suitability

Client/server is a wonderful technology. However, in spite of its power and capabilities, it is not a panacea. There are some application characteristics that suggest a client/server solution, and some that are risky to implement with client/server technology. In other words, some applications play to client/server strengths while others are at risk from its weaknesses. It is certainly worth acknowledging those strengths and weaknesses.

Some of the strengths of client/server technology are:

- Graphical presentation
- Integration of application and end-user tools
- Access to shared data
- Download for local analysis
- Single record updates

Some of the weaknesses of client/server technology are:

- Complex or long update transactions
- Distributed transaction update
- Very large database support on servers

The following application types are ranked by increasing risk in a client/server environment. The lower numbered applications are more suitable for client/server development with today's technology.

1. Information retrieval
2. Information analysis
3. Image and graphic presentation
4. Simple (single table) transaction update
5. Multimedia presentation
6. Multitable transaction update
7. Long transaction update
8. Distributed database update

Client/Server is here to stay for the long run.

The Phases of a Project

One of the ways to deliver a quality product is to follow a procedure (or methodology) that has proven to be successful at producing a quality product. There are many methodologies available that lead you through the life cycle of planning and executing application development. However, the essence of them all can be summarized into the following list of tasks to be carried out:

- Planning
- Analysis
- Design
- Construction
- Testing
- Implementation
- Maintenance

Now, each methodology probably has a different name for any one or all of these tasks, but they basically happen in some fashion. *Methodologies* are a documented path detailing what to do, how to do it, and what is delivered at each point. There is no ultimate methodology, but actual experience of implementing a methodology, and continuously refining and improving it with feedback, will result in the best methodology to suit your needs.

For the purposes of continuity, what follows is a brief description of these tasks, then we will examine how these tasks are carried out using traditional and contemporary techniques for application development.

Planning

This phase of the project is where you should determine the scope and objectives and draft the plan for the overall project. This plan is subject to change, and this is to be expected, especially if the development group is new to client/server and/or unfamiliar with the business process of the business area.

Understand the existing system. The existing business process does not necessarily have to involve computers. It could be a collection of very detailed manual operations that are carried out by individuals of various skill levels. The reason that more advanced technology is brought in is because it is widely accepted as a means to make a business more efficient, provide a better service, and therefore become more profitable. However, to suggest a new system to replace the old, you need to know and document as much as possible about the business and its existing systems.

Determine requirements. The task of determining requirements, or information gathering, typically is achieved when the systems people meet with or interview the business clients to discuss what the clients want in a new system. The meeting interview generally will flow from the description of what currently happens to what they would like to see happen with a new system and why they think it will make their jobs easier. Unfamiliar terminology or familiar words used in an unfamiliar way should be clarified when they are encountered. It might be a little difficult to begin with, especially when you have people without any knowledge of the business process. However, it will help if everybody starts to use the same words to describe the processes involved.

Technical architecture analysis. During the planning stages, you evaluate the current platform and plan for the future technical environments. To facilitate the planning and scheduling of development, it is a good idea to gather some information to quantify the project. This information can be gathered during the life of the project but normally is started during the business analysis phase. To assist in the technical evaluations, you will need to develop pilot or proof of concept applications.

The following is a list of areas that should be discussed and reviewed when developing a client/server application:

- Evaluations for: hardware, software, and the network
- Strategies for: location, migration, operation, and support

Each of these issues must be addressed for the development environment and the production environment. Each point now will be described in more detail.

Hardware evaluations. For hardware, you will need to establish the configurations and the size and type of processor, memory, and storage space for the following items or multiples thereof:

- Workstation
- File server
- Local database server
- Enterprise database server

   If any of the hardware is not currently available, you need to plan for the acquisition of it. To help in the determination of what type and size of hardware you need, you should ask questions like: How big will the database be, in the short, medium, and long term? What are the data requirements? How "big" is each table (rows × columns, including column width)? How much file server space is required for items such as the development tools, user and technical documentation, etc.?

Software. Once again, if any of the software is not currently available, you need to plan for the acquisition of it. The software list also might include standard office productivity tools for word processing, spreadsheets, presentations, electronic mail, and scheduling meetings. You also will need to consider other supporting products, such as version control, entity-relationship modeling, and database query tools. In terms of the PowerBuilder development side, here are some specific areas for consideration:

- What platform and edition of PowerBuilder (Windows, NT, Max, or UNIX)? If it's Windows, are you going to use Enterprise or Desktop?
- During development, where will the PowerBuilder development environment reside: on each developers workstation or in a directory on the shared file server?
- In the production environment, where will the PowerBuilder runtime environment reside: on each client workstation or in a directory on the shared file server?
- How many developers, testers, administration and support people (database server and file server), and end-user clients will be involved?
- What are the printing and reporting requirements? This will cover simple screen printing to possibly large outputs. How do you design a system so that your users don't need that mountain of paper anymore? If they do need a large amount of output on a daily/weekly basis, can you print it elsewhere and deliver it so that you don't tie up the local laser printer?
- You can extend the life of your product if you provide the means to export data for additional analysis with a tool like Microsoft Excel or Lotus 123. You also might want to specifically restrict this kind of process due to the sensitivity of the data.
- Discuss and establish standards to satisfy the security issues for connecting the PowerBuilder application to the database: using standard DataWindow SQL statements, using views and stored procedures to facilitate all (or possibly update) access, using cursors to populate window control and variables, and using embedded SQL.

- Plan the development library setup with respect to the number and purpose of PowerBuilder libraries and procedures for checking out entries under version control and the backup and restore procedures. (We tend to forget to test the recovery procedure until it's too late!)

- Establish development standards: guidelines for naming conventions, screen sizes, fonts, colors, and technical documentation.

- Consider the following application design issues: using and maintaining the Power-Builder catalog of extended attributes via third-party tools, the use of a multiple document interface (MDI) as a standard environment for all applications, the use of object-oriented programming, including inheritance, encapsulation, and polymorphism.

- Avoid global variables by using functions and/or a nonvisual user object to hold these variables.

- Consider the following areas to be candidates for creating common functions or objects: providing runtime context-sensitive help, application/menu/window-level security, a common login screen, and simple but familiar error handling and problem reporting in the event that something goes wrong in the production environment.

Network infrastructure. The network plays an essential part in the success of a client/server project. The product might perform perfectly under laboratory conditions and be rolled out, then have performance that is something less than desired. If you have any network engineers within reach, you should involve them from the start of the project to help with the prediction and resolution of network traffic bottlenecks. A common resolution to this is to make sure that all of the application is stored on each client machine. That way, the network isn't being flooded with requests to load application code (EXEs, DLLs, etc.) onto a client processor. It might pay to try to create a model of the application or consult with the many books that provide formulas for determining the load on networks.

Location strategy. If the project involves the implementation of a distributed system, you will need to consider the other locations and, where necessary, involve support staff in those locations to manage remote database and file servers, including backup and disaster recovery procedures for each site. You also will find it necessary to buy or construct a "watchdog" application that can alert support staff in the event of an impeding or actual failure of a component of the client/server implementation.

Migration and transition strategy. As with all software products, for the users to maximize their use of the new system, you should consider establishing some form of training prior to the production date. This education will help to smooth out the process of production and allow you to reacquaint the users with the proper procedures in the event of any real or perceived failure of the system.

If you are reengineering an existing system, you should consider whether you can and how you will migrate/replicate all of the data that exists to the new system. This might involve writing and testing conversion programs and routines or downloading or transferring the data via some other media and uploading it to the new database.

You should perform this complete exercise on several occasions to iron out any problems and get a feel for how long the process will take when the production date comes around.

Prior to the production date, you might be planning to have a subset of the production users execute a planned test drive of the new system, possibly in conjunction with the prior system, to ensure that the system is performing as expected. This user acceptance period will give you the opportunity to optimize the end-user workstation configurations as well as test the application and runtime environment software distribution techniques.

Operation strategy. Any day-to-day operations that are required in order to make the system flow smoothly, including backups and scheduling the submission of jobs, should be documented in an operations guide.

Support strategy. In the event of a failure in any part of the system, you should format a standard message with as much diagnostic material as possible to uniquely identify where the error has occurred and for what reason. For severe errors, you should consider some kind of paging utility to notify key support personnel.

However, before anything does go wrong, you should consider building in some kind of capture utility that will allow you to gather information, such as transaction usage or frequency. Reviewing this information might provide insight into improving the process the next time around.

Analysis

This task of analysis really is the structuring and organizing of the information that has been gathered by meetings or interviews with the business clients. Again there are many tools and techniques designed to do this: flow charts, information flow diagrams, entity-relationship models, etc. For more information on tools, see chapter 20, "Related Tools, Libraries, and Publications"

Design

The design task is taking the results of the analysis of the requirements and turning this into a detailed description of the new system. What are the platforms, the architecture, and the construction tools? How will it look and feel? What are the subsystems, the inputs, the processes, and the outputs?

Construction

The construction task is taking the detailed design specification and implementing it. At various points throughout the building of the application, some questions or issues will arise that might prompt a small amount of redesign, but this is not uncommon and usually is due to a misinterpretation of the requirements during the design phase. Any large-scale redesign at this point will be a major setback to the schedule for the project, obviously affecting any subsequent planning dates and ultimately the rollout date.

Testing

The testing phase is responsible for ensuring that the product that was built performs the way that the detailed design documentation specifies. There are various testing levels that typically are carried out by specific personnel during the development lifecycle. Each testing level must be successful before the next level is attempted.

At the very lowest level is *unit testing*, where the programmer that writes the code tests the code as per the detailed specification. The next level is *system testing*, where a project leader or systems analyst tests all of the components to see that they interact correctly when combined as a system. The next level is *user acceptance testing*, where the users get to exercise the product in a preproduction mode.

Quality assurance recently has begun being addressed by automated test tools. The more advanced tools today allow you to construct small enough test cases that can be grouped together to test a large piece of functionality. See chapter 13, "Testing and Verifying Applications," for more information on testing.

Implementation

The implementation phase is the rollout of the production version of the system to the client community. This involves tasks like backing up the existing system (data and programs), data conversion, producing user documentation, user training, software distribution (push, pull, e-mail, sneakernet), and the setup of the infrastructure for support of the new system. See chapter 18, "Distributing the Application," for more information on deploying an application to the client environment.

Maintenance

The maintenance phase is a post-production phase for all newly implemented systems. Maintenance can be considered a project of its own. The amount of change that is required will determine how many of the previous tasks should be repeated to implement a revision of the system.

Implementing the Plan

Now we'll review again what a methodology is going to do for us if we follow it:

> For the project to be a success, one must firmly establish the business requirements. By performing business analysis, one will document the data and process requirements. Detailed design will document how the data and process requirements are to be met. Construction will attempt to meet the requirements. Testing will ensure that construction does meet the requirements.
>
> ANON

Traditional application development

Traditional application development (see Figure 3.11) is quite simply the execution of the project tasks, as described at the beginning of this chapter, in an almost serial fashion. In other words, before you start design, you have to complete (or almost

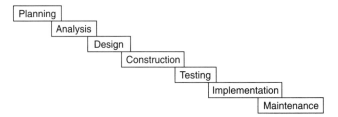

Figure 3.11 The traditional application development method.

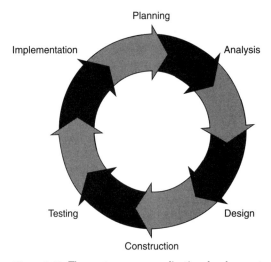

Figure 3.12 The contemporary application development method.

complete) the analysis. You have to have a detailed design specification before you start construction. At the end of the process, you deliver the complete system.

This all seems fairly logical, right? Well, a number of issues arise when you build a system in this fashion. Systems, especially large ones, invariably are delivered late, consequently with budget overruns. By the time the system is implemented, the users' needs have expanded or changed. In other words, what you give them now, they needed last year!

Contemporary application development

Rapid Application Development (RAD) and prototyping (see Figure 3.12) are techniques that allow a group of users and developers to get together and interact with the gathering and implementation of the application objectives or requirements. This will help to ensure that everybody understands what is required to be delivered. The presentations or discussions might range from stepping through a simple sequence of screens and reports to an SQL query involving user- or industry-supplied equations and calculations. There are times when Rapid Application Development (RAD), Joint Application Development (JAD) sessions, and prototyping can fill in the gaps left in the Business Analysis phase. You will find that it is very effective if you begin prototyping before completing the analysis to enable the user/client to better visualize the processes. It should be pointed out that RAD, JAD sessions, and prototyping do not necessarily replace the need for traditional business analysis.

Iterative development

In iterative development, you specify the objectives for a system, then build and deliver a series of partial but increasingly complete implementations. You can start with a shell type of application or prototype. With each successive implementation, you can add functionality.

With this style of development, it is possible to build and integrate and demonstrate the sections of the application in a short space of time, keeping everybody involved interested and providing valuable input. This early and regular integration will reduce the likelihood of encountering major problems near the end of the project. Each iteration allows you to incorporate the latest feedback and refinements from the JAD session. This regular interaction becomes part and parcel of the acceptance process.

With the eventual users of the application getting comfortable and accepting the interface, functionality, and performance during its development, the feedback becomes a part of the quality assurance process. The comments also provide feedback on the usability of the product that is being developed jointly.

During each subsequent JAD session, the prototype features are refined to a point where, piece by piece, the design is accepted. Discussing and incorporating feedback during these sessions is likely to improve the overall success of the project. Because this is the most effective way to agree on what the system should look like in production, more and more corporations have turned to this form of development.

Using a tool like PowerBuilder with RAD techniques allows the development team to quickly turn the prototype into production standard code. During this phase, it makes sense to keep any documentation up to date to prevent any creeping scope. It also is important to continue the JAD sessions throughout the construction and make an effort to record any metrics during the process. These can help to improve the process in review meetings after the project is implemented and before you embark on the next.

4

Setup Development Environment

This chapter explores the tasks involved in setting up the PowerBuilder develop-ment environment. The PowerBuilder development environment can be set up for a standalone developer workstation or in a network environment.

If you are in the Windows environment, there are two editions of PowerBuilder: Enterprise and Desktop. PowerBuilder Desktop includes all of the development painters as well as a single-user version of Watcom's relational database management system Watcom SQL. This lower cost package provides you with all that you need to start developing an application with PowerBuilder. These single-user Desktop appli-cations are fully compatible with the Enterprise edition. The Enterprise edition adds all of the large-scale enterprise-wide DBMS interfaces to the package, the capability to connect to a version control package, such as PVCS, and it also includes the Ad-vanced Developers Toolkit, which contains utilities, an application class library and additional example source code. See chapter 1, "Getting Started," for detailed infor-mation regarding the product line.

When we started to write this book, even the beta version of PowerBuilder 4.0 was not available. The announced platforms for PowerBuilder included Windows, Win-dows NT, Macintosh, and UNIX and were to be delivered in that order over the course of late 1994 and early 1995. Support for OS/2 also was promised but was never an-nounced, but you can run PowerBuilder on any OS/2 platform using WIN OS/2.

The multiplatform approach is practical because the next version of Windows re-sembles the Macintosh interface and UNIX Motif resembles Windows. This additional platform support makes PowerBuilder one of a growing number of cross-platform tools. The term *platform* usually refers to the operating system, but it also implies the processor and hardware architecture. Macintosh, which uses Motorola's 680x0 processor, until very recently was the only manufacturer of its hardware, which is tightly bound to the operating system, System 7/7.5. The Intel chip, the most popular chip for IBM and compatible PCs, can host Windows/DOS, Windows NT, and some im-plementations of UNIX.

For this particular edition of the book, we will discuss and focus on the issues with the installation and operation of PowerBuilder on the platforms available at the time the book was being written: Windows/DOS and OS/2 platforms only. We also will discuss the basic installation and setup for some of the database interfaces. If you are developing an application, your development team should be contemporaneously designing the database. In most systems development efforts, especially the larger ones, it is imperative that the database design be virtually completed before developing the application for production-level deployment. The database should be designed and the set of SQL transactions tested and benchmarked to guarantee some real proof of concept, integrity, and performance.

Planning the Development Environment

To effectively begin any application development, the hardware and software components of the development environment should be in place. Although you might have an overall project plan, as outlined in chapter 3, "Planning client/server development," it makes sense to spend some time adding some detail to the section for the acquisition, installation, and ongoing maintenance of the many elements of the actual development environment.

The plan is for large-scale application development, but can apply to smaller scale projects also. The plan that follows is based upon the assumption that the following list of hardware and software resources are, or are soon to be put, in place:

- One or more database servers (e.g., Sequent, IBM/RS6000, Sun, IBM compatible PC running Windows NT or OS/2)

Database management software (e.g., Informix, Oracle, Sybase, DB/2, Watcom)

- Network file servers with the necessary connections (e.g., routers, bridges, and gateways) and software (e.g., NetWare, Vines) are installed
- Client machines for all developers (e.g., workstation with file space and memory)
- A plan for source management (e.g., PVCS, Endeavor, LBMS, CCC, MKS software)

Sample planning chart

A sample planning chart (see Table 4.1) shows columns for task and subtask descriptions (including any prerequisites) and comments. To use this in your environment, you might add columns for human resources, scheduled completion dates, a status, or anything else pertinent to your environment.

Standards, guidelines, and good practices

A good way to start this task is to develop a framework for and subsequently add to and modify some standards, guidelines, and practices/procedures. One of the biggest mistakes is trying to come up with the ultimate standards guide before publishing it. This will not happen! This needs to be put in place early to help with productivity, es-

TABLE 4.1 A Sample Planning Chart for Development

Task		Subtask
Establish system environment for development		Acquire copies of PowerBuilder Acquire local or LAN disk space for PowerBuilder (approximatey 30MB) Setup LAN directory structure (Source, Documentation, Class) Setup backup and recovery procedures Establish source control procedures Provide copies of PowerBuilder and DB documentation to developer Prepare basic startup document for new developer
Install PowerBuilder	Local:	Run PowerBuilder setup for each developer, including DB connections
	Network:	Run PowerBuilder setup, installing to network location Setup network PowerBuilder icons to each developer Add network PowerBuilder location to PATH Modify WIN.INI, specify PowerBuilder developers INIT PATH location
Install database connection layers for developers		Determine any addressing (e.g., IP) Install transport layer (e.g., named pipes, TCP/IP) Install database connection (e.g., SQL*NET, DBLIB, Open Client) Modify WIN.INI and other configuration files Run additional PowerBuilder scripts for certain DBMSs (SQL Server, SYBASE, IBM) Test the links (e.g., use PowerBuilder, Ping, DBPing)
Configure PowerBuilder environment		Install any third-party class libraries Allocate library for reusable objects and classes Establish and publish standards and naming conventions Establish guidelines document Establish development libraries

pecially with the developers that are getting up to speed with a product like Power-Builder. After all, not everybody can, off the top of their head, remember the best technique for a given situation. The payback for this up-front administration normally comes much sooner than you might expect. The thought process will naturally slow the project down to begin with; however, too often surging ahead with what first comes to mind can come back to haunt you later on. The following are some initial thoughts to resolve:

- What can be leveraged from the organizations current standards?
- What resources can be leveraged?
- How do we implement version control?
- Naming conventions (code and database)
- What standard documentation do we require (user and technical)?
- Database resources and requirements

See chapter 21, "Standards and guidelines," for more information and examples for establishing standards on a client/server project.

Establish development team

Client/server projects, like most projects, require the bringing together of a range of skills to complete the development of an application successfully.

Larger development projects typically will include a variety of people, each specializing in one or more skills that are necessary for the development project. This usually means that the success of a project largely depends on the relationships between the team members and how well their efforts are coordinated. With smaller projects involving one or two people, the relationships still are important; however, for the smaller teams, expertise usually is easier to manage and is the main reason for success.

The skill sets that you'll typically need for most client/server development projects are listed in Table 4.2.

Dividing the work. A large application typically can be broken down into subsystems, with three to four developers per subsystem. It still is important to coordinate

TABLE 4.2 The Skill Sets Needed for Most Client/Server Development Projects

Skill area	Involves
Project management	Decision-making, scheduling, coordination
End-user representation	Understanding of what users want the application to do and how they want to interact with it
Design	Architecting of the application to meet its requirements and to fit well in the computing environment where it is intended to operate
Database administration	Development and management of test and production databases
Network administration	Configuration and monitoring of server computers and the networks that connect client computers to them
Standards and conventions	Establishment and enforcement of conventions and standards for such things as user-interface design, coding style, documentation, and error processing
Reusable object creation	Administration of the application components that developers create with PowerBuilder (with particular attention to facilitating the reuse of these components in multiple applications)
Development	Creation and maintenance of application components with PowerBuilder (which includes painting them and coding logic for them), proficiency with SQL, and familiarity with the client computer's operating system and any other programs to be accessed from the application
User and technical Documentation	Writing of comments, documents, or online Help about the application for reference by developers or end users
Multimedia	Creation of pictures, sounds, or other multimedia elements to be used in the user interface of the application
Quality assurance and testing	Test plan creation, testing and debugging of the application, and bug tracking, reporting, and resolution

the overall project and keep the channels of communication open at all times, particularly when changes in one of the subsystems affect any of the others. It's a good idea for changes to be published, through memos or e-mail, in advance so that anybody who is affected will be aware and can subsequently make the necessary adjustments when appropriate.

Code review and walkthrough. It's a good idea to institute an ongoing code review and walkthrough session during the development of an application. This can be especially helpful on large projects that have several developers with varying PowerBuilder proficiency.

For example, when a particular window or large section of functionality is coded, the code review meeting can be scheduled. At the review meeting, preferably in a conference room, the developer brings multiple copies of all of the scripts and the original design specification for the particular window or section of functionality. If possible, a quick demonstration of the code is given while the group refers to the original design specification to note any differences in functionality. If the group comes across any differences, a decision must be made as to whether to change the specification or the code. If the functionality of the code is wrong, then it must be changed and a meeting rescheduled. If there are no, or very minor, differences, then the group proceeds to look at each piece of the code in detail. There are several purposes to this scrutiny:

- To check that the code looks like it will work as per the specification.
- To examine any new techniques and transfer the knowledge to the whole group.
- To make sure that the code is up to the accepted standards and naming conventions.

For this kind of code review to work, the team must check their egos at the door so that they don't take the criticism personally. The idea is to improve the quality of the product that is being developed. Once the code has passed through this kind of review, it is no longer the sole responsibility of the original coder; it becomes the responsibility of the whole team. There will be less of the traditional "Oh, it was Dave who developed that window" if there is ever a problem with a piece of code later on.

Developers tools. It also is important to make sure that the developers have adequate hardware (e.g., high-end PCs with print capabilities), the appropriate software to produce documentation (e.g., Word, Excel), access to database administration tools (e.g., ISQL, SQL*Loader), and case tools for modelling (e.g., ERWin, LBMS). In addition to the documentation that is provided with these tools, including the Powersoft's InfoBase and Online Books, developers sometimes need access to the wealth of information available electronically through services like bulletin board systems, CompuServe, America Online, Prodigy, and the ever-increasing Internet. These services provide many forums and libraries that can be scanned for possible solutions to issues that arise during development.

Network file server access

If you are in, or plan to be in, a network environment, take some time to plan the directory structures and user groups that will access these directories on the shared file server. You might want to separate the project into coders, testers, and integrators and grant access rights accordingly. You can start with a fairly simple directory structure, such as the one shown in Figure 4.1.

You might want to establish a review committee that is responsible for, and meets periodically to discuss, any modifications to the directory structure.

Database server access

Use roles (DBO, DBA) to govern the access to the data tables.

Source control methods

Version control systems track the evolutionary history of changes to components of a software system and store this history in archives. An *archive* is a repository for the current copy of a file, as well as information leading back to the original copy of the archived file. Every time that you modify a file and check it into the archive, it becomes a new revision. Most version control systems provide disaster recovery protection, as well as a number of management functions to help you manage complex development processes.

Why use a third-party system? PowerBuilder provides check-out and check-in facilities in the Library painter that allow you to manage your objects when working on large, multideveloper projects. However, your organization might want access to the enhanced source control features available in a third-party version control system.

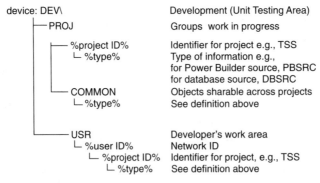

Directory Architecture

```
device: DEV\                    Development (Unit Testing Area)
        ├─ PROJ                 Groups  work in progress
        │    ├─ %project ID%    Identifier for project e.g., TSS
        │    │   └ %type%       Type of information e.g.,
        │    │                  for Power Builder source, PBSRC
        │    │                  for database source, DBSRC
        │    └─ COMMON          Objects sharable across projects
        │        └ %type%       See definition above
        │
        └─ USR                  Developer's work area
             └ %user ID%        Network ID
                └ %project ID%   Identifier for project, e.g., TSS
                   └ %type%     See definition above
```

Figure 4.1 An example of directory architecture.

How does it work? Using a version control system with PowerBuilder lets you track the development history of each object in your PowerBuilder application and restore previous revisions of objects if necessary.

Once you have installed your version control software and the PowerBuilder interface and have registered your PowerBuilder objects with the version control system, all of this can be managed automatically, provided that stringent procedures are followed by all concerned.

Backup and recovery procedures

The client/server environment is not immune to hardware failure and accidents, so design backup and recovery procedures for the network file server (if applicable) and the data server. Once the procedures are in place, make a point of testing them on a regular basis (i.e., once a month or more frequently) so that you can catch problems before they become nightmares. Keep some of the backups offsite; if the building goes up in flames, you still can operate in an emergency replacement installation.

Installing PowerBuilder

When it comes to installing development software, there are a couple of questions about the environment that need to be answered. The answers determine how you will proceed with the installation:

- Is this a standalone or a network installation?
- If it's a network installation, should the development environment be installed on each developer workstation or the network file server?

If this is a standalone installation or if the development environment is to be loaded on each developer workstation, then install PowerBuilder from the CD-ROM or diskettes. If you intend to run PowerBuilder from the LAN, then skip to the "Network File Server Access" section to continue.

Recommended workstation configuration

With the geometric advances in the speed and capacity of computers, workstations become obsolete almost overnight, but your basic hardware and software setup should be as follows:

- 486DX2 66MHz or Pentium processor
- 16MB of memory, depending on operating system (but more is always better)
- Microsoft Windows 3.1/3.11 or Windows NT 3.5
- CD-ROM drive for installation and later access to InfoBase and Online Books
- 3.5" high-density disk drive (necessary for floppy disk installation only)

- 500MB of hard disk drive (Enterprise is around 75MB with all of the options installed)

- Most recent video driver for your monitor

Tuning the configuration for performance. Table 4.3 lists some configuration ideas for the DOS/Windows 3.1 environment. There was not much evidence when this book was being written, but it is hoped that the new PowerBuilder platforms like NT and other operating systems, which support true multitasking, probably will avoid many of the memory problems associated with the PowerBuilder DOS/Windows interface.

Installing PowerBuilder Enterprise for Windows

The PowerBuilder Setup program installs PowerBuilder in the drives and directories that you specify. If a directory does not exist, PowerBuilder will create it.

If you have PowerBuilder on CD-ROM, the master Setup program displays a dialog box that lists the various products that you can install. (See Figure 4.2.) Each product has its own Setup program that is run automatically from the master Setup program when you select the product. If you have PowerBuilder on disks, there are several sets of disks, each with its own Setup program.

Perform the following steps to install PowerBuilder from CD-ROM.

Step 1 Exit any programs that are running, except for Program Manager and File Manager. If you do not, the Setup program will not be able to copy some files, such as OLE DLLs, to your Windows and Windows System directories.

Step 2 Mount the CD-ROM in your CD-ROM drive and run the PowerBuilder Setup program. To run from the Windows Program Manager, select File|Run. To run from the Windows File Manager, select SETUP.EXE in the root directory of the CD-ROM drive.

Step 3 Select PowerBuilder 4.0 (or PowerBuilder 4.0 for NT) from the list of products.

Step 4 Enter your name and your company name in the initial dialog box.

Step 5 On the main screen, check the installation options that you want. The information on the screen will help you make your choices. While the files are being installed, the program might ask some questions or display messages.

If the Setup program cannot copy some files to the specified directory because of file-sharing conflicts, it displays a message telling you where it put the files instead. Make a note of these files so that you can copy them later.

You can have PowerBuilder automatically update your AUTOEXEC.BAT and put PowerBuilder in your DOS path, or you can update your AUTOEXEC.BAT manually. In either case, you must reboot before the changes to your AUTOEXEC.BAT will take effect.

TABLE 4.3 Configuration Ideas for the DOS/Windows 3.1 Environment

Resource	Performance point	Comments
Memory	Use extended memory	Windows does not use expanded memory
	Load drivers in high memory	This frees up base memory, which is memory below the 1MB mark. With DOS 6.0, you have better control over where applications go. MemMaker and other memory managers also can provide help.
	Use disk caching	Use disk caching, and give as much memory as possible to the buffer.
	Stay away from wallpapers or anything that is form over substance	Using a wallpaper as a background can eat up a lot of memory. If you find it necessary to have a background, use a color pattern rather than a wallpaper.
CONFIG.SYS and AUTOEXEC.BAT	Understand what each item in your CONFIG.SYS and AUTOEXEC.BAT means, remove unnecessary items	You should understand the configuration of your machine to control it. Read the DOS and Windows configuration manuals.
Swap files	Use a permanent swap file	Windows knows exactly where the swap file is and how big it is.
	Do not put a swap file or TEMP directory on the network	You will be in constant contention with other network users.
Hard drive	Defragment your hard drive on a regular basis	Use DEFRAG or some other tool
	Performance will be affected by the hard drive speed and the drives interleaf setting	Both Windows and the server are hard drive intensive.
Display	Use the lowest resolution display that will meet your needs	The higher the resolution of the monitor, the slower the application will run.
WIN.INI and SYSTEM.INI	Understand what each item in your WIN.INI and SYSTEM.INI means	There are WRITE files for both of these files. The Windows Resource Kit provides documentation. Note that the 386 enhanced section can greatly affect performance.

You will be asked if you want to create a program group for the PowerBuilder 4.0 icon and other installed components. If you say yes, appropriate icons are added to the Powersoft program group. If the Powersoft group already exists, a new one is not created.

When you have finished installing PowerBuilder 4.0, the Setup program returns you to the initial list of products.

Step 6 To install another product, select it, choose Install, and make the appropriate selections in its Setup list. Repeat this step until you have installed all the products.

Step 7 Reboot your machine to make use of the AUTOEXEC.BAT changes.

Figure 4.2 The PowerBuilder Enterprise Master Setup dialog.

Perform the following steps to install PowerBuilder from disks.

Step 1 Insert Disk 1 of the PowerBuilder 4.0 disk set into your disk drive and run the PowerBuilder Setup program. To run from the Windows Program Manager, select File¦Run. To run from the Windows File Manager, select SETUP.EXE.

Step 2 If requested, enter your name and your company name in the initial dialog box.

Step 3 On the main screen, check the installation options that you want. The information on the screen will help you make your choices. While the files are being installed, the program might ask some questions or display messages.

If the Setup program cannot copy some files to the specified directory because of file-sharing conflicts, typically DLLs in Windows/System, it displays a message telling you where it put the files instead. Make a note of these files so that you can copy them later.

You can have PowerBuilder automatically update your AUTOEXEC.BAT and put PowerBuilder in your DOS path, or you can update your AUTOEXEC.BAT manually. In either case, you must reboot before the changes to your AUTOEXEC.BAT will take effect.

You will be asked if you want to create a program group for the PowerBuilder 4.0 icon and other installed components. If you say yes, appropriate icons are added to the Powersoft program group. If the Powersoft group already exists, a new one is not created.

Step 4 To install additional Powersoft products, insert Disk 1 for the product that you want, run SETUP.EXE as you did for PowerBuilder 4.0, and make appropriate selections.

Step 5 Exit to DOS. Make sure PowerBuilder is in your DOS path, then restart Windows.

Finishing the installation.   If you used the `Advanced` option to specify alternative directories for the Windows and Windows System directories or if the Setup program couldn't copy files there because of file-sharing conflicts, there are some additional steps to complete the installation.
  To move files to your Windows directories:

Step 1 Copy the files in the alternative directories to your Windows and Windows System directories.

Step 2 Edit the ODBCINST.INI file to specify the correct paths for the DLLs for the ODBC drivers that you installed.

Step 3 If the Setup program notified you that it could not copy some files to the Windows or the Windows System directory, copy those files to the expected directories now.

Your DBMS might require additional setup procedures. See "Database Connectivity" for specific information.

Additions to the PATH statement.   The installation routine adds the following directories to your PATH statement:

```
C:\PB4;C:\PB4\EXAMPLES;C:\WSQL40\BIN
```

If you install the C++ Class Builder, the installation routine adds the following entries to the PATH and creates several environment variables:

```
PATH
%PATH%;C:\WATC\BIN;C:\WATC\BINB;C:\WATC\bINW
SET EDPATH=C:\WATC\EDDAT
SET INCLUDE=C:\WATC\H;C:\WATC\H\WIN
SET Watcom=C:\WATC
```

Installing PowerBuilder to run from a LAN

In some organizations, PowerBuilder has been set up for basic evaluation for use in new development. It is stored on the LAN drive/directory probably mapped to you as something like X:\APPS\PB4. This PowerBuilder environment would be a read-only directory containing a model of the .INI files as well as the PowerBuilder software and sample applications. As the execution of PowerBuilder requires write access to certain files, you will have to copy these files to a drive that you have write-access to, either on the LAN or your local C: drive.

The following is an example of what you will have to do to set up PowerBuilder for this kind of installation.

Setting up the developer workstation. Perform the following steps to set up a developer workstation:

Step 1 Set up a directory for PowerBuilder on the LAN (e.g., F:\PROGS\PB4).

Step 2 Copy PB.INI, ODBC.INI and SAMPLE.INI from the model (location = X:\APPS \PB4) to your LAN: HOME or LOCAL:"C". PB.INI contains basic database and user profiles. ODBC.INI contains the location of ODBC database and drivers; ODBC.INI is located in \APPS\PB4\DSD_PB. Place it in your HOME\WINDOWS subdirectory. SAMPLE.INI is an example of an application .INI file and is used by the demo.

Step 3 Update your ODBC.INI to point to your local demo database. This will point at your LAN:HOME or LOCAL:"C":

```
DATABASE=F:\PB4\PBDEMODB.DB
DRIVER=X:\APPS\PB4\WSQLODBC.DLL  (in two places)
```

Make sure ODBC.INI is in your WINDOWS directory (see the example in the next section).

Step 4 Copy the demo database and log to your HOME or "C". The PBDEMODB.DB and PBDEMODB.LOG databases are located on X:\APPS\PB4 and are used by the sample application.

Step 5 Set up a program group for POWERBUILDER (optional). You can use the WINDOWS GRP POWEROF.GRP on X:\APPS\PB4.

- Setup a program item for POWERBUILDER:
  Command line: X:\APPS\PB4\PB040.EXE
  Working directory: X:\APPS\PB4

- Setup a program item for the Watcom database (note the parameter after the EXE is the DEMO DB location):
  Command line: X:\APPS\PB4\DB32W.EXE F:\PB4\PBDEMODB.DB
  Working directory: X:\APPS\PB4

Step 6 Update your WIN.INI to add a POWERBUILDER section. This will point at your LAN:HOME or LOCAL:"C".

```
[PowerBuilder]
INITPATH=F:\PB3
INIPATH040=F:\PB4  (If you are using both PB3 and PB4.)
```

At this point, you are ready to use PowerBuilder. Restart your Windows session and start PowerBuilder. See the Getting Started manual or try the sample application.

You also can use the Advanced Developers Toolkit, if it is installed, by setting up Windows program items within the PB group for:

- PEAR.EXE
- DWEAS.EXE
- PBTIPS.HLP

ODBC.INI example. The following is an example ODBC.INI file:

```
[ODBC Data Sources]
PowerBuilder Demo DB=Watcom SQL
[PowerBuilder Demo DB]
Database=f:\pb4\pbdemodb.db
UID=dba
PWD=sql
Driver=x:\apps\pb4\wsqlodbc.dll
Description=PowerBuilder Demo Database
Start=db32w %d
[Watcom SQL]
driver=x:\apps\pb4\wsqlodbc.dll
```

Installing PowerBuilder in an OS/2 environment

You can install the following Powersoft products under OS/2:

- PowerBuilder 4.0 Enterprise or Desktop InfoMaker

The following OS/2 versions are supported by Powersoft:

- OS/2 Standard Edition Version 2.1 or later (with Win-OS/2 included)
- OS/2 for Windows Version 2.1 or later
- OS/2 Warp
- OS/2 Warp Standard Edition

Note: Install all Powersoft 4.0 products under a Win-OS/2 full-screen session. As you run through the installation, use the following as a checklist:

- PowerBuilder
- Watcom SQL
- ODBC from the Powersoft Database Interfaces option
- Watcom SQL from the Open Database Connectivity Drivers option

To install PowerBuilder for a machine that runs OS/2:

Step 1 Install PowerBuilder on a machine running Windows alone, without OS/2 loaded.

Step 2 Copy the default PowerBuilder directory to the machine with OS/2.

Step 3 Copy the ODBC.INI and ODBCINST.INI files from the C:\WINDOWS directory in the Windows computer to the C:\OS2\MDOS\WINOS2 directory on the OS/2 computer.

Step 4 Copy the ODBC.DLL, ODBCINST.DLL, and MSJETDSP.DLL files from the C:\WINDOWS\SYSTEM directory in the Windows computer to the C:\OS2\MDOS\WINOS2\SYSTEM directory on the OS/2 computer.

Step 5 Copy the WSQLODBC.DLL file, which usually is found in your C:\WINDOWS\SYSTEM, PB4, directory in your Windows computer, to your C:\OS2\MDOS\WINOS2\SYSTEM in your OS/2 computer. *Note*: If the Windows machine is on the network, it might be helpful to copy the previously mentioned files to a directory on the network for others to download.

Step 6 Make sure your C:\OS2\MDOS\WINOS2, C:\OS2\MDOS\WINOS2\SYSTEM, and PB4 directories are in your OS/2 path.

Step 7 Edit the ODBCINST.INI file and make sure that the [Watcom SQL] section has both a driver and setup pointing to the location of the WSQLODBC.DLL file, which should be in your C:\OS2\MDOS\WINOS2\SYSTEM directory. For example:

```
[Watcom SQL]
DRIVER=C:\OS2\MDOS\WINOS2\SYSTEM\WSQLODBC.DLL
SETUP=C:\OS2\MDOS\WINOS2\SYSTEM\WSQLODBC.DLL
```

Step 8 Edit the ODBC.INI file and make sure that the [Watcom SQL] and your [database] profile name section have the driver pointing to the location of the WSQLODBC .DLL file, which now should be in your PB4 directory. For example:

```
[Watcom SQL]
DRIVER=C:\OS2\MDOS\WINOS2\SYSTEM\WSQLODBC.DLL
...
[PowerMaker Demo DB]
Database=c:\pm4\pmdemodb.db
UID=dba
PWD=sql
DRIVER=C:\OS2\MDOS\WINOS2\SYSTEM\WSQLODBC.DLL
Description=PowerMaker Demo Database
Start=dbstartw %d
```

The previous information is based on an installation setup at a client site. OS/2 is an unsupported platform for Powersoft products. This installation will work but is subject to changes for new releases.

Installing Powersoft 4.0 products under an OS/2 single-boot system. Your system can boot up only under OS/2. You can run Windows sessions under OS/2. The installation is simple.

Step 1 Run SETUP.EXE on Installation Disk 1 or the root directory of the CD-ROM.

Step 2 Refer to FaxLine document 4012 as the software is installed.

Installing Powersoft 4.0 products on an OS/2 dual-boot system. Dual boot systems allow the user to boot into DOS—just like a Windows PC—or OS/2—where Windows runs in a Windows session.

Running a machine with the dual-boot architecture requires two AUTOEXEC.BAT files, AUTOEXEC.DOS and AUTOEXEC.OS2, which reside in the \OS2\SYSTEM directory. When you choose the environment, the OS/2 boot manager copies the appropriate AUTOEXEC.BAT file from this directory into the root directory prior to continuing the boot.

To install into a dual-boot environment:

Step 1 Run SETUP.EXE on the Installation Disk 1 or the root directory of the CD-ROM.

Step 2 Refer to FaxLine document 4012 as the software is installed.

Step 3 If you plan on running any Powersoft products from both boot environments (OS/2 and DOS/Windows), edit the AUTOEXEC.BAT in the \OS2\SYSTEM directory and add \WSQL40\WIN, \PB4, and \IM4 (if using InfoMaker) to the PATH statement.

PowerBuilder 4.0 and the Watcom Database Engine. The PowerBuilder 4.0 and InfoMaker install programs copy the new Watcom 4.0 engine (also called DB32W .EXE) and its associated files into \WSQL40\WIN. If, while trying to connect to a Watcom 4.0 data source in PowerBuilder 4.0 or InfoMaker, you receive the following error:

```
IM003: [Microsoft][ODBC] Specified Driver could not be loaded.
```

This means that the Powersoft product can't find DB32W.EXE, the default Watcom 4.0 engine. You need to edit the current active \AUTOEXEC.BAT in the root directory and add \WSQL40\WIN and \PB4 to the DOS PATH statement, assuming you used the default installation directory names. Then you need to change the Watcom 4.0 engine for running under OS/2. Use the Watcom 4.0 16-bit engine dbstartw instead of db32w. If you try to connect using db32w, you will receive the following error dialog:

```
Application Error
db32w caused a GPF in module [unknown]
04EF:8E82DB32w will close.
```

This will cause your Windows session to close. Edit the ODBC.INI file in your \WINDOWS directory and change the start= entry for your Watcom 4.0 database profiles:

```
[Powersoft Demo DB]
start=db32w -d -c512
```

The default location for the ODBC.INI file is in the \OS2\MDOS\WINOS2 directory, if you have the Standard Edition of OS/2 2.1 or later, or in \WINDOWS, if you're using OS/2 for Windows or OS/2 Warp.

Other setup tasks

This section provides information about other situations in which you might use the Setup programs.

Creating install disks from the CD-ROM. If you have purchased a license for Power-Builder that allows multiple copies, you might want to create disks to install individual components on the CD-ROM. Powersoft provides a DOS batch program called MAKEDSKS.BAT for creating install disks.

To create installation disks for a Powersoft product:

Step 1 Find the DOS batch program MAKEDSKS.BAT on the CD-ROM.

Step 2 At the DOS prompt, run the program to display the instructions.

Step 3 Run the program again, specifying the product for which you want disks. The program will tell you how many blank formatted disks you need.

Adding options later. To add an option to your PowerBuilder installation:

Step 1 Run the Setup program as described in "Installing PowerBuilder Enterprise for Windows."

Step 2 Select the product, options, and suboptions that you want to install. You do not need to select the PowerBuilder option again—it already is installed.

Installing maintenance fixes

There are some typical problems that you should be aware of when testing and deploying multiple applications. This is important in the development environment as well as when users have multiple PowerBuilder, PowerMaker, or PowerViewer environments in addition to Powersoft applications running on the same PC.

Use RBRAND to make sure your executable is pulling in the right DLLs. Remember, to find DLLs, Windows searches in the following locations:

- Current directory

- Windows directory or the directory where WIN.COM was run from WINDOWS\ SYSTEM directory or the directory where GDI.EXE is, if different from the location in the previous item

- Directory that the .EXE file was run from, if different not the current directory
- DOS PATH, searching local directories first, then network directories

This allows you to view the DLLs that the executable will pick up *unless you're running another application* using different revision DLLs.

If you're deploying multiple applications on the same system but with different revision DLLs or perhaps even sometimes in development, you can run into several problems. To avoid these, it's best to have one set of DLLs on the system to be accessed by both applications.

While testing new DLL patches for PowerBuilder, if you exit PowerBuilder normally (without GPFing), the DLLs are unloaded so that you can stay in Windows and upgrade your DLLs. To test any new patches, it probably is safer to exit Windows to make sure that you unload/load the correct DLLs.

The program RBRAND (delivered with software releases and patches) doesn't check what currently is in memory—it basically checks the PATH for the DLLs that your executable will pick up if no other PowerBuilder application has loaded DLLs into memory. So it's not always accurate in an environment where multiple Power-Builder applications are running (unless they both source the same DLLs). The correct way to install RBRAND is to place it in the same directory as your executable so that it "sees" the same DLLs.

Database Connectivity

Powerbuilder comes with support for connecting to a database via ODBC or native (optimized) connectors.

ODBC connections

The ODBC Configuration can be performed from the Database painter in Power-Builder. This can be done as follows:

Step 1 Start the Database painter.

Step 2 Select the Configure ODBC option from the File menu. PowerBuilder then will display the Configure ODBC Selection dialog, which contains two list boxes. One is labeled `Installed Drivers` and is a list of the ODBC drivers that currently are installed. The other is labeled `Data Sources for Selected Drivers` listbox and is a list of the data sources defined for the driver selected in the Installed Drivers list.

Step 3 Select Watcom SQL from the list of Installed Drivers.

Step 4 To edit an existing data source, click the command button titled `Create`. To edit an existing data source, select the data source and click the `Edit` command button. A window titled `Watcom SQL ODBC configuration` will display. Data specified in this window is used to connect to the database.

For example, if PSDEMODB.DB is started on the server as follows:

```
DB32 PSDEMODB.DB
DBSERVER DEMO
```

then the Watcom SQL ODBC configuration data source should read as follows:

```
Data Source Name:  Powersoft Demo DB
Description:       Powersoft Demo Database
Database Information:
User Id:    dba
Password:   sql
Database:   Demo
Database Startup:
Local:      O
Network:    *
Execute:    O        dbclienw %d
```

Note that the dbclienw %d cannot be edited. The %d references Database: Demo.

Native database connections

PowerBuilder can be used to access a number of database servers, including but not limited to SYBASE SQL Server System 10. Even before the merger, PowerBuilder and SYBASE functioned well together. PowerBuilder also connects to just about every SQL-based DBMS. Each first-time organizational connection probably will present some challenge to get it working well. The real interesting part is how to detail PowerBuilder and the DBMS to ensure stabilized and reliable connections that provide the required throughput. Also of importance is the network that provides the pathway of data from and to database server and client workstation.

The following items describe the basic software setup tasks to allow PowerBuilder to access SYBASE. (Note that the following is an example using DBLIB, and not CTLIB.)

Step 1 Set up a directory for SYBASE NETLIB DLLs. For example, set up your own C:\SYBASE\BINR directory or set up a PATH to X:\APPS\NETLIBS. The later is preferable for consistency and ease of software upgrade.

Step 2 Update your WIN.INI (i.e., to identify your SYBASE database). An example is stored on X:\APPS\PB4\WINSYB.INI. Windows is aware of SQL servers—whether they be SYBASE, ORACLE, etc.—by virtue of an SQLSERVER section in the WIN.INI.

```
[SQLSERVER]
DSQUERY=WDBWSKTC,132.32.119.252,15000,urgent
; WINDOWS database socket attach for UNIX server
; includes the IP address and port number of the server
SYBDSD1_WSK=WDBWSKTC,132.32.119.252,15000,urgent
```

Step 3 End and restart your Windows session. Start PowerBuilder and set your preferences. Preference setting is done by clicking the painter of the same name and choosing Database. The settings that you choose will be stored in your PB.INI file. You also can build a profile for each database if you use more than one.

The settings for SYBASE are as follows:

```
DBMS=Sybase
Vendor=Sybase
Database=databasename
UserId=databaselogonid
DatabasePassword=
ServerName=sybdsd1
DbParm=
```

```
Prompt=0
StayConnected=0
```

DbParm is probably the most underrated parameter. Here, if you are familiar with the particular DBMS specifics, you can set parameters to help performance, target PowerBuilder catalog tables, and provide what specific database features you will need to make the application viable. For example, DbParm allows the user to choose special features of SYBASE operation (e.g., `DbParm="Async=1"` indicates asynchronous operation of SYBASE).

Note: StayConnected has important ramifications. The default is 1, and this causes PowerBuilder to open the database connection the first time that you need it and holds it until PowerBuilder is exited. A setting of 0 causes the database connection to be dropped when you close a painter or a compile is complete.

Step 4 Set up a database profile for the SYBASE database (optional). Get into the Database painter, choose `Connect` and `Setup`, and enter the following parameters:

```
[Profile Sybase System 10]
DBMS=sybase
Database=databasename
UserId=databaselogonid
DatabasePassword=
LogPassword=
ServerName=sybdsd1
StayConnected=0
DbParm=
Prompt=0
```

Step 5 Run the SQL to create the PowerBuilder special stored procedures (SP). These SP's are used by PowerBuilder to access the PowerBuilder and SYBASE system catalog tables to provide table, column, index, etc. info for PowerBuilder database administration and DataWindow painters. This needs to be done one time only, and you should have one of the Database Administrators do it as soon as possible. You must execute this SQL with the proper permissions.

Network data server access

Network support layer. There are several ways to access a database server that is connected to a network. The connection can be:

- Named pipes, which are popular for MS SQL Server.

- TCP/IP, which are popular for UNIX bases database server (e.g., Oracle and Sybase). With the TCP/IP Transport Layer, you also will need the database network support layer (e.g., WDBNOVTC).

Database layer. The database layer is unique and should be provided by each DBMS vendor. Here are some examples:

- W3DBLIB for MS SQL Server or SYBASE SQL Server 4.9.*x*

- WCTLIB for SYBASE SQL Server System 10

- SQL*NET for Oracle

WIN.INI or other .INI changes.   There also will be changes to initialization files. For example, you will need to add an [SQLSERVER] section to your WIN.INI if you are connecting to SYBASE SQL Server 4.9.*x*. For example:

```
[SQLSERVER]
DSQUERY=wdbnovtc,199.199.199.199,1024,URGENT
```

Network Considerations

This section focuses on how to set up PowerBuilder for projects that have more than one developer. Project might have multiple developers because the pilot project now is approved and additional developers are coming on to the project. It is going to be very important to PowerBuilder developers that you all work from the same playbook from now on. Make time for teamwork. The areas that we cover in this chapter are by no means all-encompassing, but our intention is to get the juices flowing and the brain cranking. The areas are:

- Tips for NetWare environments
- Multideveloper library setup
- Sharing Online Books and InfoBase CD-ROM information
- Starting PowerBuilder

Tips for NetWare environments

If you use Novell NetWare, use FLAG * . PBL +S. This allows more than one developer to save (write) to the PBL if another developer is using the PBL at the same time.

If you are having file I/O problems with PowerBuilder libraries that seem to occur *only* when the PBL is running on the network (i.e., the problem does not occur when PowerBuilder PBLs are installed locally) and you are running Novell, you need to make sure that you have installed all of the latest Novell drivers for Windows 3.1.

Multideveloper library setup

In multideveloper environments, where teams with many members are involved with the coding and testing of objects and libraries, version control is an important consideration. There are several third-party version control systems available with interfaces to PowerBuilder. See chapter 20, "*Related Tools, Libraries, and Publications,*" for more information.

To provide the team with greater security throughout the development life cycle, PowerBuilder includes check-out and check-in functionality for the PowerBuilder libraries, it is suggested that you take advantage of these capabilities. Use of the check-out and check-in functionality also includes other features designed for the protection of the development environment. Objects that have been checked out cannot be checked in when an application using that object is currently being executed. Although this feature helps to maintain the integrity of the development library, it can be frustrating trying to find out who is running the executable and asking them to stop the application so that you can check-in your work. In addition, it is recommended that you set up separate and discrete library environments for unit test (DEV), system test or quality assurance (QA), user acceptance test (UAT), as well as an actual copy of what ultimately will be migrated to production (PROD).

An example of the initial setup might be:

- The LAN administrator sets up the following directories on the network:

  H:\   *This would be distinct for each developer.*
  I:\QA   *This would be common to all developers.*
  J:\UAT   *This would be common to all developers.*
  K:\PROD   *This would be common to all developers.*

  Note: The logical mapping of H:\ would physically map to:

  ```
  ServerName/VolumeName:DEV/User]])/PBDir
  ```

  For example:

  GIANT/VOL1:DEV\ALLENP\PBSRC

- Designate two members of the team with the role of library managers (librarians). Only the librarians have the *write* privileges to the UAT and PROD libraries. They are responsible for moving the system-tested (quality-assured) objects from the QA directory to the UAT directory, ready for user acceptance testing. When this is completed satisfactorily, the objects are moved from UAT directory to the PROD directory, ready for production. The PROD libraries ultimately contain the final versions of the libraries that will be moved out to the production environments.

- The librarians create the new PowerBuilder libraries on PROD, UAT, and QA.

- The developers create their own work in progress library on H:\ and set up their library search paths. The following example assumes that there are three production libraries (applib1, applib2, applib3) in the project, there could be many more:

  H:\UNIT.PBL
  I:\QA\QA.PBL
  J:\UAT\UAT.PBL
  K:\PROD\APPLIB1.PBL
  K:\PROD\APPLIB2.PBL
  K:\PROD\APPLIB3.PBL

An example of the development procedures might be:

- *If the object exists already:*

  1. The developer requests a librarian to copy the object from the relevant PROD library to the QA.PBL.

  2. The developer then checks-out the object from the QA.PBL to their H:\UNIT .PBL and makes the necessary changes, then tests them.

  3. After successful testing, the developer checks-in the object back to the QA.PBL.

4. The system test/quality assurance team then runs the regression test(s) for the areas affected by the change (or better still has an automated testing tool that will run regression tests for the complete application overnight)

- *If the object is new:*

1. The developer creates the object in H:\UNIT.PBL, then tests it.

2. After successful testing, the developer moves the new object to the QA.PBL.

3. The system test/quality assurance team, then develops an appropriate test or tests for the new object (possibly in conjunction with the developer), runs the tests for the new object (in addition, the test team might want to run regression tests for the complete application overnight).

Once the object is considered of high enough standard (i.e., it works as expected), the test team notifies a librarian that the object (or a series of objects) is ready to be moved from the QA library to the UAT library, ready for the testing in accordance with the test plan developed by the user community. The testing probably will take place using an executable to simulate the production environment. Upon successful testing in this environment, the object (or series of objects) is ready for the PROD library. The librarian then can determine which production library that the objects must be moved to prior to building the executable (and dynamic libraries).

It is important to note that PowerBuilder is not a version control system. The success of these techniques relies, in great part, upon the cooperation of the development team as a whole.

Sharing Online Books and InfoBase CD-ROM information

This section outlines the steps necessary to run all the Powersoft Online Documentation locally or on a network instead of running it from the CD-ROM drive. This will not only free your CD-ROM drive but also will increase performance in accessing and searching the documentation. You will need approximately 91MB of free disk space available to proceed.

Step 1 Place your Powersoft product CD-ROM into your CD-ROM drive. Run SETUP .EXE from your CD-ROM drive (e.g., D:\SETUP.EXE where "D" is your CD-ROM drive).

Step 2 Install the Powersoft Online Documentation component using a destination path (e.g., C:\PBDOC).

Step 3 Manually copy all of the files in the \DOC\DOC directory from your CD-ROM drive to the destination path that was specified during the installation of the Powersoft Online Documentation component (e.g., COPY D:\DOC\DOC*.* C:\PBDOC).

Step 4 Edit the LNAME.INI file that is located in the destination path that was specified during the installation of the Powersoft Online Documentation component. Do a search and replace for the entire file. Search for D:\DOC\DOC (where "D" is your CD-ROM drive) and replace it with the destination path that was specified during the installation of the Powersoft Online Documentation component (e.g., Edit LNAME.INI, search for D:\DOC\DOC, and replace it with C:\PBDOC).

Step 5 Repeat the edit step for the VIEWS.INI file. You now are finished and will be accessing the Powersoft Online Documentation from either your local or network drive. You can take the Powersoft Product CD-ROM out of the CD-ROM drive as it is no longer needed to access the documentation.

Viewing online books using BoundViews

If you purchased PowerBuilder on CD-ROM, PowerBuilder manuals are provided on-line. You can view the manuals using BoundViews.

To install the documentation viewer:

Step 1 Run the Setup program as described in "Installing PowerBuilder Enterprise for Windows," and select Powersoft Online Documentation.

Step 2 The Setup program installs a program icon labeled BoundViews.

To view the documentation:

Step 1   Mount the PowerBuilder CD-ROM in your CD-ROM drive.

Step 2 Run BoundViews.

Step 3 Select the document that you want to view. Use the BoundViews Help to learn about the search capabilities and other features of the viewer.

Note: If you purchased PowerBuilder on disks, the printed manuals are included. The manuals are not available online.

Starting PowerBuilder

Double-click on the PowerBuilder icon in the Windows group that you specified in the installation session. If this is the first time that you have run PowerBuilder since installing it, the default application is exampl40, and your screen should resemble Figure 4.3.

Command-line parameters. There are additional parameters that can be given on the command line when starting PowerBuilder. The syntax is:

```
[WIN] PATH\PB030.EXE [/P paintername] [/L libraryname] [/O objectname] [/N] [/R] [/RO]
[/A arguments]
```

(Use WIN to start windows from the DOS prompt.) The switches are described in Table 4.4, and their parameters are described in Table 4.5.

Note: You must specify /P when using /O or /N.

Not many developers use these options to start up PowerBuilder, but the feature is there anyway. Here are some ideas, though:

- Build a front-end program that starts PowerBuilder's Project painter and regenerates and optimizes all of the libraries and rebuilds the executable over the weekend.

- Build a front-end program that accepts a string, starts the PowerBuilder Library painter scanning for any occurrence of the string, and prints the results.

Figure 4.3 The PowerBuilder initial workspace.

TABLE 4.4 The Command-Line Switches

Switch	Description
/P	Used with the *paintername* to identify the painter to launch
/L	Used with the *libraryname* to identify the library to open
/O	Used with the *objectname* to identify the object to open
/N	To create a new object
/R	Run the object and allow modifications
/RO	Run the object and do not allow modifications
/A	Used to supply arguments to a DataWindow that must be run

TABLE 4.5 The Command-Line Parameters

Parameter	Description
path	Path containing the PowerBuilder development environment
paintername	Name of the painter that you want to open. You need to specify as much of the *paintername* to be unique for PowerBuilder to determine which painter to launch
libraryname	Name of the library that you want to open
objectname	Name of the object that you want to open

Migrating from PowerBuilder 3.0 to 4.0

Migration to the new version of the software can be a simple regeneration of the compiled code or can be an involved task with much review and fixup prerequisite. We have a client who has not converted a production application that still is running in Version 2.0 of PowerBuilder. In any event, the migration should be carefully planned and completed as soon as practical. However, try to avoid making the mistake of letting too much time slip by. You will pay for it in blood, sweat, tears, time, money, and frustration. Get it out of the way, ASAP.

The basics

Before you migrate your application to 4.0, make a backup of the 3.0 PBLs. Power-Builder provides you with a warning about this prior to starting migration, but don't wait to get that far before acting. We suggest that, before you proceed, you create a new directory and copy all of the application's PBLs to it. In this way, you can fall back to the 3.0 release of an application if the 4.0 regeneration is problematic. Another tip is to do this on a local disk drive, thereby avoiding being delayed by excessive network traffic and also not creating any for everybody else.

Basic migrate

Start up PowerBuilder 4.0, and choose the application to be migrated from within the Application painter. When you try to run a 3.0 application in 4.0, you are prompted to migrate the application to 4.0. See Figure 4.4.

To migrate the application, start up PowerBuilder 4.0 and open the application object, selecting it from within either the Application painter or the Library painter. PowerBuilder 4.0 then will prompt you with a migration dialog.

If you click Yes, PowerBuilder will display a list of libraries (see Figure 4.5) that will be included in the migration process. If you press OK, you will be presented with a final confirmation message (see Figure 4.6).

Because you already have made a back up, press Yes to continue. When you elect to continue the migration, PowerBuilder will make a two-pass search through each of the libraries in the library search path for the application, converting each object in each library to 4.0 format, then will regenerate each object. This might take some time, especially if your application is large. Most of the migrated objects will perform just as they did in Version 3.0, but there are some exceptions, which are covered in the following sections.

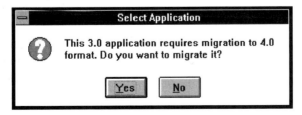

Figure 4.4 The Migration dialog.

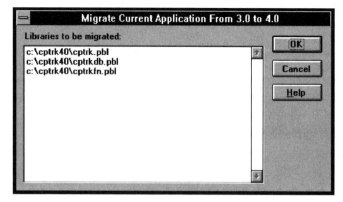

Figure 4.5 The library list for migration.

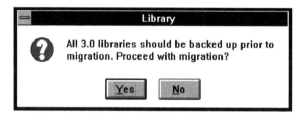

Figure 4.6 Migration confirmation.

Syntax and semantics

The example compiler error shown in Figure 4.7 is one of syntax. The latent semantic problems are the ones that you will not see in the regeneration but that might show up in the execution. Even if the application regenerates properly, regression testing should be performed.

Use the `Print` and `Copy To...` buttons to either print the compiler errors or save them to a text file (e.g., ERRORS.TXT) to refer to them later.

Migrating from earlier versions

Powersoft has a policy of supporting the current release and the prior release. This means that, if the current release is 4.0, they also will support release 3.0B. If you are migrating from Version 2.0 to Version 4.0, you will need to read "Migrating from PowerBuilder 2.0 to 3.0," which is available on CompuServe and via the BBS, before you migrate.

Realistically speaking, if this is your situation, you probably will need to do some degree of application rewriting. There are many new features available in 4.0 that were not available in 2.0.

Watcom SQL 4.0

The Watcom 4.0 installation program converts your existing Watcom 3.2 data sources to Watcom 4.0. To save a copy of these data sources in Watcom 3.2 format, click the Save Old Data Sources checkbox in the Migrate Watcom SQL Data Sources dialog. The program will save a copy of each of your Watcom 3.2 data sources in your ODBC.INI with the suffix of " 3.2."

To access your Watcom database using the 3.2 Watcom ODBC driver (WSQL ODBC.DLL), you must include DBLIBW.DLL and WSQLEN.DLL in your DOS path. These two files were installed with PowerBuilder 3.0.

AUTOEXEC.BAT changes

When you install PowerBuilder Enterprise, the setup program will add the following directories to your PATH statement in the AUTOEXEC.BAT:

```
C:\PB4; C:\PB4\EXAMPLES; C:\WSQL40\WIN
```

If you install the C++ Class Builder that comes with PowerBuilder Enterprise and tell the setup program to modify your AUTOEXEC.BAT file, the program will add these directories to your path:

```
C:\WATC\BIN; C:\WATC\BINB; C:\WATC\BINW
```

It also will add these SET statements to your AUTOEXEC.BAT:

```
SET EDPATH=C:\WATC\EDDAT
SET INCLUDE=C:\WATC\H;\WATC\H\WIN
SET Watcom=C:\WATC
```

These directories and SET statements are required only by the C++ Class Builder.

WIN/OS2

Running a machine with the dual-boot architecture requires two AUTOEXEC.BAT files (e.g., C:\DOS\AUTOEXEC.BAT and D:\OS2\AUTOEXEC.BAT). When you choose the environment, the OS/2 boot manager copies the appropriate AUTOEXEC.BAT file from this directory into the root directory prior to continuing the boot. Ensure that

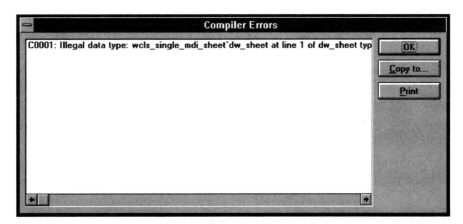

Figure 4.7 Compiler errors during migration.

the modifications that are made to the PATH statement during the installation of PowerBuilder are copied to underlying environment's AUTOEXEC.BAT files.

The 32-bit Watcom SQL engine is unstable in the Win/OS2 environment; therefore, you must use the 16-bit Watcom SQL engine in this environment.

To use the 16-bit engine:

Step 1 Select the Watcom SQL data source in the Configure ODBC dialog.

Step 2 Click Edit. The Watcom SQL ODBC Configuration dialog displays.

Step 3 Click Options. The Setup Options dialog displays.

Step 4 Change the Start Command from DB32W.EXE to DBSTARTW.EXE in the Startup Options dialog.

You must do this for all your Watcom SQL data sources that you want to access in the Win/OS2 environment.

Deploying applications against a Watcom engine

If you are deploying an application against a Watcom engine, you must copy the following files from the developer's environment to the application (deployment) directory or a directory on the DOS path:

- RTSTARTW.EXE
- RT32W.EXE
- RTSQLW.EXE

SQL Server interface

In the FaxLine document, Powersoft states the following:

> The Powersoft SQL Server interface works only with the Microsoft version of SQL Server. A Powersoft interface for the Sybase version will be forthcoming.

We have not found this to be a problem for SYBASE System 10.

Compiler change

In Version 4.0, the Powersoft compiler was enhanced to detect improper overloading and overriding of functions. As a result, any attempt to change only the return type of a function that is defined in an ancestor and a descendant will result in a compiler error as will functions that are defined in the ancestor and descendant and differ only in the pass by option (one is pass by reference, and the other is pass by value).

For example, an ancestor window class has a function defined as:

```
integer wf_init (integer AV_iIdentity)
```

and a descendant window class has this function defined as:

```
long wf_init (integer AV_iIdentify)
```

During the migration, the compiler will detect this and display the following error message:

```
C0123: Function wf_init differs from ancestor only by return type
```

This type of overloading was unintentionally supported in prior releases. Functions defined in this manner would appear to work properly at runtime but lead to improper polymorphic execution. In other words, the wrong function would be executed. Typically, the ancestor function would execute in cases where the descendant should have been executed in an .EXE. (In the development environment, the proper function would execute.) To help understand the restriction on return type overloading, think of functions in PowerBuilder as equivalent to C++ virtual functions. Overloading is done by function signature, and the signature consists of the function name and the types and numbers of arguments, not the return type.

CALL statement

The compiler also has been enhanced to detect improper use of the CALL statement. In previous versions, the compiler allowed calls to scripts that did not belong to the ancestor of the object in which the CALL statement appeared.

New reserved words

The following are new reserved words in Version 4.0:

- INDIRECT
- RPCFUNC
- ALIAS
- INTRINSIC

If you have a Version 3.0 application that uses any of these words as a variable or object name, it will cause a syntax error, and the migration will fail.

32-bit platform addressing

This is a migration issue for applications that save the result of the Handle function and plan on running this code on a 32-bit operating system. PowerBuilder handle-related variables and parameters have been changed from integer (16-bit signed integer, range: −32768 to +32767) to long (32-bit signed integer, range: −2,147,483,648 to +2,147,483,647). The following is a list of functions and objects that you should check for if you are running on a 32-bit operating system:

- DataWindowChild( )
- Handle( )
- Post( )
- PostEvent( )

- Send( )

- TriggerEvent( )

- Message standard class

For example, the following statement intends to make the window w_main scroll up one page, but it might fail if the handle to the window is greater than 64K:

```
INTEGER  L_iW_Main
L_iW_Main = Handle(w_main)
Send(L_iW_Main, 274, 2, 0)
```

In PowerBuilder 4.0, the script should be changed to:

```
LONG  L_lW_Main
L_lW_Main = Handle(w_main)
Send(L_lW_Main, 274, 2, 0)
```

or:

```
Send(Handle(w_main), 274, 2, 0)
```

CloseWithReturn

In 3.0, using the CloseWithReturn function to close a parent (or ancestor, etc.) from a response window caused unpredictable results. The system would hang, possibly experience a General Protection Fault (GPF), or seem to do nothing. A fix in PBRTF 030.DLL (30A14) prevents closing the parent (or ancestor, etc.) of a response window with CloseWithReturn.

This was documented on the 3.0a bulletin. You should refer to these bulletins for additional fixes that have been implemented in 4.0.

MDI frame windows

In PowerBuilder 4.0, MDI frame windows must have a menu assigned to them. Migration does not enforce this new requirement. If you have MDI frame windows that do not have a menu assigned to them, you must assign each frame window a menu in 3.0 before you migrate your application. If you do not, you will experience problems at runtime.

Retrieval arguments

If you create a DataWindow and define retrieval arguments for the DataWindow but do not reference them anywhere in the data source, you will get this message:

```
The columnname argument defined for the SELECT statement was not referenced. Do
you want to continue anyway?
```

If you click the Yes button to return to Design mode and then preview the DataWindow, you will be prompted for the retrieval arguments. In 3.0 and 3.0a, you were not prompted.

In 4.0, you can use retrieval arguments in Computed fields and DataWindow expressions; therefore, the arguments must be resolved before the DataWindow detail processing begins.

Edit mask keystroke behavior changes

Edit masks have been rewritten in response to user demand. Therefore, you might find that some masks that worked in 3.0a are no longer valid.

Delimiters in certain data types. Date, DateTime, and Time data types are restricted by the following rules:

- If a nonzero digit is entered in the first position of the day (*dd*) or month (*mm*) date fields or the hour (*hh*), minute (*mm*), or second (*ss*) time fields and the delimiter character is entered in the next position (for example, 3/), the EditMask will insert a zero before the digit and move the insertion point after the delimiter. For example, if you enter 12/1/, it will display 12/01/, and the insertion point will be after the second slash.

- If the user enters 00/00/00 or 00/00/0000 in Date or DateTime EditMask, the EditMask will interpret the value as a NULL value for the column.

- The user can type to the end of the EditMask. The insertion point displays after the last letter entered in the EditMask. The user can use the mouse to move the insertion point.

- You can enter AM or PM in DateTime edit masks if you include am/pm in the mask pattern. In addition, you can enter only the time in the edit mask if you specify a mask that omits the date portion of the DateTime data type. For example, if the mask is mm/dd/yy hh:mm:ss am/pm, you can enter 10/12/95 10:15:10 am. If the mask is hh:mm:ss am/pm, you can enter 12:00:00 pm. The mask pattern is not case sensitive, but the edit mask itself is case sensitive; the case is determined by the WIN.INI file setting. To move from the data portion of a DateTime edit mask to the time portion, enter a or p. The insertion point will move automatically to the time portion of the mask.

ItemFocusChanged event

The ItemFocusChanged event for a DataWindow control is triggered when the Retrieve is complete and focus is set to the first item in the first row, just as the RowFocusChanged event is triggered when the Retrieve is complete and focus is set to the first row.

Arrays

Testing an element beyond the upperbound of an unbounded array in an IF statement:

```
IF array[beyond_upperbound] = 1 THEN ...
```

results in this error message during execution:

```
ARRAY BOUNDARY EXCEEDED
```

In 3.0a, this did not result in an error; the upperbound of the array was increased automatically. Unfortunately for us, we had code to test the array item using ISNULL in one of the first scripts we ran in the new 4.0, so we got a system error (see Figure 4.8). Figure 4.9 shows the code in the debugger.

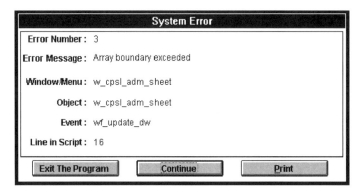

Figure 4.8 A runtime error after migration.

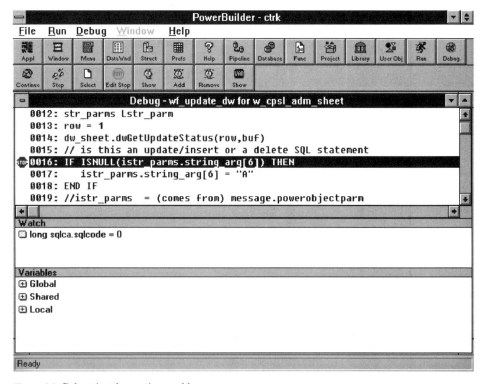

Figure 4.9 Debugging the runtime problem.

The rest of the gotch ya's

Maximum number of objects. The maximum number of objects that you can have in a class is approximately 2700. If you exceed this number, a message will display and your application will terminate.

Nested reports. Due to a bug in nested reports, the main report and all nests must use the same units. For example, if units for the main report is $\frac{1}{1000}$ inch, units for the nests also must be $\frac{1}{1000}$ inch.

Composite style reports. The Composite presentation style report relies on the print preview capability of the reports. Therefore, before you can create a Composite presentation style report, you must define a printer using the `Printers` option in the Windows Control Panel.

Using reports with external data sources or static data in composite reports. If a composite style report is composed of external data source reports, reports with static data, or any combination of the two, the DataWindow control containing the composite will display empty at runtime. To populate the report, you must call the Retrieve function. The Retrieve function requires a connected transaction object to be assigned to the DataWindow control using SetTrans or SetTransObject. This connection is used for the nested reports.

DropDownDataWindows. Dynamically changing the dataobject assigned to a DropDownDataWindow column during execution no longer automatically triggers a retrieve of data for the DropDownDataWindow.

If the new dataobject has data defined with it, the static data is used. If the existing DropDownDataWindow is shared, the new DropDownDataWindow will be shared. If the existing DropDownDataWindow has rows, the rows are copied and the update flags are reset. If none of these conditions exist, PowerBuilder attempts to retrieve data as it did in Version 3.0.

Note: In 3.0, when the dataobject was changed for a DropDownDataWindow, the old child DataWindow was destroyed (its handle released), and a new one was created. By chance, the new child often had the same handle as the old one. So, if you didn't execute the GetChild function again, you had a good chance that the original child handle still would work. In 4.0, the new child is created before the old one is destroyed so that the rows can be copied to the new one. This means that the new child handle will *never* be the same as the old one. To get the new handle, you must call GetChild after you change the dataobject. Using the old handle will have unpredictable results.

Graph sort criteria. In Version 4.0, you can specify a sort order for the data on the Category and Series axes of a graph. The choices are `Unsorted`, `Ascending`, or `Descending`, and the default is `Ascending`. In Version 3.0, graph data was always unsorted. Because migration does not add a PowerScript statement to assign a value to this new attribute, it takes on the default value (`Ascending`). If you want the graph to be unsorted, you can change the sort order after migration is complete.

Changing graph types. In 3.0, you could change the type of a DataWindow graph during execution, and it would appear to be correct. In 4.0, if you don't change the expressions at the same time, your graph might not be what you expect. For example, for most graph types, the default expression for the legend is "category." However, for pie type graphs, the default expression for the legend is "series." So, if you change the type from BarGraph to PieGraph, the legend will be incorrect. In some cases, you also will have to change the Pie expression. When you change the graph type in the development environment, the expressions are adjusted automatically; however, during execution, they are not.

New attribute. The Pie.DispAttr type attributes are new in Version 4.0. If you want to use Describe or Modify on these attributes for a DataWindow graph during execution, you first must create these attributes by saving the DataWindow in Version 4.0. If you don't, Modify and Describe will give unpredictable results.

Accelerator key change. In the Window painter:

- Ctrl–Shift–W opens the Run Window dialog; in 3.0, Ctrl–W opened this dialog
- Ctrl–W previews the current window

Project painter. Note that the `Regenerate All Objects` Project painter option only regenerates classes that can be inherited: Window, Menu, and User Objects.

Watcom 4.0 stored procedures. The IF EXISTS (SELECT ...) statement fails when used in a Watcom 4.0 stored procedure. This will be fixed in the first level 1 patch of Watcom 4.0 SQL. Check with Watcom SQL support for dates. This problem does not exist in the released NT version of Watcom 4.0 SQL.

PowerBuilder in Use

This section discusses further recommendations that cover a range of development areas. If you have an existing application developed in a prior release of PowerBuilder that you want to migrate or if you are planning to start new development, there are several things that we recommend that you should do that will ensure project success.

Developing PowerBuilder Cross-Platform Applications

When developing or distributing an application on multiple platforms, you need to consider how PowerBuilder was ported to the new platforms to make use of the features that are available across all platforms, while trying to avoid any platform-specific operating system calls.

When you use PowerBuilder to develop a Windows application that will run on another platform in the future, you need to consider the other environment when you design your application. In general, things that you typically do in a PowerBuilder application can move between platforms with little or no change. However, there are certain issues that you should be aware of and take into account when you design and build applications in PowerBuilder that you plan to deploy on multiple platforms.

How PowerBuilder was ported. When Powersoft first developed PowerBuilder, it intended to make PowerBuilder platform independent. However, there was no standard GUI interface at the time; therefore, as a start-up company, they chose the market that would show the quickest return on their investment. This platform was the PC, and after they saw a beta for Microsoft's Windows 3.0, they selected this as their API. Now Powersoft has ported their technology to other major platforms, including Macintosh and several UNIX platforms.

The UNIX version is not a total port to the UNIX operating system and Motif GUI. PowerBuilder runs natively on the UNIX platforms by using Bristol Technology, Inc.'s Wind/U portability kit. The Wind/U portability kit implements the Microsoft Windows API under Motif. Wind/U supports Win16, Win32, and the Microsoft Foundation Class Library (MFC). What Powersoft has done is to recompile the PowerBuilder source in the UNIX environment and link it with the Wind/U library. This allows the same PowerBuilder source that runs under Windows to execute in the native UNIX environment with the look and feel of Motif.

A similar port using the Altura library was carried out for the Apple Macintosh environment. When PowerBuilder issues a Windows API function call, Altura maps the call to the relevant System 7 (or 8) call for the Mac.

Platform-independent elements. When we say PowerBuilder, we really are talking about two components: the development environment, which is what you use to develop an application, and the runtime environment, which is what you use to execute the application that you have developed. Powersoft's goal is for you to be able to develop an application on one platform (e.g., Windows) and be able to execute that application on another platform (e.g., UNIX).

Powersoft supports a very large set of application and GUI functionality on the Windows, Windows NT, Macintosh, and UNIX platforms as well as some platform-specific extensions that are supported on some, but not all, platforms. For example, not all PowerScript functions are supported on all platforms. If you call a function that is not supported on a particular platform (such as the DDE function ExecRemote on the Mac), the function will return without doing anything. This is not an error, so no error code is returned and no message displayed. PowerBuilder libraries (.PBL files) and the objects stored in them are platform independent (see Figure 4.10). That is, PBLs can be moved and shared between platforms during development.

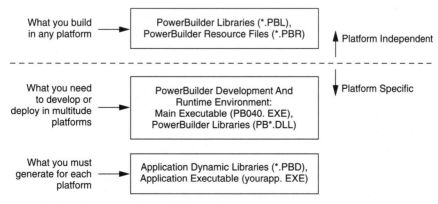

Figure 4.10 Platform independence in PowerBuilder.

Powersoft will try to make the cross-platform transition as easy as possible. Most things that you can do in Windows will work when your application is moved to any of these platforms, but if you want your application to look like a Mac or UNIX application, you should take into account the differences summarized in this section.

The user interface. Study the interface guidelines for Windows, the Mac, and UNIX. To help you, we recommend that you read:

- *The Windows Interface: An Application Design Guide*, which is available from Microsoft Press
- *Human Interface Guidelines: The Apple Desktop Interface*, which is produced by Apple Computer and published by Addison-Wesley Publishing Company
- *Motif Style Guide*, which is produced by the Open Software Foundation and published by Prentice-Hall

Database connectivity. The following database connectivity options are provided in the multiplatform environment:

- Sybase SQL Server 4.9.x and System 10
- Oracle 6.0 and 7.0 (on Windows NT, only Oracle 7 is supported)
- Watcom SQL (Windows, Windows NT Intel, and Macintosh)
- Local DBMS
- Server access (Windows NT, Novell NLM, and OS/2)
- Binary compatibility (Watcom SQL database .DB files)
- ODBC (Windows, Windows NT, and Macintosh)

Environment feature issues. The Mac platform does not support DDE. Applications ported to UNIX via third-party tools, such as Bristol's Wind/U, can support DDE, but native UNIX applications in general do not. So, if you must use DDE in your applications, obviously, you can only talk to other applications that support DDE.

If you call a function in a DLL, make certain the equivalent of the DLL is available on the target platform. If there is a Windows API call with functionality that you need on all platforms, you will have to write a DLL to call the equivalent functionality in the Mac toolbox or from Motif, then have your PowerBuilder application call the DLL function.

All of the PowerBuilder functions are supported on the Mac and UNIX platforms. However, if you use the Other event to call an external API or function, it might not behave as you expect.

User-defined events, the TriggerEvent, and PostEvent functions are supported in the Mac and UNIX. You can create user events and write scripts that are triggered by these events within your applications (for example, in a user object). You can't use user events to communicate with external APIs or other external function calls.

The WIN.INI file exists only in the Windows 3.x environment. So do not set session options for your applications in the WIN.INI file. Use your application's .INI file to set all options. On the UNIX platform, you also can use the .WindU file to set some session options.

VBX controls are supported only in Microsoft Windows 3.*x*.

Windows message IDs have no meaning on the other platforms.

Avoid fully specified path names for things such as bitmap files in scripts or attributes. The path conventions on Mac and UNIX are not the same as in Windows. If you cannot avoid specifying a path in a script, define standard functions such as GetDiskName( ) or GetDirectorySeparator( ) and build the string dynamically.

Although the Mac and UNIX support PBL and file names with more than eight characters, you should not use names that exceed eight characters if you plan to port your applications from these platforms to the DOS/Windows environment.

There is no right mouse button on the Mac mouse. The right mouse button is supported as Ctrl–Click. When you are designing a Windows application that will be ported to the Mac, you might want to avoid using the right mouse button. Most UNIX systems have three mouse buttons. Initially, all three buttons cannot be utilized.

Online help. Create your Help text on the Windows platform, save it in Rich Text Format (.RTF), and compile and run the Help. For Mac, use Microsoft's cross-platform Help compiler for the Mac Help engine. For UNIX, use Bristol Technology's HyperHelp compiler and UNIX Help engine.

Fonts. If you use the Windows system font in your applications, PowerBuilder will convert it to Chicago on the Mac. If you want to use fonts other than the Windows system font, you should select TrueType fonts. The Mac supports TrueType fonts. Even though these fonts are slightly smaller on the Mac, they look about the same as they do in Windows.

Most applications use the system font more than other fonts (for example, the window title and the text on the controls usually are in the system font). The system font on other platforms might be larger than the Windows system font, so you should allow more space in your windows and dialog boxes than Windows requires. Leave space around the edges of the windows. A good rule of thumb is to allow 20 percent more space.

Make sure that the fonts that you select are installed on all platforms; missing fonts will be mapped to fonts that are available on the system, and resulting displays might look quite different.

The UNIX .WindU file is equivalent to the Windows WIN.INI file and contains the font mappings as well as other information. These sections map groups of font name aliases to groups of font names that are found on almost all X servers and printers.

The .WindU file supplied with the UNIX version of PowerBuilder will have a set of XDISPLAY, PostScript, and PCL font values for common Microsoft Windows font names. If you use a font that is not on this list, you will have to add it to the FontSubstitute sections. The font names in the default list are:

- arial

- helv

- courier new

- times roman

- times new roman

- tms

- ms serif

- ms sans serif

Creating the deliverable files. When an application is ready to be deployed, you must create the executable program file on each platform on which you are going to deploy it. You can share Dynamic PowerBuilder Libraries (.PBD files) between platforms.

Window types. See Table 1.3 for a comparison of the Windows and Mac window types. PowerBuilder on the Mac will honor the Windows hierarchy.

Menu shortcut keys (Mac). On the Mac, PowerBuilder will substitute the Command key in place of the Ctrl key for menu shortcuts. When you do this, be careful not to use reserved command keys for other purposes. On the Mac, PowerBuilder will substitute the Option key in place of the Alt key for menu shortcuts. Powersoft does not use the Ctrl key on the Mac except for Ctrl–Click, which is used as the right mouse button.

Watch out for function and system keys. Not all of the Mac keyboards have function keys. These keys are mapped to a command key combination so that the user can get to them. However, this is not always easy for the user, so you should make function keys optional.

MDI and the Mac desktop. Windows are not clipped. Because all of the Mac windows share the Master Window, you can move a window outside of a parent window; the window will not be clipped at the edge of the parent window. For example, if you open a child window in Windows, then move the window beyond the edge of the parent, you will see only the portion of the window that is within the parent; the window is clipped. If you open a window within a window in the Mac environment and move it beyond the edge of the "parent" window, the entire window is visible; the window is not clipped.

Don't place controls in MDI frame windows. If you place controls on MDI frame windows or use floating controls and lists, they will not behave as you expect. Because the window background color on the Mac is transparent, they disappear.

Look and feel. Don't force the 3D look for controls. 3D controls are not standard on the Mac. If you accept the default border style for PowerBuilder controls, Power-Builder will convert the border to the Mac default style. If you specify 3D for your controls. Your application will display in 3D on the Mac.

Note that, because Microsoft Office has implemented 3D controls on the Mac, Powersoft will be reviewing its approach before final release and might change the default to 3D for the Mac.

Allow extra space around CommandButtons. The default CommandButton border on the Mac is much larger than the Windows button. If you do not allow extra space around CommandButtons in your Windows applications, the CommandButton border will overlay the other controls or objects when you move the applications to the Mac.

The Tab key behaves differently on the Mac. You can tab to edit controls, but you cannot tab to other controls. For example, you cannot use the Tab key to move from the OK button to the Cancel button, but you can tab between SingleLineEdits and can tab automatically at the end of an edit mask. Therefore, do not depend on events such as GetFocus that are triggered when the user tabs to a control.

Mac applications always require a mouse. When an option, object, or control is clicked, it becomes the active item. Because the user always uses the mouse to select items, there is no concept of getting or losing focus. Therefore, you should not write scripts that depend on the GetFocus and LoseFocus events. The behavior of these events will be different on the Mac than it is in Windows.

Mac windows can be zoomed up and down but do not have a minimize box to iconize (minimize) the window. Therefore, PowerBuilder will ignore the Minimize attribute of windows in your application.

The screen size (number of pixels) varies with the size of the monitor screen. Design and build your user interface for the smallest display that your users will have. The Macintosh grow box is in the bottom-right corner of the window. Do not place a control there in resizable windows.

Sketching the shape of the application

When you begin the development of a new application, you will need to think about the libraries that make up the application. This might not be known at the very beginning, particularly if this is your first application. Table 4.6 contains an example.

We recommend creating a library that contains solely the application and project objects. This helps to avoid check-in/out contention problems later. It also is a good idea to apply an extra layer of security to this library because it contains the compile definition in the project object and the global variable definition in the application object.

See chapter 6, "Defining an application," for more information on creating PowerBuilder libraries, applications, and project objects. See chapter 17, "Preparing the application for production," for more information on creating the executable.

Changing the shape of the application during development

During the development of an application, you might find it necessary to move objects around and create new libraries for additional subsystems. Bare in mind that applications that have the libraries that contain the ancestor objects, such as the cor-

TABLE 4.6 An Example Library List

Library name	Contains
TSC.PBL	Application (tsc) and project (p_tsc) objects
CORP_AFX.PBL	Corporate application framework library
TSC_MAIN.PBL	Reusable object library
TSC_TRADE.PBL	Objects for trade capture
TSC_PRTY.PBL	Objects for counterparty maintenance
TSC_ADM.PBL	Objects for static data maintenance
TSC_RPT.PBL	Objects for reporting and printing

porate application framework and the reusable object library in the previous example, at the beginning of the library list tend to perform better. If you change the structure, or shape, of the application, then don't forget to update the definition in the project object and notify the rest of the team so that they can modify the library search path for the application in their PB.INI files.

Accessing application initialization files

For each PowerBuilder application that you develop, it's a good idea to create an application initialization file (.INI) that contains a profile of the user preferences that are used during the application execution. You can get some ideas for an application initialization file by reviewing the PB.INI file that is issued with PowerBuilder itself. When you build your application, it should have its own INI file that contains the database transaction connection parameters, with the exception of password, for the applications database. PowerBuilder provides several functions for accessing data from an INI file.

The following is a sample PROFILE.INI file:

```
[Database]
DBMS= SYC Sybase System 10
ServerName=ai_pt_db
Database=db_tv
UserId=allenp
[Toolbar]
toolbarvisible=yes
toolbaralignment=top
toolbartext=no
```

The following is a sample script for reading database user information from the INI file:

```
MyTrans.DBMS = ProfileString("PROFILE.INI", "Database", "DBMS","")
MyTrans.UserId = ProfileString("PROFILE.INI", "Database", "UserID","Guest")
MyTrans.ServerName = ProfileString("PROFILE.INI", "Database", "ServerName","")
MyTrans.Database = ProfileString("PROFILE.INI", "Database", "Database","")
```

In addition to the connection information, this is a good place to store the user profile to access at execution time to make decisions about things like which database to connect to or the location of another file that contains profile information.

Windows application initialization files (those with extension .INI) commonly are placed in one of the two following locations:

- The WINDOWS directory (most often)
- The directory of the application (less often)

If you do not specify a path for the initialization file, the PowerBuilder function will look for an INI file in the following locations:

- Current directory
- The directory where Windows is installed or where WIN.COM is executed

- The SYSTEM subdirectory for Windows or where GDI.EXE is installed
- The application working directory, if not the current directory
- Sequentially through each directory listed in the PATH

Establish the use of class libraries

Developers new to PowerBuilder should consider using the application library that is supplied with the Enterprise version or purchasing one of the many third-party class libraries that are available. Then, after some experimentation and education, you might choose to add features to the library or build your own from scratch.

See chapter 20, "Related Tools, Libraries, and Publications," for more information on third-party class libraries.

User and technical documentation

Make sure that you produce the user and technical documentation as the project is in progress, because it will never be done satisfactorily after the fact.

Regeneration, optimization, and compilation

It is good practice to regenerate and optimize the PowerBuilder libraries (PBLs). It also is good practice to rebuild the executable on a regular basis. This will bring to light any problems that might have occurred during development. As a consequence, you can always pass on the latest executable to the testing team. See chapter 14, "Refining your code," for more information.

5

Developing the Application

Developing an application is one of those catch phrases that can mean a host of different things. For the purposes of this guide, we will focus on the tasks (as well as the relative sequence the tasks are undertaken) that comprise the average application development life cycle. Each of these tasks probably will be undertaken during the course of development. Some will need to be done more than once. Sometimes a whole group of tasks will be iteratively performed. This is not unique to Power-Builder. It is common in most development efforts. Effective planning and hard work can keep these reiterations to a minimum. This will save time and perhaps maintain the integrity of the objects developed. In any event, this chapter, at first, will provide a quick overview and later basic checklist of the tasks involved in PowerBuilder application development.

Prerequisites

Before you begin the actual construction portion of the development life cycle, certain prerequisite tasks should be either complete or in an advanced state. The project team should have a development approach and accompanying plan with skilled players to carry it to fruition, a database logical model and physical manifestation, and adequate workstation resources.

Logistic prerequisites

The developers must decide on the separation of the application components. As we discussed in chapter 3, "Planning client/server development," the lead developers on a larger project, say a team of more than 30 developers, will incorporate an application design based upon either a two-tier (2T) or three-tier (3T) approach. Exactly what a tier is and when it begins and ends can be a somewhat nebulous concept. In any event, the developers must decide how to break out the functional requirements into logistic tiers that promote a consistent, reusable, and maintainable application system that performs to the users satisfaction. They must consider how this can be accomplished. There are many aspects of development to consider. This will dictate the type of developers that you will staff the effort with (i.e., which skills are required to implement the architecture.

Next, what exactly is a 2T or 3T approach? It is largely in the eye of the beholder. The classic 2T approach implemented *ad infinitum* using the CICS/COBOL/MVS client with DB2/MVS server sometimes residing on the same host platform MSV includes:

Tier 1   Server   Database server: stores and requests data
Tier 2   Client   Application objects: receive and present data

The majority of the application is on the client, including the database access language (SQL). Another approach is to put the data access (e.g., stored procedures) and the database on the server and use the client as a presentation tool only. The latter approach provides more control and performance but might inhibit the use of some of PowerBuilder's most comprehensive features (i.e., the DataWindow and the extended attributes). See the PowerBuilder utility SPUD stored procedure update for some help here.

The best implementations are flexible and include the proper mix of client SQL with DataWindows and the use of stored procedures for performance-problematic functions. This approach must be made on a case-by-case basis.

To complicate further, the three-tiered (3T) development explicitly breaks out everything in the application into a separate layer. The architecture includes the following tiers:

Tier 1   Presentation logic   Developers build windows and menus to provide application presentation and navigation
Tier 2   Business rules   Separate developers build all of the business rules and processes, perhaps using PowerBuilder nonvisual objects or even using a CASE tool (e.g, LBMS)
Tier 3   Database management   DBA develop database design and access modules (e.g., stored procedures)

The 3T will require three separate teams of developers and better coordination of effort. It also will break out the types of PowerBuilder objects developed as well as which external items will have to interface with PowerBuilder. For example, the PowerBuilder objects might call external DLLs for business logic or message switching. Depending on the requirements of the application, either the 2T or 3T approach can be useful.

The vast majority of client-server systems that we have seen, including the ones that we have worked on, require an interface into a legacy system (e.g., mainframe-based application). A 2T approach is useful when the legacy system has a large amount of business rules and database access integrated together (e.g., mainframe COBOL/CICS programs with embedded SQL to access DB2). Breaking the application into separate components usually is not feasible, so development usually consists of extending or enhancing the current system to include a GUI presentation client. For example, this breakout can cause the following connections: a Power-Builder client workstation accessing a Unix-based Oracle database server and returning the data down the chain to the client for presentation. So a 2T architecture consists of business rules and database access integrated together.

A 3T approach is useful when the requirements for the application consists of migrating processing requirements from a legacy system onto the client or a middle-layer server. For example, this breakout can result in the following connections: PowerBuilder client 1 workstation to Unix Sybase server 1/client 2 to issue a remote procedure call (RPC) to a Sybase gateway server 2/client 3 to access a mainframe CICS transaction to select from a mainframe DB2 database server 3 and return the data down the chain to the client for ultimate presentation. The legacy system is being viewed mainly as a database server, with the business rules aspects of the application being moved onto an intermediate server, and presentation on the end-user client machine.

The business rules could have been placed on the client machine resulting in a physically 2T system with a 3T architecture, but security and performance concerns mandated an intermediate server to effect load balancing between database and file servers. The result has been the freeing up of a lot of expensive mainframe time (database server) and a much more efficient system.

Three-tiered development is much more complex and expensive. It also requires faster network communication to support the increase in messaging between the three tiers. Extensive planning, design, and coordination also is required. The 3T systems that we have worked on have been well over budget and behind schedule. This is not only due to a lack of appropriate planning but also undereducated and miscast management and developers. Neither approach is "better" than the other, and each should be taken on it's own merit and used where appropriate.

Physical prerequisites

Before you begin the physical construction of the application components, certain prerequisite physical items must be in place for use by the development team. Besides an adequate workstation and the appropriate servers, the project PowerBuilder libraries (PBLs) that are accessible to developers also should be available and appropriate permissions in place. You should have access to PowerBuilder with current maintenance and whatever third-party or inhouse class library software ready for use from each workstation. Developers should be aware of the guidelines and naming standards the project team has agreed to use to develop the application.

These suggestions might seem a bit pedantic, but they will save precious time later in the process. They also will reduce the start-of-project confusion. Developers will not hesitate. They can be sure that the objects (i.e., window sheets and Data-Windows that they build are named properly) inherited from the correct class library object and stored in the appropriate PBL.

Design the Database

The design process for the application database is unique to each development environment. I will discuss it in general terms. The specifics of the process might vary from shop to shop. In any event, this is a critical item, and the degree to which it is completed before full-scale development will facilitate the process greatly.

Determine the application entities

An *entity* is a person, place, object, event, or activity that is of interest to the functionality that you are creating (i.e., any noun that can represent information of interest to the organization). In the logical database design, you try to build an entity/relationship model by identifying the entities and their attributes as well as the relationships between the different entities. The database logical design starts as soon as you meet the users. Listen for entities in interviews with users. If you are developing a database to track the schedules at one television station, the entities might include series and episodes. See Figure 5.1 for an ERwin-based logical entity model. The attributes of an entity are the things that describe and define it. For example, a series has a descriptive name. Name is an attribute of series. The date that it originally was produced also might be an attribute.

Also listen for relationships in the user interviews. What is a relationship? If an entity cannot exist without a parent, it is dependent (i.e., it "belongs to" another entity). This is a relationship. Important subsets of an entity with special attributes are subentities. For example, a TV series might be of type "special" with attributes that pertain only to a "special" series. We might have a subentity called "special." "Special" is a part of a series (i.e., it could be merged with series and has the same primary key). In contrast, a dependent entity (e.g., an episode) belongs to a series and has a primary key that contains the parent key and an additional key to identify the dependent.

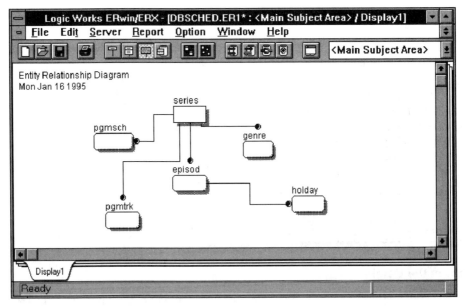

Figure 5.1 Database logical design.

Refine each entity and attribute

After you have collected the business entities and attributes from interviews with the user, check the project standards for naming conventions. (See chapter 21.) Also, if applicable, use companywide abbreviations to ensure consistent naming. Next, attempt to capture a description and validation criteria for each entity and attribute. Does the project have a data dictionary? If so, then enter the description and validation criteria here. Also check the dictionary to determine if the attribute or entity already exists. PowerBuilder has its own catalog tables (i.e., the extended attributes) that can house descriptions and validation rules. These attributes can be populated from CASE tools like ERwin or LBMS. Both of these vendor tools have interfaces to PowerBuilder that can be used to populate the extended attributes.

Determine the primary key for each entity. The primary key of an entity uniquely identifies entity instances (rows). The primary key of a dependent entity includes the parent key and descriptive column. For example, the primary key for the episode entity is the concatenation of series_code and episode_cde. Document past or future states in the description (i.e., add last_update_timestamp). The primary key will promote database integrity as it will inhibit table row duplicity and the creation of database orphans (i.e., rows in a dependent table with no parent).

Determine relationships

Here again, listen for relationships in interviews with the users. Document the roles of entities in recursive relationships. This will facilitate the choice of keys or indices to access the entity. Determine the cardinality of the relationship. For example, how many episodes are in series? Decide on a formal name by checking the standards for naming keys. Don't confuse relationships with entities or attributes. Attributes that designate entities are relationships. If the primary key of an entity consists of other primary keys, it might be a relationship. For example, the TV episode entity would have a primary key consisting of the TV series identifier and the episode identifier. The TV series identifier is the primary key of the series entity.

Create tables and columns

Typically, using the completed logical design, independent entities become independent tables. Similarly, dependent entities become dependent tables. See Figure 5.2 for an example of a physical design in Watcom of the logical model that was depicted in Figure 5.1. Before getting physical (i.e., defining the database in the development DBMS), the designers should verify that tables are in third normal form, or 3NF (i.e., every nonkey column depends on the key). The designers should attempt to retain normalized subtables unless the cost of application-required table joins is unacceptable or merging with the supertable creates few inapplicable nulls (i.e., most attributes are populated).

Denormalize for performance as a last resort. You should exhaust physical solutions first, denormalize selectively, apply updates directly to 3NF tables. The attributes of each entity usually become table columns. These table columns should have well-thought-out data types (e.g., do not use a decimal for a number that is always

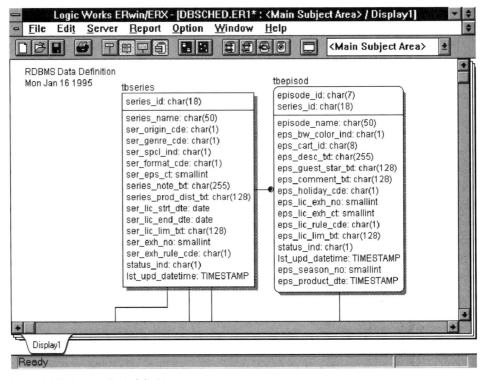

Figure 5.2 Database physical design.

an integer). These table columns should be specified as NOT NULL for all required attributes and relationships. You can cause the DBMS to enforce unique attributes/columns by defining them as an index. Attributes of relationships then go with a foreign key. Implement vectors columnwise, unless physical size, user access, or number of tables forces rowwise design. For example, a week will always have seven days; a schedule row with a week of data is seven times faster to access than a daily schedule. Where possible, avoid alternating, encoded, or overlapping columns.

Create keys

Besides the primary key and index, secondary keys and indices might be required. In a many-to-one relationship, place the foreign key in the many-side table. In a one-to-one relationship, place the foreign key in the table with fewer rows. The many-to-many relationship becomes an associative or junction table. Consider an artificial primary key such as a random number when there are many incoming foreign keys, and the natural key is null, not unique, unstable, complex, or not meaningful.

Complete database physical design

Now you have tables, columns, and a clustered index, but you are not done yet. To really know whether your design will perform, you should list, examine, and explain critical queries and transactions. Critical queries are ones that are high-volume, in which a quick response is required, or that are executed frequently. They are a point of reference for physical design. Create and use, for reference and access, a clustered index for most if not all tables (usually on primary key). Occasionally some other column is more important for access and gets the clustered index. Small or temporary tables might have no clustered index. Create nonclustered indexes (consider foreign key columns) for other columns that are used to search or order the data. Review the critical queries after you have assigned a clustered index. Can all of these queries utilize the clustered indexes for access? If not, consider nonclustered indexes on the columns specified in WHERE clauses, particularly join columns. Create a nonclustered index only when the hit ratio is low. You usually should not create more than three or four indexes per table (unless they are read-only). The rest of the physical design process is DBMS-dependent. The DBAs usually determine partitions, locking, granularity, and device assignments. Have whomever is responsible complete the physical design and notify the developers at each significant milestone.

Define the Application

After the development environment has been established, the first step is to create the application object. Defining the application not only includes the setup and definition of the application object but also the rules of interaction between developers. The developers must buy in to the sharing of objects they will develop jointly. They should check in and check out development objects and use basic teamwork to maximize project productivity.

The application object

The application object constitutes the entry point into the application. This is similar to a mainframe OLTP transaction ID in CICS. The application object names the application and specifies which libraries (i.e., PBLs) will be used to save the objects and run the application. The library list also will include class libraries used to inherit base objects from. Finally, it specifies the application-level scripts. The application Open event script usually will include a function to initialize the application's variables, test the database connection, and launch or open the application window frame (in an MDI application). Other events in the application object include Idle, System-Error, and Close. The Library and Preference painters also are used in setting up the application. Application PBLs are manipulated and default preferences are set for the application development workstation using the respective painter.

The application standards

At this point, you and your developer colleagues should be familiar with certain application defaults. The standard font and size can be set in the application object (e.g., MS sans serif, 8 point). The number and names of PowerBuilder libraries (PBLs) should be determined. You can set up libraries and store objects based on application functionality or by object type. For example, you might store all DataWindows in APPLDB.PBL. Defining an application object usually is done once for an application, but the application object can be copied onto each developer's workstation so that the developer can include their own personal PBL in the library list (usually first in the developer's application library list). This is a good technique for setting up a development environment where object sharing is accomplished (library list items 2 through N will contain project wide PBLs), and developers can test new objects without affecting other developers (library list item 1, which contains individual developer PBL). More on this later.

Create the Window/Menu Interface

After you have developed the basic presentation/navigation of the application and received user approval, you can build the windows and menus that present the data. You also develop the menus that allow the user to move from window to window and to perform application tasks. OnLine Transaction Processing applications (OLTP) should provide easy-to-understand, user-approved data-entry characteristics as well as a quickly understandable response to each user action. Note that the user-approved application presentation and navigation can and should be done at or near the beginning of the development cycle. Make sure the user has seen and used a prototype or example of how the basic system components will look and feel. Make sure they sign off on the design for that application version.

Choose an interface style

In the early days of client server development, OLTP systems would resemble either old dBASE systems or mainframe CICS implementations (i.e., single document applications—only one document or sheet open at a time). As software like Word and Excel increased in popularity, their look and feel became the de facto standard. A growing number of users are familiar and accustomed to using Wordlike application interfaces.

These applications are based upon the multiple document interface (MDI). (See Figure 5.3.) The MDI consists of a window frame to house the main menu and one or more window sheets that present the application data to the users for update and inquiry. The MDI provides the ability to open more than one window sheet at a time (i.e., work on different parts of an application at the same time). It also will provide a consistent and common interface to all of the operating system features. For example, after it has been created once, a Save menu item on an application's main menu will be used by all of the application components, and each user can access the full range of data manipulation features.

Setup the class library for the interface style

In simple terms, a class library is a collection of PowerBuilder objects (windows, menu, and user objects) that have generic functionality that the developer can use by inheriting the class object. For example, you inherit a class object menu that includes item FILE and subitem PRINT that triggers an event script to print the current window. Inheriting this class object provides all windows that use this menu with a consistent print interface. Moreover, the interface is only coded once. Each

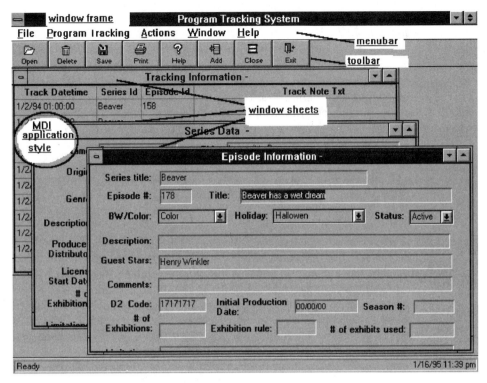

Figure 5.3 The Multiple Document Interface (MDI).

time that you inherit it, you save time and money. Eventually, the class library will pay for it's cost. PowerClass, PowerTool, and Icon Solutions are examples of robust vendor class libraries for PowerBuilder. Each contains a full set of objects to define an MDI application.

Assuming that we will use the MDI interface, the organization will have either purchased a class library that includes an MDI implementation kit or will have developed its own class libraries. This will obviate a redo of the application launching objects (window frame and base menu) that the aggressive developers will create if the class objects have not been determined and available early on. Once the base frame, menu, and sheets are created, the developers need only inherit the sheet, then they can create windows, place controls in the window, and build scripts that specify the processing that will occur when events are triggered.

Build Windows

Windows are the main interface between the user and PowerBuilder applications. Windows can display information, request information from a user, and respond to mouse or keyboard actions.

There are six types of windows. Where class libraries are used, the developer typically will be inheriting a main type window. The MDI frame with a microhelp type window usually is built once. The other four typically are used to provide information for a main type window. For example, PowerBuilder uses a child window type when you add a dropdown DataWindow to provide only valid choices for a field on a main window. Most of the windows that you develop in an MDI application will be type main.

Each Window object has a style, events, functions, and structures.

A *style* is determined by its attributes. The attributes are things that describe an object—in this case a window. The attributes of a window include but are not limited to: whether or not it is enabled, its height, the MenuName if one is associated with the window, the window title, and (for MDI frames and sheets) toolbar attributes.

Events can trigger the execution of scripts. The basic window events include Open and Close as well as user events that are defined to perform special processing in an MDI application. For example, the base menu might have a Save item that has a script to trigger event ue_filesave. It will have been defined to contain a user-defined event called ue_filesave. The script associated with this event will be executed.

Functions are part of the definition of the window and are used in scripts to change the style or behavior of the window or to obtain information about the window. The window might contain a function wf_update that contains a script that will perform update processing particular to the current window sheet.

Structures are part of the definition of the window and are used in scripts to define groups of window-pertinent variables.

Determine the type of window

The type of window that you use to implement a particular feature of the application is an important decision when trying to make your application consistent with other Windows applications. Table 5.1 lists some general considerations.

The Multiple Document Interface windows. You use a main window as the frame and sheets for an MDI application. This probably is the most common window type that you will create. The main window suits the open application because you can add user events that are common to applications (e.g., ue_filesave and ue_fileopen) and include the specific processing in a script behind the event. You then can use the same common main_menu for all the main sheet windows, saving all of the expense of a menu. For example, the menu item Save will trigger the event ue_filesave in the current window. Whatever script is embedded in that event will be executed. The script can be different for each window even though the basic function (i.e., save) is the same.

Child windows are useful when an application needs to display a variable number of subordinate entities, tables, or data views. If an application's style calls for heavy usage of response windows, try to find an open solution and use a menu or toolbar item if possible. The downside to response windows is that the approach makes the applications modal or less open (i.e., the user must go down a predefined path to perform a task).

There are few options for change. When deciding how to use response windows, look at other Windows applications for some precedents before you commit to an approach. Both child and pop-up windows can have an explicit parent window. If a par-

TABLE 5.1 Some General Considerations When Determining the Type of a Window

Window type	Window type properties
Main	Is a standalone window (i.e., has no dependencies)l. Has a title bar (Is there a project standard for setting the title?). Is independent of other windows—main sheet windows encapsulate funtionality (e.g., w_series_ sheet maintains series and w_episode_sheet maintains episodes). Is sometimes called a parent or overlapped window. Can be minimized or maximized. Can have its own menu (Is there a standard class library menu?).
Child	Is always subordinate to its parent window (e.g., dropdown DataWindow). Is never the active window. Can exist only within the parent window. Can have a title bar. Is automatically closed when its parent window is closed. Is clipped when you move it beyond the parent window. Moves with the parent window because its position is always relative to the parent window. Has no menu.
Popup	Has a parent window Can have a title bar or menu. Can display inside or outside the parent window. Can never disappear behind its parent window. Can be minimized; when minimized, it is displayed as an icon at the bottom of the the screen. A pop-up window minimizes with its parent.
Response	Obtains information from and provides information to the user (e.g., The row that you are trying to add already exists! Continue? Yes or No). Remains the active window until the user responds by clicking a control. Is application modal (i.e., fixed path, menu items disabled). The user must respond before any other action can be taken. When the response window is open, the user cannot go to other windows in the application from which the response window was opened. The window cannot be minimized but can be moved.

ent window is not named when the child or pop-up window is opened, the last active main window becomes the parent window.

The base or frame window of an MDI application. Every Windows application needs a base or frame window. This usually is the first window that you see when you invoke the application or after you have supplied logon information (for example, Word has a frame window that contains a menu, toolbars, and blank open sheet).

The base window should be a main type window because it is at the highest level in your application hierarchy. It is not subordinate to any other window in the application. This window usually remains on the screen throughout the application session. The MDI frame in an MDI application is a prime example of a base window.

The sheet windows of an MDI application. As we mentioned in "The Multiple Document Interface windows" section, after the base frame is defined, you will build as many sheets as are necessary to perform the application functionality. For example, one sheet per table for basic maintenance, plus as many others as are needed for special functions. Each sheet acts like a main window and follows most of the rules of child windows.

A sheet always is subordinate to its parent window, the MDI frame. A sheet is activated at the same time as the MDI frame. A sheet can exist only within the MDI frame. Sheets always have title bars that can be populated dynamically. Sheets are closed automatically when the MDI frame is closed. Sheets move only within the MDI frame because their position is always relative to the MDI frame. They occupy the workspace that remains after the menu and toolbar real estate is established. Sheets can be minimized. When minimized, they display as an icon inside the MDI frame. Sheets can have menus, but developers should attempt to minimize the number of menus. Find the common denominator of menu functionality in your application. Sheets are activated by the user clicking anywhere within the sheet boundary; the menu associated with the sheet also becomes active.

The rest of the windows in the MDI. Child windows are subordinate to the sheets (for example, the Table windows used in the Database painter). This nesting can continue. However, MDI does not provide for the nesting of sheets within sheets, and this should not be attempted. Pop-up windows generally are not used in MDI applications because sheets replace the need for pop-up windows.

Response windows, although modal, are used as yield or stop signs to draw the user's attention. While response windows frequently are not invoked directly from the MDI frame, they can be used to open or print application entities or to perform some similar actions. For example, a response window can be used with a DataWindow control to search for existing database rows and return the key values to the main window sheet for subsequent retrieval and update. The About box is a response window as well. Response windows usually are used within the context of a sheet, to further refine the definition of an application entity or to specify options for an action. Response windows also can be invoked from other response windows. This is useful when a generic entity interface needs to be invoked or space limitations on the surface of a response window dictate that additional information needs to be gathered elsewhere. Response windows should never be nested more than one level down.

Adding controls to a window

After the window type is chosen, one or more controls are added to enhance the functionality. In the MDI style, the number of controls should be kept to a minimum. The menu and toolbar should be used for carrying out application tasks.

The most common control will probably be the DataWindow control. It can provide a good deal of functionality. It can be used to receive, edit, validate, display, print, and maintain data. Most of the window controls can be built within a DataWindow. The DataWindow can, but does not need to, be associated with a database table. For determining an option or value, the external source DataWindow can be used. More on this later. In any event, Table 5.2 contains a brief summary of controls.

The DataWindow control should be the most common control utilized. Use it with a menu to trigger event processing on the window sheet and the DataWindow object currently associated with the control. To build a window, use the Window painter.

TABLE 5.2 A Summary of the Controls

Control	Executes a script	Determines option or value	Notes
CheckBox	No	Yes	
Button	Yes	No	Try to use the menu instead; it is common on response windows
DataWindow	Yes	Yes	Should be the most common control; you can use it as a better alternative to almost all of the other controls. The data window control includes its own control styles (e.g., dropdown list box)
DropDownListBox	Yes, but only on the editable and show list	Yes	
Edit Mask	No	No	Display and enter formatted data
Graph	Yes	No	
GroupBox	No	No	Used to group available selections
HScrollBar and VscrollBar	No	No	
ListBox	Yes	Yes	
MultiLineEdit	No	No	Used to enter data; try an external DataWindow instead
Picture	Yes	Yes	Cosmetic as well; expensive and large
RadioButton	No	Yes	
SingleLineEdit	No	No	Used to enter data; try an external (nondatabase) DataWindow instead
SpinBox	No	Yes	
StaticText	No	No	Used to display text information
User Object	Yes	Yes	

Create Menus

Menus in your windows can include a menu bar, drop-down menus, and cascading menus. You also can create pop-up menus in an application. You define the menu items and write scripts that execute when the items are selected. These scripts launch the particular application component. In the MDI application style, menu bars usually are accompanied by toolbars. Toolbar buttons map directly to menu items. Clicking a menu toolbar button is the same as clicking on its corresponding menu item (or pressing the accelerator key for that item.)

Design menu interaction

Menu development should be done carefully. Poorly designed menu handling can cause latent problems that might be detected only when the application is used heavily (e.g., the first month of production). Menus are expensive (they are one of the larger objects in a PowerBuilder library), and their misuse can seriously degrade application performance.

Poor planning with menus also can cause problems that manifest themselves as inconsistent responses to user actions. These errors are hard to detect, reproduce, and correct.

The menu bar/toolbar combination is the backbone of an MDI application. It provides a common user interface to all of the application components. If you are using a class library, you probably will build menus by inheriting a class object menu and adding your custom items to the existing list of common items (e.g., File, Window, Help). Improper handling of menus can make the trivial seem complex. You should be aware of the way that PowerBuilder sets the current menu and toolbar. You should follow some basic rules and guidelines for working with menus.

Optimize menu usage

The MDI frame always should have a menu. If the currently active sheet does not have a menu, then the menu and toolbar (if any) associated with the last active sheet remains in place and operative while that previous sheet remains open. So you can see that, to avoid unpredictable results, all sheets should have a menu.

Another nuance of PowerBuilder menu/toolbar workings is the toolbar. If the currently active sheet has a menu but no toolbar and the previously active (and still open) sheet has both a menu and a toolbar, then the menu displayed will be the menu associated with the currently active sheet, but the menu toolbar displayed will be the toolbar for the previously active sheet. This will totally confuse a user, and the situation must be avoided.

Here again, if you are using toolbars (a virtual given in the MDI application), then all sheets should have a menu toolbar. Disabling a menu item will disable its toolbar button as well but will not change the appearance of the button. If you want the button to have the gray look, you must do this programmatically. Hiding a submenu item does not cause its toolbar button to disappear or to be disabled. If you want the button to disappear or be disabled, you must do this programmatically as well. To build a menu use the Menu painter.

Create DataWindow Objects

Create DataWindow objects to retrieve data from the database, format and validate data, analyze data through graphs and crosstabs, create reports, and update the database. A DataWindow object is a special window object that allows the user to display and manipulate database information without having to code SQL statements in scripts. You build a DataWindow object in the DataWindow painter and save it in a library that is available to the application.

The DataWindow is the real "power" in PowerBuilder. The newest user can build a DataWindow in minutes. It is the equivalent of what used to take a good developer days to produce in report or display form using COBOL and embedded SQL. To build serious DataWindows (i.e., those that are used for data entry and mission-critical applications), the database design should be in the 90% complete zone. Otherwise, the windows will have to be recreated or edited with other PowerBuilder Library painter tools like Export/Import.

Build DataWindow objects with completed database entities

A good database design will make DataWindow creation easy. This is due to the fact that good design will provide column names that are consistent, datatypes that are not overly exotic, unique indices that provide uniform data distribution, and primary/foreign keys that create relationships that promote integrity and facilitate "full statement" information joins.

These are the database qualities that allow developers to easily build a usable DataWindow. If your database has these qualities, then you are ready to proceed. If not, stop here and get out your database design book and read it again carefully. Set up meetings with the database administrators. Take the time to get it right. The lack of a good database design signifies either a lack of business knowledge or paucity of database administration talent or both.

The database design is the most critical component. The presentation can be easily changed and modified; the database cannot. A poor database design can cause integrity as well as performance problems. See chapter 19 for hints on good database design techniques. Another important consideration is the extended attributes that, in effect, are information stored in PowerBuilder's catalog tables to provide labels and edits and display characteristics for the database columns.

At some point, the database design becomes workable and all developers are granted permissions and are ready to build DataWindows. To use a DataWindow object in a window, you place a DataWindow control in the window inside the Window painter, then associate a DataWindow object with the control in the Window painter or in a script. During execution, PowerBuilder creates an instance of the DataWindow object.

Every DataWindow control has:

- A style, which is determined by its attributes.

- Events, which can trigger the execution of scripts.

- Functions, which are part of the definition of the DataWindow control and are used in scripts to change the style or behavior of the DataWindow control or to obtain information about the DataWindow control.

You might want to customize the DataWindows and allow for dynamic changes in the base DataWindow SQL. PowerBuilder provides some functions that can help.

The DataWindow object is the most powerful graphical device in the PowerBuilder environment. It represents only a single Window control regardless of the number of elements placed on its surface.

DataWindows are designed to be intelligent database controls. See Figure 5.4 for an example of a data-entry DataWindow. You can include other objects in a DataWindow for cosmetic purposes. DataWindows also allow you to display columns of data in the form of an edit, CheckBox, RadioButton, DropDownListBox, or DropDownDataWindow Control. The DropDown DataWindow is a powerful edit style and can be used to create firmwide editing capabilities for code or subject area data.

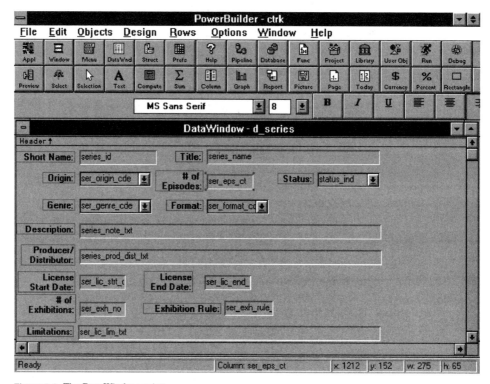

Figure 5.4 The DataWindow painter.

Uses of a DataWindow object

The primary strengths of DataWindows are discussed in the following paragraphs.

Data display. You do not have to code variables to contain column values, do data formatting, translate data values to display values, or map column values to nontext. You also can use them to display forms (pictures and OLE).

Data entry layout. To define a window with normal controls for data entry, the programmer would need to manage many separate controls collectively.

Scrolling. DataWindows deal with all of the scrolling page formatting issues without any programmer code.

Reporting. DataWindows also provide extensive reporting capabilities. Calculated columns, formatting, and grouping can all be managed by DataWindows without any coding.

Data validation. Data can be validated by the DataWindow. This is important for database validity and consistency, especially if you have used the Database painter to create edit styles and validation rules.

Automatic SQL. It is not necessary to code the appropriate SQL statements to access the data from the database.

Performance. Data entry often requires many different slots for the user to enter or display data. It would require many normal controls if you were to implement such an interface without using the DataWindow control.

When a DataWindow displays information, it doesn't use a collection of individual Windows controls; it paints the information on the screen as needed. By detecting when the user clicks the mouse, the DataWindow knows where to activate a particular column.

The more complicated a DataWindow is, the greater the performance benefits achieved. A DataWindow with 40 objects on its surface requires nearly the same resources as a DataWindow with 10 objects, or even only one object, on its surface. This is because the DataWindow actually is managed internally by PowerBuilder, not the Windows environment.

The DataWindow also provides many other performance advantages. It requires fewer resources. Because Windows paints each control separately and a DataWindow is only one control, the speed of painting is significantly increased because PowerBuilder handles it all at once. Because the DataWindow manages many form-oriented tasks internally, you write less PowerScript code to perform validation and cursor control. Windows considers the DataWindow as a single control; therefore, DataWindows use fewer resources compared to multiple standard controls.

Updates. One of the most difficult database programming problems is identifying what needs to be updated based on what the user selected and modified. How do you select the appropriate syntax that is required? The DataWindow object does this for you. The PowerScript UPDATE statement builds the correct SQL based upon the DataWindow settings.

Using DataWindow or standard controls

Some situations call for a DataWindow, some call for other controls, and some are situations where either a DataWindow or another control could be used. In general, most windows will require both DataWindows and standard controls. DataWindows improve performance and reduce programming effort for data access, presentation of data, and data entry. A large percentage of controls within an application probably will be DataWindows. Anytime you need to access the database (DB), you should use a DataWindow (DW). The external DW with no database access also is useful as a data-entry display object.

Some situations straddle the line between using a DataWindow and using a standard control. An example of this is a database logon window. There is no database information to display—none that originates from a table by using a Select statement. There is no formatting, reporting, or updating requirements. On the other hand, there is data entry in that the user is required to enter several pieces of related information onto a window, then the information must be collectively processed. This means that you should consider an external DataWindow. Either way does the job, but the code to accomplish the task will be slightly different depending on the technique you choose.

To build DataWindows, you use the DataWindow painter.

Add Scripts

Scripts determine the actions that are initiated when an event takes place. For example, when a user runs a PowerBuilder application, the system opens the application and executes a script in the application for the Open event. The application's Open event might open an application frame window and test the database connection to see if it is active before a user begins processing.

The PowerScript application Open might look like this:

```
OPEN (w_appl_frame_window)
CONNECT using SQLCA ;
IF SQLCA.SQLCODE<> 0 THEN f_db_error(SQLCA)
```

What is PowerScript?

PowerScript is the programming language for PowerBuilder. It is as simple as BASIC. It is similar to the COBOL, FORTRAN, PL/1, or C programming languages. However, it is different because it is not yet fully compilable, and as such, it must be interpreted, then executed. A PowerScript can be easily built, verified, and executed. PowerScript is supplemented by a large assortment of PowerBuilder functions.

How do you build a PowerScript?

You build these scripts in the PowerScript painter, which you can open by clicking the Script icon or selecting `Script` from the Edit menu. Scripts usually are plentiful by the end of the development cycle. They are one of the ways that developers customize an application. They help facilitate work-arounds and special processing for some of the things that you can't simply select from the other painters. For example, updating two tables in one DataWindow can be accomplished using a script to modify the "update" attributes of a DataWindow.

The script for the Open event is the only script that is required in an application. However, applications usually have a script for the Close event, which allows users to exit the application cleanly at the end of the application session (e.g., destroying transactions and connections and closing windows).

Scripts are associated with windows, menus, user objects, and functions. There are scripts behind events and functions associated with each of these PowerBuilder objects.

Building a script begins when the script painter found within the application, window, menu, and user object function painter is invoked. PowerScript code in the PowerScript painter can be directly keyed in or selected from the Objects dropdown list box, which provides for pasting SQL, functions, and statements.

Declaring object-level functions also invokes the PowerScript painter. Instances and shared variables also can be selected using the dropdown windows in the Script painter. You can copy and paste an existing script to build a new script using the clipboard. You can use context-sensitive Help by focusing on a statement and using the F1 function key. You can connect to multiple databases within a script by setting up connections to each one.

When painting an SQL statement, you can choose any one of the following data manipulation language (DML) statements: DELETE Where Current Of Cursor, DELETE Statement, FETCH From Cursor Statement, FETCH From Procedure Statement, INSERT SQL Statement, Singleton SELECT Statement, Singleton UPDATE Statement, UPDATE From Cursor Statement. This overview, while by no means exhaustive, gives you some idea of the PowerScript painter capability.

Maintaining a script is easily done with the painter bar. You can comment and uncomment lines by highlighting them and checking the painter bar. You can copy part of a script to a text file. Compiling a script is as easy as invoking the Compile dropdown box at the center of the PowerScript menu bar. When you close the Script painter, you return to the painter from which you invoked the PowerScript editor. You also can save a script as an operating system file if you are not finished or want to work on it in another editor.

Validating Your Code

You can run your application anytime during development. If you discover problems, you can debug your application by setting breakpoints, stepping through your code statement by statement, and looking at variable and structure values during execution.

When to use the debugger

When you compile a script, the compiler detects obvious errors (such as incompatible data types or a misspelled function name), and the script will not compile until you fix these errors. In addition to compiler errors, you can have errors (such as dividing by zero) that will cause errors that stop execution of the application or logical errors that might not stop the script from running but produce incorrect results.

PowerBuilder Debug helps you find these errors. Debug allows you to suspend the application at selected points in a script (stops) and review the contents of variables used in the application.

Selecting the scripts to breakpoint

In Debug (see Figure 5.5), you select the script that you want to debug, insert stops in the script, then run or single-step through the script. When PowerBuilder encounters a stop, it suspends execution of the application and displays the Debug window. Figure 5.5 shows an example of a suspended script.

In the Debug window, you can:

- Display the objects and user-defined functions in the application, the current values of the objects, the instance variables, and the attributes of the objects.

- Display the current values of the global, shared, and local variables.

- Edit stops (i.e., add or modify the existing stops).

- Select another script to debug.

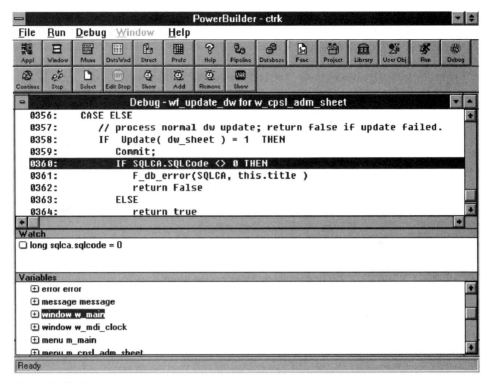

Figure 5.5 The Debugger.

- Modify variable values.
- Select the variables that you want to watch during the debug session.
- Continue executing the application to the next stop or step to the next executable statement.

The stops remain in the scripts until you remove them or exit PowerBuilder. When you close Debug, you suspend the Debug session. If you run Debug again during the same session, Debug resumes processing at the point at which you closed Debug. The Debug settings are saved for you in your .INI file so that you can continue an existing debug trail the next time you are ready.

Refining Your Code

At some point in the application development, key developers will see that certain patterns are being repeated frequently within the application. This might mean that certain application functions or database accesses are being repeated or that certain user tendencies are emerging. The developers must respond and refine those parts of the application so that they perform in an optimal fashion. This is the point in the development cycle of an application that will make or break its acceptance and use.

Things to consider for improving your code and application performance are as follows:

- Code reusability, reducing development time
- Code modularity
- Reduced maintenance costs
- Improved consistency (visual look and feel, nonvisual standards)
- Improved performance

You will accomplish these objectives by carrying out the following tasks:

- Optimizing PowerBuilder
- Removing redundant classes
- Minimizing the levels of menus and toolbar inheritance
- Minimizing the use of large bitmaps
- Minimizing or isolating array processing outside of window open processing
- Minimizing the loading of list and dropdown listboxes in the open event (use Data-Windows or dropdown DataWindows instead)
- Put inherited PBLs first in the library search path (in reverse order)
- Place the directory that contains the PowerBuilder runtime DLLs first in the network search path
- Optimize libraries (for example, if you use Novell, reset the sharable attribute after optimizing a library)

Create Functions and Structures

To support the refinement effort for your scripts, you probably want to define functions to perform processing unique to your application and structures to hold related pieces of data. If you want to be able to reuse components that are placed in windows, define them as user objects and save them in a library. Later, when you build a window, you can simply place the user object instead of having to redefine the components.

Create User Objects

In the PowerBuilder environment, one of the most commonly used techniques to implement reusability is by way of user objects. In PowerBuilder, user objects can be of two types:

- Visual
- Class (known as *nonvisual* in prior releases)

A visual user object is a control or group of controls with a defined look and behavior. You can modify its attributes, add variables or structures, put scripts behind the controls, create functions or methods, and take action on the controls, structures, or variables defined in the object. The visual user object can be placed in a window or inside another custom visual user object.

Class user objects can be used to implement functionality that does not require a visual element. Typically class user objects are used to define business rules, act as a repository for application data, or perform any other common related processing that needs to take place. Class user objects can be implemented and used with local, instance, shared, or global scope, depending on how widespread the functionality or data of the class user object is required.

Create an Executable

When your application is complete, you prepare an executable version to distribute to your users. Before you deliver your application to users, you will need to prepare a standard .EXE file in the Application painter. The .EXE file contains:

- A PowerBuilder bootstrap routine
- The application icon (optional)
- The compiled version of each object in the application

Preparing to create the executable

To create an .EXE file, you perform a series of steps that we will mention not for procedure sake but for consideration that each of these items must be fashioned properly long before this point in the development cycle is reached.

When you open the Application painter from the PowerPanel or the PowerBar, there is an icon/menu item that you select to create an executable. The Create Executable window displays the name of the current application with the file extension .EXE. It also displays the name of the current directory, a list of available directories, and the libraries in the search path for the current application. Make sure that you have considered the placement of the executable library components. Consider which libraries you plan to make dynamic libraries from the list in the Select Dynamic Libraries box. When the application executes, PowerBuilder will look for a dynamic library (a .PBD file) with the same name as the library that you select in the Select Dynamic Libraries box. If a library is a dynamic library, it must always be available to the application at execution. You create the dynamic library in the Library Manager before you create the .EXE.

Prepare the name of the PowerBuilder Resource (PBR) file that includes resources that are assigned dynamically in scripts for the application. These resources include .BMP, .RLE, .ICO, and .CUR files and DataWindows that are assigned dynamically at execution. The .PBR file is an ASCII file that includes the names of each file that contains these resources. The name of each object must exactly match the name used to reference the object in scripts (if the name is fully qualified in the script, it must be fully qualified in the .PBR file). If you do not know the name of the resource file that you want to include, click the `File` button. The Select Resource File window displays. Select a file from the list. When you do not use a .PBR file, PowerBuilder searches the operating system search path for resources that are loaded dynamically in scripts in the application.

Create the deployable application executable

PowerBuilder creates the executable, stores it in the specified directory, and closes the Create Executable window. Consider its size. How many libraries must be packaged? If the application is large, can it be broken up into smaller deliverables? Is the security in place? Has the production database been defined with the proper sizing and partitioning? Is it available for use? Are the user identifiers in place with the proper permissions? Do the users have connectivity? Has the user acceptance team been put in place? Are the database support people ready? These are the types of issues that must be addressed before deploying a production PowerBuilder application. We will expand upon each of these issues and options throughout the remainder of this book.

This chapter has been an overview and a lead-in to the next part of the book, which will "drill down" into each section in this chapter adding the next levels of detail. This iterative style hopefully will minimize the amount of time and effort required to develop applications in the client/server world.

Development

Chapter

6

Defining an Application

This chapter will take you through the creation of a new PowerBuilder application. This is a multistep process that covers library management, development preferences, and project definition as well as the actual application object itself. There basically are four PowerBuilder painters that are directly involved with the process of defining an application. They are:

- Application painter
- Project painter
- Library painter
- Preferences painter

The *Application painter* is responsible for creating and maintaining the application object. The application object is a nonvisual object that defines the central features of the application. Although the Application painter primarily is responsible for the application object definition, there are three other painters that contribute to the application.

The *Project painter* allows the developer to maintain a definition of how to package the application for runtime execution. This definition is stored in a project object, a nonvisual object that can be saved inside a PowerBuilder library.

The *Library painter* is used to create, organize, and maintain the PowerBuilder libraries, in which all of the PowerBuilder objects are stored.

The *Preferences painter* is responsible for maintaining options that the developer wants to set when developing an application. These options include default settings, such as fonts, for the following painters: Application, Window, Menu, DataWindow, Database, Library, and Debug, as well as the general PowerBuilder environment.

The Application Painter

If you are developing a new application in PowerBuilder, the first step typically is to create an application object. In the application object painter you:

- Assign the name of the application
- Build the scripts that execute when the application is opened, idle, closed, or if a system error is encountered during its execution
- Assign a default icon that appears on the Windows Task List or on the desktop when the application is minimized
- Establish defaults (e.g., text font and color)
- Specify the library search path, which includes the libraries that PowerBuilder is to search through to find an object (this is similar to the DOS PATH statement)
- Default global variable types (SQLCA, SQLDA, SQLSA, Error, and Message)
- Define the executable file name (.EXE)

An application is a collection of PowerBuilder windows that perform related activities, such as order-entry, accounting, or manufacturing activities. It is what you deliver to your users. The application object is the entry point into the windows that perform these activities. It is a discrete object that is saved in a PowerBuilder library (see Figure 6.1), just like the other classes: a window, menu, function, or DataWindow object.

The application object defines application-level behavior, such as which libraries contain the classes that are used in the application, which fonts are used by default for text, and what processing should occur that occur when the application begins, ends, is idle for a period of time, and in the event of an error. The only processing that is required is what should happen when the application begins; this is coded in the Open event. The following sections describe the complete list of standard application events.

Open

When a PowerBuilder application is started, the Open event is triggered in the application object. In this script, you could open a login window, load any user preferences, and open an MDI frame or main window. This code is more commonly moved to a global function, such as f_app_open( ). This reduces the code inside the application object to a simple call to this function.

Close

When the MDI frame or the last window is closed in an application, the Close event in the application object is triggered. In the script, you typically would do all of the clean-up required, such as closing any database connections, destroying nonvisual class objects or saving the user's settings to a preferences file. Once again, for simplicity, this code probably would be placed in a function, such as f_app_close, and called from the Close event.

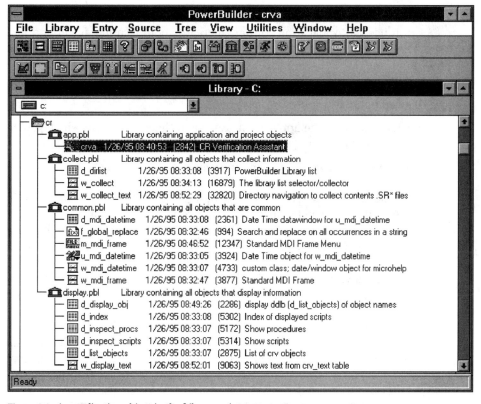

Figure 6.1 An application object in the Library painter.

Idle

If you want to make use of the Idle event, you will need to call the Idle( ) function, which you could place in the application Open event. In the Idle( ) function, you specify the number of seconds of inactivity (i.e., no mouse or keyboard activity) before the Idle event is triggered. This can be useful as a security feature of the application. If this event gets triggered, you could minimize or hide any open sheets and display a login window again, securing any sensitive application or information from unauthorized use or display.

SystemError

If there are serious errors during execution, the application object's SystemError event is triggered. In this event, you could place some generic error-handling function that could open a window and display as much diagnostic information (e.g., window name, function name, error code, line number, etc.) as possible to the user. This information then can be relayed back to the development group for investigation.

Creating a new application object

You use the Application painter to create an application object and modify the following properties within it:

- Icon

- Default text colors, sizes, styles, and fonts

- Libraries that the application can use in the sequence in which you want them to be searched during execution

- Application-level scripts and functions

Within the PowerBuilder development environment, the application object is the context in which you work. When you start PowerBuilder, it requires that you select an application object for the session. If no applications have been defined or the previously selected application is no longer available, then you will be prompted when you first start PowerBuilder to select an application via the Select Application Library dialog (see Figure 6.2). If you click Cancel and do not select an existing application, you will be prompted to create a new one (see Figure 6.3).

If you choose Open, then the Select Application dialog will display again. If you choose Exit, then the PowerBuilder environment will close. Choose New to create a new application, and the Select New Application Library dialog will display.

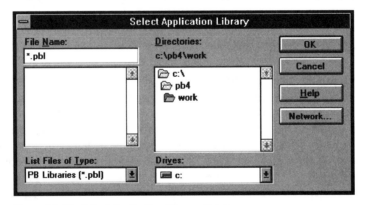

Figure 6.2 The Select Application Library dialog.

Figure 6.3 The Required Application dialog.

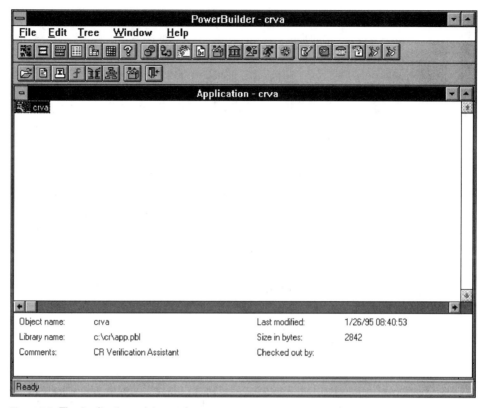

Figure 6.4 The Application painter workspace.

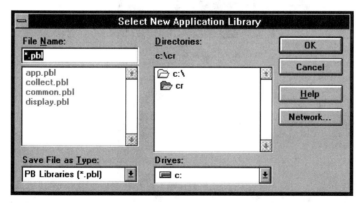

Figure 6.5 The Select New Application Generator dialog.

If you already have an application, click the Application painter icon in the Power-Bar or the PowerPanel, and the current application object will be displayed in the Application painter workspace (see Figure 6.4).

From within the Application painter workspace, click New from the File menu, and the Select New Application Library dialog will display (see Figure 6.5).

In the Select New Application Library dialog, you:

Step 1 Specify the PowerBuilder library in which you want to store the application object. (The application itself can use multiple libraries. The library that you are specifying here is the library in which to store the application object.)

Step 2 Click OK, and you will be presented with the Save Application dialog (see Figure 6.6).

In the Save Application dialog, you:

Step 1 Name the application object by entering a 1- to 40-character name in the Application edit box. This name is what will display in the PowerBuilder caption while you are working with the application.

Step 2 Enter comments by entering them into the Comments box. It is a good practice to document every object in a library to help other developers understand the purpose of it. These comments display in the Library painter, possibly obviating the need for any developer to open and inspect the object to determine it's purpose.

Step 3 Click OK, and you will be presented with the Quick Application Generator dialog (see Figure 6.7).

The Quick Application Generator dialog allow you to decide if you would like PowerBuilder to automatically generate a template for your application.

In the Quick Application Generator dialog, you specify:

- Yes to automatically copy into the library the objects for a basic MDI application, including some elementary scripts. If you are new to PowerBuilder, you might find

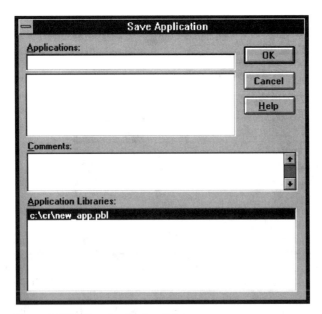

Figure 6.6 The Save Application dialog.

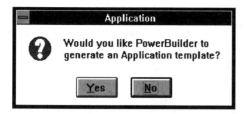

Figure 6.7 The Quick Application Generator dialog.

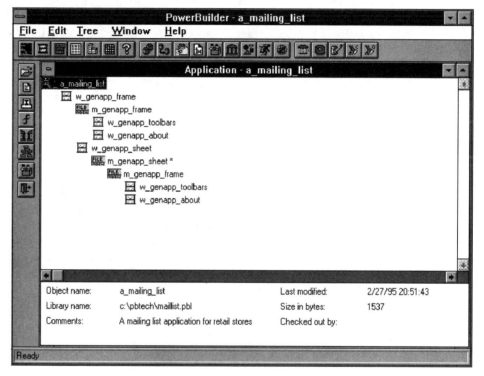

Figure 6.8 The Quick Application workspace.

it useful to reply yes at this point to take a look at the generated code. You can always delete what you do not need later.

- No to bypass copying any predefined PowerBuilder objects and code.

You then will be presented with the Application painter workspace. The new application object is displayed as an icon in the workspace. See Figure 6.4 for an example of the workspace without no Quick Application code; see Figure 6.8 for an example of the Quick Application workspace.

You now have created the application object and placed it in a PowerBuilder library. You might find that there is nothing else that you would like to do to the application at this point. If you are done, you can close the Application painter. If you want to continue with the finetuning of the application object's properties, read on through the remainder of this section.

Specifying application properties

The application object specifies the following properties of the application:

- The library search path for the application
- The icon for the application
- Default text attributes (font, style, size, and color)

Defining the library search path. The objects that you create in painters are stored in PowerBuilder libraries. You can use objects from one library or multiple libraries in an application. You define each library that the application uses in the library search path. PowerBuilder uses the search path to find referenced objects during execution. When a new object is referenced, PowerBuilder looks through the libraries in the order in which they are specified in the library search path until it finds the object.

To modify/define the library search path, click the Library Search Path icon. The Select Libraries dialog (see Figure 6.9) will display the current library search path and lists the PowerBuilder libraries in the current directory.

To add a library to the search path, double-click the name of the library that you want to include in the search path in the Paste Libraries listbox. Each time you double-click a library name, PowerBuilder appends it to the list in the Library Search Path listbox. You can include libraries from different drives and directories in the search path.

To delete a library from the search path, select the library from the list in the Library Search Path listbox and press the Delete key.

Click OK, and PowerBuilder will update the search path for the application.

There are several strategies that you can use to organize your application into libraries and optimize your environment to work with multiple developers on a large-scale application development. See chapter 4, "Setup Development Environment," for more information on this topic.

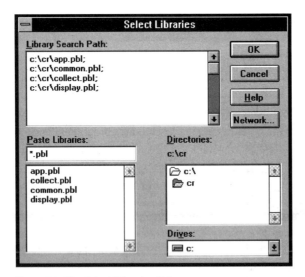

Figure 6.9 The Select Libraries dialog.

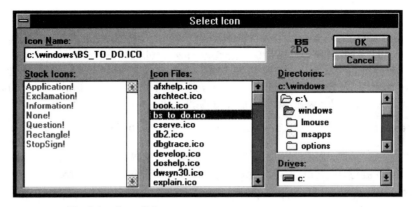

Figure 6.10 The Select Icon dialog.

Specifying the default icon. Users might minimize your application during execution. If you specify an icon in the Application painter, the icon will display when the application is minimized.

To associate an icon with an application:

Step 1 Click the Icon icon, and the Select Icon dialog displays (see Figure 6.10).

Step 2 Specify a file that contains an icon (an ICO file). The icon displays at the right of the Icon Name box.

Step 3 Click the OK button to associate the icon with the application.

Note: If you assign an icon to the application, the icon displays instead of the Run icon in the PowerPanel.

Specifying default text attributes. You should establish a standard look for text that is in your application. There are four kinds of text whose properties you can specify in the Application painter. See Table 6.1.

PowerBuilder provides default settings for the font, size, and style for each of these and a default color for text and the background. You can change these settings for an application in the Application painter and can override the settings for a window, user object, or DataWindow object.

**TABLE 6.1 The Kinds of Text Whose Properties
You Can Specify in the Application Painter**

Type	Where used
Text	Static text in windows, user objects, and DataWindow objects
Data	Data retrieved in a DataWindow
Heading	Column headings that display above the column data in tabular and grid DataWindow objects
Label	Column headings that display next to column data in freeform DataWindow objects

Perform the following step to change the text defaults for an application.

Step 1 Click the Fonts icon. The Select Default Fonts dialog (see Figure 6.11) will display the current settings for the font, size, style, and color for text. When creating a new application, PowerBuilder uses what is specified in the Microsoft Windows Control Panel for the color for text and background. The sample group box text at the bottom of the window in Figure 6.9 provides an example of the current settings.

Step 2 Select Text, Data, Headings, or Labels in the Default For group.

Step 3 Review the settings and make any necessary changes:

- To change the font, select one from the list in the Font listbox.
- To change the font size, select a size from the list in the Size listbox or type a valid size in the listbox.
- To change the font style, click one or more checkboxes (Bold, Italic, and Underline).
- To change the text color, select a color from the Text Color listbox. You cannot specify colors for DataWidow data, headings, and labels here. This is done within the DataWindow painter.

Step 4 When you are satisfied with the setting, click OK.

Note: When specifying a text color, you can choose a custom color. You define custom colors in the Window or DataWindow painters.

Setting application attributes

The application object has the application-level attributes or properties that are shown in Table 6.2.

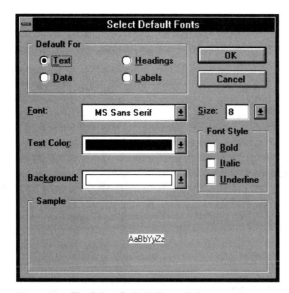

Figure 6.11 The Select Default Fonts dialog.

TABLE 6.2 The Application Object's Application-Level Attributes and Properties

Attribute	Description
Appname	A string that contains the name of the application object.
DDETimeOut	An integer that contains the number of seconds PowerBuilder, as a DDE client, waits before giving up when trying to communicate with a DDE server. The default is 10 seconds.
dwMessageTitle	A string that contains the default title that displays in DataWindow message boxes during execution. You can override this default for a specific Data-Window as follows: `dwControl.dwModify ("DataWindow.MessageTitle = 'New Title' ")`
MicroHelpDefault	A string that contains the default text that displays for MicroHelp in an MDI application. The default is `Ready`.
ToolbarText	A boolean that determines whether to display text associated with items in the toolbar in an MDI application.

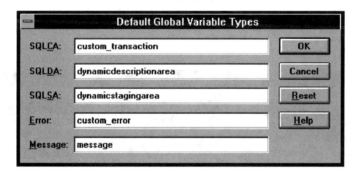

Figure 6.12 The Default Global Variable Types dialog.

You can reference these attributes in any script in the application using the syntax:

AppName.attribute

(*Note*: If the script is in the application object itself, there is no need to qualify the attribute name with the application name.)

Default global variable types

In the Application painter, you can modify the default global variables that are used in the application. To change the default global variables for an application:

Step 1 Click the VarTypes icon, and the Default Global Variables Types dialog will display (see Figure 6.12).

Step 2 Modify the defaults, then click OK.

You can always reset the global variable types back to the PowerBuilder standard settings by pressing the Reset button.

Looking at the application's structure

Once you have selected an application object, it displays as an icon in the Application painter workspace. The workspace displays referenced objects in an outline format. If you are working with an application that references one or more objects in an application-level script, you can look at the application's structure in the Application painter.

To display the application's structure:

Step 1 Open the Application painter, and select the application object that you want to work with. The application object displays as an icon in the workspace. Information about the object displays in the bottom of the window. (See Figure 6.13.)

Step 2 Double-click the icon. PowerBuilder expands the display to show all of the global objects that are referenced in a script for the application object. (See Figure 6.14.)

Using the pop-up menu. The Application painter workspace provides a pop-up menu that offers shortcuts to working with displayed objects in the workspace. To use the pop-up menu:

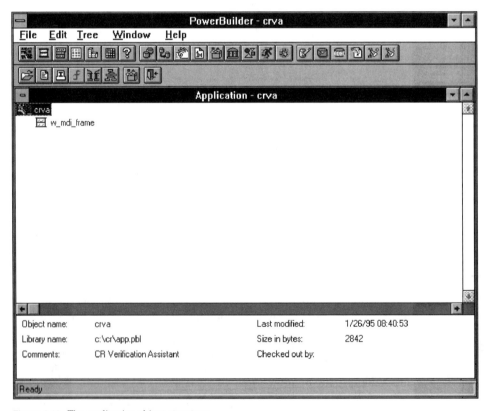

Figure 6.13 The application object structure.

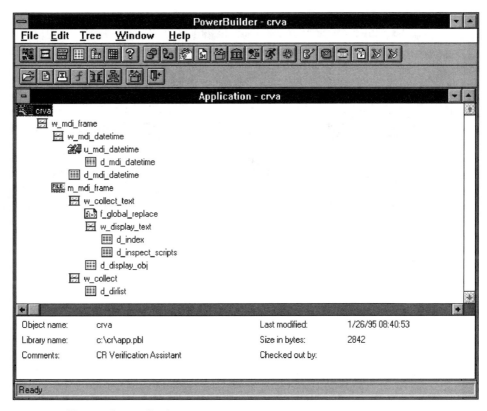

Figure 6.14 The complete application structure.

Step 1 Position the mouse pointer over an object.

Step 2 Click the right mouse button, and the pop-up menu will display.

Step 3 Select one of the items on the menu.

Changing the display of objects. See Table 6.3 for a list of ways to change the way that the objects are displayed.

TABLE 6.3 Ways to Change the Way that the Objects Are Displayed

To	Do this
Display the objects referenced by an object	Double-click the object, select Expand Branch from the pop-up menu, or press +
Hide the objects referenced by an object	Double-click an expanded object, select Collapse Branch from the pop-up menu, or press -
Go to a painter for an object	Press Shift and double-click an object, or select Go To Painter from the pop-up menu

Inherited objects. If an asterisk appears at the end of an object name, see Figure 6.15. This asterisk indicates that the object is a descendant of another object.

To see the inheritance hierarchy for a descendant object, select Object Hierarchy from the pop-up menu, and PowerBuilder displays a window showing the inheritance hierarchy for the selected object. (See Figure 6.16.)

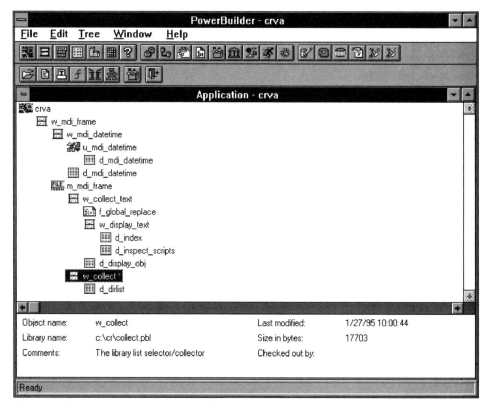

Figure 6.15 Depicting inheritance in the Application painter.

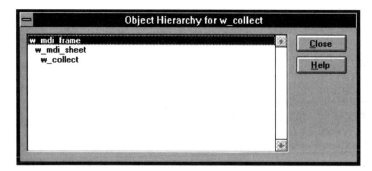

Figure 6.16 The Object Hierarchy dialog.

Which object references are displayed?   The Application painter workspace shows global objects that are referenced in your application. It shows the same types of objects that you can see in the Library painter. It will display the following types of references for an object when the object is expanded: objects that are referenced in painters and objects that are directly referenced in scripts.

The following are several examples of objects that are referenced in painters:

- If a menu is associated with a window in the Window painter, the menu displays when the window is expanded.
- If a DataWindow object is associated with a DataWindow control in the Window painter, the DataWindow object displays when the window is expanded.
- If a window contains a custom user object that includes another user object, the custom user object displays when the window is expanded, and the other user object displays when the custom user object is expanded.

The following are several examples of objects that are directly referenced in scripts:

- If a window script contains the statement, `Open(w_continue)`, then w_continue displays when the window is opened.
- If an object's script refers to a global function:

```
L_sUserID = f_GetUserName(L_sUserID)
```

- If a window uses a pop-up menu through the following statements:

```
M_RMB L_mRMB
L_mRMB = CREATE m_rmb
L_mRMB.m_search.PopMenu( PointerX(), PointerY() )
```

then m_rmb will display when the window is expanded.

Which object references will not display?   The workspace does not show entities that are defined within other objects, such as controls and object-level functions. Also, it does not display the following types of references: objects that are referenced only through attributes and objects that are referenced dynamically through string variables.

The following is an example of objects that are referenced only through attributes. If w_currency has the following statement (and no other reference to w_currency _list):

```
w_currency_list.Title = "Active Currency List"
```

then w_currency_list will not appear as a reference for w_currency.

The following are examples of objects that are referenced dynamically through string variables:

- If a window w_currency_list contains a script with the following code:

```
WINDOW L_wWindow
STRING L_sName = "w_currency_history"
Open(L_wWindow, L_sName)
```

then the window w_go does not display when the window is expanded. The window w_go is named only in a string.

- If the DataWindow object is dynamically associated with a DataWindow control in a window:

```
dw_info.DataObject = "d_emp"
```

then Datawindow d_currency_list will not show when the window is expanded.

The Project Painter

The Project painter allows you to create a definition for the building of the executable file and PowerBuilder dynamic libraries. You use the Project painter to create and maintain PowerBuilder project objects. Project objects contain information for building executable files, such as:

- Executable file name
- PowerBuilder dynamic libraries (.PBD files)
- PowerBuilder resources and resource file names (.PBR files)

Once defined, you can rebuild your application from the Project painter by clicking a single button or by selecting `Build Project` from the Project painter File menu. Building a project object for your application can greatly reduce the amount of time spent creating an executable, PBDs, and PBRs for every build that you want to generate.

To start the Project painter, click the Project painter button on the PowerBar. If the Project painter button doesn't appear on the PowerBar, select `Toolbars` from the Window menu, click `Customize`, and click and drag the Project painter button into the current toolbar space.

Creating a project object

To create a project object, perform the following steps.

Step 1 Open the Project painter by clicking on the `Project` button in the PowerBar. The Select Project dialog box appears. (See Figure 6.17.)

Step 2 Click `New`, and the Select Executable File dialog box will appear. (See Figure 6.18.)

Step 3 Enter a file name for the executable file that you want to create, and click `OK`. The Project painter workspace (see Figure 6.19) appears with the executable file name that you specified appearing in the Executable File Name text entry box.

Step 4 If you want to include resources or dynamically referenced DataWindows into the executable, then you must enter a resource file name in the Resource File Name text entry box, or select `Paste Executable` from the Edit menu to open the Select Resource File dialog (see Figure 6.20), which can be used to browse your directories for the resource file name that you want to include in the project object definition.

Step 5 Check `Prompt For Overwrite` if you want PowerBuilder to prompt you before overwriting any files it creates when building the executable (.EXE) and dynamic library (.PBD) files.

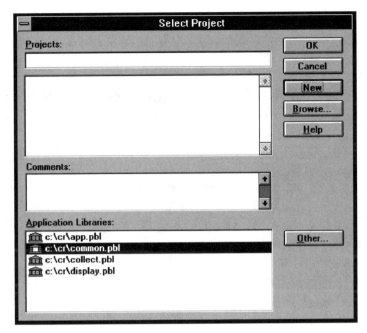

Figure 6.17 The Select Project Object dialog.

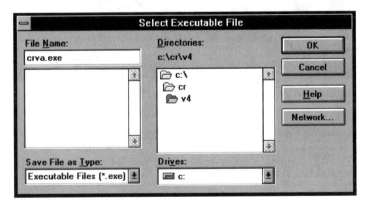

Figure 6.18 The Select Executable File dialog.

Step 6 Check `Regenerate All Objects` if you want PowerBuilder to regenerate all of the window, menu, and user-object classes in the libraries before the executable and dynamic libraries are built. Generally, this is a good practice prior to rebuilding the EXEs and PBDs because it will ensure that the inheritance links still are in good stead.

Step 7 In the Library column in the Project painter workspace, PowerBuilder lists the libraries defined in the library search path for the current application. To define a library as a PowerBuilder dynamic library to be included in the build, check the PBD checkbox.

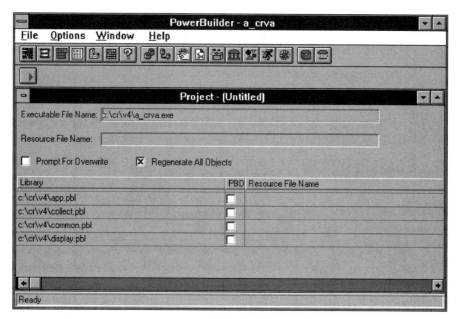

Figure 6.19 Project painter workspace.

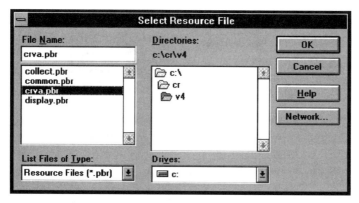

Figure 6.20 The Select Resource File dialog (for executable).

Step 8 You also can add resource file names as necessary to each individual library name. This is done by entering the file name directly into the Resource File Name column or by selecting `Paste Dynamic Library's Resource` from the Edit menu to open the Select Resource File dialog (see Figure 6.21). This dialog will allow you to browse your directories for the resource that you want to add to a particular PowerBuilder dynamic library (PBD).

Step 9 When you have finished defining the project object, save the object by selecting `Save` or `Save As` from the File menu. The Save Project dialog will appear. (See Figure 6.22.)

After saving the project, you can either close the Project painter by selecting `Close` from the File menu or the Control menu, or you can choose to build the application. See the section "Creating an executable" for more information on building the executable and dynamic libraries from within the Library painter.

Maintaining project objects

To change the information contained in a project object:

Step 1 Select the project object that you want to edit, either by double-clicking on the project object in the Library painter or by clicking the project icon on the Power-

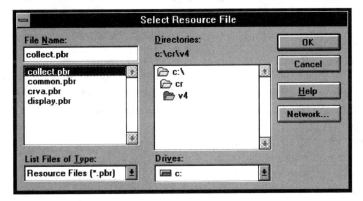

Figure 6.21 The Select Resource File dialog (for dynamic library).

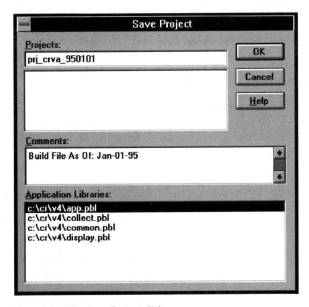

Figure 6.22 The Save Project dialog.

Bar and selecting the project object in the Select Project dialog. The Project painter opens with the settings defined for the executable file name, resource file names, dynamic libraries, and library names.

Step 2 Edit the project object settings as necessary.

Step 3 Save the object definition by selecting Save from the File menu. (To save the object under a new name, select Save As from the File menu and enter the name for the new project object.) You might choose to create several project objects for an application—one for each type of build (along with separate library lists for the application object.

Note: As with all objects that are contained in a PowerBuilder library, you can delete them from within the Library painter by selecting them and pressing the Delete key, clicking the Delete icon, or selecting Delete from the Entry menu.

Creating an executable. There are two ways to produce executables in PowerBuilder. You can use the Project painter to create a project object that defines the executable file name, PBRs, and PBDs. This method allows you to create a new executable and PBDs with complete resource referencing without having to redefine the executable each time you want to create it.

The other method is to use the Create EXE button in the Application painter to define how PowerBuilder will search for application objects as it creates an executable. With this approach, you would create PBDs by using the Build Dynamic Library option in the Utilities menu of the Library painter.

If you are working on a substantial project that includes PBDs that you expect to build and rebuild a number of times, using the Project painter to create a project object will save you a great deal of time and effort.

To create an executable using an existing project object:

Step 1 Open the Project painter, and select the required project object.

Step 2 Inspect the workspace, and make sure that you are satisfied with the project object definition. Then change the definition if necessary.

Step 3 Click the Build button in the PainterBar, or select Build Project from the Options menu. PowerBuilder then will proceed with the creation of the executable file (.EXE) and any dynamic libraries (.PBDs), regenerating objects (if specified). Any errors that are encountered appear in a message box.

Step 4 Once the process is complete, you can close the Project painter. If you have made any changes to the project object, PowerBuilder will prompt you to save them.

The Library Painter

PowerBuilder uses libraries to store object (source and compiled) definitions and their associated scripts. When you create an application, you specify the default libraries that you want PowerBuilder to use for the application. When you save an object from within a painter, you save the object definition and any of its scripts as a single entry inside one of the application libraries.

The Library painter is the painter that you use to manipulate these PowerBuilder libraries and their entries. This includes a facility that allows a developer in a workgroup environment to take a make a copy of the object in their working library and lock the original, protecting against the situation of multiple developers having an updatable copy of the same object. This is implemented with the "Check in" and "Check out" functions. The painter also allows you to build dynamic libraries (PBDs) and produce a report on library entries.

Library painter workspace

When you open the Library painter by clicking on the Library painter icon on the PowerBar or PowerPanel, you are presented with the library painter workspace (see Figure 6.23).

The workspace consists of two sections: the libraries and directories of the current drive and the drive selection dropdown list. The menu choices that relate to the Library painter are shown in Figure 6.24.

From within the Library painter workspace, using the mouse or keyboard, you can:

- Maintain the libraries (create, add comments, print directory, optimize, and delete).
- Open libraries and display their entries.
- Maintain library entries (add comments, copy, move, regenerate, and delete).

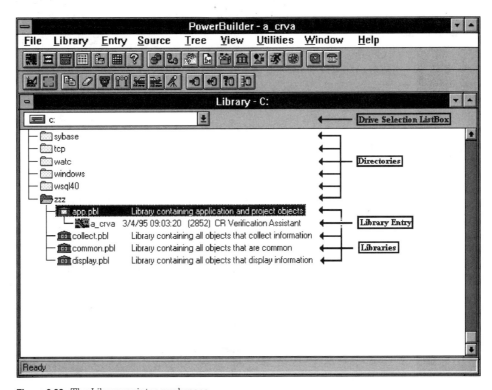

Figure 6.23 The Library painter workspace.

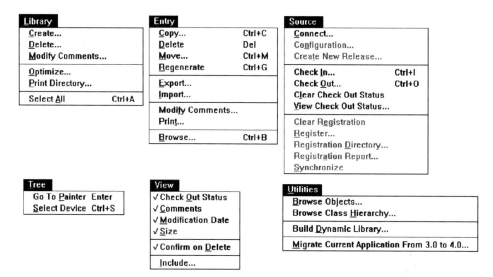

Figure 6.24 The Library painter menu choices.

The Library painter provides a convenient browse utility for you to open the respective painter and edit an object entry that exists within a library. Full keyboard support for the cursor, Enter, and Delete keys has been implemented.

Maintaining libraries

The following is a list of library maintenance features that are available from within the library painter workspace. You can:

- Create a new library.
- Add comments to a library.
- Print the directory listing of a library.
- Optimize, or defragment, a library.
- Delete a library.

We now will show you each feature in more detail.

Creating a new library. To create a new library:

Step 1 Select Create from the Library menu, or select an existing library and select Create from the pop-up menu. The Create Library dialog (see Figure 6.25) will display.

Step 2 Enter the new library name, click OK, and the Modify Library Comments dialog (see Figure 6.26) will display.

Step 3 Enter a comment for the library (it is a good idea to document the purpose of the library, especially if other developers are going to share it), and click OK. The new library name will appear in the workspace.

Adding comments. If you want to add, or change, a comment:

Step 1 Select the library name in the workspace.

Step 2 Select `Modify Comments` from the Library menu, or select `Modify Comments` from the pop-up menu. The Modify Library Comments dialog (see Figure 6.26) will display.

Step 3 Enter a new or modified comment for the library, and click OK. The new comment will appear in the workspace.

Printing the directory. If you want to print the directory for a library:

Step 1 Select the library to be printed (optional).

Step 2 Select `Print Directory` from the Library menu, or select `Print Directory` from the pop-up menu. The Modify Library Comments dialog (see Figure 6.27) will display.

Step 3 Confirm or reselect the library name to be printed, and click >OK. Power-Builder will print the library directory.

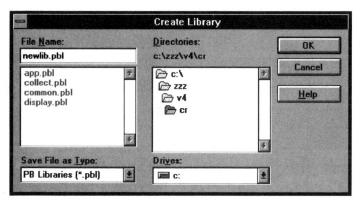

Figure 6.25 The Create Library dialog.

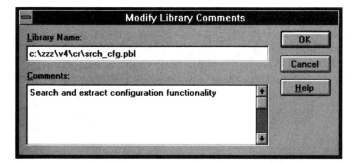

Figure 6.26 The Modify Library Comments dialog.

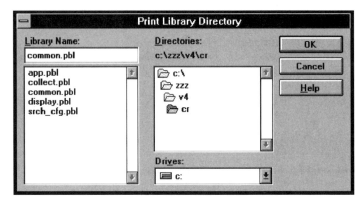

Figure 6.27 The Print Library Directory dialog.

Optimizing. Just like the files in file systems (e.g., DOS), objects in libraries become fragmented. The object no longer occupies contiguous space. This typically happens if you modify an object several times, adding or deleting scripts or functionality, making the object grow or shrink in size. Periodically (weekly or monthly), it pays to optimize libraries that contain objects that have been modified. This will help maintain a consistant load time of objects while testing the application in the development environment. This also should be done prior to producing the executable.

To optimize a library:

Step 1 Select the library to be optimized (optional).

Step 2 Select Optimize Library from the Library menu, or select Optimize Library from the pop-up menu. The Optimize Library dialog (see Figure 6.28) will display.

Step 3 Confirm or reselect the library name to be optimized.

Step 4 If you want to keep the prior copy as a backup, then check the Save Original As .BAK File CheckBox, and click OK. PowerBuilder will optimize the library.

Generating a dynamic library. Dynamic libraries (.PBDs) are used in the runtime environment along with the executable file. To build a dynamic library:

Step 1 Select the source library name for the dynamic runtime library (optional).

Step 2 Select Build Dynamic Library from the Utilities menu and the Build Dynamic Runtime Library dialog (see Figure 6.29) will display.

Step 3 Confirm or reselect the source library name.

Step 4 If you want to include a resource file name for the build of the dynamic runtime library, then enter the file name in the Resource File Name edit box, or click the Files button to display the Select Resource File Name dialog (see Figure 6.30). In this dialog, you can select the name of the resource file, and click OK to return to the Build Dynamic Runtime Library dialog, pasting the selected name into the edit box.

Step 5 Click OK, and PowerBuilder will build the dynamic library.

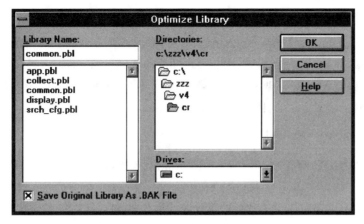

Figure 6.28 The Optimize Library dialog.

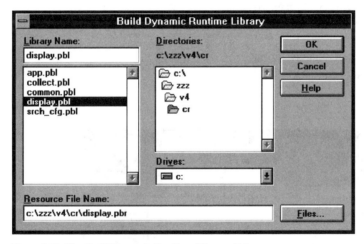

Figure 6.29 The Build Dynamic Runtime Library dialog.

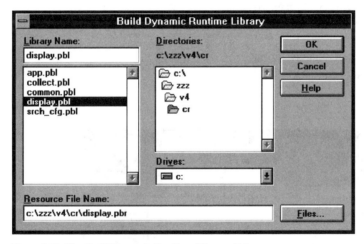

Figure 6.30 The Select Resource File dialog.

Deleting a library. To delete an existing library:

Step 1 Select the library to be delete (optional).

Step 2 Select `Delete Library` from the Library menu, or select `Delete Library` from the pop-up menu. The Delete Library dialog (see Figure 6.31) will display.

Step 3 Confirm or reselect the library name to be deleted, and click `OK`.

Step 4 If you have the Confirm On Delete option off, PowerBuilder will delete the library. If delete confirmation is on, PowerBuilder will display the Delete Library dialog (see Figure 6.32). If you choose `Yes` from this dialog, PowerBuilder will delete the library.

Maintaining library entries

The following is a list of library-entry maintenance features that are available from within the Library painter workspace. You can:

- Navigate the entries
- Select and/or open an entry
- Add comments
- Print

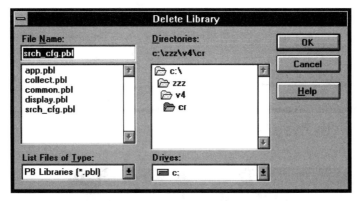

Figure 6.31 The Delete Library dialog.

Figure 6.32 The Delete Library Confirmation dialog.

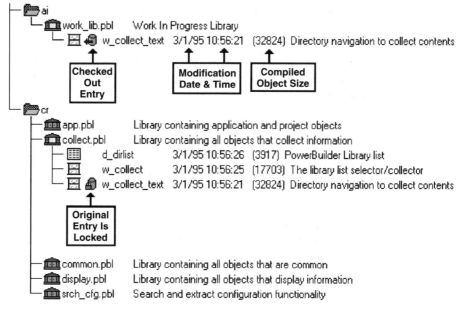

Figure 6.33 The workspace viewing options.

- Delete
- Copy or move
- Check-in or check-out
- Export or import
- Regenerate
- Browse, scan, and report

Navigating the library. There are several ways to navigate the file system and the PowerBuilder libraries. As well as mouse support, you also can use the keyboard within the library painter to:

- Navigate the focus to the a directory or library name using either the mouse or the up and down cursor keys; double-clicking or pressing the Enter key will toggle between opening and closing directories and libraries.

- Determine what you see inside a library when it is open. Select the required viewing options from the View menu. The menu contains toggle options for displaying information (see Figure 6.33) for the library entries: Check Out Status, Comments, Modification Date, Size, Confirm On Delete, and an Include dialog that allows you to include or exclude any types of objects from the workspace.

Selecting and opening an entry. To open a library entry, double-click the entry, or select the entry and press the Enter key.

Adding comments. If you want to add or change a library entry comment:

Step 1 Select the object entry name in the library.

Step 2 Select `Modify Comments` from the Entry menu, or select `Modify Comments` from the pop-up menu. The Modify Library Entry Comments dialog (see Figure 6.34) will display.

Step 3 Enter a new or modified comment for the library, and click OK. The new comment will appear in the workspace.

Printing entries. If you want to print one or more library entries:

Step 1 Select one or more entries from the library to be printed.

Step 2 Select `Print` from the Entry menu, or select `Print` from the pop-up menu. The Print Options dialog (see Figure 6.35) will display.

Step 3 Check or uncheck the required options, and click OK. PowerBuilder will print the selected entries.

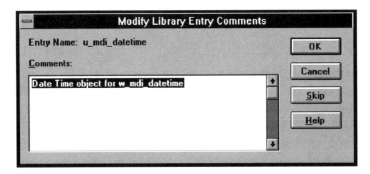

Figure 6.34 The Modify Library Entry Comments dialog.

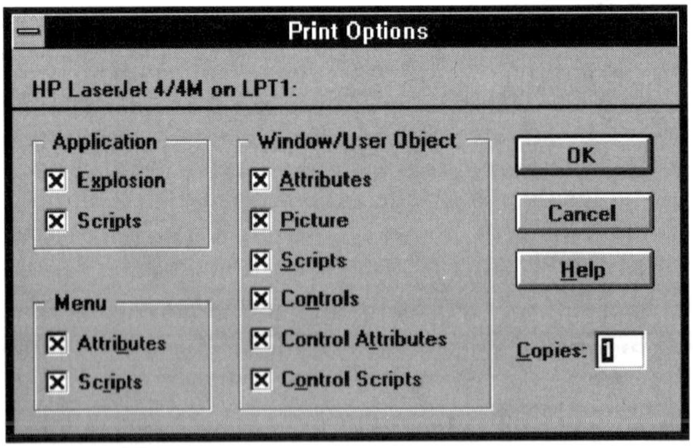

Figure 6.35 The Library Entry Print Options dialog.

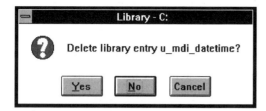

Figure 6.36 The delete library entry confirmation dialog.

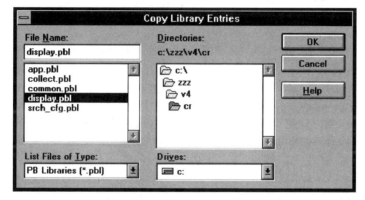

Figure 6.37 The Copy Library Entries dialog.

Deleting entries. If you want to delete one or more library entries:

Step 1 Select one or more entries from the library to be deleted.

Step 2 Select Delete from the Entry menu, or if you only need to delete a single entry, select Delete from the pop-up menu or press the Delete key.

Step 3 If you have the Confirm On Delete option off, PowerBuilder will delete the selected entries from the library. If delete confirmation is on, for each selected library entry, PowerBuilder will display a delete library entry confirmation dialog (see Figure 6.36).

Step 4 If you choose Yes from this dialog, PowerBuilder will delete the library entry. If you choose No, PowerBuilder will bypass deleting the current library entry and continue on to the next selected entry (if any). If you choose Cancel, PowerBuilder will abort the delete process for the library entry and any subsequent selected library entries.

Copying and moving entries. If you want to copy one or more library entries to another library:

Step 1 Select one or more entries from the library to be copied.

Step 2 Select Copy from the Entry menu, or if you only need to copy a single item, select Copy from the pop-up menu or press the Ctrl–C. The Copy Library Entries dialog (see Figure 6.37) will display.

Step 3 Select the destination library, and click OK. PowerBuilder will copy the select entries to the destination library.

If you want to move one or more library entries to another library:

Step 1 Select one or more entries from the library.

Step 2 Select Move from the Entry menu, or if you only need to move a single item, select Move from the pop-up menu or press the Ctrl–M. The Move Library Entries dialog (see Figure 6.38) will display.

Step 3 Select the destination library, and click OK. PowerBuilder will move the select entries to the destination library.

Check In and Check Out

The Check In and Check Out options help ensure that only one user at a time is working on the master copy of a library entry.

For a more substantial source version control package, you will need to purchase one of the supported products and its corresponding PowerBuilder interface. See chapter 20, "PowerBuilder-related tools," for more information on the supported packages.

If you want to check out one or more library entries to another library:

Step 1 Select one or more entries to be checked out from the library.

Step 2 Select Check Out from the Source menu, or if you only need to check out a single item, select Check Out from the pop-up menu or press the Ctrl–O.

Step 3 If you have not already set the current user ID from within the Preferences painter, PowerBuilder will request this information by displaying the Set Current User ID dialog (see Figure 6.39) before allowing you to continue.

Step 4 Enter your user ID, and click OK. PowerBuilder will display the Check Out Library Entries dialog (see Figure 6.40).

Step 5 Enter the destination library, and click OK. PowerBuilder will copy the selected entries to the destination library and "lock" the entries in the original library.

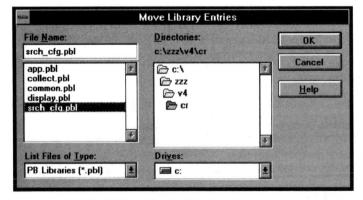

Figure 6.38 The Move Library Entries dialog.

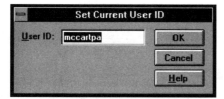

Figure 6.39 The Set Current User ID dialog.

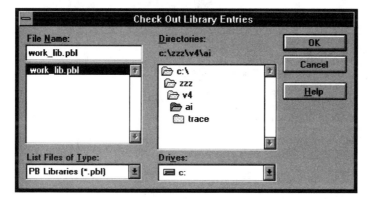

Figure 6.40 The Check Out Library Entries dialog.

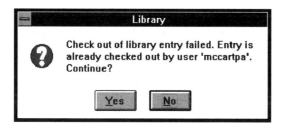

Figure 6.41 The Already Checked Out dialog.

For every entry that you have chosen that already is checked out, you will receive a failure dialog (see Figure 6.41).

Step 6 If you choose No from the dialog, PowerBuilder aborts the check-out process. If you choose Yes PowerBuilder bypasses the current entry and continues trying to check out the remaining selected entries (if any). This situation can be avoided if the Check Out Status under the View menu is on, because the entry will display a locked status.

If you want to see what you or any other developer has currently checked out:

Step 1 Select View Check Out Status from the Source menu, and PowerBuilder will display View Entries Check Out Status dialog, which contains the list of the library entries that you have checked out.

Step 2 If you want to see the complete list of objects that are checked out for this application, select the Show All Users checkbox (see Figure 6.42).

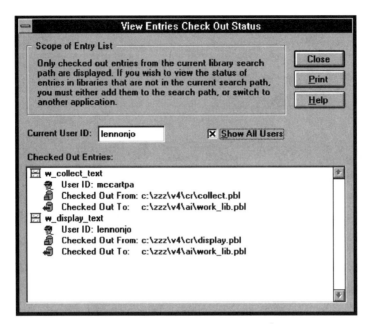

Figure 6.42 The View Entries Check Out Status dialog.

When you have finished making changes to one or more checked out objects and you want to check them back in to their respective original libraries:

Step 1 Select the modified entries to be checked in from your library.

Step 2 Select Check In from the Source menu, or if you only need to check in a single item, select Check In from the pop-up menu or press the Ctrl–I. PowerBuilder will check the entries back into their respective original libraries.

Note: When you develop a new object, there is no need to check it into the network library from your work library; you can either move it or copy it to the network library.

If you find that you need to cancel a check out of a library entry:

Step 1 Select the library entries that need to be cleared from check out.

Step 2 Select Clear Check Out Status from the Source menu, and PowerBuilder will clear the check out status from the entries. When clearing the check out status, PowerBuilder will prompt you to delete the checked out copy (see Figure 6.43).

Step 3 If you choose No from the dialog, PowerBuilder will leave the library entry in your working library. If you choose Yes, PowerBuilder will delete it.

Note: You can only clear the checked out status from entries with the same preference user Id.

Exporting and importing entries. In the Library painter, you can export and import library entries to and from text files. If you haven't purchased one of the many version control interfaces available, you can use these text files and simulate what a version control package typically does: keep text archives of every object and produce reports on the differences (often called *deltas*). This whole process might prove a little cumbersome without some form of database and a management tool (possibly yet another PowerBuilder project!).

To export one or more library entries:

Step 1 Select one or more entries from the library.

Step 2 Select `Export` from the Entry menu, or if you only need to move a single item, select `Export` from the pop-up menu. The Export Library Entry dialog (see Figure 6.44) will display.

Step 3 Accept the PowerBuilder-generated name or enter a new name for the export file, and click `OK`. PowerBuilder will export the entry. This dialog will repeat until all of the selected entries are exported. If you want to abort the export process, press `Cancel`. If you want to skip the entry but continue the export process, press `Skip`, and PowerBuilder will bypass the object an continue with the next entry (if any).

PowerBuilder generates the export file name in the format *filename*.SR*x*, where *filename* is first eight characters of the entry name and *x* is a letter that identifies the type of object exported:

a—Application	q—Query
d—DataWindow	s—Structure
f—Function	u—User object
j—Project	w—Window

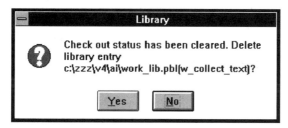

Figure 6.43 Delete the checked out entry.

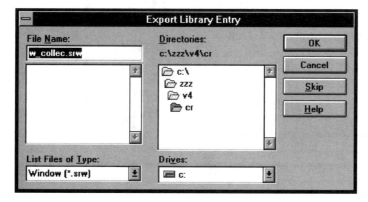

Figure 6.44 The Export Library Entry dialog.

To import one or more text files into a library:

Step 1 Select `Import` from the Entry menu, or if you are positioned on the library name, select `Import` from the pop-up menu. The Import Library Entries dialog (see Figure 6.45) will display.

Step 2 Select one or more the the listed (.SR*) files, and click OK. The Import File Into Library Entry dialog (see Figure 6.46) will display.

Step 3 Select the destination library, and click OK. PowerBuilder will import the files into the selected library.

Note: When you import a file, PowerBuilder automatically regenerates it.

Regenerating entries. Occasionally, you will need to regenerate library entries to ensure that descendant objects in an inheritance chain have the most up-to-date linkages to their respective ancestor objects. This can be done via two methods: using the `Regenerate` option in the library painter or through the Class Browser dialog, which will be covered in the next section, "Browse facilities."

To regenerate one or more entries in a library:

Step 1 Select one or more entries to be regenerated from the library.

Step 2 Select `Regenerate` from the Entry menu, or if you only need to regenerate a single item, select `Regenerate` from the pop-up menu or press the Ctrl–G. PowerBuilder will regenerate each of the selected entries. The current name of entry being regenerated will be displayed in the StatusBar.

Browse facilities. In PowerBuilder, there are three browse facilities that allow you to scan through your application libraries for occurrences of a search string, walk through the inheritance chain, or display the attributes and methods of the object types within your application.

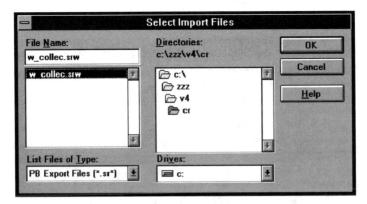

Figure 6.45 The Select Import Files dialog.

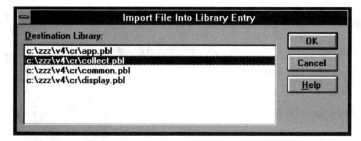

Figure 6.46 The Import File Into Library Entry dialog.

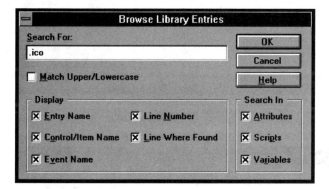

Figure 6.47 The Browse Library Entries dialog.

To search entries in a library for all occurrences of a search string:

Step 1 Select a library to be searched, closing and opening it again to ensure that you have an up-to-date list of entries.

Step 2 Select the entries that you want to scan.

Step 3 Select Browse from the Entry menu, select Browse from the library's pop-up menu, or press Ctrl–B. The Browse Library Entries dialog (see Figure 6.47) will display.

Step 4 Enter the search string, and select/deselect any options. Then, click OK, and PowerBuilder will scan the selected entries, based on your search criteria. If the search string is found, the matching information will be displayed in the Matching Library Entries dialog (see Figure 6.48).

Step 5 From this dialog, you can print the results of the scan by clicking the Print button, you can copy the results to a text file by clicking the Copy To button, or you can select a line in the listbox and open the related object in its respective painter by clicking the Go To Painter button.

Browsing class hierarchy. The Browse Class Hierarchy function allows you to view the inheritance relationship among a set of classes in your application. The inheri-

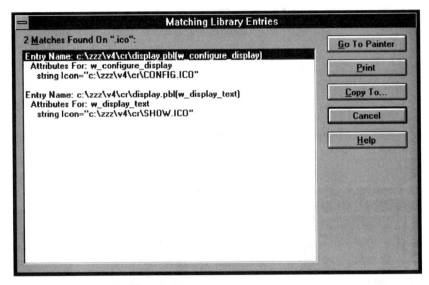

Figure 6.48 The Matching Library Entries dialog.

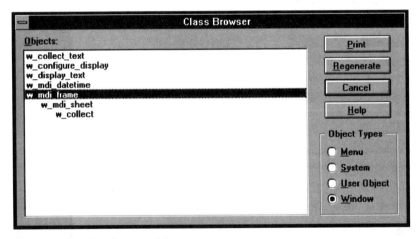

Figure 6.49 The Class Browser dialog.

tance is represented in a indented treelike fashion. The class hierarchies have a single left-most root node and an unlimited number of descendant class levels and descendant classes at each level.

To view the class hierarchy for you application:

Step 1 Select Browse Class Hierarchy from the Utilities menu. The Class Browser dialog displays (see Figure 6.49).

Step 2 From the Class Browser dialog, you can select from four object types. For three of them, you can see the inheritance chain for the objects that you define in the Menu, User Object, and Window painters. The other, System, shows the inheritance chain for the classes that are predefined for you in the PowerBuilder environment (they are the ultimate parent classes from which you inherit when creating all objects and controls).

Step 3 Another useful feature is the ability to regenerate all or some of the inheritance chain. Selecting an ancestor object clicking on the `Regenerate` button will prompt PowerBuilder to regenerate the selected class, walk down the inheritance chain, and regenerate all its descendants.

Note: This method of regeneration is more reliable than selecting all of the entries in a library and using the `Regenerate` option, because you can use it to regenerate the complete inheritance chain in the correct sequence.

Browsing objects. To display the attributes and methods of the objects within an application:

Step 1 Select `Browse Objects` from the Utilities menu, and the Browse Objects dialog displays (see Figure 6.50).

Step 2 From the Browse Objects dialog, you can select from 10 object types and up to 8 different categories of information for the object type. In Figure 6.50, you can see some of the function signatures for the w_collect_text window object within the application.

This dialog is particularly useful when opened in the Script painter so that you can find those hidden ancestor functions and attributes.

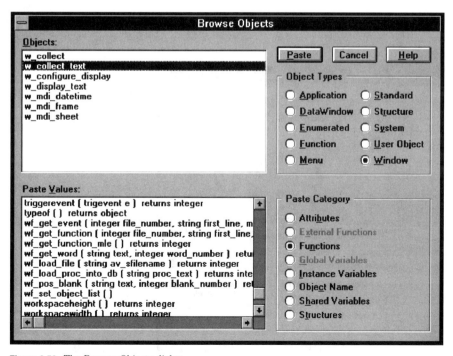

Figure 6.50 The Browse Objects dialog.

The Preferences Painter

The Preferences painter (see Figure 6.51) is essentially the editor for the Power-Builder initialization file (PB.INI). The Preferences painter lets you set and maintain preference variables for the general PowerBuilder environment and specify the following painters: Application, Database, DataWindow, Debug, Library, Menu, and Window. As mentioned earlier, the Preferences painter stores your changes in the PowerBuilder initialization file, PB.INI.

What follows is essentially a series of reference tables that show the entries within the PB.INI that can be set via the Preferences painter. The series will start with the preferences that effect the overall environment, then move progressively through the preferences for each of the painters.

PowerBuilder preferences

The preference entries listed in Table 6.4 apply to the PowerBuilder environment.

Application preferences

Application preference variables specify information about your PowerBuilder applications. You typically specify these options (see Table 6.5) in the Application painter; however, you can specify them in Preferences. When you specify them in the Application painter, the values display in Preferences.

Database preferences

Database preference variables identify the default database and specify defaults for the Database painter. These options depend on your database management system

Figure 6.51 The Preferences painter.

TABLE 6.4   The PowerBuilder Preference Entries

Variable	Description/setting
CompilerWarnings	0=suppress; 1=display
DashesInIdentifiers	0=prohibit; 1=allow
DatabaseWarnings	0=suppress; 1=display
FontBold	0=off; 1=on
FontFixed	0=variable; 1=fixed (if available for family)
FontHeight	Point size (e.g., 8)
FontName	Font family (e.g., MS Sans Serif)
Layer	Painters: 0=cascade; 1=layer
Maximized	0=previous position; 1=maximized
Object(n)	Last four objects references
PowerPanel	0=PowerBar; 1=PowerPanel
PromptOnExit	0=no; 1=yes
SharedIni	Shared .INI file name for database profile (e.g., P:\PUBLIC\PB.INI)
StripComments	Database administration painter: 0=keep; 1=strip
ToolbarFontHeight	Height in points (e.g., 6)
ToolbarFontName	Font family (e.g., Small Fonts)
UserHelpFile	Help (.HLP) file name for User icon
UserHelpPrefix	Search keyword prefix (e.g., uf_)
Window	PowerBuilder environment frame size and position (e.g., 0 0 587 402)

TABLE 6.5   The Application Preference Variables

Variable	Description/setting
AppName	Default application name
AppLib	Default application library list
DefLib	Default library for saving objects
Library path for each application	List of runtime search libraries for application

(DBMS). The variables described in Table 6.6 are common variables that might or might not be valid for your DBMS.

DataWindow preferences

The DataWindow preference variables are described in Table 6.7.

Debug preferences

The debugger has several more preferences that also can be set. The Debug preference variables are described in Table 6.8.

TABLE 6.6 Common Database Preference Variables

Variable	Description/setting
AutoCommit	FALSE=Automatic Begin Transaction following a Connect, Commit, or Rollback statements; TRUE=Manual, under explicit application or stored procedure control
AutoQuote	Strings in SQL: 0=no; 1=yes
Columns	Number of table or view columns to automatically display
Database	Default database name
DatabasePassword	Database password
DBMS	Default database management system vendor
DbParm	Database dependent
ForeignKeyLineColor	RGB color value used for line in display
IndexKeyLineColor	RGB color value used for line in display
LEXICON	Not documented
Lock	The isolation level. Database dependent
LogId	Logon ID
LogPassword	Password
NoCatalog	Catalog access. No=create the PB Catalog tables automatically the first time user connects to database; Yes=do not create PB Catalog tables
PrimaryKeyLineColor	RGB color value used for line in display
Prompt	0=no; 1=prompt for database information on connection
ReadOnly	Database access. 0=create the PB Catalog tables automatically the first time user connects to database; 1=do not create them. If the tables exist, they will be used but information in tables cannot be modified.
ServerName	Name of the server
ShowIndexKeys	0=no; 1=yes
ShowReflnt	Referential integrity, or RI (i.e., foreign keys, primary keys, and associations). 0=do not show; 1=show
StayConnected	Keep transaction open: 0=no; 1=yes
TableDir	0=prompt for table name; 1=display table list
TableListCache	Cache table list for specified seconds before refresh
TableColumnNameTextColor	Text color for column list window Column Name column in detail
TableDetailColor	Background color for column list window detail band
TableDetailTextColor	Text color for column list window detail band
TableHeaderColor	Background color for column list window header band
TableHeaderTextColor	Text color for column list window header band
TableSpace	Database dependent
TerminatorCharacter	Character used to terminate a SQL statement (e.g., a semicolon)
UserID	User ID
Vendors	List of available DBMS vendors

TABLE 6.7 The DataWindow Preference Variables

Variable	Description/setting
DefaultFileOrLib	0=display only entries in the current PBL; 1=display only PSR files in current directory; 2=display entries in current PBL and PSR files
GridOn	Snap to grid: 0=no; 1=yes
GridShow	0=no; 1=yes
GridX	Width in pixels (e.g., 8)
GridY	Heigth in pixels (e.g., 8)
new_default_datasource	Default new DataWindow data source: 1=SQL Select; 2=Query; 3=Stored Procedure; 4=Script; 5=Quick Select
new_default_presentation	Default new DataWindow presentation style: 1=Tabular; 2=Freeform; 3=Grid; 4=Label; 5=N-Up; 6=Crosstab; 7=Graph; 8=Group
new_form_color	Freeform: Default background color
new_form_column_border	Freeform: Default column border
new_form_column_color	Freeform: Default column color
new_form_text_border	Freeform: Default text border
new_form_text_color	Freeform: Default text color
new_grid_color	Grid: Default background color
new_grid_column_border	Grid: Default column border
new_grid_column_color	Grid: Default column color
new_grid_text_border	Grid: Default text border
new_grid_text_color	Grid: Default text color
new_label_color	Label: Default background color
new_label_column_border	Label: Default column border
new_label_column_color	Label: Default column color
new_label_text_border	Label: Default text border
new_label_text_color	Label: Default text color
new_tabular_color	Tabular: Default background color
new_tabular_column_border	Tabular: Default column border
new_tabular_column_color	Tabular: Default column color
new_tabular_text_border	Tabular: Default text border
new_tabular_text_color	Tabular: Default text color
Outline_Objects	0=no; 1=yes
PreviewOnNew	0=no; 1=yes
PreviewRetrieve	0=no; 1=yes
Preview_RetainData	0=no; 1=yes, keep in temporary file (needs SHARE)
PrintOnNew	0=no; 1=yes
PrintPreviewRulers	0=no; 1=yes
PrintPreviewZoom	Zoom percentage (e.g., 100)
Ruler	No=do not show; Yes=show
Status	0=do not show; 1=show
stored_procedure_build	0=prompt; 1=execute procedure to get result set

TABLE 6.8 The Debug Preference Variables

Variable	Description/setting
Stop*n*	Stops set in Debug (*n* is the sequence number of the stop)
	Format: STATE, ONAME, CONTROL, ENAME, LINENO
	STATE: e=enabled or d=disabled
	ONAME: object name
	CONTROL: control name
	ENAME: event name
	LINENO: line number for stop
	(e.g., Stop1=e,m_mdi_first_next,mf_is_open,,4)
VariablesWindow	0=do not show, 1=show
WatchWindow	0=do not show, 1=show

Library preferences

The Library preferences usually are set in the Library painter. If you change the default values in the Library painter, PowerBuilder changes the values in Preferences. Table 6.9 lists the variables that display in Preferences.

TABLE 6.9 The Library Preference Variables

Variable	Description/setting
ApplicationExplosion	0=exclude; 1=include in printed reports
ApplicationScripts	0=exclude; 1=include in printed reports
CondensedFont	The font used for printed reports. Determined by print driver and the fonts installed.
DeletePrompt	Library/Library entry delete confirmation (0=no; 1=yes)
DisplayComments	0=no; 1=yes
DisplayDates	Modification date/time (0=no; 1=yes)
DisplaySizes	Display file sizes (0=no; 1=yes)
IncludeApplications	0=no; 1=yes
IncludeDataWindows	0=no; 1=yes
IncludeFunctions	0=no; 1=yes
IncludeMenus	0=no; 1=yes
IncludePipeLines	0=no; 1=yes
IncludeQueries	0=no; 1=yes
IncludeStructures	0=no; 1=yes
IncludeUserObjects	0=no; 1=yes
IncludeWindows	0=no; 1=yes

MenuAttributes	0=exclude; 1=include in printed reports
MenuScripts	0=exclude; 1=include in printed reports
NormalFont	The font used for printed reports. Determined by print driver and the fonts installed.
SaveBackupsOnOptimize	0=no; 1=yes
SourceVendor	Source control vendor (e.g., PVCS)
UserID	Check in/out User ID
WindowAttributes	0=exclude; 1=include in printed reports
WindowObjects	0=exclude; 1=include in printed reports
WindowObjectsAttributes	0=exclude; 1=include in printed reports
WindowObjectsScripts	0=exclude; 1=include in printed reports
WindowPicture	0=exclude; 1=include in printed reports
WindowScripts	0=exclude; 1=include in printed reports
SourceVendors	CCC,ENDEVOR,LBMS,PVCS,RCS

Menu preferences

The Menu painter has only one preference entry, the prefix for MenuItem names, which is m_. Although you can change it, it is not advisable to do so.

Window preferences

Window preference variables control the use of the painting grid and the default prefixes for window object names. The grid options usually are set in the Window painter. The name prefixes can be changed only in Preferences. (See Table 6.10.)

TABLE 6.10 The Window Preference Variables

Variable	Description/setting
Control names...	Default prefix for all 22 possible controls (e.g., "ListBox=cbx_")
Default3D	0=white window; 1=grey window and controls have 3D option on
GridOn	Snap to grid: 0=no; 1=yes
GridShow	0=no; 1=yes
GridX	Width in pixels (e.g., 8)
GridY	Height in pixels (e.g., 8)
Status	Option no longer used, but still present

7

Creating a Window/Menu Interface

The presentation of the application is effected by creating the menus and windows that facilitate navigation through the application functionality and that display the resultant data and graphical representations in response to the invoked functionality.

The Graphical User Interface (GUI) and Application Style

Some early Online Transaction Processing (OLTP) applications, circa 1972, were run on IBM's CICS, a transaction processing program environment. It became the most popular mainframe OLTP development environment. As graphic-capable front-end environments have become more popular, character-based systems development using CICS has been limited. Character-based systems have data-entry and presentation limitations; you are limited to a small set of keyboard-based controls and can only display in character. The GUI enables you to dictate actions like Save and Print by pointing the mouse arrow and clicking on symbols, icons, or data as well as the basic keyboard interfacing. The older OLTP equivalent was the program function key ("PFkey") whose meanings also had to be standardized to promote ease of use and end user acceptance.

The typical GUI Window (e.g., Word) is navigable by way of a menu bar/toolbar running along the top of the window. The bar will contain items like File, Edit, Windows, and Help. By clicking on a menu item or its toolbar counterpart (a picture or symbol), the application will respond in kind (e.g., open a new window).

Within an enterprise, developing standards of presentation and user appeal for this new GUI interaction is important. We can look at other popular GUI applications (e.g., Word or Excel). They give us some ideas about the look and feel of the GUI, and both conform to a standard. They both use the Multiple Document Interface style (MDI).

The limitations of character-based transaction systems like CICS have fostered the need to develop new applications using graphical user interface (GUI) front-end tools like PowerBuilder. CICS did teach us some important lessons about large-scale OLTP development. OLTP applications should have a consistent look and feel across an enterprise. The windows, menus, and controls should look and function consistently. The obvious prerequisite to accomplishing consistency would be that OLTP development should be standardized within an organization. Developing firmwide standards and guidelines for OLTP and building firmwide libraries containing shareable class objects, functions, and database interfaces will be both practical and cost effective. It also will promote consistency. An organization does not evolve to that level after one project, but strategy and appropriate initiatives should be deployed early enough to facilitate the transition.

Overview of the Multiple Document Interface

Multiple Document Interface (MDI) is an application style that you can use to open multiple window sheets in a single window frame. The user can navigate between the open sheets by focusing on the sheet with a click of the mouse button. An MDI frame window can be divided into three parts: a frame, a client area, and sheets opened within the client area (i.e., the frame is the shell). (See Figure 7.1.) This shell typically will contain a menu, a toolbar, maximize/minimize buttons, and Micro-Help. It acts as a main window that helps the user to navigate through the application components and to provide the capability to have multiple application components

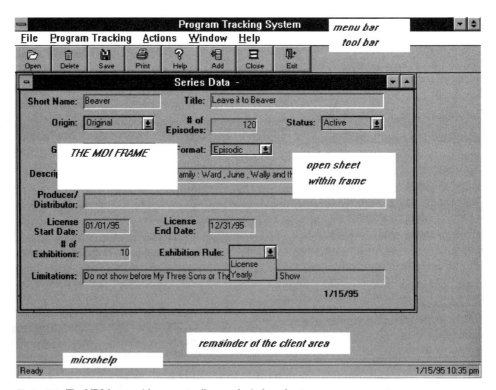

Figure 7.1 The MDI frame with menu, toolbar, and window sheet.

(window sheets) in a partial state of execution. The sheets represent application components and are manipulated using the menu associated with them. The menu of the active sheet displays in the frame's menu bar. It is a good idea, if practical for the application, to have one menu (attached to the frame) for the entire application and to have each window enable/disable pertinent menu items. This will promote consistency as well as help performance. You also can have a menu (inherited from a base menu and extended) for custom sheets within the application. More on this later.

To the extent that it is possible, an organization should try to create a client/server and even a PowerBuilder developer support group, consisting of the firm's best application developers. Included in this group individuals who are knowledgeable in the firm's client/server environment and who can set up procedures to facilitate PowerBuilder setup and DBMS connectivity. Network and connectivity knowledge will help to develop firmwide procedures for software and data distribution. Probably the most important function and the most difficult to install on a firmwide basis would be a set of libraries containing class objects that can be used by all developers to create the components of the MDI application. Today it is *pro forma* to develop all large-scale client/server applications as MDI applications. For example, Power-Builder is also an MDI application.

The frame

The MDI frame is built using the Window painter to define a window with the style MDI frame with or without MicroHelp. In effect, it is, from a presentation perspective, the outside area of the MDI window that contains the client area. The client area is the remaining space left after the menu and sheet border are displayed. The MDI frames can be standard or customized. Here you ideally would create the application frame by inheriting it from a class object library.

The following PowerBuilder statement is used to open a frame:

```
Open ( MdiFrameWindowName )
```

A standard MDI frame window usually has a menu bar and a status area for displaying MicroHelp. The client area is empty, except when sheets are open. Sheets can have their own menus, or they can use the menus associated with the MDI frame. Menu bars in MDI applications always display in the frame, never in a sheet. The menu bar in an MDI application typically has an item that lists all open sheets and another item (e.g., Window to tile, cascade, or layer the open sheets). The movement and positioning of each sheet as it is opened typically is done in a cascaded or layered style for an MDI application, but it can be controlled programmatically with the PowerBuilder OpenSheet and Move functions (i.e., the developer can open and position each sheet).

Using menus

Although it is not required, all MDI frame windows should have menus. If the user has closed all of the sheets, a menu provides a nice way to close the frame. If the sheets do not have a menu, they inherit the frame menu.

Here again, the mature application development environment should use a standard menu that has been set up as a base class object to be inherited. It should contain all of the standard menu items—File, Window, Edit—as well as filler slots for application-specific processing.

Like a standard frame, a custom frame window usually has a menu bar and a status area. The difference between standard and custom frames is in the client area. In standard frames, the client area contains only open sheets. In a custom frame, the client area contains the open sheets as well as other objects, such as buttons and StaticText, that you add to meet the needs of the application. Another difference is that, in a standard frame window, PowerBuilder sizes the client area automatically and the open sheets display within the client area. In custom frame windows containing objects in the client area, you must size the client area yourself. If you do not size the client area, the sheets will open but might not be visible.

Providing a toolbar

Often you want to provide a toolbar for users of an MDI application. Toolbars contain icons that you can use to obviate, or at least duplicate, menu items such as opening a window, saving database rows, and executing commands such as run the current report, delete the selected records, or exit the window. You can have PowerBuilder automatically create and manage a toolbar that is based on the current menu, or you can create your own custom toolbar (generally as a user object) and size the client area yourself. As you are building the menu, PowerBuilder gives the opportunity to associate a toolbar graphic. For an example of this menu bar/toolbar combination, look at Word or Excel. The toolbar becomes even more popular now that PowerBuilder provides focus-only toolbar text, known as Power Tips.

About the client area

The client area is the area within the MDI frame in which open sheets display. In a standard MDI frame, PowerBuilder sizes the client area automatically so that it fills the space inside the frame. For example, if the frame has a menu bar and MicroHelp, the client area fills the space between the sides of the frame and the space below the menu bar and above the MicroHelp.

In a custom MDI frame window, you determine the size of the client area. For example, if the frame has buttons below the frame menu bar, you size the client area so that it begins below the buttons.

As it does when you create any object when you build an MDI frame window, PowerBuilder creates a control with a name consisting of its standard object abbreviation and _1 (i.e., MDI_1), which it uses to identify the client area of the frame window. In standard frames, PowerBuilder manages MDI_1 automatically. In custom frames, you write a script for the frame's Resize event to size MDI_1 appropriately.

A nice PowerBuilder feature is the Object Browser. You can see the attributes and related functions for MDI_1 in the Object Browser. Open the browser from within the PowerScript painter, and double-click the MDI window. The browser lists MDI_1 as one of the controls. Select MDI_1 and click Attributes or Functions as the Paste Category to see the information.

About MDI sheets

Sheets are windows that can be opened in the client area of an MDI frame. You can use any type of window except an MDI frame as a sheet in an MDI application. Typically they will be window type Main for reasons that will be discussed later.

To open a sheet, use the OpenSheet function:

```
OpenSheet ( sheet {, windowname }, mdiframewindowname {, position {, arrangeopen } } )
```

This command opens *sheet* in the application's *mdiframe* as specified in *arrangeopen* (cascaded or layered) and appends the name of *sheet* to *position* (1-*n* where *n* is the number of menu items starting left counting from 1). In a mature development environment, the MDI sheet will be inherited from a class object library. Fortunately, there are only a finite number of requests that a user can have. For this reason, the sheets available for inheritance can be broken up by the type of control contained on the sheet: one for a single database row update, one for multiple row update, one with a grid datawindow control, etc.

Although the application can have many sheets, the number of sheets can and should be reduced by developing the application to use a sheet with data window control containing a base of data functionality (i.e., insert, delete, select, and browse). This will improve performance because the application size will be smaller. Application maintenance will be easier because it will involve a smaller number of components. Then the developers can build the data-entry portion of the application quickly without the use of a varied and consistent assortment of base window sheets. Some class libraries like PowerClass provide one datawindow user object that is used to provide all of the database functionality in one control.

Building the Frame

The mechanics of building a frame window follow, but the bulk of the task is planning a framework for the entire application. Decisions on the style of the application—what the base application processing will consist of, the organization, and the presentation to the users—should be resolved to a good degree before proceeding.

Building an MDI frame window

So once you reach this point, perform the following steps to build an MDI frame window.

Step 1 Open the Window painter.

Step 2 The Select Window window displays. (See Figure 7.2.)

Step 3 Click the New button or Inherit to work with the class object. When you chose Inherit, you will be prompted to provide the source for the ancestor window. Check the project guidelines and standards for establishing a window frame. (See Figure 7.3.) In any event, the Window painter workspace ultimately displays.

Step 4 Double-click in the window or select Window style from the Design menu. The Window Style window displays. (See Figure 7.4.)

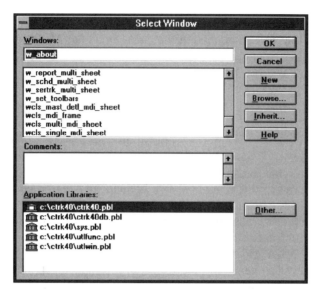

Figure 7.2 The Window painter's Select Window dialog.

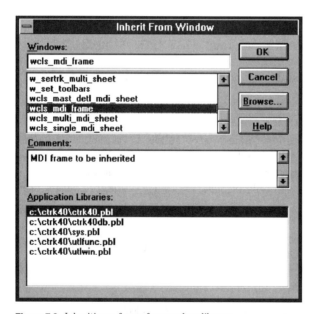

Figure 7.3 Inheriting a frame from a class library.

Step 5 Select the type of MDI frame that you want to create: MDI frame or MDI frame with MicroHelp.

Step 6 Select the style options that you want for the MDI frame.

Step 7 Click the Menu checkbox and enter the name of a menu if you want to associate a menu with the frame. It is good practice to associate a menu with every MDI frame and include items in the menu to open sheets in the frame. Use the Menu painter to build the menu.

Step 8 Click OK to return to the Window painter workspace.

Step 9 Build scripts to open the sheets in the frame and to perform other processing if appropriate. The scripts can be triggered by events in the frame or in the Menu-Items in the menu associated with the frame.

Step 10 If you are adding objects to the client area (that is, building a custom frame), you must size the client area in the script for the Resize event in the frame window.

Step 11 Save the MDI window.

Using menus within the frame

When you build an MDI frame window, you associate a menu with the frame. If the user closes all the sheets, a menu provides a nice way to close the frame. When a sheet without a menu is opened, it inherits the current menu.

For example, assume the frame and w_sheet_1 have menus but w_sheet_2 does not have a menu. The order in which you open the sheets determines which menu w_sheet_2 will have:

- If w_sheet_1 is opened before sheet_2, sheet_2 will inherit the menu from sheet_1.

- If W_sheet_2 is opened before w_sheet_1, w_sheet_2 will inherit the menu from the frame.

As long as you do not close the sheet, the menu that the sheet inherited when it was opened is the menu that displays when that sheet is the active sheet. When you close a sheet without a menu and reopen it, the sheet will inherit the menu that is current when it is opened.

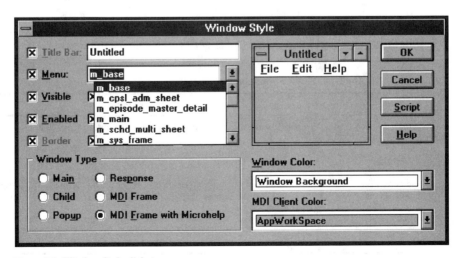

Figure 7.4 Window Style dialog.

Working with Sheets within the Frame

In an MDI frame window, users can open windows (sheets) to perform activities. For example, in an electronic mail application, an MDI frame might have sheets that the users open to create and send messages, read messages that they have received, and reply to these messages. All sheets can be open at the same time, and the user can move among the sheets, performing different activities in each sheet.

Opening sheets

To open a sheet in the client area of an MDI frame, use the OpenSheet function in a script for an event in a MenuItem, an event in another sheet, or an event in any object in the frame.

OpenSheet has the following syntax:

```
OpenSheet ( sheet, {, window }, mdiframe {, position {, arrangeopen } } )
```

The OpenSheet parameters are described in Table 7.1.

Opening instances of windows

Typically in an MDI application, you will allow your users to open more than one instance of a particular window type. For example, in an television station program-tracking application, users probably can look at several different episodes in a series at the same time. Each of these episodes displays in a separate window (sheet). When you open a sheet in the client area, you can display the title of the window (sheet) in a list at the end of a dropdown menu.

To list open sheets in a dropdown menu, specify the number of the menu bar item (the leftmost item is 1) in which you want the open sheets listed when you call the OpenSheet function to open each sheet. If more than nine sheets are open at one time, the first nine sheets are listed in the menu and More Windows displays in the tenth position. When you click More Windows, the Select window lists the open sheets so that users can select the sheet they want to activate.

TABLE 7.1 The OpenSheet Parameters

Parameter	Description
sheet	As a windowsheet in the frame, it can be any window type except an MDI frame.
window	An optional string that contains the name of the window to open.
mdiframe	The name of the MDI frame in which you are opening the sheet.
position	An optional number that contains the number of the menu bar item to which you want to append the names of the open sheets. Menu bar items are numbered from the left beginning with 1.
arrangeopen	An optional enumerated data type specifying how you want the sheets arranged in the MDI frame when they are opened: cascaded.

An example of sheet management

There are situations when using an MDI application where a finer degree of window sheet identification and management is required. For example, let's imagine that you have created a window that will be used to maintain a table of currencies. This window is a sheet in an MDI application, and you want to give the user the ability to open the sheet several times so that they can work with multiple currencies. However, you probably do not want to open a second sheet for the same currency because it already is open. How can this be done? We now will show you some code that can be used to provide this kind of sheet management. The following example code is taken from five objects that could be used to manage the sheets inside an MDI application. The example uses two new 4.0 functions, GetFirstSheet( ) and GetNextSheet( ), to prevent an application opening the second sheet for the same "key" information.

Application object. In the application object, define a global variable of the type of the sheet manager:

```
u_mdi_sheet_manager  G_uoMDI
```

Instantiate the global instance of the sheet manager in the application Open event:

```
G_uoMDI = CREATE u_mdi_sheet_manager
Open(w_mdi_frame)
```

Don't forget to destroy this instance in the application close event:

```
DESTROY G_uoMDI
```

User object for sheet management. In the user object, define a instance variable of the type of the MDI frame:

```
W_MDI_FRAME    I_wFrame
```

Add the subroutines and functions shown in Figure 7.5 to the user object.

MDI frame object. Register the MDI frame object with the sheet manager in the frame's Open event:

```
//Pass handle to the frame to the manager
G_uoMDI.uf_register_frame(THIS)
```

MDI sheet object (ancestor). In the ancestor object for all MDI sheets, code the following in the Open event:

```
IF Len(Message.StringParm) > 0 THEN
THIS.Title = THIS.Title + " - " + Message.StringParm
END IF
```

The code in action. To make the sheet manager user object manage the sheets in your MDI application, all you will have to do is make a simple call to a single function:

```
//Open the currency maintenance sheet for Pounds Sterling...
G_uoMDI.uf_open_sheet("w_mdi_currency",  "GBP")
```

Figure 7.5 The subroutines and functions to add.

```
public subroutine uf_open_sheet (string av_ssheet, &
      string av_skey);
W_MDI_SHEET L_wInstance
IF Len(AV_sKey) = 0 THEN
   // If a title parameter does not exist, make it <Untitled>
     AV_sKey = "<Untitled>"
END IF
IF uf_sheet_is_open(AV_sKey, L_wInstance) THEN
   // If it already is open, check if minimized...
  IF L_wInstance.Windowstate = Minimized! THEN
      // Restore it...
      L_wInstance.Windowstate = Normal!
   END IF
   // Now set focus on this sheet
   L_wInstance.SetFocus()
ELSE
   OpenSheetWithParm(L_wInstance, AV_sKey, AV_sSheet, &
         I_wFrame, 0, Original!)
END IF
end subroutine


public function boolean uf_sheet_is_open (string av_skey, &
      ref w_mdi_sheet ar_wsheet);
BOOLEAN      L_boReturn = FALSE
W_MDI_SHEET  L_wSheet
// Get the first sheet
L_wSheet = w_mdi_frame.GetFirstSheet()
DO WHILE IsValid(L_wSheet)
   // If we have a valid sheet, check its title after the "- "
   IF Mid(L_wSheet.Title,Pos(L_wSheet.Title,"- ")+2)= AV_sKey THEN
      // If the title matches, set return to TRUE...
      L_boReturn = TRUE
      // Pass handle of the found sheet back to caller...
      AR_wSheet = L_wSheet
      // And exit the loop
      EXIT
   END IF
   // Get the next sheet
   L_wSheet = w_mdi_frame.GetNextSheet(L_wSheet)
LOOP
RETURN L_boReturn
end function


public subroutine uf_register_frame (window av_wframe);
//Store the handle to the frame in an instance variable
I_wframe = AV_wFrame
end subroutine
```

For example, this function could be called when the user double-clicks on a row within a DataWindow list of currencies in a sheet.

Passing parameters between windows

You can pass parameters between windows and sheets by opening them with the functions OpenWithParm and OpenSheetWithParm. You can return parameters from response windows by closing them with CloseWithReturn function. You also can define your own window-level functions to make it easier to pass information to them from other objects that are contained within the window.

Window event map

When you develop applications in PowerBuilder, you will find that you need to know what events get triggered (e.g., what events get triggered when you open a sheet and subsequently close that sheet). The sequence of events is as shown in Table 7.2.

Arranging sheets

After you open sheets in an MDI frame, you can change the way that the sheets are arranged in the frame. To arrange the sheets, use the Arrange-Sheets function. To allow the user to arrange the sheets, create a MenuItem (typically on a menu bar item named Window), and use the ArrangeSheets function to arrange the sheets when the user selects a MenuItem.

Maximizing sheets

If sheets opened in an MDI window have a control menu, users can maximize the sheets. This is what happens when the active sheet is maximized:

- If another sheet becomes the active sheet, that sheet is maximized (the sheet inherits the state of the previous sheet).

- If a new sheet is opened, the current sheet is restored to its previous size and the new sheet is opened in its original size.

Closing sheets

To close the active window (sheet), users can press Ctrl–F4. In addition, you can write a script for a MenuItem that closes the parent window of the menu. Make sure the menu is associated with the sheet, not the frame. For example:

```
Close(ParentWindow)
```

To close all of the sheets, the users can press Alt–F4. In addition, you can write a script to keep track of the open sheets in an array and then use a loop structure to close them.

Providing MicroHelp

MDI provides a MicroHelp facility that you can use to display information to the user in the status area at the bottom of the frame. You can define MicroHelp for Menu-Items and for controls in custom frame windows. You specify the text for the Micro-Help associated with a MenuItem for an MDI frame or sheet in the Menu painter. To change the text of the MicroHelp in a script for a MenuItem, use the SetMicroHelp function. You can associate MicroHelp with a control in a custom frame window by using the control's Tag attribute. For example, say you have added a `Print` button to the client area. To display MicroHelp for the button, write a script for the button's

TABLE 7.2 The Sequence of Events

Seq#	Event	Object	PB Statement	Description
1	open	application	Open(w_mdi_frame)	
2	resize	w_mdi_frame		
3	open	w_mdi_frame		
4	activate	w_mdi_frame		
5	show	w_mdi_frame		
6	resize	w_mdi_frame		
7	selected	m_mdi_frame.m_adm.m_ccy		
8	clicked	m_mdi_frame.m_adm.m_ccy	w_currency L_wSheet "OpenSheet(L_wSheet, w_mdi_frame, 0, Original!)"	
9	deactivate	w_mdi_frame		
10	activate	w_mdi_frame		All objects within the sheet are instantiated. This is carried out using the create statement (see exported definition). The sequence is typically in the reverse order that they were placed onto the the window using the window painter
11	constructor	w_currency.mle_1		
12	constructor	w_currency.dw_1		
13	constructor	w_currency.cb_1		
14	constructor	w_currency.lb_1		
15	constructor	w_currency.ddlb_1		
16	constructor	u_custom_search		
17	constructor	w_currency.uo_1		
18	constructor	u_custom_search.cb_1		
19	constructor	w_currency.sle_1		
20	constructor	w_currency.cbx_mouse		
21	constructor	w_currency.rb_2		
22	open	w_currency	dw_1.SetTransObject (SQLCA) dw_1.Retrieve( )	
23	toolbarmoved	w_mdi_frame		
24	toolbarmoved	w_mdi_frame		
25	retrievestart	w_currency.dw_1		Begin retrieval of data
26	sqlpreview	w_currency.dw_1		Send the SELECT statement
27	retrieverow	w_currency.dw_1		Retrieve rows until...
28	retrieverow	w_currency.dw_1		
29	retrieverow	w_currency.dw_1		"The DataWindow is full, so..."
30	resize	w_currency.dw_1		Add vertical scroll bar (if allowed)
31	resize	w_currency.dw_1		Add horizontal scroll bar (if allowed)
32	retrieverow	w_currency.dw_1		Continue retrieval...
33	retrieverow	w_currency.dw_1		

34	retrieverow	w_currency.dw_1	
35	retrieverow	w_currency.dw_1	
36	rowfocuschanged	w_currency.dw_1	Establish row focus (if control is enabled)
37	itemfocuschanged	w_currency.dw_1	Establish column focus (this only occurs if tab order > 0 and control is enabled)
38	retrieveend	w_currency.dw_1	The retrieval is complete
39	resize	w_currency	Resize the window
40	show	w_currency	Show the window
41	getfocus	w_currency.dw_1	Establish focus on DataWindow (only if the DataWindow is lowest tab order or a dw_1.SetFocus( ) is coded)
42	selected	m_mdi_frame.m_close	
43	clicked	m_mdi_frame.m_close	Close(w_mdi_frame.Get ActiveSheet( ))
44	closequery	w_currency	
45	close	w_currency	
46	hide	w_currency	
47	deactivate	w_currency	
48	losefocus	w_currency.dw_1	
49	destructor	w_currency.mle_1	
50	destructor	w_currency.dw_1	
51	destructor	w_currency.cb_1	
52	destructor	w_currency.lb_1	
53	destructor	w_currency.ddlb_1	
54	destructor	u_custom_search	
55	destructor	w_currency.uo_1	
56	destructor	u_custom_search.cb_1	
57	destructor	w_currency.sle_1	
58	destructor	w_currency.cbx_mouse	
59	destructor	w_currency.rb_2	All window objects are destroyed
60	selected	m_mdi_frame.m_exit	
61	clicked	m_mdi_frame.m_exit	Close(w_mdi_frame)
62	clicked	m_frame.m_exit	
63	closequery	w_mdi_frame	
64	close	w_mdi_frame	
65	close	application	

GetFocus event that sets the Tag attribute to the desired text, then uses SetMicro-Help to display the text. For example:

```
cb_print.Tag="Prints information about current episode "
w_frame.SetMicroHelp(This.Tag)
```

You also can set a control's Tag attribute in the Tag window. In the LoseFocus event, you should restore the MicroHelp, such as:

```
w_frame.SetMicroHelp("Ready")
```

Building Toolbars

To make your MDI application easy to use, you might want to add a toolbar with icons that users can click as a shortcut for choosing an item from a menu. Power-Builder provides an easy way for you to add a toolbar to an MDI frame window. When you define a MenuItem in the Menu painter, you simply specify that you want the MenuItem to display in the toolbar with a specific picture. During execution, PowerBuilder automatically generates a toolbar for the MDI frame window containing the menu.

The toolbar works the same as the PowerBuilder toolbars. Your users can select items from the toolbar, choose to display or not display text in the toolbar, move the toolbar around the frame, make the toolbar floating, and so on, and all without your writing a line of code. If you provide a toolbar this way, PowerBuilder automatically manages the client area of the MDI window, so you don't need to resize the client area based on the toolbar.

Adding a toolbar to a menu

To add a toolbar to an MDI window:

Step 1 In the Menu painter, associate pictures with the MenuItems that you want to display in the toolbar.

Step 2 In the Window painter, associate the menu with the window and turn on the display of the toolbar.

Step 3 In the Application painter, specify whether you want text to display below the pictures.

In the Menu painter, you specify which MenuItems you want to display in the toolbar and which pictures to use to represent the MenuItems.

Associating a toolbar item with a particular menu item

To associate a toolbar picture with a MenuItem:

Step 1 Open the menu in the Menu painter.

Step 2 Select the MenuItem that you want to display in the toolbar.

Step 3 Click the `Change` button shown in Figure 7.6. The Toolbar Item window displays.

Step 4 To specify the picture displayed in the toolbar, click `Change Picture`. The Toolbar Item Picture window displays. (See Figure 7.7.)

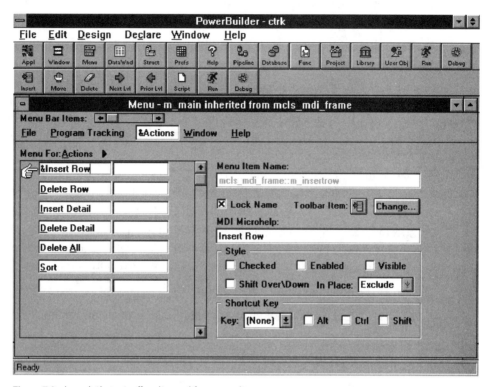

Figure 7.6 Associating a toolbar item with a menu item.

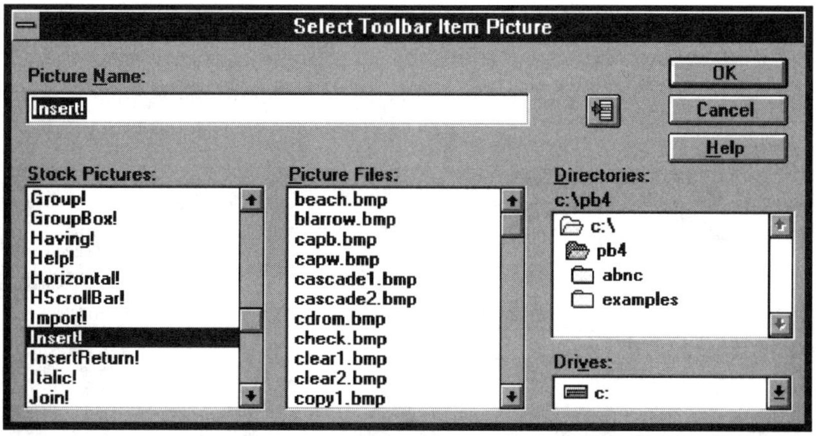

Figure 7.7 Toolbar item picture selection.

Step 5 Specify the picture to display in the toolbar. You can choose a stock picture or a BMP or RLE file. If you choose a stock picture, PowerBuilder uses the up version when the item is not clicked and the down version when the item is clicked.

Step 6 If you chose a BMP or RLE file as the picture and want a different picture to display when the item is clicked, click `Change Down Picture` and specify the picture.

Step 7 In the Text box in the Toolbar Item window, specify the text to display below the picture when text is displayed in the toolbar.

Step 8 If you want to leave space before the picture in the toolbar, specify a value in the Space Before box. You can specify any integer in this box. Experiment with values to get the spacing the way that you want it. If you leave the value 0, there will be no spacing before the picture. (Note that spacing is used only when the toolbar is not displaying text.)

Step 9 In the Order box, specify the order in which the MenuItem displays in the toolbar. If you leave the value 0, PowerBuilder places the MenuItem in the order in which it goes through the menu to build the toolbar. (See Figure 7.8.)

Step 10 If you want the item to stay down until the user performs an action, click the Display Down checkbox. The item stays down after it is selected until you set it up in a script (set the MenuItem's ToolbarItemDown attribute to False).

Step 11 Preview the menu. The currently defined toolbar displays below the menu.

Step 12 Save the menu. Check the naming standards if a new menu is being built.

Associating Menus with Windows

In the Window painter, you associate the menu with the MDI frame window and specify that the window should display the toolbar. To use the toolbar in a window:

Step 1 Open the MDI frame window that is to include the menu and associated toolbars.

Step 2 Associate the menu with the window using the dropdown window.

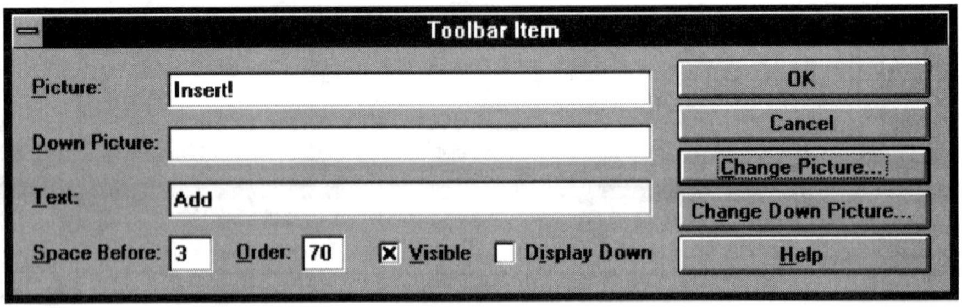

Figure 7.8 Refining the position of the toolbar item.

Basic menu/window association and rules for interaction

When working with menus, you should be aware of the rules of window menu interaction within an MDI application. These rules will facilitate development and avoid latent and patent problems that will be hard to find and debug, especially if the development is in an advanced state.

- The MDI frame should always have a menu. This will avoid potential problems because, if the currently active sheet does not have a menu, then the menu and toolbar (if any) associated with the last active sheet remains in place and operative while that previous sheet remains open.

- If any one sheet has a menu toolbar, then all sheets should have a menu toolbar. This will avoid a potential problem in the making. For example, if the currently active sheet has a menu but no toolbar and the previously active (and still open) sheet has both a menu and a toolbar, then the menu displayed will be the menu associated with the currently active sheet, but the menu toolbar displayed will be the toolbar for the previously active sheet

- Menu toolbars work only on MDI frame and MDI sheet windows. If you open a non-MDI window with a menu that has a toolbar, the toolbar will not show. Menu toolbar buttons map directly to menu items. Clicking a menu toolbar button is the same as clicking on its corresponding menu item.

- Disabling a menu item will disable its toolbar button as well but will not change the appearance of the button. If you want the button to "look" disabled, you must do this programmatically. Hiding a submenu item does not cause its toolbar button to disappear or to be disabled. If you want the button to disappear or be disabled, you must do this programmatically. Hiding a main menu item does not cause the submenu item toolbar buttons to disappear; however, it does disable them. Again, to gray out the buttons, you must do this programmatically in the associated script.

- A double toolbar effect will be achieved if you have a menu with a toolbar on both the frame and the sheet. You can align these toolbars any way that you like. If both the sheet and the frame have menu toolbars and the sheet is open, then the menu that is displayed will be the menu for the sheet, but both toolbars will appear and be operative. If the main menu item under which you want your open sheet list to be displayed does not have any submenu items under it, the open sheet list will not appear there. To make it appear there, either add some submenu items under the main menu item or add a single menu item with text consisting of a single dash as a submenu item.

Putting the Window menu association in motion

Working in the Application Script painter, you can set the basic frame appearance at the start of the application execution. For example, in the Application painter, you can invoke the Script painter and add the following line of script to specify whether to display text in the toolbar. To display in the toolbar, code `ToolBarText = TRUE`. To suppress the text display, code `ToolBarText = FALSE`. When the user runs the application, the toolbar displays as you have defined it.

Toolbars are friendly, and displaying the text helps the new user gain familiarity with the toolbar items, thereby allowing the user to quickly master the application. Clicking a picture is the same as choosing the corresponding MenuItem. Power-Builder automatically provides a pop-up menu for the toolbar, which users can use to move the toolbar or change its properties. You also can manipulate the toolbar in scripts during execution.

The window/menu interface is the crux of the application presentation level. PowerBuilder's comprehensive Window and Menu painters facilitate the development. With proper planning and control, the development team can work on different parts of the application all navigated and launched from within a single application shell.

8

Building Windows

A window is the main conversation medium between an application and a user. It is used to display information to the user and can accept information from a user via the keyboard and/or the mouse. This chapter will take you through the various options available when creating and/or modifying windows. The areas that will be covered are:

- Creating the window definition
- Adding controls to the surface of the window
- Adding scripts and variables
- Saving and previewing the window
- Using the window

Creating a Window

You design windows with PowerBuilder's Window painter. The Window painter gives you the ability to assign starting values for the attributes of the window. These values also can be changed during execution via PowerScript.

Opening the Window painter

To open the Window painter:

Step 1 Click the window painter icon in the PowerBar or the PowerPanel. The Select Window dialog appears (see Figure 8.1), listing the windows in the current library.

Step 2 Now click the New button to build a new window. The Window painter workspace displays (see Figure 8.2).

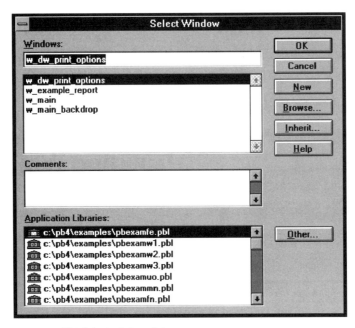

Figure 8.1 The Select window dialog.

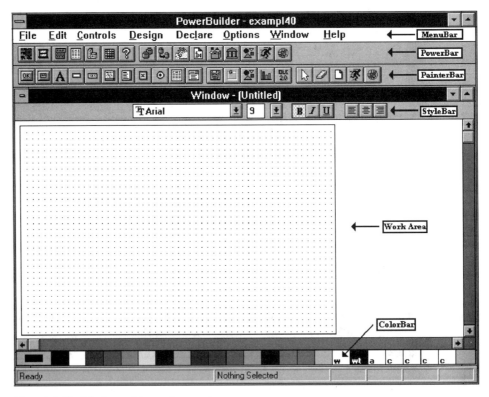

Figure 8.2 The Window painter environment.

The Window painter can be divided into five parts or sections: the ColorBar, the Menu Bar, the PainterBar, the StyleBar, and finally the work area itself, where you actually paint the window surface.

The ColorBar. The ColorBar is used to assign colors to window elements. You can choose to hide the ColorBar, or you can make it display in the Window painter window or in the PowerBuilder frame, which encompasses all windows.

To specify the appearance and position of the ColorBar:

Step 1 Select `Color Toolbar` from the Options menu.

Step 2 Choose the location of the toolbar from the cascading menu:

- `Hide`

- `Show` on `Frame` (will not disappear when the window painter is minimized)

- `Show` on `painter` (disappears when the window painter is minimized)

The MenuBar. The MenuBar for the Window painter consists of the following options: File, Edit, Controls, Design, Declare, Options, Window, and Help.

The PainterBar. The PainterBar in the Window painter works the same as in the other painters. You can move it around and customize it. One customization that you might want to do specifically in the Window painter is add particular user objects to the PainterBar so that you can place a frequently used (i.e., popular) user object in a window by simply clicking an icon in the PainterBar.

To add a user object to the PainterBar:

Step 1 Click the right mouse button in the PainterBar.

Step 2 Select `Customize` from the PainterBar's pop-up menu. The Customize dialog displays. (See Figure 8.3.)

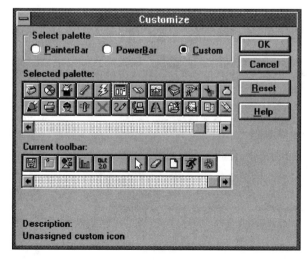

Figure 8.3 The Customize Toolbar dialog.

Step 3 Click the Custom button in the Select palette group. PowerBuilder displays a set of custom icons that you can place in the PainterBar.

Step 4 Drag one of the unassigned custom icons into the Current Toolbar box, and release the mouse button. PowerBuilder places the custom icon in the Current Toolbar box and displays the Toolbar Item Command dialog. (See Figure 8.4.)

Step 5 Click the UserObject button in the Special Command box. The Select User Object window displays.

Step 6 Select the user object that you want, and click OK. PowerBuilder fills in the Command Line box.

Step 7 Type the text that you want to appear in the icon and as the icon's MicroHelp.

Step 8 Click OK. PowerBuilder adds the icon to the PainterBar. To place the user object in the window, simply click the icon.

The StyleBar. The StyleBar is used to assign attributes to text. Similar to the Color-Bar, you can choose to make the StyleBar display in the Window painter window or in the PowerBuilder frame, encompassing all windows. However, you cannot hide the StyleBar.

To specify the position of the StyleBar:

Step 1 Select Text Style Toolbar from the Options menu.

Step 2 Choose the location of the toolbar from the cascading menu:

- Show on Frame (will not disappear when the Window painter is minimized)
- Show on painter (disappears when the Window painter is minimized)

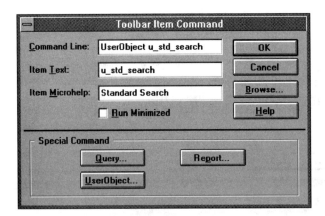

Figure 8.4 The Toolbar Item Setup dialog.

Using the Window painter. The Window painter is a flexible environment. You can use:

- Pop-up menus to specify a style for a control or the window.
- Icons in the PainterBar or the items on the Controls menu to place controls in the window.
- Items on the Design menu to specify the appearance and behavior of the window.
- The mouse to size and position the window and its controls.
- The PowerScript icon to build scripts for the window and its controls.
- Items on the Declare menu to declare variables, functions, structures, and events for the window and its controls.

Window painter shortcut keys

If you're a big fan of using the keyboard instead of the mouse, then you'll be pleased to know that you can use keyboard shortcuts to carry out many of the tasks. Table 8.1 lists the keyboard shortcuts available for the Window painter.

Window appearance

Each window has attributes that define how a window will appear to the user. The appearance of the window can be defined in the following major areas:

- Window type
- Windows control menu functions (min, max, size)
- Initial position on the screen
- Icon when minimized
- Style of mouse pointer

You can modify a window's style at anytime by displaying the Window Style dialog and changing the properties. To define a window's style, double-click the window's background, select `Window Style` from the Design menu, or select `Style` from the pop-up menu. The Window Style window displays. (See Figure 8.5.)

From within the Window Style dialog, you can:

- Specify the window type.
- Specify miscellaneous window properties, such as control menu, resizable, etc.
- Associate a menu with the window (if appropriate).
- Choose a color for the window background and, in the case of an MDI window, the MDI client color.

TABLE 8.1   The Keyboard Shortcuts Available for the Window Painter

Action	Keystroke	Description
Bold text	Ctrl–B	Toggles bold on and off
Center text	Ctrl–N	Centers text
Close	Ctrl–F4	Close active painter
Copy	Ctrl–C	Copy selected control or text to the clipboard
Cut	Ctrl–X	Cut selected control or text to the clipboard
Debug	Ctrl–D	Open Debug painter
Delete	Del	Deletes all selected controls
File editor	Shift–F6	Open File Editor
Duplicate	Ctrl–T	Duplicate selected control
Edit text	Ctrl–E	Move focus to the Text box in the StyleBar
Exit	Alt–F4	Exit PowerBuilder
Font face	Ctrl–F	Move focus to the Font box in the StyleBar
Italic text	Ctrl–I	Toggles italics on and off
Left-justify text	Ctrl–L	Left aligns text
Next window	Ctrl–F6	Switch to next window in Window menu list
Paste	Ctrl–V	Paste control or text from the clipboard
PowerPanel	Ctrl–P	Open the PowerPanel dialog
Preview	Ctrl–W	Toggle window preview mode
Return to control	Ctrl–O	Return focus to control from the StyleBar
Right-justify text	Ctrl–G	Right aligns text
Run	Ctrl–R	Run the current application
Run window	Ctrl–Shift–W	Open the Run Window dialog
Script	Ctrl–S	Open the Script painter for the selected control
Select all	Ctrl–A	Select all controls in the window
Switch	Ctrl–Esc	Open the Task List window
	Alt–Esc	Switch to next task in Task List
	Alt–Tab	Toggle through Task List
Tab	Tab	Moves to next control in the window
Back tab	Shift–Tab	Moves to previous control in the window
Underline text	Ctrl–U	Toggles underline on and off
Undo/redo	Ctrl–Z	Undo last action, or redo last undo

When you have finished with the window style, click the OK button to return to the Window painter.

By selecting and deselecting checkboxes in the Window Style window, you can specify whether the window is sizable or minimizable, whether it has scroll bars, and so on. Note the following:

Figure 8.5 The Window Style dialog.

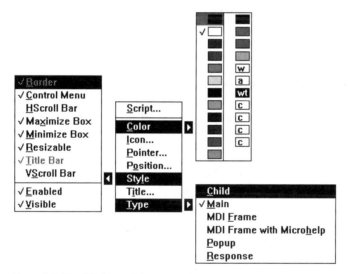

Figure 8.6 The Window painter pop-up menu.

- Main windows must have a title bar.
- Child windows cannot have a menu.
- Response windows cannot have a menu, minimize box, or maximize box.

Using the pop-up menu. You also can modify a window's attributes by clicking the right mouse button on the window background and choosing the attribute from the window's pop-up menu. (See Figure 8.6.)

Types of Windows. One of the first things that you must do is specify the type of window that you are creating. Depending on the type of window, PowerBuilder enables or disables certain checkboxes in the Window Style dialog that specify the other properties of the window. For example, when you create a Main window, the Title Bar checkbox is disabled because a Main window must always have a title bar; therefore, this checkbox option cannot be deselected.

PowerBuilder has the following types of windows:

Main

Child

Pop-up

Response

MDI frame

MDI frame with MicroHelp

To specify the window's type, click the appropriate radio button in the Window Type group box in the Window Style window or the pop-up menu. The features of each type of window are described in the following sections.

Main window. A main window (see Figure 8.7) is an top-level (parent) or stand-alone window that is independent of all other windows. It can overlap and be overlapped by other windows. It has a title bar and can have a menu, and it also can be minimized, maximized, and resized.

Child window. Child windows (see Figure 8.8) are opened from within a main or pop-up window, which becomes the child window's parent. Child windows always are associated with and can exist only within a parent window. If you move a portion of a child window beyond the parent, it is clipped so that only the portion within the parent window is visible. If you move the parent window, the child window moves with the parent and maintains the same position relative to the parent.

They can have title bars and can be minimizable, maximizable, and resizable. When they are maximized, they fill the space of their parent; when they are mini-

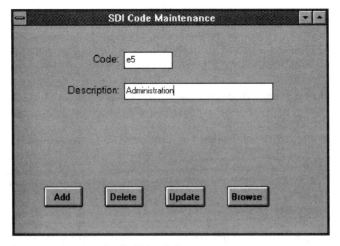

Figure 8.7 An example of a Main window.

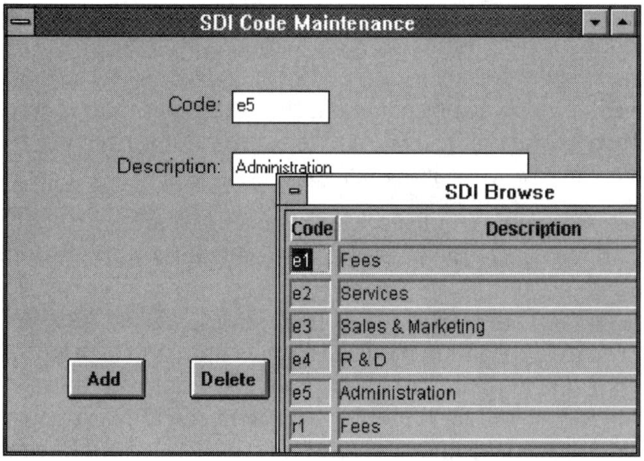

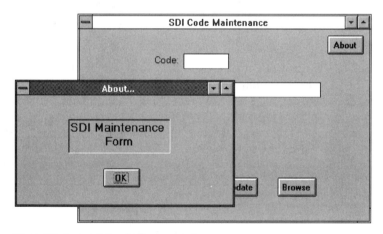

Figure 8.8 An example of a Child window.

Figure 8.9 An example of a Pop-up window.

mized, their icon displays at the bottom of their parent. Child windows do not have menus and are never considered the active window (the parent is). The initial position of the child is relative to the parent and not the entire screen. When the parent window is closed, the child window closes along with it.

Pop-up window. Pop-up windows (see Figure 8.9) are very similar to child windows in that they always are associated with a parent window. However, unlike child windows, pop-up windows can display outside the boundaries of their parent. They can never be overlapped by their parent and are hidden when its parent is minimized. When the parent window is closed, the pop-up window closes along with it. When you minimize a pop-up window, the icon for the window displays at the bottom of the screen.

Pop-up windows are useful when the application needs to show extra information about a field or row that is being displayed on the parent window. This feature commonly is implemented in most applications via a pop-up menu that appears when the right mouse button is pressed. For more information on this technique, see chapter 9, "Building menus."

Note: If the parent window is not named in the statement that opens a child or a pop-up window, then by default, the last active main window becomes the parent of the child or pop-up window when it is opened.

Response window. Response windows (see Figure 8.10) are used to display information to a user and to request the next action to be taken by presenting a choice of command buttons. They always are opened from within another window (its parent). They can be moved, but they cannot be minimized. A key feature of response windows is that they are application modal. An application modal window is the only window that is accessible in the entire application. That is, until the user chooses to respond to this window, it will be the only window in the application that the user can interact with via the mouse and keyboard. The user can switch to another Windows application, but, when he or she returns to this application the Response window still will be active.

For example, a common use for displaying a response window could be when the user closes a window with unsaved changes. You can display a response window like the one shown in Figure 8.10. The user cannot proceed until he or she has chosen Yes, No, or Cancel.

PowerBuilder also provides an alternative to a response window. It is called a *message box*. (See Figure 8.11.) You open message boxes through the PowerScript function MessageBox. The message box is a predefined window dialog that acts just like a response window in that it also is application modal. You are limited in the combinations and text values of the command buttons that can be displayed, but the combinations are fairly extensive and make the message box a useful debugging tool, besides the debugger itself, when testing scripts and displaying values of variables. Be careful, though; some unprintable characters might prevent the dialog from appearing, leading you to make incorrect assumptions about what is going behind the scenes.

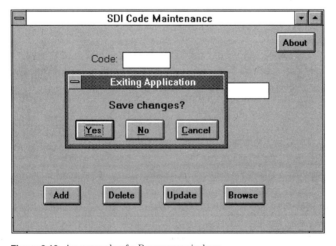

Figure 8.10 An example of a Response window.

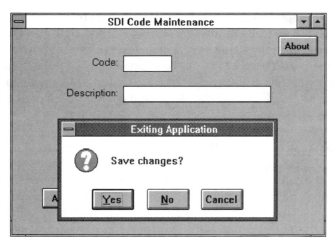

Figure 8.11 An example of a MessageBox dialog.

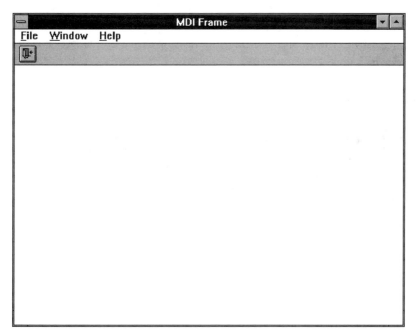

Figure 8.12 An example of an MDI frame window.

MDI frame window. An MDI frame window (see Figure 8.12) is the Multiple Document Interface window in which you can open many other windows, which commonly are referred to as *sheets*, and allow the user to move around the sheets that they have opened within the frame. This type of application is ideal if users need to have several of the application's screens open at one time, usually so they can reference information across screens. With the MDI application, they do not have to close one screen before opening another.

MDI frame with MicroHelp window. An MDI frame with MicroHelp (see Figure 8.13) includes all of the functionality of the MDI frame described in the previous section; however, at the bottom of the frame is an area that can be used to provide additional information to the user. This could be status information, like the current date and time or the identity of the currently selected DataWindow row, or it could be textual help that appears when the user moves the mouse pointer over a particular area of the screen.

Specifying window colors. To specify the color of a window background, specify the background color of the window from the Window Color listbox in the Window Style dialog, or select the color from the `Color` menu option on the pop-up menu.

For main, child, pop-up, and response windows, the default color is Window Background, which is the color that the user has specified in the Windows Control Panel for Window Background.

Sizing, positioning, and scrolling of the window. To determine the size and position of a window when it will open during execution, you:

Step 1 Select `Position` from the window's pop-up menu, or select `Window Position` from the Design menu. The Window Position dialog displays (see Figure 8.14).

Step 2 Move the window to the location required. You can do this by either entering the values into the appropriate X, Y, Width, and Height boxes or by dragging the rep-

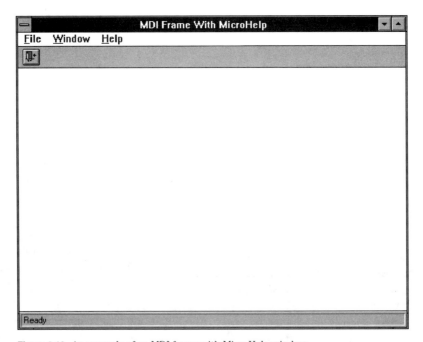

Figure 8.13 An example of an MDI frame with MicroHelp window.

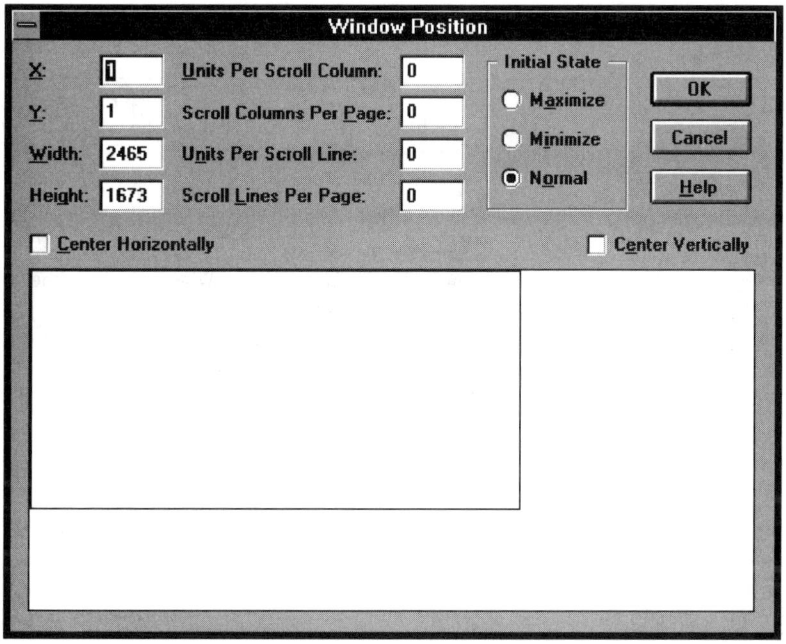

Figure 8.14 The Window Position dialog.

resentation of the window, and/or its edges, with the mouse. You also can use the checkbox fields to center the window in the *X* and *Y* axes.

Step 3 Click OK.

For main, pop-up, response, and MDI frame windows, *X* and *Y* locations are relative to the upper-left corner of the screen. For child windows, *X* and *Y* are relative to the parent.

About PowerBuilder units. By using PowerBuilder Units (PBU), it is possible to build windows that are scaled appropriately for the video resolution of client screens. The resolutions are more commonly 640×480, 800×600, or 1024×768. Bear in mind that you probably will want to develop your windows with the lowest common denominator of the anticipated production environment (i.e., 640×480). A horizontal PBU is $\frac{1}{32}$ of the width of an average character in the System font. A vertical PBU is $\frac{1}{64}$ of the System font height. Sizes in the Window painter and in scripts are expressed as PBUs. (The two exceptions are text size, which is expressed in points, and the grid size in the Window and DataWindow painters, which is in pixels.)

Specifying window scrolling. If your window is resizable, it is possible that not all of the window's contents are visible during execution. In such cases, you should make the window scrollable by providing scroll bars. You specify that a window has scroll bars in the Window Style window. By default, PowerBuilder controls scrolling when scroll bars are present. If you want, you can control the amount of scrolling by specifying values for attributes in the Window Position window, as shown in Table 8.2.

TABLE 8.2 Controlling the Amount of Scrolling

Option	Meaning
Units Per Scroll Column	The number of PBUs to scroll right or left when the user clicks the right or left arrow in the horizontal scrollbar. When the value is 0 (the default), it scrolls ⅟₁₀₀ the width of the window.
Scroll Columns Per Page	The number of columns to scroll when the user clicks the horizontal scrollbar itself. When value is 0 (the default), it scrolls 10 columns.
Units Per Scroll Line	The number of PBUs to scroll up or down when the user clicks the up or down arrow in the vertical scroll bar. When value is 0 (the default), it scrolls ⅟₁₀₀ the height of the window.
Scroll Lines Per Page	The number of lines to scroll when the user clicks the vertical scroll bar itself. When value is 0 (the default), it scrolls 10 lines.

Specifying the pointer. There might be situations where you need to display a nonstandard mouse pointer, different from the default arrow, whenever the mouse is over the window area. This is done by specifying either one of the supplied pointers or by choosing an external Microsoft Windows cursor resource for the window pointer.

To choose the window pointer:

Step 1 Select `Pointer` from the window's pop-up menu. The Select Pointer window displays. (See Figure 8.15.)

Step 2 Choose the pointer either from the Stock Pointers list, or, if you have files containing pointer definitions (.CUR files), choose one from the Pointer Files list. The chosen pointer displays next to the Pointer Name box.

Step 3 Click OK.

Note: You also can specify the pointer that displays when the mouse is moved over any individual control by using the control's pop-up menu in the Window painter.

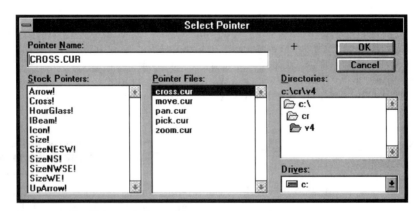

Figure 8.15 Specifying a window pointer.

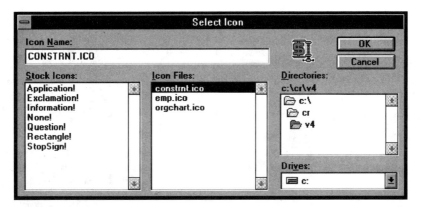

Figure 8.16 Specifying a window icon.

Specifying an icon. If the window is minimizable, you can specify an icon to represent the minimized window. If you don't choose an icon, PowerBuilder uses the application icon for the minimized window.

To choose the window icon:

Step 1 Select Icon from the window's pop-up menu. The Select Icon window displays. (See Figure 8.16.)

Step 2 Choose the icon either from the Stock Icons list or from the Icon Files list if you have .ICO files containing icon definitions. The chosen icon is shown to the right of the Icon Name box.

Step 3 Click OK.

Note: You can change the window icon during execution by assigning the name of the icon file to the window's Icon attribute.

Placing controls in the window

A window is the vehicle that is used to show information to a user and to collect data from a user, via keyboard or mouse clicks. It does this via objects, know as *controls*, that are painted onto the surface of the window. A window must have these controls to be of any use. An example of all of the controls that can be placed onto a window is shown in Figure 8.17.

To add a control to a window:

Step 1 Select the control from the PainterBar or from the Controls menu.

Step 2 Click the location where you want to place the control.

DataWindow (dw_). DataWindows are the best way, in PowerBuilder, to display any information to, or capture information from, the user. Every visual control for a Window can be inserted into a DataWindow control, except the GroupBox, which can be simulated with a combination of Rectangle and StaticText objects. In PowerBuilder,

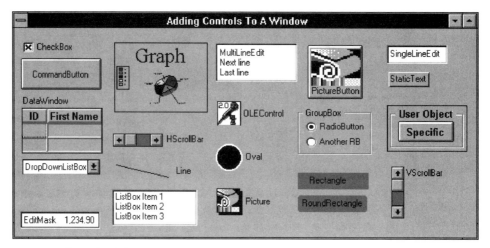

Figure 8.17 Example window controls.

the DataWindow has its own dedicated engine in the runtime environment and is processed considerably faster than any of the other window controls. This is because it does not matter how many controls exist within a DataWindow, Microsoft Windows needs to deal with only one control. If this were implemented with nonDataWindow controls inside a window, Microsoft Windows would need to manage each control, consequently using more of the valuable Graphics Device Interface (GDI) resources. When you first place a DataWindow control in a window, no DataWindow object has yet been specified for the control, so an empty box appears in the area representing the DataWindow. Although the DataWindow control is the most powerful control in PowerBuilder, you might find that you still need to use some of the other controls list in the following sections.

CheckBox (cbx_). Checkboxes are square boxes that display one of two states: checked (x) or unchecked (blank). These states typically represent options such as yes or no, or on or off. However, a CheckBox also can be used to represent a third state (gray). For example, a window containing medical information for a patient has a CheckBox to indicate whether the patient has been immunized for Cholera. In certain situations, the information might not be known, so the third state of the Checkbox can represent the unknown state.

CommandButton (cb_). CommandButtons typically are used to initiate or confirm an action (e.g., Cancel or OK). When clicked, they visually simulate a pushed-down look during the time that the mouse button is held down. Because of the amount of window real estate that a CommandButton uses, it would make sense to try to avoid using them on most windows, except response windows that cannot make use of the menu. For common functionality, such as saving the current sheet's data or closing the current sheet, you should look to implementing this logic via the menu and/or its associated toolbar.

DropDownListBox (ddlb_). A DropDownListBox is similar to a SingleLineEdit. However, when the user clicks on the down arrow, a list of data items is displayed. These items can either be specified at design time or added via the PowerScript AddItem( ) function at execution time.

EditMask (em_). An EditMask is visually similar to a SingleLineEdit, but it allows the developer to apply a specific mask or picture to the values that are entered during execution (e.g., adding a spin control edit mask for entering dates).

Graph (gr_). The graph control can be used to display data in a graphical form. A format of the graph is determined by the graph type (see Figure 8.18). This formatting and display of graphs is not covered in this edition of the book.

GroupBox (gb_). A GroupBox is used to visually group controls, typically RadioButtons, that are closely related. For example, you might have three RadioButtons inside a GroupBox to indicate that the user can select only one RadioButton at a time.

HScrollBar (hsb_). The HScrollBar (horizontal) control can be used to provide relative information that pertains to a combination of controls that are being displayed in a window.

Line (ln_). The line control is one of the drawing objects that can be used to make a window more interesting and visually appealing.

ListBox (lb_). A ListBox can be used to display a list of data items. These items can either be specified at design time or added via the PowerScript AddItem( ) function at execution time.

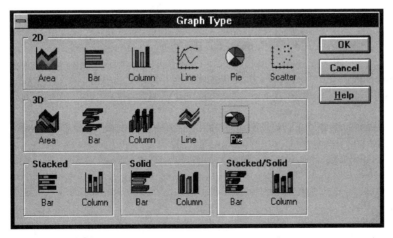

Figure 8.18 Graph types.

MultiLineEdit (mle_). These are SingleLineEdits that allow the window to display or allow the entry of multiple lines. You typically use a MultiLineEdit as a simple data entry field for a large amount of text.

OLEControl (ole_). An OLE 2.0 control contains an linked or embedded object, such as a spreadsheet or word processing document, that was created by an OLE 2.0-compliant application. The user can activate the object and edit it in the application in which it was originally created.

Oval (oval_). The oval control is one of the drawing objects that can be used to make a window more interesting and visually appealing.

Picture (p_). A Picture is a control in which you can display a bitmap. When you first place a picture, no picture has yet been specified for the control, so an empty box will appear in the relevant area representing the unallocated object.

PictureButton (pb_). A PictureButton is a CommandButton with a picture on it. You can associate two pictures to a PictureButton: one for the "enabled" state, when the user has the ability to press on the control, and another for the "disabled" state, when the user is notable to press-down the control. When you first place a Picture-Button in a window, a space will appear in the button representing the area to be populated when the picture is added.

   Tip: Convert the enabled picture to gray scales, using a utility such as PaintShop, and use it for the disabled picture. The absence of color will visually simulate the disabled look.

RadioButton (rb_). A RadioButton is a round object that is used to indicate a selection: on and off. When the option is on, the button has a dark center. When the option is off, the center is blank. RadioButtons often are grouped in a GroupBox so that the user can only select one button from the group.

Rectangle (r_). The line control is one of the drawing objects that can be used to make a window more interesting and visually appealing.

RoundRectangle (rr_). The line control is one of the drawing objects that can be used to make a window more interesting and visually appealing.

SingleLineEdit (sle_). A SingleLineEdit is a box in which the user can enter a single line of text. You typically use a SingleLineEdit as a simple data entry field.

StaticText (st_). StaticText is useful for describing the contents of other window controls (e.g., see the SingleLineEdit or the Picture control in Figure 8.17) or read-only data.

UserObject (uo_). When you choose to place a user object control, the Select User Object dialog will display, listing the user objects defined for the application.

VScrollBar (vsb_). The VScrollBar (vertical) control can be used to provide relative information that pertains to a combination of controls that are being displayed in a window.

Control definition and appearance

Once you have placed a control in a window, you can modify its style and appearance. This is done by changing its attributes, moving and resizing it, and writing scripts to determine the processing that takes place when an event occurs in the control. However, you first must identify the control that you want to change.

Selecting an existing control. To select a single control, click on it, and the control displays with handles on it. Previously selected controls are no longer selected.
     To select multiple controls that are close by:

Step 1 Press and hold the left mouse button at one corner of the neighboring controls.

Step 2 Drag the mouse over the controls that you want to select, in a rectangular fashion. PowerBuilder will display a box that will lasso the controls.

Step 3 Release the mouse button, and all of the controls within the box are selected and will display handles.

     To select multiple controls that are not close by:

Step 1 Click the first control.

Step 2 Press and hold the Ctrl key, and click additional controls.

     All the controls are selected and have handles.

Control status. When a control is selected, its name, location (x: and y:), and size (w: and h:) are displayed in the MDI status bar at the bottom of the PowerBuilder frame window (see Figure 8.19). This can help you when moving, sizing, and aligning controls.
     The values change dynamically as you manipulate the control. This information is only displayed when a single control is selected. If more that one control is selected, then a message Group Selected will display instead.

Acting on multiple controls. You can act on all selected controls as a unit. For example, you can move all of them or change the fonts for all the text displayed in the controls.
     You also can display a list of controls and select one from the list by selecting Control List from the Edit menu. You can select all controls by selecting Select All from the Edit menu.

Figure 8.19 The window control status.

Modify a control's attributes. The way to modify a control's attributes is by using the control's pop-up menu.

Each distinct control has its own set of attributes and, therefore, its own pop-up menu. You select items on the pop-up menu to change the control's definition.

To modify a control's attributes:

Step 1 Display the control's pop-up menu by either clicking the right mouse button inside the control or selecting Control Style from the Design menu. The selected control's pop-up menu will display.

Step 2 Use this menu to change the control's attributes.

Duplicating controls. To duplicate an existing control or group of controls:

Step 1 Select the control or group of controls.

Step 2 Press Ctrl–T, or select Duplicate from the Edit menu or from the control's pop-up menu.

The new duplicate controls are placed under the original selection and are automatically selected for you so that you can move them to the required location using the mouse or the arrow keys.

Displaying the grid. The Window painter also provides a grid to help you with the alignment of controls. To use the grid, select Grid from the Design menu. The Alignment Grid dialog displays. (See Figure 8.20).

The grid options allow you to:

- Make controls snap to a grid position when you place them or move them.
- Show or hide the grid when the workspace displays.
- Specify the width (X) and height (Y) of the grid cells, in pixels.

Note: You can specify a default grid size in the Preferences painter.

Window painting can be slower when the grid is displayed, so display the grid only when necessary.

Aligning, spacing, and sizing window controls. When you first create a new window and place several controls on it, you might find that, prior to spending some time on the cosmetics, it looks like the window shown in Figure 8.21.

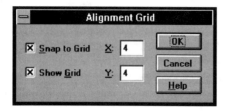

Figure 8.20 The Alignment Grid dialog.

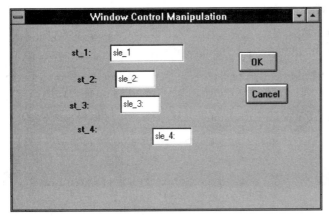

Figure 8.21 An example window with controls.

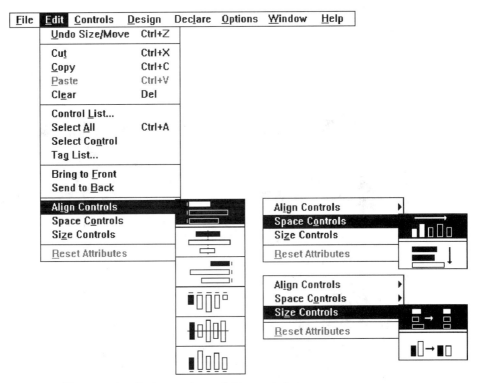

Figure 8.22 The menus for aligning, spacing, and sizing controls.

Thankfully, PowerBuilder provides some powerful editing features that allow you to quickly remedy the "ugly screen syndrome." The features are located in the Edit menu (see Figure 8.22), which shows the three cascading menus that will display if you choose the Align Controls, Space Controls, or Size Controls option.

Aligning controls. It is easy to align two or more controls:

Step 1 Select the control whose position you want to use to align the others. Power-Builder displays handles around the selected control.

Step 2 Press and hold the Ctrl key, and click the controls that you want to align with the first one. All of the selected controls have handles on them.

Step 3 Select `Align Controls` from the Edit menu. (See Figure 8.22.)

Step 4 From the cascading menu, select the axis along which you want to align the controls.

In our example, we want to align the static text boxes along the left side, so select the first choice on the cascading menu. See Figure 8.23 for the result.

Spacing controls. You can move controls manually by dragging them with the mouse. You also can easily equalize the spacing around specified controls.

To equalize the space between controls:

Step 1 Select the two controls whose spacing is correct (select one control, then press and hold Ctrl and click the second control).

Step 2 Select the other controls whose spacing you want to be the same as the first two controls by pressing Ctrl and clicking.

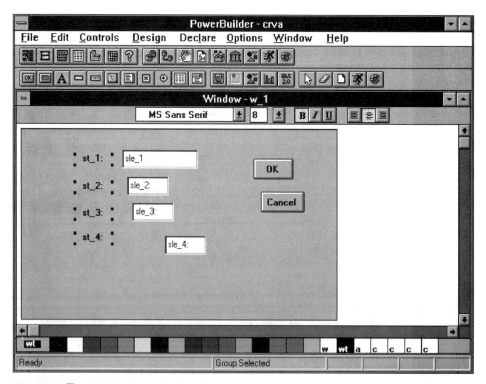

Figure 8.23 The static text controls after alignment.

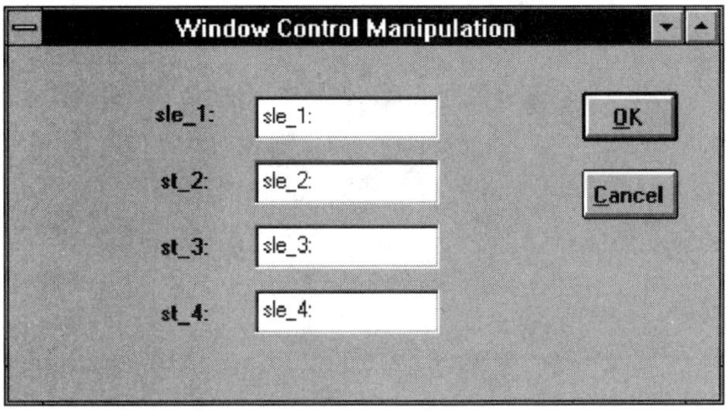

Figure 8.24 The window after manipulation.

Step 3 Select Space Controls from the Edit menu.

Step 4 From the cascading menu, select the dimension whose spacing you want to equalize.

Sizing controls. Let's assume that you have several CommandButtons and want them to be the same size. You can accomplish this manually or by using the Edit menu.

To equalize the size of controls:

Step 1 Select the control whose size is correct.

Step 2 Select the other controls whose size you want to match the first control by pressing and holding Ctrl and clicking.

Step 3 Select Size Controls from the Edit menu.

Step 4 From the cascading menu, select the dimension whose size you want to equalize.

After careful use of the alignment, spacing, and sizing features of the Window painter, you can see how the window looks now in Figure 8.24.

Tab order. When you place controls in a window, PowerBuilder assigns them a default tab order, the default sequence in which focus moves from control to control when the user presses the Tab key.

PowerBuilder establishes this default tab order by looking at the relative positions of controls in a window. It assigns the tab order in a left-to-right, top-to-bottom fashion. See Figure 8.25, which shows the tab order after window construction. Note that the StaticText objects have a zero value assigned. This is because there is no need to tab to this type of field. With a zero value, it will be skipped. The zero tab value also applies to the drawing objects and RadioButtons in a GroupBox.

To change the tab order:

Step 1 Select Tab Order from the Design menu. The current tab order will display.

Step 2 Use the mouse or the Tab key to position the focus to the tab value that you want to change.

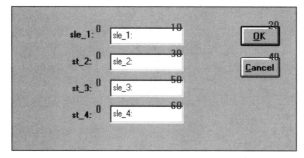

Figure 8.25 The initial tab order.

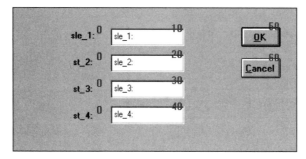

Figure 8.26 The revised tab order.

Step 3 Enter a new tab value (0-9999); 0 removes the control from the tab order. If you want the user to tab to control Y after control X but before control Z, set the tab value for control Y so that it is between the value for control X and the value for control Z.

Step 4 To allow tabbing between controls in a group box, assign nonzero tab values to the controls in the group box.

Repeat this procedure until you have the tab order that you want, then select Tab Order from the Design menu, and PowerBuilder will save the new tab order. See Figure 8.26, which shows the revised tab order for the example window.

Each time you select Tab Order, PowerBuilder, in increments of 10, renumbers the tabs to include any controls that have been added to the window and to allow space to insert new controls in the tab order.

Note: When the user tabs to the first control in a custom user object in a window and presses the Tab key, focus moves to the next control in the order established for the user object. When the user has tabbed through all of the controls of the user object, focus moves to the first control in the window tab order.

Accelerator keys. You can define accelerator keys for your controls to allow users to change focus to the control by pressing Alt plus the accelerator key. How you do it depends on whether the type of control has displayed text associated with it. Be aware that these accelerators will work only if they do not clash with the accelerators attached to the MenuBar. If you use the same accelerator key, the menu will be the option that is taken not the window control.

To define an accelerator key for a CommandButton, CheckBox, or RadioButton, precede the accelerator key with an ampersand character (&) when adding the text that displays for the control.

To define an accelerator key for a SingleLineEdit, MultiLineEdit, ListBox, or Drop-DownListBox:

Step 1 Double-click the control to display the Style window, choose `Control Style` from the Design menu, or choose `Style` from the pop-up menu.

Step 2 Type the letter of the accelerator key in the Accelerator box.

Step 3 Click OK, and you have defined the accelerator key.

Step 4 To give the user a visual clue that the control has an accelerator, place a StaticText control in the vicinity of the control that you just assigned the accelerator key. When defining the text for the StaticText control, precede the accelerator key with an ampersand character (&).

PowerBuilder will display an underline to visually indicate the accelerator key. Now your user knows that there is an accelerator key associated with the control.

Choosing colors. As described earlier, the Window painter has a ColorBar, which displays colors that you can use for components of the window. Initially, the Color-Bar displays the following color selections:

- 16 predefined colors
- Window color (labeled w)
- Window Text color (labeled wt)
- Application Workspace color (labeled a)
- Four custom colors (labeled c)

The Window, Window Text, and Application Workspace colors are those defined by the user in the Microsoft Windows Control Panel. So if you use these colors in your window, the window colors will change to match the user's settings during execution.

Assigning colors to a control. There are two ways to assign colors to controls. To assign a color using the pop-up menu:

Step 1 Click the right mouse button in a control, and the pop-up menu displays.

Step 2 Select `Color`, and a cascading menu displays.

Step 3 Choose the part of the control that you want to specify a color for and select the color.

To assign a color using the ColorBar:

Step 1 Select the control.

Step 2 Click either the left or right mouse button on the appropriate color in the ColorBar, as described in the next section.

Selecting colors from the ColorBar. You can select two colors from the ColorBar for a window component: one by clicking the left mouse button and the other by clicking the right mouse button.

When you select a color, the color displays in the first space in the ColorBar. The color that you select by clicking the left mouse button displays in the center. The color that you select with the right mouse button displays in the border area. Where these color apply is dependent on the type of control. See Table 8.3.

Creating custom colors. You can define your own custom colors for use in windows, user objects, and DataWindow objects.

To maintain your custom colors:

Step 1 Double-click in a custom color area in the ColorBar. The Color window displays.

Step 2 Choose an existing color or create the color that you want. You can start with one of the basic colors and customize it in the palette to the right by dragging the color indicator with the mouse. You also can specify precise values to define the color.

Step 3 When you have the color you want, click Add to Custom Colors. The new color displays in the list of custom colors.

Step 4 Select the new color in the list of custom colors, click OK.

The new color displays in the ColorBar and is available in all windows, user objects, and DataWindow objects you create.

Note: PowerBuilder saves custom colors in the [Colors] section of the PB.INI file, so they are available across sessions. Also, you cannot change the color of a CommandButton.

Providing access to a control. Controls have two boolean attributes that affect the accessibility of the control:

- Visible
- Enabled

The Visible attribute. If the Visible attribute is selected, the control displays in the window. If you want a control to be initially invisible, uncheck the Visible attribute. Hidden controls do not display by default in the Window painter. To display hidden controls in the painter, select Show Invisibles from the Design menu. To display a control during execution, assign the TRUE value to the Visible attribute, such as:

```
p_logo.Visible = TRUE
```

TABLE 8.3 Where the Colors Apply

Type of control	Left mouse color	Right mouse color
Control with event	Text	Background
Drawing object	Fill (the color inside the object); for objects with a pattern; this is the background color for the pattern	The outline; for object with a pattern; this is the color of the pattern

The Enabled attribute. If the Enabled attribute is selected, the control is active. For example, an enabled CommandButton can be clicked.

If you want a control to display but be inactive, uncheck the Enabled attribute. For example, a CommandButton might be active only after the user has selected an option. In this case, display the CommandButton initially disabled (it appears grayed out), then when the user selects the option, enable the CommandButton in a script:

```
cb_ok.Enabled = TRUE
```

Naming controls. Each type of control has a default prefix for its name. The default prefixes are set in the Preferences painter and saved in the PB.INI file. When you place a control in a window, PowerBuilder automatically assigns it a unique name. The name is generated by joining the default prefix for the control name with the lowest number that will make the name unique.

Although you can change the default prefixes for controls in the Window section of the Preferences painter, it is not advisable and the defaults are clear enough. You can change the generated number to a suffix that is meaningful (e.g., change cb_2 to cb_cancel).

Using meaningful names, instead of generated numbers makes it easier to identify the controls when writing scripts in the script painter.

To change a control's name:

Step 1 Display the control's pop-up menu, or double-click the control.

Step 2 Select Name from the menu and the control's Style dialog will display with the generated number suffix selected.

Step 3 Type in a meaningful suffix. You can use any valid PowerBuilder identifier with up to 40 characters.

Step 4 Click OK.

Repeat this procedure for all of the controls that are to be manipulated. You need not bother doing this for controls that are not manipulated in PowerScript. An example might be StaticText or the drawing objects.

Changing controls that display text. By using the StyleBar in the Window painter, you can change the:

- Text
- Font name
- Font size
- Bold, italic, and underline attributes
- Alignment of text within the control

To change textual attributes of controls, select each control whose attributes you want to change, and specify the new attributes using the StyleBar.

Font name. Make sure that the fonts that you pick will be available to your users when you distribute your application. If you pick a font that is on your computer but not on your user's computer, Windows will use the font it considers closest to the one you specified, which might not look very good.

Font size. The font size is stored in the control's TextSize attribute. PowerBuilder saves the font size in points, using negative numbers. Positive numbers indicate the font size in pixels, for compatibility with previous releases. For example, if you define the text for the StaticText control st_identity to be font size 8, PowerBuilder sets the value of st_identity's TextSize attribute to –8. If you want to change the point size of text during execution in a script, remember to specify a negative value:

```
//Change the font size to 12 points
st_identity.TextSize = -12
```

You can continue to specify font size in pixels if you want, by using positive numbers:

```
//Change the font size to 12 pixels
st_identity.TextSize = 12
```

Moving and resizing controls. You can move or resize a control using the mouse or the keyboard.

Using the mouse. To move a control, drag it with the mouse to the desired location. To resize a control, select it, then grab an edge and drag it with the mouse.

Using the keyboard. To move a control, select it, then press an arrow key to move it in the corresponding direction. To resize a control, select it, then use the key combinations listed in Table 8.4 to adjust the size of the control.

3D look. More and more of the commercial applications developed today have a three-dimensional look. If you make your window color gray and select a 3D border for your controls, your applications also can look this way. You can make the 3D look the default by selecting `Default to 3D` from the Options menu.

With this option enabled, when you build a new window, PowerBuilder will automatically set the window background color to gray and set the 3D attribute on for controls that support it. PowerBuilder records this preference in the Default3D variable in the [Window] section of PB.INI, so the preference is maintained across sessions.

**TABLE 8.4 Adjusting
the size of the control**

Press	To make the control
Shift–Right arrow	Wider
Shift–Left arrow	Narrower
Shift–Down arrow	Taller
Shift–Up arrow	Shorter

Saving the window

You can save the window that you are working on at anytime. To save a window:

Step 1 Select Save from the File menu. If you *have* previously saved the window, PowerBuilder saves the new version in the same library and returns you to the Window painter workspace. If you *have not* previously saved the window, PowerBuilder displays the Save Window dialog.

Step 2 Name the window in the Windows box.

Step 3 Write comments to describe the window. These comments display in the Select Window window and in the Library painter. It is a good idea to use comments so that you and others can easily remember the purpose of the window later.

Step 4 Specify the library to save the window in.

Step 5 Click OK to save the window.

A recommendation. The window name can be any valid PowerBuilder identifier with up to 40 characters. When you name windows, you should use a two-part name: a standard prefix that identifies the object as a window (such as w_) and a suffix that helps you identify the particular window (e.g., for a window that displays customer data, you might use the name w_customer_data).

How window classes are stored. When you save a window, PowerBuilder generates two entities within the class. Look at the following excerpt from an exported window definition:

```
$PBExportHeader$w_exported.srw
forward
global type w_exported from Window
int X=910
...
end type
...
global w_exported w_exported
```

A new data type is used:

```
global type w_exported from Window
```

The name of the data type is the name of the window, w_exported. Also note that it is inherited from the PowerBuilder Window data type.

The following is a new global variable of the new data type:

```
global w_exported w_exported
```

The name of the global variable is also the same as the new data type.

By duplicating the name of the data type and variable, you can refer to windows easily through their global variables and ignore the concept of data type. This concept will need to become more familiar when you need to open multiple instances of the same window. This concept will be covered in more detail later in this chapter, see the section, "Using the window."

Reviewing the Window

Once you have started to build a window, you might want to review the window to see what it will look like when you open it within an application and that it is evolving as required. With PowerBuilder, there are several ways to do this. You can:

- Preview the window
- Print the window definition
- Run the window
- Export the window

Previewing a window

As you develop your window, you can preview its appearance from within the Window painter. By previewing the window, you get a good idea of how it will feel during execution.

To preview a window, select Preview from the Design menu or press Ctrl–W. The window displays with the attributes that you have defined, such as a title bar, menu, minimize box, and so on.

What you can do. While previewing the window, you can get a sense of its look and feel. You can:

- Move the window
- Resize it (if the window is resizable)
- Maximize and restore it (if these properties were enabled)
- Tab around the window
- Select controls

What you cannot do. You cannot:

- Change attributes of the window (changes you make while previewing the window, such as resizing it, are not saved)
- Trigger events (for example, clicking a CommandButton while previewing a window does not trigger its Clicked event)
- Connect to a database

To return to the Window painter, select Preview from the Design menu again.

Printing a window

The printed definition provides you with a simple representation of the window and the controls that have placed on the window. The information that is printed is dependent on variables specified in the Library section of the PB.INI file. The print settings can be changed in the Library painter (select Print from the Entry menu) or in the Preferences painter. Printing the window's definition can be useful for documentation purposes.

To print information about the window:

Step 1 Open the window

Step 2 Select Print from the File menu.

Information about the current window then is sent to the printer specified in Printer Setup.

Running a window

You can test a window without running the whole application. To run a window:

Step 1 From within the Window painter, press Ctrl–Shift–W. PowerBuilder will prompt you to save any changes in any of the open painters before you can run a window. If there are no outstanding changes to be saved, then the Run Window dialog will display.

Step 2 Select the window that you want to run, then click the Start button, or just double-click the window, and PowerBuilder will run the window.

When you run a window it is possible to trigger events, including ancestor code, open other windows, connect to a database. However, the window does not have access to global variables that you have defined for the application. Also, the System-Error event is not triggered if there is an error, because it is an event at the application-object level.

If you use this facility frequently, you will find it useful to add it to the toolbar. The icon is in the PowerBar palette and looks like the Window painter icon without the blue and white coloring for the glass.

Exporting the window

A very useful feature in PowerBuilder is the ability to export the window definition to a text file. This text file can be modified and imported back into the PowerBuilder library. Figure 8.27 is a sample export of a simple window.

Adding Events, Functions, and Variables

The Window painter provides you with the capability to add scripts (also known as PowerScript), events, functions, and variables to a window and its controls. Power-Script is the programming glue that allows PowerBuilder objects to interact with each other. The scripts can be added to either events or functions. For more detailed information on scripts and related material, see chapter 12, "Adding scripts."

Events

An *event* is the notification of either a predefined or user-defined occurrence, such as a mouse click on a CommandButton. PowerBuilder windows and controls come

Figure 8.27 A sample export of a simple window.

```
$PBExportHeader$w_exported.srw
forward
global type w_exported from Window
end type
type st_1 from statictext within w_exported
end type
type cb_1 from commandbutton within w_exported
end type
type sle_1 from singlelineedit within w_exported
end type
end forward

global type w_exported from Window
int X=910
int Y=769
int Width=1482
int Height=377
boolean TitleBar=true
string Title="Window To Be Exported"
long BackColor=12632256
boolean ControlMenu=true
boolean MinBox=true
boolean MaxBox=true
boolean Resizable=true
st_1 st_1
cb_1 cb_1
sle_1 sle_1
end type
global w_exported w_exported

on w_exported.create
this.st_1=create st_1
this.cb_1=create cb_1
this.sle_1=create sle_1
this.Control[]={ this.st_1,&
this.cb_1,&
this.sle_1}
end on

on w_exported.destroy
destroy(this.st_1)
destroy(this.cb_1)
destroy(this.sle_1)
end on

type st_1 from statictext within w_exported
int X=124
int Y=109
int Width=247
int Height=73
boolean Enabled=false
string Text="sle_1:"
Alignment Alignment=Center!
boolean FocusRectangle=false
long TextColor=33554432
long BackColor=12632256
int TextSize=-8
int Weight=700
string FaceName="MS Sans Serif"
FontFamily FontFamily=Swiss!
FontPitch FontPitch=Variable!
end type
```

```
type cb_1 from commandbutton within w_exported
int X=1084
int Y=89
int Width=247
int Height=109
int TabOrder=20
string Text="&OK"
boolean Default=true
int TextSize=-8
int Weight=700
string FaceName="MS Sans Serif"
FontFamily FontFamily=Swiss!
FontPitch FontPitch=Variable!
end type

on clicked;MessageBox("cb_1","clicked")
end on

type sle_1 from singlelineedit within w_exported
int X=426
int Y=101
int Width=462
int Height=89
int TabOrder=10
BorderStyle BorderStyle=StyleLowered!
boolean AutoHScroll=false
string Text="sle_1:"
long TextColor=33554432
int TextSize=-8
int Weight=400
string FaceName="MS Sans Serif"
FontFamily FontFamily=Swiss!
FontPitch FontPitch=Variable!
end type
```

with a set of predefined events into which you can insert script to carry out some action. These events are familiar, in name and purpose, to the underlying Microsoft Windows messages and its event-driven programming model. The events are Power-Builder's hooks into this messaging environment. In addition to the predefined events, you also can define your own user events. These provide you with the flexibility to trap any of the countless PowerBuilder and Microsoft Windows messages, as well as your own custom events, that are listed in the User Event dialog. The window has its own set of events (for example, Open, which is triggered when the window is opened, and Close, which is triggered when the window is closed).

An example of a user-defined event in a window might be ue_move, attached to the pbm_move message, which is triggered when a window is moved. Every type of control also has its own set of events (for example, a CommandButton has a Clicked event, which is triggered when a user clicks on the button). A SingleLineEdit and a MultiLineEdit have Modified events, which trigger when the contents of the edit box is changed.

Functions

PowerBuilder provides built-in functions that act on windows and built-in functions that act on types of controls. You can use these functions in scripts to manipulate your windows and controls. For example, to open a window, you use the built-in window-level function Open.

Variables

Along with the ability to add script to events and functions, you often will have the need to be able to store data in an area that is accessible to various scripts within the window. In PowerBuilder, there are several ways to implement this, you can declare a:

- Global variable, then all scripts in the application have access to this variable.
- Instance variable within the window, then all scripts for the window and for controls in the window have access to this variable.

When declaring variables, it is important that you consider what the scope of the variable is. If the variable is only likely to be used within a window, declare it as an instance variable. For a variable that is likely to be used throughout the entire application, you should consider creating a class user object that contains all application-wide variables and instantiate the user object at start-up instead of just declaring it as a global variable.

Using the Window

If you construct a Single Document Interface (SDI) application, you need to consider whether or not it is able to display multiple copies of the same window, displaying different data values. This type of functionality is ideally suited to an Multiple Document Interface (MDI) implemention; however, this functionality is available in the SDI. See chapter 7, "Creating a window/menu interface," for more information on MDI implementations. For example, you have a window, w_currency, that displays information about a currency, see Figure 8.28.

During execution, you want the ability to display information for multiple currencies at the same time by opening multiple copies (instances) of the w_currency window. Let's walk through some of the possibilities.

Opening windows

If you open the w_currency window with the Open function:

```
Open(w_currency)
```

Figure 8.28 The Currency Information window.

this creates an instance of the data type w_customer and assign it a reference to the global variable named w_customer. If you execute the Open statement again without closing the first instance, it will appear as if nothing has happened. PowerBuilder has simply activated the existing window and not opened a new instance of the w_currency window. This is because the argument to the Open function is a window variable (in this case, the global variable w_currency) that is already pointing to the window that you have open.

In the previous example, a CommandButton, cb_close, was placed in the w_currency window, which has the following code in the Clicked event:

```
Close(Parent)
```

This closes the *parent* of the button, which is the window in which the button displays (i.e., w_currency).

Using discardable reference variables

A quick way to open multiple instances of the same window is to declare reference variables of the same type of the window. When you save the window, its name automatically becomes a new global data type. You can declare a reference variable of the window data type just like any other data type. The following statement declares a reference variable named L_wWorkCurrency of type w_currency and uses it in the Open function to open a window instance:

```
W_CURRENCY    L_wWorkCurrency
Open(L_wWorkCurrency)
```

The Open function determines that the data type of the variable L_wWorkCurrency is w_currency. It then creates an instance of w_currency and assigns a reference to the L_wWorkCurrency variable (hence the name reference variable). Each time that you execute this script, a new instance of w_currency will be created, and a new window will be opened.

By creating and using these discardable reference variables whose data type is the name of a window, you can open multiple instances of that window. Discardable reference variables are easy, and PowerBuilder manages them automatically. However, you cannot manipulate particular instances of windows created using reference variables.

Using persistent window arrays

The drawback with the reference variable technique is that the instances are created using a local variable that is discarded at the end of the script, consequently; there is no way to explicitly refer to a particular instance of the window from another window. However, by using a *global* (or preferably, a nonvisual user object class) persistent array of windows, you can maintain a "handle" to the window instances.

To create a global array of windows, click on Global Variables in the Declare menu, and declare an array of the data type of the window. The array can be of a finite length:

```
W_CURRENCY G_wWorkCurrencyArray[10]
```

The array also can be unbounded if the number of instances to be opened is not known or fixed:

```
W_CURRENCY G_wWorkCurrencyArray[]
```

To open an instance of a window in an array, use the Open function and pass the array index to it:

```
Open(G_wWorkCurrencyArray[1])    // Open 1st instance
Open(G_wWorkCurrencyArray[2])    // Open 2nd instance
```

Note: The second instance will appear at the same location as the first instance. By using window arrays, you can manipulate any instance by using its array index:

```
G_wWorkCurrencyArray[2].Sle_1 = "USD"
G_wWorkCurrencyArray[2].Title = "Window 2"
```

When you open or close a large number of instances of a window, you might want to use a FOR NEXT loop to open or close the instances. For example:

```
w_currency  G_wWorkCurrencyArray[10]
int  i_ctr, i_max = Upperbound(G_wWorkCurrencyArray)
for i_ctr = 1 to i_max
  Open(G_wWorkCurrencyArray[i_ctr])
next
```

Opening different windows using arrays. In the prior example, all windows in the array are the same type. You will more than likely need to manage several different types of windows. To do this, you must know one more thing about window classes that you create in PowerBuilder. All windows that you define actually are descendants of the built-in system data type *window*.

In the following example, we have three windows: w_ancestor_win, w_currency, and w_country. w_currency and w_country are both inherited from w_ancestor_win. See Figure 8.29 for the complete inheritance hierarchy.

Notice that, in PowerBuilder, the system "window" class is the true ancestor of all window classes that you define in the Window painter. The following code assumes that there are two global arrays (one for of the type window, and the other for the type string):

```
WINDOW  G_wWinArray[]
STRING  G_sNameArray[]
```

The G_wWinArray can reference any type of window, because if you declare a variable of type window, you can reference any other window type because its ultimate parent is type window itself. For the same reason, G_sNameArray can reference any type of string. The following code will open three windows (an instance of w_currency, an second instance of w_currency, and an instance of w_country):

```
INTEGER  L_iCounter
G_sNameArray[1] = "w_currency"
G_sNameArray[2] = "w_currency"
G_sNameArray[3] = "w_country"
```

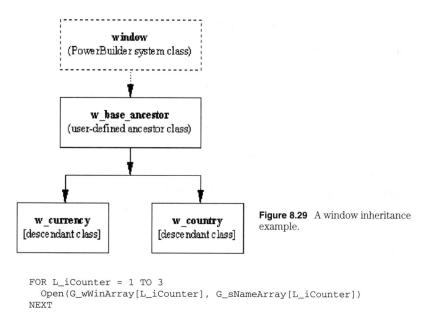

Figure 8.29 A window inheritance example.

```
FOR L_iCounter = 1 TO 3
  Open(G_wWinArray[L_iCounter], G_sNameArray[L_iCounter])
NEXT
```

Notice that this code uses a alternative form of the Open function:

```
Open(windowvar, windowtype)
```

where *windowvar* is the window variable and *windowtype* is a string whose value is the data type of the window that you want to open. The data type of *windowtype* must be the same or a descendant of *windowvar*.

In a real application, you will need to manage this array. Here is some code to open an instance using an available slot in the global (or class object) array. Gaps within the array indicate that the slot was used by a window that has been closed. The following function will find you a space in the array:

```
integer f_open_slot()
INTEGER L_iPointer, L_iMax, L_iAvailable
L_iMax = UpperBound(G_wWinArray)
WHILE L_iPointer < L_iMax
 //Is the slot in use by a window?
  IF IsValid (G_wWinArray[L_iPointer]) = FALSE THEN
    //No, this is available
   L_iAvailable = L_iPointer
    //Drop out of the loop
    EXIT
  END IF
  //Increment the pointer
  L_iPointer++
LOOP
//Did we find a opening?
IF L_iAvailable = 0 THEN
  //If not let's return a number that will extend
  //the array by one entry...
  L_iAvailable = L_iMax + 1
END IF
//Return the array address of any empty slot
RETURN L_iAvailable
```

Then the Open statement can fill the array address with the next window instance:

```
INTEGER L_iOpenSlot
L_iOpenSlot = f_open_slot()
//Load the name of the window you want to open into the window name array
G_sNameArray[L_iOpenSlot] = "w_next_window"
Open(G_wWinArray[L_iOpenSlot], G_sNameArray[L_iOpenSlot])
```

Window arrays versus reference variables. You have a choice: use discardable reference variables or arrays to manipulate window instances. With arrays, you can refer to particular instances, but because you must manage the arrays yourself, you have a little more coding to do.

In conclusion, if you do not need to refer to instances, use discardable reference variables. If you need to refer to window instances, use arrays.

9

Building Menus

This chapter explains the features of the Menu painter, which is used to create and maintain menus for an application. Menus provide the user with a easy way to issue commands and select options in an application. Menus are composed of three parts:

- Menu bar—The horizontal grouping of general functions (e.g., File)
- Dropdown or cascaded menu—The vertical group of specific functions (e.g., Exit)
- ToolBar—A graphical representation of selected menu items (e.g., Open and Close)

Menus typically are featured in an Multiple Document Interface (MDI) type application, with a menu for the frame and a menu for each sheet.

The *menu bar* contains the menu items that describe the menu headings, like File, Window, and Help. The *dropdown menu* is the list of menu items that appear when a menu item item is selected from the menu bar. The *cascading menu* is a menu that is attached to the side of an menu item in a dropdown menu. The *menu items* are the commands or options that the user chooses to perform an action in the application or currently active window. The menu items that appear in the menu bar are grouped together logically to make them a little easier to find. Menus appear in most windows, except the child and response type, in which they would not be appropriate. See chapters 7, "Creating a Window/Menu Interface," and 8, "Building Windows," for more information on the various window types in PowerBuilder.

As with all standard Windows applications, you can select PowerBuilder menu items with either the mouse or with the keyboard. To make the application keyboard enabled, you must define "accelerator keys" for the menu headings and subsequent menu items.

When designing menus, you should follow the layout and structure of other leading Windows programs (e.g., Microsoft Excel or Word), making it easier for the user to learn how to use the new application.

As you build the menu, you:

- Set the menu attributes, specifying the appearance and behavior of the menu items.
- Add scripts to determine how the application responds to events in the menu items. Along with these scripts, you can declare functions, structures, and variables for the menu.

There are two ways to build a menu. You can:

- Build a new menu
- Inherit from an existing menu, such as one provided by a framework or object library (e.g., Powersoft's Application Library, PowerTool, or ObjectStart)

Framework and class libraries can provide a more productive way to create a consistant look and feel for the application. See chapter 20, "Related Tools, Libraries, and Publications," for more information on framework and class libraries.

Opening the Menu Painter

To open the Menu painter:

Step 1 Click the Menu painter icon in the PowerBar, or double-click the Menu painter icon in the PowerPanel, and the Select Menu window lists the menus in the current library. (See Figure 9.1.)

Step 2 From this dialog, you can browse other libraries by clicking the Browse button, or you can inherit the definition of an existing menu by pressing the Inherit button.

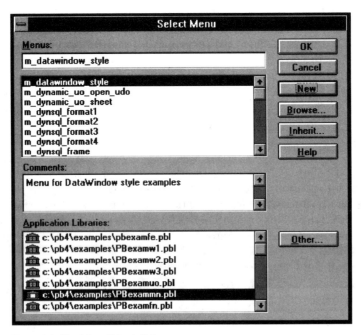

Figure 9.1 The Menu Select dialog.

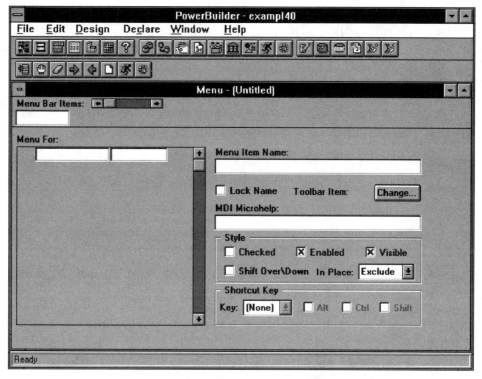

Figure 9.2 The Menu painter workspace.

Step 3 Click the New button to build a new menu, and the Menu painter workspace displays. (See Figure 9.2.)

From within the Menu painter, you specify the:

- The menu items that display in the menu bar (the bar at the top of the window), and the menu items that display under each item in the menu bar
- Attributes of the menu items: how they display (e.g., initially disabled or gray)
- Accelerator and shortcut keys (Ctrl–key or Alt–key combinations)
- Scripts for menu item events
- Attributes for Toolbar items (bitmaps, enabled, visible)

Adding Menu Items

Each menu consists of at least one menu item on the menu bar and menu items in a dropdown menu.

- To the menu bar
- To a dropdown menu
- To a cascading menu

To add menu items to the menu bar:

Step 1 Click the empty space to the right of the last defined menu item on the menu bar at the top of the painter workspace, and PowerBuilder displays an empty box. (See Figure 9.3.)

Step 2 Type the text that will display for the menu item.

Step 3 To add another menu item to the menu bar, click to the right of the menu item that you just defined, and PowerBuilder displays another empty box.

Step 4 Type the text for the new menu item.

Step 5 Repeat these steps to add additional items to the menu bar.

To add menu items to a dropdown menu:

Step 1 Click in the box for the item in the menu bar, and PowerBuilder displays the dropdown menu for the selected menu item. (See Figure 9.4.)

Step 2 Press Tab to go to the first empty box under the Menu For heading.

Step 3 Type the text that will display for the menu item.

Step 4 Repeat these steps to add additional items in the dropdown menu.

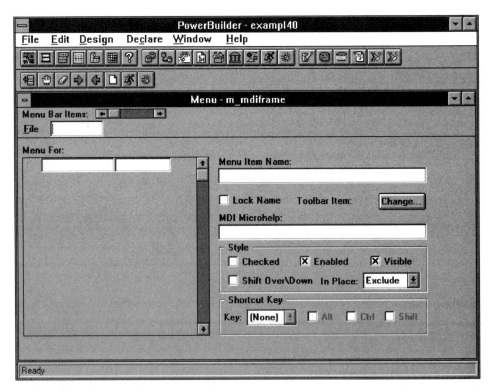

Figure 9.3 Adding a new menu item to the menu bar.

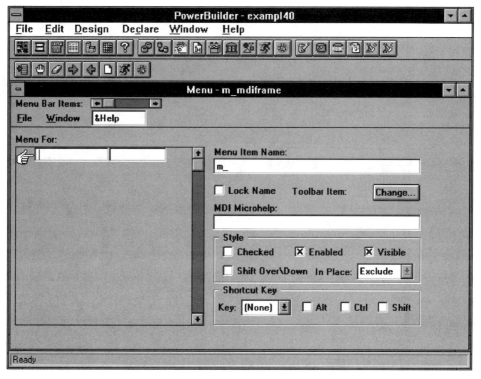

Figure 9.4 Adding a menu item to a dropdown menu.

To add menu items to a cascading menu:

Step 1 Click in the box for the item in a dropdown menu that you want to attach a cascading menu to.

Step 2 Click the Next Level icon in the painter, or select Next Level from the Edit menu. An empty box displays under the Menu For heading, and the pointer moves to the box so that you can build the cascading menu. (See Figure 9.5.) Note that the Menu For heading displays the name of the menu item, a right triangle, the menu item that you selected, and another right triangle. This is to remind you that you are entering items in a cascading menu.

Step 3 Enter items in the menu the same way that you enter items in the dropdown menu.

Step 4 To return to the previous menu level, click the Prior Level icon, or select Previous Level from the Edit menu.

Menu item names

As you add a menu item, PowerBuilder assigns it a default name, which is displayed in the Menu Item Name box. (See Figure 9.6.) This is the name that you specify if you refer to a menu item from a script.

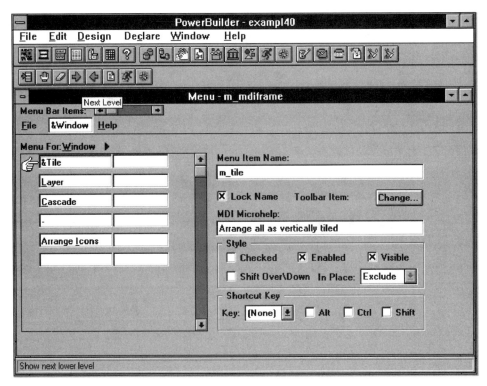

Figure 9.5 Adding a menu item to a cascading menu.

The default name is a concatenation of the text specified for the Prefix variable in the Menu section of the Preferences painter (initially the default prefix is m_) and the valid PowerBuilder characters and symbols in the text that you typed for the menu item.

If there are no valid characters or symbols in the text that you typed for the menu item, PowerBuilder creates a unique name prefix_n, where n is lowest number that can be combined with the prefix to create a unique name. The complete menu item name (prefix and suffix) can be up to 40 characters. If the prefix and suffix exceed this size, PowerBuilder uses only the first 40 characters (without displaying a warning message).

If you add a menu item to the menu and the name that PowerBuilder assigns by default already has been used in the menu, PowerBuilder displays a window and suggests a unique name for the menu item. (See Figure 9.7.)

After you add a menu item and move to another item, the name that PowerBuilder assigns to the menu item is locked. Even if you later change the text that displays for the menu item, PowerBuilder will not rename the menu item. This is so that you can change the text that displays in a menu without having to revise all your scripts that reference the menu item (remember, you reference a menu item through the name that PowerBuilder assigns to it).

If you want to change the text that displays for a menu item and have Power-Builder rename the menu item based on the new text, click the Lock Name checkbox to deselect it, then change the text that displays for the menu item. Be aware that, if you change the name of a menu item, PowerBuilder will not change any script that refers to the menu item to the new name.

Inserting menu items

You can insert menu items between existing menu items on the menu bar or in drop-down and cascading menus. To insert a menu item:

Step 1 Select the menu bar item before which you want to insert an item.

Step 2 Click the Insert icon in the PainterBar, press the Ins key, or select `Insert` from the Edit menu, and an empty box will display ready for you to insert the test of the new menu item.

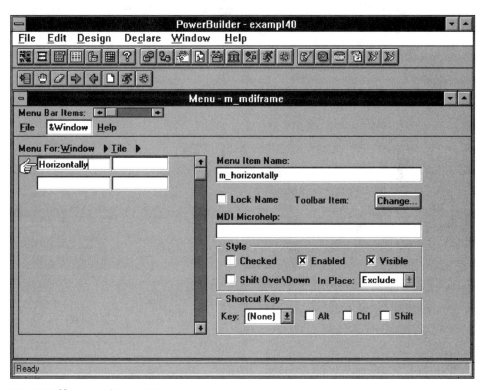

Figure 9.6 New menu item names.

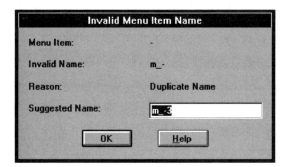

Figure 9.7 Conflicting menu items.

Moving menu items

To change the order of items in the menu bar or in a dropdown or cascading menu, you can drag the items to the desired order within their current menu. You cannot drag items from one menu to another (for example, you cannot drag an item in the menu bar to a dropdown menu).

To move a menu item:

Step 1 Click the Move icon in the PainterBar, or select Move from the Edit menu. You are now in Move mode.

Step 2 Press and hold the left mouse button on the menu item that you want to move. The pointer becomes a hand pointer.

Step 3 Drag the item to a new location in its menu and release the mouse button. The menu item displays in its location, and you leave Move mode.

Deleting menu items

To delete a menu item:

Step 1 Select the menu item that you want to delete.

Step 2 Click the Delete icon in the PainterBar, or select Delete from the Edit menu. The selected item is deleted.

Defining the appearance

By selecting checkboxes in the Menu painter, you can specify how a menu item appears during execution. Each of the checkboxes corresponds to an attribute of a menu item. (See Table 9.1.)

The settings that you specify here determine how the menu items display by default when the window opens. The values of these attributes can be changed easily from within scripts during execution.

Assigning accelerators and shortcuts

All menu items should have an accelerator key. An accelerator key allows a user to choose items from the menu using the keyboard. Menu bar items can be chosen by pressing Alt–key, and the dropdown and cascading items can be chosen with a key when the menu is displayed. Accelerator keys are identified by an underline in the

TABLE 9.1 The Menu Item Attributes that the Checkboxes Refer to

Attribute	Meaning
Checked	Menu item displays with a checkmark next to it
Enabled	Menu item can be selected
Visible	Menu item is visible

menu item's text. Shortcut keys are function keys or combinations of keys that a user can press to select a dropdown or cascading menu item directly without first selecting the related menu bar menu item.

You should adopt conventions for using accelerator and shortcut keys in your applications. All items should have accelerator keys, and commonly used items should have shortcut keys.

To assign an accelerator key, type an ampersand before the letter in the menu item text that you want to designate as the accelerator key. Accelerator keys display as underlined letters in the menu during execution.

To assign a shortcut key:

Step 1 Select the menu item that you want to assign a shortcut key to.

Step 2 Select a key from the Key dropdown listbox in the Shortcut Key group.

Step 3 If you want, select Alt, Ctrl, and/or Shift to create a key combination.

Shortcut keys display to the right of the menu item text during execution.

To create a separation line in a menu, type a single dash as the menu item text. This will separate groups of related menu items with lines.

Defining MicroHelp text and toolbar items

Two properties of menu items are used in Multiple Document Interface (MDI) applications are:

- MicroHelp text
- Association of a menu item with an icon in a toolbar

Using Inheritance to Build the Menu

When you build a menu that inherits its style, events, functions, structures, variables, and scripts from an existing menu, you save coding time. All that you have to do is modify the descendant object to meet the requirements of the current situation.

To use inheritance to build a descendant menu:

Step 1 Open the Menu painter, and the Select Menu window displays.

Step 2 Click the `Inherit` button, and the Inherit From Menu window lists the menus in the current library. (See Figure 9.8.)

Step 3 Select the menu that you want to use to create the descendant, and the selected menu displays in the workspace. The title of the workspace indicates that the menu is a descendant. For example, if the new menu inherits from the existing menu m_update_file, the title bar will look like Figure 9.9.

Step 4 Make the changes that you want to the descendant menu as described in the next section.

Step 5 Save the menu under a new name.

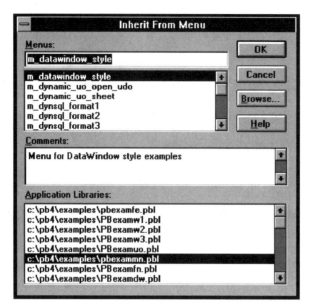

Figure 9.8 Inherit from a menu dialog.

Figure 9.9 An inherited menu Titlebar.

When you build and save a menu, PowerBuilder treats the menu as a unit that includes:

- All menu items and their scripts
- Any variables, functions, and structures declared for the menu

When you use inheritance to build a menu, everything in the ancestor menu is inherited in all of its descendants.

In a descendant window, you can do the following:

- Add menu items
- Modify existing menu items (for example, you can change the text displayed for a menu item or change its initial appearance, such as making it disabled)
- Build scripts for menu items that don't have scripts in the ancestor menu
- Extend or override inherited scripts
- Declare functions, structures, and variables for the menu

However, you cannot:

- Change the order of inherited menu items
- Delete an inherited menu item

Inherited menu item names

PowerBuilder uses the following syntax to show names of inherited menu items:

```
ancestormenu::menuitem
```

For example, if a menu, m_mdi_sheet, is inherited from m_mdi_frame, you will see something like the following for the m_open menu item, which is defined in the title bar of the menu:

Menu—m_mdi_sheet inherited from m_mdi_frame

See chapter 14, "Refining Your Code," for more information on inheritance

Saving Menus

You can save the menu that you are working on anytime. When you save a menu, Power-Builder saves the compiled menu items and scripts in the library that you specify.

To save a menu:

Step 1 Select Save from the File menu. If you have previously saved the menu, PowerBuilder saves the new version in the same library and returns you to the Menu painter. If you have not previously saved the menu, PowerBuilder displays the Save Menu window.

Step 2 Name the menu in the Menus box. (See Figure 9.10.)

Step 3 Write comments to describe the menu. These comments display in the Select Menu window and in the Library painter. It is a good idea to use comments so that you and others can easily remember the purpose of the menu later.

Step 4 Specify the library in which to save the menu, and click OK to save the menu.

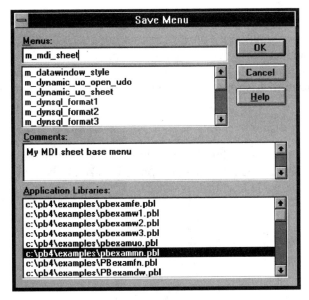

Figure 9.10 The Save Menu dialog.

Naming the Menu

The menu name can be any valid PowerBuilder identifier up to 40 characters. For information about PowerBuilder identifiers, see chapter 12, "Adding Scripts."

We recommend that, when you name menus, you should use a two-part name: a standard prefix that identifies the object as a menu (such as m_) and a suffix that helps you identify the particular menu. For example, you might name a menu used in a trade capture application m_trade_capture.

Reviewing Your Menu

Once you have started to build a menu, you might want to review the menu to see what it will look like when you open it within an application and that it is evolving as required. With PowerBuilder there are several ways to do this. You can:

- Preview the menu
- Print the menu definition
- Export the menu

Previewing a menu

You can visually preview a menu anytime to see how it looks. To preview a menu, select Preview from the Design menu or press Ctrl–W.

The menu will display in a dummy window. You can navigate through the menu using the mouse or the keyboard. You cannot trigger events in the menu items. For example, clicking a menu item while previewing does not trigger the item's Clicked event.

To return to the Menu painter, select Preview from the Design menu, or select Close from the preview window's Control menu.

Printing a menu

You can print a menu's definition for documentation purposes. To print information about the current menu, select Print from the File menu.

Information about the current menu is sent to the printer specified in Printer Setup. The information that is sent to the printer depends on variables specified in the Library section of the PB.INI file.

Exporting the menu

A very useful feature in PowerBuilder is the ability to export the menu definition to a text file. This text file can be modified and imported back into the PowerBuilder library. Figure 9.11 is an example of the exported text file.

Adding Scripts to Menu Items

You write scripts that specify what happens when users select a menu item. To write a script for a menu item:

Step 1 Select the menu item.

Step 2 Click the Script icon in the PainterBar. The PowerScript painter opens.

Figure 9.11 An example of the exported text file.

```
$PBExportHeader$m_mdi_frame.srm
$PBExportComments$Standard MDI frame menu
forward
global type m_mdi_frame from menu
end type
type m_file from menu within m_mdi_frame
end type
type m_open from menu within m_file
end type
type m_-1 from menu within m_file
end type
type m_close from menu within m_file
end type
type m_exit from menu within m_file
end type
type m_file from menu within m_mdi_frame
m_open m_open
m_-1 m_-1
m_close m_close
m_exit m_exit
end type
type m_window from menu within m_mdi_frame
end type
type m_tile from menu within m_window
end type
type m_horizontal from menu within m_window
end type
type m_layer from menu within m_window
end type
type m_cascade from menu within m_window
end type
type m_- from menu within m_window
end type
type m_arrangeicons from menu within m_window
end type
type m_window from menu within m_mdi_frame
m_tile m_tile
m_horizontal m_horizontal
m_layer m_layer
m_cascade m_cascade
m_- m_-
m_arrangeicons m_arrangeicons
end type
end forward

global type m_mdi_frame from menu
m_file m_file
m_window m_window
end type
global m_mdi_frame m_mdi_frame

on m_mdi_frame.create
m_mdi_frame=this
this.m_file=create m_file
this.m_window=create m_window
this.Item[]={this.m_file, &
this.m_window}
end on

on m_mdi_frame.destroy
destroy(this.m_file)
destroy(this.m_window)
end on
```

Figure 9.11 *Continued.*

```
type m_file from menu within m_mdi_frame
m_open m_open
m_-1 m_-1
m_close m_close
m_exit m_exit
end type

on selected;WINDOW L_wWindow
// Do we have an active (i.e. open) sheet?
L_wWindow = ParentWindow.GetActiveSheet()
// if we do, enable close menu item, otherwise disable it
m_file.m_close.enabled = IsValid(L_wWindow)

end on
on m_file.create
this.Text="&File"
this.Microhelp="Make a Choice or Exit Application"
this.m_open=create m_open
this.m_-1=create m_-1
this.m_close=create m_close
this.m_exit=create m_exit
this.Item[]={this.m_open, &
this.m_-1, &
this.m_close, &
this.m_exit}
end on

on m_file.destroy
destroy(this.m_open)
destroy(this.m_-1)
destroy(this.m_close)
destroy(this.m_exit)
end on

type m_open from menu within m_file
end type

on clicked;G_uoMDI.uf_open_sheet("w_mdi_document", "")
end on

on m_open.create
this.Text="Open"
end on
type m_-1 from menu within m_file
end type

on m_-1.create
this.Text="-"
end on

type m_close from menu within m_file
end type

on clicked;// Close the currently active sheet
WINDOW L_wWindow
L_wWindow = ParentWindow.GetActiveSheet()
IF IsValid(L_wWindow) THEN
        Close(L_wWindow)
END IF
end on

on m_close.create
this.Text="&Close ~tCtrl+F4"
```

```
this.Microhelp="Close the current sheet"
this.Shortcut=371
end on

type m_exit from menu within m_file
end type

on clicked;//Clicked script for m_exit (i.e. close the frame)
WINDOW  L_wWindow
L_wWindow = ParentWindow.GetActiveSheet()
IF IsValid(L_wWindow) THEN
        L_wWindow = ParentWindow(L_wWindow)
ELSE
        L_wWindow = ParentWindow
END IF

Close(L_wWindow)
end on

on m_exit.create
this.Text="E&xit"
this.Microhelp="Exit application"
end on

type m_window from menu within m_mdi_frame
m_tile m_tile
m_horizontal m_horizontal
m_layer m_layer
m_cascade m_cascade
m_- m_-
m_arrangeicons m_arrangeicons
end type

on m_window.create
this.Text="&Window"
this.m_tile=create m_tile
this.m_horizontal=create m_horizontal
this.m_layer=create m_layer
this.m_cascade=create m_cascade
this.m_-=create m_-
this.m_arrangeicons=create m_arrangeicons
this.Item[]={this.m_tile, &
this.m_horizontal, &
this.m_layer, &
this.m_cascade, &
this.m_-, &
this.m_arrangeicons}
end on

on m_window.destroy
destroy(this.m_tile)
destroy(this.m_horizontal)
destroy(this.m_layer)
destroy(this.m_cascade)
destroy(this.m_-)
destroy(this.m_arrangeicons)
end on

type m_tile from menu within m_window
end type

on clicked;//Clicked script for m_tile

ParentWindow.ArrangeSheets(Tile!)
end on
```

Figure 9.11 *Continued.*

```
on m_tile.create
this.Text="&Tile Vertical"
this.Microhelp="Arrange all as vertically tiled"
end on

type m_horizontal from menu within m_window
end type

on clicked;ParentWindow.ArrangeSheets(TileHorizontal!)
end on

on m_horizontal.create
this.Text="Tile &Horizontal"
this.Microhelp="Arrange all as horizontally tiled"
end on

type m_layer from menu within m_window
end type

on clicked;//Clicked script for m_layer

ParentWindow.ArrangeSheets(Layer!)end on

on m_layer.create
this.Text="&Layer"
this.Microhelp="Arrange all as layered"
end on

type m_cascade from menu within m_window
end type

on clicked;//Clicked script for m_cascade

ParentWindow.ArrangeSheets(Cascade!)
end on

on m_cascade.create
this.Text="&Cascade"
this.Microhelp="Arrange all as cascaded"
end on

type m_- from menu within m_window
end type

on m_-.create
this.Text="-"
end on

type m_arrangeicons from menu within m_window
end type

on clicked;//Clicked script for m_arrangeicons

ParentWindow.ArrangeSheets(Icons!)
end on

on m_arrangeicons.create
this.Text="Arrange &Icons"
this.Microhelp="Arrange all icons"
end on
```

Menu items have the following events:

- Clicked
- Selected

The Clicked event is triggered in the following situations:
The menu item is clicked with the mouse.
The menu item is selected (highlighted) using the keyboard and then Enter is pressed.
The shortcut key for the menu item is pressed.
The menu containing the menu item is displayed and the accelerator key is pressed.
A menu item responds to a mouse click or the keyboard only if both its Visible and Enabled attributes are true. If the menu item has a dropdown or cascading menu under it, the script for its Clicked event (if any) is executed when the mouse button is pressed, then the dropdown or cascading menu displays. If the menu item does not have a menu under it, the script for the Clicked event is executed when the mouse button is released. A typical script for the Clicked event for an Open menu item on the File menu will present an open file dialog.
The Selected event is triggered when the user selects (highlights) a menu item. You will not use the Selected scripts much because users don't expect things to happen when they just highlight a menu item, but changing the MicroHelp that is displayed in an MDI application is a good use for the Selected script.

Functions and variables

Using functions. PowerBuilder provides built-in functions that act on menu items. You can use these functions in scripts to manipulate menu items during execution. For example, to hide a menu, you can use the Hide built-in function.

Using variables. Scripts for menu items have access to all global variables defined for the application. You also can define local variables that are accessible only in the script where they are defined.
You also can define instance variables for the menu when you have data that needs to be accessible to scripts in several menu items in a menu. Instance variables are accessible to all menu items in the menu.

Referring to objects

You can refer to any object in the application in scripts for menu items. You must fully qualify the reference, using the object name, as described in the following sections.

Referring to windows. When referring to a window, you simply name the window:

```
w_currency
```

When referring to an attribute in a window, you must always qualify the attribute with the window's name:

```
window.attribute
```

For example:

```
w_currency.Title = "Currency Information"
```

To move the window w_order from within a menu item script, code:

```
w_order.Move(200, 100)
```

To maximize w_order, code:

```
w_order.WindowState = Maximized!
```

You can use the reserved word ParentWindow to refer to the window that the menu is associated with during execution. For example, the following statement closes the window the menu is associated with:

```
Close(ParentWindow)
```

You also can use ParentWindow to refer to attributes of the window that a menu is associated with but not to refer to attributes of controls or user objects in the window.

For example, the following statement is valid, because it refers to attributes of the window itself:

```
ParentWindow.Height = ParentWindow.Height/2
```

However, the following statement is invalid, because it refers to a control in the window:

```
ParentWindow.sle_result.Text = "Statement invalid"
```

Referring to controls and user objects in windows. When referring to a control or user object, you must always qualify the control or user object with the name of the window:

```
window.control.attribute.
window.userobject.attribute
```

For example, to enable a CommandButton in window w_cust from a menu item script, code:

```
w_cust.cb_print.Enabled = TRUE
```

Referring to menu items. When referring to a menu item, use this syntax:

```
menu.menuitem menu.menuitem.attribute
```

When referring to a menu item within the same menu, you don't have to qualify the reference with the menu name. When referring to a menu item in a dropdown or cascading menu, you must specify each menu item on the path to the menu item that you are referencing, separating each name with a period.

For example, to place a checkmark next to the menu item m_bold, which is on a dropdown menu under m_text in the menu saved in the library as m_menu, code:

```
m_menu.m_text.m_bold.Check( )
```

If the previous script were for a menu item in the same menu (m_menu), you wouldn't need to qualify the menu item with the name of the menu. You could simply code:

```
m_text.m_bold.Check( )
```

Using the Menu

With PowerBuilder, you can display menus in two ways:

- In a window
- As a pop-up menu

Adding a menu to a window

To display a menu bar when the window is opened, you associate a menu with the window in the Window painter. To associate a menu with a window:

Step 1 Open the Window painter, and select the window that you want to associate the menu with.

Step 2 Display the Window Style window by either double-clicking the window's background or selecting `Window Style` from the Design menu.

Step 3 Select the Menu checkbox, and pick the menu from the dropdown listbox, which lists all menus available to the application.

Identifying menu items in window scripts

You can reference menu items in scripts in windows and controls using the following syntax:

```
menu.menuitem
```

You must always fully qualify the menu item with the name of the menu. When referring to a menu item in a dropdown or cascading menu, you must specify each menu item on the path to the menu item that you are referencing, separating each name with a period.

For example, to refer to the Enabled attribute of menu item m_open, which is under the menu bar item m_file in the menu saved in the library as m_menu, code:

```
m_menu.m_file.m_open.Enabled
```

Changing menus during execution

You can use the ChangeMenu function in a script to change the menu associated with a window during execution.

Displaying pop-up menus

To display a pop-up menu in a window, use the PopMenu function to identify the menu and the location at which you want to display the menu.

If the menu is currently associated with the window, you can simply call the Pop-Menu function. The following CommandButton script displays m_main.m_view as a pop-up menu at the current pointer position (assuming the menu m_main already is associated with the window):

```
m_main.m_view.PopMenu( PointerX(), PointerY())
```

If the menu is not already associated with the window, you must do a little more work and create an instance of the menu before you can display it as a pop-up menu. The following code creates an instance of the menu m_search (this menu is not associated with the window containing the code) and will pop up the menu m_search.m_view at the current pointer location:

```
m_search  L_mPopup
L_mPopup = CREATE m_search
L_mPopup.m_view.PopMenu( PointerX(), PointerY() )
```

This kind of pop-up menu typically is associated with a click of the right mouse button anywhere within a window (rbuttondown) to enable some advanced functions that might be specific to the window or the clicked location.

Note: Don't forget to clean up the pop-up menu instance by destroying it when you are finished. For example:

```
DESTROY  L_mPopup
```

Chapter

10

Building DataWindows

The hub of the typical application is the database. The database contains the entities and relationships required to satisfy the application data objective. The relational database consists of the tables/views, columns, indices, etc. The DataWindow is used to access, maintain, and display the data. While the DataWindow is the primary vehicle for interfacing with the database, it is not the exclusive one (e.g., embedded SQL in an event script can be used to access the database).

PowerBuilder's DataWindow sets it apart from tools like Visual Basic. The Visual Basic 3.0 user must acquire add-on software to paint windows that access, edit, and display database data. Visual Basic 4.0 has some database connectivity but still requires a good amount of program code to provide comprehensive and effective data access. PowerBuilder's DataWindow painter, in concert with its Database painter, provides the ability to easily define, index, populate, manipulate, and display database data for virtually all of the relational DBMS platforms popular today. Moreover, its popularity has created an industry requirement for CASE and other third-party tools to interface with the PowerBuilder database extended attributes; this combination can facilitate development by enhancing the power of the DataWindow.

Overview

The DataWindow object is used to access, maintain, and display data from a data source. During window development, it is associated (statically or dynamically) with the DataWindow control. The control contains all of the events used to manipulate the object during execution. Together they provide a full-function SQL interface to the developer's relational DBMS platform. The platform preference as well as the specific database parameters for each development DBMS can be preset using the Database or Preference painters. This allows the developer to be insulated from entering database logon details and facilitates the desired objective: a powerful window into the database. Take care not to logon as the database owner (dbo) when developing an application (especially for Sybase and SQL Server); PowerBuilder will omit the creator name when building internal SQL. This will be problematic when a developer works with the DataWindow. PowerBuilder then will use the developers logon ID in place of the dbo causing a "table not found" database error.

The DataWindow object used with the Database painter and PowerBuilder catalog tables can create validation (pbcatvld), display (pbcatfmt), and edit styles (pbcatedt) that can be associated with DataWindow columns to automatically provide the ability to:

- Validate input data using the `Design¦Object Style¦Edit Styles` menu option of the DataWindow painter, where you can associate an edit style (e.g., a dropdown DataWindow). Using this technique, you create an edit style in the Database painter that enforces validation using a DataWindow on a code table, thereby permitting valid choices only for the column.

- Display data in specialized formats using the display formats defined in the Database painter and associated with a column using the `Design¦Object Style¦Format`.

- Use various Database painter-defined validation rules (e.g., vr_multiple_of_100) for data entry and associate them with a column using the `Design¦Object Style¦Edit Style¦Edit` or `Edit Mask`.

This comprehensive array of external DataWindow functionality is complemented by the internal capability of the PowerBuilder DataWindow to communicate with most of the available relational DBMS's platforms. It is important that full-scale DataWindow development is preceded by a sound and near-complete database design. This will obviate the need to extensively rework DataWindows to accommodate database changes.

The DataWindow painter provides an easy-to-use methodology for choosing a database source.

The developer can select among the following source options:

- Quick Select (one table or tables related with common key)
- SQL Select (one or more tables/SQL predicates)
- Query (existing SQL developed using the Query painter)
- External (nonrelational data source; a good substitute for other window controls)
- Stored Procedure (prefabricated SQL; only available for DBMSs that support the stored procedure; for example, Sybase, Oracle, and Watcom)
- English Wizard (not Paul Allen) where common words stored in a user dictionary are used to ask questions about data from tables and columns to create a query. The user does not need to know the details about composing SQL. This is an optional data source.

After the source has been chosen, the developer then selects a presentation style:

- Free form (columns movable window; typically used for data entry)
- Grid form (columns across the page; typically used for reporting)

- Tabular (same as grid only different, i.e., no grid lines and columns are movable)
- Labels, N-Up (use database query to produce labels)
- Composite (combining base and dependent DataWindows to form a new one; added in PowerBuilder 4.0)
- Graph, Group, Crosstab (bar graphs, pie charts, etc.)

To use DataWindows objects within an application, the developer typically will perform the following steps:

Step 1 Create the DataWindow object using the DataWindow painter. In this painter, you define the data source, presentation style, and all other attributes of the object, such as display formats, validation rules, and sorting and filtering criteria.

Step 2 Place a new DataWindow control in the window or user object. The DataWindow control is the communication layer between the application and the database. It is a buffer where database data is sent, received, and massaged.

Step 3 Associate the DataWindow control with the DataWindow object. This can be done at define time or dynamically during execution. If a DataWindow control has generic scripting behind the control events, one DataWindow control can be used for many DataWindow objects.

Step 4 Write PowerScripts using the Window painter to manipulate the DataWindow control that houses the DataWindow object. The developer might have a user object DataWindow control that contains custom events that correspond to typical data transactions (e.g., ue_filesave will save the current row on the DataWindow object).

The DataWindow control can be operated on by a window or menu control. For example, a Save menu item can be used to trigger a control event script and cause the current contents of the DataWindow control to be verified and then written to the DBMS database table.

Creating a New DataWindow Object

To create a new DataWindow object:

Step 1 Click the DataWindow icon in the PowerBar, or double-click the icon in the PowerPanel. The Select DataWindow window lists the DataWindowobjects in the current library.

Step 2 Click the New button. The window shown in Figure 10.1 will be displayed.

Step 3 Select a data source for the DataWindow object. (We will review this in detail later on.) Be careful to connect to the ultimate DBMS if you are using a special feature such as the stored procedure. This source option will not present itself if the current DBMS connection does not provide support for the stored procedure.

Step 4 Select a presentation style. This is how you want the data to be arranged on the DataWindow object. The most common are Freeform, Grid, or Tabular. The Freeform typically is used for data entry for tables with more than ten columns (e.g.,

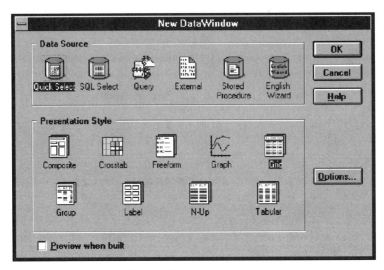

Figure 10.1 The New DataWindow dialog.

wider than the width of a page). Grid and Tabular are used for reporting in a spreadsheet format. Grid and Tabular also are used for code table updates (i.e., tables with fewer that 10 columns). Tabular is closer to Freeform because columns can be rearranged. The Grid style comes complete with the grid lines, hence the name.

Step 5 Select options for the DataWindow object. This is a nice place to set the font and other style defaults for this entire application. This is an opportunity to promote a "look and feel" for the application. Once set, it becomes the default for every object built in the particular presentation style.

Step 6 Select `Preview when built` to see what the basic DataWindow object will look like during actual execution. If data is available, it will be accessed and presented based upon the SQL generated by the DataWindow Painter.

Step 7 Enhance the basic DataWindow object. After adding and previewing the presentation style and data source, the developer can add additional cosmetic enhancements, such as text and/or bitmaps to make the window more readable and user-friendly. This is a point where edit style, display format, and validation rules can be applied to columns on the DataWindow to make it a complete data object—where the data object provides data entry, access, and presentation all in one object definition (i.e., the PowerBuilder DataWindow). The DataWindow now is ready to be used in the application contained within a control that includes scripts to retrieve, present, and maintain application data.

Step 8 Save the basic DataWindow object. After the developer is satisfied with the DataWindow object, it should be saved in the appropriate PowerBuilder library (PBL) with a standard name. A typical convention is to name the object "d_" followed by a meaningful name using corporate-wide business name abbreviations. For example d_upd_mm_px might be a standard corporate name for an object that updates (upd) money market (mm) prices (px). The project usually will designate a PBL for DataWindow objects.

Presenting the Data

The choices for presenting a DataWindow object are described in the following sections.

The Freeform and Tabular styles

The Freeform style presents data with the data columns going down the page vertically and labels next to each column. You can reorganize the data/column order by moving columns and text. Freeform style often is used for data-entry forms. This presentation style usually provides the ability to access, present, and maintain one database row per DataWindow control.

The Tabular form is similar in that you can reorganize the data. It is different in that it presumes a horizontal display of the columns with more than one row per DataWindow control. The individual database columns can be protected or updatable using the window Tab feature (zero for protected; nonzero for relative tab order and updatable).

The Grid style

The Grid style presents data in a row-and-column format with grid lines separating rows and columns. Everything that you place in a grid-style DataWindow object must fit in one cell in the grid. You cannot move columns and headings around as you can in the tabular and freeform styles. However, unlike the other styles, users can reorder and resize columns with the mouse in a grid-style DataWindow object during execution.

Other

The other styles present data in specialized formats, such as labels and graphs. The setup and use of these styles, while interesting and useful, will not be addressed in this book. The reasoning is that Freeform, Tabular, and Grid represent the majority of DataWindow styles developed in the typical application. Moreover, after becoming familiar with these styles, labels and graph-based presentation should be easily accomplished.

Select Options for the DataWindow Object

When you begin creating DataWindow objects for the development effort, you can specify default colors and borders by clicking the Options button after selecting a presentation style. You can have different default settings for tabular, freeform, grid, N-Up, and label DataWindow objects. This is a good idea because you do it once, then it will be the default for each new DataWindow that you create. In an application, DataWindows probably are the most frequently occurring object. Before setting the default, determine if there are any firmwide or project standards for the background colors and borders.

The options for DataWindow objects can be set up to provide:

- `Background Color`: Select the color that you want to use for the background of the DataWindow object from the list in the dropdown listbox. The default is the window background color specified in the Windows Control Panel.
- `Text Border` and `Color for Text`: Select the border and color that you want to use for display text (such as headers and labels) in the DataWindow object from the list in the dropdown listbox(s).
- `Text Border` and `Color for Columns`: Select the border that you want to use for all column data in the DataWindow object from the list in the dropdown listbox.

To specify default colors and borders, click the `Options` button (bottom right) in the New DataWindow window.

Selecting the Data Source

The data source specifies where the data (used in the DataWindow object) resides and how you will access it. You can select from the following data sources when first defining your DataWindow object in the New DataWindow window:

- Quick Select (one table or base and dependent tables)
- SQL Select (multiple tables)
- Query (previously defined SQL Select)
- External (data from a nonrelational source)
- Stored Procedure (precompiled SQL procedure residing on the DBMS)

The DataWindow Update function (source: Quick SELECT) always updates the database by dynamically, generating its own SQL INSERT, DELETE, and UPDATE statements. This can be an issue when your organization's standards require that stored procedures perform all database updates. The use of the Stored Procedure is a powerful feature both from a performance and development point of view. Because the Stored Procedure is written in the specific DBMS transaction language (e.g., the TRANSACT-SQL program in Sybase), it can be developed by the designated database programmer or administrator to ensure integrity and consistent database access. It also can be tuned for performance. The Stored Procedure obviates sending a long stream of dynamic SQL (i.e., less network traffic), and it does not need to be compiled at execution time. It can be recompiled (off hours) if the database statistics change and warrant that the access paths change to effect good performance.

Tip If the data for the DataWindow object will be retrieved from a relational database, then the possible choices for the data source are:

- Quick Select
- SQL Select

- Query
- Stored Procedure

To make the best choice review the following considerations:

- If the data is coming from one table and you only need to select columns, selection criteria, and sorting and you don't need to specify grouping, computed columns, and so on, choose Quick Select.
- If the data is coming from multiple tables or your objective implies the need to specify grouping, computed columns, and so on, choose SQL Select.
- If the SQL already has been developed using the Query painter, choose Query. The Query painter presents the user with the same options as SQL Select (i.e., the SQL Select and Query choices are essentially the same).
- If the data is coming from a database that supports the Stored Procedure (e.g., Sybase, Oracle, and now Watcom SQL) and the applications performance is critical to its viability, or the organization has separated the presentation and business tiers, then choose Stored Procedure. You also can use SPUD to develop the DataWindow using SQL Select, then creating the stored procedure later in development when the solution has stabilized. See the discussion on stored procedure update utility SPUD later in this chapter.

Using Quick Select

The easiest way to define a data source is using Quick Select. With Quick Select, you can choose columns from multiple tables associated by common key (a new Power-Builder 4.0 feature). After you select the columns that you require, you can:

- Specify whether you want to sort the retrieved rows (e.g., SQL clause ORDER BY).
- Specify criteria that a row must meet to be retrieved (e.g., SQL clause WHERE).
- Specify how to group data (e.g., SQL clause GROUP BY).
- Specify additional criteria for the grouped data (e.g., SQL clause HAVING).

To define the data source using Quick Select:

Step 1 Select the Quick Select icon on the New DataWindow. The window shown in Figure 10.2 will be displayed.

Step 2 Select the tables that you want to display/manipulate.

Step 3 Select the columns that you want to display/manipulate.

PowerBuilder's extended attribute Catalog tables provide a good way to maintain database dictionary information on the table columns such as description, default labels and headings, edit masks, etc. If populated, the design of a new SQL query is greatly facilitated, especially for those unfamiliar with the database tables/columns. The column name, heading label, data type, and comments are automatically

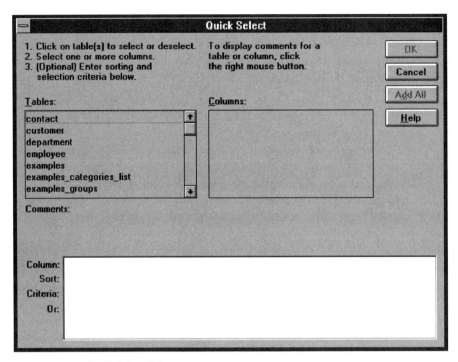

Figure 10.2 The Quick Select dialog.

displayed. This information can demystify the table content and speed up the development process:

- To add columns, select them in the Columns box.
- To add all columns, click Add All.
- To remove columns, deselect them in the Column box.

Work in the grid to finalize column ordering, add sorting criteria, and add selection criteria:

- To reorder a column, move the pointer to the column, press the left mouse button, and drag the column to a new position.
- To specify sorting criteria, enter the criteria in the grid.
- To specify selection criteria, enter the criteria in the grid.

Step 4 Click OK when you are satisfied with your selections

You go to the DataWindow painter workspace (unless you are defining a label or N-Up DataWindow object, in which case you need to provide additional information).

Specifying sorting criteria (ORDER BY). You can specify in the grid whether you want the retrieved rows to be sorted. As you specify sorting criteria, PowerBuilder builds an ORDER BY clause for the SELECT statement. If many rows will be retrieved, try to select columns that are indices as well.

Specifying selection criteria (WHERE).   You can specify selection criteria in the grid to determine which rows to retrieve. As you specify selection criteria, PowerBuilder builds a WHERE clause for the SELECT statement.

To specify selection criteria, enter the criteria as expressions in the grid below the column names starting in the row below the Sort row. If the column is too narrow for the criteria, drag the grid line to enlarge the column.

Use the PowerBuilder extended attributes.   If your database design is done by a data administration group familiar with the using and populating the PowerBuilder Catalog tables, then you can use the PowerBuilder extended attributes (stored in the PB Catalog tables) to provide the database columns' edit style, display format, and validation rules at DataWindow object definition time. For example, associate an edit style with a column at definition (i.e., when the table is created in the DBMS). So, if a column has an edit style format and/or validation rules associated with it in the PowerBuilder Catalog tables (i.e., the association was made in the Database painter), the edit style automatically is used in the DataWindow. This insulates the developer from having to revisit each column and its particular validation rules when building the DataWindow. This is all done at Create time. It can be Altered later if required.

Using SQL Select

When you choose SQL Select as the data source, you go to the Select painter, where you can paint a SELECT statement that includes the following:

- More than one table/view (FROM clause)
- Selection criteria (WHERE clause)
- Sorting criteria (ORDER BY clause)
- Grouping criteria (GROUP BY and HAVING clauses).
- Computed columns (PowerBuilder functions that can operate on a database column to produce a derivation (e.g., a datetime column can be used twice once in its native display form 1994-11-18 and as a computed column day of the week)
- One or more arguments to be supplied during execution (host variables).

SQL Select is a comprehensive option whereby you can quickly and easily develop a full-function SQL statement without concern for the syntactic requirements. This does not mean that the developer can be SQL illiterate. The prudent developer should focus upon creating optimal SQL to satisfy the user objective. A good practice might be to work in the Query painter, then EXPLAIN the SQL to ensure that it will perform (i.e., that indices are being utilized and database scans are not producing Cartesian products). EXPLAIN is a commonly available DBMS tool that can analyze SQL using the DBMS system catalog tables to predict the performance of the query based upon the currently available database statistics on the subject tables.

To define the data using SQL Select:

Step 1 Click SQL Select in the New DataWindow window, and click OK. The Select Tables window displays. It lists all tables and views defined in the current database.

Step 2 Select the tables and/or views that you will use in the DataWindow object by doing one of the following:

- Click the name of each table or view that you want to open in the list displayed in the Select Tables window, then click the Open button to open them.
- Double-click the name of each table or view that you want to open. Each object is opened immediately. Then click the Cancel button to close the Select Tables window. The window shown in Figure 10.3 will be displayed.

Step 3 Select the column to be retrieved from the database. Double-click on the desired columns; use the left mouse button to drag and drop.

Step 4 Join the tables if you have selected more than one. Double-click on the Join toolbar.

Step 5. Select retrieval arguments if appropriate. Click on the Object menu bar. Retrieval argument is the only choice.

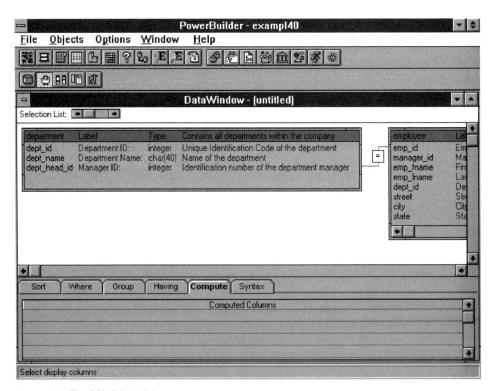

Figure 10.3 The SQL Select dialog.

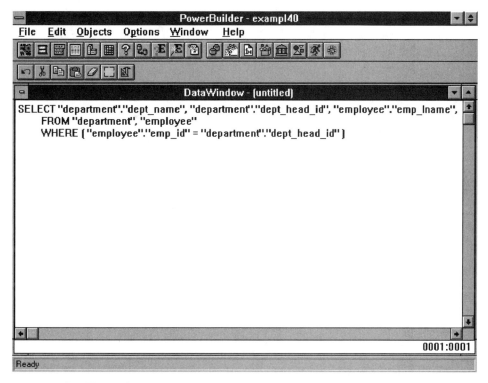

Figure 10.4 DataWindow Select syntax.

Step 6 Specify WHERE, ORDER BY, GROUP BY, and HAVING criteria if appropriate. Click on the toolbar toolbox icon to display the toolbox that contains tabs for the criteria (details are provided later in this chapter).

Step 7 If you want to eliminate duplicate rows, select `Distinct` from the Options menu. (*SQL note*: This adds the DISTINCT keyword to the SELECT statement.)

Step 8 When you have finished defining the data source, click the Design icon in the PainterBar. The DataWindow painter workspace displays (unless you are defining a label or N-Up DataWindow object, in which case you need to provide more information). (*SQL note*: Instead of modifying the data source, you can directly edit the SELECT statement. This is the primary technique for amending the SQL as the DataWindow is modified based upon changing application requirements.

To specify the data source syntax:

Step 1 When in the Datawindow Design painter, select `Edit data source¦Convert to Syntax` from the Options menu. PowerBuilder then displays the SELECT statement in a text window. (See Figure 10.4.)

Step 2 Edit the SELECT statement in the painter. You can develop the SQL using a more comprehensive Editor or using Word and cut and paste. You can use Word as an editor, then `Select All` and `Paste` to quickly amend a DataWindow.

Step 3 Do one of the following:

- Select Convert to Graphics from the Options menu to return to the Select painter.
- Click the Design icon to go the DataWindow painter workspace.

    To select all columns from a table, Select All from the table's control menu.
    To include a computed column:

Step 1 Click the Computed Column icon in the PainterBar, or select Create Computed Column from the Objects menu. The window shown in Figure 10.5 will appear.

Step 2 Enter the expression for the Computed Column. You can paste the following into the expression:

- Names of columns
- Supported functions (the day of the week based on a date column: day (d))
- Supported DBMS operators
- Retrieval arguments

Step 3 Click OK. The computed column is added to the list of columns to select from.

Joining tables. In the more comprehensive SQL queries, data from more than one table might be required. If the tables contain columns with the same name PowerBuilder will develop natural joins on these columns. Make sure that the join columns are keys, especially where the database tables contain a large number of rows (more than 100,000). This will ensure some degree of performance when deployed in a production environment.

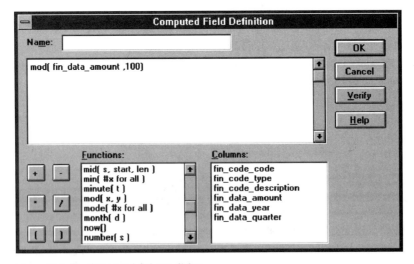

Figure 10.5 The Computed Column dialog.

To join tables:

Step 1 Click the Join icon.

Step 2 Click the columns on which you want to join the tables.

Step 3 To create a join other than the equality join, click the join operator in the workspace.

Select the join operator that you want from the Join window. You also can choose an outer join column if it is supported in your DBMS. Sybase and Oracle support the outer join. The new IBM DBMSs and DB2/MVS will provide support for the outer join soon.

Using retrieval arguments. If you know which rows will be retrieved into the Data-Window object during execution (i.e., if you can fully specify the SELECT statement without having to provide a variable), then you don't need to specify retrieval arguments. If you want to limit the result set, then you must provide a host variable to the WHERE clause of the SQL Select. Use the Object menu item to specify `Retrieval Arguments`. (*Note*: When it appears in the SQL syntax, the argument must be preceded by a colon.)

Amending your query to use arguments. If you decide later that you need selection refinements, you can return to the Select painter from the DataWindow painter workspace to define the arguments as described in this section. If criteria will be provided during execution that determine which rows are retrieved, you need to define retrieval arguments when defining the SQL SELECT. For example, consider these situations:

- The user might key the date into an edit box and click a button to retrieve the checks (rows) in the checkbook table written on that date. You don't know the date when you are defining the DataWindow object in the DataWindow painter, so you must have that information passed to the SELECT statement as an argument during execution.

- The user will select a state code from a dropdown listbox and click a button to retrieve all rows from a table for that state. The state code (e.g., NY will be passed as an argument during execution).

To define retrieval arguments:

Step 1 Select `Retrieval Arguments` from the Objects menu. The window shown in Figure 10.6 will be displayed.

Step 2 Enter a name and data type for each argument.

You can enter any valid SQL identifier for the argument name. This name must match in the actual SQL statement to the defined retrieval argument. The position number identifies the position of the argument in the Retrieve PowerScript function that you would code in a script to retrieve data into the DataWindow object. For ex-

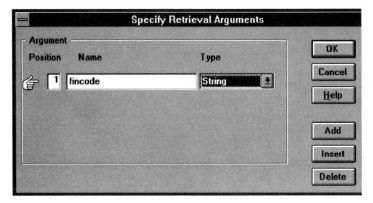

Figure 10.6 The Specify Retrieval Arguments dialog.

ample, `dw_sheet.Retrieve (is_cde1, is_cde2)` will pass two arguments to the DataWindow object associated with the DataWindow control dw_sheet. The argument is_cde1 will be used as the first retrieval argument, and is_cde2 will be the second even if the retrieval arguments have different names in the DataWindow (i.e., position is the determining factor.)

Step 3 Click OK when completed.

You return to the Select painter workspace. After you select the columns in the Select arguments painter, you reference the arguments in the WHERE or HAVING clause of the SELECT Statement, as described in the following section.

Specifying selection, sorting, and grouping criteria. In the SELECT statement associated with a DataWindow object, you can use the following SQL constructs to fashion and refine the result set:

- A WHERE clause to limit the data that is retrieved from the database
- An ORDER BY clause to sort the retrieved data before it is brought into the Data-Window object
- A GROUP BY clause to group the retrieved data before it is brought into the Data-Window object
- A HAVING clause to limit the groups specified in the GROUP BY clause

To specify the various criteria:

Step 1 Click the Where Criteria icon in the PainterBar, or select Where from the Objects menu. The Where Criteria window displays. (See Figure 10.7.)

Step 2 Specify Expression 1 and/or Expression 2. You can:

- Paste names of columns in the tables used in the DataWindow object.
- Paste functions supported by the DBMS. Only supported functions will appear. Be careful. If you begin using Watcom as a prototype and switch to Sybase, the func-

tion might not be available in the ultimate target production DBMS. Be aware of the target function set possible with the ultimate DBMS as early in the development cycle as possible. This will avoid redesign and reimplementation of DataWindow objects.

- Paste argument names if you have specified retrieval arguments. The arguments are listed in the Retrieve Arguments box. The argument names are prefaced with colons, because they are used as SQL host variables.

- Click the Select button to paint a Select statement for the expression (a nested subquery). You go to another painter where you can paint the nested SELECT statement. When you have completed it, you return to the Where Criteria window.

- Type the expression.

Step 3 If you have specified two expressions, select an operator from the Operator dropdown listbox.

Step 4 If your WHERE clause consists of more than one predicate, select the AND or OR logical operator from the Logical listbox.

Step 5 Click OK. You return to the Select painter.

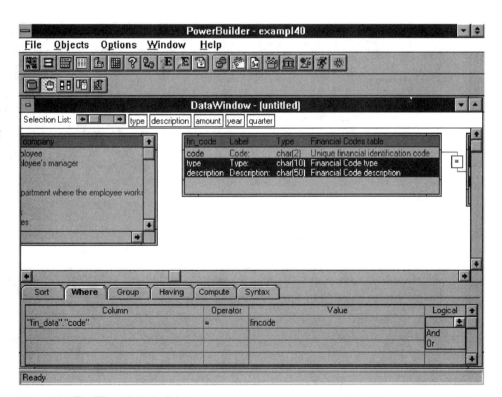

Figure 10.7 The Where Criteria dialog.

To define ORDER BY/GROUP BY criteria perform the following steps:

(*Note*: ORDER BY determines the sort sequence for data being retrieved; GROUP BY determines the way that the data will be grouped. Data columns retrieved that are not objects of the GROUP BY must be the constants or objects of a SCALAR function.)

Step 1   Click the Sort/Group icon in the PaintBar, or select `Columns` from the Objects menu. The Columns window displays. (See Figure 10.8.) It displays the first table selected for the DataWindow object and lists the columns in that table from the drop-down listbox.

Step 2   Click the columns that you want to use to form the groups or sort on. You can Select as many columns as you want. The selected columns display in the Column Name box. The columns are grouped/sorted in the order in which you selected them. For example, if you select the column dept_id and then the column dept_mgr, the grouping will be by dept_id and, within dept_id, by dept_mgr.

Step 3   Click OK. You return to the Select painter.

Defining HAVING criteria.   If you have defined groups, you can define HAVING criteria to restrict the retrieved groups. For example, if you group employees by department, you can restrict the retrieved groups to equities that have closing prices that are 15% greater than the opening price.

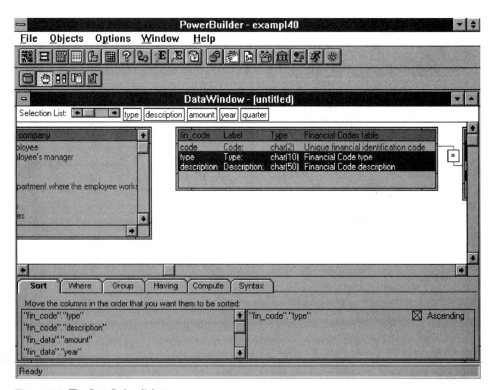

Figure 10.8 The Sort Order dialog.

To define HAVING criteria:

Step 1 Click the Having icon in the PainterBar, or select `Having Criteria` from the Objects menu.

Step 2 Follow the instructions for specifying a WHERE clause.

Using stored procedures

You can specify that the data for a DataWindow object be retrieved through a stored procedure if your DBMS supports stored procedures. The stored procedure is basically a database program incorporating a series of SQL commands in concert with modal statements to test and record database access results. Multiple SQL statements can be executed with a single command from PowerBuilder.

The development standard might require that the presentation layer and the data layer should be separated. The stored procedure provides a tool to create the separation of the two layers. This can be productive in some environments because it insulates the developer where advanced SQL expertise is required. However, it does require additional data structures be created to house the data passed to and from the stored procedure. See chapter 15 for more on structures.

In large database environments (more than 500,000 rows per table) the stored procedure is a virtual "must have" to provide acceptable response to the user. Stored procedures are compiled and thereby eliminate the time and resources required by the DBMS to compile the SQL passed by PowerBuilder. They also reduce the message size passed by PowerBuilder (e.g., `EXECUTE` procedure instead of `SELECT a,b,c,d,e,f,g,h,i,j,k FROM x,y,z WHERE a=b and b=c and e=f` and so and so on).

To define the data source using Stored Procedure:

Step 1 Select `Stored Procedure` as the data source in the New DataWindow window. The Select Stored Procedure window lists the stored procedures in the current database. The stored procedure typically is developed using the DBMS platform prior to generating a DataWindow object.

Step 2 Select a stored procedure from the list. The syntax of the selected stored procedure displays in the Source box. If this is not the source that you want to use, select another procedure.

Step 3 Click OK.

Step 4 Define the result set. This is a PowerBuilder structure that mirrors the database schema. Be careful to match the appropriate PowerBuilder datatype with the DBMS datatype. For example, integer in PowerBuilder is a two-byte integer. Integer in Sybase is a four-byte integer. The correct PowerBuilder data type for Sybase would be Long (i.e., PowerBuilder's four-byte integer).

Another approach that ultimately uses stored procedures is to begin developing the DataWindow using the SQL SELECT mode and, when development is complete, create the stored procedures and use the PowerBuilder Enterprise utility SPUD (Stored Procedure Update), which generates PowerScript statements that you can use to override default DataWindow behavior and update the database through stored procedures. The benefit of this approach is that you don't need to create stored procedures until all DataWindows have been tested completely, and you do not lose the benefit of extended attributes and other DataWindow features that usually are not available when using the stored procedure as a data source. This also will save you the time expended revising stored procedures due to DataWindow design changes. The DBAs that are developing the stored procedures will appreciate your completed specification. Obviously, to use this utility, your DBMS must support stored procedures.

Because the DataWindow Update function always updates the database by dynamically generating INSERT, DELETE, and UPDATE SQL statements, PowerBuilder provides the SQLPreview event, which is invoked just before it submits a SQL statement to the database. This event allows you to override the default DataWindow update capability by creating a script that updates the database through a stored procedure. The SPUD utility can be used to create PowerScript statements that you can use in a DataWindow's SQLPreview event to perform database updates through stored procedures. Stored Procedure Update generates PowerScript statements based on information that you provide. These statements override default DataWindow database update processing and invoke your stored procedures instead. You then paste or import the PowerScript statements into your DataWindow's SQLPreview event.

Saving a DataWindow Object

Once you have selected a presentation style and data source, PowerBuilder generates the DataWindow object. At this point, you have a functioning DataWindow object. You should save it before making any changes.

To save a DataWindow object:

Step 1 Select Save from the File menu. If you have previously saved the DataWindow object, PowerBuilder saves the new version in the same library and returns you to the DataWindow painter workspace. If you have not previously saved the DataWindow object, PowerBuilder displays the Save DataWindow window.

Step 2 Name the DataWindow object in the DataWindows box. (See Figure 10.9.)

Step 3 Write comments to describe the DataWindow object. These comments display in the Library painter. It is a good idea to use comments so that you and others can easily remember the purpose of the object later.

Step 4 Specify the library in which to save the object.

Step 5 Click OK.

The DataWindow object now is stored in the PBL and has the basic presentation and data layer in place. Depending on the particular intended use of the object, enhancements will be added to provide edit, display, and validation beyond that which you might have included by virtue of the extended column attributes. Moreover the data layer can be augmented to provide additional dynamics (e.g., modifying the

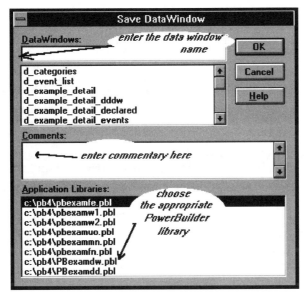

Figure 10.9 Saving the DataWindow.

SQL to change the selected columns or the source tables and even the WHERE predicates to use the DataWindow to answer a multitude of user questions thereby creating a powerful while flexible view of the business data).

The Format of the DataWindow

After specifying your presentation style and data source, you will be presented with the DataWindow painter where you can create and customize the view of the data as needed. Here you will use the available workspace (real estate) to arrange the data (i.e., columns and computed columns) and insert other information (e.g., text) to make the DataWindow easy to use and understand.

Depending on the type of use that the DataWindow will have, certain features are used more often. For example, a DataWindow used for data entry might use an edit style DropDownDataWindow to provide only the valid choices for a column entry. This edit style can display text and store a code in the data entry column. You also might use edit style DropDownListBox, which has been defined using the database painter to provide firmwide code lists that are small and static (e.g., gender).

The DataWindow Workspace

The first time that you see it, the workspace might appear somewhat cryptic. You will see the columns that you have chosen in the initial setup of the DataWindow arranged horizontally for the grid and tabular style and vertically for the free form. The columns will have headings/labels based upon the database definition. If you have populated the extended attribute, then you will see that default heading and any other defaults. The database extended attributes are a powerful way to set up data for the DataWindow build. Proper database setup will facilitate this next refinement step greatly. Use of the extended attributes also will promote consistency.

DataWindow bands

The DataWindow is divided into bands. They appear above a gray bar that identifies the band by name and with an upward pointing arrow. Each band has a different responsibility. See Figure 10.10. for a graphical view of the bands that are described in the following sections.

This is used to display information, like report title and column headings, at the top of each page or screen. You will use this with data presented with the horizontal alignment such as the grid or tabular form.

Group Header band. This band is used to define the heading to be displayed before the group information, such as series_code and series_name if grouping by series in our television network example. This band, along with the Group Trailer, appears only if you choose to create groups (Rows|Create Group).

Detail band. The Detail band displays the retrieved data. It also is where the user will input and/or update any information. The initial contents of this band are determined by the presentation style that was chosen:

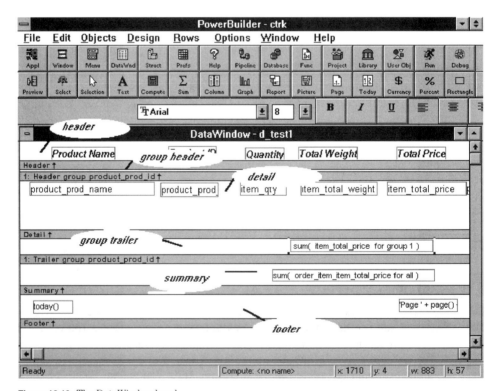

Figure 10.10 The DataWindow band.

- If the presentation style is Grid, Label or N-Up, then this band will contain a row of boxes representing column data. You have less flexibility here, and this style is best suited for the basic report type DataWindow.

- If the presentation style is freeform, then this band will contain a label for each column and a box representing the column data to the right. Here you have the most flexibility to easily rearrange the data columns in any way you like. This is a popular style for data entry. You can use the Tab feature to order the way that the input fields will be entered. The column with the lowest nonzero value will be the initial position for the cursor. The cursor then will tab to the next higher Tab and so on. A column with a Tab value of zero is protected from user data entry.

You can specify display formats and validation criteria for each of the columns in the detail band. Here again, if you have properly set up the extended attributes for the columns, then you can quickly proceed with the next steps because the edit validation and display are set per the project team standards. You can add drawing objects, graphs, and pictures as well as text.

Group Trailer band. This band is used to define what you want to see displayed after the last item in the group is displayed, such as total number of episodes in a series group. This band, along with the Group Header, appears only if you choose to create groups (Rows ¦ Create Group).

Summary band. This band is used to define any summary information that will appear on only the last page or screen. An example might be to display the total amount of profit or loss in U.S. dollars, using the prevailing commercial spot rates for each episode airdate.

Footer band. This band is used to display information—like the date, page number and report name—at the bottom of each page or screen.

The bands in the DataWindow can be resized to allow more room for placing columns while you are designing. The bands then can be resized again to bring them closer together ready for runtime presentation. Just move the cursor to the band and drag in the desired direction.

Manipulating objects in the DataWindow

Once selected, an object or a group of objects in a DataWindow can be manipulated in several ways. Once selected, an object or a group of objects can be repositioned, and you can change the foreground or background color, change the font, or adjust the font size.

Before you can perform any enhancements to an object in a DataWindow, you first must select it. An object that is selected will display small squares, which commonly are called *handles*, in each corner. PowerBuilder provides you with several ways to select objects for manipulation. You can select a single object or multiple objects. Selecting multiple objects is useful for moving or changing the colors and fonts for several objects at once.

Selecting a single object. A single object can be selected by clicking on it with the left mouse button. After selecting an object, any previously selected objects are deselected. If you have a group of objects selected and you want to select just a single object that happens to be in the group that already is selected, just clicking on it does not deselect the other members of the group. What you should do is click anywhere outside of the selected group, then click on the required object.

Selecting multiple objects. Multiple objects can be selected by holding down the Ctrl key while clicking the new object with the left mouse button. All of the selected objects then are treated as a group. To deselect a single object in this group, click on it once more while still holding down the Ctrl key.

"Lassoing" objects. You can select multiple objects by a "lasso" technique. Position the mouse pointer near the objects that you would like to select. Then, while holding down the left mouse button, drag the mouse from left to right a little and you will see a box appear. By moving the mouse, you can make this box grow or shrink so that is covers or touches objects in the DataWindow. When you stop holding down the left mouse button, every object that is covered or touched by the lasso box area is selected.

Reorganizing objects

There are several tools within the DataWindow painter environment that deal with the reorganizing objects in the DataWindow.

Displaying boundaries for objects. It often is useful to see how large an object is, particularly when it is in close proximity to another. Select Show Edges from the Design menu, and PowerBuilder will display the boundary for all objects in the DataWindow. These do not appear during the execution of the application, so you might as well leave this feature on until it gets in the way.

Grid/Ruler. This is one of the features that will help you to align objects. Select Grid/Ruler from the Design menu, and the Alignment Grid window will appear. (See Figure 10.11.) When selected, it will force the controls that subsequently are placed or moved to snap to the grid that has been defined by the X and Y values.

Show Grid When selected, Show Grid will show the grid that has been defined by the X and Y values.

Show Ruler When selected, it will show the ruler.

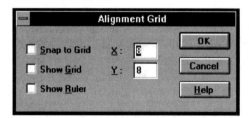

Figure 10.11 Snap to grid.

X This control specifies the width of each cell of the grid in pixels.

Y This control specifies the height of each cell of the grid in pixels.

These settings are saved in the PowerBuilder PB.INI file, and the settings will be in place the next time that you start PowerBuilder.

Deleting objects. To delete objects in the DataWindow Painter:

Step 1 Select the objects.

Step 2 Press the Del key, click on the Delete icon, or select `Delete` from the Edit menu.

Moving objects. With the exception of the Grid presentation style, you can move an object anywhere that you want. To move objects:

Step 1 Select the objects.

Step 2 Either drag the object using the mouse or press an arrow key to move the object in that direction.

Resizing objects. Resizing of an object can be done using either the mouse or the keyboard.

Using the mouse:

Step 1 Select the object.

Step 2 Grab an edge and drag it with the mouse.

See Table 10.1 for a list of the keys to use to resize an object.

Aligning objects. You can align several objects at the same time. You can use the Grid method, as described earlier in this section, or you can let PowerBuilder align them for you. To align objects:

Step 1 First select the master object, the one whose position you want to use to align the other objects.

Step 2 While holding the Ctrl key down, select the other objects by clicking on them with the left mouse key.

**TABLE 10.1 A List of Keys
to Use to Resize an Object**

Press	To make the object
Shift–Right arrow	Wider
Shift–Left arrow	Narrower
Shift–Up arrow	Taller
Shift–Down arrow	Shorter

Step 3 Select `Align Objects` from the Edit menu.

Step 4 On the cascading menu, select the dimension along which you want to align the objects (e.g., to align the objects along the left side, select the first choice from the menu).

PowerBuilder then will align all of the objects with the master object.

Spacing objects. It is possible to equalize the spacing between objects. To space objects:

Step 1 Select the master objects, two objects whose spacing is as desired. Click on first object, then hold down the Ctrl key while you click on the second.

Step 2 Select the other objects whose spacing you want to be the same as the first two objects.

Step 3 Select `Space Objects` from the Edit menu.

Step 4 On the cascading menu, select the dimension in which you want to equalize the spacing.

Sizing objects. You can set objects to have the same dimensions to obtain a consistent look and feel on the DataWindow. To size objects:

Step 1 Select the master object—the object that is the required size.

Step 2 Select the other objects whose size you want to set to match the master by holding down the Ctrl key while clicking on the next object.

Step 3 Select `Size Objects` from the Edit menu.

Step 4. On the cascading menu, select the dimension whose size you want to equalize.

Modifying general attributes of the DataWindow

There are several general DataWindow attributes that can be modified in the DataWindow Painter.

The DataWindow object style. A DataWindow object has a Style window (see Figure 10.12) that defines:

- The unit of measure used in the DataWindow
- A timer interval for events in the DataWindow
- A background color for the DataWindow

When the DataWindow is first generated, PowerBuilder assigns defaults that you can change:

Step 1 Double-click the background of the DataWindow, or select `DataWindow Style` from the Design menu.

Step 2 Click the unit of measure that you would like to use for the DataWindow object.

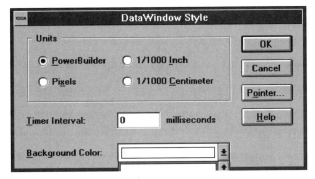

Figure 10.12 The DataWindow object styles.

Step 3 Specify the number of milliseconds that you require between internal timer events for the DataWindow. This value determines how often PowerBuilder updates the time fields in the DataWindow.

Step 4 Select a background color from the dropdown listbox.

Step 5 Click OK to save your selections and return to the painter.

The look and feel of the DataWindow

You also can improve the appearance of a DataWindow by using colors and well-chosen borders. The following sections provide some suggestions.

Setting colors. To enhance the appearance of the DataWindow, PowerBuilder gives you the ability to change the colors of the display. Table 10.2 shows how to do this.

Specifying the display of grid lines. With the Grid Presentation Style, you can define whether grid lines are always displayed, never displayed, displayed only when the DataWindow displays online, or displayed only when the contents of the DataWindow are printed. To change this:

Step 1 Click the right mouse button on the background of a Grid DataWindow.

Step 2 Select Grid Lines from the pop-up menu.

Step 3 On the cascading menu, select the option that you want.

TABLE 10.2 Changing the Colors of the Display

To set the color for	Do
DataWindow background	Click in an empty spot in the DataWindow object, and select Color from the pop-up menu
A band	Position the mouse pointer on the gray bar that describes the band, and select the color from the pop-up menu
An object	Position the mouse pointer on the object, and select the color from the pop-up menu

Specifying pointers. It is possible to configure the style of pointer that is displayed when the mouse passes over specific, or all, areas the DataWindow object during execution. To change the mouse pointer:

Step 1 Move the mouse to the object whose pointer you would like to define.

Step 2 Click on the right mouse button, and select `Pointer` from the pop-up menu.

Step 3 Choose from the list of PowerBuilder pointers that are available or, if you have files containing pointer definitions (.CUR files), choose from the file list.

Step 4 Click `OK` to return to the painter.

Modifying text. When the DataWindow first is generated, PowerBuilder sets up the following text defaults:

- For the text and alignment of column headings, PowerBuilder uses the extended column attributes made in the Database painter. These definitions are set by selecting `Header` from the column's pop-up menu in the Database painter.

- For fonts, PowerBuilder uses the extended column attributes made in the Database painter. These definitions are set by selecting `Fonts` from the column's pop-up menu in the Database painter.

These defaults can be re-configured. To change the text:

Step 1 Click on the text object.

Step 2 The left-hand box of the StyleBar now will have focus, and you can type the new text to replace the old text. The characters ~n~r can be used to insert a new line and carriage return in the text.

To change the attributes of text objects:

Step 1 Click on the text object.

Step 2 Either change the attributes using the StyleBar, or click on the right mouse button and select `Font` from the pop-up menu and change the attributes from the Font window.

Datawindow data entry

In the early days of online data entry, when there was mostly character-based data entry, the main data-entry format questions concerning the developer revolved around whether or not a field or column was keyable (i.e., protected), its order, and what variable contained the entry content when the user hit the Enter key. Now, using GUI front ends, we have a host of new considerations, but we still need to concern ourselves with the data-entry order, variable name, and whether a column is protected or updatable. We will discuss your options in the following sections.

Setting the tab order. Taking care of the data-entry order is simple enough. PowerBuilder assigns columns a default tab order. When an application displays a window that contains a DataWindow that is ready for data entry, if the user presses the Tab key, the cursor will focus on the next column in the tab order sequence. (See Figure 10.13, which illustrates five data-entry fields with tabs of 10 through 50.) The tab order is assigned in increments of 10 in a left-to-right, top-to-bottom order. After some redesigning, you arrange the columns in a new fashion; it might be necessary to change the sequence. You need only open the DataWindow and edit the tabs to effect the desired sequencing.

To change the tab order, do the following:

Step 1 Select Tab Order from the Design menu, and the current tab order will be displayed.

Step 2 Either click on or use the Tab key to select a tab value to be changed.

Step 3 Enter a new tab value (range of 0 to 9999). Entering 0 will prevent the user from tabbing to the column. This is a good technique for protecting a field from being updated. For example, the DataWindow might be used for add and update. On an update, simply modify the Tab order of the column to zero. In an MDI application, only that instance wil be modified. Be sure to restore the tab to a nonzero value to accomodate the user who chooses the INSERT menu/toolbar.

All Tab numbers are relative, making it easy to insert a column within an existing tab sequence. For example, suppose you have three columns—A (with a tab value of 10), B (with a tab value of 30), and C (with a tab value of 20)—and the desired tab

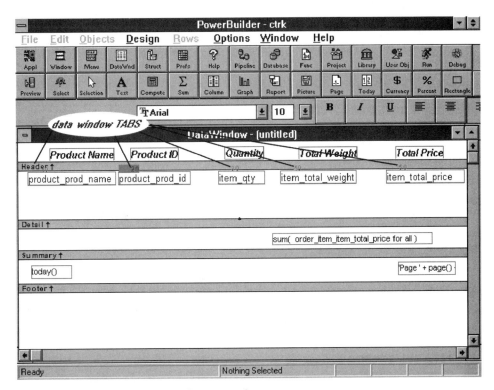

Figure 10.13 Assigning a tab order to data-entry columns.

sequence was A, B, then C, all you need to do is select the B column and change it's tab value to 15. When you switch off tab order mode, all tab values, except those with a value of 0, are resequenced in increments of 10.

Naming objects.   You can use names to identify objects on the DataWindow. To specify a name:

Step 1   Select the object.

Step 2   Click on the right mouse button, and select Name from the menu, then type the name.

This name is important, especially when you advance to using PowerBuilder functions to dynamically modify the DataWindow during execution. It will default to the database column name. If the DataWindow joins more than one table, the table name will be appended to the front of the object name separated by an underbar (e.g., series_series_cde is series_cde in the series table).

Using borders.   It is possible to display borders around certain objects (e.g., a column). Check your development standards manual. There usually are standards for borders based upon the type of data displayed (e.g., read only, update, etc.). PowerBuilder has different types of borders:

- Underline
- Box
- Resize—Allow a user to resize the object during execution; useful for graphs
- Shadow box
- 3D raised—A popular choice for display
- 3D lowered—A popular choice for columns that are enterable

To specify a border:

Step 1   Select the objects around which you would like to place a border.

Step 2   Click on the right mouse key, and select Border from the pop-up menu

Step 3   On the cascading menu, select the border that you want.

Modifying the Data Source

When modifying a DataWindow object, you might realize that you haven't included all of the columns that you need, or you might need to define retrieval arguments. You can modify the data source from the DataWindow painter workspace. How you do it depends on the data source.

Modifying SQL SELECT statements

If the data source is Quick Select, SQL Select, or Query, you can graphically modify the SQL SELECT statement. To modify the SQL data source:

Step 1 Click the Select (SQL) icon in the PainterBar or select `Edit Data Source` from the Design menu. PowerBuilder returns you to the Select painter.

Step 2 Modify the SELECT statement graphically using the same techniques as when creating it. Select `Convert to Syntax` from the Options menu to modify the SELECT statement syntactically.

Step 3 Click the Design icon to return to the workspace. Some changes that you make (such as adding or removing columns) require PowerBuilder to modify the update capabilities of the DataWindow object.

Changing the table. If you change the table referenced in the SELECT statement, PowerBuilder maintains the columns in the workspace (now from a different table) only if they match the data types and order of the columns in the original table. If you change the table name, then you will have to map the selected columns to those already present in the DataWindow. Use the EXPORT object utility in the Library painter to see the table columns that correspond to the DataWindow items. EXPORT also is a somewhat tricky but useful tool to effect global changes to a DataWindow. For example, if the database column names changed but all else remained static, you can export the DataWindow and use an editing tool (e.g., Word) macro to globally change a column name.

Modifying the retrieval arguments. You can add, modify, or delete retrieval arguments when modifying your data source. Retrieval arguments are tantamount to host variables that are used to refine the WHERE clause to SELECT particular rows from the data source. To modify the retrieval arguments:

Step 1 In the Select painter, select `Retrieval Arguments` from the Objects menu. The Specify Retrieval Arguments window displays the existing arguments. (See Figure 10.14.)

Step 2 Add, modify, or delete the arguments.

Step 3 Click OK. You return to the Select painter or to the text window displaying the SELECT statement if you are modifying the SQL syntactically.

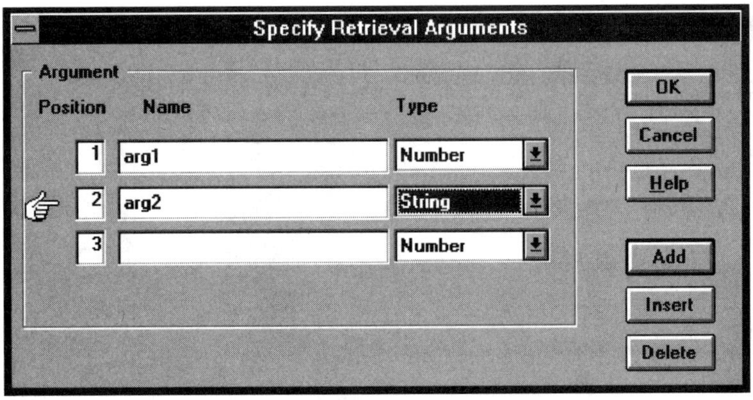

Figure 10.14 Setting up retreival arguments or host variables.

Reference any new arguments in the WHERE or HAVING clause of the SELECT statement. Retrieval arguments are added to the SELECT/WHERE clause and preceded by a colon to identify and distinguish them from table columns or scalars. For example:

```
SELECT series_nme FROM series WHERE series_id = :arg1
```

Modifying the result set. If the data source is external or a stored procedure, you can modify the result set description. To modify a result set:

Step 1 Click the Select icon in the PainterBar, or select `Edit Data Source` from the Design menu. The Modify Result Set Description window displays.

Step 2 Review the description, and make any necessary changes.

Step 3 Click OK. You return to the workspace.

If the data source is a stored procedure. If you are modifying the result set for a DataWindow object whose data source is a stored procedure, the Modify Result Set window contains a `More` button. Click `More` to edit the Execute statement, select another stored procedure, or add arguments. As we discussed earlier, SPUD, the stored procedure update utility (Enterprise only), allows the developer to work with a native SELECT DataWindow and, when it is completed and tested, it can be converted to interface via stored procedure avoiding all of the DataWindow rework if stored procedures are used from the start.

Prompting for retrieval criteria

You can define your DataWindow object so that it always prompts the user for retrieval criteria just before it retrieves data. (See Figure 10.15.) This is similar to the way in which the Database painter data manipulation window operates. In some cases, you might not want the user to be prompted in quite this way. You can avoid the prompting by coding a preretrieval event script to retrieve the DataWindow using a default key.

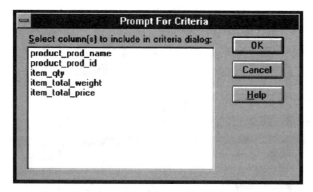

Figure 10.15 The Prompt For Criteria dialog.

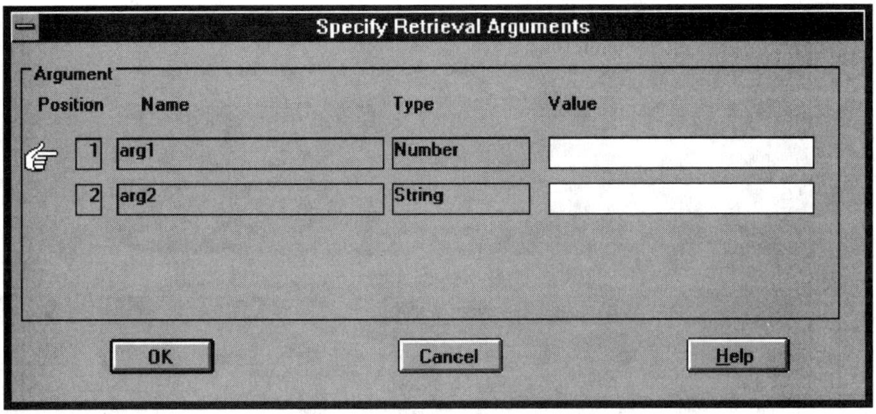

Figure 10.16 The execution-time window for retrieval arguments.

To prompt for retrieval criteria:

Step 1 Select the columns that you want the user to be able to specify retrieval criteria for during execution. The selected columns are highlighted.

Step 2 Click OK.

What happens. When you specify prompting for criteria during execution, Power-Builder displays the window shown in Figure 10.16 to the user just before a retrieval is to be done (it is the last thing that happens before the SQLPreview event). You can avoid this by coding a script to preselect the data row in the window open event for the window that contains the DataWindow control. See chapter 11 for an example.

Each column that you selected in the Prompt for Criteria window displays in the grid. Users can specify criteria here exactly as you do in the grid with the Quick Select DataWindow data source. Criteria specified here is added to the WHERE clause for the SQL SELECT statement defined for the DataWindow object, providing the SQL search predicate. (See Figure 10.17.)

Using edit styles. If a column uses a dropdown DataWindow as a reference/code table or the Radio Button, Check Box, or DropDownListBox edit style, it is standard to have an arrow display in the column header, signifying that users can select a value from a dropdown list box during execution.

If you don't want the dropdown list box used for a column when the user specifies retrieval criteria, select the particular column, choose Design Object Style Query Criteria, and choose Override Edit from the column's pop-up menu in the DataWindow painter workspace. Doing so provides a standard edit control for the column.

Forcing use of equality. You can force users to use the equal sign operator in a criteria for a column by selecting Query Criteria Equality Required from the column's pop-up menu in the workspace. PowerBuilder will underline the column header

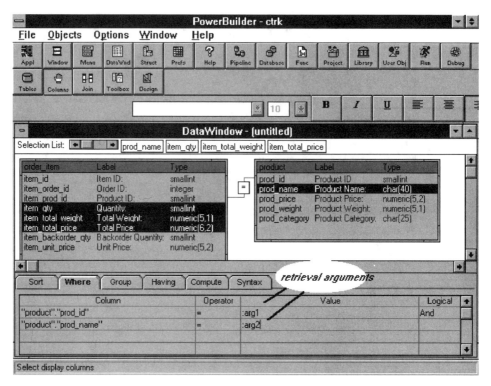

Figure 10.17 A WHERE clause with host/retrieval variables.

in the grid during execution. Doing this ensures that criteria specified for the column use the equal sign rather than other operators, such as the greater than or less than symbols.

Adding objects to the DataWindow

You can add PowerBuilder objects to improve your DataWindow. New to Power-Builder 4.0 was the addition of a DataWindow within the DataWindow, or a *report* or *nested DataWindow*. This obviated the extra code required in earlier releases to print two DataWindows with one invocation of the Print(DataWindow) functionality.

You also can add, amend, or delete columns, text, drawing objects, pictures, computed fields, graphs, crosstabs, and of course another DataWindow. (See Figure 10.18 for the dropdown list.)

The layering of objects

Each object has a *specified layering*—how it is positioned within the DataWindow object. An object's layering is specified by the Layer cascading menu in the object's pop-up menu. See Table 10.3.

The default attributes for a Graph object are Foreground, Moveable, and Resizeable. The default attributes for all other objects are Band, not Moveable, and not Resizeable.

These defaults in PowerBuilder normally are what is most suitable. However, you can change the settings using the Layer menu

Adding objects

During the course of DataWindow development, you will be enhancing your presentation with other objects. See Figure 10.18 for the dropdown list of objects that can be added.

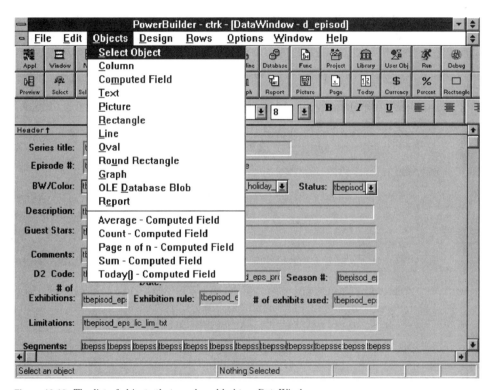

Figure 10.18 The list of objects that can be added to a DataWindow.

TABLE 10.3 The Type of Layering

Attribute	Meaning
Background	Object is always behind other objects. It is not restricted to single band.
Band	Object is within one band. It does not extend beyond the band's border.
Foreground	Object is in front of other objects and is not restricted to one band.
Moveable	Object is be moveable during execution
Resizeable	Object is resizeable during execution

Adding data columns. This is a fairly common type of update. Take care when you add or change column specifications; the DataWindow update specifications might change in response. To add a data column to a DataWindow object:

Step 1 Click the Column icon on the PainterBar, or select Column from the Objects menu.

Step 2 Click where you want to place the column. The Select Column window displays, listing all columns included in the DataWindow object.

Step 3 Select the column, and click OK.

Adding text. When PowerBuilder generates a basic DataWindow object from a presentation style and data source, it places columns and their headings in the workspace. The headings can be primed with the heading value for the column as specified in the extended attributes row. You also can add text to describe a column or anywhere else that you want to the DataWindow. To add text:

Step 1 Click the Text icon on the PainterBar, or select Text from the Objects menu.

Step 2 Click where you want to place the text. The text object will appear in the DataWindow displaying the word text.

Step 3 Overwrite the text in the left-hand box of the StyleBar.

You also can change the font, size, style, and alignment for the text using the Style-Bar.

Adding drawing objects. You can add drawing objects to a DataWindow object to enhance its appearance. The possible list includes: Rectangle, RoundRectangle, Line, and Oval.

Drawing objects are useful in grouping objects in a DataWindow object or providing design highlights. For example, you can place a colored rectangle behind a group of objects to group them. To place a drawing object:

Step 1 Select the drawing object from the PowerBar or from the Objects menu.

Step 2 Click where you want the object to display.

Step 3 Resize or move the drawing object as needed.

Step 4 Use the drawing object's pop-up menu to change its attributes as needed. For example, you might want to specify a fill color for a rectangle or thickness for a line.

Adding pictures. You can place pictures, such as your company logo, in a DataWindow object to enhance its appearance. If you place a picture in the header, summary, or footer band of the DataWindow object, the picture displays each time the contents of that band displays. If you place the picture in the detail band of the DataWindow object, it displays in each row.

Adding computed fields. You can use computed fields in any band of the DataWindow object. Typical uses of computed fields include:

- Calculations based on column data that change for each retrieved row. For example, if you are retrieving annual salary, you could define a computed field in the detail band that displays monthly salary (defined as Salary/12).

- Summary statistics of the data. If you have a grouped DataWindow object, you can use a computed field to calculate the totals of a column for each group.

- Concatenated fields. If you are retrieving first name and last name, you can define a computed field that concatenates the values as they appear with only one space between them (defined as FirstName + " " + LastName).

- System information. You could place the current page and page count in a DataWindow object's footer by using computed fields Page( ) and PageCount( ).

About defining computed columns and computed fields. When creating a DataWindow object, you can define computed columns and computed fields as follows:

- In the Select painter, you can define computed columns when you are defining the SELECT statement that will be used to retrieve data into the DataWindow object.

- In the DataWindow painter workspace, you can define computed fields after you have defined the SELECT statement (or other data source).

To define a computed field in the workspace. Perform the following steps to define a computed field in the workspace:

Step 1 Click the Compute icon in the PainterBar, or select Computed Field from the Objects menu.

Step 2 Click where you want the computed field. If the calculation is to be based on column data that changes for each row, make sure that you place the computed field in the detail band. The Computed Field Definition window displays (see Figure 10.19) and lists:

- Built-in PowerScript functions that you can use in the computed field

- The columns in the DataWindow object

- Operators and parentheses

Step 3 Name the computed field.

Step 4 Enter the expression that defines the computed field. You can enter any valid PowerScript expression when defining a computed field. You can paste operators, columns, and PowerScript functions into the expression from information in the Computed Field Definition window.

Step 5 You can click Verify to test the expression. PowerBuilder then will analyze the expression.

Step 6 Click OK. PowerBuilder returns you to the workspace with the computed field in place.

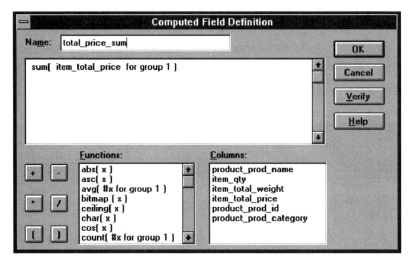

Figure 10.19 A computed field definition.

Note: The expression that you are entering is a PowerScript expression is not an SQL expression processed by the DBMS, so the expression follows PowerScript rules. You can use any non-object-level PowerScript function (built-in or user-defined) in an expression. You can use the plus sign operator to concatenate strings.

You also can refer to other rows in a computed field. This is particularly useful in N-Up DataWindow objects when you want to refer to another row in the detail band. Use this syntax:

```
ColumnName[x]
```

where x is an integer. A 0 refers to the current row (or first row in the detail band), a 1 refers to the next row, a –1 refers to the previous row, and so on.

Some examples of computed fields and columns are shown in Table 10.4.

Summary functions. Select one or more columns in the DataWindow object's detail band. Place the computed field by doing one of the steps shown in Table 10.5.

PowerBuilder places a computed field in the summary band or in the Group trailer band if the DataWindow object is grouped. The band is resized automatically to hold the computed field.

TABLE 10.4 Computed Fields and Columns

To display	Enter this expression	In this band
Current date at top of each page	Today( )	Header
Current time at top of each page	Now( )	Header
Current page at bottom of each page	Page( )	Footer
Total page count at bottom of each page	PageCount( )	Footer
Average price of all returned rows	Avg(Price)	Summary

TABLE 10.5 Placing the Computed Field

Function	Step
Average	Click the Average icon, or select `Average Computed Field` from the Object menu
Count	Click the Count icon, or select, `Count-Computed Field` from the Object menu
Sum	Click the Sum icon, or select `Sum-Computed Field` from the Object menu

Adding a graph. Graphs are perhaps the best way to present information. If your application displays information over the course of a year, instead of displaying rows and columns of data that is difficult to interpret, you can easily build a graph in a DataWindow object to display the information visually. PowerBuilder offers many types of graphs and provides you with the ability to control the appearance of a graph to best meet your application's needs.

Useful features in the DataWindow

The DataWindow is a comprehensive tool for accessing relational DBMSs, but it also is useful in other ways.

Static data in a DataWindow object. In an application, you typically retrieve data into a DataWindow object during execution. Data also can be modified and saved. However, sometimes the data that you display in a DataWindow object is static; it doesn't need to change.

A typical use of this feature is during Rapid Application Development (RAD), where you might not have the database table ready to use. So, PowerBuilder can help you by allowing you to store the data in the DataWindow object itself.

Another good reason could be where the data that is to be displayed is not going to change. For example, you could display a list of state code abbreviations for a user entering values in a State column in a DataWindow object. Those State codes can be stored in a dropdown DataWindow edit style. To store data in a DataWindow object:

Step 1 Select Data from the Rows menu. The Data Retained on Save window displays. All columns defined for the DataWindow object are listed at the top.

Step 2 Do one of the following:

- Click `Add` to create an empty row, and type a row of data into the window. You can enter as many rows as you want.
- Click `Retrieve` to retrieve all of the rows of data from the database. If you want, you can delete rows you don't want to save or manually add new rows.

Step 3 Click `OK`. PowerBuilder saves the rows.

Data changes are local to the DataWindow object. Adding or deleting data here does not change the data in the database. It only determines what data will be stored with the DataWindow object when you save it.

When you save the DataWindow object, the data is stored in the DataWindow object in the PowerBuilder library.

Note: Storing data in a DataWindow object is a good way to share data and its definition with other developers. They can simply open the DataWindow object on their computer to get the data and all its attributes.

During execution. Data stored in a DataWindow object is stored within the actual object itself. So when a window opens showing such a DataWindow, the data already is there. There is no need to issue Retrieve to get the data, with one exception.

If you reissue the Retrieve for a DataWindow stored with data, PowerBuilder handles it the same as a DataWindow that is not stored with data. PowerBuilder gets the latest data by retrieving rows from the database. PowerBuilder never retrieves data into a dropdown DataWindow that already contains data.

Retrieving data as needed. If your DataWindow object retrieves an enormous number of rows, there can be a noticeable delay during execution while all of the rows are retrieved and before control returns to the user. In these DataWindow objects, you can specify that PowerBuilder retrieves only as many rows as it has to before displaying data and returning control to the user.

For example, if your DataWindow displays only 10 rows at a time, it might make sense to have PowerBuilder retrieve only a small number of rows before presenting the data. Then, as the user pages through the data, PowerBuilder continues to retrieve what is necessary to display the new information. There might be slight pauses while PowerBuilder retrieves the additional rows, but the pauses might be worth it if the user doesn't have to wait a long time to start working with data.

To specify that a DataWindow object retrieve only as many rows as it needs to, select `Retrieve Only As Needed` from the Rows menu. With this setting, PowerBuilder presents data and returns control to the user when it has retrieved enough rows to display in the DataWindow object.

Limitations. `Retrieve Only As Needed` is overridden if you have specified sorting or have used aggregate functions, such as Avg and Sum, in the DataWindow object. This is because PowerBuilder must retrieve every row before it can sort or perform aggregates.

How the database is updated through the DataWindow

When PowerBuilder generates the basic DataWindow object, it defines whether the data is updatable by default as follows:

- If the DataWindow contains columns from a single table and includes that table's key columns, PowerBuilder defines all columns as updatable and specifies a non-zero tab order for each column, allowing the user to tab to the columns.

- If the DataWindow contains columns from two or more tables or from a view, PowerBuilder defines all columns as not being updatable and sets all tab orders to zero, preventing users from tabbing to them.

You can accept the default settings or modify the update characteristics for a DataWindow object.

If you are using a stored procedure or external data source, you can use the dwGetNextModified function to write your own update script.

How you can affect the update. You can affect the update in the following ways:

- Allow updates in a DataWindow object associated with multiple tables or a view; you can define one of the tables as being updatable
- Prevent updates in a DataWindow object associated with one table
- Prevent updates to specific columns in a DataWindow object that is associated with an updatable table
- Specify which columns uniquely identify a row to be updated
- Specify which columns will be included in the WHERE clause of the UPDATE or DELETE statement PowerBuilder generates to update the database
- Specify whether PowerBuilder generates an UPDATE statement, or a DELETE then an INSERT statement, to update the database when the user modifies the values in a key column

Update capability of views. Some views are logically updatable; some are not. For the rules that your DBMS follows regarding updating of views, see your DBMS's documentation.

To specify update characteristics for a DataWindow object:

Step 1 Select Update from the Rows menu. The Specify Update Characteristics window displays. (See Figure 10.20.)

Step 2 To prevent updates to the data, make sure the Allow Updates box is not selected. Click OK to return to the workspace. To allow updates, select the Allow Updates box and specify the other settings.

Step 3 Click OK to return to the workspace.

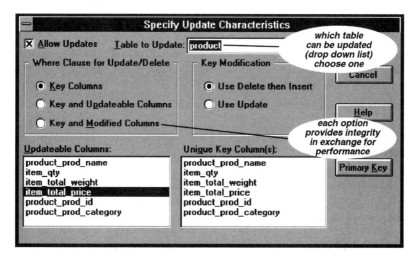

Figure 10.20 Updating specifications for a DataWindow.

Changing tab values. PowerBuilder does not change the tab values associated with columns after you change the update characteristics of the DataWindow object. So if you have allowed updates to a table in a multitable DataWindow object, you should change the tab values for the updatable columns so that users can tab to them.

Tailoring the update.

Specifying the table to update. Each DataWindow object can update one table. To specify the table that can be updated, select the table from the Table to Update box. If more than one table needs to be updated, a DataWindow control script can modify the update table and columns to perform additional updates.

Specifying the unique key columns. The Unique Key Columns box specifies which columns PowerBuilder uses to identify a row being updated. PowerBuilder uses the column or columns that you specify here as the key columns when generating the WHERE clause to update the database, as described later in this chapter.

The key columns that you select here must uniquely identify a row in the table. They can be the tables primary key; however, they don't have to be.

Using the primary key. Clicking the `Primary Key` button cancels any changes in the Unique Key Columns box and highlights the primary key for the updatable table.

Specifying updatable columns. You can specify that all or some of the columns in a table are updatable. Updatable columns are displayed highlighted. Click a nonupdatable column to make it updatable. Click an updatable column to make it nonupdatable.

Changing tab values. If you have changed the update attribute of a column, you should change its tab value in the workspace. For example, if you have allowed a column to be updated, you should change its tab value to a nonzero number so that the user can tab to it.

Specifying the WHERE clause for update/delete. Sometimes multiple users are accessing the same tables at the same time. In these situations, you need to decide where to allow your application to update the database. If you allow your application to always update the database, it could overwrite changes made by other users.

Generally, the more columns there are in the WHERE clause, the more integrity and the less performance you get. Nonkey columns might require entire scans of the table to resolve. You can control which updates to perform by specifying which columns PowerBuilder includes in the WHERE clause in the UPDATE or DELETE statement used to update the database:

```
UPDATE table.
SET column = newvalue
WHERE col1 = value1
AND col2 = value2...

DELETE
FROM table
WHERE col1 = value1
AND col2 = value2...
```

Using timestamps. Some DBMSs maintain a timestamp for each row of a table so that you can ensure that users are working with the most current data. If the SE-

LECT statement for the DataWindow object contains a timestamp column, Power-Builder includes the key column and the timestamp column in the WHERE clause for an UPDATE or DELETE statement regardless of which columns you specify in the WHERE clause for Update/Delete box. If the value in the timestamp column changes (possibly due to another user modifying the row), the update fails. To see whether you can use this timestamp with your DBMS, see the PowerBuilder interface manual for your DBMS.

Choose one of the options in the Where Clause for Update/Delete box. The results are illustrated by an example in Table 10.6.

Example. Consider this situation: a DataWindow object is updating a Counterparty table, whose key is Cpt_ID; all columns in the table are updatable. If the user changes the exposure limit of counterparty 123 from $60,000 to $100,000, the following paragraphs describe what happens with the various styles for the WHERE clause columns.

If you choose Key Columns for the WHERE clause, the UPDATE statement looks like this:

```
UPDATE Counterparty
SET ExposureLimit = 100000
WHERE Cpt_ID = 123
```

This statement succeeds regardless of whether other users have modified the row since your application retrieved the row. For example, if another user had modified the exposure limit to $75,000, that change will be overwritten when your application updates the database.

If you choose Key and Modified Columns for the WHERE clause, the UPDATE statement looks like this:

```
UPDATE counterparty
SET ExposureLimit = 100000
WHERE Cpt_ID = 123 AND ExposureLimit = 60000
```

TABLE 10.6 The Results of Selecting an Option in the Where Clause for Update/Delete Box

Option	Result
Key Columns	The WHERE clause includes the key columns only. The values in the originally retrieved key columns for the row are compared against the key columns in the database. If the values match, the update succeeds.
Key and Updatable Columns	The WHERE clause includes all key and updatable columns. The values in the originally retrieved key columns and the originally retrieved updatable columns are compared against the values in the database. If any of the columns have changed in the database since the row was retrieved, the update fails. This can seriously degrade performance.
Key and Modified Columns	The WHERE clause includes all key and modified columns. The values in the originally retrieved key columns and the modified columns are compared against the values in the database. If any of the columns have changed in the database since the row was retrieved, the update fails. Likewise, this also can degrade performance but does provide some integrity.

Here the UPDATE statement also is checking the original value of the modified column in the WHERE clause. The update fails if another user changed the exposure limit of counterparty 123 since your application retrieved the row.

If you choose `Key and Updatable Columns` for the WHERE clause, the UPDATE statement looks like this:

```
UPDATE counterparty
SET ExposureLimit = 100000
WHERE Cpt_ID = 123 AND ExposureLimit = 60000
   AND CptName = 'The International Corporation, Inc.'
```

When the user modifies the key. The key modification attribute determines the SQL statements that PowerBuilder generates whenever a key column, specified in the Unique Key Columns list box, is changed. The options are:

- Use DELETE, then INSERT (this is the default, and certain DBMSs, such as Sybase, will perform the two SQL actions anyway even if you specify UPDATE)
- Use UPDATE

How to choose which option to use:

- If your application allows primary key values to change, then DELETE followed by INSERT should be chosen.
- If only nonkey columns in a row can be updated, use UPDATE; it's faster for most DBMSs (e.g., DB2/MVS or ORACLE).

Summary

As you can see, the DataWindow is a comprehensive database interface that can be easily constructed using only the painter and not much else. This is only part of the story. If you want to provide additional functionality (e.g., multiple-table updates with one DataWindow), the DataWindow format and presentation options also can be amended and controlled using scripts and PowerBuilder DataWindow functions. We will discuss these techniques in detail later in the book.

The Database Transaction

A sometimes-gray area in application design is the database transaction. Where does it start, and where does it end? Should we use stored procedures, or do we let Power-Builder access and update the database? Stored procedures afford you the advantage of being independent of the front-end GUI, but they neutralize some of the benefits that developers can derive from developing native DataWindows, especially where the extended attributes have been populated with edit, display, and validation information about the database table columns. While you can use stored procedures with Power-Builder, it requires a good deal of coding, especially in a multiple row datawindow. For this reason, they should be used for complex or performance-problematic updates, which hopefully do not represent more than 20% of the application SQL.

There is a new utility that PowerBuilder provides with the Enterprise edition called SPUD (stored procedure update). The basic idea is that you develop the DataWindow in a native SQL Select form and, when development is complete, use SPUD to create scripts that you insert in the SQLPREVIEW event of a DataWindow control to execute the appropriate stored procedure instead of the PowerBuilder generated SQL. It still requires some cutting and pasting, but a least you only do it once or twice. The next sections will deal mostly with the native DataWindow and the control and use of same.

When developing the application with native DataWindows, the prudent developer must consider how to manage database transactions and database access during application execution. There are a number of things to consider:

- The options available for connecting to the database
- How to manage database-specific logical units of work
- How to control and avoid performance problematic database operations
- How and when to use techniques for dynamically modifying the database interaction
- How to control and provide viable and concurrent access by multiple users

Connecting to the Database

In PowerBuilder, all database connections are managed using a transaction object. Figure 11.1 depicts the transaction object SQLCA that contains all fields used to manage the database access (e.g., user login, database return codes, etc.). The default transaction object SQLCA is created when the application is invoked and is destroyed when the application terminates. You can create and destroy your own transaction objects and name them any way that you find appropriate (e.g., CONNECT2 as opposed to SQLCA). During any discussion, SQLCA means any generic database connection.

You can prime SQLCA (i.e., set up the connect to a database; see Figures 11.2 and 11.3) by using one or more of the following techniques:

- Loading values from an application .INI file (static server name, database name, and specifics)
- Prompting the user for values using a logon screen (userid and password)
- Coding the values in a script (varying between servers based upon availability)

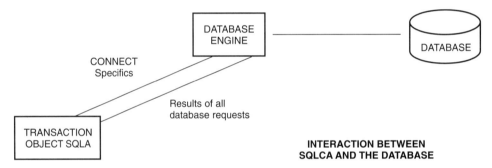

Figure 11.1 A diagram of the SQLCA.

Figure 11.2 The layout of the SQLCA.

SQLCA attributes

```
DBMS—Which relational database engine will be used ( Sybase, Oracle, MDIDB2)
Database—The name of the database where SYSPB catalog tables will be built
UserID—The database user ID
DBPass—The database passwords
Lock—The type of locking
LogID—The user ID
LogPass—The user password
ServerName—The name of the server (usually a symbolic assignment to a remote con-
nection)
AutoCommit—How and if PowerBuilder should COMMIT your work
DBParm—The database parameters specific to the DBMS
SQLReturnData
SQLCode—The return code from the last SQL access; always check this after each ac-
cess
SQLNRows
SQLDBCode—A database-specific return code
SQLErrText—Database-specific error text
```

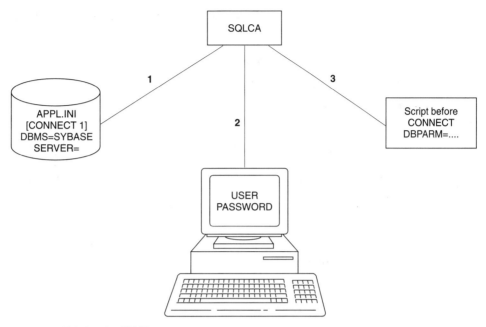

Figure 11.3 Priming the SQLCA.

A database CONNECT is generally an expensive operation and should be managed carefully. Try to optimize its invocation. Sometimes it is unavoidable. For example, in Sybase, if you are using a cursor to traverse one table and you want to do INSERTs on another table while continuing to FETCH, Sybase requires a second database thread or connection. You would have to manage the second transaction within a script containing embedded SQL.

The transaction object

In PowerBuilder, all database connections are managed using a transaction object. (See Figure 11.2.) Although PowerBuilder provides one (SQLCA), you might need to create your own.

If you are accessing more than one database at a time or performing updates, use a second transaction while scrolling through the result set with the first transaction (i.e., you can create your own transaction object):

```
Example Script  to create transaction and perform Connect
Transaction CONNECT1
CONNECT1 = Create Transaction
CONNECT USING CONNECT1;
```

Priming transaction objects

Before connecting to a database, an application must prime the transaction object (SQLCA or user-defined) with the attribute values required by the target database.

(See Figure 11.3.) Review the particular attribute settings for each DBMS to ensure the proper connection.

```
sqlca.dbms        = "Sybase"
sqlca.database    = "ABCDB"
sqlca.logid       = "JProgrammer"
sqlca.logpass     = "blackeye"
sqlca.servername  = "BUBBA"
sqlca.autocommit  = "FALSE"
```

These are the basic SQLCA parameters. See chapter 19 for specifics for each DBMS supported by PowerBuilder. The ideal technique is to read most of these attribute values from an application .INI file and prompt the user for LOGINID and PASSWORD.

You can use one, two, or a combination of all three methods depending on the requirements of your site.

Managing database connections

At various times within the course of development (for example, embedded SQL development) when you invoke the DataWindow or Database painter and from within an application execution, PowerBuilder connects to the database. The connection takes place when:

- The CONNECT verb is executed

- A SetTransObject function coded by the programmer is executed and the DataWindow Retrieve or Update function is called

SetTransObject function. The SetTransObject function also associates a transaction object with a DataWindow, but the programmer is responsible for issuing all transaction verbs (CONNECT, DISCONNECT, ROLLBACK, COMMIT). The programmer has control over when and how often connects take place. The programmer must understand and utilize the transaction implications of COMMIT and ROLLBACK.

Logical units of work

Once connected, you will need to manage the database transactions (i.e., logical units of work). A logical unit of work is a set of database operations that must be completed or rejected together (e.g., debiting one account and crediting another). For example, the SQL might look like the following:

```
UPDATE tb_acct  SET balance_qty = balance_qty + :arg1_qty
  WHERE acct_no = :arg2_acct;
IF Sql_code <> 0 ......quit transaction ; return to caller
UPDATE tb_acct  SET balance_qty = balance_qty - :arg1_qty
  WHERE acct_no = :arg3_acct;
IF Sql_code <> 0
  ROLLBACK
ELSE
  COMMIT;
```

The developer needs to recognize what constitutes a logical unit of work within the context of the application to guarantee the integrity of the data. For example, if we are deleting a TV series, we must delete all of its episodes first before we can delete the series or else we will have orphan episodes.

When several users can access the same data at the same time, you must take precautions to prevent any collisions. Concurrency is a database issue rather than a PowerBuilder issue, but that does not relieve the developer from understanding the implications of the SQL that is generated. The prudent developer must be aware of the various types of concurrent transactions: retrieve only, single-row retrieval with single-row update, multiple-row retrieval with single-row (or limited) update, and multiple-row retrieval with multiple-row update. Each of these will have an effect on how you will manage the logical unit of work. A well-placed stored procedure or a well-constructed user object with embedded SQL script can overcome shortcomings or semantic PowerBuilder snafus.

Where is the database data stored within the context of PowerBuilder?

A buffer is the storage area where data is staged before and after a database access. We will see how these buffers interact with the database and DataWindow. (See Figure 11.4.) We will begin with definitions, and the next sections will add increasing detail about the buffers and their use and status.

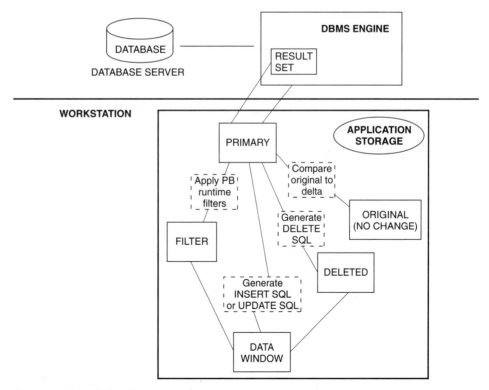

Figure 11.4 DataWindow filters.

There are four buffers associated with a DataWindow:

- Primary buffer contains data that has not been deleted or filtered out. The data is placed in this buffer through the Retrieve and InsertRow functions (i.e., after a database access and before a database insert, respectively). Only data that is contained in the primary buffer is visible to the user.

- Filter buffer contains data that was filtered out at runtime through the Filter function. A PowerBuilder filter is, in effect, a locally performed WHERE clause that further re-fines the result set returned by the database. For example, `dw_test` `.Filter("color=purple")` would populate the Filter buffer with rows that are the color purple.

- Delete buffer contains data that has been deleted from the DataWindow but not yet deleted from the database. It is a log of the database before image. The data is placed in this buffer through the DeleteRow function. A PowerBuilder UPDATE function will generate SQL DELETE statements using the information stored in this buffer.

- Original buffer contains data provided by the original RETRIEVE function. This data is used to generate the WHERE clause for an Update or Delete statement. For example, you might not want to perform an update if the data has changed since the point at which you retrieved it. A WHERE clause then is added to the UPDATE such that the update will take place only if the contents of the database are equal to the original buffer values.

When you define a DataWindow, you can specify the type of WHERE clause that PowerBuilder will build when you update a row. The WHERE clause can contain:

- Key—This is quick because the index is scanned to find the page where the subject row resides; it provides no integrity that some other user might have changed the row.

- Key and modified columns—This is more time-consuming because the entire table might be scanned (more than once) to find the target row; it provides integrity, letting the user know if the particular columns changed. The original buffer is used to determine data modified row status.

- Key and updateable columns—this is most time-consuming because the entire table might be scanned for each updateable column to find the target row; it provides integrity, letting the user know if any updateable column in the row has changed.

There are tradeoffs among the options as to concurrency and data consistency. Which buffers are used, as well as the SQL created by PowerBuilder, is determined by the options chosen and the techniques employed by the developer. As we shall see in the following sections, there is a comprehensive suite of techniques available, but care must be taken to ensure database integrity and avoid performance degradation.

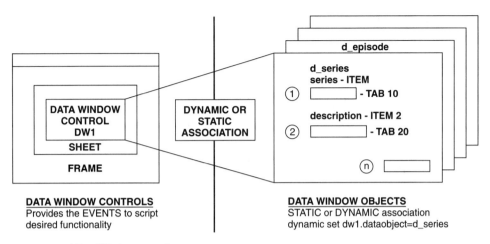

Figure 11.5 A DataWindow control.

Basic DataWindow Control Behavior

A DataWindow control (see Figure 11.5) is a PowerBuilder control that allows a user to display, manipulate, and update database information. It occupies some portion of a window, and it can be statically or dynamically associated with a DataWindow object. Like other controls, it has events and functions that can be associated with it. As you probably are aware, an edit control is a text field that acts as an overlay to hold information as it is entered until it can be validated. Each DataWindow control has and equals one window edit control, notwithstanding the fact that it can contain multiple items with the control. If you click on Tab to show the sequence of data-enterable controls within a window containing a data window control, you will see one nonzero Tab representing the DataWindow.

Items

The items (or cells) in a DataWindow can be of several data types and are stored in the DataWindow object buffers using the client's memory. As you probably know by now, you can use the PowerScript functions GetItemdatatype and SetItem in a DataWindow to access and update the contents of the PowerBuilder data buffers. An item also has a status associated with it. When a datawindow item is entered or modified, the item's status indicates the change. Is it new? Has it been modified? This item status dictates the SQL to be generated. New data will generate an INSERT. A item that is a table primary key field and has been modified might cause a DELETE, then an INSERT of the same row. A good developer understands the update ramifications of an item and its status. This is not unlike the IBM mainframe OLTP monitor CICS modified data tags used to control whether or not a data record should be updated. The developer who chooses to get behind the data window control and add functionality must carefully plan, implement, and test the scripts to ensure that they not only produce the right result but also do it wisely.

Validating the user-entered data

PowerBuilder validates the data as it moves it from the edit control into the underlying items in the buffer. Validation begins when the user modifies data in the edit control and one of these conditions occurs:

- The Enter key or its equivalent has been activated.
- The user moves (changes focus) to a different item (field) in the DataWindow control
- A script executes the AcceptText function.

During the validation procedure, the values in the item buffer and the edit control might be different. The edit control receives the user entered data and holds it until the data is validated. The information in the item comes from the database and is updated only after the new data in the edit field has passed all levels of validation. As each column passes a data validation test, it continues to the next test until it passes all levels. When the contents of the edit control passes all validation levels, the item and its status are updated, but the database does not change because no SQL has been submitted for execution. *Note:* Use a DataWindow function, GETSQLSYNTAX, in the SQLPREVIEW event of a DataWindow control to view the actual SQL submitted to the database engine.

To update the database, you must successfully execute the Update function or issue /execute a stored procedure call. This will cause the actual SQL to be built and sent to the database for execution. An Update will generate an SQL INSERT or UPDATE depending on the status of the data buffer

Did the item change? In the first validation test, the DataWindow control examines the content of the edit control to determine if they have changed from the item in the buffer. When the contents of the edit control are different, this condition is satisfied and additional edit checks and validation are performed depending on the datatype.

When you use the Tab key or the mouse to move away from a field, the DataWindow control determines that there has been no change and the validation stops. If the value has changed, the validation continues to the next level.

Is the entered data of the correct datatype? In the second validation test, PowerBuilder checks to see if the data type of the entry in the edit control matches the datatype of the item. For example, if a numeric column of type integer contains 123 and the user attempts to enter nonnumeric characters into the edit control (e.g., ABC), this action passes the first-level validation (something changed) but does not pass the second level validation because ABC is not a valid integer.

If datatype validation fails then what happens? When the data type validation fails, an ItemError event occurs. You can let PowerBuilder handle the error, or you can develop a script to handle the error and perform additional processing. When you let PowerBuilder handle the validation error, the user receives a standard message that the entry did not pass the validation rules. The cursor returns to the edit control. To discard the entry and start over, the user can press the Esc key. This restores the current item value to the edit control.

You can perform your own custom error handling. When you write a custom error message, you might need to know what the user has entered in the edit control. To retrieve the value of the edit control, use the function GetText( ). To compare the value of the edit control with the DataWindow item, use one of the GetItemxxx functions, where xxx is based on the data type. (You must know the underlying data type or use Describe( ) to determine the data type.)

The edit control itself is always defined as data type string. PowerBuilder always compares what is in the edit control (i.e., what the user has entered) to what is in the item (e.g., what was in the database originally). The value of the item might not be what you think it is, especially when you use code tables in a dropdown DataWindow or list box. What you see displayed in the edit control is not necessarily what is in the actual data item. You might want to do a GetItemxxx( ) to see what is in the item before you continue.

The user might get an error message when trying to delete a value from an edit control. The empty string has a data type of text, because it is a string. This level of validation stops if the underlying item data type is anything other than string. To work around this, set the column back to NULL and allow the focus to move out of the column.

Validation rules: beyond just data type

The third validation test checks for any validation rules that you define for a column in the DataWindow object. These validation rules can be set for the database column using the extended attributes (i.e., the PowerBuilder system catalog tables). They can be populated in a number of ways, prior to DataWindow development using CASE design tools such as ERWIN and LBMS (both of which contain a PowerBuilder interface) or using the Database painter. You also can use DataWindow object validation rules for anything that is appropriate:

- Range validation: column1 > 10000 and column1 < 100000
- Cross-column validation: If column1 is 1, then column2 must be greater than 1
- Specific value checks: column1 must be A or B or C

When a column fails a DataWindow control validation rule, an ItemError event occurs.

The PowerBuilder Extended Attributes (catalog tables)

One of the features often overlooked in PowerBuilder is Extended Attributes. This feature allows you to define edit styles, display formats, and validation rules to store them as rows in a set of tables, known as the PowerBuilder catalog. These entries can go some way to making a column's visual look and feel and associated business rules external to an application. That is to say, one can use a "data-driven" approach to presentation and validation.

Having defined an entry, you can associate it with an actual column of a table in the database. If a column has extended attributes, they are included automatically in the syntax of any new DataWindow that is created, either in the DataWindow painter or dynamically through PowerScript. This does not apply to any DataWindows that already have be defined and saved in a Library, but you can use the PowerBuilder Enterprise utility DWEAS.EXE in order to synchronize this pre-existing DataWindow with the new attributes definitions.

The PowerBuilder Catalog is comprised of 5 tables (see Table 11.1).

When defining an edit style, display format, or a validation rule, a good practice is to use the PB catalog three-character suffix as the prefix for the name of the entry. We like to use the conventions shown in the following sections.

Edit style

```
edt_SSS_xxxx
```

where *SSS* is the style (there are six styles of edit style available: CheckBox, DropDownDataWindow, DropDownListBox, Edit, EditMask, and RadioButton) and *xxxx* is a meaningful, user-defined name.

For example:

```
edt_cbx_health_ins—Yes (Y), No (N)
edt_dddw_customers—Database list of customers
edt_ddlb_quarters—List of yearly quarters (Q1, Q2, Q3, Q4)
edt_e_up_req—Uppercase, required field
edt_em_sdate_time—[SHORTDATE] HH:MM
edt_rb_sex—Yes (Y), No (N), Male (M), Female (F)
```

It is a good idea to turn on the Auto Selection checkbox and supply a Format when defining edit styles. That way, when the column with this edit style receives focus, it will highlight the current contents as opposed to deleting it.

Display format

```
fmt_TT_xxxx
```

TABLE 11.1 The Five PowerBuilder Catalog Tables

Table	Content
pbcatcol	Column information
pbcatedt	Edit styles
pbcatfmt	Display formats
pbcattbl	Table information
pbcatvld	Validation rules

where *TT* is the type (there are 5 types of display format available: Date, DateTime, Number, String, and Time) and *xxxx* is a meaningful, user-defined name.

For example:

```
fmt_d_ldate—[LONGDATE]
fmt_dt_sdate_time—[SHORTDATE] HH:MM
fmt_n_unit_price—$###.00
fmt_s_ssn—@@@-@@-@@@@
fmt_t_time—HH:MM
```

Validation rules

```
vld_TT_xxxx
```

where *TT* is the type (there are 5 types of display format available: Date, DateTime, Number, String, and Time) and *xxxx* is a meaningful, user-defined name.

For example:

```
vld_d_future—@col > today()
vld_dt_sdate_time—month(@col) = 'November'
vld_n_positive—@col > 0
vld_s_y_or_n—match(@col, "^[YNyn]$")
```

Production migration/transition of Extended Attributes

These attributes (i.e., the PowerBuilder catalog tables and their row content) also must be migrated to the production database if an application uses the dynamic DataWindow technique. Even if your application does not use this technique (i.e., an active dictionary), it still pays to migrate these entries (tables and rows) because they play a role in the presentation and validation of your application database columns and as such should be maintained as production source code.

The following are some suggestions for migrating the entries. These suggestions relate to SYBASE SQL Server but are applicable to Oracle and other DBMSs like DB2/MVS.

For edit styles, display formats, and validation rules:

Step 1 Unload the extended attribute data definition language (DDL) from the test. Do this one time only.

Step 2 Define the PowerBuilder catalog in production. Do this one time only. Have an authorized DBA run the DDL to create the catalog tables.

Step 3 Use BCP (DBMS bulk copy program) to unload PowerBuilder tables pbcatedt, pbcatfmt, and pbcatvld rows from the test database.

Step 4 Use BCP to load PowerBuilder tables pbcatedt, pbcatfmt, and pbcatvld data to previously defined production catalog tables.

For table and column associations:

Step 1 Unload DDL for tables pbcattbl and pbcatcol from the test. Do this one time only.

Step 2 Define the PowerBuilder catalog tables in production. Do this one time only. Have an authorized DBA run the DDL to create the tables.

Step 3 BCP unload the PowerBuilder-specific entries from pbcattbl and pbcatcol in test.

Step 4 Use BCP to load the PowerBuilder-specific entries into pbcattbl and pbcatcol in production.

Step 5 For SYBASE SQL Server, run the stored procedure to refresh the table IDs (TID):

```
UPDATE pbcattbl
  SET pbt_tid = object_id ('dbo.'+pbt_tnam)
UPDATE pbcatcol
  SET pbc_tid = object_id ('dbo.'+pbc_tnam)
```

Repeat steps 3 through 5 when necessary. (Check your particular DBMS for required variations on the basic theme.)

ItemChanged event

You might be wondering when you can get your opportunity to perform specific or custom edits. Behind the DataWindow control are events. One of them is the Item-Changed event. The ItemChanged event is triggered when a column in a DataWindow has been modified and loses focus. This event is the final level of validation and is used for integrity checking and cross-table validations.

When a user makes a change in a DataWindow, you can add a script to this event to determine which column has changed, then, based upon that determination, perform the appropriate action. For example, you can write a script in the ItemChanged event to edit the data, then set the action code as well as trigger an ItemError event. The ItemChanged event is not triggered if the input fails either data type validation or a validation rule. The ItemFocusChanged event is triggered after the ItemChanged event.

Changing the behavior of a DataWindow event

The SetActionCode function allows you to accept or reject values based on script code within an event. It is a fancy validation technique to be used in special cases. The value that you pass to SetActionCode() depends upon the event in which you call this function. For example, when you set the action code to 1 in an ItemChanged event script, you cause an ItemError event:

```
this.SetActionCode(1)
```

The ItemChanged event has the following action codes:

0   Accept the data value
1   Reject the data value
2   Reject the data value but allow the focus to change

The ItemError event has the following action codes:

0   Reject the data value and show an error message box
1   Reject the data value with no message box
2   Accept the data value
3   Reject the data value but allow focus to change

Some DataWindow control functions can reset the action code. If the SetActionCode( ) command is not the last line in your script, enter a Return command after the last line to terminate the script. Otherwise, you might not get the result you expect.

Techniques for validating data

There are several things to be aware of when validating data in DataWindow controls such as validating the last column of the DataWindow control. A DataWindow control has LoseFocus and GetFocus events. Use these events to ensure that all DataWindow items have been validated. Be careful when using the mouse (rather than the Tab key) to move out of a DataWindow control onto another window control. The DataWindow object does not realize that you have moved because the row and column focus remains as before. Because focus has not changed from the last item in the DataWindow object, no action (such as validation) will take place.

For example, you can create a user-defined event containing a script to ensure DataWindow object validation is done before an UPDATE is invoked:

```
// issue AcceptText function call
DataWindow control.AcceptText()
// IF the data is not valid THEN return to the caller ELSE perform the update
IF dw_sheet.AcceptText( ) = -1 then
   Return
ELSE
   // update the datawindow using the window function: wf_update_dw
   SetPointer(HourGlass!)
   iw_frame.SetMicroHelp("Updating data..." )
   IF wf_update_dw () THEN
     iw_frame.SetMicroHelp( "Data updated successfully.")
   ELSE
     iw_frame.SetMicroHelp( "Data not updated." )
     return
   END IF
END IF
```

You also can post to the user-defined event in the LoseFocus event of the DataWindow or at anytime as long as it is before you issue a PowerBuilder UPDATE or invoke a stored procedure. Sometimes, you, as a developer, need to prime a DataWindow item.

You can bypass all validation except data type checking by putting a value into an item:

```
dw_sheet.SetItem(row, col, value)
```

where *dw_sheet* is the datawindow (dw) control name.

Call SetItem( ) when you want to set the value of an item in a DataWindow control event that has a user-developed script as the source. For example, you can use it to set the static part of a key in a multiple row dw control. You also can call it to set the value for the item in the script for the DataWindowItemChanged Event when the action code is 2 (i.e., reject the value) or in the script for the DataWindowItemError event when the action code is 3. These action codes reject the data but allow the focus to change. Be careful with the SetItem function; it signals a change in the buffer. If you setting a key value in a two-table update database object, PowerBuilder might delete and reinsert a row that has not changed. You can reset the item status to avoid this.

Displaying the value in an edit control. In certain situations, you might want to alter the value that the user enters. For example, a user schedules television programs using a one-week model where Monday is the week start date. When the user creates actual schedules, the application alters that date to be the day the month begins on. In an ItemChanged event, the SetItem function will change only the DataWindow item in the buffer; it will not change the value in the edit control. To display the new value in the edit control, you can use SetText( ) to update the edit control after SetItem( ) updates the DataWindow buffer item.

Reference/code tables as a technique for validation. In database applications, there often is a need to minimize the amount of data stored in the database. For example, for holiday information, it is not necessary to store the entire holiday name (`Halloween`). By storing an alternative representation (`HA`), the amount of space required to store a row is reduced. As the number or rows increases, this savings can become significant.

It's the responsibility of the application that uses the data to provide an alternative representation and display and edit accordingly. In DataWindows, using an object style to associate a column with a reference table (see Figure 11.6) will provide the ability to handle coded data values at the column level. When coded data values are retrieved from the database, DataWindows can display the complete value that the user expects to see. For example, when the `HA` is retrieved, the DataWindow displays `Halloween`. Likewise, when data is entered, DataWindows can validate the entered data against the code table value and perform any required translation.

In the DataWindow painter, you can associate code tables with the database columns. Note that, as mentioned, you can create an edit style (to be stored in a PowerBuilder catalog table row) using the database painter. These edit styles should be created at database design time. However, most development teams are not aware or do not choose this powerful technique of database validation. In any event, you choose a DataWindow column and, using the right mouse button or the menu

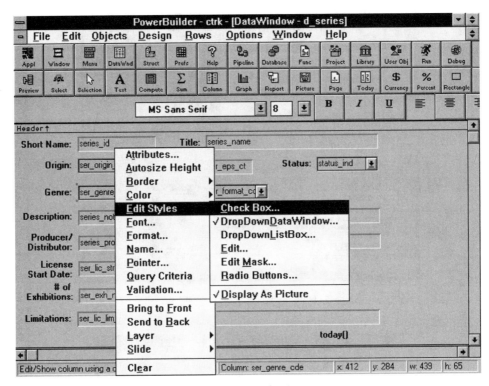

Figure 11.6 The object styles associated with a DataWindow item.

option, choose Edit Styles and specify the edit style for the column. The choices are as follows:

- CheckBox
- DropDownDataWindow (This is the most powerful option)
- DropDownListBox (Use this only if there are only a few values)
- Edit
- RadioButton
- Edit mask

Note: As mentioned, you might want to build/create these edit styles when the database design is completed and before actual development. This will facilitate the process. See Figure 11.7 for the edit styles stored in the extended attribute tables. They are maintained within the Database painter; invoke the Objects menu item Edit style.

To obtain the display value in the code table associated with a particular column, use the LookUpDisplay function. Once you have chosen a style, a specific Edit Style window displays depending on the type of edit style you chose. You are presented with options pertaining to the type of control that will display within the DataWin-

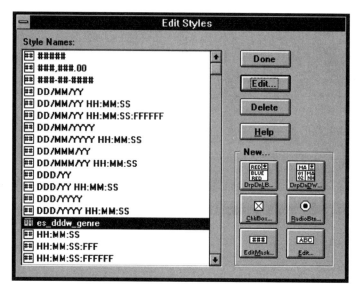

Figure 11.7 Database painter edit style maintenance.

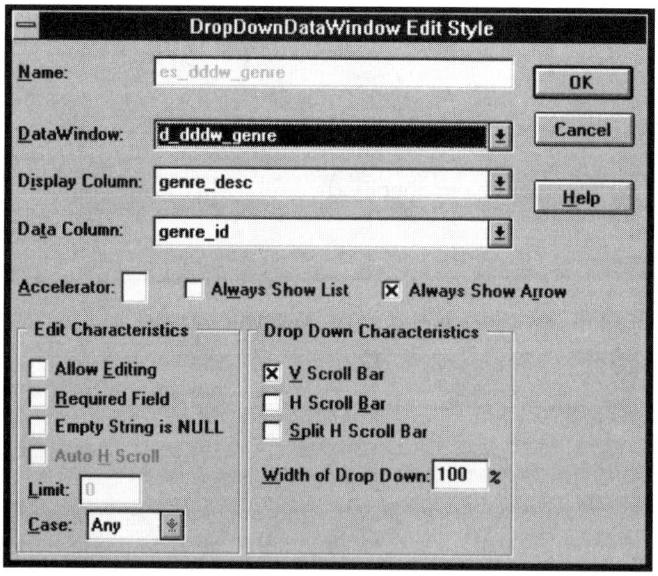

Figure 11.8 The DropDownDataWindow Edit Style dialog.

dow when the user is focused on that database column. (See Figure 11.8.) If you have wisely used the Database painter and defined the styles on a project-wide basis, you need choose only the one that pertains to you. All database edit styles will be displayed in the dropdown list box at the top of the Edit Style window.

For an edit-style column, you can define a code table by clicking on the Code Table check box. This enables the display code table capabilities that take a coded data value from the database and display it in a translated form. Enter the pairs of display and data values to define the code table.

By default, no validation is performed. (This is represented by the unchecked state of the Validate using code table check box.) When no validation is performed, PowerBuilder performs only display translation. When the column is first retrieved, the code table is searched from the top down for a matching data value. If a match is found, PowerBuilder displays the matching display value. If no match is found, PowerBuilder displays the coded data value.

When data is entered, the value is compared against the data values in the code table when the user leaves the database column display field. If a match is found, the entered value is translated to the display value and then displayed. For dropdowns with a large number of items, use the following features. A dropdown DataWindow with a "sorted" code table will retrieve and display the first code table value that matches the keyed letter. Repeating this letter will scroll through the table to the next item beginning with that letter. If no match is found in the code table, the display remains as is.

Validate using code table. When `Validate using code table` is selected, the run-time engine reports an error if the data entered does not match a value in the code table. PowerBuilder compares the entered value against both data values and display values in the code table. By default, if a validation error occurs, PowerBuilder displays a MessageBox indicating that a validation rule has been violated. You can trap this error by coding an ItemError event script for the DataWindow control. All data values are case sensitive. You need to guarantee that all acceptable coded data values are translated correctly when defining the set of coded data values.

Storing data with a DataWindow object. A DropDownDataWindow can be populated dynamically from the database every time it is used, or you can store data with the DataWindow object. When you store data with the DataWindow, you eliminate the need to access the database. The data will be stored in the PBL as a snapshot and is a static part of the definition.

Code table considerations. For CheckBox and RadioButton styles, you can associate an accelerator key with each code value by placing an ampersand (&) before the desired accelerator letter. For Edit and DropDownListBox styles, you can assign an accelerator key in the Accelerator attribute. Typically, you would identify this accelerator for the user by placing a text item above or to the left of the column and placing an ampersand before the appropriate letter in this text item.

Because the less users have to key, the fewer errors they will make, you should take advantage of the CheckBox, RadioButton, DropDownDataWindow, and DropDownListBox styles wherever possible. Even though any number of data values can be retrieved dynamically from the database through the use of a DropDownData Window, graphical user interface design guidelines suggest that you limit the number of items that a user must choose from. Dynamically loading a large DropDown-Widow code table is faster than running a SQL script to load the table. Sorting (i.e., using the ORDER BY clause) in the DataWindow data source SQL will facilitate data entry by causing the keystroke to position the user within the code list. It is not feasible for the user to search through a large number of values in a code table. "Large" of course is a relative term. Use good judgment.

Because the RadioButton style should display all available values, it usually is appropriate only for data columns that have a relatively small number of values. For example, using the RadioButton style for a state data column (male or female) is perfect.

Validation rules. Reference tables provide a good technique for validating data in a DataWindow. Reference tables compare what the user enters in a column against a list of valid values for that column. When entered, if the data does not pass validation, an error status message box is displayed, or the ItemError event is triggered (if a script is coded).

Why use validation rules as opposed to reference tables? Sometimes verifying data values with a reference table is impractical (for example, if a coded number needs to fall in some range, but the range is very large). While it is possible to prime the reference table with the valid values, it is impractical for performance reasons. For such situations, DataWindow validation rules often can be used to achieve the same result.

Validation rules are simple expressions that result in a Boolean (TRUE or FALSE) value. When you build a rule, you should form the expression so that it will validate the data while resulting in a Boolean value. You can think of a validation rule as an IF statement:

if validation rule (returns TRUE)
  then let the data pass
  else issue an error message
or ItemError event occurs

Validation rules are triggered automatically for a modified column when:

- The Enter key interrupt is invoked

- Focus leaves the column because the user pressed Tab or an arrow key

- Focus leaves when the user clicks the mouse in another DataWindow column

Thereafter an Update( ) or AcceptText( ) is processed causing the current input to be validated.

Building validation rules. You specify validation rules at the column level in the DataWindow painter by selecting the `Validation...` menu item. (See Figure 11.9.) This displays the Column Validation Definition window. In this window, you can specify a validation rule to be used by the DataWindow to validate values that the user enters in this column.

Here again, it is advisable to define validation rules in the Database painter as Extended Column Attributes. When you define the validation rules in the Database painter, the rules are copied only to new DataWindow objects. Existing DataWindow objects remain unchanged. However, you can edit the existing DataWindows

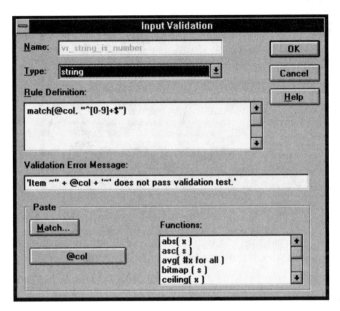

Figure 11.9 Validation rules.

and choose the new validation rules. Therefore, if you plan to use them throughout a project, enter the validation rules during database design phase and before actual development.

Note: Because the user might have just entered a value in the column, validation rules that need to refer to the current data value should use the GetText DataWindow function to validate the input.

When validation rules are coded, you also can reference other data values in the DataWindow. This guarantees that related data columns are validated against each other before the value is accepted. The Error Message Expression depicted at the bottom of the column validation definition window allows the developer to change the default error message that PowerBuilder displays if an ItemError event is not coded. Any DataWindow validation expression can have an error message. In the Column Validation Definition window, you can define an Error Message Expression that will be displayed if a validation rule error occurs. For example:

```
Episode code must be a number greater than 1 and less than 1000
```

To include the invalid value in the display, code the following:

```
'" + GetText() + " ' is an invalid value,  Episode must be between 1 and 1000
```

Validating input through an edit mask. An edit mask specifies the format of a field to make it easier for users to enter values that have a fixed format. (See Figure 11.10.) An edit mask consists of special characters that determine what can be entered. It also can contain punctuation characters to help the user, such as dd/mm/yy to indicate that a date should be entered.

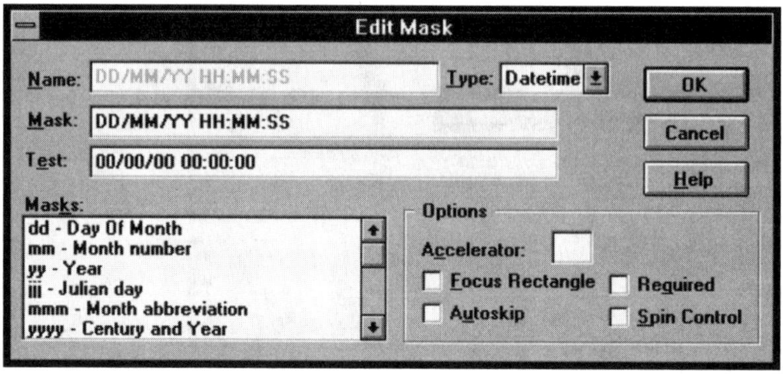

Figure 11.10 The Edit Mask dialog.

The edit mask sets formatting when the field has focus. In the DataWindow painter, you can override an edit mask that has been defined through the Database painter.

Performing the Actual Database Update

Thus far, we have considered only updates to a single table and data window (i.e., basic DataWindow processing). The application might require that two data windows be updated together (e.g., parent and child) or that one data window that contains information from two or more tables cause updates to both tables within the same transaction. To do this properly, the updates must be coordinated.

Coordinating database updates

Although PowerBuilder does provide some information that can help, the developer must use code that can fallback to the before image of the database if a problem occurs. For example, DataWindows maintain update flags for each row within a DataWindow buffer. If a new row has been inserted or an existing row has been deleted or modified, an update flag is maintained, indicating that a change has occurred. These flags are reset (or cleared) when the Update function executes successfully. Once these flags have been reset, the DataWindow thinks that a given row in the DataWindow buffer is in the same state as on the database. You need to guarantee that these flags accurately reflect the state of the database.

To manage this in a multiple DataWindow situation, you need to use two optional parameters for Update(*parameter1, parameter2*):

- *Parameter1*—AcceptText(TRUE or FALSE, the default is TRUE)
- *Parameter2*—Reset update flags (TRUE or FALSE, the default is TRUE)

AcceptText. The AcceptText parameter controls whether the contents of the edit control (where newly entered data resides) are sent to the DataWindow as part of the update. In most cases, this parameter is TRUE—accept the text into the current column, then send the data to the DataWindow.

Reset flag. The Reset flag parameter in the Update function controls resetting the update flags. When the reset parameter is TRUE, the update flags are reset if an update is completed successfully. If you update two data windows, there is the risk of clearing the update flags in the DataWindow, but rolling back the changes made to the database in the second data window update fails.

For example:

```
// Update the episode only if the series update is successful (i.e., rc=1)
Li_rc=dw_series.Update()
if Li_rc=1 then
  Li_rc=dw_episode.Update()
  if Li_rc=1 then Commit using SQLCA;
else
    Rollback using SQLCA;
end if
else
    Rollback using SQLCA;
end if
```

While the Rollback SQL statement causes changes to be removed from the database and original values to be restored, it does not cause a DataWindow to turn on the update flags that were on when the Update function call was processed.

Managing the flags. You manage these flags by setting the Reset option to FALSE, then resetting the flag explicitly later with the ResetUpdate function:

```
//Variable to hold return from update function
integer li_rc
//Update the series; do AcceptText,
//but don't reset the update flags
li_rc = dw_series.Update(TRUE,FALSE)
//Did it work?
if  li_rc = 1 then
//Yes, try to update the series episode using
//same options as above
  li_rc = dw_episode.Update(TRUE,FALSE)
//Did it work?
  if li_rc = 1 then
//Yes, commit changes to the database
    Commit using SQLCA;
//Clear the flags for both DataWindows
    dw_series.ResetUpdate( )
    dw_episode.ResetUpdate( )
  else
//No, make sure everything is cleared
    Rollback using SQLCA;
  end if
else
//No, make sure everything is cleared
  Rollback using SQLCA;
end if
```

Multiple row updates

Unlike the single row update where any database error can be associated readily with only the row currently displayed, when updating multiple rows, the user needs to know the row in which the error actually occurred. You can trap database errors in the DBError event for a DataWindow. You can use a similar technique not only to report that a database error has occurred, but also to identify the row in which the error occurred.

GetUpdateStatus function. When the DBError event is triggered in a multiple-row DataWindow, dwGetUpdateStatus( ) returns the number of the row in which the error occurred. Using this number, you then can set that row as the current row.

GetUpdateStatus( ) returns the number of the first row in which an error was encountered. Processing stops at that point allowing the user to correct the error.

Example. The following example is a script from a DBError event. This script retrieves the error text and the row in error. It then issues a message to the user and makes the row in error the current row. Finally, it tells the DataWindow that the default message should not be displayed. (ErrorRow and ErrorBuffer are passed by reference.)

```
Buffer dwErrorBuffer
long   ll_ErrorRow
string ls_DatabaseErrorText
//Get the error text
ls_DatabaseErrorText = DBErrorMessage( )
//Get the row in error
li_Result = this.GetUpdateStatus(ll_ErrorRow, ErrorBuffer)
///Let the user know what happened
MessageBox("DatabaseError in Row" + String(ll_ErrorRow), ls_DatabaseErrorText)
//Make it the current row
this.SetRow(ll_ErrorRow)
//Let the DataWindow know that its message shouldn't be displayed
this.SetActionCode(1)
```

The mysterious Update function

You might wonder how PowerBuilder builds the correct SQL when you just say UPDATE. An UPDATE will cause one or more instances of SQL INSERT, UPDATE, or DELETE to be built. Furthermore the columns that will be included in either of these statements will be based upon whether the row or column has been modified and whether the row is new. PowerBuilder data windows provide status for row/column information. PowerBuilder identifies the kind of SQL statement to generate by determining the status of each row In the DataWindow buffers. (See Table 11.2.)

How does this status work? When a row is retrieved into a DataWindow, it has a row status of NotModified!; all columns have a column status of NotModified!. When a

TABLE 11.2 The DataWindow Buffer Status

Status	What can have this status
New!	Rows only
NewModified!	Rows only
NotModified!	Rows and columns
DataModified!	Rows and columns

column is changed, either by user entry or the SetItem function, the column status for that column is changed to DataModified! and the status of the row in which the column resides is changed to DataModified!. (See Table 11.3.)

When you insert a row into a DataWindow, the row has a row status of New!, and all columns in that row have a column status of NotModified!. After a column in the inserted row is updated, by user entry, the SetItem function, or default values placed in the column, the column status for that column changes to DataModified!. When the status for any column in the new row changes to DataModified!, the row status changes to NewModified!. (See Table 11.4.)

If you use SetItemStatus to change the status of a row to NotModified! or New!, all columns in that row will have a column status of NotModified!.

Generating the SQL statement. Once the row status has been established, it is fairly simple for PowerBuilder to generate the SQL INSERT, UPDATE, and DELETE statements. When the DataWindow Update function is called, SQL statements are generated for rows in the primary or filter buffer of the DataWindow based on the row status shown in Table 11.5.

Delete statements are generated for any rows that were moved into the delete buffer of the DataWindow via the Delete Row function. A row that was added to the DataWindow via InsertRow( ) or ImportFile( ) and then deleted using DeleteRow( ) will not be placed in the delete buffer because it never reached the DBMS storage. In general, only rows with a status of DataModified! or NotModified! are placed in the delete buffer. Once the SQL INSERT or UPDATE is chosen, then column selection is

**TABLE 11.3 Column and Row Status
of a Modified Column**

Activity	Column status	Row status
Row retrieved	NotModified!	NotModified!
Column changed	DataModified!	DataModified!

TABLE 11.4 Column and Row Status of a New Row

Activity	Column status	Row status
Row inserted	NotModified!	New!
New column changed	DataModified!	NewModified!

TABLE 11.5 The Row Status

If the row status is:	Then generate:
NewModified!	An Insert statement
DataModified!	An Update statement

handled. A column is included in the INSERT/UPDATE statements generated by the DataWindow if it is on the updatable column list maintained by the DataWindow and has a column status of DataModified!.

When a SQL INSERT statement is generated, all columns in the row are included as part of the INSERT statement. If a column has no value, the DataWindow attempts to insert a NULL value into column for that row. This might cause a database error if the database table definition does not allow NULL values for that column (i.e., NOT NULL). Typically keys and required data columns are not nullable.

Changing the status programmatically. You might need to change the status of a row or column programmatically. For example, you might present a row from the database as a template for the user. The user makes changes to the template. You want to store this row with a different key (in effect, a copy function) as a new row in the database. However, right now, the row status is DataModified! and, based on this row status, an UPDATE statement would be generated updating the row used as the template. You must change the row status to NewModified! so that an INSERT statement will be generated. You also would use SETITEM to enter the new key in the appropriate columns. Use the SetItemStatus function to change the status of a DataWindow row or column. Use the GetItemStatus function to determine the current status of a row or column.

Changing column status is very simple; changing row status can be more complex.

Table 11.6 shows the effect of changing from one row status to another and whether that change can be made.

Yes. The change is valid. For example, if you issue a SetItemStatus on a row that has a status of NotModified! to change that status to New!, the status is changed. Always check the return code.

No. The change is not valid. For example, if you issue a SetItemStatus on a row that has a status of New! to change that status to NotModified!, nothing happens.

Issuing a SetItemStatus( ) to change a row status from DataModified! to New! actually changes the row status to NewModified!. Issuing a SetItemStatus( ) to change a row status from NewModified! to NotModified! actually changes the row status to New!.

Note: If you cannot achieve the desired status directly, you usually can achieve it indirectly through chained status changes (for example, New! to DataModified! to NotModified!).

TABLE 11.6 The Effect of Changing from One Row Status to Another

Original status	New!	NewModified!	DataModified!	NotModified!
New!	—	Yes	Yes	No
NewModified!	No	—	Yes	New!
DataModified!	NewModified!	Yes	—	Yes
NotModified!	Yes	Yes	Yes	—

Controlling the Cost of the Transaction

The DataWindow painter facilitates access to the Relational Database Management system (RDMS) used in your application. The basic language of the RDMS is SQL (an acronym for structured query language). SQL uses only four verbs—SELECT, INSERT, DELETE, and UPDATE—to perform data manipulation language (DML).

SQL is a set-oriented language rather than a record-oriented language. In record-oriented systems, such as IBM's virtual sequential access method (VSAM), the programmer controls file access by getting the first record, getting the next record, and so on. In most cases, the programmer also knows how many records can be traversed in a transaction and, therefore, can identify potentially expensive operations. These operations then can be stopped before they start, or the user can be warned that a particular operation might take time to complete. When the program issues an SQL data manipulation statement (SELECT, INSERT, DELETE, or UPDATE), the programmer usually doesn't know how many rows will be returned and how much time on CPU the statement will take to complete. In addition, RDMS databases, in general, don't provide a way to estimate the cost of execution or determine how many rows will be affected. Some RDMSs, such as DB2/MVS, do supply EXPLAIN utilities that provide some resource requirement information based upon the current state of the database objects to be accessed.

Use unique keys

You can control the effect of nonretrieval SQL (e.g., update) verbs by including a unique primary key in the WHERE clause for the target table:

```
UPDATE series
  WHERE series_cde  ='BEAVER'
```

For example, deleting series rows based on a single unique key series_cde guarantees that only one row will be accessed to complete the statement. Retrieving a series row by series_cde will have the same limiting effect as in the nonretrieval case:

```
SELECT * FROM EPISODE WHERE SERIES_CDE= "LUCY" AND EPISODE_CDE= "225"
```

However, most retrieval situations don't fit into this category.

Frequently, the search criteria are supplied entirely by the user in an *ad hoc* fashion. It is the programmer's responsibility to provide governing mechanisms to prevent a user from executing a potentially expensive retrieval. For example:

```
SELECT * FROM episode
```

This query will retrieve all rows in the episode table. If the table is large, this query could degrade system performance significantly and provide more rows than any user could possibly scroll through (i.e., wasted resources).

Limit the user to a specific WHERE clause

Limiting the user to a specific WHERE requires that the programmer prevent the user from executing any query that might result in retrieving a large number of rows. You need to include some form of WHERE criteria in the SELECT regardless of what options the user is able to specify. Because the programmer is in control during development, the programmer can make a reasonable estimate of the data to be returned.

For example, instead of allowing a user to retrieve information for all episodes in all series, the application would allow the user to retrieve only episodes associated with a particular television series. This option has a disadvantage. It limits the flexibility for the user. In many situations, it is difficult for the programmer to anticipate how the user will want to use the application. For example, some user requirements might be satisfied viewing episodes one series at a time, but others might need to view them based on a holiday or genre. In a addition, this option doesn't consider growth. It is possible that even limiting the user to accessing episodes by series would eventually return a large amount of data.

Perform a Count(*) calculation

To provide flexibility for the user while limiting the number of rows retrieved, you can query the database server to determine how many rows will be retrieved. This provides an accurate count of the rows that will be sent to the client requester once the completed query is processed.

For example, if you provide users with the capability of retrieving episode rows completely *ad hoc*, they might end up executing a wide range of queries:

```
SELECT episode_name, series_name, episode_holiday
  FROM episode
  WHERE series_cde LIKE "L%";
```

It would by difficult to estimate the number of rows that might be retrieved for any of these queries. If, however, the query is executed with a COUNT(*) and no other columns, the single value returned will determine the total number of rows that meet the criteria and should provide you with an accurate estimate of the expense of the query:

```
SELECT count(*) FROM series WHERE series_cde="LUCY"
```

or, if you are using a query-mode DataWindow, the following code could determine the row count:

```
mode = dw_1.describe('datawindow.querymode')
if mode = 'yes' then
  wf_set_buttons(false)
  ib_query_mode = false
  dw_1.modify('datawindow.querymode = no datawindow.readonly = yes')
// check to make sure that the select will not bring back too many rows
  old_sql = dw_1.describe('datawindow.table.select')
  posi = pos(lower(old_sql),' from ')
```

```
    new_sql = 'select count(*) '+mid(old_sql,posi)
    posi =  pos(lower(new_sql),' order ')
    if posi > 0 then new_sql = left(new_sql,posi - 1)
    if not wf_check_row_count(new_sql) then
      ib_query_mode = true
      dw_1.modify('datawindow.querymode = yes datawindow.readonly = no')
      return
    end if

// window function :wf_check_row_count(new_sql)
// Determine the row count from the selection criteria
// The SQL is passed to as_sql.
integer  li_count
setmicrohelp ( "Checking number of records to be selected" )
as_sql = f_global_replace(as_sql,'~~"','"')
DECLARE sel_ll_cnt DYNAMIC CURSOR for SQLSA;
PREPARE SQLSA from :as_sql;
if sqlca.sqlcode <> 0 then
  f_db_error(sqlca,"Error on PREPARE with SQL = "+as_sql)
 return false
end if
OPEN DYNAMIC sel_ll_cnt;
if sqlca.sqlcode <> 0 then
  f_db_error(sqlca,"Error on OPEN with SQL = "+as_sql)
  return false
end if
FETCH sel_ll_cnt INTO :li_count;
if sqlca.sqlcode <> 0 then
  f_db_error(sqlca,"Error on FETCH with SQL = "+as_sql)
  return false
end if
CLOSE sel_ll_cnt;
if li_count > ii_max_rows then
  if MessageBox ( this.title , "This select will cause " + String ( li_count )
+ " rows to be returned.~r~nDo you really want to do this?" ,question! , okcancel! , 2 )
= 2 then
     return false
     else
    return true
  end if
end if
if li_count = 0 then

MessageBox ( this.title , "No information found for search criteria entered." )
  return true
end if
setmicrohelp ( "" )
return true
```

Because there are no columns in the column list, the database can process the request without sending a lot of data to the client. Once the count is known, you or the educated consumer can decide that any query resulting in more than a certain number of rows will be disallowed. This technique is not always the answer. Depending on the volume of data and configuration of the database, the COUNT(*) request can be costly in terms of server time and, therefore, might not be feasible. For example, the WHERE predicate column, especially in the query-mode example, might not be an index, and an entire table scan might be required to determine the COUNT. In addition, if the retrieval subsequently is issued, the server must obtain the rows that meet the WHERE criteria again.

Use the RetrieveRow event

A RetrieveRow event occurs as each row is returned from the query and is placed in memory on the client machine. If there are a number of rows or is a limited amount of client memory, it might be necessary to limit the total number of rows returned by coding a script in the RetrieveRow event that counts the number of rows already retrieved from the server and stops the retrieval after a certain point. If any script (even comments) is coded in the RetrieveRow event, the event is triggered each time the Data Window receives a new row from the database server.

In a window, define an instance variable:

```
Integer li_counter
```

When the window is opened, this variable has a default value of zero. In the RetrieveStart event, initialize the counter variable, then code a RetrieveRow event for the DataWindow control:

```
//Bump up the total count
li_counter = li_counter + 1
//Is the limit reached?
if li_counter >= 100 then
  //Yes, tell the DataWindow to stop retrieving
  this SetActionCode(1)
  //inform the user
MessageBox("Retrieve Notify", "Maximum allowable number of rows retrieved")
  end if
```

This approach gives you complete control over the number of rows that the user is able to retrieve. Users, therefore, have more flexibility with the type of queries they can execute. When a DataWindow only needs to copy each retrieved row into memory on the client machine, it can do this very quickly. The speed of execution of the query is driven by the server's ability to send rows to the client, and not the processing requirements on the client machine itself. However, if a RetrieveRow event is triggered for each one of these rows, the speed of execution is degraded because more work has to be performed on the client machine. This additional processing can become a bottleneck, greatly increasing the time that it takes to execute a query. Once a retrieval has been stopped by calling the SetActionCode function, the retrieval cannot be resumed.

Use a cursor

Because the DataWindow Retrieve function is a bulk operation, you can only terminate the process (as in the previous example). To have complete control over the retrieval and be able to resume the retrieval after determining that the user wants more rows, you can load the DataWindow directly from an SQL cursor. Each row retrieved by a FETCH then must be sent to the DataWindow with a series of SetItem function calls. The SetItem can prime any data window column with data returned via FETCH.

By defining a cursor and issuing each FETCH explicitly, you can count the number or rows and determine when to prompt the user. For example, if you want to prompt the user after the first 100 rows, you suspend FETCHes from the server by popping up a MessageBox to the user:

```
Continue? Yes  No
```

If the user responds Yes, then the FETCH loop continues until the next point at which you want to ask if the retrieval should continue. If the user responds No, the cursor is closed and no more rows are sent to the DataWindow. You are not only in complete control of the number of rows retrieved but also can periodically prompt the user to determine whether to continue.

For example:

```
DECLARE C1 CURSOR FOR
SELECT epsseg.series_cde,
  epsseg.episode_cde,
  epsseg.eps_seg_num,
  epsseg.eps_seg_len
FROM  epsseg
WHERE episode_cde = :ls_episode_cde AND
  series_cde = :ls_series_cde ;
//
// check the return code to verify whether the cursor was successfully created.
// If not successful display error message
IF sqlca.sqlcode <>  0 THEN &
   f_db_error( sqlca," in epsseg CURSOR build ")
 SetPointer(HourGlass!)
 li_counter = 0
OPEN C1;
  IF sqlca.sqlcode <  0 THEN &
    f_db_error( sqlca," epsseg CURSOR OPEN ")
// Set the values in the data entry window with the values retrieved
// from the database. Pass through the loop while the FETCH
// is successful
// FETCH result ends with sqlcode = 100
  li_sqlcode = 0
  DO WHILE li_sqlcode = 0
    FETCH C1 INTO :ls_series_cde,
                  :ls_episode_cde,
                  :li_seg_num,
                  :li_seg_len;

    IF sqlca.sqlcode <> 0  and sqlca.sqlcode <> 100 THEN &
      f_db_error( sqlca," epsseg FETCH error ")
   IF sqlca.sqlcode = 100 THEN &
      li_sqlcode = sqlca.sqlcode
   IF sqlca.sqlcode <> 100 THEN &
     li_counter = li_counter + 1
   IF sqlca.sqlcode <>  100 AND li_counter > 64 THEN &
     MessageBox ( this.title , "This select will caused " + &
      String ( li_counter ) + " rows to be returned.~r~nDo you want to continue?", &
      question!, okcancel!, 2 ) = 2 then li_counter = 0
  LOOP
CLOSE  C1;
```

Using a cursor in a conversational mode can be very expensive due to the additional overhead on the client. Processing queries through a cursor, retrieving the values into local variables, then setting them into a DataWindow is not very efficient compared to a direct DataWindow retrieval. It is cumbersome to code and maintain the DataWindow control scripts. Also, the cursor remains open while you are prompting the user whether to continue. This not only ties up resources on the server but can cause locks on the retrieved records. This can interfere with other users' database access.

Specifying update characteristics

As previously mentioned, SQL UPDATE, INSERT, and DELETE statements are created (the PowerBuilder Update function) based on the status of data in the primary and delete buffers. Use the GetSqlPreview function within a SqlPreview event to view the SQL created by an UPDATE or INSERT PowerBuilder function. If the DataWindow does not have update capability, neither the delete nor the original buffers are maintained, and no SQL statements are generated by the Update function.

When you define a DataWindow in the DataWindow painter, you can allow updates and specify the table that you want to update. You also can specify what kind of SQL UPDATE statement PowerBuilder will build (WHERE clause for Update/Delete) and how the modification will be performed (Key Modification).

WHERE clause for Update/Delete. You choose one of the following three options in the Where Clause for Update/Delete group box:

- `Key columns` works well if dirty read is not problematic
- `Key and Updateable Columns` can be very expensive and invariably requires scan of the entire table
- `Key and Modified Columns` can be expensive but provides integrity and protection against another intermittent update to the target row

Using each of these options, PowerBuilder creates an SQL statement that compares the value of the originally retrieved key and other column in the row against the current value of the key and other column for that row in the database. If the key values match, the update takes place. This key option usually is adequate with most user applications. However, you might use KEY and MODIFIED columns in a TICK ETRON application where the KEY and EVENT_CDE and LOCATION_CDE and AVAILABLE_IND indicated that the event still was available for a particular location (e.g., seat number). This will protect against the "dirty read" (i.e., a user has updated the table rows after you have read its values into your buffer).

Example. If the `Key and Modified Columns` option has been chosen, when Transaction 2 wants to update the database, PowerBuilder builds a SQL statement such as:

```
UPDATE  TBEVENTS
SET AVAILABLE_IND=NO
  WHERE EVENT_CDE='CLAPTON'
  AND LOCATION_CDE='1'
  AND AVAILABLE_IND = "YES";
```

This statement compares the key and column with the original key and column and finds that they match, so the update takes place. If the keys do not match, the update does not take place, and PowerBuilder returns an error.

Timestamps are maintained in certain databases (for example, Sybase) so that you can ensure that your users are working with the most current data. They act as an alternate technique to providing concurrent access, allowing you to track database changes. Timestamps are database-specific. The Sybase implementation of TIMESTAMP is different than DB2/MVS. Sybase automatically sets the TIMESTAMP after each UPDATE or INSERT.

PowerBuilder supports timestamp checking in DataWindows by using the Transact SQL function TSEQUAL( ) in the WHERE clause for Update and Delete statements. It returns the same errors as it does for the Update Characteristics Where Clause for Update/Delete. To implement timestamp checking, you need to include a column called timestamp (with a data type of timestamp) on the table and in the SELECT statement of the DataWindow.

The DBError event of the DataWindow is invoked if a timestamp has changed while updating or deleting a row. You can add processing here to send a response window to the user to determine next steps to be taken by the application. The timestamp overrides the setting in the Specify Update Characteristics window.

DataWindow testing techniques

Building DataWindows also encompasses testing the SQL for correct results and performance. Use the `Database Administration` option within the Database painter to try out and verify SQL statements before generating the DataWindow. It also is very useful for testing embedded SQL. You can code the SQL using PASTE functions to develop basic syntax. Copy and paste to your favorite editor, then refine the syntax until it works well.

Explain SQL

After you get the desired result, use the `Explain SQL` option in the Database Administrator's tool to examine the SQL. `Explain SQL` displays information about the path that PowerBuilder will use to access the data. Sometimes there is more than one way to code an SQL statement to obtain the desired result. `Explain SQL` (on the Objects menu) can help you select the more efficient method. This is most useful when you are retrieving or updating data in an indexed column or using multiple tables. You also can copy the SQL to an external file and pass it to a specific DBMS EXPLAIN utility (e.g., Platinum and BMC provide one for DB2/MVS).

Preview SQL

Use the SQLPreview event and the GetSQLPreview function to trap and display SQL. An SQLPreview event occurs after a Retrieve, Update, or ReselectRow function call and immediately before the function is executed. The SQL that you see is what will be executed. The SQLPreview event has action codes that specify the action that takes place when the event occurs. To set the action code, call the SetActionCode function. The action codes are:

- 0—Continue (Default)
- 1—Stop processing
- 2—Skip this request and execute the next request

Note: When the Retrieve function triggers the SQLPreview event, the DataWindow control already has been reset. When the Update function triggers the SQLPreview event, the DataWindow control has not been reset.

Dynamically Changing a DataWindow

Sometimes an application needs to provide the user with the ability to create or modify DataWindows results themselves. Typically, with this type of requirement, the developer cannot anticipate the result set that the user will need or when the number of potential result sets is so large that it would be impractical to create them ahead of time.

Dynamically creating a DataWindow is accomplished by first dynamically creating a data object, then attaching it to a preexisting DataWindow control at runtime. For the sake of simplicity, we will call this two-step process creating a DataWindow. After creating the DataWindow, the user might want to print the contents as a report and save the DataWindow in a library for use in future queries and reports.

Dynamic DataWindow creation

To create a DataWindow dynamically, the application must:

- Build the SQL statement for the data object and describe the form and style of the data object.
- Associate the new data object with a DataWindow control.

The SQL statement and the presentation style are combined to produce the syntax for a data object via the SyntaxFromSQL function. This function is always associated with an existing transaction object (for example, `connect1.SyntaxFrom SQL(...)`), and the application must be connected using that transaction object before the function is executed.

To build the data object syntax:

Step 1 Declare a string to hold the SQL statement. The SQL statement must be a complete, executable statement. Arguments are not allowed. If the result set of selected columns will stay the same but the WHERE clause or constant values in the WHERE clause might change, build the SQL statement without a WHERE clause initially, then append one after the DataWindow has been created via the dwModify function.

Step 2 Declare a string variable to hold the presentation string. The presentation string gives information on how the DataWindow should look: freeform, grid, fonts, units of measure, color, etc.

Step 3 Provide a string variable to hold any errors returned.

Step 4 Create the data object syntax by executing SyntaxFromSQL function:

```
String ls_sql_select, ls_present_str, ls_errmsg, ls_syntax_str
ls_sql_select="select series name from series where series_name like "%BEAVER%"
```

```
ls_present_str="style (type=form)"
ls_syntax_str=SyntaxFromSQL(CONNECT1, ls_sql_select, ls_present_str, ls_errmsg)
```

The data object created by SyntaxFromSQL( ) is a runtime data object only.

The presentation string holds information on what you want the DataWindow to look like. The following presentation string takes the following defaults: a tabular DataWindow and default fonts, colors, validation rules, etc. These were taken from the PowerBuilder system tables.

```
string ls_present_str=""
```

There are four DataWindow style attributes that you can specify in the presentation string in SyntaxFromSQL( ):

- DataWindow
- Style
- Column
- Text

Note: Information retrieved from the PowerBuilder catalog tables will take precedence over conflicting values specified through the presentation style string. To override PowerBuilder system table information, use the Modify function after the DataWindow has been created.

Creating a DataWindow object in a DataWindow control

The DataWindow control must exist already on the window. You are dynamically creating the data object, not the control. The control can be hidden, of course. To associate the new syntax with an existing DataWindow control, use the Create function:

```
// ls_syntax_str contains valid data object syntax.
dw_series.Create(ls_syntax_str, ls_errmsg)
dw_series.SetTransObject(CONNECT1)
```

This syntax is most commonly derived as output from the SyntaxFromSQL function but also can be derived from the Library Export function or be created by the developer from a number of different sources.

The Create( ) statement must be followed by a new SetTransObject( ) statement because Create( ) destroys any previous association between the DataWindow and a transaction object.

If you distribute an application that dynamically creates DataWindows and you want default information to be retrieved from the PowerBuilder system tables, make sure that those tables exist in the target production database. This was discussed earlier in this chapter.

If you want to save the data object into a library for reuse later, use the Library Import function.

The Library Export function can be used to bring the syntax for a preexisting data object into a .PBL. You then can make modifications to the string and dynamically create a DataWindow that is more complex than that allowed by the SyntaxFrom-SQL function. See the PowerBuilder documentation for information on Syntax FromSQL( ) limitations. You cannot issue a Modify( ) statement until after the Create( ) statement.

Modify existing DataWindows dynamically

All of the DataWindow examples so far have used features available in the DataWindow painter or through PowerScript functions. In the DataWindow painter, you define result sets, set fonts, set colors, and prime code tables. With PowerScript functions, you populate code tables and set validation rules. Both of these interfaces make the programmer's job easier because they are at a relatively high level. Underlying this is a DataWindow engine that manipulates entities at a much lower level than the programmer sees. The dynamic DataWindow interface deals directly with this lower level and, therefore, provides the programmer with a powerful tool for manipulating DataWindows at execution.

You can modify DataWindows dynamically, as well. Conditionally set the display of the DataWindow in the Open event of the window that it resides in. This could be used to give additional information relevant to a particular user or a particular piece of data. Allow the user to alter the display of DataWindows through a menu item or some other interface. Save the display state in an .INI file and automatically start there the next time the user invokes that window. You might have a user profile (i.e., only select and display certain information from a large database).

Deploying dynamic DataWindows

Using PowerBuilder, we have several approaches for displaying the data in a dynamic fashion. The solutions range from a "hardcoded" solution to a "data-driven" solution. However, it is not as simple as that; we also have to consider the future maintenance, including any additional tables, and the dynamics of data presentation.

What follows is a brief description of the approaches and a list of the pros and cons of each:

The "hardcoded" approach. This involves developing a database view and a PowerBuilder DataWindow for each of the tables to be displayed. The DataWindow contains a selection of all of the columns from the view and formats them according to the established project standards (i.e., dates, numeric amounts, prices, etc.).

Pros. This solution does not require that the PowerBuilder catalog table entries (pbcatcol, pbcatedt, pbcatfmt, pbcattbl, and pbcatvld) be migrated to the production database servers.

Cons. Table and/or column maintenance requires changes to the DataWindow and redeployment of the affected dynamic library (.PBD) to each client workstation.

The "middle-of-the-road" approach. This involves developing a database view for each of the tables to be displayed. A dynamic DataWindow is constructed on client demand and contains a selection of all of the columns from the view. Additional PowerScript logic would loop through the DataWindow columns and format the column according to the established project standards (i.e., dates, numeric amounts, prices, etc.).

Pros. Table and/or column maintenance does not require a redeployment of dynamic library (appl1dw.pbd). This might not be the case if the formatting is "column name" specific.

Smaller dynamic library (appl1dw.pbd) are distributed because the DataWindows are dynamic.

It does not rely on PowerBuilder catalog table entries (pbcatcol, pbcatedt, pbcatfmt, pbcattbl, and pbcatvld) being migrated to the production database servers.

Cons. "Hardcoding" the formatting of the columns in PowerScript will affect the performance and might not be possible without specifying the exact column names. How do you tell the difference between an amount and a price, in order to apply the correct decimal place format?

The "data-driven" approach. This involves developing a Sybase base view (v1) for each of the tables to be displayed. The dynamic DataWindow is constructed on client demand and uses a selection of the columns from the base table. Prior to submitting the SQL to the engine, the table name is switched to a view by the application. During this dynamic construction process, PowerBuilder's DataWindow engine refers to its catalog entries to format the column accordingly.

Pros. Table and/or column maintenance typically does not require a redeployment of the dynamic library.

The catalog entries allow the definition for each column's alignment, display mask, and heading.

Cons. It still needs SELECT access to the base tables. Then, at the point of actually submitting data manipulation language (DML) to the server, the table names are switched to the view names. Using this technique avoids the need to grant any additional permissions to the base tables.

The PowerBuilder catalog table entries (pbcatcol, pbcatedt, pbcatfmt, pbcattbl, and pbcatvld) must be migrated to the production database servers for the correct formatting to take place. Even if this does not happen, the data is still displayed!

The DataWindow Object

When you create a DataWindow using the DataWindow painter, everything on that window is an object. Headings and columns on the DataWindow are given names; other objects (such as drawing objects, picture objects, etc.) are not given names; however, you can name them yourself. Every object on the DataWindow has attributes associated with it. The DataWindow object has the attributes of its own.

Attributes

There is a corresponding set of attributes for each of the objects. (These attributes are documented in the PowerBuilder documentation.) When you manipulate a

DataWindow object through the DataWindow painter or through a PowerScript function, you refer to the column name and attribute.

For example, the following code is used to set the reference table for the genre column in the d_Series DataWindow in the TV Program Tracking application. The SetValue function is coded as follows:

```
//Set the genre code table value
dw_sheet.SetValue("genre" Counter, Name + "~t"+ Code)
```

Exported syntax

If you EXPORT a DataWindow object using the Library painter, you will see a series of attribute assignments for each object in the DataWindow definition.

The following is the exported syntax for the city_t(header) column in the d_customer_query DataWindow in the class OrderEntry application

```
text(band=header color="0" alignment="2"border="0" x="1779"
y="4" height="53" width="115" text="City" name=city_t
font.face="MS Sans Serif" font.height="53"font.weight="700
font.family="2" font.pitch="2"font.charset="0"
background.mode="1" background.color="536870912")
```

Using the dynamic DataWindow interface, you can manipulate these attributes directly. This is a very powerful tool; however, it is up to the programmer to provide accurate syntax so that the modifications will work.

Displaying object attributes

The PowerBuilder documentation contains a list of DataWindow object attributes. You also can access these attributes using the Object Browser in the Script painter. In the Object Browser, select the DataWindow Object Type, then select the Attributes Paste Category. As each DataWindow object is highlighted in the Objects List-Box, the supported attributes display in the Paste values ListBox.

The dynamic DataWindow interface

There are two PowerScript functions that allow you to access and manipulate DataWindow objects attributes:

- Describe( ) is used to access the current value for attributes.
- Modify( ) is used to change the current value for attributes.

To find the X coordinate of the picture TVlogo_pic, in a DataWindow, you use the Describe function:

```
string ls_star_val
ls_star_val = dw_sheet.Describe("TVlogo_pic.x")
```

All attributes are built as a string. You can get the attributes for all the objects by using parameters:

```
.obj+"x"
```

where *obj* contains the name of a DataWindow object.

To describe attributes for the DataWindow object itself, use the following syntax:

```
("datawindow<attribute>")
```

The following example would return the background color of the data object associated with dw_emp:

```
string ls_colorval
ls_colorval = dw_sheet.Describe ("datawindow.color")
```

Dynamically changing a WHERE clause

You might need to add or modify a WHERE clause in a DataWindow dynamically from variables in a script. In the Window event script, retrieve the current WHERE clause using Describe( ) and modify it with as you require. Be careful; test out the code to ensure proper SQL is being built. Use the SQL preview event to sight verify.

The following is an example script:

```
// WF_MODIFY_DW
// this window function will add some predicates
// to the WHERE clause of a SQL SELECT statement = the report request
string ls_sql_src
string ls_date1,ls_date2, ls_sql_new,ls_series, :ls_dwmod_status
string ls_where_src1, ls_where_src2, ls_order_src1
long    ll_rc
//GET THE DATAWINDOW BASE SQL
ls_sql_src = dw_sheet.GetSQLSelect()
/////////////////////////////////
CHOOSE CASE istr_parms.string_arg[3]
  CASE   "tbrept02", "tbrept03"
 // add code to perform dw_modify
  // prime the predicates with the instance variables
    ls_series =  "'" + istr_parms.string_arg[1] + "'"
    ls_date1  = "'" + string(istr_parms.datetime_arg[1]) + "'"
    ls_date2  = "'" + string(istr_parms.datetime_arg[2]) + "'"
  // setup SQL syntax
    ls_where_src1 = " AND episod.series_cde = "
    ls_where_src2 = " AND pgmtrk.track_datetime between "
    ls_order_src1 = " ORDER BY episod.series_cde ASC, &
                    pgmtrk.track_datetime ASC"
  // Did they choose ALL as opposed to a particular tv series from the ddlb
    ll_rc = POS(ls_series,"ALL")
  // If they choose ALL then leave out the series portion of the WHERE
    IF ll_rc > 0 THEN
      ls_sql_new = ls_sql_src + ls_where_src2 + ls_date1 + &
                    " AND " + ls_date2 + ls_order_src1
    ELSE
      ls_sql_new = ls_sql_src + ls_where_src1 + ls_series + &
                  ls_where_src2 + ls_date1 + " AND " +   &
                  ls_date2 + ls_order_src1
    END IF
  CASE   "tbrept03"
// add code to perform dw_modify
  CASE   "tbrept04"
// add code to perform dw_modify
  CASE ELSE
END CHOOSE
// dwModify the stuff
ls_sql_new = "datawindow.Table.Select = ~"" + ls_sql_new + "~""
```

```
ls_dwmod_status = dw_sheet.Modify( ls_sql_new )
//
return true
IF ls_dwmod_status  = "" THEN
  dw_sheet.Retrieve()
ELSE
  MessageBox("Modify Failed", rc)
END IF
```

Prompt for criteria

Another option for changing the WHERE clause is to prompt for criteria. This attribute is set on a column-by-column basis using Modify( ) and `criteria.dialog=yes`.

In the DataWindow painter by selecting columns for which you want the user to be prompted for criteria (`Prompt for Criteria...` option in the Rows menu). You use this option to bring up the same dialog box that you see in the DataWindow painter when you paint a DataWindow using the Quick Select option.

Example. To display a dialog box that allows you to enter criteria for the series column, code the following:

```
dw_1.Modify("series.criteria.dialog=yes")
```

or specify it in the DataWindow painter.

The same operators that you can use in query mode (i.e., >, <, =, etc.) can be used in prompt for criteria.

Notes. The prompt-for-criteria generated WHERE clause is dynamically synthesized each time that you do a new retrieve. Therefore, a Describe( ) of datawindow.table.select will not show this WHERE clause.

You cannot specify sort criteria from prompt for criteria. Although not required, datawindow.querymode should be equal to `no` (the default) when using the prompt-for-criteria approach. If you allow the user to enter criteria using query mode and using prompt for criteria, you might have conflicting WHERE clause criteria. If you want your user to be able to specify sort criteria as part of the SELECT, use query mode. If sorting is not an issue or you intend to do client-side sorting (that is, the DataWindow SetSort function) and/or you want to limit the number of fields for which the user can specify criteria, use prompt for criteria.

Using query mode to dynamically change the WHERE clause

There are two additional approaches to dynamically modifying a DataWindow WHERE clause: query mode and prompt for criteria. Although these methods are slightly less flexible than a Modify( ).

To set datawindow.querymode to `yes`:

```
dw_1.Modify("datawindow.querymode=yes")
```

When you do this, any data in your DataWindow will seem to disappear, and you will see what looks like blank rows. The data still is there, but is not hidden from view.

Identifying the conditions. To build the WHERE clause for the SELECT associated with the DataWindow, the user tabs into columns for which he wants to specify a condition and types in the condition.

You should note the following when using query mode:

- The Valid operators that can be used in a column in query mode are: like, in, >, <, >=, <=, <>, =
- AND conditions are built between columns on the same row.
- OR conditions are built between columns on different rows. There is an implicit == if you type in a value without an operator.

Specifying sort criteria. To allow the user to specify sort criteria, set datawindow .querysort to yes via Modify( ):

```
dw_1.Modify("datawindow.querysort=yes')
```

Even if you are not already in query mode, setting datawindow.querysort to yes will force a DataWindow into query mode. When datawindow.querysort=yes, the first row of the DataWindow is dedicated to specifying sort criteria. All subsequent rows are dedicated to specifying where criteria.

Retrieving the new data. The criteria/sort specification is not added/modified until the user tabs or clicks away from the column or presses Enter. To bring back a new result set based upon your new WHERE clause, you must do a Retrieve( ). To get the data to reappear, set datawindow.querymode to no using Modify( ).

Note: When using query mode, take care that your DataWindow is built as a SELECT without a WHERE clause, otherwise your criteria will be appended without an AND or an OR to the existing WHERE clause, and you will an SQL error and get no results from your Retrieve( ).

DataWindows versus Embedded SQL

DataWindows provide powerful and highly efficient database access for just about all of your application requirements. Sometimes performance requirements dictate the need to use embedded SQL (not generated bu PowerBuilder). For example, a stored procedure, which is a recompiled collection of SQL.

Embedded SQL requires that you create your own SQL statements. You will use embedded SQL whenever you want something you cannot easily do with a DataWindow (for example, adding rows to another table in the database not associated with this datawindow), or you are explicitly specifying CREATE, DROP, GRANT, and REVOKE SQL statements.

In general, you will use embedded SQL when the data is brought in to be manipulated rather than displayed. When using embedded SQL, you must always check the SQLCode from the transaction object to determine whether the SQL statement executed successfully or not.

Embedded SQL can take several forms:

- Static SQL, including cursors
- Stored procedures
- Dynamic SQL

Embedded static SQL

Use embedded static SQL when the components of the SQL statement do not change; only the values passed as arguments to the WHERE clause change. Remember to use the USING clause to associate the SQL statement with a particular transaction object.

For example:

```
SELECT series_cde, series_name
FROM dbo.series  WHERE series_cde = :ls_series_cde
USING Connect1;
```

Host variables are prefixed with a colon and must be declared before being referenced in SQL statements. It is not necessary to use the & character to continue the line when the SQL statement wraps across multiple lines. Always check the SQLCode attribute of your transaction object after executing the SQL statement to verify success or failure. If you do not prefix a table with the owner name, PowerBuilder assumes that the owner of the table is whatever was specified in your logon_id or userid.

It is a good idea always to use the USING clause, even when the transaction object is SQLCA.

Stored procedures

Stored procedures are named, precompiled sets of modal SQL (e.g., PL/SQL for Oracle or TRANSACT-SQL for Sybase). Stored procedures hit the ground running. Unlike dynamic SQL, which must be parsed, validated, optimized, and compiled before the request can be executed, database stored procedures allow you to define procedural SQL statements in the database for use by all applications. Using stored procedures to perform database updates allows you to enhance database security, integrity, and performance. Because stored procedures provide for conditional execution, you also can use them to enforce additional business rules.

The remainder of this chapter contains some examples of Sybase stored procedures that use popular combinations of:

- Result set (rs)—The result of the SQL statement execution of a FETCH or SELECT.
- Input Parameter (ip)—A parameter or search argument passed to the stored procedure.
- Return Value (rv)—A return value for the caller to determine if the stored procedure was successful.
- Output Parameter (op)—A parameter returned to the caller.

The Transact SQL procedure language is used in the example stored procedure syntax. The PUBS database, which is the Sybase/SQLServer introductory database, was used to allow developers to easily recreate and execute the stored procedures.

Transact SQL procedure type 1. Result set, no input parameter, no return value, output parameter

```
CREATE PROCEDURE rs_nip_nrv_op
  @outparm1 int OUTPUT,
  @outparm2 int OUTPUT
AS
SELECT series_id, series_name from .series
SELECT @outparm1 = @@rowcount,
  @outparm2 = @@error;
```

PowerScript execution syntax

```
LONG    outparm1, outparm2, num
STRING  id, name
DECLARE TYPE1_proc PROCEDURE FOR rs_nip_nrv_op
  @outparm1 = :outparm1 output,
  @outparm2 = :outparm2 output
USING SQLCA;

EXECUTE TYPE1_proc;

IF SQLCA.SQLCode = 0 THEN
  DO
    //Loop to get the query result set from the table SELECT...
    FETCH TYPE1_proc INTO :id, :name;
    CHOOSE CASE SQLCA.SQLCode
    CASE 0
      num = num + 1
    CASE 100
     MessageBox ("End of Result", STRING (num) + " rows fetched")
    CASE -1
     MessageBox ("Fetch Failed", STRING (SQLCA.SQLDBcode) + " = " +&
      SQLCA.SQLErrText)
    END CHOOSE
  LOOP while SQLCA.SQLCode = 0
   // An extra fetch to get the output parameter(s).
   FETCH TYPE1_proc INTO :outparm1, :outparm2;
  CHOOSE CASE SQLCA.SQLCode
   CASE 0
     MessageBox ("Fetch Output Parms SUCCESSFUL","Results are: " + &
     STRING (outparm1) + " " + STRING (outparm2))
   CASE 100
     MessageBox ("Fetch Output Parms NOT FOUND", "")
   CASE ELSE
     MessageBox ("Fetch Output Parms FAILED", "SQLDBcode is " + &
     STRING (SQLCA.SQLDBcode) + " = " + SQLCA.SQLErrText)
   END CHOOSE
   CLOSE TYPE1_proc;
ELSE
  MessageBox ("Execute Failed", STRING (SQLCA.SQLDBcode) + &
  " = " + SQLCA.SQLErrText)
END IF
```

Transact SQL procedure type 2. Result set, no input parameter, return value, no output parameter

```
CREATE PROCEDURE rs_nip_rv_nop
AS
SELECT series_id, series_name FROM .series
RETURN 999;
```

PowerScript execution syntax

```
LONG    rv, num
STRING  id, name

DECLARE TYPE2_proc PROCEDURE FOR
 @rv = rs_nip_rv_nop
USING SQLCA;

EXECUTE TYPE2_proc;

IF SQLCA.SQLCode = 0 THEN
  DO
    //Loop to get the query result set from the table SELECT...
    FETCH TYPE2_proc INTO :id, :name;
    CHOOSE CASE SQLCA.SQLCode
   CASE 0
     num = num + 1
   CASE 100
     MessageBox ("End of Result", STRING (num) + " rows fetched")
    CASE -1
      MessageBox ("Fetch Failed", STRING (SQLCA.SQLDBcode) + " = " +&
      SQLCA.SQLErrText)
    END CHOOSE
  LOOP while SQLCA.SQLCode = 0
  // An extra fetch to get the RETURN VALUE.
  FETCH TYPE2_proc INTO :rv;
  CHOOSE CASE SQLCA.SQLCode
  CASE 0
    MessageBox ("Fetch Return Value SUCCESSFUL", "Return Value is: " &
    + STRING (rv))
  CASE 100
    MessageBox ("Fetch Return Value NOT FOUND",  "")
  CASE ELSE
    MessageBox ("Fetch Return Value FAILED", &
    "SQLDBcode is " + STRING (SQLCA.SQLDBcode) + " = " +  &
   SQLCA.SQLErrText)
  END CHOOSE
ELSE
  MessageBox ("Execute Failed", STRING (SQLCA.SQLDBcode) + &
" = " + SQLCA.SQLErrText)
END IF
```

Transact SQL procedure type 3. Result set, no input parameter, return value, output parameter

```
CREATE PROCEDURE rs_nip_rv_op
  @outparm1 int OUTPUT,
  @outparm2 int OUTPUT
AS
SELECT series_id, series_name from .series
SELECT @outparm1 = @@rowcount,
  @outparm2 = @@error
RETURN 999;
```

PowerScript execute syntax

```
LONG    num, outparm1, outparm2, rv
STRING  id, name

DECLARE TYPE3_proc PROCEDURE FOR @rv = rs_nip_rv_op &
 @outparm1 = :outparm1 output,
 @outparm2 = :outparm2 output ;
EXECUTE TYPE3_proc;
CHOOSE CASE SQLCA.SQLCode
CASE 0
 // Execute successful; at least one result set.
  // Loop to get the query result set from the table SELECT...
  DO
    FETCH TYPE3_proc INTO :id, :name;
    CHOOSE CASE SQLCA.SQLCode
    CASE 0
      num = num + 1
    CASE 100
      MessageBox ("End of Result", STRING (num) + " rows fetched")
    CASE -1
      MessageBox ("Fetch Failed",STRING (SQLCA.SQLDBcode) + " = " + &
      SQLCA.SQLErrText)
    END CHOOSE
  LOOP while SQLCA.SQLCode = 0
  // An extra fetch to get the RETURN VALUE and OUTPUT PARMS.
  FETCH TYPE3_proc INTO :rv, :outparm1, :outparm2;
  CHOOSE CASE SQLCA.SQLCode
  CASE 0
   MessageBox ("Fetch Return Value & Output Parms SUCCESSFUL", &
     "Return Value is: " + STRING (rv) + "~r~nOutput Parms are: " + &
     STRING (outparm1) + " and " + STRING (outparm2))
  CASE 100
    MessageBox ("Return Value & Output Parms NOT FOUND",  "")
  CASE ELSE
   MessageBox ("Fetch Return Value & Output Parms FAILED", &
     "SQLDBcode is " + STRING (SQLCA.SQLDBcode) + " = " + SQLCA.SQLErrText)
  END CHOOSE
  CLOSE TYPE3_proc;
CASE 100
  // Execute successful; no result set; do not try to close.
  MessageBox ("Execute successful", "No result set")
CASE ELSE
  MessageBox ("Execute Failed", STRING (SQLCA.SQLDBcode) &
 + " = " + SQLCA.SQLErrText)
END CHOOSE
```

12

Adding Scripts

PowerBuilder applications are event-driven. After constructing the basic application objects (i.e., windows, DataWindows, and menus), we need a mechanism to control the way in which these objects will interact. That is to say, we need to specify the processing that takes place when an event within one of these objects occurs. We do this by writing in a free-form language known as PowerScript. PowerScript is similar to Basic and is not unlike most high-level languages. It includes many high-level programming language constructs familiar to mainframe and client/server developers. For this reason, PowerScript is relatively easy to learn for an experienced developer. Moreover, PowerBuilder provides a good script development environment from which you can open, edit, compile, and save scripts. The PowerScript editor is comprehensive and even provides a paste facility to easily access any script construct, PowerBuilder function, SQL statement, or scope variable.

PowerScripts Are Executed When an Event Is Triggered

Determining which events to work with is your job as a developer. You must figure out all of the events that might occur in your application and provide appropriate processing logic for each event in its script. To do that, you've got to know more about the various kinds of events that there are. Each kind of user-interface component has its own set of events that occur during program execution.

For example, Table 12.1 lists some components (objects and controls) and associated events. There are even some events that apply to your application as a whole, including:

TABLE 12.1 Some Components and Their Associated Events

Component	Events associated with the component
CommandButton control	Events including: Clicked, GetFocus, and LoseFocus
Menu item	Events: Clicked and Selected
DataWindow control	Events including: SQLPreview, RowFocusChanged, and Updatestart
Window	Many different events, including: Open, Close, Resize, Timer, and Clicked

- One that's triggered when the application starts: the Open event. You normally will use the script for this event to specify the initial window that you want the application to display.

- One that's triggered when the application ends: the Close event.

In many cases, you'll need to write scripts for just one or two of the events of a particular component. Mostly, users drive the flow of processing; however, on occasion, you'll want the application to take control. In these situations, you can write code in the script of one event that manually causes another event to occur. When doing this, you can either:

- *Trigger* the event so that its script executes right away.

- *Post* the event to a queue so that its script execution is deferred until after the scripts of any earlier events have executed.

You also can define your own events for any particular component, then manually trigger or post them to execute their scripts. These are called *user events*, and they can be useful for such things as:

- Extending the processing of other event scripts by serving as subroutines.

- Responding to messages from your operating environment that PowerBuilder doesn't provide as standard events.

In Figure 12.1, we have a window object and its DataWindow control opened and the events within the datawindow control listed in the dropdown list. Events, as they occur within the course of application execution, might cause an associated script to execute (scripts also can be executed via a function). The events in Figure 12.1, with the script box to the left, have scripts associated with them. The scripts are executed as the events are triggered either explicitly (called by another script) or implicitly by the user's actions. For example, the sqlpreview event is implicitly triggered when the user causes a PowerBuilder Update function.

The sqlpreview event in this window contains an inherited script that is contained in a user object that was encapsulated in the ancestor window (see Figure 12.2). This script can be extended or overridden by the descendant event script.

PowerScript Can Be Used to Define Functions

In addition to event scripting, functions can be composed using PowerScript statements. You can use the PowerBuilder Function painter to write functions to perform

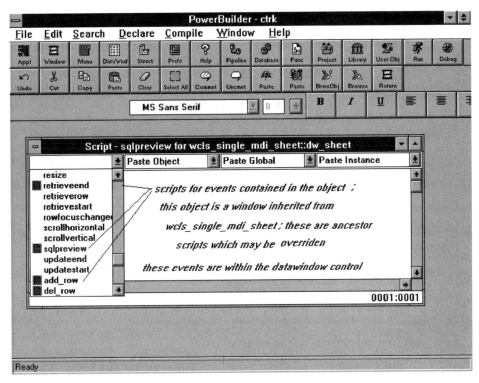

Figure 12.1 The events associated with an object.

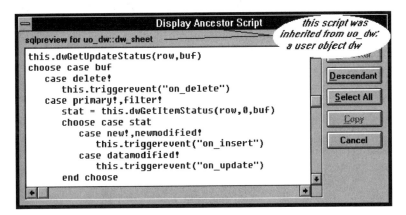

Figure 12.2 The ancestor script for the object event.

processing that is common within your application. You can write global user-defined functions or object-level functions. Object-level functions can be written for an application, a window, user objects, and menu objects. They become part of the object (i.e., they are encapsulated). If your environment is experienced in developing with PowerBuilder, there probably is a firmwide function library that contains common development scripts. These function libraries also are available in vendor tools, such as PowerClass, PowerTool, or PowerFrame.

PowerScript Basics

PowerScript is the high-level language that you use to specify the processing that you want your PowerBuilder application to perform. It provides language constructs such as IF/THEN/ELSE to control the flow of processing in the script. It also provides built-in functions to perform commonly used operations. A good PowerBuilder development environment will probably develop a rich PowerScript function library to facilitate consistent PowerBuilder applications.

PowerScript is a free form language (i.e., spacing and statement position are meaningless). This does not mean that the old tried-and-true standards of aligning blocks of code should be discontinued. It only means that the PowerScript compiler, as any good compiler would, does not hold a lack of neatness against the developer. PowerScript is not case-sensitive. You can enter statements, functions, and variables in any combination of upper- and lowercase that you want. For example, the following statements are equivalent:

```
name = Rosanna
NAME = Rosanna
Name = Rosanna
```

They all assign the value Rosanna to the variable string Name.

How do you reference PowerBuilder objects?

You define objects (such as windows, DataWindow objects, menus, and user objects) and controls (such as CommandButtons and RadioButtons) in PowerBuilder painters. In your scripts, you respond to events in those objects and controls (such as a button being clicked). The scripts use PowerScript code to specify the processing that will occur in response to each of these events. The script gets control when the event takes place. For example, a user clicks the left mouse button while positioned over a menu item. The script behind that menu item associated with the "clicked" event is given control at that time. So it is through scripts that you can open and close windows, enable and disable controls, change the menu associated with a window, or retrieve data into a DataWindow.

The PowerScript statements accomplish these tasks by referring to controls and objects defined in the application. Each object and control has a set of attributes, which are specialized variables from a PowerScript point of view that specify its behavior and appearance. By setting the values of attributes, you can modify the behavior and appearance of any object or control in your application. You refer to attributes of an object or control using the following syntax, called dot notation:

```
object.attribute
control.attribute
```

For example, to refer to an attribute in a window, you specify the name of the window, followed by a period (the dot), followed by the attribute name.

To change the behavior or appearance of a window, set the value of one of its attributes:

```
window.attribute = value
```

Similarly, to change the behavior or appearance of a CommandButton, write:

```
CommandButton.attribute = value
```

The behavior and appearance of a control is determined by the values of its attributes. To change the behavior of a control, you change its attributes. For example, a DropDownListBox control has an attribute named Text, which defines the text that appears in the box.

Exactly how you refer to a control depends on the relationship between the control and the script that you are writing. For example, the following script associated with a command button will assign the text and the item in two dropdown list boxes:

```
string ls_yr,ls_mo,ls_wk
integer ln_wk_p1
// change the text (i.e., what appears in the dropdown list box control DDLB1)
// ddlb1.text is the control.attribute object reference discussed earlier
ddlb_1.text  = string(in_no)
// change what appears in the DDLB1 to the item referenced by the in_num2)
ddlb_2.SelectItem(in_num2)
ln_wk_p1 = in_num3 + 1
ddlb_3.SelectItem(ln_wk_p1)
// likewise you can set a local string variable to the value in a ddlb
ls_yr = ddlb_1.text
ls_mo = ddlb_2.text
ls_wk = ddlb_3.text
```

To reference a window, enter the name of the window. The window must be defined, and the library containing the window must be included in the library search path for the application. *Note*: If the object appears more than once within the application (i.e., in two or more libraries in the application search list), the first copy of the object found will be used (i.e., the object found in the library closest to the top of the application library list).

For example, to open window w_main, write the following PowerScript statement to execute a PowerBuilder Open function, which implicitly executes all of the event scripts associated with the opening of a window object:

```
Open(w_main)
```

By assigning a value to a window's attribute, you can modify the behavior or appearance of the window. For example, the text that appears in a window's title bar is the value of the window's Title attribute. So to change the text in the title bar for w_main, modify the value of its Title attribute, such as:

```
w_main.Title = "LARGE CLIENT SERVER APPLICATION"
```

As in the previous example, you can simply specify the name of the control if the script is behind or associated with one of the following:

- The control itself
- The window or user object containing the control
- Another control in the same window or user object as the control you are referencing

For example, if you are writing a script for a CommandButton in window w_cust and need to refer to a SingleLineEdit named sle_output, also in window w_cust, you can simply use the control's name:

```
sle_output.Text = "Vanessa"
```

You must fully qualify the control name with the name of the window it is in when you write scripts that are not in the window. You use this syntax:

```
window.control.attribute
```

For example, if you are writing a script for window w_main and you meant to allow updates under the present circumstances in another window and need to reference the CommandButton cb_update in window w_sales, you will need to fully qualify the control name by adding its window name:

```
w_sales.cb_update.Enabled = TRUE
```

Say you are writing a script for a MenuItem and that, as part of the processing, you want to change the SingleLineEdit control named sle_files in w_output to be read-only. You would code:

```
w_output.sle_files.DisplayOnly = TRUE
```

To reference a MenuItem, use the name of the MenuItem and the name of each item above it in the menu hierarchy. You must combine the items in succession (beginning with the name of the menu and ending with the name of the item being identified) and separate the item names with periods. For example, to identify the item m_new under the item m_file in the menu bar of the menu m_main, enter:

```
m_main.m_file.m_new
```

You don't need to include the name of the menu if the script referencing this object is for a MenuItem in the menu itself.

What does PowerScript provide in the way of development variables?

You define variables to hold values in your scripts. PowerScript provides many data types, including: INTEGER, LONG, REAL, DECIMAL, CHAR, STRING, DATE, TIME, and BLOB. These will be described in detail later. However, as they say in Latin, *res ipsa loquitor* or "the thing speaks for itself." You also can create arrays and structures of these aforementioned variable types.

What is the scope or accessibility of each variable?

As with most client/server development environments, each variable has a scope, which specifies where in the application the variable can be used. PowerBuilder supports the following:

- Global variables, accessible anywhere in your application
- Local variables, accessible only in the script in which they are declared

- Instance variables, associated with one instance of an object, such as a window

- Shared variables, which are associated with a type of object

Which type of variable should be used in a development situation, as well as the properties of each type, will be in more detail later, but the choice depends upon some of the following considerations.

To some, global variables are a no-no. They are difficult to maintain, and amendments to an application's global variable list require tedious change management to control affected objects. While global variables are accessible anywhere in the application, the storage used is unavailable for other competing resources within the client workstation. Because it can affect all parts of the application, the global variables' pool (if implemented) should be set up, kept small in size, and maintained by the lead development team with a plan on how to update and distribute the application object that contains the globals. Also if you are using a class object base for development, it might require a global variable structure as part of the implementation. Global variables should be used judiciously, and all developers should be aware of the meaning of the global variables, their content, as well as the ramifications caused by changes made to their structure.

Instance variables provide a better alternative to globals if information needs to be shared between objects. Each object will include instance variables/structure. The PowerBuilder message object can be used to house the information as it is passed between objects. You could build a structure (see chapter 15) that would house the variables that you want to pass to the called object. The called object then would retrieve the Message.PowerObjectParm and store the structure into an instance based structure within the receiving object.

Shared variables are associated with an object class. They retain their value when an object is closed and then opened again. They should be called *object* or *class variables* as they are visible and updateable by all instances of a class. They are limited in use for the same reasons as the global variable (e.g., shared variables are hard to manage).

Local variables are those unique to the script in which they are contained. They are used to stage and store variables within a particular script. Their lifetime is the duration of the script execution. As such, they are visible only to the script in which they are declared.

Suffice it to say that we have written entire applications using instance and local variables only.

How does the developer access PowerBuilder functions?

PowerScript provides two kinds of built-in functions: global functions and object-level functions.

Global functions are not associated with a particular PowerBuilder object type. Global functions are available anywhere in an application. PowerBuilder also provides global functions that manipulate external files. You might want to open a local user profile. The following example opens for a read operation:

```
FileOpen("user.pif",StreamMode!,Read!)
```

Note: because it is not fully qualified, the directory where USER.PIF resides must be in the operating system PATH.

Object-level functions are associated with particular types of PowerBuilder objects and controls.

For example, some functions manipulate windows (such as resizing and moving windows), other functions manipulate DataWindow controls (such as retrieving data into a DataWindow control or scrolling a DataWindow control), while other functions manipulate CommandButtons (such as moving or hiding a CommandButton). You always call object-level functions with reference to an instance of an object; their scope is at the object level. Think of an object-level function as being a message to an object. As we did with objects and controls, we use dot notation to call object-level functions. The syntax is:

```
object.function(arguments)
```

To retrieve data into a DataWindow control named dw_sheet, passing one argument, you code:

```
dw_sheet.Retrieve(Series_id)
```

Each PowerBuilder built-in function is described in the Function Reference. There are over 500 functions, not to mention whatever functions your organization might have stored in a firmwide or vendor class library. Built-in functions that are associated with particular object or control types are listed by type in Objects and Controls in the Class Browser.

How do we use PowerScript statements?

PowerScript provides most of what you need to gain a desired result. It is not unlike other programming/development languages. To cut to the chase, we have included a script example (see Figure 12.3) that hopefully will illustrate things to be mindful of before you start serious coding. Things like:

- Naming conventions
- How to continue a statement across lines
- The built-in data types
- How to declare variables (and the types of variables that you can declare)
- How to use mathematical and logical operators and expressions
- The PowerScript statements
- How to embed SQL statements in scripts

How to create a PowerScript

In a large organization, you probably will be using a class library. As such, the developer needs to be familiar with how the class objects scripts work before they can code additional scripts to extend or override the ancestors.

Figure 12.3 An example script.

```
//////////////////////////////////////////////////////////////////////
//      Script: CREATE A SCHEDULE for Program Tracking
//      Date: October 6, 1993
//      Purpose: Fills the normalized pgmtrk table from the
//               denormalized program schedule pgmsch table.
// Log of Updates:
//   DATE          WHO         WHAT
//   --------      -----       -------------------------------------------
//////////////////////////////////////////////////////////////////////
// declare some variables --- use convention for the naming
//    li - local integer
//    ls - local string
//    ld - local date
integer li_counter, li_dayct, li_end_day, li_sqlcode, li_hour,li_rc
string  ls_codedesc, ls_codevalue, ls_series[7],ls_dte, ls_day
string  ls_strt_dte, ls_end_dte
string  ls_year, ls_month, ls_week, ls_hour, ls_min, ls_tim, ls_datetime
date ld_dte, ls_date
time ld_tim
datetime ldt_dtetim
//////////////////////////////////////////////////////////////////////
// Purpose of the code to follow:
// it will set the values in CONNECT2 based on what
// was in SQLCA  and attempt to connect to the database.
//////////////////////////////////////////////
// trigger and event (i.e., the script behind it)
li_rc = parent.triggerevent("ue_filesave")
// Set up a second database connection to perform updates
// out of a cursor
// Set new values in transaction object
transaction  connect2
// connect2 should have the same value as sqlca
Connect2               = Create transaction
connect2.DBMS          = sqlca.DBMS
connect2.database      = sqlca.database
connect2.servername    = sqlca.servername
connect2.dbparm        = sqlca.dbparm
connect2.logid         = sqlca.logid
connect2.logpass       = sqlca.logpass
CONNECT using connect2;
if connect2.sqlcode < 0 then &
  f_db_error( connect2," in 2nd dbms connect ")
// Declare a cursor, C1, for the program schedule
// to fetch each weeks schedule on a week by week basis to
// build the actual data
is_no   = in_yr
is_num2 = in_mo
is_num3 = in_wk
DECLARE C1 CURSOR FOR
  SELECT pgmsch.sch_year,
         pgmsch.sch_month,
         pgmsch.sch_week,
         pgmsch.sch_time,
         pgmsch.sunday_series_cde,
         pgmsch.monday_series_cde,
         ...
         pgmsch.saturday_series_cde
    FROM pgmsch
         WHERE sch_year  = :is_no AND
               sch_month = :is_num2 AND
               sch_week  = :is_num3;
// check the return code to verify whether the declare was successful.
// If not successful, display error message.
        IF sqlca.sqlcode <> 0 THEN &
```

Figure 12.3 *Continued.*

```
            f_db_error( sqlca," in pgmsch CURSOR build ")
// build month date range
// setup for start of month
// use default of day 1 for start of month
// (e.g., NOVEMBER 1994 would be 1994-11-01)
// convert an integer to a string with the String PowerBuilder function
ls_year  = String(is_no)
ls_month = String(is_num2)
ls_day   =  String( 1 )
// the + sign concatenates variables
ls_strt_dte = ls_year + "-" + ls_month + "-" + ls_day
// the & continues a line
IF is_num2 = 1 or &
   is_num2 = 3 or &
...
   is_num2 = 12 &
     THEN li_end_day = 31
IF is_num2  = 2 and is_no  <> 1996 or 2000 &
     THEN li_end_day = 28
ELSE li_end_day = 29
END IF
ls_day      = string(li_end_day)
ls_end_dte = ls_year + "-" + ls_month + "-" + ls_day
// Delete any existing schedule for this month
// You might add code to determine if rows exist for this month
// a SQL statement like  select count(*) where,
// if rows exist, as a precaution you can send a warning response window
DELETE FROM  pgmtrk
WHERE ( track_datetime >= :ls_strt_dte ) AND
      ( track_datetime <= :ls_end_dte ) USING CONNECT2   ;
IF connect2.sqlcode <> 0 THEN &
  f_db_error( connect2," in pgmtrk DELETE ")
// this might take some time, so let user know by displaying
// the hour glass symbol
  SetPointer(HourGlass!)
// Open the cursor (embedded SQL)
OPEN C1;
IF sqlca.sqlcode <> 0 THEN &
  f_db_error( sqlca," pgmsch CURSOR OPEN ")
// Pass through the loop while the FETCH is successful
// FETCH result ends with sqlcode = 100
  li_sqlcode = 0
// Use a DO WHILE loop to walk through an entire schedule. Expand the
// seven-day denormalized schedule table into a normalized table for
// each slot
DO WHILE li_sqlcode = 0
  FETCH C1 INTO :istr_sch.sch_year,
        :istr_sch.sch_month,
        :istr_sch.sch_week,
        :istr_sch.sch_time,
        :istr_sch.sunday_series_cde,
        :istr_sch.monday_series_cde,
        ...
        :istr_sch.saturday_series_cde ;
IF sqlca.sqlcode <> 0  and sqlca.sqlcode <> 100 THEN &
  f_db_error( sqlca," pgmsch FETCH error ")
IF sqlca.sqlcode = 100 THEN &
  li_sqlcode = sqlca.sqlcode
// prime the index with the series to be run
  ls_series[1] = istr_sch.sunday_series_cde
  ls_series[2] = istr_sch.monday_series_cde
  ...
```

```
   ls_series[7] =  istr_sch.saturday_series_cde
// setup date and time
ls_year  = string(istr_sch.sch_year)
ls_month = string(istr_sch.sch_month)
ls_day   = string((istr_sch.sch_week * 1) + 1)
ls_day   = string((Integer(ls_day) - 1))
ls_dte   = ls_year + "-" + ls_month + "-" + ls_day
li_hour  = istr_sch.sch_time/100
ls_hour  = String(li_hour )
// the mod function divides the first number by the second with no remainder
ls_min = String(mod(istr_sch.sch_time,100))
ls_tim = ls_hour + ":" +  ls_min
IF SQLCA.sqlcode = 0 THEN
  li_counter = 1
// use a DO WHILE loop to build all of the rows in a month
  DO WHILE li_counter <= li_end_day
// build date time for sybase pgmtrk insert
  ls_day      = string((Integer(ls_day) + 1))
  ls_dte      = ls_year + "-" + ls_month + "-" + ls_day
  ls_datetime = ls_dte + " " + ls_tim
// here are some PowerBuilder built in functions
  ld_dte   = Date(ls_dte)
  li_dayct = DayNumber(ld_dte)
// PowerBuilder DayNumber function does not align w. our 7 occurs
// hence the code to realign and save the correct day in the slot
// 0 is saturday ; 1 is sunday
  IF li_dayct > 1 THEN li_dayct = li_dayct - 1
  IF li_dayct = 0 THEN li_dayct = 7
// build row in actual tracking table using a second database connection
// (required in Sybase while using an OPEN cursor )
  INSERT INTO pgmtrk
    ( track_datetime,
      series_cde,
      episode_cde,
      track_note_txt,
      channel_cde,
      last_upd_datetime )
      VALUES ( :ls_datetime,
               :ls_series[li_dayct],
               null,
               ...
               null ) USING CONNECT2;
  IF connect2.sqlcode <> 0 THEN &
    f_db_error( sqlca, "pgmtrk INSERT using connect2  ")
    li_counter = li_counter + 1
  // end of the inner INSERT loop used to add one month's data
    LOOP
  END IF
// end of the first or outer DO WHILE loop
LOOP
// close the cursor when complted
CLOSE  C1;

// disconnect the second database connection
// COMMIT USING CONNECT2; obviated - disconnect does implicit COMMIT
DISCONNECT USING CONNECT2  ;
// destroy the CONNECT2 transaction created above
DESTROY CONNECT2;
IF connect2.sqlcode <> 0 THEN &
  f_db_error( sqlca," in pgmtrk COMMIT/DISCONNECT")

// destroy the CONNECT2 transaction created earlier
DESTROY CONNECT2;
RETURN
```

The basic steps to creating a PowerScript "script" are as follows:

Step 1 Determine what processing your application component needs to accomplish in the event.

Step 2 Review the available PowerScript and internal functions that facilitate this response.

Step 3 Sketch out the statements/functions to be utilized; desk check the new script.

Step 4 Open the PowerScript painter from the object that the script is for.

Step 5 Insert (key or copy) the statement/function syntax for the script based upon your application requirement.

Step 6 Compile the script iteratively until syntactically correct; semantic check later (see chapter 13).

Step 7 Return to the previous painter.

Opening the PowerScript painter

You can open the PowerScript painter (see Figure 12.4) from the Application, Window, Menu, or User Object painter (that's because you can attach scripts only to ap-

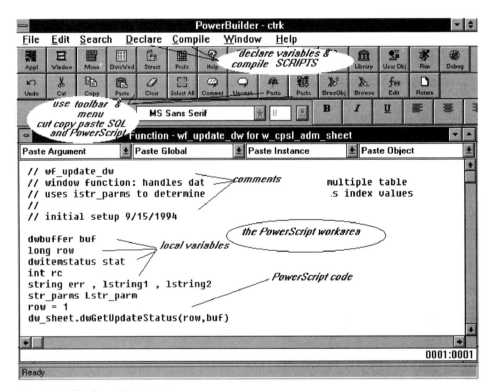

Figure 12.4 The PowerScript painter.

plication objects, windows and their controls, menus, and user objects). You also set up breakpoints to debug your application.

Go to the appropriate painter and select the object or control that you want to write a script for. Do one of the following:

- Click the Script icon in the PainterBar, which is discussed later.

- Use the pop-up menu, which is discussed later.

- Select Script from the Edit menu.

- Press Ctrl–S.

Using the Script icon is the most popular form. The icon is a sheetlike object with the right corner folded. The Script icon has two appearances:

- An empty icon indicates that the currently selected object or control has no scripts.

- An icon containing a text representation (i.e., horizontal lines) indicates that the current object or control has at least one script.

Using the pop-up menu also is a convenient way to quickly access the PowerScript painter.

You also can select an object or control and open the painter in one step. Click the right mouse button on the object or control to display the pop-up menu (see Figure 12.5), and choose Script from the menu. This will cause the PowerScript painter to open in a separate sheet.

When you open the PowerScript painter, the following information appears:

- The name of the current event displays in the painter's title bar. This is important to note as an object can have many events and you don't want to add the script to the wrong one, so always be conscious of which event is current. If multiple events can occur in the object that you are working with, the current event is the last event for which a script was displayed. If there is no script, the current event is an event that typically has a script.

- The name of the current object or control also is displayed in the title bar. For example, the title bar might say script - dragdrop for dw_1. The name of the current object or control is dw_1.

- A Select Event dropdown listbox, which lists events for the current object or control.

- A Paste Object dropdown listbox, which lists objects and controls whose names you can paste into the script.

- A Paste Global dropdown listbox, which lists global variables that you can use in the script.

- A Paste Instance dropdown listbox, which lists instance variables usable in the script.

- The script for the current event. If there is no script, the workspace is blank.

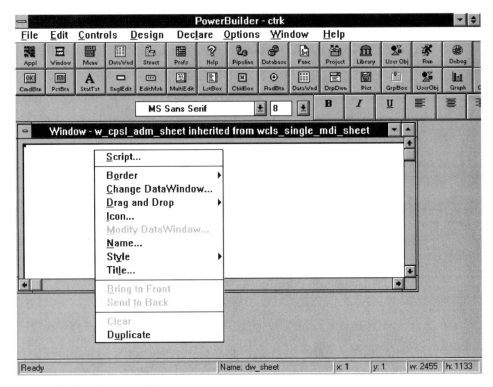

Figure 12.5 The right mouse button pop-up menu.

Changing events

If the object or control has multiple events, you can change the current event by selecting an event from the list in the Select Event dropdown listbox. (Refer back to
Figure 12.1.) The PowerScript painter indicates which events have scripts as follows:

- If the event has a script written for the object or control that you are working with,
  a script icon appears next to the event.

- If the event has a script in an ancestor object or control only, the script icon in the
  Select Event dropdown listbox is displayed in color.

- If the event has a script in an ancestor as well as in the object or control you are
  working with, the icon is displayed half in color.

Editing scripts

You write scripts in the PowerScript painter. It provides all of the features needed for
writing and modifying scripts. For example, you can cut, copy, and paste, search for,
and replace text. The painter also provides many features that make it easy to use
the PowerScript language, such as facilities for pasting information into scripts. Like
the other painters, the PowerScript painter has a PainterBar that provides a short-

cut for performing frequently used activities. There also is a menu item corresponding to each activity. If you have code in one script that you want to use in another script, you can copy it to the clipboard, then paste it in the second script. You can choose the items from the Search menu to find specific text in the script and optionally replace the text.

You can print the current script on the default printer by selecting Print from the File menu. To change the printer or its settings, select Printer Setup from the File menu before printing.

In addition to accessing Help through the Help menu and F1 key, you can use context-sensitive Help in the PowerScript painter to display Help for reserved words and built-in functions.

To use context-sensitive Help:

Step 1 Click to insert within a reserved word or built-in function.

Step 2 Press Shift–F1. The window displays information about the reserved word or function.

You can copy text from the Help window into the PowerScript painter. This is an easy way to get information about parameters required by the built-in functions. This will facilitate development because it will reduce the need to access the reference guide as well as save keying and syntax errors associated with the frequent use of a PowerBuilder function or PowerScript statement.

Scripts frequently reference objects and controls or the names of variables and built-in functions. To quickly access these entities, you can paste information directly into scripts.

If you paste information into your script by mistake, immediately click the Undo icon or select Undo from the Edit menu to delete the paste.

You also can use the Paste dropdown listboxes just above the painter workspace to paste the name of an object, control, or variable that is currently available. The listboxes are accessible using the mouse or the keyboard.

To use the Paste listboxes using the mouse:

Step 1 Move the cursor where you want to paste the object, control, or variable.

Step 2 Click the Paste dropdown listbox for the type of information that you want to paste. A list of available objects and controls or variables displays.

Step 3 Click the entity that you want to paste. PowerBuilder closes the list and pastes the selected object, control, or variable at the insertion point in the script.

The Paste Instance listbox displays all instance variables defined for the corresponding application object, window, menu, user object, or one of its ancestors. (To define instance variables, choose Instance Variables from the Declare menu.)

Shared variables are not displayed in the listbox. To access them, choose Shared Variables from the Declare menu or use the Object browser (see Figure 12.6). You can use the Object browser to paste the name of any attribute, data type, function, structure, variable, or object in the application.

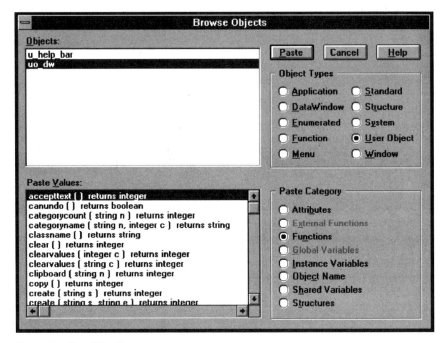

Figure 12.6 The Object browser.

You also can paste PowerScript statements.

You can paste a template for the following PowerScript statements:

- IF THEN
- DO LOOP
- FOR NEXT
- CHOOSE CASE

When you paste these statements into a script (see Figure 12.7), prototype values display in the syntax to indicate conditions or actions.

To paste a PowerScript statement into the script:

Step 1 Move the cursor to where you want to paste the function.

Step 2 Select the Paste Statement icon from the PainterBar, or choose Paste State-ment from the Edit menu. The Paste Statement window displays.

Step 3 Select the statement that you want to paste into the script, and click OK. The statement prototype displays at the insertion point in the script.

Step 4 Replace the prototype values with the conditions that you want to test and the actions that you want to take based on the test results.

You can paste an SQL statement into your script instead of typing the statement. To paste an SQL statement:

Step 1 Within the script, click the insertion point where you want to execute the SQL statement in the script.

Step 2 Do one of the following:

- Click the Paste SQL icon in the PainterBar
- Press Ctrl–Q
- Select `Paste SQL` from the Edit menu.

The SQL Statement Type window displays. (See Figure 12.8.)

Step 3 Select the type of statement that you want to insert by double-clicking the icon. The appropriate window displays so that you can paint the SQL statement.

Step 4 Paint the statement, then return to the PowerScript painter.

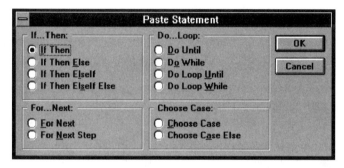

Figure 12.7 Pasting a PowerScript statement.

Figure 12.8 Pasting an SQL statement.

You can paste the name of any function into a script. To paste a function name into a script:

Step 1 Select `Paste Function` from the Edit menu. The Paste Function window displays.

Step 2 Choose the type of function that you want to paste: built-in, user-defined, or external.

Step 3 Double-click the function that you want.

PowerBuilder pastes the name of the function into the script and places the cursor within the parentheses for you to define any needed arguments. You can read the contents of an external text file into the PowerScript painter or save the contents of the script to a text file.

For example, you or your fellow developers might have code that is common across different scripts; you can keep that code in a text file, then read it into new scripts you write.

To read the contents of a file into the PowerScript painter:

Step 1 Place the insertion point where you want the file contents pasted.

Step 2 Select `Paste From` from the Edit menu. A dialog box appears.

Step 3 Choose the file that contains the code that you want. You can change the type of files displayed by changing the file specification in the File Name box. Power-Builder copies the file into the PowerScript painter at the current insertion point.

Before you can execute a script, you must compile it. To compile the script, choose `Script` from the Compile menu, or press Ctrl–L. If problems occur when a script is compiled, PowerBuilder displays messages in a window below the script.

To leave the PowerScript painter, click the last icon in the PainterBar (the Return icon). The Return icon pictures the painter that you came from. For example, if you are writing a script for a control in a window, a window is pictured in the Return icon. When you click the Return icon, PowerBuilder compiles the script.

If there are problems, PowerBuilder reports them. You usually have to make a choice to leave without saving the uncompilable script code. As development continues, you probably will comment out code that is syntactically problematic and maintain whatever status offers the development effort has achieved.

If there are no problems, the PowerScript painter closes, the script is saved temporarily in a buffer, and you return to the painter from which you opened the PowerScript painter.

When you save the object (such as the window containing a control you wrote a script for), PowerBuilder saves the script in the library with the object. To leave the PowerScript painter without saving your changes, select `Close` from the File menu. You are asked whether you want to save your changes. Click `No` to discard your changes. PowerBuilder returns you to the painter from which you opened the PowerScript painter.

If you are having difficulty because PowerBuilder functionality is problematic (e.g., the PBL is on a network file server that just came down), you can copy the script to a clipboard and save it in platform-based flat text file.

The PowerScript Language

This section will describe the conventions and techniques that PowerScript uses for identifiers, statement labels, statement continuation, and reserved words. These rules and conventions should seem familiar and similar to those of other established computer languages (e.g., BASIC).

Identifiers

Identifiers have the following traits:

- Must start with a letter
- Can have up to 40 characters, but no spaces
- Are case-insensitive (PART, Part, and part are identical)
- Can include any combination of letters, numbers, and the following special characters:

-	Dash	for COBOL programmers
_	Underscore	for SQL people
$	Dollar sign	for consultants
#	Number sign	for accountants
%	Percent sign	for those planning to use the SQL LIKE operator

Labels

You can include labels in scripts for use with GOTO statements. A label can be any valid identifier followed by a colon. You can enter it on a line by itself or at the start of the line preceding a statement.

ASCII characters

You can include special ASCII characters that format strings. For example, you might want to include a tab in a string to ensure proper spacing when a string is displayed or printed.

See Table 12.2 for instructions on how to specify special ASCII characters.

Reserved words

Parent, This, ParentWindow, and Super are PowerScript reserved words. When you use any of these to make a general reference to an object or control, the reference is correct even if the name of the object or control changes. This will reduce potential maintenance. You can use these pronouns in functions to cause an event in an object or control or to manipulate or change an object or control. You also can use these pronouns to obtain or change the setting of an attribute. Each of these pronouns has a specific meaning and use.

**TABLE 12.2 Specifying
Special ASCII Characters**

Special character	How to specify it
Newline	~n
Tab	~t
Vertical tab	~v
Carriage return	~r
Formfeed	~f
Backspace	~b
Double quote	~"
Single quote	~'
Tilde	~~

Parent. You can use the pronoun Parent in the following scripts (where you use Parent determines what it references):

- Scripts for a control in a window
- Scripts for a custom user object
- Scripts for a MenuItem

When you use Parent in a script for a control (such as a CommandButton), Parent refers to the window that contains the control. When you use Parent in a script for a control in a custom user object, Parent refers to the user object.

When you use Parent in the script for a MenuItem, Parent refers to the MenuItem on the level above the MenuItem the script is for.

This. The pronoun This refers to the window, user object, MenuItem, application object, or control itself. In the script for an object or control, you can refer to the attributes of the object or control without qualification. However, it is good programming practice to include This to make the script clear and easier to maintain.

ParentWindow. The pronoun ParentWindow refers to the window that a menu is associated with at execution time. ParentWindow can be used only in scripts for MenuItems.

Super. When you write a script for a descendant object or control, you can call scripts written for any ancestor. You can directly name the ancestor in the call, or you can use the reserved word Super to reference the immediate ancestor (parent). When you print out a script to review, you will see a statement embedded in the first line by PowerBuilder to execute the super (ancestor) script.

Continuation character

The PowerScript continuation character is the ampersand. To continue a statement to another line, insert an ampersand wherever there is white space at the end of a line, then start the new line. The ampersand must be the last nonwhite character on the line (or the compiler will consider it part of the statement).

White space

Blanks, tabs, formfeeds, and comments are forms of white space. The compiler ignores them unless they are part of a string literal (enclosed in single or double quotation marks).

Data types

The standard data types are the familiar data types that are used in many programming languages, including char, integer, decimal, long, and string. In PowerScript, you use these data types when you declare variables or arrays.

Table 12.3 lists all standard PowerScript data types.

You use literals to assign values to variables of the standard data types. PowerScript supports the following types of literals: date, decimal, integer, real, string, and time. You use integer literals to assign values to data types that can contain only whole numbers and real literals to assign values to the data types real and double.

Most of the character-based data in your application—such as names, addresses, and so on—will be defined as strings. PowerScript provides many functions that you can use to manipulate strings, such as a function to convert characters in a string to

TABLE 12.3 The Standard PowerScript Data Types

Data type	Description
Blob	Binary large object. Used to store an unbounded amount of data (for example, an image).
Boolean	Contains TRUE or FALSE.
Char or character	A single ASCII character.
Date	The date, including the full year (1000 to 3000), the month (01 to 12), and the day (01 to 31).
DateTime	The date and time in a single data type.
Decimal or Dec	Signed decimal numbers with up to 18 digits.
Double	A signed floating-point number with 15 digits of precision and a range from 2.2^{-308} to 1.7^{+308}.
Integer or Int	16-bit signed integers, from –32,768 to +32,767.
Long	32-bit signed integers, from –2,147,483,648 to +2,147,483,647.
Real	A signed floating-point number with six digits of precision and a range from 1.17^{-38} to 3.4^{+38}.
String	Any ASCII characters with variable length (0 to 60,000).
Time	Hour (00 to 23), minute (00 to 59), second (00 to 59), and fraction of second (up to six digits).
UnsignedInteger, UnsignedInt or UInt	16-bit unsigned integers, from 0 to 65,535.
UnsignedLong or ULong	32-bit unsigned integers, from 0 to 4,294,967,295.

uppercase and functions to remove leading and trailing blanks. When working with a string, you need only use the Help menu's `Search` option and enter the string `sharing functions` to quickly get a context sensitive list of function names and description of their action. Click on the green function name to display detail syntax and examples.

Additionally, you can use the `Browse Object` option under the Script painter's Edit menu item.

Declarations

As with most languages except perhaps Fortran, before you use a variable or array in a script, you must declare it (give it a type and a name). Here it is important that you review the standards and guidelines of the organization before declaring the variables. Check the naming conventions for naming each type of variable. Global strings might begin with gs_. Check to see if the application already has defined global variables. There might be existing structures that you will update. The change that you make might affect other application components. What you need already might exist or be derivable from existing information in an existing variable. For example, before you can use an integer variable, you must identify it as an integer and assign it a name:

```
Integer I, J, K
```

PowerScript recognizes four types of variables:

- Global variables, which are accessible anywhere in an application
- Instance variables, which are associated with one instance of an object
- Shared variables, which are associated with a type of object
- Local variables, which are accessible only in one script

Global variables. You use global variables when you have data that needs to be available anywhere. Global variables can be used without qualification in any script in an application.

For example, if you have defined a global integer variable named GI_Sequence, you can reference the variable directly in any script, such as:

```
GI_Sequence = GI_Sequence + 1
```

To declare global variables, select `Global Variables` from the Declare menu in the Application Window, User Object, Menu, or PowerScript painter. (See Figure 12.9.)

Instance variables. You use instance variables when you have variables that need to be accessible in more than one script within an object. This is a good space saving technique. For example, several scripts for a window might reference a Cusip number. You can declare in_CusipNum as an instance variable for that window; all scripts in that window have access to that variable. In effect, instance variables are attributes of the object. As previously mentioned, instance variables stored in the form of

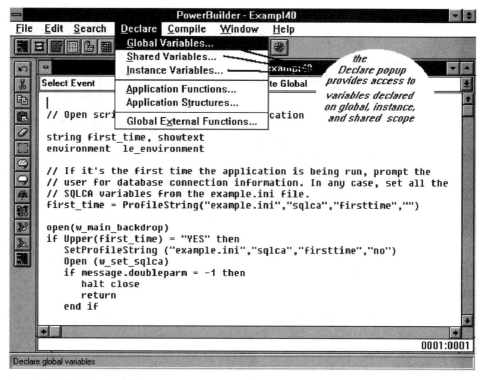

Figure 12.9 Declaring variables.

a structure also provide a good technique for passing information between application objects without resorting to global variables, which are hard to maintain.

Instance variables can be application-level, window-level, user-object-level, or menu-level variables:

Application-level variables are declared within the application object. They are always available in any scripts for the application object. In addition, you can choose to make access to them available throughout the application.

Window-level variables are declared within a window. They are always available in any scripts for the window in which they are declared and the controls in that window. In addition, you can choose to make access to them available throughout the application (i.e., public, private, protected). More on this later.

User-object-level variables are declared within a user object. They are always available in any scripts for the user object in which they are declared and the controls in that user object. Likewise, you can choose the access type throughout the application.

Menu-level variables are declared within a menu. They are always available in any scripts for the menu in which they are declared and its MenuItems. In addition, you can choose to make access to them available throughout the application.

Declaring instance variables. To declare instance variables, select `Instance Variables` from the Declare menu in the Window, User Object, Menu, or PowerScript painter. (Refer back to Figure 12.9.)

Specifying access to instance variables. When you declare an instance variable, you also can specify the access level for the variable (i.e., you can specify which scripts have access to the instance variable). See Table 12.4.

To specify an access level when you declare an instance variable, include the access level in the declaration. If you don't specify an access level, the variable is defined as Public.

When you define an instance variable for a window, menu, or application object, the instance variable is initialized when the object is opened. Its initial value is the default value for its data type or the value specified in the variable declarations.

When you close the object, the instance variable ceases to exist. If you open the object again, the instance variable is initialized again. If you need a variable that continues to exist after the object is closed, use a shared variable or save the instance variables within the PowerBuilder message object.

When using multiple instances of windows (e.g., the order-entry window is open more than once), each window has its own instance variables. You can refer to instance variables in scripts if there is an instance of the object open in the application. Depending on the situation, you might need to qualify the name of the instance variable with the name of the object defining it.

Shared variables. Shared variables, like instance variables, can be application-level, window-level, user-object level, or menu-level variables. Shared variables are associated with the object definition, rather than an instance of the object. Therefore, all instances of the object type share the same block of storage.

Shared variables retain their value when an object is closed and then opened again.

When you use a shared variable in the script for a window or menu, the variable is initialized when the first instance of the window is opened. When you close the window, the shared variable continues to exist until you exit the application. If you open the window again without exiting the application, the shared variable will have the value it had when you closed the window.

Because shared variables are shared among all instances of the window and use the same block of storage, changing a variable in any instance of the window changes it for all instances.

Local variables. Use local variables when you need a temporary variable to hold some value. Local variables are declared in a script and can be used only in that script.

TABLE 12.4 Specifying the Access Level for a Variable

Access	You can reference the instance variable in:
Public	Any script in the application.
Private	Scripts for events in the object for which the variable is declared. You cannot reference the variable in descendants of the object.
Protected	Scripts for the object for which the variable is declared and its descendants.

Search order for PowerScript variables.   PowerBuilder has a search order for finding a variable. This is a good reason for using naming conventions to avoid duplicate names and the resulting inconsistent results.

When PowerBuilder executes a script and finds an unqualified reference to a variable, it looks for the variable in the following order:

- A local variable
- A shared variable
- A global variable
- An instance variable

   As soon as PowerBuilder finds a variable with the specified name, it uses the variable's value. Here again, the proper use of naming conventions can avoid confusion and conflict in a script.

Declaring variables.   Typically, in the development cycle, you will be using a DBMS. Be sure you understand the meaning of each of the DBMS data types that you will access. Find the equivalent PowerBuilder data type. For example, a Sybase INTEGER is a PowerBuilder LONG. A PowerBuilder INTEGER is a Sybase SMALLINT. There are two sets of syntax for declaring variables: a standard syntax for all variable data types except blob and decimal, and a syntax for blob and decimal variables.

   Standard declarations.   To declare any variable except a blob or decimal, enter the data type followed by one or more spaces and the variable name with a standard (if you decide to use it) prefix:

```
int gi_count            // Declares count as a global integer
long sl_comment_length  // Declares comment-length as a shared long
string ls_first-name    // Declares first-name as a local string
```

You can declare multiple variables of the same data type on one line. To declare additional variables of the same type on the same line, enter a comma and the next variable name:

```
int li_a,li_b, li_c   // Declares a, b, and c as local integers
```

   Blob declarations.   To declare a blob variable, enter `Blob` followed by the length of the blob (in bytes) enclosed in curly braces and the variable name. The length is optional, and braces are required only if you specify the length. If you enter the length and exceed the declared length in a script, PowerBuilder will truncate the blob. If you do not enter the length in the declaration, the blob has an initial length of 0 and PowerBuilder will define its size by use at execution time.

   Decimal declarations.   To declare a decimal variable, enter `Dec` or `Decimal` followed by the number of digits after the decimal point (the precision) enclosed in curly braces and the variable name. The braces are required only if you enter the precision. If you do not enter the precision in the declaration, the variable takes the precision assigned to it in the script.

Initial values. When you declare a variable, you can assign an initial value to the variable or accept the default initial value. To assign a value to a variable when you declare it, place an equal sign and a literal appropriate for that variable data type after the variable:

```
int li_a=5, li_b=10
string ls_name ="Michael S. Bambara"
date ld_StartDate = 1982-05-28
```

Using default values. If you do not assign a value to a variable when you declare it, PowerBuilder sets the variable to the default value for its data type. Table 12.5 lists the default values for variable data types.

Declaring arrays. Anyone who has ever used a programming language is familiar with the array. An array is an indexed collection of elements of a single data type. An array can be single- or multidimensional. Single-dimensional arrays can have a fixed or variable size, and single-dimensional arrays without a range can have as many as 65,534 elements. Each dimension of a multidimensional array can have 65,534 (–32,767 to +32,767) elements.

To declare an array, enclose the sizes of the array in square brackets after the variable name. Here is an example of a single-dimensional array of three integers named Ii_array:

```
int Ii_array[3]  // Declares an array of 3 integers
```

To refer to individual array elements, use square brackets and the element number, such as Ii_array[1], Ii_array[2], and Ii_array[3].

Array defaults. PowerBuilder initializes each element of an array to the same default value as its underlying data type. For example, in the integer array are all initialized to zero.

To override the default values, initialize the elements of the array when you declare the array by specifying a comma-separated list of values enclosed in braces.

TABLE 12.5 Arithmetic Operators

Variable data type	Default value
Blob	A blob of 0 length; an empty blob
Char	ASCII value 0
Boolean	FALSE
Date	1900-01-01 (January 1, 1900)
DateTime	1900-01-01 00:00:00
Numeric, integer, long	0 (zero)
Decimal, real, double	0 (zero)
UnsignedInteger, UnsignedLong	0 (zero)
String	Empty string ("")
Time	00:00:00 (midnight)

Variable-size arrays. A variable-size array variable consists of a variable name followed by square brackets but no number. PowerBuilder defines it by use at execution time (subject only to memory constraints). Only one-dimensional arrays can be variable-size arrays. It is a performance point to initialize the average number of array elements at the start of the script.

For example:

```
int li_ld_Price[ ]
// Declares a variable-size array of any quantity of integers
ld_Price[100]=2000
// This will allocate 100 slots for the ld_Price array, avoiding
// memory allocation for each array element. 100 should be the
// average number of array slots the script used in a
// normal execution
```

When the previous statements first execute, they allocate memory as follows. The statement `ld_Price[100]=2000` will allocate memory for 100 integers ld_Price[1] to ld_Price[100], then assign 0 (the default for numbers) to ld_Price[1] through ld_Price[99] and assign 2000 to ld_Price[100].

Multidimensional arrays. A fixed-size array can have more than one dimension. To specify additional dimensions, use a comma-separated list. The amount of memory in your system is the only limit to the number of dimensions for an array. You cannot initialize multidimensional arrays.

Decimal arrays. To declare a decimal array, enter `Dec` or `Decimal`, followed by the number of digits after the decimal point (the precision) enclosed in curly braces, the array name, and the dimensions of the array enclosed in square brackets.

If you do not enter the precision in the declaration, the variable takes the precision assigned to it in the script.

The following example declares an array of 10 decimal numbers each with two digits to the right of the decimal:

```
dec{2} ld_Cost[10]
```

Operators and expressions

Operators perform arithmetic calculations; compare numbers, text, and Boolean values; execute logical operations on Boolean values; and manipulate text strings. This section describes the operators supported in PowerScript and shows how you can manipulate strings in expressions.

PowerScript supports the following types of operators:

- Arithmetic
- Relational
- Logical
- Arithmetic

Arithmetic operators. Table 12.6 lists the arithmetic operators in descending order of precedence.

TABLE 12.6 Relational Operators

Operator	Meaning	Example
+	Addition	`li_Count=li_SubCount1+li_Tax`
—	Subtraction	`Ld_Price=Ld_Price - ld_Discount`
*	Multiplication	`ld_Total=ld_Quantity*Ld_Price`
/	Division	`ld_Factor=ld_Discount/Ld_Price`
^	Exponentiation	`ld_grade=ld_grade^2.5`

TABLE 12.7 Logical Operators

Operator	Meaning	Example
=	Equals	`if Ld_grade=100 then Ld_allowance_rate=.05`
>	Greater than	`if Ld_grade>100 then Ld_allowance_rate=.05`
<	Less than	`if Ld_grade<100 then Ld_allowance_rate=.05`
>=	Greater than or equal	`if Ld_grade>=100 then Ld_allowance_rate=.05`
<=	Less than or equal	`if Ld_grade<=100 then Ld_allowance_rate=.05`
<>	Not equal	`if Ld_grade<>100 then Ld_allowance_rate=.05`

TABLE 12.8 The Operators in Descending Order of Precedence

Operator	Meaning	Example
NOT	Logical negation	`if NOT Ld_grade=100 then Ld_allowance_rate=.05`
AND	Logical and	`if Tax>3 AND Ship<5 then Ld_Rate=.05`
OR	Logical or	`if Tax>3 OR Ship<5 then Ld_Rate=.05`

Relational operators. PowerBuilder uses relational operators in relational expressions to evaluate two or more operands. The result is always TRUE or FALSE. Table 12.7 lists the relational operators in descending order of precedence.

Logical operators. PowerBuilder uses logical operators to form Boolean expressions. The result of evaluating a Boolean expression is always TRUE or FALSE. Table 12.8 lists the logical operators in descending order of precedence.

Operator precedence. To ensure predictable results, all operators in a PowerBuilder expression are evaluated in a specific order of precedence. You remember this from grammar school. It was referred to as the *order of operations*. When the operators have the same precedence, PowerBuilder evaluates them left to right. Table 12.9 lists the operators in descending order of precedence.

String concatenation. To concatenate strings, use the plus sign operator between the strings:

TABLE 12.9 The CALL Statement Parameters

Operator	Purpose
( )	Grouping
+, —	Unary plus and unary minus
^	Exponentiation
*, /	Multiplication and division
+, —	Addition and subtraction; string concatenation
=, >, <, <=, >=, <>	Relational operators
NOT	Negation
AND	Logical and
OR	Logical or

```
string ls_Lname, ls_Fname, ls_FullName
// Set up ls_FullName to contain last name and first name,
// separated by a comma.
ls_FullName = ls_Lname + ',' + ls_Fname
```

String comparison. When PowerBuilder compares strings, the comparison is case-sensitive. Trailing blanks are significant. For example:

```
ls_Friend1="Vanessa"
ls_Friend2="VANESSA"
if ls_Friend1=ls_Friend2 ...              // Will return FALSE
if UPPER(ls_Friend1)=UPPER(ls_Friend2)... // Will return TRUE
```

To compare strings regardless of case, use the UPPER or LOWER function.

Statements

The good news is that there are only eight PowerScript statements (not counting the GO TO, CREATE, and DESTROY). This small set of statements, coupled with the fact that you can paste any of them using the editor, greatly facilitates the coding of scripts. As simple as PowerScript is, the good developer still needs to plan what each script is intended to do and to use the proper combination of script statements coupled with PowerBuilder and user defined functions. For example, to avoid coding GOTOs, code user-defined global or object-based functions to execute a common set of script code over and over again.

There are no new language constructs in PowerBuilder. The statements are all borrowed from existing programming languages. You can make use of the following statements in a script:

- CALL
- CHOOSE CASE
- CONTINUE
- DO...LOOP

- EXIT
- FOR...NEXT
- HALT and RETURN
- IF...THEN

CALL. CALL calls an ancestor script from a script for a descendant object. The syntax is:

```
CALL ancestorobject {controlname}::event
```

The CALL statement parameters are listed in Table 12.10.

For example, the following statement calls a script for an event in an ancestor window:

```
CALL w_emp::Open
```

CHOOSE CASE. Use the CHOOSE CASE control structure to direct program execution based on the value of a test expression (usually a variable). It is not unlike the computed GOTO used in some older languages (for example, FORTRAN). The syntax is:

```
CHOOSE CASE testexpression
CASE expressionlist
        statementblock
{CASE expressionlist
        statementblock
............
CASE expressionlist
        statementblock}
{CASE ELSE
        statementblock}
END CHOOSE
```

The CHOOSE CASE statement parameters are listed in Table 12.11.

At least one CASE clause is required. You must end a CHOOSE CASE control structure with END CHOOSE.

If test expression at the beginning of the CHOOSE CASE statement matches a value in *expressionlist* for a CASE clause, the statements immediately following the CASE clause are executed. Control then passes to the first statement after the END CHOOSE clause.

If multiple CASE expressions exist, then *testexpression* is compared to each *expressionlist* until a match is found or the CASE ELSE or END CHOOSE is encountered.

TABLE 12.10 The CHOOSE CASE Statement Parameters

Parameter	Description
ancestorobject	An ancestor of the descendant object
controlname	The name of a control in an ancestor window or custom user object
event	An event in the ancestor object

TABLE 12.11 The FOR...NEXT Statement Parameters

Parameter	Description
testexpression	The expression on which you want to base the execution of the script.
expressionlist	One of the following expressions: a single value, a list of values separated by commas, a TO clause (for example, 1 TO 30), IS followed by a relational-operator and comparison value (for example, IS>5). Any combination of the above with an implied OR between expressions (for example, 1, 3, 5, 7, 9, 27 TO 33, IS >42)
statementblock	The block of statements you want PowerBuilder to execute if the test-expression matches the value in expressionlist.

If there is a CASE ELSE clause and the test value does not match any of the expressions, the `statementblock` in the CASE ELSE clause is executed. If no CASE ELSE clause exists and a match is not found, the first statement after the END CHOOSE clause is executed.

The following is an example in which, based upon which table we are accessing, we want to execute a different data retrieve based upon the value of an array instance structure string argument:

```
CHOOSE CASE istr_parms.string_arg[3]
  CASE "tbseries"
   if dw_sheet.retrieve(is_id) < 0 then
     message.returnvalue = 1
    return
    end if
  CASE "tbepisod"
    if dw_sheet.retrieve(is_id,is_id2) < 0 then
    message.returnvalue = 1
    return
    end if
  ....
CASE ELSE
if dw_sheet.retrieve(is_id) < 0 then
    message.returnvalue = 1
    return
    end if
END CHOOSE
```

CONTINUE. Use the CONTINUE statement in a DO...LOOP or a FOR...NEXT control structure. CONTINUE takes no parameters.

In a DO...LOOP structure. When PowerBuilder encounters a CONTINUE statement in a DO...LOOP, control passes to the next LOOP statement. The statements between the CONTINUE statement and the LOOP statement are skipped in the current iteration of DO...LOOP. In a nested DO...LOOP structure, a CONTINUE statement bypasses statements in the current DO...LOOP structure.

In a FOR...NEXT structure. When PowerBuilder encounters a CONTINUE statement in a FOR...NEXT control structure, control passes to the following NEXT statement; the statements between the CONTINUE statement and the NEXT statement are skipped in the current iteration of FOR...NEXT.

DO...LOOP. Many times, when developing, you want to repeat a bunch of code with a changing value (e.g., fetching a cursor that contains all of the television series to be scheduled in a particular month). The DO...LOOP control structure is a general-purpose iteration statement. Use DO...LOOP to execute a block of statements while or until a condition is true. DO...LOOP has four formats.

In all four formats of the DO...LOOP control structure, DO marks the beginning of the statement block that you want to repeat. The LOOP statement marks the end.

Use DO WHILE or DO UNTIL when you want to execute a block of statements only if a condition is TRUE (for WHILE) or FALSE (for UNTIL). DO WHILE and DO UNTIL test the condition before executing the block of statements.

Use LOOP WHILE or LOOP UNTIL when you want to execute a block of statements at least once. LOOP WHILE and LOOP UNTIL test the condition after the block of statements has been executed.

See Figure 12.3 for an example of a script that uses embedded SQL within a DO WHILE...LOOP to fetch all of the rows in a cursor that is declared to bring back all the rows for a week's worth of television programming and INSERT rows into another table, one for each day of the week. The example also contains a FOR...NEXT.

EXIT. Use the EXIT statement in a DO...LOOP or a FOR..NEXT control structure to pass control out of the current loop. EXIT takes no parameters. An EXIT statement in a DO...LOOP control structure causes control to pass to the statement following the LOOP statement. In a nested DO...LOOP structure, an EXIT statement passes control out of the current DO...LOOP structure.

FOR...NEXT. The FOR...NEXT control structure is a numerical iteration. Use FOR...NEXT to execute one or more statements a specified number of times. The syntax is:

```
FOR variablename = start TO end {STEP increment}
        statementblock
NEXT
```

The FOR...NEXT statement parameters are described in Table 12.12.

For a positive increment, *end* must be greater than *start*. For a negative increment, *end* must be less than *start*. When *increment* is positive and *start* is

TABLE 12.12 The IF...NEXT Single-Line Format Parameters

Parameter	Description
variablename	The name of the iteration counter variable. It can be any numerical type (integer, double, real, long, or decimal), but integers provide the fastest performance.
start	Starting value of *variablename*.
end	Ending value of *variablename*.
increment	(Optional) The increment value or variable. *increment* must be the same data type as *variablename*. If you enter an increment, STEP is required. +1 is the default increment.
statementblock	The block of statements you want to repeat.

greater than *end*, *statementblock* does not execute. When *increment* is negative and *start* is less than *end*, *statementblock* does not execute.

You can nest FOR...NEXT statements. You must have a NEXT for each FOR.

HALT. Use the HALT statement without any associated keywords to terminate the application immediately.

When PowerBuilder encounters HALT without the keyword CLOSE, it immediately terminates the application. When PowerBuilder encounters HALT with the keyword CLOSE, it immediately executes the script for the Close event for the application, then terminates the application. If there is no script for the Close event at the application level, PowerBuilder immediately terminates the application. HALT obviously should be used with great care.

The following statement executes the script for the Close event for the application before it terminates the application if the user enters a password in the sle_password that does not match the value stored in the string CorrectPassword:

```
if sle_password.Text <> CorrectPassword &
then HALT CLOSE
//          BEGINNING of EXAMPLE
///////////////////////////////////////////////////////////////
//    User Event: UE_FILENEW
//    Description: This user event will create 48 new rows/records.
///////////////////////////////////////////////////////////////
int ln_timeslots = 48 , ln_yr = 1994, ln_mo = 1, ln_wk = 0 , &
    ln_min = 30 , ln_hr = 05 , ln_ct, ln_time
boolean lb_stat
integer li_response
long ll_cur_row
ib_data_ok = false
if dw_sheet.accepttext() = -1 then return
long ll_ct
ln_ct = RowCount( dw_sheet )
If ln_ct <> 0 Then Return
is_id = ""
// insert 48 rows
FOR ll_ct = 1 TO ln_timeslots
  InsertRow(dw_sheet,ll_ct)
  ll_cur_row = RowCount( dw_sheet )
  dw_sheet.SetItem(ll_cur_row, "sch_year",ln_yr)
  dw_sheet.SetItem(ll_cur_row, "sch_month",ln_mo)
  dw_sheet.SetItem(ll_cur_row, "sch_week",ln_wk)
  ln_ct = ll_ct
  IF Mod ( ln_ct , 2 ) = 1 THEN
    ln_min = 0
    ln_hr = ln_hr + 1
    ln_time = ((ln_hr * 100) + ln_min)
    dw_sheet.SetItem(ll_cur_row  ,"sch_time",ln_time)
  ELSE
    ln_min = 30
    ln_time = ((ln_hr * 100) + ln_min)
    dw_sheet.SetItem(ll_cur_row  ,"sch_time",ln_time)
  END IF
  IF ln_hr = 23 AND ln_min = 30 THEN ln_hr = -1
NEXT
ll_cur_row = RowCount( dw_sheet )
iw_frame.SetMicroHelp( " Week of Planned Scheduling Inserted.")
ll_cur_row = 1
il_current_row = ll_cur_row
SetRow( dw_sheet, 1 )
```

```
// set the active focus to this data window sheet control
SetFocus(dw_sheet)
dw_sheet.enabled = True
/////////////////////////////////////////// end of example
```

RETURN. Use the RETURN statement to stop the execution of a script or function immediately. In a script, just code RETURN. In a function, code RETURN `expression` where `expression` is any value (or expression) that you want the function to return. The return value must be the same data type specified as the return type in the function.

When PowerBuilder encounters RETURN in a script, it terminates execution of that script immediately and waits for the next user action. When PowerBuilder encounters RETURN in a function, RETURN transfers (returns) control to the point at which the function was called.

IF...THEN. This is the classic Aristotelian syllogism that is the most common programming construct in existence. Use the IF...THEN control structure to cause the script to perform a specified action if a stated condition is true. IF...THEN has a single-line format and a multiple-line format.

Using the single-line format. The syntax for the IF...THEN single-line format is:

```
IF condition THEN action1 {ELSE action2}
```

The IF...THEN single-line statement parameters are described in Table 12.13.

Using the multiple-line format. The syntax for the IF...THEN multiple-line format is:

```
IF condition1 THEN
        action1
{ELSEIF condition2 THEN
        action2}
{ELSE
        action3}
END IF
```

The IF...THEN multiple-line statement parameters are described in Table 12.14. You must end a multiline IF..THEN control structure with END IF (i.e., two words).

Built-in PowerScript functions

Much of the power of the PowerScript language resides in the built-in PowerScript functions that you can use in expressions and assignment statements. To call a func-

TABLE 12.13 The IF...NEXT Multiple-Line Format Parameters

Parameter	Description
condition	The condition you want to test.
action1	The action you want performed if the condition is TRUE. The action must be a single statement on the same line as the rest of the IF statement.
action2	(Optional) The action you want performed if the condition is FALSE. The action must be a single statement on the same line as the rest of the IF statement.

TABLE 12.14 The Built-In PowerScript Functions

Parameter	Description
condition1	The first condition you want to test.
action1	The action you want performed if condition1 is TRUE. The action can be a statement or multiple statements that are separated by semicolons or placed on separate lines. At least one action is required.
condition2	(Optional) The condition you want to test if condition1 is FALSE. You can have multiple ELSEIF...THEN statements in an IF...THEN control structure.
action2	The action you want performed if condition2 is TRUE. The action can be a statement or multiple statements that are separated by semicolons or placed on separate lines.
action3	(Optional) The action you want performed if none of the preceding conditions is true. The action can be a statement or multiple statements that are separated by semicolons or placed on separate lines.

tion, you specify the function name, followed by an open parenthesis, zero or more arguments, and a close parenthesis:

```
function({argument1,argument2,...})
```

Most PowerScript functions require a specific number of arguments. However, some take optional arguments. The arguments can be literals, variables, other functions, or expressions. Function names are not case sensitive. The PowerBuilder documentation shows built-in functions with uppercase letters for the first character of each word in the function name, such as MessageBox.

The built-in PowerScript functions include object functions, which act on an instance of a particular object, and system functions, whose effects are independent of any object.

You can list all the functions that apply to a particular object in the Object browser. See Figure 12.10 for the Object browse of the functions that can be executed within a datawindow control.

Open the PowerScript painter and click the Browse icon, or select the `Browse Object` option from the Edit menu in the menu bar. Click the function's radio but-

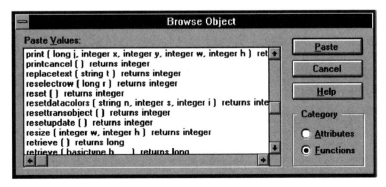

Figure 12.10 Browse Object for data window control.

ton. Likewise, open the Library painter, and select the `Browse Object` option from the Utilities menu.

Closing Remarks

The PowerScript language should be fairly easy for an experienced developer to learn. We will use PowerScript examples in most sections within this book. This chapter is a mere introduction. It will take a fair amount of development experience with PowerBuilder to become familiar with the total extent of its built-in functionality. However, it is simple enough for any developer to just dive in as soon as possible and start coding away.

13

Testing and Verifying Applications

Testing and verifying (i.e., debugging) an application is as much a part of the development cycle as any other. The debugging phase of the application also should be planned. Should we use a separate group to test the application? Should we use a tool that records user keystrokes and allows you to replay it for regression and performance testing? The answers to these questions depend upon your environment and the size of the application. However, in essence, to verify an application, you must have a plan that can test each component of an application in the environment in which it will be used. We will discuss techniques for debugging using Power-Builder, its painters, its debugger, and third-party tools that can be used to augment the testing process.

Overview

After you build all or part of an application and save its objects, you can begin to execute and test the application components. This is helpful at various junctures in the application development cycle to establish the credibility of the code developed thus far. For example, early in development after the basic navigation and framework is set up, you can try it out, then feel confident to develop the DataWindows and customized scripting that usually follows in a typical development cycle. More often than not, frequent use of a debugging tool happens later in the development cycle. In either event, PowerBuilder provides an easy to use debugging tool with well-conceived features.

There also are other not-so-obvious debugging techniques. Besides the debugging tool, there are other utilities that can identify the faulty application part. For example, the suspected object can be exported from within the Library painter. The exported object can be reviewed and even edited. In any event, the Debugging painter is a primary, but not the sole, debugging tool. More on this later. The PowerBuilder development environment provides two ways to run an application: in debug mode and in regular mode.

In debug mode, you can insert stops (breakpoints) in scripts and functions, single-step through code, and display the contents of variables to locate logic errors and mistakes that will result in errors during execution. This is similar to the MVS/CICS vendor debugging tool Intertest or the Microfocus COBOL tool known as the Animator. If you are familiar with tools like these, then you will become proficient at using the debugger in no time at all. Everyone else will take a little longer. One thing is certain: while developing your first serious application (i.e., business application) with a time deadline, you will become proficient at the debugger.

In regular mode, the application responds to user interaction and runs until the user stops it or until an execution-time error occurs. Regular mode creates the appearance and result of the actual application execution. An executable (EXE) would be physically different. It would consist of an EXE, some PBDs, and perhaps a PBR.

The Basics of Testing an Application

It is invariable that, during the development, you will spend some time debugging unforeseen responses by your application as its executes. Perhaps a variable is not being assigned the value that you expect or a script doesn't seem to do what you want it to. In these situations, you can closely examine the execution of particular scripts in your application by running it in debug mode.

Running the application in debug mode

You use debug mode to set stops (breakpoints). When you run your application in debug mode, PowerBuilder stops execution just before it hits a line containing a stop. You then can look at (and change) the values of variables. A good strategy is to review the scripts that you are verifying or suspect to have problems and choose breakpoints that are revealing. For example, data is not being written to a window control properly. You suspect the retrieve is not executing properly. You can set breakpoints before and after the retrieve to examine and even change the retrieval arguments.

Setting up to perform basic testing

The first phase of testing application components that you are developing usually is done by the developer working on those components for which the developer is responsible. The developers should periodically take a timeout and test and verify the components that they have developed. Here we are discussing basic first-level unit tests. More involved systems testing, using some regression capable tool (e.g., SQA Team Test), will be discussed later.

To debug (i.e., unit test and verify an application), you would:

Step 1 Determine which parts of the application you want to test or verify (i.e., event scripts or object function scripts).

Step 2 Determine if you need to add code to illustrate the content of variables. For example, you might want to determine the actual SQL being issued by PowerBuilder. You could use GetSQLPreview into a local variable and set a breakpoint there.

Step 3 Open the Debug window.

Step 4 Set breakpoints at places in the application that you want to verify or debug.

Step 5 Run the application in debug mode. Go to the Run menu, and choose the `Start` option. When execution is suspended at a stop (breakpoint), look at the values of variables or change values.

Step 6 Step through the code line by line if you want.

Step 7 As needed, add, modify, or delete stops (breakpoints) in the middle of running your application.

Step 8 When you uncover the problem, switch back to the Library painter and double-check the suspected problem object.

These steps are all described later in this chapter.

The Debug Painter

To run an application other than the current application, change the application before you open the Debug window. PowerBuilder will read you PB.INI and restore the existing breakpoints.

To begin debugging your application:

Step 1 Open the Debug painter by clicking the Debug icon (the icon with the bug in the circle with the bar) in the PowerBar, double-clicking the icon in the PowerPanel, or selecting `Debug` from the File menu. You can do this from almost anywhere in PowerBuilder.

Step 2 If you are in a painter with unsaved work, you are asked whether you want to save the object. If you are in a script you must close it first. If necessary, save your work. Typically you have just added code to fix the problem.

Step 3 After you respond, the PowerBuilder Debug window appears.

Step 4 If no stops (breakpoints) currently are defined, the Select Script window displays (see Figure 13.1.)

Step 5 If one or more stops (breakpoints) are defined, the Edit Stops window displays.

Adding stops or breakpoints

To add a breakpoint, you first use the Select Script window to specify the script that contains the line that you want to stop execution at. Here again, a little planning goes a long way. Ill-considered choices will slow down the process. Concentrate on what you think is wrong. Review the path of scripts that are executed to gain a result. Know the order in which event scripts will be executed. Know where each object function script is executed. Then you will quickly and efficiently select scripts for debugging the code.

Sometimes you need to debug something that is happening in an ancestor script. If so, then edit the script, select it all, bring it down to the descendant, and override the ancestor.

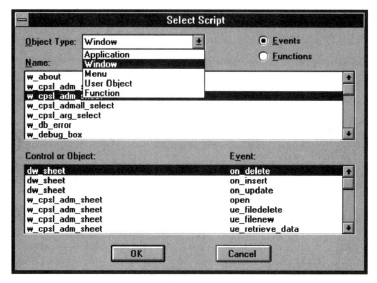

Figure 13.1 Selecting a script for animation.

Initially, the Select Script window lists the windows in the current application and the controls in the selected window that have scripts (only events having scripts are listed).

To add a stop (breakpoint):

Step 1 Select the object type in the Select Script window. To add a stop (breakpoint) in a window, leave the value in the Object Type box as is. You also can choose to add a stop (breakpoint) to a menu, user object, global function, or application object by changing the selection in the Object Type box.

Step 2 Specify whether you want to add a stop (breakpoint) in a script for an event or in an object-level function by selecting the Events or Functions button.

Step 3 Select the object that contains the script or function that you want to add the stop (breakpoint) for in the Name box.

Step 4 If you are adding a stop for a script, select the control and event in the Control or Object box.

Step 5 If you are adding a stop for an object-level function, choose the function in the Function box.

Step 6 Click OK. The Debug window displays with the script or function listed.

Step 7 Double-click in each line in which you want to insert a stop (breakpoint). A stop sign displays at the start of each line that has a stop (breakpoint). (*Note*: Select executable lines. Insert breakpoints in lines that contain an executable statement; do not insert stops in variable-declaration lines, comment lines, or blank lines.)

To remove an existing stop, double-click on the line containing the stop.

When PowerBuilder runs your application in debug mode, it stops just before executing a line containing a stop. (See Figure 13.2.)

Sometimes it seems that, for no reason, you single step and the application goes into a hard loop. For instance, do not set a breakpoint in the Activate or GetFocus event. The constant going to and returning from the Debug window can cause the recursive triggering of the events. To be able to see values for variables assigned in the last line of a script, add an executable line at the end of the script and set a breakpoint there. Perhaps set a variable equal to itself LI_CT = LI_CT. A real nice feature of PowerBuilder's debugger is its ability to save settings (breakpoints) between debugging sessions.

When you close Debug, PowerBuilder saves the information about the stops (breakpoints) as Debug variables in PB.INI. The next time that you debug your application, whether in the current PowerBuilder session or another one, the stops will be used.

Editing stops (breakpoints)

As you proceed through a debugging session, you will solve some problems and discover some new ones. You can add and modify or delete stops (breakpoints) when you first go to the Debug window or anytime in a debugging session. In either case, you use the Edit Stops window. (See Figure 13.3.)

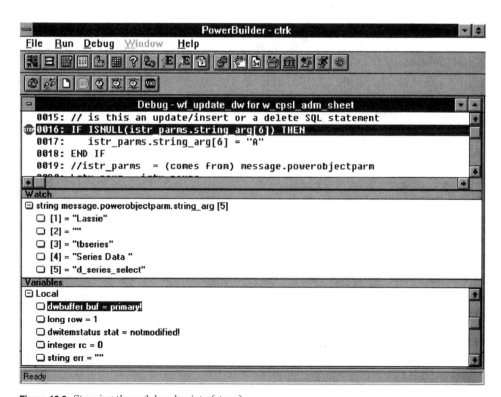

Figure 13.2 Stepping through breakpoints (stops).

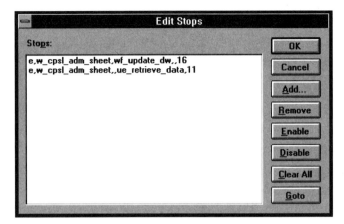

Figure 13.3 Editing stops.

To open the Edit Stops window, open the Debug window, as described previously. If you already are in the Debug window and want to set a new stop (breakpoint) or modify an existing one, click the Edit Stops icon in the PainterBar.

To add a new stop (breakpoint) from within the Debug window workspace, you also can click the Select Script icon in the PainterBar, which displays the Select Script window.

The Edit Stops window displays, listing the defined stops. Add a new stop (breakpoint) by clicking the Add button and following the procedure. To modify an existing stop, select the stop, then click the Goto button. Enable or disable a stop by selecting the stop, then clicking the Enable or Disable button. Delete a stop by selecting the stop, then click the Remove button, or delete all stops by clicking the Clear All button.

The Edit Stops window lists all stops currently defined using the following format:

```
state, object, control, event, lineno
```

where *state* is the state of the stop (enabled or disabled); *object* is the name of the object that contains the stop (a window, menu, user object, global function, or the application object); *control* is the name of the control, MenuItem, or user object whose script contains the stop; *event* is the name of the event with the stop; and *lineno* is the number of the line in the script at which the stop is set. (*Note*: *control* and *event* are not used when showing stops for functions.)

When you click Goto in the Edit Stops window, the script or function displays. You add or remove stops by double-clicking on the appropriate lines.

You can disable stops without deleting them. PowerBuilder will not stop execution at disabled stops. Later you can enable the stop again. To disable a stop, select the stop in the Edit Stops window and click Disable. PowerBuilder grays the Stop Sign icon indicating disabled stops when displaying scripts. To enable a disabled stop, select the stop in the Edit Stops window and click Enable. The stop is active again. PowerBuilder will stop execution just before it hits the stop.

Deleting stops

You can remove stops that you have set. To remove one stop:

- In the Edit Stops window, select the stop and click the `Remove` button.
- When looking at the script or function itself in the Debug window's workspace, double-click on the line containing the stop.

  To remove all stops, click the `Clear All` button in the Edit Stops window.

Running in Debug Mode

Running in debug mode is the same as the normal execution, but you also have the ability to pause and check variables and other status items. This is not a technique for performance debugging. Remote terminal emulators, such as Performix EM-POWER, can capture user keystrokes and emulate multiple users to determine response time statistics. This type of debug mode usually follows systems testing and precedes full scale user testing thereby avoiding latent and patent performance problems.

Launching the application with debug

Once you have set your stops, you can run the application in debug mode. The application will proceed as normal until it hits a line containing a stop.
  To run in debug mode:

Step 1 If necessary, open the Debug window by clicking the Debug icon.

Step 2 Click the Start icon in the PainterBar, or select `Start` from the Run menu. The application starts and proceeds until it hits a stop. The application then is suspended, and you return to the Debug window with the line containing the stop displayed. You can examine the state of the application at this point.

Step 3 To execute the next statement and stop, click the Step icon. Debug executes the current line, then stops and returns you to the Debug window.

Step 4 To continue execution, click the Continue icon. The application continues until the next stop is hit.

Step 5 To leave the Debug window, select `Close` from the File menu. The Debug window closes (but the information about all of the stops is retained).

Viewing information while stopped

When Debug encounters a stop, it suspends the application before executing the statement with the stop, then displays the Debug window. The statement that will be executed next is highlighted.

At this point, you can look at the state of your application. You can:

- Display objects in the current application and the current values of the instance variables and attributes of the objects.
- Display the current values of the global, shared, and local variables, but not instance variables.
- Change the values of variables.
- Select the variables that you want to watch.
- Edit the stops.
- Print the variables and watch variables lists.

You also can continue executing the application (either one step at a time or at normal speed) or select another script to debug.

To display the current values of variables, click the Show Variables icon in the PainterBar or select Show Variables from the Debug menu. The Variables window displays. When you close Debug, PowerBuilder saves the setting of the Variables option as a Debug variable in PB.INI. This variable determines whether the Variables window displays when the Debug painter opens.

Display the variables whose values you want to look at, as described in Table 13.1.

The Variables window displays information in an expandable outline. If there is information below a displayed entry, the entry displays with a plus sign next to it. Double-click the entry to see the information. Note the following:

- The Debug window displays the first 128 characters of a variable's value. If you want to see a value that exceeds 128 characters, double-click the variable as if you were going to modify the value. You can scroll through the contents in the resulting window.
- Instance variables are perhaps not so easily found. Instance variables are part of an object's definition, so PowerBuilder lists instance variables as attributes of the object itself.

TABLE 13.1 Displaying the Variables Whose Values You Want to Look at

Variable type	Action	Description
Global variables	Double-click the Global icon	Displays all global variables defined for the application and lists all objects (such as windows) that are open.
Shared variables	Double-click the Shared icon	Displays all objects that have been opened so far. Click an object.
Local variables	Double-click the Local icon	Displays all objects that have been opened so far to the current script or function.
Instance variables	Locate the variable in the object itself	This is sometimes difficult with inherited windows; you also can set up a local variable to store the instance variable, then easily view for debugging.

To look at instance variables and attributes for an object:

Step 1 Double-click the Global icon. All global variables and open objects display.

Step 2 Double-click the object that contains the instance variable. All attributes for the selected object display. Instance variables are displayed at the end of the list.

Step 3 Scroll to the end of the list to examine the instance variables.

Watching variables as they change

You can select the variables that you want to watch as the application proceeds. PowerBuilder displays these variables in a Watch window and updates their values as the application runs.

There are two ways to create a watch list. Use the first method to add a few watch variables one at a time. Use the second method to add groups of variables at once, then remove the ones that you don't want.

To select the variables you want to watch one at a time:

Step 1 From the Debug window, open the Variables window by clicking the Show Variables icon in the PainterBar or by selecting Show Variables from the Debug menu.

Step 2 Click the Show Watch icon in the PainterBar or select Show Watch from the Debug menu. The Watch window displays.

Step 3 Select a variable that you want to watch by clicking the variable name in the Variables window.

Step 4 Click the Add icon in the PainterBar. PowerBuilder adds the variable to the watch list and displays it in the Watch window.

You can Shift–Click a variable in the Variables window to add it to the Watch window in one step.

Note: When you close Debug, PowerBuilder saves the setting of the Watch window option as a debug variable in PB.INI. This variable determines whether the Watch window displays the next time the Debug painter displays.

To select the variables you want to watch by group:

Step 1 From the Debug window, open the Variables window by clicking the Show Variables icon in the PainterBar or by selecting Show Variables from the Debug menu.

Step 2 Display the Watch window by clicking the Show Watch icon in the PainterBar or by selecting Show Watch from the Debug menu.

In the Variables window, click the name of the variable type that you want to watch (Global, Shared, or Local).

Step 3 Select Add Watch from the Debug menu. PowerBuilder displays the name of the selected variable type in the Watch window.

Step 4 Expand the variable list in the Watch window by clicking the icon next to the name of the variable type.

Step 5 Remove the variables you do not want to watch from the list by selecting the variable and clicking the Remove icon or selecting `Remove Watch` from the Debug menu. PowerBuilder removes the selected variables from the watch list.

To see more lines in the script, you can close the Variables window after selecting the watch variables. To size the Watch window, drag the bar at the top of the Watch window.

Changing variable values

While running an application in debug mode, you can change the values of variables, then continue the application. You can use this technique to easily examine different flows throughout the application.

To change a variable's value:

Step 1 Run the application in debug mode.

Step 2 When at a stop, display the variable whose value you want to change in either the Watch window or the Variables window.

Step 3 Double-click the variable. The Modify Variable window displays. (See Figure 13.4.)

Step 4 Enter the new value for the variable.

Step 5 Click OK. PowerBuilder closes the Modify Variable window and changes the value of the selected variable.

When you continue the application, the new value will be used.

Amending the application. When you discover the problem and decide where to amend the scripts to correct it, you must leave the debugger to correct it. Be careful to exit the application that is being tested and also exit the debugger before going to an object painter (the reverse also is true):

Step 1 Close the Debug window by selecting `Close` from the File menu. (Be sure to close the Debug window before making any changes to your application.)

Step 2 Open the appropriate painter. Working from the Library painter is convenient.

Step 3 Correct the event script or function script. Compile and save it.

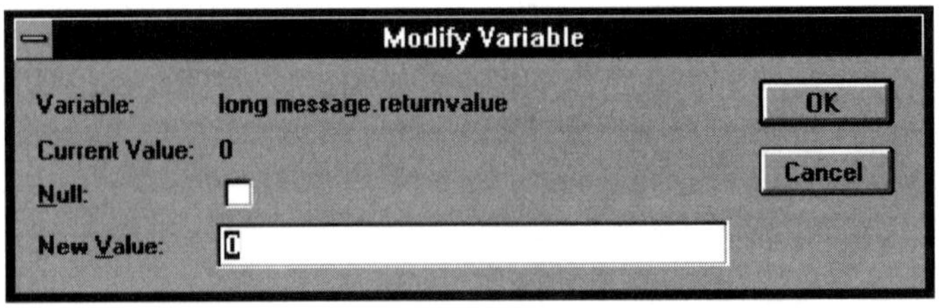

Figure 13.4 Modifying a variable.

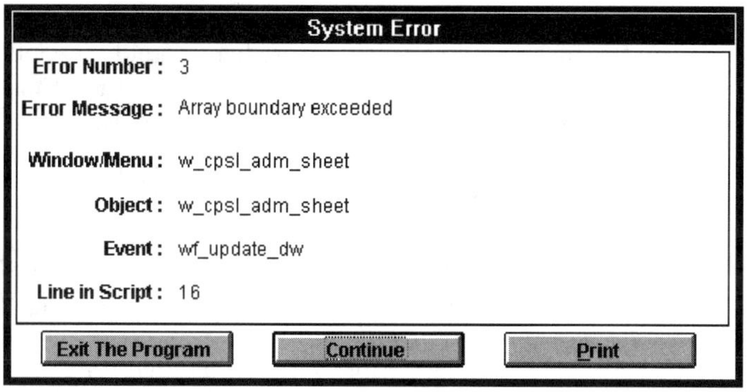

Figure 13.5 Error handling.

To check the fix, you can run the application in debug mode again by clicking the Debug icon in the PowerBar and clicking the Start button. All stops that you previously set still are defined.

When the application seems fine, you are ready to run it in regular mode. In regular mode, the application responds to user interaction and continues to run until the user exits the application or an execution-time error occurs. You can rely on the default execution-time error reporting by PowerBuilder or write a script that specifies your own error processing.

Running the application. To run the current application, do one of the following:

- Click the Run icon in the PowerBar.
- Double-click the application icon (the Run icon if the application does not have an icon) in the PowerPanel.
- Press Ctrl–R.
- Select Run from the File menu.

PowerBuilder becomes minimized (its icon displays at the bottom of the screen along with the icons of other minimized applications), and your application executes.

Handling errors during execution

A serious error during execution (such as attempting to access a window that has not been opened) will cause a SystemError event at the application level; that is, it triggers the SystemError event in the application object. (See Figure 13.5.)

If you do not build a script to handle these errors, PowerBuilder displays a message box containing the following information:

- The number and text of the error message
- The line number, event, and object in which the error occurred

There also is an OK button that closes the message box and stops the application.

If there is a script for the SystemError event, PowerBuilder executes the script and does not display the message box. It is a good idea to build an application-level script for the SystemError event to trap and process any execution-time errors.

In the script for the SystemError event, you can access the Error object to learn which error occurred and where it occurred. The Error object contains the attributes listed in Table 13.2.

Execution-time error numbers. Table 13.3 lists the execution-time error numbers returned in the Number attribute of the Error object and the meaning of each number.

SystemError event scripts. A typical script for the SystemError event includes a CHOOSE CASE control structure to handle specific errors. When the execution of the script is complete, PowerBuilder executes the next statement in the application. To stop the application, include a HALT statement in the SystemError script.

To test the SystemError event script:

Step 1 Assign values to the attributes of the Error object by using an assignment statement and PowerBuilder dot notation (for example, `Error.Line=45`).

Step 2 Call the SignalError function to trigger the SystemError event.

The script for the SystemError event executes.

Comprehensive Tests for Your Application

There are other tools that come within and without PowerBuilder that can facilitate the testing of your application. SQA Team Test, Mercury's TestDirector, and Performix Empower are tools that can capture keystrokes and emulate a user. They primarily are for system testing and regression testing. SQA Team Test and Test Director allow you to capture keystrokes as well as track individual errors and their resolution. (See Figure 13.6.) Performix Empower can provide a facility to evaluate performance especially for large scale OLTP and DSS systems. Both of these tools are vendor tools and are add-ons to your base PowerBuilder environment. PowerBuilder comes with some testing and tracing tools as well. We will discuss them briefly in the following sections.

TABLE 13.2 The Error Object Attributes

Attribute	Data type	Description
Number	Integer	Identifies the PowerBuilder error.
Text	String	Contains the text of the error message.
WindowMenu	String	Contains the name of the window or menu in which the error occurred.
Object	String	Contains the name of the object in which the error occurred. If the error occurred in a window or menu, Object will be the same as WindowMenu.
ObjectEvent	String	Contains the event for which the error occurred.
Line	Integer	Identifies the line in the script at which the error occurred.

**TABLE 13.3 The Execution-Time
Error Numbers Returned in the Number Attribute**

Number	Message text
1	Divide by zero
2	Null object reference
3	Array boundary exceeded
4	Enumerated value is out of range for function
5	Negative value encountered in function
6	Invalid DataWindow row/column specified
7	Unresolvable external when linking reference
8	Reference of array with NULL subscript
9	DLL function not found in current application
10	Unsupported argument type in DLL function
12	DataWindow column type does not match GetItem type
13	Unresolved attribute reference
14	Error opening DLL library for external function
15	Error calling external function
16	Maximum string size exceeded
17	DataWindow referenced in DataWindow object does not exist
50	Application reference could not be resolved
51	Failure loading dynamic library

The new direction is to create a customizable test repository that can manage and integrate your entire testing process from start to finish.

SQA Team Test amd Mercury Interactive's TestDirector are automated test-management tools for quality-assurance workgroups. They both provide a customizable test repository to manage and integrate the entire testing process, from planning and design to execution, bug tracking, and analysis.

Planning the testing process

Test management is a difficult and complicated task. The first step is to plan the entire testing process, then determine how to control and monitor test execution, and organize and analyze thousands of tests.

At best, manual test management is inefficient. At worst, application quality is sacrificed. Automating test management, using an open test repository, allows the testing team to organize and store manual and automated test scripts, results, and documentation for different application versions, releases, and configurations. We require a tool to allow users to view, analyze, share, and exchange all test information. To ensure comprehensive and effective testing, it is essential to plan the process carefully.

Both SQA Team Test and the TestDirector provide an automated solution for allocating testing tasks. You can assign resources and testing tasks, with deadlines and

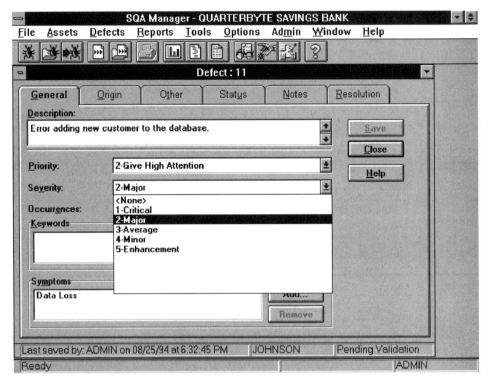

Figure 13.6 The SQA test manager.

priority rankings, to each test engineer. All the test engineer needs to do is open the test log, see what he/she has been assigned, and execute the tests.

To keep track of testing progress and to identify bottlenecks and problem areas, these tools provide online, detailed, fully customizable reports, graphs, and statistics of all the test data that accumulates during the testing process. These include tests to be executed, tests that have passed, those that have failed and need to be rerun, as well as bug-tracking information etc.

SQA Team Test and the TestDirector integrate test execution with bug tracking and keep a precise record of failures. Tests are executed, bugs are identified and logged for tracking, and results are reported. Both tools provide reports on "open" and "closed" bugs for each testing cycle, including bugs by status, severity and criticality, functional area, software module, person responsible, fix time per bug, and date.

Managing the testing process

The following list is a nonexhaustive checklist to consider when you are ready for full-scale systems testing. You should be able to automate all of the following testing functions before you get to this critical stage in the implementation:

- Integrate and manage the entire quality process.
- Manage thousands of tests for different versions, platforms, and configurations.

- Organize test data in a single test repository.
- Improve teamwork and integrate application development with quality assurance.
- Monitor and control automated and manual test execution.
- Manage concurrent test cycles.
- Pinpoint version-, platform-, or configuration-specific problems.
- Allocate test tasks to QA team members.
- Analyze test data indepth, using customizable reports, graphs, and statistics.
- Zoom into the exact test script line where the failure occurred.
- Identify bottlenecks and problem areas.
- Instantly assess application quality and progress towards release.
- Define test repository fields.
- Create queries to analyze test data.
- Enter test failures into the centralized bug-tracking system.
- Present general and detailed reports on bugs.
- Log and track bugs until closed.

PowerBuilder database trace

You might have a database problem that is latent and hard to isolate. There is a database trace facility that can be initiated to record database server and workstation interaction.

Starting the Database Trace tool. To trace your database connection, you must start the Database Trace tool (see Figure 13.7). There are two ways to start the Database Trace tool in PowerBuilder as summarized in the following paragraphs. The information displayed can help track the actual SQL and the time expended on each statement. Figure 13.8 shows a sample of the trace.

Starting the Database Trace tool by editing a database profile. The Database Profiles dialog box appears, listing the names of existing profiles. If you currently are connected to a database profile, its name is highlighted. Edit the profile by typing the word `trace` followed by one space to the left of the DBMS name. A message box appears stating that database tracing is enabled and that output will be written to the PBTRACE.LOG file in your Windows directory.

Figure 13.7 Database trace notification.

Figure 13.8 A sample trace.

```
DIALOG CONNECT TO TRACE ODBC:
USERID=dba
DATA=ABNC Main DB (v4)
DBPARM=ConnectString='DSN=ABNC Main DB (v4);UID=dba;PWD=sql' (5383 MilliSeconds)
  TABLE LIST: (220 MilliSeconds)
  PREPARE:
SELECT "prod_id", "prod_name", "prod_price", "prod_weight", "prod_category" FROM
"product" (55 MilliSeconds)
  DESCRIBE: (0 MilliSeconds)
name=prod_id,len=40,type=INT,pbt6,dbt5,ct0,dec0
name=prod_name,len=41,type=????,pbt2,dbt12,ct0,dec0
name=prod_price,len=40,type=DECIMAL,pbt4,dbt2,ct0,dec2
name=prod_weight,len=40,type=DECIMAL,pbt4,dbt2,ct0,dec1
name=prod_category,len=26,type=????,pbt2,dbt12,ct0,dec0
  BIND SELECT OUTPUT BUFFER (DataWindow): (0 MilliSeconds)
name=prod_id,len=40,type=FLOAT,pbt3,dbt5,ct0,dec0
name=prod_name,len=41,type=CHAR,pbt1,dbt12,ct0,dec0
name=prod_price,len=40,type=DECIMAL,pbt4,dbt2,ct0,dec2
name=prod_weight,len=40,type=DECIMAL,pbt4,dbt2,ct0,dec1
name=prod_category,len=26,type=CHAR,pbt1,dbt12,ct0,dec0
  EXECUTE: (0 MilliSeconds)
  FETCH NEXT: (55 MilliSeconds)
    prod_id= prod_name=Pecans on Parade prod_price=15.95 prod_weight=4.2
prod_category=General
  FETCH NEXT: (0 MilliSeconds)
    prod_id= prod_name=Sunflower Surprise prod_price=14.95 prod_weight=3.7
prod_category=General
```

If you want to trace a database connection in a PowerBuilder application script, you must specify the required connection parameters in the appropriate script. For example, you might specify connection parameters in the script that opens the application.

To trace a database connection in a PowerBuilder script, you specify the name of the DBMS preceded by the word `trace` and a single space. One way to start the Database Trace tool in a PowerBuilder script is to specify it as part of the DBMS attribute of the default transaction object.

PowerBuilder uses a special, nongraphic object called a transaction object to communicate with the database. The default transaction object is named SQLCA, which stands for SQL Communications Area. SQLCA has 15 attributes, 10 of which are used to connect to your database. One of the 10 connection attributes is DBMS. The DBMS attribute contains the name of the database to which you want to connect. Use the following PowerScript syntax to specify the DBMS attribute (this syntax assumes you are using the default transaction object SQLCA):

```
sqlca.DBMS = "trace DBMS_name"
```

Unfortunately, once you start tracing a particular database connection, PowerBuilder continues sending trace output to the PBTRACE.LOG file until you do one of the following:

- Reconnect to the same database with tracing stopped (i.e., remove the word `trace`).
- Connect to another database for which you have not enabled tracing.

PowerBuilder writes the output of the Database Trace tool to the PBTRACE.LOG file in your Windows directory (see Figure 13.9). You can display the contents of the PBTRACE.LOG file anytime during a PowerBuilder session. If you want, you can leave the PBTRACE.LOG file open as you work in PowerBuilder. However, the Database Trace tool does not update the PBTRACE.LOG file if you leave it open.

When you use the PBTRACE.LOG file as a troubleshooting tool, it might be helpful to add your own comments or notes to the file. For example, you can specify the date and time of a particular connection, the versions of database software that you used, or any other useful information.

To add notes to the PBTRACE.LOG file:

Step 1 Open the PBTRACE.LOG file using any text editor. The PBTRACE.LOG file is in your Windows directory. (See Figure 13.9.)

Step 2 Edit the log file with your comments and save your changes.

Each time that you connect to a database with tracing enabled, PowerBuilder appends the trace output of your connection to the existing PBTRACE.LOG file. As a result, the log file can become very large over time, especially if you frequently enable tracing when connected to a database in PowerBuilder. To keep the size of the PBTRACE.LOG file manageable, you must clear it of unneeded trace information. To do this, you can open the PBTRACE.LOG file, clear its contents, and save the empty file. You also can delete the PBTRACE.LOG file; PowerBuilder automatically will create a new PBTRACE.LOG file the next time you connect to a database with tracing enabled.

PowerBuilder and GPFs

The following is a checklist to help track down the cause of a General Protection Fault (GPF) in Windows. A GPF occurs when a code, typically in a DLL, tries to write outside of its boundary within memory. This causes uncertain behavior, and the ap-

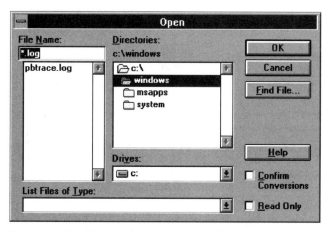

Figure 13.9 The Windows location of PBTRACE.LOG.

plication cannot continue. The application might give you a choice as to whether or not to continue, but it often merely terminates. At this point, it is a good practice to save any other work (if you can) and exit and restart Windows before continuing.

There are two ways to help resolve the problem. The first step is to explore, document, and, if possible, resolve a machine configuration problem. If this does not resolve the GPF, then you will need to obtain some more information and report the problem to Powersoft.

Explore and document the configuration

Step 1 Check for, rename, or delete any duplicate PowerBuilder DLLs.

Step 2 Ensure that you have the latest PowerBuilder fixes (downloaded from the BBS, FTP site, or CompuServe). The fix files contain RBRAND.EXE, which, when executed, creates a list of the PowerBuilder DLLs that the executable is finding and loading (along with dates, sizes, and release information). (See Figure 13.10.) Place this executable in the same directory as your PowerBuilder executable, and run it to display the information.

Step 3 Capture the complete error message, including the DLL name and the address of the GPF. If the GPF occurs in a user-written or third-party DLL, it is possible that it is caused by user error or a bug within the DLL.

File	Path	Date	Length	Brand	
PBAPL030.DLL	C:\PB3\PBAPL030.DLL	1/31/94 03:00:00	87856	no brand	
PBBGR030.DLL	C:\PB3\PBBGR030.DLL	1/31/94 03:00:00	394368	no brand	
PBCMP030.DLL	C:\PB3\PBCMP030.DLL	1/31/94 03:00:00	157936	no brand	
PBCTL030.DLL	C:\PB3\PBCTL030.DLL	1/31/94 03:00:00	357680	no brand	
PBDBI030.DLL	C:\PB3\PBDBI030.DLL	1/31/94 03:00:00	66304	no brand	
PBDBL030.DLL	C:\PB3\PBDBL030.DLL	1/31/94 03:00:00	5235	no brand	
PBDEC030.DLL	C:\PB3\PBDEC030.DLL	1/31/94 03:00:00	38640	no brand	
PBDTP030.DLL	C:\PB3\PBDTP030.DLL	1/31/94 03:00:00	241808	no brand	
PBDTS030.DLL	C:\PB3\PBDTS030.DLL	1/31/94 03:00:00	52848	no brand	
PBDWD030.DLL	C:\PB3\PBDWD030.DLL	1/31/94 03:00:00	152976	no brand	
PBDWE030.DLL	C:\PB3\PBDWE030.DLL	1/31/94 03:00:00	833696	no brand	
PBDWO030.DLL	C:\PB3\PBDWO030.DLL	1/31/94 03:00:00	22016	no brand	
PBDWP030.DLL	C:\PB3\PBDWP030.DLL	1/31/94 03:00:00	440224	no brand	
PBDWT030.DLL	C:\PB3\PBDWT030.DLL	1/31/94 03:00:00	31184	no brand	
PBECT030.DLL	C:\PB3\PBECT030.DLL	1/31/94 03:00:00	55744	no brand	
PBFRM030.DLL	C:\PB3\PBFRM030.DLL	1/31/94 03:00:00	122544	no brand	
PBGUP030.DLL	file not found				

Figure 13.10 RBRAND report of PowerBuilder DLL.

Step 4 Search the Infobase CD-ROM for a similar problem.

Step 5 Search the Powersoft forum on CompuServe for a similar problem.

Step 6 Check the video board. Systems must have the latest software drivers (from the board manufacturer) that are configured correctly.

Reporting the bug to Powersoft

Step 1 Create a library that contains the smallest excerpt of your code that still continues to GPF, with text files that contain any database definition language (DDL) and database manipulation language (DML) to construct the database (if necessary).

Step 2 Run Dr. Watson before starting your application, using these WIN.INI settings:

```
[Dr. Watson]
ShowInfo=dis err loc mod
DisStack=30
TrapZero=0
```

When Dr. Watson takes over after the GPF, you will be asked to input a comment. Enter the description of the problem and the address of the GPF into this comment. Double-click on the Dr. Watson icon to find the name and location of the generated log.

Step 3 Run RBRAND.EXE, and save the output as a text file, using the File menu Save option.

Step 4 Compress the PBL, DDL, DML, and TXT files; the RBRAND output; and the Dr. Watson log. In the package, include a README.TXT file that explains how to reproduce the GPF.

Step 5 Upload the compressed file to the BBS, after having called Tech Support and been assigned a bug-tracking number for the issue. Even if you do not have a support agreement, you can report a bug or GPF by using the BUGReport form (PBBUG.WRI) from the BBS or CompuServe.

14

Refining Your Code

We now assume that you have covered the fundamentals of the PowerBuilder environment and played with it, possibly having developed a simple application that was not intended for a prime-time production audience. Well, now you need to examine, in greater detail, some of the more advanced concepts within PowerBuilder, allowing you to create a larger or more complicated application, building it and refining it to take advantage of the object-oriented techniques that are available. This chapter reiterates the object-oriented programming aspects of PowerBuilder. It will cover using additional material, objects, classes, instantiation, inheritance, encapsulation, and polymorphism, which were introduced in chapter 2, "The PowerBuilder environment." It then will cover the areas for additionally improving the performance of a PowerBuilder application, by tuning the client workstation and/or the database servers that house the data.

Object-Oriented Programming

The most powerful way of refining your code is to make a conscious decision, at the planning stage of a project, to take advantage of the object-oriented programming (OOP) features that are provided in PowerBuilder. These features, along with Powersoft's DataWindow technology, give PowerBuilder the biggest advantage over its competition for developing and delivering client/server applications in a rapid fashion. To properly take advantage of something, however, you first must understand its principles. This section will attempt to provide you an understanding of object-oriented programming and how it is applied in the PowerBuilder environment. We hope to achieve this by covering the following topics:

- Objects versus classes

- Object-oriented programming in PowerBuilder

- The impact of object-oriented programming

Objects versus classes

If you are new to object-oriented programming in PowerBuilder, then what you must do first is to understand some of the terminology. (For example, what is the difference between an object and a class?) These terms are commonly used interchangeably amongst developers, but there is a subtle difference. What follows are simple definitions that should help to explain the difference to you.

Classes in PowerBuilder.   In PowerBuilder, a class is the definition of a collection of characteristics, which can be attributes, controls, events, functions, structures, or variables. PowerBuilder ships with a set of predefined standard classes (or types).
   The classes can be separated into two categories:

- Visual—Those that can be seen (e.g., CheckBox, CommandButton, and SingleLine Edit)
- Nonvisual—Those that cannot be seen (e.g., Error, Message, and Transaction)

By using the PowerBuilder painters, these PowerBuilder predefined system classes can be inherited from and modified to create more specific or complex "user-defined" classes. For example, when you create a new window with some controls, instance variables, and window functions and save it as w_base_ancestor (see Figure 14.1), you are defining a new "user-defined" class to PowerBuilder, called w_base_ ancestor, that is inherited from the standard class window.
   This is known as *single inheritance*. PowerBuilder does not support multiple inheritance.
   (*Note*: Multiple inheritance is similar to inheritance within humans, where the parents' characteristics—recorded in the genetic alleles—are passed on, and Mother Nature determines which characteristics are dominant and consequently manifested in the descendant. Likewise, the software developer has to pick and choose which characteristics are manifested in the descendant.)
   A class is what is saved into the PowerBuilder libraries. It can be considered a blueprint (or model) of something. However, a class does not actually exist, nor can it be referred to, during execution. This might seem possible when you first start to develop classes in PowerBuilder. This is because, when you create and save a win-

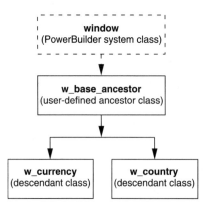

Figure 14.1 Direct and indirect system class inheritance.

dow, you will find that you can immediately refer to it by name in a script that is contained in another window. However, behind the scenes, what actually happens is that, when you create the window class, PowerBuilder automatically creates a global variable with exactly the same name as the window class, allowing the script to compile correctly. However, the script will fail at runtime if there is no object instance of the window class available (see the section "Instantiation"). This automatic variable creation is done as a shortcut for you so that you do not have to do it yourself within the application.

In summary, a class:

- Is inherited from a predefined "system" or user-defined class.
- Defines characteristics: attributes, controls, events, functions, structures, and variables.
- Can have a visual or nonvisual definition.
- Must be instantiated to be referenced during execution (see the section "Instantiation" for a complete list of the classes that PowerBuilder does not automatically instantiate).

Objects in PowerBuilder. In PowerBuilder, an *object* is an instantiation (or an instance) of a class. The object has all of the characteristics that have been defined in the class blueprint. Only, in this case, the instantiated object exists; it can be referred to and manipulated during execution of the application.

In summary, an object:

- Is an instance of a visual or nonvisual class.
- Can be referenced during execution (can receive and process messages).
- Derives initial attributes, controls, functions, structures, and variables from its class.

To see the class hierarchy for the current application select `Browse Class Hierarchy` from the Utilities menu in the Library painter.

Instantiation. During execution, all classes must be instantiated (CREATE an object instance of) before they can be referenced. In PowerBuilder, instantiation occurs:

- Automatically
- Implicitly
- Explicitly

Automatic instantiation. There are five built-in global objects that PowerBuilder will instantiate automatically. (See Table 14.1.) They are the default global variable types defined in the Application painter. You can replace these defaults with classes created in the User Object painter. (See chapter 16, "Building a user object," for more information about this technique.)

PowerBuilder will automatically create these global variables when you start any PowerBuilder application.

TABLE 14.1 The Built-In Global Objects

Global object	Description
SQLCA	The default transaction object, used to communicate with a database
SQLDA	The dynamic description area, used in dynamic SQL
SQLSA	The dynamic staging area, used in dynamic SQL
Error	Used to report errors during execution
Message	Used to process Microsoft Windows messages and pass parameters between windows

Implicit instantiation. Classes are implicitly instantiated if you use the following functions to open a window in PowerScript:

- Open
- OpenWithParm
- OpenSheet
- OpenSheetWithParm

When you open a window, PowerBuilder will implicitly instantiate the window and any controls or menus attached to it. Also when you close the window, PowerBuilder will perform the clean-up process by destroying all of the objects that it instantiated for you.

Explicit instantiation. In certain situations, you will need to explicitly instantiate a class that you have constructed. This is done using the CREATE statement. Typically, you will explicitly instantiate user objects that are built to handle some business function or provide some central place for interaction with external functionality (e.g., the Microsoft Windows API). Unlike automatic and implicit instantiation, when you explicitly instantiate an object, you also must take care of the destruction of the object instance when you are finished with it. This is done via the DESTROY statement, which will allow Windows to reclaim the resource areas allocated to the object.

(*Note*: If you do not perform this clean-up, you will lose access to the blocks of Windows resources (GDI and user stacks) allocated to the object and possibly run out of memory for the Windows session.)

For example, you might build a (nonvisual) class user object (u_WinSDK) that handles all interaction with the Microsoft Windows API. To instantiate this class for use globally within an application:

Step 1 Define a global variable for the instance of the class. Select the `Global Variables` option under the Declare menu (in any script painter) and add:

```
u_WinSDK  G_uoWinSDK
```

Then in a script that is executed at the start of the application—possibly the application open event or a function called in this event (e.g., f_app_open( ))—add:

```
G_uoWinSDK = CREATE u_WinSDK
```

This will instantiate the u_WinSDK object so that it now can be referenced.

Within this user object class is an encapsulated function, uf_GetWindowsDirectory, which returns the path of where Windows is installed. It does this by calling the Microsoft Windows SDK function GetWindowsDirectory.

To call this function from within a script that you code:

```
//Declare a local string to hold the Windows Directory
INTEGER L_iLenWinDir=144          //Maximum length of result
STRING  L_sWinDir                 //Result string
L_sWinDir = SPACE(L_iLenWinDir)   //Pre-allocate enough space
//L_sWinDir will contain the path where Windows is installed and
//L_iLenWinDir will contain the length of the path
L_iLenWinDir = &
  G_uoWinSDK.uf_GetWindowsDirectory(L_sWinDir, L_iLenWinDir)
```

As mentioned earlier, when you have finished with the object instance, you need to perform the clean-up task. This is performed by the DESTROY statement.

To destroy an object instance, code:

```
DESTROY G_uoWinSDK
```

Where this takes place depends on the scope of the object instance. In the previous example, the application is calling the Windows API. The Windows API typically is called in several places within an application, so it makes sense to instantiate it with a global scope.

Another situation might not require an object instance with such a widespread scope. In this case, it would make sense to declare it either at the instance level (i.e., a window) or local level (i.e., an event or function). It then can be used and later destroyed (when the window closes or the event/function script finishes) to free up the resources and valuable memory. For global object instances, perform the clean-up in the application close event or a function that is called from the close event (e.g., f_app_close).

Inheritance

Inheritance is an object-oriented programming technique that allows you to build a new class, the *descendant*, by deriving its initial characteristics from another class, the *ancestor*. The inheritance chain (or line) can be continued so as to define a hierarchy of classes, where each descendant class "inherits" the characteristics of its immediate and distant ancestor classes. You can use inheritance with the following PowerBuilder classes:

- Menus
- User objects
- Windows

As mentioned at the start of this chapter, the characteristics can be a combination of attributes, controls, events, functions, scripts, structures, or variables. In a well-designed PowerBuilder application, inheritance can be used as a vehicle for code reusability (elimination of duplicate code). (For example, an ancestor class can provide a piece of common or reusable code for descendant classes.) When developing the descendant class, the developer can concentrate on either adding or extending functionality or overriding any code that is inherited from the ancestor.

If you find that you seem to be overriding the majority of the ancestor's code, you probably are being too specific with the code that is functioning at the ancestor level. In this case, you should think about reengineering the inheritance tree. By bringing the often overriden code down an additional level, you might be able to avoid this problem.

For an application with many windows that have very similar functionality (i.e. a maintenance window with insert, update, and delete capability), it is possible that, if the application is developed using inheritance, it will yield significantly faster run-time performance than the same application developed by duplicating the code for each window. With the advent of version 3.0 came some improvements in the loading of inherited objects. This has been vastly improved in the object manager for version 4.0; so much so that you should not be afraid of establishing reasonably deep (greater than five) levels of inheritance hierarchies.

Consider the window class inheritance tree shown in Figure 14.2.

During execution, the user action determines that an instance of w_customer gets loaded, along with its ancestor code, which is inherited from w_cls_single_dw and wcls_base_sheet. Then subsequent user action determines that an instance of w_product gets loaded. In this case, however, the only code that PowerBuilder needs to load into memory is any of the additional and overridden functionality that is coded in the w_product class.

Although this shows what will happen in just two window classes, if an even greater number of window classes are inherited from the same (or distant) ancestor, inheri-

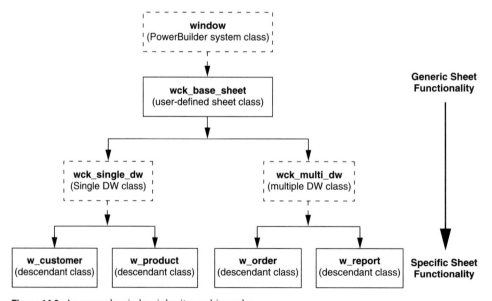

Figure 14.2 An example window inheritance hierarchy.

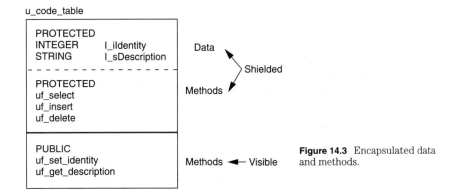

Figure 14.3 Encapsulated data and methods.

tance really will improve the performance of loading and displaying of these classes when compared to simply copying the code to each of the new windows.

Encapsulation

Encapsulation is an object-oriented programming technique that allows you to combine methods, in the form of scripts in functions and events, and data, in the form of variables and structures, together into a single class. (See Figure 14.3.) This feature allows you to shield any internal complexity from the external domain by defining appropriate access to the data and methods. An "instantiated class" (object) can present public data and methods for access by other objects, while keeping as private for itself or protected for itself and any of its descendants the specifics of what it knows, or contains, and how it functions.

In PowerBuilder, you can encapsulate data and methods into many of its classes. When you encapsulate functions, structures, or variables inside the class, you can decide to what extent they are available to other objects during execution. When they are declared public, they are accessible by other objects. When declared protected, they are accessible only to that class and its descendants. When declared private, they are accessible only to that class. However, there are some exceptions to these definitions. Please note them:

- An instance variable in any class is directly accessible from other class because they are public by default.
- Controls that are internal to custom (or combination) user-objects are protected but still can be accessed by other objects through previously defined user object functions and events.

It sometimes can be useful to think of a class, especially a nonvisual user object class, as a server class. The client, or calling, class can interact with the server class through the defined interface (API), which in this case are the public data and methods encapsulated into the server class definition.

The benefit of encapsulation is that it allows you to hide information or shield complexity. When you embed the functions that operate on an object in the object class itself and only interact with that object through this defined interface, other system components are insulated from the details of these operations. It does not matter if the details of the operation or the data change. As long as the interface (function calls and associated parameters) does not change, the user of the object will not be affected. This is because, from the client's perspective, the server class still performs exactly the same function or functions as before.

Encapsulation has far-reaching implications in code maintenance and quality. When used properly, simple changes to systems will no longer cause other pieces of the system to break unexpectedly.

Polymorphism

Polymorphism literally means "many forms." It is implemented in PowerBuilder through the sending of messages as a means of communication between classes.

Sending messages. Polymorphism involves sending the same message to classes of similar but unknown type. With polymorphism, the communication is generic enough so that the sender does not need to know about the specific type of class that is the recipient of the "message." As long as the message is meaningful to the receiving class, the sender can trust that the receiving class will interpret the message in a manner that makes sense for it. You can send messages to classes in PowerBuilder by triggering events, with TriggerEvent and PostEvent, using the Send or Post functions, or by calling system functions like Open or Close.

CheckBoxes and RadioButtons are part of the same *polymorphic family*. They are different object types inherited from the same base class. Both can receive the Windows message bm_getcheck to find out if the object is checked and the message bm_setcheck to check the object. Windows does not have to send a specific type of message to RadioButtons and a different message to CheckBoxes; the same message works for both.

An example of using events. In PowerBuilder, for example, you might have an MDI frame with a menu option named Print. When the w_currency_list sheet is active, clicking the Print menu option will print the contents of the DataWindow. When the w_currency sheet is active, clicking `Print` the sheet to be printed.

The clicked event script for the Print menuitem is:

```
w_mdi_frame.GetActiveSheet().TriggerEvent("ue_print")
```

Both sheets have a user-defined event called ue_print that has been defined using one of the custom events, but the scripts coded for the event are different in the two sheets.

The following code is the ue_print event for w_currency_list:

```
dw_ccy.Print()     //DW print
```

The following code is the ue_print event for w_currency:

```
INTEGER L_iJob
L_iJob = PrintOpen("Currency")  //Open print job
```

```
PARENT.Print (li_pjob, 1, 1)    //Print Window
PrintClose(li_pjob)             //Close the print job
```

Using functions. Another aspect of polymorphism is called *function overloading*. Function overloading allows you to define the script in functions with the same name, but with different signatures: arguments and return values. Based on the argument list passed to the function, the appropriate version of the function is called.

Function overloading is used internally by PowerBuilder in many of its built-in functions. For example, the STRING( ) function converts a number, a date, or a time to a string. The MessageBox function accepts a string or a number as its second argument.

You can implement function overloading in PowerBuilder by using:

- Inheritance
- External functions

Using external functions. If you are using an external dynamic link library (DLL) that has implemented function overloading for one or more functions, define those functions as external functions to PowerBuilder multiple times, once for each possible argument list. Use the same function name each time, but use a different argument signature:

```
Function long GetHandle(string name) Library "EXTL.DLL"
Function long GetHandle(int id, string name) Library "EXTL.DLL"
```

Using inheritance. To implement overloading in PowerBuilder functions, you must use inheritance. This is because you cannot define multiple versions of the function name at the same object level. You must define one version of the function in an ancestor object and the other version in a descendant. For example, you have defined two functions, both named uf_initialize. The first version of uf_initialize takes one argument of type string:

```
uf_initialize("country")
```

The second version of uf_initialize takes a numeric argument:

```
uf_initialize(44)
```

Based upon the argument list passed to uf_initialize and depending from where uf_initialize is called from, PowerBuilder will search up the inheritance hierarchy, from the descendant to the ancestor, for the first version of uf_initialize that it finds matching the specified argument signature.

Impact of OOP

The object-oriented programming (OOP) features of PowerBuilder, if implemented carefully, can minimize duplication of code and effort. However, just because you are going to use an object-oriented programming language to develop your application, this does not guarantee that you will benefit from them.

> . . . if I give you a blowgun that has hit 200 gazelles without missing, there is no guarantee that you will hit the next gazelle with it . . . alternately, if I give you a blowgun that leaks air, you still might hit every gazelle in the plains, because you superbly compensate for the blowgun's obvious deficiencies . . .."
>
> Roland Racko, Software Development, July 1994

In other words, to be really successful with OOP, you first must understand it, then accept it, and above all invest up-front with the planning of its implementation, and continue practicing it *ad infinitum*.

In summary, if you decide to utilize the object-oriented programming features included with PowerBuilder, you might receive the potential benefits listed in Table 14.2.

It should be noted that it takes time to learn and subsequently apply these techniques effectively. However, do not pass up on the potentially positive impact that the object-oriented features have on the development cycles, execution performance, and ongoing upkeep of an application.

Optimizing PowerBuilder

This section deals with what can be done to squeeze every last drop of performance out of your PowerBuilder application.

Removing redundant classes

In the heat of development, developers build lots of classes, then they modify them, rewrite them, or build better ones to replace the old ones. However, developers tend to not get rid of the ones that are superseded. So consequently, towards the end of a project, there comes a time when a good clean-up of the libraries is necessary.

Unfortunately, this is a tedious, but risky, task that must be handled in a careful manner. If you delete the wrong class, you'll have to restore it from a backup (if you have one, that is). A better way of cleaning up is to identify the redundant classes and move them to a different library that you create specifically for the clean-up task.

First, you can use the class browser that is part of PowerBuilder to print the list of menu, user object, and window classes that are in the library list of the current application. Then, for each of these classes, you must check to see if it still is being

TABLE 14.2 The Potential Benefits of OOP

Potential benefit	Reason
Reduction of development time	Code reusability
Enabling plug-and-play development	Code modularity
Reduced ongoing maintenance costs	Changes made at an ancestor level will ripple throughout the descendant hierarchy
User familiarity and comfort	Consistent look and feel to an application
Improved performance	Avoiding duplicate code

used in the application. You can search through the libraries by using the Browse Library Entries in the Library painter. To do this:

Step 1 Open the Library Painter.

Step 2 Open one of the libraries in the application's search path by double-clicking on the line that contains the library, or use the arrow keys to position the highlight bar on the library name, then press Enter.

Step 3 Highlight all of the entries in the library by selecting Select All from the Library menu or pressing Ctrl–A.

Step 4 Select Browse from the Entry menu, or press Ctrl–B.

Step 5 Enter the class name, and press OK. Note the result on the print-out. If there are no matches, then a "Match not found" dialog will display; if there are matches, then a "Matching Libraries Entries" dialog will be displayed.

Step 6 Repeat these steps for each library in the applications library list, building up your list.

If you find that the class is no longer being used, you should move it to another library (e.g., not_used.pbl) that is not a part of the current application's library path. By moving it to an unused library instead of deleting it, you can continue to refer to it or, if necessary, include it back into the application.

Note: You also can run the cross-referencing utility (XREF.EXE) that comes with the Developer's Toolkit. The cross-reference utility checks the association among classes that make up an application. For example:

- DataWindows (d_),
- Global functions (f_)
- Global (G_), Shared (S_) and Instance variables (I_)
- Menus (m_) and menu functions (mf_)
- User objects (u_) and user object functions (uf, cf_)
- Windows (w_) and window functions (wf_)

Once you have run the utility (which will take some time), you can review, sort, save, and print the associations.

More performance tips

There are other things besides eliminating unused code that will help make your application run, or appear to run, quicker:

- Minimize levels of menus and toolbar inheritance. Inheritance is more sluggish for menus/toolbars than for window and user object classes.
- Minimize the use of large bitmaps. They make the application bigger and slower to load. When loaded, they use up large amounts memory and, if you don't have much memory to spare, might cause Windows to frequently swap out.

- Minimize or isolate array or other costly processing from the window open processing. Create a custom event (e.g., ue_post_open) that contains the slower processing, and add a PostEvent ("ue_post_open") function to the end of the Open script. This will execute the ue_post_open event after the window has appeared on the screen. That way, the user will at least see the window and not just the hourglass.

- Minimize the loading of a large amount of items into List and Drop Down List boxes. If you have to, use a DataWindow or DropDown DataWindow instead. The DataWindow manager loads data and generally performs much faster than the standard object manager. In practice, you can develop any screen using the DataWindow technology instead of standard window controls.

- Minimize use of database cursors. Replace the cursor logic with either a nonvisual DataWindow user object or an invisible DataWindow instead.

- Utilize DBMS processing power by replacing SQL-based DataWindows access with Stored Procedure-based DataWindows using the utility SPUD.EXE, which comes with the Developer's Toolkit.

- Make the database server perform as much selection, sorting, and aggregation of data as possible prior to returning the information to the client.

- Order the application library search path in the "most referred to" sequence. Put the libraries that contain the classes that referred to (used) the most first in the library search path.

- Minimize placing complex (i.e., time-consuming) code in the Activate and Open events, and avoid coding "user-interrupt" logic in the RetrieveRow event unless it is specifically required.

- Destroy all explicitly created user objects when they are no longer required, or at least before exiting the application. This will free up resources for use by other functionality within the application and/or other Windows applications.

- Place the directory that contains the PowerBuilder Deployment Kit and the runtime DLLs first in the search path before any of the network search paths. This will prevent the runtime application from adding to the network traffic by searching for a PowerBuilder DLL that might be placed on the client workstation.

- Optimize PowerBuilder libraries regularly. If these libraries are stored on a Novell file server, reset the Sharable attribute after optimizing a library to avoid locking problems with other developers; use `FLAG * . PBL +S`.

Optimizing Clients and Servers

If you have a badly tuned car, it will not give you the optimum performance when you drive it. In the client/server environment, the same can be said of a badly tuned workstation that is used to either develop an application on or to deploy an application to and of database servers that store and retrieve the information. The following section contains a few pointers to tuning the configuration and subsequently improving the performance of the client workstation and the database server.

Optimizing the workstation

Here is a list of things to check and configure for the IBM-compatible PC:

- Use DOS 6.22 or later.
- Use Windows 3.11, then Windows '95 when it is released. Make sure that you have and use a permanent swap file for Windows that is twice as big as the amount of RAM on the workstation.
- Defragment the hard drive regularly, organizing the disk in the order of the path and with the following file extensions at the front of the disk: .EXE, .DLL, .COM, and .BAT.
- Run an extended memory manager (e.g., EMM386) with the appropriate areas of high memory excluded (typically for the network card).
- Run a disk caching utility (e.g., SmartDrive for DOS). If you have a large amount of RAM (12MB or more), run the caching utility with a larger buffer size to improve disk reading for data that is stored together (i.e., the Windows swap file).
- Run a memory manager (e.g., MEMMAKER) to squeeze as many TSRs and device drivers into the high memory block as possible, leaving as much of the 640K available as possible.
- Use a permanent Windows swap file with 32-bit access. For laptops, disable the 32-bit access.
- Remove unnecessary TSRs and device drivers.

Optimizing the database server

With your attention now coming to the database server, you will find there are a multitude of possibilities that affect its performance. This includes the tuning of the DBMS, the devices allocated to the database, the structure of the tables and indexes, and also the SQL that is being issued by the application. There are several publications that discuss the tuning and performance aspects for the specific DBMS that you are using on the database server.

The administration of the database server is best left to an experienced database administrator (DBA). On larger projects, this typically will be one or more specialized individuals that is skilled in tuning the DBMS. For smaller projects, it might be you, the developer, that is doing the DBA work, in which case see chapter 19, "Managing the database," for more information regarding database administration and how you can improve performance (e.g., with secondary indices).

15

User-Defined Functions and Structures

User-defined functions and structures in PowerBuilder are no different than the functions (i.e., subroutines or subprograms) and copybooks (i.e., DSECTs) that we built in the online and batch systems of the 1970s and 1980s. The typical development team would have one or two individuals who loved to code and devise the best solution to common problems. These individuals would be given the task of developing all of the code, which frequently was used by the other developers to develop the multitude of CICS/VSAM and eventually DB2 systems. The functions would be coded, tested, documented, and hopefully stored in the firm's "PROD" LOADLIB and be accessible to all. For example, in a financial house, computing the settlement day for a securities exchange would be one of the functions that you would find in a copy of the firms "Programming Standards and Guidelines." These functions were important because they could save development time and provide consistency. User-defined functions and structures can provide the same benefits.

How Are Functions Deployed

To be useful, functions that you or your organization decide to implement should be flexible and well-documented. To be used on a large project, they also must be published and maintainable. The PowerScript language itself provides many built-in functions. However, as you develop applications to satisfy your particular requirements, you might find certain code (i.e., a blend of your own script mixed with PowerBuilder functions and/or SQL) is used a dozen times, warranting the need to create a callable routine. Ideally you develop and maintain this routine only once with a single source that you invoke from various places in the application.

For example, you might need to perform a function like "convert Sybase data type datetime to DB2/MVS data type timestamp" in several places in an application or in different applications. In these situations, you will want to create a user-defined function to perform the processing. It should be noted that there are a growing number of third-party tools, the so-called "class libraries" that come equipped with fairly comprehensive function libraries. Here again, they are useful only if they are maintained and documented. The advantage of third-party tools is they facilitate maintenance and documentation. They obviously are more useful at the beginning of an organization's PowerBuilder development cycle. It is recommended that any common functions be identified and named during the design phase, thus allowing function development to be assigned as a separate project task, and other developers can stub these function calls during script development based on argument listings.

What Is a User-Defined PowerBuilder Function?

A user-defined function is a collection of PowerScript statements (SQL as well) that perform some processing. You use the Function painter to define user-defined functions. You define and code the user-defined function within the painter. When you are finished, you save it in a library either as a global function or as part of an object, perhaps a class object to be reused by many members of the development team. In any case, any application that accesses that library can use the function or inherit the object.

Types of Functions

When you are developing an application and a coding situation calls for a function (i.e., code that will be reused frequently) as the solution, you then must decide the best way to define the function (i.e, how will this function be used).

Types of functions

There are two types of user-defined functions: global functions and object-level functions.

Global functions are not associated with any object in your application and are always accessible anywhere in the application. These correspond to the PowerBuilder built-in functions that are not associated with an object, such as the mathematical and string-handling functions. Note that global functions, etc. should be placed in specific PBL files (such as FIRMFUNC.PBL or PROJFUNC.PBL) that should exist in all application library lists.

Object-level functions are defined for a particular type of window, menu, or user object or for the application object. To be utilized more than once, they usually are part of class objects that are inherited. For example, the class window sheet might contain a window function to update a row in the database. Object-level functions are part of the object's definition and can always be used in scripts for the object itself. You also can choose to make these functions accessible to other scripts as well. These functions are effectively built-in functions that are defined for windows, menus, user objects, or the application object.

Which type of function should be used?

As you develop your application, it usually becomes apparent that a function might make the code more readable and maintainable. If a function is general-purpose and might be used throughout the application, then it is a global function. Check the available application or maybe even firmwide directory of functions. Determine if someone else already has solved the problem before you continue.

If a function applies only to a particular kind of object, make it an object-level function (you still can call the function from anywhere in the application; it is just that the function acts on a particular object type). This might be a window function that performs a single table update for the DataWindow object. The window function might be inherited from an ancestor window, and you want to change it to update multiple tables using the same call.

Two or more objects can have functions with the same name that do different things (in object-oriented terms, this is called *polymorphism*). For example, each window can have its own window data row update, which performs processing unique to it. You might inherit a window with a window function and extend or change the basic function for this particular window object.

There is never a conflict about which function is being called because you always specify the object's name when you call an object-level function. If the function with the same name exists in the ancestor and its issue (i.e., children), the function contained in the issue (i.e., the younger object's function) is used.

Creating a User-Defined Function

To create a user-defined function:

Step 1 Open the Function painter. Its the one with the f(x).

Step 2 Name the function. First check the naming convention.

Step 3 Define a return type.

Step 4 For object-level functions, define an access level. (Will it be used by all or is it private?)

Step 5 Define arguments for the function. Develop a flexible list of parameters.

Step 6 Code the function. Use PowerScript and even SQL to effect the desired result.

Each of these steps is described in the following sections.

Opening the Function painter

Opening the Function painter (see Figure 15.1) depends on whether you are defining a global function or an object-level function.

To open the Function painter for a global function:

Step 1 Click the Function painter icon in the PowerBar or double-click the icon in the PowerPanel. The first window that displays is the Select Function window.

Step 2 Click the New button to declare a new function. The New Function window displays. (See Figure 15.2.)

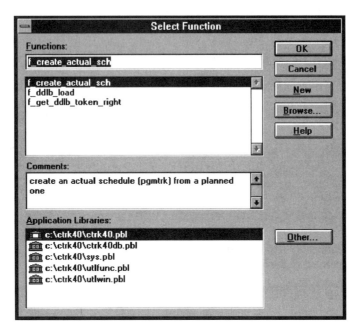

Figure 15.1 The Function painter.

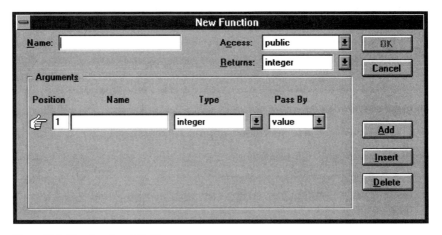

Figure 15.2 New function definition.

To open the Function painter for an object-level function:

Step 1 Open the painter for the object in which you want to define a function.

Step 2 From the Declare menu, select the menu item: X Functions, where X is Menu, User Object, or Application. You also can declare structures for the function from the same menu.

Step 3 You can use the Declare menu in the Window, Menu, User Object, or Power-Script painter. A Select Function window displays. (See Figure 15.3.) You can select and edit an existing function in the current object or define a new function for that object.

Step 4 To define a new function, click the New button. The New Function window displays.

Naming the function

Function names can have up to 40 characters. As noted previously, it is a good idea to develop and use a naming convention for all objects, including user-defined functions. This will allow that you to recognize them easily and distinguish them from built-in PowerScript functions. Your project team and hopefully your organization should have published naming standards for PowerBuilder development. A quick reference table should be handy for the developer to facilitate the process.

A global function name should have a prefix (i.e., first character of its name such as f_). If the name is a conglomerate of a multiword description, the various words should have their first letters capitalized. If the name contains an abbreviation or word commonly displayed as all upper case, it should be named consistently. Use the firm's abbreviation list. Object-level functions should be named with the object type and the fact that it is a function. For example, a window function should begin with the prefix wf_. Likewise, a menu function should begin with the prefix mf_. For example, f_ExcelPromptSave would be a global function to prompt for the name and save the data to an Excel spreadsheet as that name, and wf_SetBaseWhere would be a window function to set the base portion of the WHERE clause of a SQL SELECT statement to be executed to retrieve the data for the subject window.

Because built-in functions do not have underscores in their names, this convention makes it easy for you to identify functions as user-defined.

Naming object-level functions

You also might want to adopt a naming convention to distinguish global functions from object-level functions. Doing this makes it easier for you to identify functions. Table 15.1 contains a suggested naming convention.

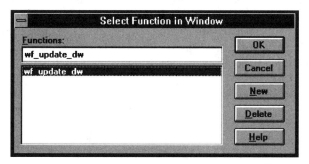

Figure 15.3 Object-level function definition.

**TABLE 15.1 Suggested Naming
Standards for User-Defined Functions**

Type of function	Name prefix
Global	f_
Window level	wf_
Menu level	mf_
User-object level	uf_
Application-object level	af_
C++ user-object level	cf_

Defining a return type

Typically a function performs some special processing. It might return a value (e.g., a date converted from one form into one that is acceptable to Sybase for insert or update; for example, YYYY-MM-DD). It is prudent to also provide a return code. The return code is a value that indicates whether the function executed successfully or not. To have your function return a value or a return code, you need to define its return type, which specifies the data type of the returned value.

For example, the following function returns the result of the conversion of a string arg1 into a date form acceptable to Sybase. A string containing a valid date is the argument that you want returned as a date. If the date is invalid, then the string 99-99-99 is returned so that the caller can take the appropriate action. You can let function update the actual value (reference) or pass it a copy of the value itself.

```
// function f_CONVERTDATE(arg1)
// The PowerBuilder DATE function converts strings
// (such as Jan 1, 1998, or 12-31-99) into YYYY-MM-DD format
// if the string contains a valid date else it returns 01-01-0
If DATE(arg1) <> 01-01-0 then
  Return arg1
else
  arg1 = '99-99-99'
  Return arg1
end if
```

You code a RETURN statement in the function that specifies the value to return. When you call the function in a script or another function, you can use an assignment statement to assign the returned value to a variable in the calling script or function. The date returned in the function can be used as input to a Sybase table update. You also can use the returned value directly in an expression in place of a variable of the same type.

```
ls_date1 = f_CONVERTDATE(ls_date1)
IF ls_date1 <> 99-99-99
THEN sybase_date = ls_date1
```

To define a function's return type, you select the return type from the Returns dropdown listbox in the New Function window. You can specify any PowerBuilder data type. To indicate that a function does not return a value, you select None from the Returns list.

Another consideration is who is permitted to use the function. The New Function window has a listbox named Access. This box specifies the access level of the function (i.e., it specifies where you can call the function in the application). Global functions can be called from anywhere in the application. They are public by definition. So when you are defining a global function, you cannot modify Access; the box is read-only. For object-level functions, you can restrict access to an object- level function by setting its access level, as shown in Table 15.2.

Defining function arguments

Like built-in functions, user-defined functions can have any number of arguments, including none. You declare the arguments and their types when you define a function.
To define arguments:

Step 1 Name the argument. Declare the argument's type. This can be almost anything, including an array of a particular data type. The brackets must be included. The order in which you specify arguments here is the order that you use when calling the function. If you are not using a reference argument, then the names do not have to match but the data types must match the corresponding argument. For example, if the first argument in the caller's list is an integer, the function expects the first argument to be an integer and will use it as such even if the variable name is different from the invoker to the invoked function.

Step 2 Declare how you want the argument passed (by reference or by value).

Step 3 If you want to add another argument, click the Add button and repeat the process.

In user-defined functions, you can pass arguments by reference or by value. You specify this property for each argument in the function definition Pass By listbox.

By reference. When you pass an argument by reference, the function has access to the original argument and can change it directly (i.e., it changes in the invoker's copy of the data).

By value. When you pass by value, you are passing the function a temporary local copy of the argument. The function can alter the value of the local copy within the function, but the value of the argument is not changed in the calling script or function.
The choice here comes down to whether or not you want the function to update some variable within the caller scripts memory. You can return only one value, and it

TABLE 15.2 Access Choices for User-Defined Functions

Access	When you can access the function
Public	In any script in the application.
Private	Only in scripts for events in the object in which the function is defined. You cannot call the function from descendants of the object.
Protected	Only in scripts for the object in which the function is defined and its descendants.

is prudent to use the return type for return code. Therefore, to modify and use more than variable, use the "reference" address to update the argument in place.

Coding the function

The Function painter workspace (see Figure 15.4) displays after you finish declaring the function's name, return type, access level, and arguments. The Function painter workspace is functionally the same as the PowerScript painter. In it, you key in or copy PowerScript statements that hopefully carry out the desired results for the function, just as you specify the script for an event in the PowerScript painter. See chapter 12.

The Function painter workspace looks like the PowerScript painter; it includes listboxes that can be used to paste arguments or variables as well as PowerScript statements.

For example, the Paste Argument dropdown listbox lists the arguments defined for the function. The Paste Global dropdown listbox lists the global variables defined in the application. You can paste arguments and variables from the lists into the statements in the function that you are building.

When you declare an object-level function, the workspace displays the name of the current object in the title and four listboxes. The first two listboxes are the same as in the workspace for global functions. The other two are Paste Instance and Paste

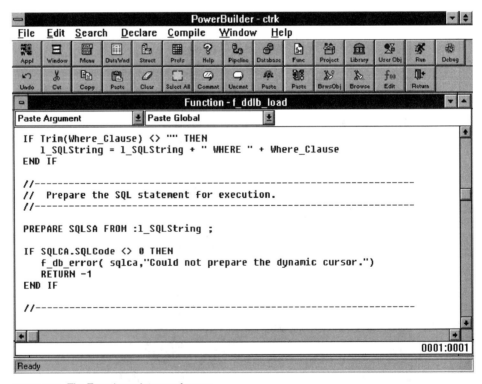

Figure 15.4 The Function painter workspace.

Object. You can use these listboxes to paste names of instance variables, objects, and controls in the current object. User-defined functions can include PowerScript statements, embedded SQL statements, and calls to built-in, user-defined, and external functions. You can type the statements in the workspace or use the icons in the PainterBar or items on the Edit menu to insert them into the function. If you defined a return type for your function, you must return a value in the body of the function or an error condition will result.

To return a value in a function, use the RETURN statement:

```
RETURN expression
```

where *expression* is the value that you want returned by the function. The data type of the expression must be the data type that you specified for the return value for the function. It can be as simple as a boolean true or false or an elaborate scheme for an involved function using an integer return code using degrees of severity (e.g., 4, 8, 12, and 16) depending on the result of the script execution.

Compiling, saving, and modifying the function

When you finish building a function, compile it and save it in a library. Then you can use it in scripts or other user-defined functions in any application that includes the library that contains the function in its library search path. Compiling a function works the same as any PowerScript compile. You can either compile the function without leaving the painter or compile the function in the process of saving it. You can change the definition of a user-defined function anytime. You change the processing performed by the function by simply modifying the statements in the workspace. You also can change the return type, argument list, or access level for a function. You can change a function's arguments anytime. Add an argument by clicking the Add button. The next position number and boxes for defining the new argument display below the last argument in the list. Insert an argument by moving the pointer to the argument before which you want to insert the argument and clicking the Insert button. Delete an argument by selecting it and clicking the Delete button.

As with any other component that can have a global impact, the proper change control must be in place. On a large project, a change to a global function should be planned with all developers alerted of the change and appropriate fallback and backup procedures in place.

The responsible developer, upon notification and after locating the new version, should recompile and verify any script in which the function is used. Regression testing will increase the reliability of scripts and functions. Proper change management will guarantee that the scripts and functions work correctly during execution.

Finding all of the objects that invoke a particular function can be accomplished with the Library painter. Click the Browse icon in the Library PainterBar entries and use the Browse Library Entries window. Specify the user-defined function as the search text and specify the types of components that you want to search. The window will allow you to print or save or go directly to the affected script to make amendments.

How are functions used

Now that we know how to name, build, compile, and amend user-defined functions, this section is just a note on how to use them. You use user-defined functions the same way that you use built-in functions. You can call them in scripts or in other user-defined functions. When calling a user-defined function, enclose the arguments in parentheses immediately after the function name. The arguments must agree in position and type with those defined for the function. If there are no arguments, you must enter parentheses after the function name to identify it as a function.

Creating and Working with Structures

A *structure* is a group or collection of one or more related variables of the same or different data types identified by a single name. A structure was called a copybook in COBOL or a DSECT in Assembly language. It provides a single name to refer to a block of contiguous storage. It allows you to refer to related entities as a unit rather than individually. You could define the columns in a database table as a structure.

For example, a database table (tbpgmsch) that represents the program schedule that an ice rink will offer for a particular time each day of the week might be represented by a PowerBuilder global structure called str_tbpgmsch consisting of the following variables:

```
date sch_week_end_date
time sch_time
string sch_program_cde_mon
string sch_program_cde_tue
string sch_program_cde_wed
string sch_program_cde_thur
string sch_program_cde_fri
string sch_program_cde_sat
string sch_program_cde_sun
```

The global structure then can be used in a script to instantiate instances of the structure:

```
str_tbpgmsch lstr_old_str_tbpgmsch
str_tbpgmsch lstr_new_str_tbpgmsch
```

This is not a new concept. In the mainframe development cycle, we used the following syntax to create an instance of the COBOL base copy book:

```
COPY tbpgmsch PREFIX old
```

You then can move the whole row from one location to another with one assignment statement:

```
lstr_new_str_tbpgmsch = lstr_old_str_tbpgmsch
```

Types of structures

As with user-defined functions, there are two kinds of structures: global structures and object-level structures.

Global structures are not associated with any object in your application. You can directly reference these structures anywhere in your application. Note that global structures, etc. should be placed in a specific PBL file (such as FIRMSTR.PBL or PROJSTR.PBL) that should exist in all application library lists.

Object-level structures are associated with a particular type of window, menu, or user object or with the application object. These structures can always be used in scripts for the object itself. You also can choose to make the structures accessible from other scripts.

As you develop your application, think about how the structures you are defining will be used:

- If the structure is general-purpose and applies throughout the application, make it a global structure.
- If the structure applies only to a particular type of object, make it an object-level structure.

Creating structures

Defining a structure is as simple a task as you could have in PowerBuilder. The planning and proper deployment is the real trick. Structures have many uses (e.g., an all-purpose parameter list that contains an unbound array of each data type). For example, a str_parms structure is used in the application developer class PBLs (in the Enterprise edition of PowerBuilder) that consists of unbounded arrays of each PowerBuilder data type:

```
string string_arg[]
char char_arg[]
int integer_arg[]
long long_arg[]
date date_arg[]
datetime datetime_arg[]
time time_arg[]
boolean boolean_arg[]
real real_arg[]
decimal {2} decimal_arg[]
double double_arg[]
```

Structures are important enough for PowerBuilder to have an entire painter devoted to them. The Structure painter is the easiest, and perhaps least used, painter; however, structures are useful in facilitating development and promoting efficient use of storage.

Creating a structure. To create a structure, you would perform the following steps:

Step 1 Open the Structure painter.

Step 2 Define the variables that comprise the structure. Check and use the firm/project naming convention for a variable. Review how the data will be used and determine the appropriate PowerBuilder data types; if the structure is a file or database row layout, take care to match PowerBuilder data types to the file system or database data types.

Step 3 Save the structure.

You should note the following:

- Check and use the firm/project naming convention for a structure.
- Once you have built a base structure, you can use it to define the same structure with a different prefix (i.e., it can be used to instantiate another structure).
- Each variable in the instantiated structure will be prefixed accordingly.
- Instantiation allows you to use the structure more than once in the same script.

Opening the Structure painter. How you open the Structure painter depends on whether you are defining a global structure or an object-level structure.

To open the Structure painter for a global structure:

Step 1 Click the Structure painter icon in the PainterBar or PowerPanel. The Select Structure window displays. (See Figure 15.5.)

Step 2 Click the New button. The New Structure window displays.

To open the Structure painter for an object-level structure:

Step 1 Open the painter for the object that you want to define the structure for (i.e., window, menu, or userobject) or from within any PowerScript painter instance.

Step 2 From the Declare menu, select the appropriate menu item: Window Structures, Menu Structures, User Object Structures, or Application Structures.

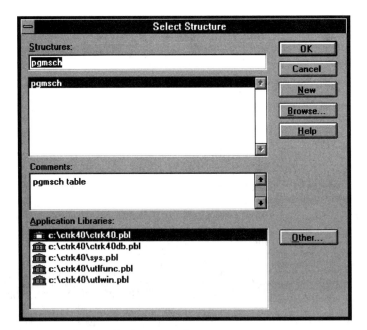

Figure 15.5 Opening the Structure painter.

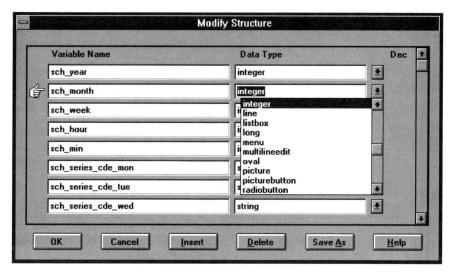

Figure 15.6 Defining and modifying structure variables.

Step 3 You can use the Declare menu in the Window, Menu, User Object, or Power-Script painter. A Select Structure window displays.

Step 4 Here you can select a structure for the current object or declare a new structure for the object.

Step 5 To define a new structure, click the New button. The New Structure window displays.

Defining the variables. Whether you are first defining the variables or modifying an existing structure, you will perform the following steps. (See Figure 15.6.)
   To define the variables that comprise the structure:

Step 1 Enter the name of a variable that you want to include in the structure. Enter the data type of the variable in the Data Type box, or select a data type from the Data Type dropdown listbox. The default for the first variable is string; the default for subsequent variables is the data type of the previous variable. Because a structure can be a group of structures (i.e., a structure can be a variable within a structure), follow the naming convention, but it also is a good idea to specify the parent structure's name as the variable's data type.

Step 2 Enter the number of decimal places in the Dec box (data type: decimal.) The default is 2.

Step 3 Repeat until you have entered all the variables.

Step 4 Save the structure. How you save the structure depends on whether it is a global structure or an object-level structure.

To save a global structure:

Step 1 Click OK in the New Structure window. The Save Structure window displays.

Step 2 Name the structure. Names can have up to 40 characters. Check the project naming standard.

Step 3 Add comments to describe your structure.

Step 4 Choose the library to save the structure in, and click OK.

PowerBuilder stores the structure in the specified library. You can view the structure as an independent entry in the Library painter.

To save an object-level structure:

Step 1 Click OK in the New Structure window. The Save Structure in ObjectType window displays.

Step 2 Name the structure, and click OK.

PowerBuilder saves the structure as part of the object in the object's library.

As with most editors, to create a structure that is similar to an existing structure, modify the existing structure, then click Save As to save the structure under another name (or in another library for global structures).

Using structures

After you define the structure, you can:

- Reference the structure in scripts and functions
- Pass the structure to functions
- Display and paste information about structures by using the Object browser

Referencing structures. When you define a structure in the Structure painter, you are defining a new data type. You can use this new data type in scripts and user-defined functions as long as the structure definition is stored in a library in the application's library search path.

To use a structure in a script or user-defined function:

Step 1 Declare a variable of the structure type.

Step 2 Reference the variables in the structure.

Referencing global structures. The variables in a structure are similar to the attributes of a PowerBuilder object. To reference a global structure's variable, use dot notation:

```
structure.variable
```

For example, assume that str_reference_table is a global structure with the variables cde_id, refer_cde, refer_long_txt, and refer_shrt_txt. To use this structure definition, declare a variable of type str_reference_table, and use dot notation to reference the structure's variables, as shown in the following script:

```
str_reference_table lstr_genre, lstr_holiday
lstr_genre.cde_id   = 01
lstr_holiday.cde_id = 02
```

Referencing object-level structures. You reference object-level structures in scripts for the object itself exactly as you do global structures: you declare a variable of the structure type, then use dot notation. For example:

```
structure.variable
```

As an example, assume that the structure wstr_schedule is defined for the window w_schedule and that you are writing a script for a CommandButton in the window. To use the structure definition in the script, you write:

```
wstr_schedule  lstr_schedule1
lstr_schedule1.series_id = "Beaver"
```

which allows access to object-level structures outside the object.

You also can choose to make object-level structures accessible outside the object. To reference object-level structures outside the object:

Step 1 In the object that defines the structure, declare an instance variable of the structure type.

Step 2 In any script or user-defined function in the application, reference a variable in the structure using the following syntax:

```
object.instance_variable.variable
```

For example, assume that you have defined a structure for the window w_schedule named wstr_schedule1 and that you want to be able to use it anywhere in your application. Define an instance variable of type wstr_schedule for w_schedule:

```
wstr_schedule1  winstruct
```

In other scripts, reference the window structure through the instance variable, such as:

```
w_schedule.winstruct.name
```

To copy the values of a structure to another structure of the same type, assign the structure to be copied to the other structure using this syntax:

```
lstr_schedule1 = lstr_schedule2
```

PowerBuilder copies all of the variable values from lstr_schedule2 to lstr _schedule1.

Using structures with functions. You can pass structures as arguments in user-defined functions. Simply name the structure as the data type when defining the argument. Similarly, user-defined functions can return structures. Name the structure as the return type for the function.

In PowerBuilder, you can define external functions that take structures as arguments.

For example, assume the following:

- ef_Revise is an external function that expects a structure as its argument.

- Emp_data is a declared variable of a structure data type.

You can call the function as follows:

```
ef_Revise(emp_data)
```

The external function must be declared before you can reference it in a script. You can display the names and variables of defined structures in the Object browser. You also can paste these entries into a script.

To display structure information:

- To display a global structure, choose Structure as the object type.

- To display an object-level structure, choose the corresponding object (such as the name of the window) as the object type.

- When displaying a global structure, choose Attributes as the Paste Category to display the names of the variables in the structure or select Object Name to display the name of the structure.

- When displaying an object-level structure, choose Structures as the Paste Category. PowerBuilder displays both the structure name and the variables.

To paste the information into a script, double-click the item in the Paste Values box or select the item and click Paste. The item displays at the insertion point in your script.

16

Building a User Object

"Reduce, Reuse, Recycle."   Anon

One of the key features of object-oriented programming techniques is reuse. Reuse is the ability to define a class once, then use it many times over again without having to recreate (or code) the class over and over again. This OOP technique is similar to "including" predefined working storage layout and subroutine copybooks that have been coded beforehand and stored in a shareable library into an application program being developed in other programming languages (e.g., CICS/COBOL or C).

In the PowerBuilder environment, one of the most commonly used techniques to implement reusability is by way of user objects. This chapter will provide an overview of the different types of user objects, present the steps involved with building a new user object (either from scratch or by inheriting from an existing user object), and finally show how to use and communicate with a user object within an application.

Introducing User Objects

Throughout the history of programming, application programs often have had features in common with other application programs (e.g., database layouts, working storage, and trade date to settlement date calculation routines). In the new object-oriented environments, these common storage areas and functions, also known as *attributes* and *methods*, still exist and also apply to the visible parts of objects in an application developed with a Graphical User Interface (GUI).

User objects (see Figure 16.1), like many other PowerBuilder objects, are created and maintained in their own painter: the User Object painter. Once you have created and saved the user object, you then can use it in your application. The user object

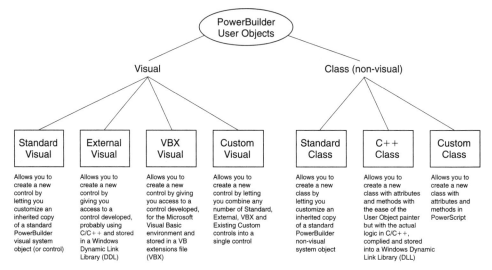

Figure 16.1 User objects in PowerBuilder.

can be used as many times as you want; there is no need to redefine it each time that you want to use it. In PowerBuilder, user objects can be one of two types:

- Visual
- Class (known as "nonvisual" in prior releases)

Visual user object

A visual user object is a control or bunch of controls with a defined look and behavior. You can modify its attributes, add variables or structures, and put scripts behind the controls, and you can create functions, or methods, that take action on the controls, structures, or variables defined in the object. The visual user object can be placed in a window or inside another custom visual user object.

In PowerBuilder, there are four types of visual user object:

- Standard
- Custom
- External
- VBX

Standard visual user object. The standard visual user object is one that is based on one of the following standard PowerBuilder controls: CheckBox, CommandButton, DataWindow, DropDownListBox, EditMask, Graph, GroupBox, HScrollBar, ListBox, MultiLineEdit, OLEControl, Picture, PictureButton, RadioButton, SingleLineEdit, StaticText, or VScrollBar.

The user object actually inherits the standard object's definition of attributes and methods, which then can be modified or tailored to suit the specific requirements of the object. So, if you find that you are repeatedly picking a standard PowerBuilder control and adjusting its attributes or methods to specific settings, then you should consider creating a standard visual user object with these settings and use it instead.

For instance, you discover that your user community finds an application visibly more pleasing and easier to use if all of the command buttons are the same dimensions, with the same size text font. Well, rather than painstakingly making sure that each button is the same, you could define one user object button in your application and reuse it as a model for every subsequent button in the application.

As with all tasks, a little planning and effort up front with user objects can reap dividends in the future.

Custom visual user object. A custom visual user object can be considered similar to a window, in that it is an arrangement of several controls that are put together to function as required in a single control. If you group together several controls to act as a single unit, then it might be worth creating a custom visual user object with these attributes and methods. If you build the user object generically enough, it probably can be used again in the future. For example, you might have a collection of query/reporting screens that use several DataWindows and dropdown DataWindows, which contain interdependent data, to specify selection criteria. Well, rather than coding all of these controls in each window, construct a custom visual object. The custom visual object would have the controls and necessary functions to allow the calling window to:

- Initialize, or set, the user object with opening defaults, such as each of the DataWindow's DataObjects and the initially selected row.

- Determine the currently selected criteria, to build a retrieval statement for the query or report.

External visual user object. External user objects allow you to make use of Microsoft Windows standard controls built in programing languages outside of PowerBuilder, such as in a C or C++ module, and stored in a Windows Dynamic Link Library (DLL).

To use the DLL, you need to know the names of the classes in the DLL, the messages the DLL responds to, and the style bits that can be set in the DLL. In the sample application (Exampl40), window w_progress_meter (see Figure 16.2) contains an external visual user object, u_3d_meter, that uses the cpalette Windows DLL.

VBX visual user object. VBX visual user objects are similar to external visual user objects in that they use controls constructed in an external library (a .VBX this time). However, the external libraries originally were written to extend the Microsoft Visual Basic environment. Many third-party component developers have released a myriad of specialized controls, such as the Diamond Arrow Pad, in file VBDIA.VBX that comes with the PowerBuilder examples.

You can purchase or build the files that define the VBX controls and use them in your PowerBuilder applications. Please note that only VBX version 1.0 controls are supported by PowerBuilder and experience has shown them to be unstable in certain installations. Evaluate them for use in the development and production envi-

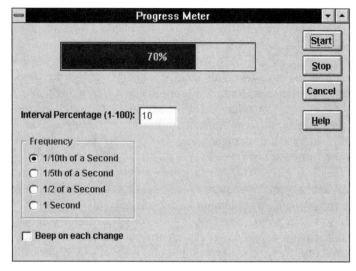

Figure 16.2 An external visual user object.

ronment before committing to them. If at all possible, develop your own objects in either PowerBuilder or C/C++.

Class user object

Class user objects can be used to implement functionality that does not require a visual element. Typically, class user objects are used to define business rules, act as a repository for application data, or perform any other common related processing that needs to take place (e.g., corporate date routines such as the trade date to settlement date calculation that was mentioned in the introduction to this chapter).

Class user objects can be implemented and used with local, instance, shared, or global scope, depending on how widespread the functionality or data of the class user object is required. For example, you might have a class user object that is concerned with application entry security and, as such, is defined locally to the application login window, whereas a Class user object that is used to return the application's current business date is available globally throughout the application. PowerBuilder is a flexible enough environment to allow the developer to define the scope (or availability) of the Class user object.

In PowerBuilder Enterprise, there are three types of Class user objects:

- Standard
- Custom
- C++ (available only if you install the Watcom C++ DLL Builder)

Standard class user object. A standard class user object inherits its definition from one of the PowerBuilder-supplied, nonvisual system objects. These are: DynamicDescriptionArea, DynamicStagingArea, Error, MailSession, Message, OLEObject, OLE Storage, OLEStream, PipeLine, and Transaction. You then can tailor the standard definition by adding variables and functions to enhance the behavior of the built-in system object to make the new class that is specific for your application. In the Application painter, there is a dialog that will allow you to directly replace system objects with new definitions of the standard class user object. This is a very advanced feature, so take great care when replacing these built-in system objects.

An example is to define a user object inherited from the built-in transaction object and add functions that make calls to database stored procedures. These calls are known as *database remote procedure calls* (RPCs). See "Database Remote Procedure Calls" later in this chapter for more information on building and executing database RPCs.

Custom class user object. Custom class user objects are classes that encapsulate data attributes (structures and variables) and methods (functions). They are not derived from, nor do they contain, other PowerBuilder objects, because they are invisible to the user. Custom class user objects can be used to define business rules or logic. Here are some examples:

- A class that is responsible for MDI sheet management, navigation, and communication
- A class that contains standard date routines for a securities trading firm
- A class that contains the rules for maintaining customer information (see example application EXAMPL40; Topic: User Objects, Example: Business Class)

C++ class user object. The C++ class user object is available in the PowerBuilder environment only if you have chosen to install it from the PowerBuilder Enterprise CD-ROM or disks. See chapter 4, "Setup development environment," for more information about installing this product.

The C++ class user object uses the Watcom C++ Class Builder, which is a set of tools that allows the developer to create and convert PowerBuilder function and variable definitions into a standard Windows DLL. This is a multistep process that takes you from constructing the user object functions and variable definitions in PowerBuilder, through generating the comparable C++ classes and framework code, to writing the actual function code in C/C++. This feature combines the ease of use of the PowerBuilder environment with the speed and efficiency of the C/C++ programming language.

The C++ Class Builder takes care of the mechanics of creating a Windows DLL, leaving the developer to concentrate on coding the function logic.

For some time, the ability to call DLLs has been, and continues to be, available from an external user object; however, with this feature, it makes the whole process easier, allowing the developer to concentrate on the logic rather than the mechanics of setting up the calls to the DLL.

Building User Objects

There are two ways to build a user object. You can either:

- Create a new user object.
- Use inheritance to build a new user object.

The following section looks at what is involved in creating a new user object, then looks at how to build a new user object with inheritance. See chapter 14, "Refining your code," for more information on inheritance.

Opening the User Object painter

To work with user objects, you must open the User Object painter. To open the User Object painter, click the User Object painter icon in the PowerBar or the Power-Panel. The Select User Object dialog (see Figure 16.3) will appear, showing a list, if it contains any, of the current library's user objects.

From here, you have the choice of either selecting another library from the current application by clicking on its entry in the Application Libraries listbox, selecting a user object to open for modification, creating a new user object by pressing the New button, or inheriting from an existing user object by pressing the Inherit button.

Creating a new user object

From the Select User Object dialog, click the button labelled New, and the New User Object dialog displays (see Figure 16.4). Select the type of user object that you want to build, and press the OK button.

Functions, structures, and variables

You declare functions, structures, and variables by selecting them from the Declare menu or by clicking the right mouse key in the workspace.

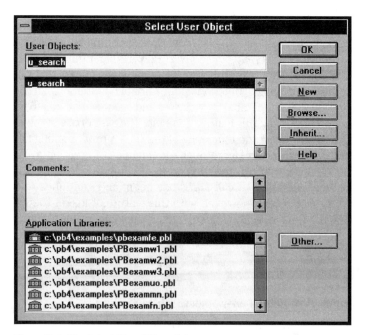

Figure 16.3 The Select User Object dialog.

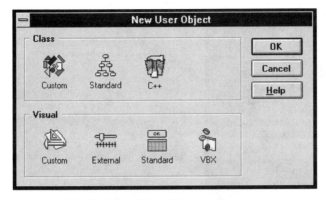

Figure 16.4 The New User Object dialog.

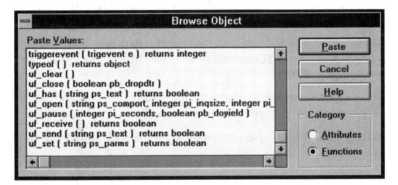

Figure 16.5 The Browse Object dialog.

In the PowerScript painter, to see a list of all the built-in attributes and functions of the ancestor object that you inherit from, you can use the Browse Object dialog (see Figure 16.5).

To display the Browse Object dialog, select Browse Object from the Edit menu, press Ctrl–O, or click the icon in the PainterBar.

Skip to the relevant section that follows to continue building a new user object of the type you have selected.

Standard visual

When you select Standard from the Visual group in the New User Object dialog, PowerBuilder displays the Select Standard Visual Type dialog (see Figure 16.6), which contains the list of standard PowerBuilder control types.

To continue building a new standard visual user object:

Step 1 Click the type of standard PowerBuilder control that you want to use to build, and press OK, or just double-click the selection. The new user object will display in the User Object painter workspace with the same attributes and events of the ancestor standard PowerBuilder control.

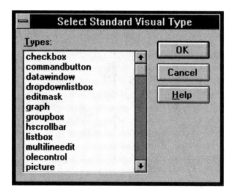

Figure 16.6 The Select Standard Visual Type dialog.

Step 2 You can modify the control exactly as you can do with the standard control in the Window painter. Press the right mouse button inside the object, or click the User Object Style option in the Design menu, to display the object's Style menu. With this pop-up menu, you can look at the current attribute settings and make the necessary adjustments.

Step 3 From the Declare menu, you can declare any functions, structures, variables, and user events that you need for the user object.

Step 4 Save the user object (see "Saving the user object" later on in this chapter).

Standard visual user objects have the same events as the ancestor PowerBuilder control that was selected to create the class. In addition, when you place the user object on a window or a custom user object, you can define your own events to further customize the user object. To do this, select User Events from the Declare menu, and the Events dialog will display showing a list of Event Names and IDs associated with the object. At the end of the list, you can add your own Event Name (typically prefixed ue_ for clarity) and Event ID taken from the list of events displayed in the Paste Event ID listbox.

Custom visual

When you select Custom from the Visual group in the New User Object dialog, Power-Builder will display an (Untitled) User Object painter workspace (see Figure 16.7). It looks like the Window painter workspace; the empty box towards the upper-left corner is the custom visual user object.

The procedure for building a custom visual user object is similar to the process of building a window. To build a custom visual user object:

Step 1 Place the controls in the custom visual user object.

Step 2 Define the attributes of the controls just as you do in the Window painter.

Step 3 Declare any functions, structures, or variables that you need for the user object. You can declare functions, structures, and variables for the user object in the User Object painter workspace or in the PowerScript painter.

Step 4 Declare any needed events for the user object or its controls.

Step 5 Build and compile the scripts for the user object or its controls.

Step 6 Save the user object (see "Saving the user object" later on in this chapter).

In custom visual user objects, the events shown in Table 16.1 are associated with the collection of controls. Each individual control within the custom visual has its

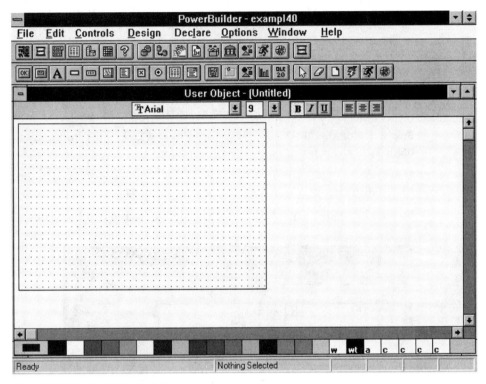

Figure 16.7 The User Object painter workspace.

TABLE 16.1 The Events Associated with Custom Visual Objects.

Event	Occurs
Constructor	When a class is instantiated (object instance). If placed on a window, it occurs before the Open event or if dynamically placed on a window via OpenUserObject() or OpenUserObjectParm().
Destructor	When an object instance is destroyed. If placed on a window, it occurs after the window's Close event or is removed dynamically via CloseUserObject().
DragDrop	When a dragged object is dropped on the user object.
DragEnter	When a dragged object enters the user object.
DragLeave	When a dragged object leaves the user object.
DragWithin	When a dragged object is moved within the user object.
Other	When a Windows message occurs that is not a PowerBuilder event.
RButtonDown	When the right mouse button is pressed inside the user object.

own particular set of events that relate to what type of control it is. In addition, when you place the user object on a window or another custom user object, you can define your own events to further customize the user object.

External visual

When you select External from the Visual group in the New User Object dialog and click OK, the Select Custom Control DLL dialog displays (see Figure 16.8).

The workspace that is displayed behind the dialog has a small rectangle in the upper-left corner and looks like the workspace used to build the custom visual user object.

To build an external user object:

Step 1 Specify the DLL that defines the user object, and click OK. The External User Object Style dialog displays (see Figure 16.9).

Step 2 Enter the class name registered in the DLL. This information about class name typically is provided by the DLL vendor.

Step 3 Enter text in the Text box. The text attribute is displayed if the object has a text style attribute.

Step 4 Modify the display attributes (border and scroll bars) as required.

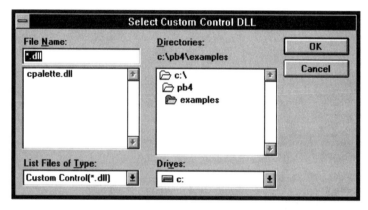

Figure 16.8 The Select Custom Control DLL dialog.

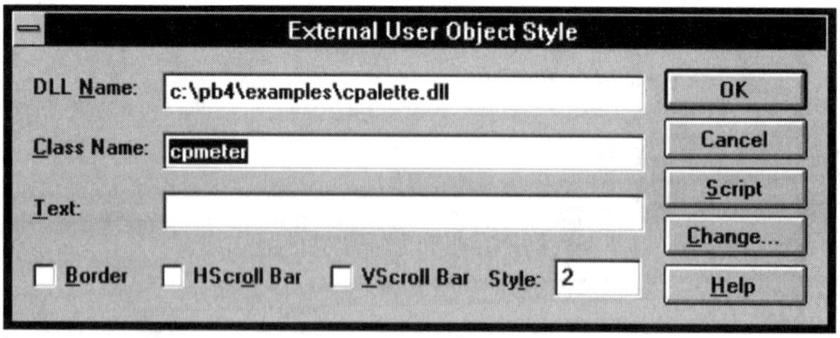

Figure 16.9 The External User Object Style dialog.

TABLE 16.2 The Events Associated with External User Objects

Event	Occurs
Constructor	When a class is instantiated (object instance). If placed on a window, it occurs before the Open event or if dynamically placed on a window via OpenUserObject( ) or OpenUserObjectParm( ).
Destructor	When an object instance is destroyed. If placed on a window, it occurs after the window's Close event or is removed dynamically via CloseUserObject( ).
DragDrop	When a dragged object is dropped on the user object.
DragEnter	When a dragged object enters the user object.
DragLeave	When a dragged object leaves the user object.
DragWithin	When a dragged object is moved within the user object.
Other	When a Windows message occurs that is not a PowerBuilder event.
RButtonDown	When the right mouse button is pressed inside the user object.

Step 5 Enter decimal values for the style bits associated with the class. Again this information is provided by the DLL vendor. PowerBuilder will OR these values with the values selected in the display attributes for the control.

Step 6 Click the OK button, and the external object will display in the User Object painter workspace.

Step 7 Declare any functions, structures, or variables that you need to declare for the user object (information about functions usually is provided by the vendor of the purchased DLL). You can declare functions, structures, and variables for the user object in the User Object painter workspace or in the PowerScript painter.

Step 8 Declare any needed events for the user object.

Step 9 Create and compile the scripts for the user object.

Step 10 Save the user object (see "Saving the user object" later on in this chapter).

The events shown in Table 16.2 are associated with external user objects. In addition, you can write scripts for each of the controls in a custom user event.

VBX visual

When you select VBX from the Visual group in the New User Object dialog and click OK, the Select VBX Control window displays (see Figure 16.10).

To continue building a VBX user object:

Step 1 Select the VBX file that defines the VBX control. When you select the VBX, the list of Class Names gets populated.

Step 2 Select the class name for the control in the Class Name box, and click OK. The functionality of the VBX should appear in the vendor's documentation. PowerBuilder will display the VBX control in the user object workspace.

Step 3 Specify the attributes for the user object (see the following paragraph).

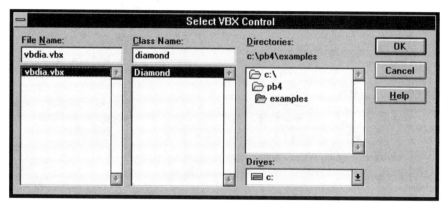

Figure 16.10 The Select VBX Control dialog.

Step 4 Build and compile the scripts for the user object.

Step 5 Save the user object (see "Saving the user object" later on in this chapter).

Each type of VBX control has its own set of attributes (also called *properties*). When you define a VBX user object, PowerBuilder reads the definition from the VBX file and builds an attribute list.

To define a VBX user object's attributes, double-click the object in the Window or User Object painter workspace. The VBX window displays the attributes unique to the VBX control (see Figure 16.11). Change values for the attributes as needed, and click OK.

For complete information about the attributes for a specific VBX control, see the documentation from the VBX control's vendor. You also can assign values to the attributes in a script. You also can see the list of the attributes in the Object browser.

VBX visual user objects have the same events as custom visual and external visual user objects, plus events that are specific to the VBX user object. When you define a VBX user object in the User Object painter, PowerBuilder reads in all of the events defined in the VBX file. It prefixes VB to the name of each event and lists them in the Select Event listbox in the PowerScript painter. For complete information about the events for a specific VBX control, see the documentation from the VBX control's vendor.

If a VBX user object event takes parameters, you can supply the parameters through the PowerScript functions EventParmDouble and EventParmString.

Standard class

When you select the standard class user object type in the New User Object dialog box and click OK, the Select Standard Class Type dialog box displays (see Figure 16.12).

To build a standard class user object:

Step 1 Select the built-in system object, click OK, and the User Object painter workspace will display.

Step 2 Declare any events, functions, structures, or variables required.

Step 3 Build and compile the scripts for the user object.

Step 4 Save the user object (see "Saving the user object" later on in this chapter).

The events shown in Table 16.3 are associated with standard class user objects.

Database remote procedure calls (RPCs)

A new feature in PowerBuilder is the ability to make a direct call to a database to execute a stored procedure. This is known as a *database remote procedure call* (RPC). Currently, stored procedures are supported in Informix, Oracle, Sybase, Wat-

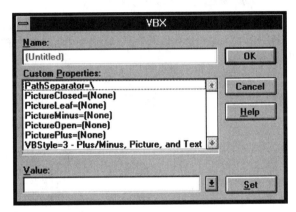

Figure 16.11 An example VBX Attributes dialog.

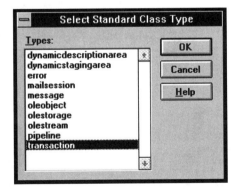

Figure 16.12 The Select Standard Class Type dialog.

TABLE 16.3 The Events Associated with Standard Class User Objects

Event	Occurs
Constructor	When a class is instantiated (object instance), either automatically when the application is opened or explicitly using the CREATE statement.
Destructor	When an object is destroyed, either automatically when the application is closed or explicitly using the DESTROY statement.

com, and other ODBC databases. Database RPCs are executed through a customized transaction class that has the appropriate function declarations for the stored procedures that are to be called.

Note: The stored procedure cannot return a result set using this method. If a result set is required, use either a DataWindow or a Cursor Declare, Execute, and Fetch sequence to retrieve it.

To set up a transaction object to be able to do this:

Step 1 Create a standard class user object inherited from the transaction class.

Step 2 Select Local External Functions from the Declare menu, and the Declare Local External Functions dialog (see Figure 16.13) will display.

Step 3 Click the button labelled Procedures, and the Remote Stored Procedures dialog (see Figure 16.14) will display, listing the names of the stored procedures available in the current database.

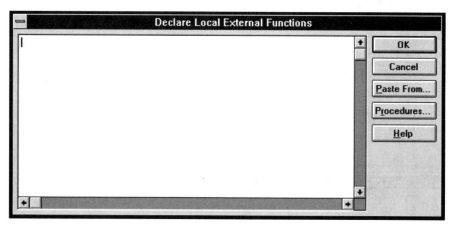

Figure 16.13 The Declare Local External Functions dialog.

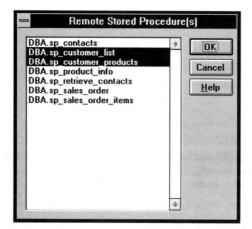

Figure 16.14 The Remote Stored Procedure dialog.

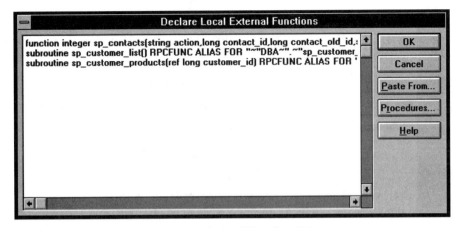

Figure 16.15 The Populated Declare Local External Functions dialog.

Step 4 Select the names of one of more procedures to be declared as functions, and click OK. PowerBuilder will paste the declaration for each selected procedure back into the Declare Local External Functions dialog (see Figure 16.15).

Step 5 Edit the declarations as required, and click OK to return to the workspace.

The syntax for declaring database remote procedure call can be either a function call or a subroutine. The only difference is that subroutines do not return a value:

```
FUNCTION ReturnType FunctionName (
   [REF] [Type1 Argument1, ..., TypeN ArgumentN]
) RPCFUNC [ALIAS FOR AliasName]

SUBROUTINE SubroutineName (
   [REF] [Type1 Argument1, ..., TypeN ArgumentN]
) RPCFUNC [ALIAS FOR AliasName]
```

where *FunctionName* and *SubroutineName* are the names that you want to use in your scripts and the *AliasName* is the actual procedure name in the database.

To call the database RPC in PowerScript, assuming that you replace the standard transaction (SQLCA) with the customized transaction:

```
INTEGER  L_iResult
L_iResult = SQLCA.pr_employee('I', 21, 21, "Martha", "Allen")
IF SQLCA.SqlCode <> 0 THEN
  MessageBox("Error calling RPC pr_employee", SQLCA.sqlerrtext)
END IF
```

See chapter 6, "Defining an application," for more information on replacing the default transaction object with a customized transaction object.

Custom class

When you select the custom class visual user object type in the New User Object dialog box and click OK, the User Object painter workspace displays.

To build a custom class user object:

Step 1 Declare any functions, structures, or variables that you need for the user object.

Step 2 Build and compile the scripts for the user object.

Step 3 Save the user object (see "Saving the user object" later on in this chapter).

The events shown in Table 16.4 are associated with class user objects.

C++ class

When you select the C++ class user object type in the New User Object dialog box and click OK, the Select C++ DLL Name dialog box displays (see Figure 16.16).
To build a C++ class user object:

Step 1 Enter the name of the DLL to be created, click OK, and the User Object painter workspace will display.

Step 2 Declare any functions and variables you need for the user object (see "Declaring shared and instance C++ variables").

Step 3 Build and compile the C++ scripts for the user object, using the Watcom IDE and Watcom Text Editor (see "Building and compiling C++").

Step 4 Save the user object (see "Saving the user object" later on in this chapter).

TABLE 16.4 The Events Associated with Class User Objects

Event	Occurs
Constructor	When a class is instantiated (object instance) using the CREATE statement.
Destructor	When an object is destroyed using the DESTROY statement.

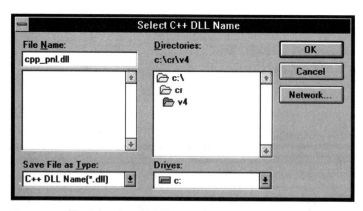

Figure 16.16 The Select C++ DLL Name dialog.

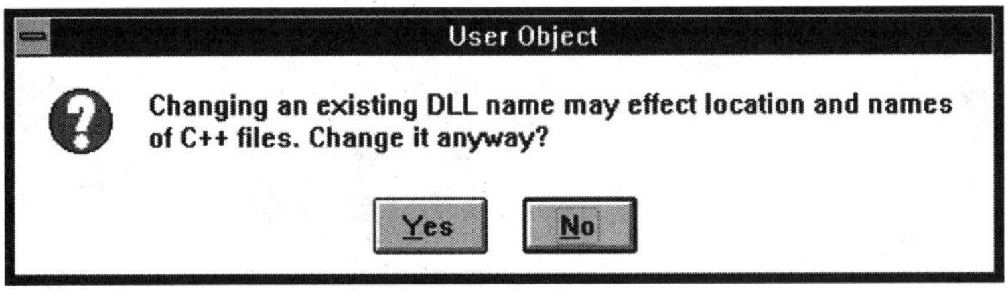

Figure 16.17 The Replace DLL Name dialog.

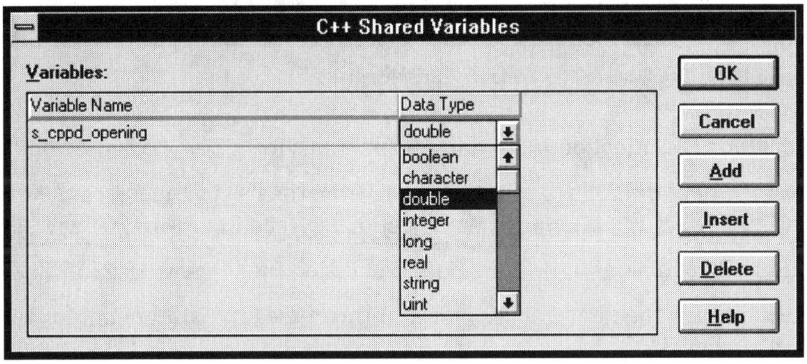

Figure 16.18 The Declare C++ Shared Variables dialog.

Later on, if you attempt to rename the DLL by selecting Change DLL from the Design menu or the pop-up menu, you will be prompted with the dialog as shown in Figure 16.17.

Declaring shared and instance C++ variables.   To declare Shared variables for a C++ class user object:

Step 1 Select `Shared Variables` from the Declare menu or the pop-up menu, and the C++ Shared Variables dialog (see Figure 16.18) will display.

Step 2 Enter the name for the shared variable along with the type.

To declare Instance variables for a C++ class user object:

Step 1 Select `Instance Variables` from the Declare menu or the pop-up menu, and the C++ Instance Variables dialog (see Figure 16.19) will display.

Step 2 Enter the name for the instance variable along with the type and access level.

Note: C++ does not support the same list of data types as PowerScript (e.g., datetime). However, there are alternative types that can be used (i.e., a string with some string manipulation within the C++ module). C++ Shared and Instance variables are not available to PowerScript, and variables in PowerBuilder are not available to C++ user objects. Use functions to pass information back and forth.

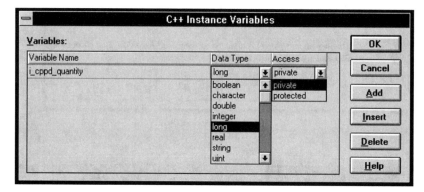

Figure 16.19 The Declare C++ Instance Variables dialog.

Declaring C++ functions. To declare functions for a C++ class user object:

Step 1 Select User Object Functions from the Declare menu or the pop-up menu, and the Select Function in User Object dialog (see Figure 16.20) will display.

Step 2 Click New, and the New Function dialog (see Figure 16.21) will display.

Step 3 Enter the name, access level, return type, and arguments for the new function, and click OK.

Once you have defined the necessary variables and function signatures, you now need to dig out your C++ manual, if necessary, and write the C++ code. When you are ready to do this, you need to invoke the Watcom Integrated Development Environment, or IDE.

To invoke the Watcom IDE:

Step 1 Select Invoke C++ Editor from the Design menu or the pop-up menu, or click the bolt of lightning on the PainterBar. If you have not saved and, therefore, named the C++ user object yet, you will be prompted with the dialog shown in Figure 16.22.

Step 2 Select Yes from the dialog, and the Save User Object dialog (see Figure 16.26) will display.

Step 3 Once you enter the name for the C++ user object and click OK, the Watcom IDE will start and you will be presented with a list of source files (see Figure 16.23).

Figure 16.23 shows the names of four files that were generated by PowerBuilder:

- CU_CPP0Y.CPP contains interface code called by PowerBuilder.

- LMAIN.CPP contains the LibMain and WEP functions required by all Windows DLLs.

- U_CPP_0Y.CPP contains the function stubs that you defined in the user object. Typically, in a simple routine, this is the only place where you need to do any coding in C++.

- U_CPP_0Y.HPP contains the the C++ class definition for the user object and the declarations for the Shared and Instance variables.

Building and compiling C++. When you are ready to code the C++ part, you need to open the file that contains the function stubs in the Watcom Windows Editor and insert the logic.

To open the Watcom Windows Editor:

Step 1 From the Watcom IDE, double-click on the file name to be opened, and the Watcom Windows Editor (see Figure 16.24) will display showing the source for the

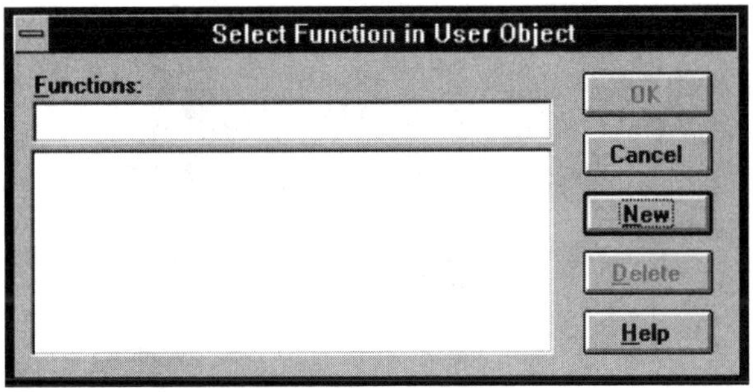

Figure 16.20 The Select Function In User Object dialog.

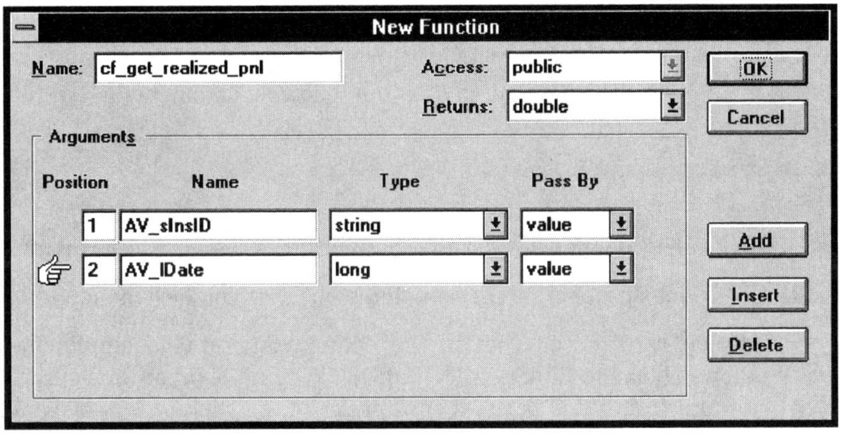

Figure 16.21 The Declare New Function dialog.

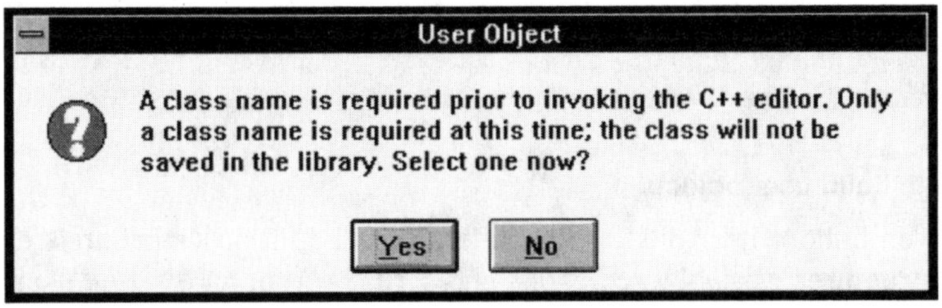

Figure 16.22 The Untitled User Object prompt.

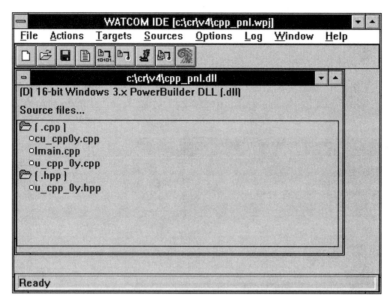

Figure 16.23 The Watcom IDE environment.

selected file. You will find that the source file will contain lines of code with several comments that PowerBuilder has generated for you.

Step 2 Look for the lines that contain the following comments:

```
/*
* PUT YOUR DECLARATIONS HERE
*/
```

Replace this comment with the logic to perform the necessary function.

Step 3 Repeat this for all of the function stubs that you have defined.

With all of the functions completely coded, you now can compile the source into a Windows Dynamic Link Library (DLL). To compile all of the source into a DLL, select Make from the Targets menu, press F4, or click on the Make all targets in the project icon. The IDE will compile the source. If successful, link it into a DLL. Monitor the IDE Log (see Figure 16.25) for the results of the compile and link phases.

Now you can use the C++ user object just like any other Class user object. See "Using a class user object" for more information on how to use Class user objects within an application.

Using inheritance to build user objects

When you build a user object that inherits its definition (attributes, events, functions, structures, variables, controls, and scripts) from an existing user object, you can save a lot of coding time. All you have to do is modify the inherited definition to meet the requirements of the current application.

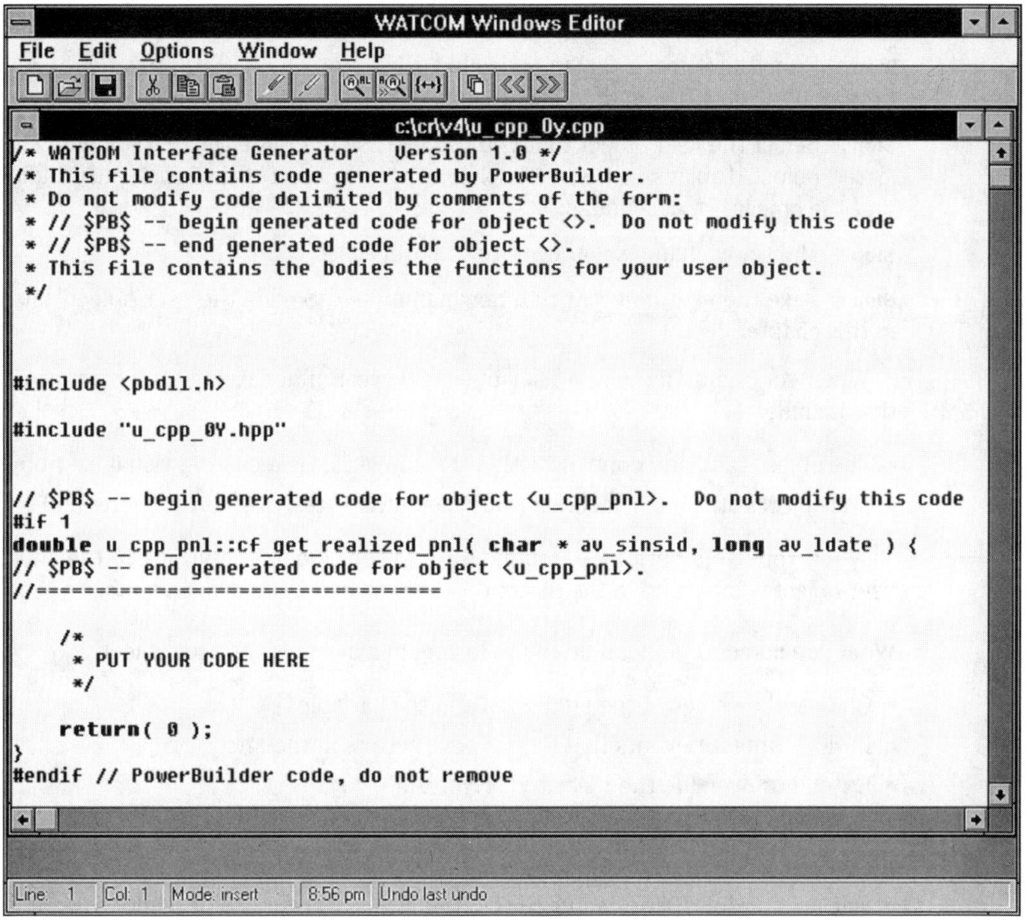

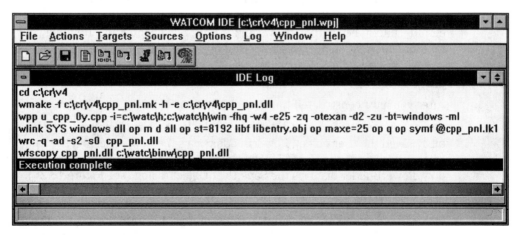

Figure 16.24 Watcom Windows editor.

Figure 16.25 An example IDE log.

To use inheritance to build a descendant user object:

Step 1 From the Select User Object dialog, click the Inherit button, and the Inherit From User Object dialog then lists the user objects in the current library.

Step 2 Select the user object that you want to use to create the descendant. The selected object displays in the workspace. The title bar for the workspace indicates that the object is a descendant.

Step 3 Make any changes you want to the user object.

Step 4 Save the user object with a new name (see "Saving the user object" later on in this chapter).

When you build and save a user object, PowerBuilder treats the object as a unit that includes:

- The object (and any controls within the object if it is a custom visual user object)
- The object's attributes, including variables, structures, events, functions, and scripts

When you use inheritance to build a new user object, everything in the ancestor user object is inherited in the direct descendant and in its descendants.

What you can do. You can do the following in a descendant user object:

- Change the values of the attributes and the variables.
- Build scripts for events that do not have scripts in the ancestor.
- Extend or override the inherited scripts.
- Add controls (if it is a custom visual user object).
- Reference the ancestor's functions, events, and structures.
- Declare variables, events, functions, and structures for the descendant.

What you cannot do. You cannot delete controls from an inherited custom control. If you want an ancestor's control in the descendant, make it invisible.

The issues concerning inheritance with user objects are the same as the issues concerning inheritance with windows and menus. See chapter 14, "Refining your code," for more information on inheritance and object-oriented programming techniques.

Saving the user object

After you have constructed the user object, to save it:

Step 1 Select Save from the File menu in the User Object painter. If you have previously saved the user object, PowerBuilder saves the new version in the same library and returns you to the User Object painter. If you have not previously saved the window, PowerBuilder displays the Save User Object dialog (see Figure 16.26).

Step 2 Name the user object in the User Objects box (see "Naming conventions").

Step 3 Write comments to describe the user object. These comments display in the Select User Object window and in the Library painter. It is a good idea to use comments so that you and others can easily determine the purpose of the user object later.

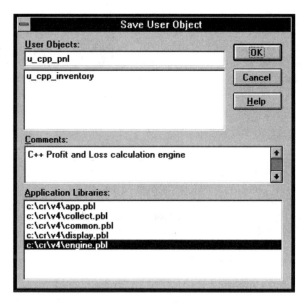

Figure 16.26 The Save User Object dialog.

Step 4 Specify the library in which to save the user object.

Step 5 Click OK to save the user object.

Naming conventions

The user object name can be any valid PowerBuilder identifier up to 40 characters. However, you should adopt naming conventions when you create user objects to make it easier to understand a user object's type and purpose. Table 16.5 contains some ideas for a naming convention. Note that all user objects basically begin with u_ and end with a descriptive purpose.

See chapter 21, "Standards and guidelines," for more information on naming conventions and standards.

TABLE 16.5 Some Ideas for a Naming Convention

User object	Format	Example
Standard visual	u_controlprefix_purpose	u_cb_close is a CommandButton that closes the parent.
Custom visual	u_cv_purpose	u_cv_toolbar is a toolbar.
External visual	u_ex_purpose	u_ex_datefunc handles date calculations.
VBX visual	u_vbx_purpose	u_vbx_gauge displays a gauge.
Standard class	u_sc_purpose	u_sc_db_rpc is a transaction with database remote procedure calls (RPCs).
Custom class	u_cc_purpose	u_cc_custodian is a business class that handles custodian information.
C++ class	u_cpp_purpose	u_cpp_pnl is a C++ class that handles trading profit and loss calculations.

Using a User Object in an Application

You use visual user objects by either placing them in a window or another custom visual user object or by dynamically opening them. You use class user objects by creating an instance of the class. Now let's deal more specifically with the two different types of user objects.

Using a visual user object

To place a visual user object into a window or a custom visual user object:

Step 1 Open the required painter: Window painter or User Object painter.

Step 2 Click the User Object icon in the PainterBar, or select User Object from the Controls menu. The Select User Object window will display.

Step 3 Select the user object that you want to use.

Step 4 Click the area where you want the user object to be placed, and PowerBuilder then creates a descendant user object that inherits its definition from the chosen user object and places it in the window or custom visual user object.

Frequently used visual user objects. You can place icons for the visual user objects that you use frequently in the PainterBar in the Window painter and User Object painter. Then you can simply click the icon to place a user object in the window or custom visual user object.

After you place a user object in a window or a custom visual user object, you can rename it (recommended), size it, position it, and write scripts for it (see "Adding scripts to the descendant" later in this chapter) just like any other control.

Using a visual user object dynamically. You can add a user object to a window during execution using the PowerScript functions OpenUserObject and OpenUserObjectWithParm in a script. You can remove a user object from a window using the CloseUserObject function.

Adding scripts to the descendant visual user object. As you can see, when you place a visual user object in a window or a custom visual user object, you actually are creating a descendant of the visual user object. All scripts defined for the ancestor user object are inherited by the descendant. These can be overridden or extended if required. However, you cannot access and subsequently add new, or override existing, scripts for individual controls in a custom visual user object after placing it in a window or custom visual user object. All you can see are the events that apply to the custom visual user object itself. If you need to do something in particular, then it must be done within the custom visual user object in the User Object painter.

Using a class user object

Class user objects are not visible, so they cannot be placed on a window or other visual object directly. To use a existing Class user object within your application, you must do the following:

Step 1 Create a variable of the same type as the user object required, with global, instance, shared, or local scope:

```
u_custodian_class  G_uoCustodian
```

With this example code, a global variable is declared so that the user object that handles custodian information can be accessed from anywhere within the application.

Step 2 Instantiate the user object in a script. For global scope, instantiate user objects in the application Open event or a function called from it, for example, f_app_open():

```
G_uoCustodian = CREATE u_custodian_class
```

Step 3 Once it is instantiated, you can call the public function or access its public variables:

```
L_sInsDesc = G_uoCustodian.uf_get_desc(I_sInsCd)
```

or:

```
L_sInsCd = G_uoCustodian.I_sInsCd
```

It is important to note that, when you are finished with the object, you must free its memory allocation by destroying the object instance variable:

```
DESTROY G_uoCustodian
```

In this example, the global variable would be destroyed in the application Close event or a function called from it, for example, f_app_close().

Class user objects are not tied to either the PowerBuilder or Windows message system and, therefore, do not have a message queue. As a result, you can issue a TriggerEvent(), but you cannot issue a PostEvent() to a Class user object.

Communicating with a user object

Frequently, you will need to pass data between a window and a user object. The user object can be either a visual user object placed in the window or a class user object that is within the access scope of the window. There are two main ways of communicating between classes (e.g., a user object and a window). You can use:

- Functions
- User events

Communicating via a function. To pass information from one class to another: In the receiving class, define a function with public access that takes as arguments the information needed from the sending class.

For example, if you need to pass information from a window, named w_customer_list, to a user object, called uo_search, placed in the window, you call the user object's function (in this case, uf_set_criteria) from a script in the window:

```
uo_search.uf_set_criteria(sle_search_string.Text)
```

Communicating via a user event. You can define events, called user events, to communicate between classes. You can declare user events for any PowerBuilder class or control. In many cases, you will not need to define user events, because they already are inherited from the underlying ancestor system class. You will find, however, that custom visual user objects often need user events. When you place a custom visual user object in a window or in another custom visual user object, you can write scripts only for events that occur for the custom user object itself. You cannot access and, therefore, code scripts for events in the individual controls that make up the custom user object. To overcome this, you define your user events for the custom user object and trigger these events, where necessary, from the controls within the user object. For example:

```
parent.TriggerEvent("ue_selected")
```

where *parent* refers to parent class of the individual control, which is the custom user object itself.

(*Note*: TriggerEvent is synchronous; the event is triggered immediately. PostEvent is asynchronous; the event is posted to the end of the event queue.)

Then, once the custom user object is placed in the window, you code scripts for these user events. This is done by selecting the user object, opening the PowerScript painter, selecting the user event (in this case, ue_selected), and coding the script.

The suitability of each communication technique is summarized in Table 16.6.

TABLE 16.6 The Suitability of Each Communication Technique

Technique	Advantages	Disadvantages
Using functions	1. Easy to pass information in both directions	1. Processing overhead
	2. Strong type checking	2. Operate synchronously
	3. Supports encapsulation	
Using events	1. Supports asynchronous (using PostEvent) and synchronous (using TriggerEvent) operation	1. No type checking
	2. No easy way of passing information	

Deployment

17

Preparing the
Application for Production

There hopefully comes a time in most development efforts when the application is approaching the ready state for production implementation. At this point, it should be both user tested and approved as well as quality assured. This chapter will review steps that should be taken to prepare the application for this stage of the cycle (i.e., production implementation). The environment hopefully has other production applications that have established the *de facto* standards for the operational hand-off from developer to operations and system assurance.

Overview

There are two ways to produce executables in PowerBuilder:

- You can use the Project painter to create a project object that specifies the executable file name, PowerBuilder Dynamic Libraries (PBD files), and PowerBuilder resource files (PBR files). This method allows you to create a new executable file and Dynamic Libraries without having to redefine the components of the application each time you build it. See chapter 6 for a description of the Project painter.

- Use the Application painter and specify which libraries are dynamic each time. Then go to the Library painter and build each of the Dynamic Libraries that you need.

Preparing the Application for Production

Preparing an application for production encompasses changes to a number of components in the environment. The items described in the following paragraphs are but a sample of the considerations.

The user's workstation must be able to execute the application. In a single-user environment, the workstation should have adequate processing strength (CPU) and disk space to house the PowerBuilder executable runtime files and the database. In a multiuser network-based application, the workstation should have adequate CPU, connectivity to the LAN, and enough disk space to house the application components. Determining the user's workstation adequacy should be done early in the development cycle to allow time to procure hardware, software, and administrative services to prepare the workstation for production.

The PowerBuilder and vendor software used to create the production executable should be the latest stable release available. The project team should be in contact with the organization's software administrators to verify and maintain the currency of the PowerBuilder and vendor software used in the implementation. In mature environments, this can be done *pro forma*, but sometimes each individual developer will each have his or her own copy of PowerBuilder, and the maintenance level of each is in question.

The database should be prepared for production. The database sizing should be revisited to ensure that it has the capacity to support the application without a near-term need for reorganization. The QA/development database objects must be migrated to the production environment. The objects to be migrated must be reviewed to ensure that they reflect the current state of the database. Use data definition (DDL) that is derived from the DBMS catalog to ensure accuracy. Check to ensure that extended attribute tables have been populated. This is necessary for dynamic DataWindows that use the extended attributes for display and validation. Check all referential integrity declarations. Prepare the database backup and recovery procedures.

Review each PBL and its members. Clean up "dirty" code. Remove commented code. Add commentary to scripts. This will help later on in the maintenance cycle.

Regenerate and optimize the PowerBuilder libraries. This will highlight any incorrect objects. This should be done periodically throughout development. Make a habit of optimizing your libraries (in the Library painter) on a regular basis. Library (PBL) files can become internally fragmented over time, especially when you make a lot of changes to the objects in them. Fragmentation means that the PBLs contain gaps of unused space with objects residing in noncontiguous areas of storage. This can affect performance when you're working in the PowerBuilder development environment. PowerBuilder optimizing will unfragment the internal storage of PBL files. (It doesn't alter the contents of objects or cause them to be recompiled.) To ensure good performance, consider optimizing any libraries that you're actively working on about once a week.

Correct regeneration problems. Pass the errors on to those who are responsible.

Freeze PBLs in preparation of building an executable.

Now you are ready to build the first draft of a PowerBuilder executable. We will review the PowerBuilder library types, which are precursors to creating an executable (.EXE). At this time, the project also should prepare a "problem log" to identify and track responses to problems that will arise as each different user begins to access the new software. Some third-party tools (e.g., SQA Team Test) have such a problem log facility built in. (See Figure 17.1.)

Problem number	Priority	Description component name/location	Responsible Developer	Date reported	Date resolved
1	1	DataWindow d_test in appldb1.pbl does not include vertical scroll bar	Dee Betoo	1/16/95	
2	2	Menu m_test in appl1.pbl does not include SAVE item and toolbar	Em Deye	1/17/95	

Figure 17.1 An example problem log.

The PowerBuilder Executable

An .EXE file is a compact, fully functional version of your application that is ready to deliver to your users. The .EXE file contains:

- A platform-dependent executable bootstrap routine.
- The compiled version of all referenced objects in the application and also PBL files, except those that reside in the .PBD files. .PBD files are similar to Dynamic Link Libraries (DLLs) in that they are linked to your application at execution time. Unlike your executable file, PBD files don't include any startup code. That's because they can't be executed independently. Instead, they are accessed when needed as an application executes to provide objects it requires (if it can't find those objects in the executable file). Typically, you will create a PBD for each PBL.
- Any resource objects that are put into the file by the PowerBuilder Resource file (.PBR)

Note: Maintain the size of your .EXE files so that they are 1.5MB or smaller.

How is the executable composed

When you invoke the Application painter to build the executable file:

- PowerBuilder locates all of the PowerBuilder libraries in the Library Search Path in the order listed. You then will specify the associated DYNAMIC libraries (PBD).
- If you are not using a PBD for a particular PBL, PowerBuilder copies all the referenced compiled objects from these libraries.
- PowerBuilder creates a file with an .EXE file extension in the directory where the PBL file is located. (You can indicate a different directory when you create the file. The PBL directory is the default location.)

Take care to know all of the objects to be included and their location. An .EXE file does not automatically include items like:

- Any item that is not referenced in the application scripts or is not assigned in a painter (for example, pictures, bitmaps, pointers, or icons that are dynamically referenced in scripts).
- Any objects that are dynamically referenced in your application scripts (e.g., a DataWindow object).

PowerBuilder does not copy objects to the .EXE file from libraries declared to be the PowerBuilder Dynamic Library (.PBD) files. Instead, objects in the PBD files are linked to the application at runtime.

If you have other files (non-PowerBuilder), you can include these items in the .EXE file, using a PowerBuilder Resource File (.PBR), which basically contains the name of the files and their location.

To create an .EXE file, you need to know the name and file location of:

- The PowerBuilder library or libraries where all of the PowerBuilder objects for your application are stored. Do not forget class libraries if they are used in development.

- Any DataWindows objects that are referenced dynamically in your application scripts.

- Any resources (other than PowerBuilder objects) that your application needs to run, such as bitmaps or icons.

- The application icon (optional).

As you can see, building the productive executable requires planning and organization. If you have taken care to locate and maintain all of the application components in a secure and reliable fashion, then building a production executable should not be problematic. If you have not been careful, then creating the executable can be difficult and resource-consuming. The use of PowerBuilder Dynamic Libraries generally avoids many of the location problems, especially with inherited and dynamically linked objects.

The contents of PowerBuilder libraries (.PBL)

As previously mentioned, a PowerBuilder library (.PBL file) contains only PowerBuilder objects such as an application, window, menu, DataWindow, function, structure, or user object. Each of the objects has two parts: the source object and the compiled object. (See Figure 17.2.)

The *source object* is a syntactic representation of the object that includes the script code. You create and modify it with the painters. You can export it and view the syntax. The *compiled object* is a binary representation of the object, similar to a .OBJ file in the C language. PowerBuilder creates the compiled object automatically each time you close the painter or issue the `Save` or `Save As` command from the File menu.

As we have mentioned, try to keep your PowerBuilder libraries (.PBL files) smaller than 800K and with fewer than 50 to 60 objects. This will facilitate an object search as well as PBL maintenance. Also be careful with the names of the PBL directories. For instance, when creating .PBD files to deliver with your .EXE, if the directory

DATAWINDOW
source
compiled object

Figure 17.2 The parts of an object.

structure contains a directory with a dot-notated name, then the .PBD file will not be created. Avoid using a directory structure with a dot notation or, if you must, then prior to creating the PBD files, copy PBLs in this directory to a directory that does not contain the dot naming convention. Then using the Library painter, point at the PBLs in this other directory to create the PBDs. This will not affect the running of the application because the directory structure at runtime is immaterial as long as the PBD files can be found as the application executes.

The content of a PowerBuilder Dynamic Library (.PBD)

A PowerBuilder Dynamic Library is not unlike a DLL or, for mainframe people, an object library that is used to build the load module or executable mainframe object. When you build a PBD, PowerBuilder automatically includes only directly referenced objects. Some of the objects that you use in your application might be referenced dynamically (e.g., a DataWindow object).

You can store these objects in a PowerBuilder Dynamic Library (a .PBD file). A .PBD file:

- Contains all of the compiled objects that the .PBL file contains. Like an .EXE file, it does not have any source code.

- Must be used with a PowerBuilder .EXE file. It cannot be run alone.

- Must be identified in the Library Search Path. Keep frequently used objects at or near the top.

- Works like a Windows Dynamic Link Library (.DLL file); however, they are not interchangeable.

    Using .PBD files allows you to:

- Break your application into smaller segments that are easier to manage.

- Distribute your application components separately (for example, to distribute an upgrade or an individual bug fix, you can send one .PBD file instead of the entire application).

- Share components among several applications.

    Note: PowerBuilder does not load the entire .PBD file into memory at once. The individual objects in a .PBD file are loaded on demand.

How does the PBD work with the PowerBuilder executable?

Like a steplib or joblib data definition in the mainframe world, a PBD is an execution library searched to find the next component to be acted upon. PowerBuilder searches through the list of execution libraries starting with the .EXE. If PowerBuilder does not find an object in the .EXE file, it searches the .PBD files in the order listed in the Library Search Path. Therefore, put the .PBL files with the most frequently called objects at the top of the Library Search Path.

Building a .PBD file

To build a PowerBuilder Dynamic library, in the Library painter:

Step 1 Select `Build Dynamic Runtime Library` from the Utilities Menu. (See Figure 17.3.)

Step 2 Select the library that you want to use as a Dynamic Library.

Step 3 Click OK.

PowerBuilder creates a dynamic execution library with the same filename as the selected library, with the file extension changed to .PBD. This file is in the directory where the .PBL file is stored. PowerBuilder copies all compiled objects in the .PBL file to the .PBD file.

Note: To run the application, you must include all .PBD files in directories in an operating system library search list (e.g. DOS path).

What is a PowerBuilder Resource file (.PBR)?

The PowerBuilder Resource file (.PBR) allows you to include in the .EXE file or the .PBD file any object that is dynamically referenced and any object that Power-Builder does not automatically include. The benefit of a .PBR file is that you can avoid having to distribute each of your resource files separately with your application. We recommend that you use the file extension .PBR for the PowerBuilder Resource file.

You create the .PBR file by listing the file name for each resource on a separate line in an ASCII file. Be sure to include the file name for each resource that is not a Power-Builder object and is not declared as an attribute of an object or control, such as:

- Bitmaps (.BMP)
- Compressed bitmaps (.RLE)

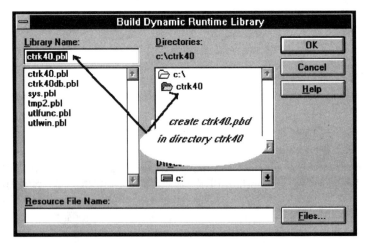

Figure 17.3 Library Utility PBD build.

- Windows Meta file (.WMF)
- Icons (.ICO)
- Cursors (.CUR)
- Any resources that you assigned dynamically in scripts for the application
- Any resources that are conditionally referenced in a script

The file name for the resource can include the drive and path name. If the resource is in the same directory where you will build the .EXE file, you need to use only the file name. If the resource is in a different directory, you obviously must qualify the file name with the drive and path name.

So, if you are using a PBL, you must plan the distribution of the application such that you are aware of the users' file access environment, especially if they run the application from their local disk drive. (More on this later.) If at all possible, make sure that all resources (usually bitmaps) are in the current directory when you create the .EXE file.

It is a good idea to create a document and perhaps a utility to track the files required in an application especially dynamic resources, unless you have a large number of dynamically called data windows (DW), in which case the DWs should be stored in a PBD. You might have a separate PBD for the dynamic PBDs and place it near the top of the search list. This will cut down on the time it takes for PowerBuilder to search and find objects used in the application. When you assign resources dynamically in scripts, without using a .PBR file, PowerBuilder tries to find the resource files somewhere on the operating system search path. When the resource is in a directory specified in the search path, PowerBuilder loads and displays the resource in the application.

If the resource does not exist in a directory in the operating system search path, you cannot use the resource in the application. Therefore, if you do not use a .PBR file, you must:

- Distribute resource files separately when you distribute the application.
- Place any dynamically called DataWindow objects in a .PBD file, and distribute the file.

To specify a DataWindow object in a .PBR file, enclose the DataWindow objects name in parentheses immediately after the complete path name for the .PBL file. For example:

```
C:\APPLIB\TVDYNDW.PBL
```

The DataWindow d_series is located in the PowerBuilder Library TVDYNDW.PBL and is qualified with the drive and complete path name.

When you specify a .PBR file in the Additional Resources File Name box on the Create Executable dialog or the Build Dynamic Runtime Library dialog, Power-Builder finds the resources listed in the .PBR file and stores them in the .EXE (or .PBD) file with the same resource names.

PowerBuilder assigns the file name that appears in the .PBR file as a name in the .EXE or .PBD file. In the application scripts, you must refer to the resource by the exact name.

When the user runs your application and dynamically specifies a resource, as shown in the examples that follow, PowerBuilder searches the .EXE or .PBD file for an exact string match, including the path. When PowerBuilder finds a match, it loads that resource from the .EXE file.

When PowerBuilder does not find a match, it searches the directories listed in the user's Windows search path. If no match is found, then no picture displays.

Before you deliver your application to users, you will need to prepare a standard .EXE file in the Application painter. Again this involves creating PBDs from PBLs as well as the other items mentioned at the start of the chapter. The next few items relate to PBLs directly.

Before you can build an executable (.EXE), however, you need to plan for and finalize the PowerBuilder components. Some additional considerations are covered in the following paragraphs.

As mentioned earlier, ensure that the latest PowerBuilder fixes have been installed. The project's software administrator should be responsible for this task.

Regenerate all .PBLs. If your application contains inheritance, make sure the ancestors are regenerated prior to regenerating the descendants, or regenerate all .PBLs twice. Optimize all .PBLs after regenerating them but before creating the .EXE.

Prioritize the order of the .PBLs in the Library Search Path. The .PBLs that contain objects that are used more often should be at the head of the library search path. Typically, 80% of the work that an application does uses about 20% of the library objects. These 20% objects should be at the front of the library list. If possible and feasible, have the .PBLs that contain the ancestors listed before the .PBLs that contain the descendants.

Return all "checked out" items to the appropriate PBL. As part of the cleanup, review all "checked out" items and resolve their status. If possible, avoid having objects checked out of your .PBLs when creating your .EXE.

Check that all required objects are in the .PBR file. Objects that are referenced dynamically in the application are not automatically included in the .EXE. Such objects should be included using a .PBR file. The advantage of a .PBR file is that each object does not have to be distributed separately with the .EXE. Some objects that you might include in a .PBR file would be bitmaps (.BMP), compressed bitmaps (.RLE), icons (.ICO), and cursors (.CUR). You also will want to include objects that are referenced dynamically or are changed conditionally.

When building an .EXE, the amount of real memory (RAM) available must be at least equal to the combined total size of all of the .PBLs that make up the application. Also check prospective user workstations to ensure that the required storage space is available.

Check the workstation memory and, if needed, increase its size. If you do not have enough memory, your machine might be thrashing while trying to create the .EXE. Try increasing the amount of memory that is available. If that does not work, try increasing the size of the operating system page or swap file.

Include all necessary objects in .PBDs. Make sure that all objects that are referenced dynamically are included in .PBDs or in .PBRs.

Creating a Simple .EXE File

Step 1 From the Power Panel or PowerBar, open the Application painter. (See Figure 17.4.) If the desired application is not the default, then select your application from the list in the Select Library and Select Application dialog boxes. Click OK.

Step 2 Verify that all .PBL files are in the Library Search path. Within the Application painter, choose LibList. (See Figure 17.5.) Amend PowerBuilder libraries as required. Click OK.

Step 3 Create the executable (.EXE) file. Within Application painter, click Create-Exe. Select libraries that have been converted to PowerBuilder Dynamic Libraries list. Click OK in the Create Executable dialog. (See Figure 17.6.)

This builds the executable file by copying or linking the compiled form of each referenced object from the PowerBuilder libraries or .PBDs in the Library Search Path to a file with an .EXE file extension. The new .EXE file is built in the directory that you specified.

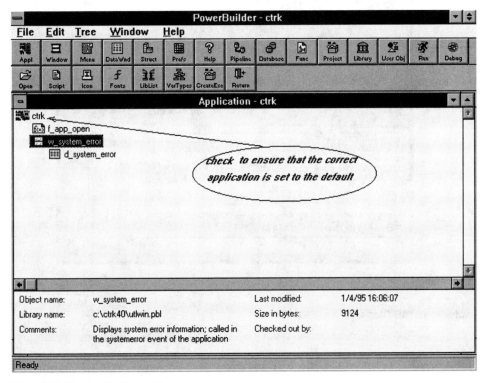

Figure 17.4 The Application painter.

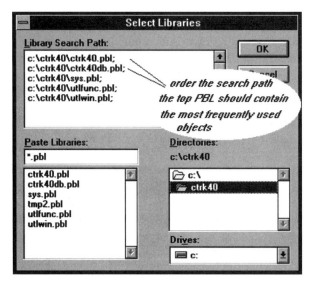

Figure 17.5 Selecting libraries for the application.

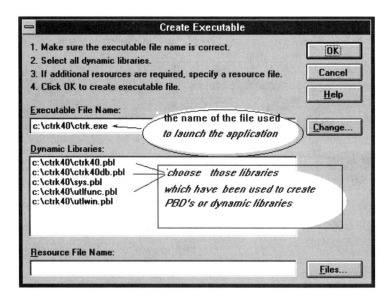

Figure 17.6 Creating an executable.

Including .PBD files with an .EXE file

Before building the executable, you must create the PBD using the Library painter Utility menu item and selecting the Build Dynamic Library option. (See Figure 17.7.)

Step 1 From the Power Panel, open the Application painter. Select your application from the list in the Select Application dialog box. Click OK.

Step 2 Verify that all .PBLs are in the Library Search path. Click Libraries in the Modify Application dialog. Verify that all of the .PBL files that you need are in the Library Search path. Add any libraries that are missing. Click OK.

Step 3 Select Dynamic Libraries. Click Runtime on the Modify Application dialog. Select all of the .PBL files in the Dynamic Libraries that you made into .PBD files for this application. (The compiled objects found in these selected .PBLs will not be copied into the .EXE file.)

Step 4 Create the .EXE file by clicking OK in the Create Executable dialog.

This builds the executable file by copying the compiled form of each referenced object that is not in a Dynamic Library from the libraries in the Library Search Path to a file with an .EXE file extension.

Including .PBR files with an .EXE file

Use your favorite ASCII text editor to create the .PBR file.

Step 1 From the Power Panel, open the Application painter. Select your application from the list in the Select Application dialog box. Click OK.

Step 2 Verify that all .PBL files are in Library Search path. Click Libraries on the Modify Application dialog. Add any libraries that are missing. Click OK.

Step 3 Add the .PBR file. Click Runtime in the Modify Application dialog. Enter the name of the .PBR file in the box Additional Resources File Name.

Step 4 Create the .EXE file by clicking OK in the Create Executable dialog.

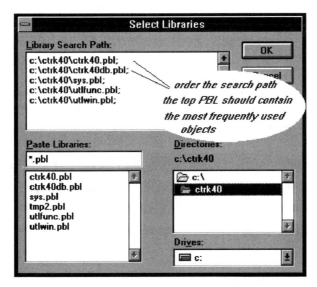

Figure 17.7 Building a dynamic PowerBuilder LIbrary (PBD).

This builds the executable file by copying the compiled form of each referenced object from the libraries in the Library Search Path and the objects named in the .PBR files to a file with an .EXE file extension. The new .EXE file is built in the directory that you specified.

Including .PBD files and .PBR files with an .EXE file

Step 1 Use your favorite ASCII text editor to create the .PBR file.

Step 2 From the Power Panel, open the Application painter. Select your application from the list in the Select Application dialog box. Click OK.

Step 3 Verify that all .PBLs are in the Library Search path. Click Libraries in the Modify Application dialog. Verify that all of the .PBL files you need are in the Library Search path. Add any libraries that are missing. Click OK.

Step 4 Select Dynamic Libraries. Click Runtime in the Modify Application dialog. Select all of the .PBL files in the Dynamic Libraries that you made into .PBD files for this application. (The compiled objects found in these selected .PBLs will not be copied into the .EXE file.)

Step 5 Add the .PBR file by entering the name of the .PBR file in the Additional Resources File Name dialog box.

Step 6 Create the .EXE file by clicking OK in the Create Executable dialog.

This builds the executable file by copying the compiled form of each referenced object from the libraries in the Library Search Path and the objects in the named .PBR files to a file with an .EXE file extension. The new .EXE file is built in the directory that you specified.

Testing the Executable Application

Once you create the executable version of your application, you'll want to test how it runs before proceeding with distribution. You might already have executed the application many times within the PowerBuilder development environment, but it still is very important to run the executable version as an independent application—just the way end users will.
To do this:

Step 1 Leave PowerBuilder and go to your operating (windowing) environment.

Step 2 Run the application's executable file as you run any native application. See Figure 17.8.

What to look for during a test run

As the application executes, you should monitor its behavior closely to uncover any problems. Here are some things to look for:

- Can the application access all of its objects? Pay special attention to those that are referenced dynamically (through string variables in scripts).

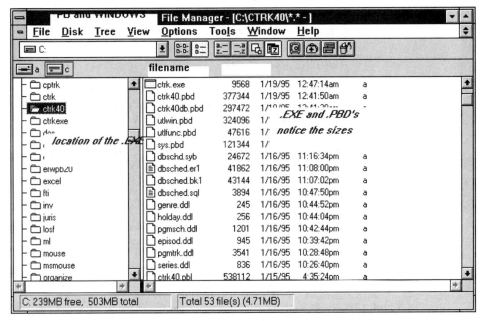

Figure 17.8 The executable files .EXE and .PBDs in Microsoft's Windows.

- Can the application access all of its resources? Pay special attention to those that are referenced dynamically (through string variables in scripts) and those that are needed by objects in your PBD files.

- Can the application access the production databases that it needs to?

- Can the application access any external programs or files that it needs to?

- Do all of the features of the application work as they did when you tested them in the PowerBuilder development environment?

- Is the performance of the application acceptable, given your requirements and expectations?

For example, maybe the application takes longer than you like getting loaded into memory (because you created a really large executable file), or maybe the application has to do too much searching for particular resources (because you've kept them in separate files instead of copying them into the executable or .PBD files). In cases such as these, it might help you to repackage the application using a different packaging model.

Tracing the application's execution

To help you track down problems, PowerBuilder provides an execution trace facility that you can use when running the executable version of an application. This facility records the application's activities, including:

- The creation and destruction of objects

- The execution of event scripts and functions

To invoke the trace facility, you will need to append the `/pdebug` switch to the command line for the executable. For example:

```
c:\pbapps\pubs.exe /pdebug
```

Now, when you run the application using this option, it stores the trace information in a text file that you can read in a text editor. The text file is generated in the same directory as the executable and has the same name as the executable with a .DBG extension.

Even if your application's executable is problem-free, you might consider using this facility to generate an audit trail of its operation.

Conducting a beta test with users

After the executable application passes your tests, you might want to conduct beta tests of it with actual end users. This typically involves:

- Distributing the application on a very limited basis (to a subset of its ultimate audience).

- Monitoring usage closely.

- Restricting usage to nonproduction work.

- Running in parallel with any existing production applications until the decision is made to go final.

Testing on user computers often can uncover problems that don't reveal themselves on developer computers. In many cases, this is due to hardware and software differences between those two environments:

- Hardware differences—For instance, developers might have more powerful processors or larger monitors than end users have. Developers also might have different network connections and peripherals.

- Software differences—For instance, developers already have all of the Power-Builder deployment DLLs needed to run the executable application independently (because those DLLs get installed along with the PowerBuilder development environment). In contrast, you must install the PowerBuilder deployment DLLs on user computers yourself when distributing the application.

- Developer and user computers also might differ in which version of the operating system they're using, how that operating system is tuned and configured, and which applications, databases, or utilities are installed.

18

Distributing the Application

After developing the application and creating an executable, you need to consider the distribution of the application. (For more detailed information on creating the executable, see chapter 6, "Defining an Application," and chapter 17, "Preparing the Application for Production.") To do this, you need to know how the application is configured so that you can determine what files are to be distributed. Also you need to understand the end-user production environment so that you can determine where the components of the application are going to reside.

This chapter is going to recap the various components that can be configured to create the application. With the configuration of the application defined, we'll discuss the what, where, and how of distribution: what needs to be delivered, where it is to be delivered, and how to get it there.

Once you have determined the delivery mechanism and procedures, it still is very important to carry out extensive testing on a subset of the production environment prior to the complete rollout. This not will only tell you whether or not the process works, but it also will allow you to make the necessary adjustments and document them accordingly.

Application Configurations

In PowerBuilder, the development team has several choices in the way that the application can be configured and, therefore, delivered to the client workstations. The choices for distribution can range from a small executable (.EXE) that references and uses objects that are stored in several PowerBuilder Dynamic Libraries (.PBD's) to a single, consequently larger, executable that contains everything. Let's recap the components of the PowerBuilder environment that are used in determining the optimum "shape" for the application configuration.

PowerBuilder Library (.PBL)

The PowerBuilder Library (.PBL) contains both a copy of the source (human read-able) object and the runtime p-code (intermediate, not-quite-executable code) ob-ject. (See Figure 18.1.)

All of the classes that can be defined using the PowerBuilder painters are stored within the PBL. The classes are Application, Data Pipeline, DataWindow, Function, Menu, Project, Structure, User Object, Query, and Window. The English Wizard also can be added to the list and is available as a additional purchase.

You should keep the following performance tips in mind:

- Put no more than 40 items, or classes, in a single PowerBuilder Library (.PBL). and try to keep the size of the PBL below 800K.

- Defragment the PowerBuilder Libraries (.PBLs) by "optimizing" them using the Li-brary painter. This should be done on a regular basis in off-peak hours—about once per week/month depending on the activity (Check-In/Out, Save, Save As, etc.).

- Regenerate prior to generating the executable (.EXE) or Dynamic Library (.PBD). This will ensure that the linkages between classes still are valid and intact.

PowerBuilder Dynamic Library (PBD)

The PowerBuilder Dynamic Library (.PBD) is like a Windows Dynamic Link Li-brary (.DLL), although they are not exactly the same. A PBD (see Figure 18.2) is created using the Library or Project painter and contains a copy of all of the com-piled objects, or runtime p-code, that is in the PowerBuilder Library (.PBL) from which it was generated. The PBD does not contain any source code and cannot be executed directly.

During runtime, the classes are loaded from the PBD via the runtime engine on an as-needed basis. The PBD is a convenient way of bundling enterprise-wide common

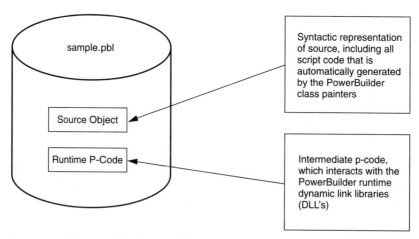

Figure 18.1 A PowerBuilder Library (.PBL).

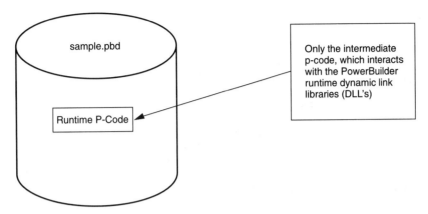

Figure 18.2 A PowerBuilder Dynamic Library (.PBD).

w_show_retrieve_arg	11/2/94 11:22:02	(17267)
w_sort_and_filter	11/2/94 11:22:08	(32753)
w_sp_update	11/2/94 11:22:13	(14993)

Figure 18.3 Object Sizes in the Library painter.

application components, thereby reducing redundant code that is present in multiple applications. The PBD also allows you to distribute upgrades to subsections of the system without a complete recompilation.

The number that is displayed within parentheses to the right of the date and time stamp is the size in bytes of the runtime p-code (compiled) object. (See Figure 18.3.)

You should keep the following performance tips in mind:

- Put the frequently referenced classes into a library at the beginning of the application Library Search Path. This path is included in the executable file; the runtime engine searches serially through this path to determine the library location of the required class.

- Application Library Search Paths are not stored in PBLs. They are maintained in each developer's PB.INI. If the application is moved, the search path must be reconstructed for each developer.

- Keep the size of the runtime p-code (compiled) window class to less than 100K. If the size gets above 100K, the time required to load the window from an .EXE or .PBD significantly increases. Don't forget to include the size of any user objects on the window and the size of any ancestor window in this calculation.

PowerBuilder Resource File (.PBR)

The PowerBuilder Resource File (.PBR) is a text file that contains the path names of Windows resource files that are referenced in the application and/or PowerBuilder DataWindows dynamically assigned using strings. (See Figure 18.4.)

```
cust.bmp
order.bmp
dyn_ref.pbl(d_customers)
dyn_ref.pbl(d_items)
dyn_ref.pbl(d_orders)
```

Figure 18.4 A PowerBuilder
Resource File (.PBR).

Windows resource files. The Windows resource files that you can use in your application are:

- RGB encoded bitmaps (.BMP)
- Compressed run-length encoded bitmaps (.RLE)
- Cursors (.CUR)
- Icons (.ICO)
- Windows meta-files (.WMF)

For example, when you insert a bitmap onto the surface of a window, the path name is stored in the container for the bitmap. So, when you run the application from within the development or runtime environment, the bitmap file can be retrieved from the same place that you referred to when you defined the picture in the Window painter. However, if you forget to copy the bitmap file to the production environment, when you run the application, the bitmap can no longer be found and will not be displayed. If you include it in a resource file with exactly the same path name, the runtime engine will make a match with the object and consequently find it in the specified file, either in the executable (.EXE) or dynamic library (.PBD).

Dynamically assigned DataWindows. In PowerScript, if you dynamically assign the DataWindow that is loaded into a DataWindow, the compiler does not automatically include this DataWindow into the compiled executable. In short, the compiler does not inspect strings for DataWindow names. So, in the runtime environment, when you run the application, these dynamically assigned DataWindows will not be available and cannot be displayed. This is one of the more frequently asked questions (FAQ) on all of the PowerBuilder forums and bulletin boards. It's a common omission by developers that are new to PowerBuilder because, when they run the application in the development environment, PowerBuilder treats the libraries in the search path as PBDs and consequently can always find the DataWindows.

If you have many dynamically referenced DataWindows or many complicated bitmaps, then you might find that the executable file will increase in size quite quickly. This can be addressed in several ways:

- Use a PBR file for a separate PBL and make this into a PBD using the Project painter or Library painter.
- Create a PBD for the DataWindows that are dynamically referred to, and add the PBL to the application Library Search Path.

- Reference the DataWindows in a script that is never executed (ue_dr_dw) so that the compiler can "see" them, or put all of these dynamically referenced DataWindows into a single PBL that you add to the application library path, then generate a PBD for this library using the Library painter.

PowerBuilder application executable (.EXE)

When you create a PowerBuilder application, the referenced runtime p-code (compiled) classes, from the nonhighlighted libraries in the Library Search Path and the resource and DataWindow items listed in a PBR file, are copied into the executable (.EXE) file. The format of the executable file is shown in Figure 18.5.

The first part of the executable file is a true Windows .EXE that has one function call to the PowerBuilder runtime engine (PBRTF040.DLL), which loads the application object and starts its Open event, etc. Frequently used (noninherited or complete inheritance chain) components and common functions are candidates for the executable.

See chapter 17, "Preparing the Application for Production," for more information on the roles of the Object Manager and the DataWindow Engine.

Executable versus small executable and Dynamic Libraries.   If you choose to compile and deliver the application in a single executable, then consider the following:

- If the executable is small enough, it probably will execute faster, because everything will be in memory after you load it.
- It requires complete application build and distribution for any change—even a one liner!

If you choose to break the application into a small executable with several Dynamic Libraries, then consider the following:

- You need to split the application into smaller, more manageable subsystems.
- The subsystems can be distributed separately (e.g., a bug fix or subsystem upgrade).
- There might be an increase in the time required to find and load objects that are located in several dynamic libraries.

Recommendation.   Try a recompile on a weekly/biweekly basis to ensure that the application still can be compiled (it's more difficult to determine what has caused a

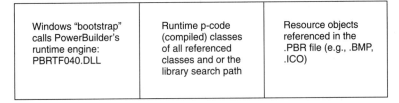

Windows "bootstrap" calls PowerBuilder's runtime engine: PBRTF040.DLL	Runtime p-code (compiled) classes of all referenced classes and or the library search path	Resource objects referenced in the .PBR file (e.g., .BMP, .ICO)

Figure 18.5 A PowerBuilder application executable (.EXE).

compilation error with no idea how many and what changes have been made). Make the testing team use the executable version, not the development environment. This minimizes check-in/out locking and contention problems, and it simulates the production environment.

What Do We Need to Distribute?

Having decided the configuration of the application, you need to consider exactly what is to be distributed. This can be broken down into two categories. The first category is what the client needs to run an executable developed using PowerBuilder in the production environment. The second is the parts of the application that are needed in the production environment.

PowerBuilder runtime requirements

Table 18.1 lists the runtime files that are needed to deploy an application developed in PowerBuilder.

The .INI files go into the Windows directory, and the non-PowerBuilder .DLL files go into the WINDOWS\SYSTEM directory of the client PC.

For databases other than Watcom, you should refer to the documentation provided in the ODBC Driver Pack. For Watcom SQL 4.0, you need to modify the database section of your C:\WINDOWS\ODBC.INI file to point to the runtime engine. For example:

```
[ODBC Data Sources]
MS Access Databases=Access Data (*.mdb)
Powersoft Demo DB=Watcom SQL 4.0

[MS Access Databases]
Driver=C:\WINDOWS\SYSTEM\SIMBA.DLL
FileType=RedISAM
SingleUser=False
UseSystemDB=False

[Watcom SQL 4.0]
driver=c:\windows\system\WOD40W.DLL

[Powersoft Demo DB]
DatabaseFile=c:\pb4\PSDEMODB.DB
DatabaseName=PSDEMODB
UID=dba
PWD=sql
Driver=c:\windows\system\WOD40W.DLL
Start=c:\wsql40\win\db32w -d
AutoStop=yes
```

The following files are common to all MS ODBC drivers:

- CTL3D.DLL

- MSJETDSP.DLL

- ODBC.DLL

- ODBCINST.DLL

- SIMADMIN.DLL

**TABLE 18.1 The Runtime Files that are Needed
to Deploy an Application Developed in PowerBuilder**

PowerBuilder files	Description
PBBGR040.DLL	Business Graphics Engine Library
PBCMP040.DLL	Compiler Library
PBDBI040.DLL	DB Interface Library
PBDBL040.DLL	DB Library
PBDEC040.DLL	Decimal Library
PBDWE040.DLL	DataWindow Routines Library
PBDWO040.DLL	DataWindow object PBL disguised as a DLL
PBECT040.DLL	Super Edit Library
PBIDBF40.DLL	DataWindow Import DBASE II and III File Library
PBITXT40.DLL	DataWindow Import Text File Library
PBLMI040.DLL	Library Manager
PBOUI040.DLL	OLE 2.0 Interface Library
PBPRT040.DLL	Print Services Library
PBRTE040.DLL	Runtime Engine Library
PBRTF040.DLL	Runtime Functions Library
PBSHR040.DLL	Utilities Library
PBTYP040.DLL	Type Definitions Library
PBVBX040.DLL	VBX Support Library

Database Interface Connection

PBxxx040.DLL	Database Interface Library, where xxx is replaced by the DBMS name (e.g., PBSYB040.DLL for Sybase and PBOR7040.DLL for Oracle)

ODBC Files

ODBC.INI	
ODBCINST.INI	
ODBC.DLL	
ODBCINST.DLL	
CPN16UT.DLL	
CTL3DV2.DLL	
ODBC16UT.DLL	
ODBC32.DLL	
ODBCCP32.DLL	
ODBCCURS.DLL	
PBODB040.DLL	ODBC Interface Library
PBODB040.INI	ODBC initialization file
Other files	There will be other files required, depending on the database source chosen (e.g., BTRV110.DLL for Btrieve databases)

- SIMBA.DLL
- ODBC.INI
- ODBCINST.INI
- ODBCISAM.INI

Table 18.2 list the files for specific Microsoft ODBC drivers.

Examples. For ODBCINST.INI:

```
[ODBC Drivers]
Access Data (*.mdb)=Installed
Watcom SQL 4.0=Installed
[Access Data (*.mdb)]
Driver=C:\WINDOWS\SYSTEM\SIMBA.DLL
Setup=C:\WINDOWS\SYSTEM\SIMADMIN.DLL
[Watcom SQL 4.0]
Driver=c:\windows\system\WOD40W.DLL
Setup=c:\windows\system\WOD40W.DLL
```

For ODBCISAM.INI:

```
[Installable ISAMS]
RedISAM=red110.dll
FoxPro 2.5=xbs110.dll
dBase4=xbs110.dll
Paradox=pdx110.dll
```

For SYBASE 4.9.x Database Network Access: Table 18-3 lists the files required to connect to SYBASE 4.9.x using LAN WorkPlace.

TABLE 18.2 The Files for Specific Microsoft ODBC Drivers

Driver	Files
MS Access	RED110.DLL, DRVACCSS.HLP
Btrieve	BTRV110.DLL, DRVBTRV.HLP
dBASE	XBS110.DLL, DRVDBASE.HLP
MS Excel	XLS110.DLL, DRVEXCEL.HLP
MS FoxPro	XBS110.DLL, DRVFOX.HLP
Borland Paradox	PDX110.DLL, DRVPARDX.HLP
Text	TXTISAM.DLL, DRVTEXT.HLP

TABLE 18.3 Files Required to Connect to Sybase 4.9.x Using LAN WorkPlace.

Filename	Description
W3DBLIB.DLL	DBLIB Layer
WDBNOVTC.DLL	LAN WorkPlace TCP/IP Layer

Add an [SQLServer] section to WIN.INI with entries for the database servers. For example:

```
[SQLServer]
genesis=wdbnovtc,106.105.100.104,2048
```

For Novell network using LAN WorkPlace: Install LAN WorkPlace into the C:\TCP directory. After the install, LANWP.BAT will be called from the AUTOEXEC.BAT. It will run the programs listed in Table 18.4 using the NET.CFG file.

Application runtime requirements

The runtime files needed to deploy an application developed in PowerBuilder are:

- .DLL—The PowerBuilder Deployment Kit and any other third-party DLLs
- .EXE—The application executable file
- .PBD—The PowerBuilder Dynamic Libraries
- .BMP—Bitmaps
- .CUR—Cursors
- .ICO—Icons
- .INI—The application INI files
- .RLE—Run-length encoded bitmaps (compressed)
- .WMF—Windows Meta files

Where Is It Going To?

The environment in which you will run the application is called the *production environment*. The design of the environment is a major factor in determining how you "shape" the application and, consequently, how you distribute it.

TABLE 18.4 The Programs Run by LANWP.BAT

Program	Description
LSL.COM	NetWare Link Support Layer
3C507.COM	Network Card Support (3COM 3C507 EtherLink/16 MLID)
IPXODI.COM	NetWare IPX/SPX Protocol Layer
NETX.COM	NetWare Workstation Shell for DOS (up to version $5.x$)
NETX.EXE	NetWare Workstation Shell for DOS (version $6.x$ or greater)
TCPIP.EXE	Novell TCP/IP Transport Layer
HOSTS	Textfile with IP addresses for UNIX servers
device=vtcpip.386	Ensure that this entry is in [Enhanced] of SYSTEM.INI

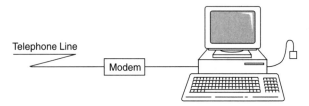

Figure 18.6 A typical standalone workstation.

We now are going to review the major elements of a production environment, which can range from a standalone workstation to a more complicated Local Area Network (LAN) or a collection of LANs spread over a wide area (WAN).

What follows is a more detailed description of the workstation environments that you might encounter when deploying a PowerBuilder application.

Standalone client workstation

The standalone client workstation is the most straightforward hardware configuration to deal with when considering software distribution. It is either an IBM-compatible Personal Computer, Apple Macintosh, or a UNIX Workstation with its own hard disk for storing programs and data. (See Figure 18.6.)

By definition, a standalone workstation is not continuously connected to any other workstations or servers (i.e. a LAN), so the methods available for distribution typically are restricted to what media devices are installed on the workstation. You can distribute the software using:

- Floppy disk

- CD-ROM

- Magnetic tape

This is provided that the client workstation has the media device for the same size and format media chosen. The most common media are 3.5" floppy disks and CD-ROMs, which are appropriate for larger products.

However, this restriction need not apply if the workstation has a modem installed with access to a telephone line. With the appropriate communications software, a modem and telephone line provide you with many more options for distributing the application software:

- You can dial in to your client using a remote communications package (e.g. Norton pcANYWHERE) to transfer applications.

- There also are bulletin boards and services that can provide the client with the capability to dial in and download the latest version of software that you have previously uploaded. This is very popular today with services like CompuServe, Prodigy, and America Online.

- Additionally, if you and your client workstation have access to the Internet, the client can use FTP (File Transfer Protocol) to obtain the latest copy from a directory on your distribution machine.

With all of these techniques for getting the software to the workstation, it still must be installed and/or configured correctly. This can be done with something as simple as enclosing a text file of written instructions for the client user to carry out. This is somewhat susceptible to human error and likely to dissatisfy the client. You also could make a simple script that creates the appropriate directories, then copies the files to these directories. You can use one of the many third-party tools that will allow you to completely script an installation of your product. See chapter 20, "Related Tools, Libraries, and Publications," for more information on distribution tools.

Local Area Network (LAN)

A Local Area Network (LAN) is a collection of client workstations and file and database servers that are all connected together. (See Figure 18.7.)

The distribution methods for a client workstation on a Local Area Network include all of the methods available for a standalone workstation, as described in the previous section. However, if you've got the LAN it makes sense to use it, doesn't it? If you do, however, there are other considerations:

- Does every client workstation run the application from a shared storage device on a "file server?" The answer is definitely "yes" if the client is a diskless workstation.
- Does every client workstation run the application from its local storage device?
- Does your user community need a mixture of both?

Let's examine the various scenarios.

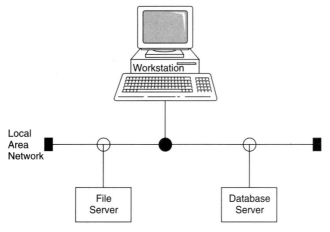

Figure 18.7 A simplified Local Area Network (LAN).

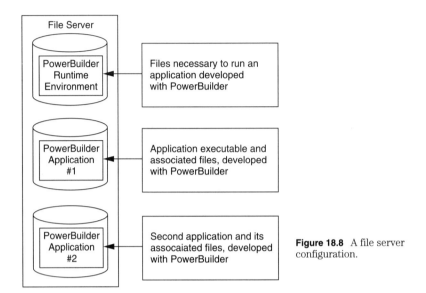

Figure 18.8 A file server configuration.

Running from the server. The pros of running the application from the server (see Figure 18.8) are:

- You can distribute any application updates quicker.
- Reduced administration. There's no need for an additional distribution process to each client workstation.
- Reduced duplication. A single copy of the application can be held on the server.
- It is a solution for diskless or space-restricted workstations.

The single biggest drawback of running the application from the server is network traffic. The application and its supporting files have to be loaded from the network to the workstation for every client. If everybody chooses to load the application at the same time, it might impact the response on the network temporarily.

Running from the client. Here are the pros of running the applications from the client workstation (see Figure 18.9):

- Reduced traffic on the network.
- If the file server goes down, the application still will be available.
- The loading of the application will not be affected by the network traffic.

Here are the cons of running the applications from the client workstation:

- Additional distribution process to each client workstation.
- Widespread duplication.
- Client machines need disks and, therefore, disk space for applications.

Wide Area Network (WAN)

Catering for the Wide Area Network (WAN) is practically the same as the Local Area Network (LAN), but you need to take into account that the routers, bridges, and gateways that connect the LANs will allow the traffic to flow from the distribution server to the client workstations. (See Figure 18.10.)

The distribution methods for a client workstation on a Wide Area Network include all of the methods available for the Local Area Network and standalone workstation,

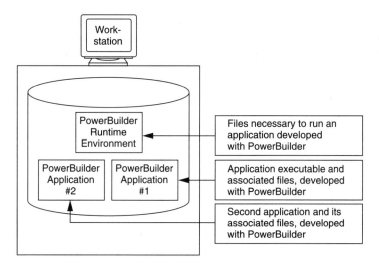

Figure 18.9 A client workstation configuration.

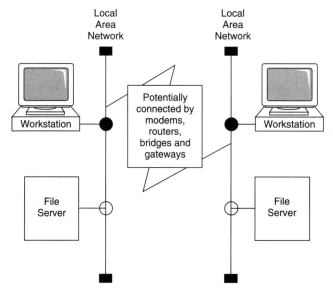

Figure 18.10 A simplified Wide Area Network (WAN).

as described earlier. The only additional process is copying the distribution package from the distribution server to each of the LAN's file servers.

How Do We Get It There?

Having decided on the destinations for the distribution package, how are you going to deploy the software files to the client workstation? For the first time? For any subsequent times? See chapter 20, "Related Tools, Libraries, and Publications," for more information on commercial software distribution products. If you do not use a commercial product, then you have to develop your own methods for getting the files to the client environments. Depending on the network size, product size, and the general accessibility of the clients, you will have to consider what one or a combination of delivery methods are best suited for this assignment. These methods are typically:

- Server-to-server copy
- Server-to-client copy
- Removable media, or floppy, copy
- Modem copy

Server-to-server copy (WAN)

The server-to-server copy is useful in a situation involving clients on a Wide Area Network (WAN). The software is copied, or pushed, from the development file server, or distribution server, to the production file servers, or staging servers. This can be achieved using the following types of commands and utilities:

- DOS XCOPY
- Windows LZCopy
- UNIX FTP

Server-to-client copy (LAN)

Once the software is loaded onto the file server that serves the Local Area Network (LAN), the server-to-client copy method can be used to load the software onto each workstation. The software is copied, or pulled, from the local file server, or staging server, to the client workstations.

Removable media copy (floppy)

If you have limited access to the client machines or you are distributing a commercial product, then the good old floppy disk might be what you need to use. If you do use this method, then make a note of the following:

- Installation can be from one or more floppy disks (a.k.a. The SneakerNet).
- Floppy disks must be loaded onto each workstation, typically, carried out during off-peak hours. What about emergency fixes?

- Very human-resource intensive and, subsequently, prone to error
- Floppy disk management and version control
- Floppy disks wear out!

Modem copy

With more workstations gaining access to external services, such as CompuServe, another method has become available for delivering software to clients that are remote. The modem connection brings multiple possibilities that range from dial-up remote control to third-party service providers.

Remote control products, like Norton pcANYWHERE for DOS, allow you to take control of a remote client workstation and its resources, including file services, from your workstation. You then can copy and install the software remotely.

Service providers, like CompuServe, allow you to send information to subscribing clients via an upload or simple mail attachments. Upon receipt, the client can download and install the files accordingly.

Installation/setup routines

Although the software has been distributed to the client, it still must be correctly set up or installed. This might be as simple as a copy of all the files from the floppy disk to standard directory and clicking an icon in Windows that starts the executable. There also are more advanced, therefore more complicated, installation routines that must be carefully constructed by the development team, taking into account the various combinations of hardware configurations of the client workstations. These install scripts can be created using countless third-party tools that are available. Some of the more popular ones are mentioned later in this chapter.

Distribution Tools

Now that you know that you will need some kind of tool, you will have to decide whether to use the Install Disk Builder that came with PowerBuilder, purchase a third-party software distribution tool, construct your own software distribution utility, or use a combination of all of these.

If you want to distribute a commercial package or one that is targeted for stand-alone workstations, then it probably will make sense either to use the Install Disk builder or to buy a third-party tool. If the target audience is predominantly on a LAN or WAN, then you probably will need to purchase a tool and possibly supplement its features with your own routines.

Using the Install Disk Builder

The Advanced Developer Toolkit includes an application called Install Disk Builder, which is a convenient way of deploying a PowerBuilder application. It creates install disks and a Setup program, just like the one used to install PowerBuilder itself, for your application. It includes ODBC configuration using your data source definitions as templates and can install the DLLs in the Deployment Kit. The Advanced Developer Toolkit is part of PowerBuilder Enterprise and PowerBuilder Team/ODBC and can be purchased separately for PowerBuilder Desktop.

Purchasing third-party tools

See chapter 20. "Related Tools, Libraries, and Publications," for more information on commercial software distribution tools.

Building a distribution tool

This applies to the client configurations that are linked by a network and run the application from a local disk. It does not apply to the client configurations that run software from a shared network device; this type of distribution method only requires the server-to-server or file distribution technique.

If you are planning on building you own distribution tool, the following is a list of areas that might or might not apply to your product:

- Auditing—Create/Maintain, Print/Display, and Purge/Cleanup.
- Scheduling/Connection/Transmission
- Packaging—Development issue/role
- Configuration management—File distribution only

In addition, the following is a list of the types of tool you might consider creating:

- A client workstation agent
- A software load program
- Application functions

Client workstation agent. This type of distribution tool is started on the client workstation and waits for the notification of change to the managed software. This can be implemented using one or more of the Windows notification messages, which will prompt the tool to copy the latest software from a shared network device to the client workstation. This probably would require the workstation to be left powered on during the nonbusiness hours when the update is most likely to receive the latest software.

Software load program. This type of distribution tool would be started when the user on the client machine selects to execute an application. It typically is installed in the application icon's start-up command line.

For example, if you had an application that had the following properties:

- Command line: C:\PBAPP\CRVA\CRVA.EXE ALLENPA
- Working directory: S:\DATA\CRVA

It could be replaced with an icon with the following properties:

- Command line: C:\SL\SLOADER.EXE
- C:\PBAPP\CRVA\CRVA.EXE
- ALLENPA S:\DATA\CRVA
- Working directory: C:\SL

The software load program, SLOADER.EXE, would parse the command line and extract the program path name (C:\PBAPP\CRVA\CRVA.EXE), optional parameters (ALLENPA), and the working directory. Using the program name, the software loader could check that the software on the C: drive was the same (date, time, and file size checks) as the network copy and download accordingly. When the download was complete, or if no download was necessary, the software loader would start the application.

Application functions. These would be several application functions that would be responsible for checking that the software on the C: drive was the same (date, time, and file size checks) as the network copy and downloading any necessary changes accordingly. The following is the list of possible functions and some pseudo-code for them:

f_distribution( )

```
IF f_upgrade_required (THIS) = TRUE THEN
  IF f_perform_upgrade(THIS) = TRUE THEN
    MessageBox("Distribution Control","Upgrade Successful.")
  ELSE
    MessageBox("Distribution Control","Upgrade Failed.")
  END IF
END IF
```

f_upgrade_required( )

- Check dates of all EXE, PBD, and other associated files with entries in the current applications DC table (or .INI file).
- Call f_get_current_version for each PowerBuilder library (or PBD) and compare with entries in the DC table (or .INI file).

Return TRUE if the version numbers or the dates are different.

f_perform_upgrade( )

- Run the home-grown installation routine to install the latest version of the application.
- Run the third-party installation routine to install the latest version of the application.
- Wait for this utility to complete before continuing with the application.

19

Managing the Database

The hub of the typical application, especially one developed using PowerBuilder, is the database. This chapter describes how you can design, administer, and manage the database from within PowerBuilder. It also covers other tools that can facilitate database design and maintenance. Depending on the DBMS that is deployed, PowerBuilder can be used to perform some, if not most, of the database management functionality. For example, small applications using Watcom as the DBMS can be managed using PowerBuilder exclusively. While larger deployments where the DBMS is Sybase or Oracle might be managed by a central database group using a database administration tool, PowerBuilder still provides some useful database functions. For example, PowerBuilder's internal catalog tables in concert with the PowerBuilder object painters (DataWindow) can provide the ability to format, edit, and validate a particular table column in a consistent fashion.

Overview

Before we move on to technical material, let's look briefly at the administrative issues. Most organizations have several database administrators who design, implement, and manage data residing on one or more DBMSs. The responsibilities of the database administrator include design and construction of database objects, performance monitoring, tuning, and data security.

Data administration

In the 1980s, a new organizational role emerged within information services; it was commonly known as *data administration*. Despite the similarity of names, this activity is quite different from database administration. The data administrator does not focus on a specific database and DBMS. The emphasis is on early life-cycle phases (analysis) and a global view of data. Responsibilities include naming standards, data models that cut across organizational boundaries, and long-range planning.

Nowadays, most large organizations have a data administration function, perhaps under a different job title. We address functions of both data administration (analysis) and database administration (design, construction, and maintenance). As we saw in our discussion of the development life cycle, all of these activities are related and covered by the term *database design*.

Both data and database administrators rely on a dictionary to document their designs and models. A dictionary stores data (meta data) about your data-table specifications, columns, indexes, even specifications for application software and hardware. The early difficulties with data dictionaries involved problems in translating the dictionary meta data into usable development objects (e.g., data definition language). Because the dictionary database is one level above the humble operational database, it sometimes is called a *meta-database*.

Some CASE tools bridge the translation gap. PowerBuilder has its own system tables, which are a form of dictionary database. They can be populated from vendor CASE tools, such as ERwin and LBMS. These catalog tables augment the RDBMS system catalog tables to provide data that can describe rules for editing, validating, and displaying database table and column information.

Dictionaries and system catalog tables

There are many alternate terms for a dictionary. Vendors of CASE (computer-aided software engineering) tools (e.g., ADW and LBMS) often refer to the internal CASE dictionary as an *encyclopedia* or *repository*. Repository is more or less synonymous to encyclopedia. Relational DBMSs have an internal catalog that contains limited but critical data about user tables, columns, indexes and security. Although these terms differ in some respects, they all maintain meta data—data about your data.

In PowerBuilder development, if you are using a tool such as ERwin or LBMS, you can use the logical model to create the DDL to define the database. Using LBMS or ERwin, you also can populate the PowerBuilder catalog tables, which can be used to store attributes of the tables and columns of the application database. This information is used when painting a new DataWindow or when building a dynamic DataWindow. It facilitates consistent validation, display, and editing of the application database elements. (*Note*: ERwin for PowerBuilder provides the most comprehensive set of PowerBuilder interface functionality.)

For the purposes of this discussion, we will assume that you have a dictionary of some kind. This is your database; it stores all information about your emerging design. If you do not have a true dictionary, simply use PowerBuilder's extended attribute tables to record names, definitions, and data types. This is not a comprehensive solution to the dictionary problem, but it is simple to implement and cost effective.

Dictionaries can either be online or offline to development and production systems. A dictionary that is actively referenced during data entry is *dynamic*. One that is offline and used strictly for documentation is *passive*. An active dictionary is online to development but not to production systems (e.g., Brownstone data dictionary for DB2/MVS). The direction of the technology is moving towards active dictionaries. PowerBuilder's catalog tables are active during development, and if they are populated prior to development, they will increase productivity significantly. They also are active in that dynamic DataWindows used in production can be constructed using the PowerBuilder catalog tables.

Dictionary technology is in a state of flux today, with a number of official and *de facto* standards emerging. LBMS and ADW are two of the more popular CASE tool dictionaries in use today; LBMS on the Windows/NT side, and ADW on the OS/2 platform. In any CASE, it is the usual start point for large system development.

Now what do we do with this data dictionary meta data? In basic relational design, we convert data dictionary entities, relationships, and attributes to physical database tables, foreign keys, and columns. Our goal is simply to move from the language of analysis suitable for client interviews to the language of relational database demanded by the computer. If the tools and methods used do not produce this result, it will severely impact the development. Ensure that proper target DBMS translation is possible before proceeding with a particular data dictionary tool; otherwise, all of the analysis work will amount to a lost effort and a waste of time and resources.

Physical database objects

Once we start to get physical, the application's database will consist of the components described in the following sections.

Tables and columns. Tables and columns are the basic building blocks of a good relational database design. They should be grouped by usage and named in a standard way. They start off as entities and attributes in the logical model where they are arranged to satisfy the business processes. A large application usually will begin with a CASE tool that will be used to develop the entity relationship diagram whose entities and attributes will be converted to physical tables and columns. Conversion to the physical requires an understanding of the target DBMS datatypes and integrity rules. ERwin, a third-party tool, can convert a logical model into any one of 15 physical DBMSs, including Sybase, Oracle, DB2, Informix, and Watcom.

Indexes. As the name implies, indexes provide a way to search, and sometimes control, the data rows within a table. One or more columns can be grouped together to form an index. Most tables should have a unique index that can serve not only as a search mechanism but also as a control to avoid duplication. For example, a table that contains employee information should use a unique index to ensure that information about a particular employee is not entered twice. An index also can be clustered to maintain the physical placement of inserted rows in a specified order. For example, at a television station, an acquired television series will include one or more episodes. A clustered unique index for the episode table might be series_code and episode_code concatenated. This would group all of a series' episodes on database pages stored in close proximity. This would speed up any access involving all of the episodes within a series.

Keys (primary and foreign). Keys are indexes that provide for database integrity. For example, the series table would have a "primary" key of series_code. The primary key typically is a unique table row identifier. It also establishes the first part of the key in any dependent table (e.g., episodes belong to and depend on a series). The episode table would have a "foreign" key of series_code to connect the episode to the series and also to ensure that a series cannot be deleted if any episodes belonging to the series exist. Design tools such as ERwin can be used to define the database logical model and also create the physical components including the referential definitions required to enforce database integrity.

Views. The name *view* describes its object's function: to provide a particular view of base tables. Views are vertical tables made up of columns from one or more tables that usually are joined by the same key or keys that they share in common. Views facilitate access to the data. They can provide security as well (e.g., you can restrict the selection of employee column data such as salary). Views that contain columns from more than one table typically are not updateable; check the target DBMS for specifics.

As mentioned, PowerBuilder also provides a catalog of internal tables that provide extended attributes. These tables are managed by PowerBuilder and allow you to store application-based information about your table's columns in the database for use in your application. For example, you can define validation rules for a column. Once they are defined, anytime you use that column in a PowerBuilder application, each entry in the column is checked against the validation rule. If the entry doesn't pass validation, the user is informed. You also can manage database security from within PowerBuilder.

PowerBuilder supports many database management systems (DBMSs). For the most part, development work is the same in PowerBuilder for each DBMS. However, because each DBMS provides some unique functionality (which PowerBuilder makes use of), there are some issues that are specific to a particular DBMS. Of particular importance are the data types that are supported by each DBMS. The database design and physical manifestation must consider which data types are available in the target DBMS. For example, date and time datatypes vary widely from DBMS to DBMS. Application requirements might necessitate the use of a time or date function. Watcom supports date, time, and datetime datatypes. Sybase supports only datetime. Applications that begin development on Watcom and are to be migrated to Sybase should avoid the use of date and time and use datetime only. If your organization allows, you can do most of your database work using the Database painter. This painter also is the launching point for other painters concerned with database issues.

The Database painter

Database administrators have been waiting for comprehensive database administration and maintenance software for a long time. The advent of menu- and GUI-based software has provided some help. For the large organization, it might not be suitable; however, for the small developer, it is more than adequate and fairly easy to use. In the Database painter, you can:

- Create, alter, and drop tables
- Drop views

- Create and drop indexes
- Create, alter, and drop primary and foreign keys
- Define and modify extended attributes for columns

From the Database painter, you also can open three related painters:

- The Data Manipulation painter, where you retrieve and manipulate data from the database.
- The View painter, where you create views.
- The Database Administration painter, where you control access to the database and execute SQL directly.

You also can do some other fairly useful things like:

- Create database profiles to quickly connect to any of the databases that you might be using or supporting in development and production. These connections can not only span databases but also can include different profiles (i.e., connection parameters) for each of the DBMSs supported by PowerBuilder.
- Add edit styles, display formats, and validation maintenance (i.e., the extended attributes that have been mentioned in other parts of this book). See the Objects menu item. These features often are overlooked but can increase development productivity significantly, especially when using DataWindows. More on this later.

Invoking the Database painter

To open the Database painter:

Step 1 Click the Database icon in the PowerBar, or double-click the Database icon in the PowerPanel. The Select Tables window displays. (See Figure 19.1.)

Step 2 You can select tables to work on now, or click Cancel to go to the painter workspace. You can open tables later from the workspace.

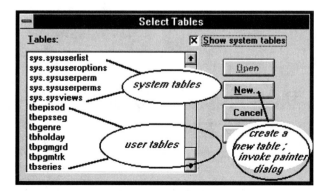

Figure 19.1 The painter displays the preference database.

Like the other PowerBuilder painters, the Database painter contains a menu bar, a customizable PainterBar, and a workspace. (See Figure 19.2.) To work with database components, you open them in the workspace.

Tables are expanded, so they show the table's columns, keys, and indexes. You can move objects around the workspace by dragging them with the mouse. For example, to move a table, press the left mouse button on the title bar for the table and drag the table. You also can select and modify objects in the workspace by pointing and clicking them with the mouse, as described throughout this chapter. Select the table for which you want to display or alter the information, then press Enter. Scroll in the painter workspace. If you open more tables and views than can be displayed in the Database painter workspace at one time, you can scroll up or down to view all the tables and views.

First-time users should build a test table with each possible data type in the target DBMS. Experiment with the DBMS before beginning serious development. As you work with your database, you probably will generate SQL/DDL statements. You might want to save a copy of the SQL statements generated by PowerBuilder. They might be helpful if you have to migrate or rebuild a database object. For example, as you define a new table in the Create Table dialog in the Database painter, Power-Builder is building an SQL CREATE TABLE statement internally. When you click the Create button, PowerBuilder sends the SQL statement to the DBMS to create the

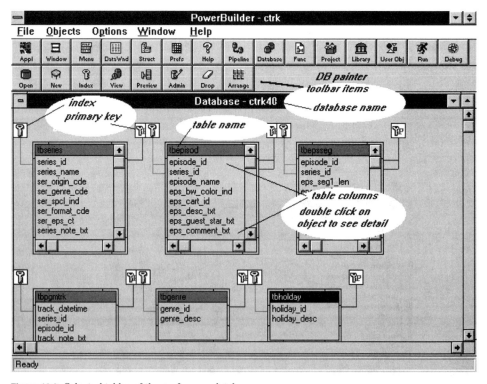

Figure 19.2 Selected tables of the preference database.

table. Similarly, when you add an index, PowerBuilder is building a CREATE INDEX statement.

You can record all SQL generated in a painter session in a log file. This allows you to have a record of your work and also makes it easy to duplicate the work if you need to create the same or similar tables in another database. In addition, each time you create or modify a database component such as a table, you have the option of generating the SQL only to a log file. You then can submit the statement to the database at a later date.

To start logging your work in a text file:

Step 1 Open the Database painter.

Step 2 Select Start/Stop Log from the Options menu.

PowerBuilder opens a log file and displays the Activity Log icon at the bottom of the screen. From this point on, all of your work will be saved in a temporary file.

To save the log to a permanent text file:

Step 1 Select Save Log As from the Options menu. The Save the Log window displays.

Step 2 Name the file, and click OK. The default file extension is .SQL, but you can change that if you want.

PowerBuilder saves the log as a text file with the specified name. You can open a saved log file later and submit it to your DBMS in the Database Administration painter. Using the log might be helpful if you have been developing in one DBMS (e.g., Watcom) and migrating to a new platform (e.g., Sybase system 10 on a UNIX machine). You could use the log to create new Sybase DDL or perhaps as input to a reengineering tool like ERwin that will accept DDL from one DBMS, build a model, then convert it to another DBMS syntactically.

To clear the log, select Clear Log from the Options menu. PowerBuilder deletes all statements in the log but leaves the log open.

To stop the log, select Start/Stop Log from the Options menu, or close the Activity Log window. PowerBuilder closes the log. Your work will no longer be logged. However, the log file still exists. You can open it again and continue logging from where you left off.

The Database painter's database connection

Always be mindful that, when you open the Database painter or DataWindow painter, PowerBuilder connects you to the preference DBMS (i.e., the database that you used last; the information is recorded in the PB.INI file). Be careful; you also are not necessarily connected to the database used in your default application. You can change to a different DBMS and/or to a different database anytime. See the end of this chapter for connection specifics for Sybase, Oracle, and Informix.

There are two ways to change your database connection:

- By being prompted for the connection parameters
- By defining and using database profiles

To change the database connection through prompts:

Step 1 Open the Database painter or DataWindow painter.

Step 2 Select `Connect` from the File menu. A cascading menu displays.

Step 3 Select `Prompt` for existing profiles from the menu. You are prompted to specify the DBMS.

Step 4 Select the DBMS. The installed DBMS interfaces are listed in the DBMS dropdown listbox.

Step 5 PowerBuilder displays additional windows asking you to specify connection parameters. Specify all the appropriate parameters.

For complete information about the connection parameters required by your DBMS, see the end of this chapter or the PowerBuilder interface manual for your DBMS. Once you have answered all the prompts, you are connected to the database and can work with its tables.

If you are working with multiple DBMSs or databases, the easiest way to move between them is by defining and using database profiles, which are named sets of parameters that specify a particular database connection. They are saved in your PB.INI file.

To define a database profile:

Step 1 Open the Database painter or DataWindow painter.

Step 2 Select `Connect` from the File menu. A cascading menu displays.

Step 3 Select `Setup` from the menu. The Database Profiles window displays. (See Figure 19.3.) It lists the existing profiles and allows you to edit or delete them or to define a new one.

Step 4 Click New to create a new profile. The Database Profile Setup window displays. (See Figure 19.4.)

Step 5 Specify a name for the profile. The name that you enter here will display on the File/Connect menu in the Database painter and DataWindow painter.

Step 6 Specify the DBMS. The installed DBMS interfaces are listed in the DBMS dropdown listbox.

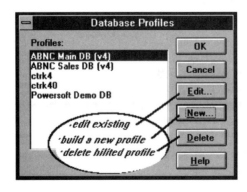

Figure 19.3 Connecting to a database using an existing profile.

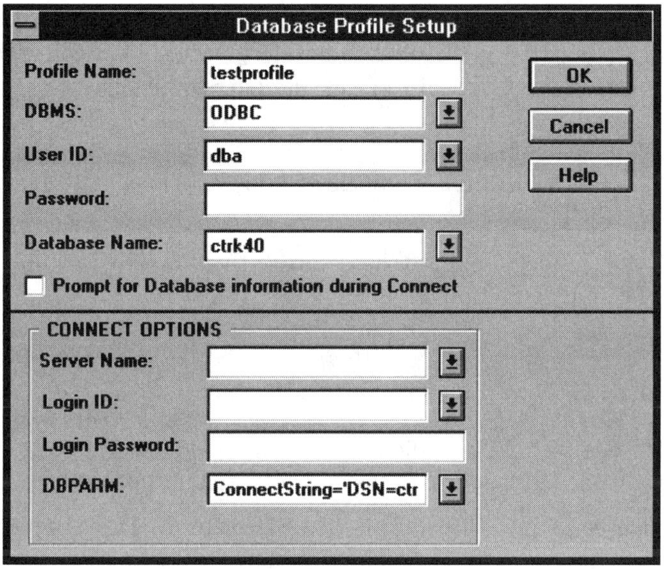

Figure 19.4 Specifying a new database profile.

Step 7 Click OK. PowerBuilder displays additional windows, asking you to specify needed connection parameters.

Step 8 Specify all of the appropriate parameters. Once you have answered all the prompts, you return to the Database Profiles window, with the new profile listed. Note whether PowerBuilder tries to make the connection to verify the profile. This sometimes causes response delays, especially with a new and untried connection.

Step 9 To connect to the database, select the appropriate profile and click OK.

To connect to a database using a database profile:

Step 1 Open the Database painter or DataWindow painter.

Step 2 Select Connect from the File menu. A cascading menu displays. It lists the defined profiles.

Step 3 Select the appropriate profile. PowerBuilder connects you to the specified database and returns you to the painter workspace. You also can customize your PowerBar with an icon to perform database connects from anywhere in Power-Builder.

Building a physical database

In PowerBuilder, you work within an existing database. With one exception (i.e., a Watcom local database), creating and deleting databases are administrative tasks that are not performed directly in PowerBuilder. For information about creating and deleting databases, see your DBMS documentation.

Creating and deleting a database

The one exception is that you can create and delete a local Watcom SQL database from within PowerBuilder. To create a local Watcom SQL database:

Step 1 Open the Database painter.

Step 2 Select Create Database from the File menu. The Create Local Database window displays. (See Figure 19.5.)

Step 3 Specify the name and path of the database that you are creating. Use a standard name. Make sure you retain the default file extension .DB.

Step 4 Click OK.

When you click OK, PowerBuilder:

- Creates a database with the specified name in the specified directory. If a database with the same name exists, you are asked whether you want to replace it.

- Adds a data source to the ODBC.INI file. The data source has the same name as the database unless one with the same name already exists, in which case a suffix is appended.

- Creates a database profile and adds it to the PB.INI file. The profile has the same name as the database unless one with the same name already exists, in which case a suffix is appended.

- Connects to the new database.

When you open the Database painter, the Select Tables window lists all of the tables and views in the current database (including tables and views that were not cre-

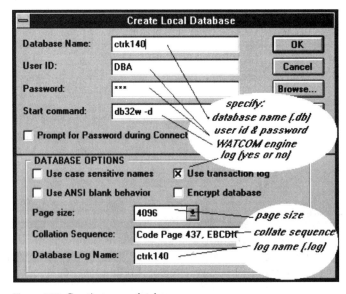

Figure 19.5 Creating a new database.

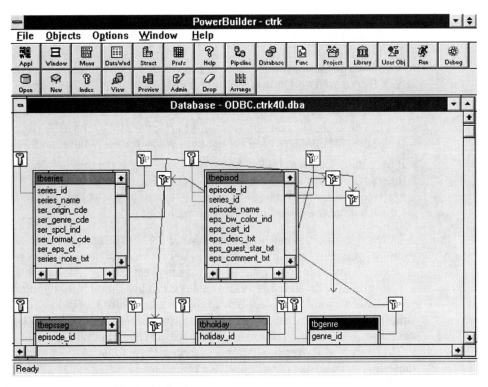

Figure 19.6 Selected tables in the database.

ated using PowerBuilder). You can create a new table or open existing tables. If you set the TableDir variable in the [Database] section of PB.INI to zero, PowerBuilder does not display the table list when you open the Database painter.

Opening tables

To open a database table:

Step 1 If the Select Tables window is not displayed, open it by clicking the Open icon in the PainterBar or by selecting Tables from the Objects menu. To display system tables, select the Show system tables checkbox.

Step 2 Select the tables to open by doing one of the following:

- Click the name of each table that you want to open in the list displayed in the Select Tables window, then click Open to open the selected tables.
- Double-click the name of each table that you want to open. Each table is opened immediately.
- Click Cancel to close the Select Tables window.

The selected tables display in the Database painter workspace. (See Figure 19.6.) By default, PowerBuilder shows only user-created tables in the Select Tables window. There are many techniques for limiting what to access and see. They typically are parameters in the DBPARM section of the database profile as specified in the PB.INI or application.INI file.

If you select Show system tables in the window, PowerBuilder also shows system tables. There are two kinds of system tables:

- System tables provided by your DBMS (see your DBMS documentation for details). These usually contain the object particulars for each DBMS. For example, in DB2/MVS, SYSIBM.SYSTABLES contains a row for each database table.

- PowerBuilder system tables. Likewise, these tables contain the object particulars for each PowerBuilder defined or PowerBuilder interface (ERwin and LBMS) generated object in the particular DBMS. For example, project.pbcattbl contains a row for each database table known to PowerBuilder.

DBMS system tables can be used to develop DBMS-specific system applications. For example, you could set up an application to provide statistical reports on your DBMS space capacity, performance, or anything of interest for the system maintenance.

PowerBuilder extended attribute tables store information that you provide when you create or modify a table (such as the text to use for labels and headings for the columns, validation rules, display formats, and edit styles) in system tables in your database. As mentioned, these system tables are a kind of database dictionary.

There are five PowerBuilder system tables. (See Table 19.1.) You can open these tables in the Database painter just like other tables.

When you open a table, PowerBuilder shows only the name of the table in a windowlike representation. You can expand the representation to show the rest of the information.

To show information about the table, click the up arrow in the upper-right corner of the table's title bar. PowerBuilder expands the display to illustrate the columns in the table in a list format.

Creating a table and its columns

Analyzing the data: the entity/attribute relationship. Your organization might have used the entity-relationship approach to data analysis. Entity-relationship has two

TABLE 19.1 The PowerBuilder System Tables

PowerBuilder extended attribute table name	Stores information about
pbcatcol	Columns
pbcatedt	Edits
pbcatfmt	Formats
pbcattbl	Tables
pbcatvld	Validation

major advantages. First, it is very close to natural language. An entity is like a noun, a relationship is like a verb, and an attribute is like a prepositional phrase. This makes it easy to convert any information gleaned in an interview with the user into a data model. Second, most CASE tools have adopted this approach. Learning entity-relationship is good preparation for CASE.

An entity is a person, place, object, concept, activity, or event of interest to your organization. You can determine entities within an application by listening for important nouns during interviews with the users.

An entity type is a set of objects. TV Series and Episode are each different entity types. An entity instance is an element of the set. "Leave It To Beaver" the series and "Beaver flunks math" the episode are instances of our entity types.

Entity types usually become tables in relational design. Entity instances usually become rows. However, entities and tables are not identical. We might split an entity into several tables for better performance. Alternatively, we might merge several entities in one table. Occasionally entities are listed merely for documentation and disappear in relational design.

Designing tables.   The formal definition of a table, according to relational godfathers Codd and Date, consists of two parts: a heading and a body. The heading is the specification for the table and does not change in time. The body, or contents of the table, is a time-varying set of rows. Each row is a set of column-value pairs.

This definition has three important consequences. Most significantly, a table is defined as a set of rows, and each row is defined as a set of column-value pairs. Because elements of a set are not ordered, the rows and columns of a table have no logical order. For example, it is impossible to refer to the "fourth row" or the "second column" of a table in SQL. Of course, rows and columns are ordered internally on storage media, but this physical order is always invisible to the user in a relational DBMS. This is called *physical data independence*.

In addition, sets cannot contain duplicate elements. Consequently, tables cannot contain duplicate rows or column names in theory. In practice, most systems allow unstructured tables with duplicate rows, but this is not particularly useful. After all, it is impossible to distinguish duplicate rows. One could not delete the "first" duplicate and retain the "second," because rows have no logical order. In practice as well as in theory, tables should have unique primary keys and, therefore, cannot have duplicate rows.

Third, the definition implies that each row-column cell contains exactly one value, not several. This point is fundamental to database design. It means that plural attributes are harder to implement than singular attributes. This rule sometimes is broken to solve performance problems. Sometimes a column is pluralized into a repeating value (i.e., an array) for performance purposes. Natural arrays are the best because they do not change in time. For example, there will always be seven days in a week and twelve months in a year. A table with seven columns, each representing a day of the week, can reduce the physical I/O by 84% (i.e., you get all the data in one access instead of seven). Moreover, it can reduce the physical storage required as well.

Another concept of the relational data structure is the null value. A null is a special symbol that means either "unknown" or "inapplicable." These two meanings are different. A null social security number for an employee means unknown presumably, but a null commission for a salesperson means inapplicable. Regardless of meaning, null is always represented as the same symbol, "NULL." This symbol is the same regardless of data type. "NULL" is used for integers and characters alike. With null values, a new arithmetic and logic is necessary. What is the value of the expression `10 + null`? In SQL, the answer is null, or unknown. What about `10 > null`? Again, the answer is null. Any arithmetic or comparative expression involving null evaluates to null.

Creating the table within PowerBuilder. Although, in a large environment, table definition will be done by central DBA group, we will review the process using Power-Builder. This exercise also will give developers who are new to SQL and relational databases a sense of how database objects are created and maintained.

You can create tables from within PowerBuilder. Before proceeding, you should know what you are going to define and whatever standards are applicable. To create a table in the current database, click the New icon in the PainterBar. The Create Table window displays. (See Figure 19.7.) Enter the following required information in the table once and once for each column:

- The name of the table that you are creating. Check the naming standards.

- The name of each column in the table. Check the naming standards as well as the project recommendations regarding data types. (*Note*: If the database will be migrated to another DBMS, use common data types.)

- The data type and other required information for each column (such as column length, number of decimal places, and whether NULL values are allowed). All data types supported by the current DBMS are displayed in the Type dropdown listbox.

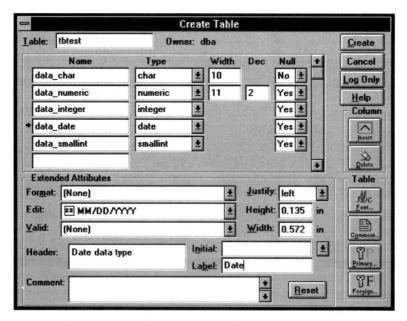

Figure 19.7 Creating a new table.

Specifying No in the NULL dropdown listbox means NULLs are not allowed; users must supply a value. Index fields usually are specified as not nullable.

Optionally, you can specify the following information now or later when you modify the table:

- The fonts used to display the headings and data for the table when it is used in a DataWindow object (Font button in the Table group).

- Comments about the table (Comment button in the Table group).

- The keys used to control and access the table. Keys (Primary and Foreign Key buttons in the Table group). Although keys can be modified later, you should spend the time to analyze the database relationships and define them before any serious development begins. This will provide you with the basic referential integrity. Again, in a large environment, the keys primary and foreign probably will be defined by the central DBA group, which will choose between the DBMS declarative referential integrity or the use of database triggers to effect same.

- The extended attributes for columns, which specify how data for the columns is displayed and validated and specifies the text that is used to label the columns in DataWindow objects.

Notes about the extended attributes. The extended attributes are an often-overlooked feature of PowerBuilder. This is something that the development team should embrace. The central DBA group can help, but this is where the developers can define the format, editing, and validation rules for each column in each table in the database. You can click the Object menu item to define edit styles and to display formats and validation rules. Once they are defined, you can use the extended attribute dropdown list boxes to associate them with database columns. Doing this early in the development process will greatly facilitate DataWindow creation.

Next, after the definition is completed, save your work by doing one of the following:

- Click the Create button. PowerBuilder submits the CREATE TABLE statement that it generated to the DBMS. The table is created in the DBMS.

- Click the Log Only button. The CREATE TABLE statement is written only to the log file; it is not submitted to the DBMS. You can later submit the statement if you choose.

You return to the Database painter workspace.

Altering a table within PowerBuilder. Once a table has been created, you can do the following:

- Append columns to the table. Appended columns must allow NULL values.

- In some DBMSs, you also can increase the number of characters allowed for data in an existing character column and allow NULL values. However, you cannot prohibit NULL values in a column that had been defined to allow NULL values.

- Add or modify all PowerBuilder-specific information about the table and its columns.

To alter a table:

Step 1 Open the table in the Database painter.

Step 2 Double-click the name of the table as represented in the workspace.

The Alter Table window displays. (See Figure 19.8.) Make your changes and do one of the following:

- Click the `Alter` button. PowerBuilder submits the ALTER TABLE statement that it generated to the DBMS. The table is altered in the DBMS.
- Click the `Log Only` button. The ALTER TABLE statement is written only to the log file; it is not submitted to the DBMS. You can later submit the statement if you choose.

You return to the Database painter workspace.

Specifying the extended attributes. The extended attributes act as the default or standard for all development. Time spent on the extended attributes for each database item (column) is well spent and can significantly enhance developer productivity. When you create or alter a table, you can choose the fonts used to display information from the table in a DataWindow object in your application. If you don't specify fonts for a table, PowerBuilder uses the font information specified in the application object. As we mentioned before, in addition to providing the information required to create a table, you can specify extended attributes for each column in the table. An extended attribute is PowerBuilder-specific information that enhances the definition of the column. The following extended attributes listed in Table 19.2 are provided by PowerBuilder for a column.

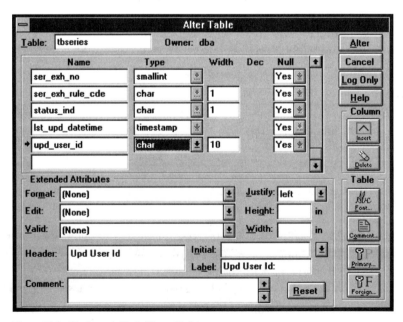

Figure 19.8 Altering a table in PowerBuilder.

TABLE 19.2 PowerBuilder's Column Extended Attributes

Extended attribute	Meaning
Comment (Comment:)	Describes the column. Whenever the table is opened in the Database painter, you can see the comment to understand the purpose of the column.
Heading and label (Header:, Label:)	Text that is used in DataWindow objects to identify columns.
Alignment and size (Justify:, Height:, Width:)	How data is aligned and how much space to allocate to the data in a DataWindow object.
Display format (Format:)	How the data is formatted in a DataWindow object.
Edit style (Edit:)	How the column is presented to the user in a DataWindow object. For example, you can display column values as radio buttons or in a dropdown listbox.
Validation rule (Valid:)	Criteria that a value must pass to be accepted in a DataWindow object.
Initial value (Initial:)	Specifies the initial value for the column (choices include: Fill with spaces, Set to zero, Set to today, and Set to null).

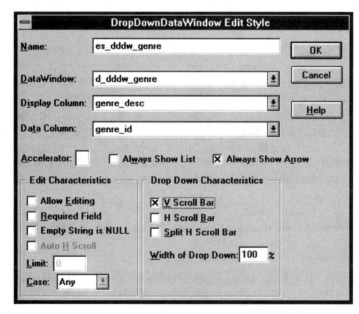

Figure 19.9 Specifying an edit style (extended attribute).

Extended attributes are stored in the repository—that is, in the PowerBuilder system tables in the database. PowerBuilder uses the information to display and validate data in the Data Manipulation painter, in the DataWindow painter, and during execution. When you create a view, the extended attributes defined for the table columns used in the view are used by default.

You can create extended attributes in the Database painter Object menu item under edit style, display format, and validation maintenance. An example of edit style extended attribute specification is depicted in Figure 19.9.

Accessing column comments in a DataWindow object. A column's comments are generated as the column's Tag attribute in a DataWindow object. You can access the comments through the DataWindow Describe PowerScript function. For example, to access the comments for the column series_code in a DataWindow object, code:

```
string ls_string
ls_string = dw_sheet.Describe("series_code.Tag")
```

You can use this technique to display comments to your users and hopefully make the application easier to use.

Creating indexes

Data in tables has both a relational and a physical order. The relational order of values is the usual arithmetic sequence for numbers, or dictionary sequence for character data. The physical order of rows in a table is the combination of the sequence of pages on the disk drive and the sequence of rows within each page. Of course, disk drives are not serial devices; pages are spread across tracks and around sectors.

A table is clustered on a column when the physical order of rows matches the relational order of values in the column. For example, SERIES is clustered on SERIES_CDE. Series that begin with the same letter will be physically located in adjacent pages. In some database systems clustering can be imperfect; a table is considered clustered even when some rows are on the wrong page. MVS/DB2 maintains a cluster ratio or the percent of rows that are clustered.

An index on a column is a list of column values, with pointers to the location (page number) of the row that contains each value. A composite index is defined over several columns. A clustering index, sometimes called a primary index, is defined on a clustering column (i.e., a column ideally with a uniform distribution of values with which to group rows together for common/fast access). A nonclustering index, sometimes called a *secondary index*, is not defined on a clustering column.

A *dense index* contains one entry for each row of the table. A *nondense index* contains one entry for each page of the table with the low and high value index values. Nondense indexes are possible only on clustered columns. Nondense indexes have a great advantage over dense indexes: they have far fewer entries and, therefore, occupy fewer pages. As a result, they are more efficient. In Sybase, for example, clustered indexes are nondense. In some other database systems, rows can be out of sequence, so a clustering index must be dense. How does this structure handle insertions and updates? Sybase places a new row on the correct page based on its clustering column. If this page is full, it splits in two to create free space, and a new entry is inserted at the bottom level of the index. If this index page is full it splits to create more space, and another entry is necessary at the next higher level of the index. In the worst case, these splits propagate all the way through the top of the index, and a new level is created. Because the new level is created at the top of the index, all branches of the index tree are always the same length. Consequently, this kind of index often is called a *B-tree*. The "B" stands for "balanced." In theory, the system could reverse the process when rows are deleted, merging pages and reducing the index.

However, this is not supported by Sybase and other vendors, because deletions are less frequent than insertions.

Occasionally a table will not have a clustering index. In this case, new rows are always inserted at the end of the table. When a row is deleted, the empty slot is not reused until the table is physically reorganized. Because there is no clustering index, rows remain in order of initial load or insertion. Because no meaningful order is maintained, this structure has limited utility. It is useful for tables of five pages or less; after all, if a table is small, the system can scan it quickly without an index. It also is useful for archival or temporary tables.

A table can have only one clustering index, but any number of nonclustering indexes. Nonclustering indexes are necessarily dense. When and how can nonclustering indexes accelerate queries? A critical factor is percentage of rows selected by a query, variously known as *hit ratio, filter factor*, or *selectivity*. When the hit ratio is high, nonclustering indexes are useless. For example, suppose we set up a nonclustering index on the holiday column within the TV EPISODE table. The holiday column contains a code that lets us know which episodes have a holiday theme (e.g., Halloween). Suppose we select all episodes not associated with a holiday (i.e., a normal day). The hit ratio is quite high; most or all pages contain qualifying rows because most days are not holidays. It is faster to ignore the index and scan the entire table. In contrast, if we select all episodes associated with the holiday of Halloween, the hit ratio is low. Less than five percent of episodes qualify. A nonclustering index on HOLIDAY quickly locates the few pages of interest.

In the Database painter workspace, you can create as many single- or multivalued indexes for a database table as you need and can drop indexes that are no longer needed. As we mentioned, indexes can facilitate integrity rules. They also are added for performance. An index and a table works like a book's index. Rather than scanning the entire table's data to find a particular piece of information, the DBMS looks for the value in the index and follows a page pointer directly to its location. Well-designed indexes can save I/O and processing time because the DBMS SQL optimizer will use the indexes to quickly access the database rows. The choices that developers make in designing indexes determines how well the database will perform. Note: you can update a table in a DataWindow object only if it has a unique index or primary key.

Creating an index using the PowerBuilder database painter.   To create an index:

Step 1 Select the table that you want to create an index for.

Step 2 Click the Index icon in the PainterBar, or select Index from the New cascading menu on the table's pop-up menu. The Create Index window displays. (See Figure 19.10.)

Step 3 Enter a name for the index. Check the naming conventions.

Step 4 Select whether or not to allow duplicate values for the index.

Step 5 Specify any other information required for your database (for example, in SQL Server, specify whether the index is clustered, and in SQLBase or ORACLE, specify the order of the index).

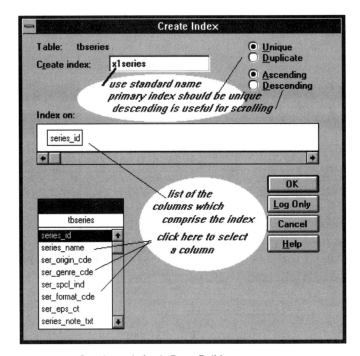

Figure 19.10 Creating an index in PowerBuilder.

Step 6 Click the names of the columns that make up the index. The selected column names display in the Index On box.

Step 7 Save your work by doing one of the following:

- Click the OK button. PowerBuilder submits to the DBMS the CREATE INDEX statement that it generated. The index is created in the DBMS.
- Click the Log Only button. The CREATE INDEX statement is written only to the log file; it is not submitted to the DBMS. You can later submit the statement if you choose.

After this is done, you return to the Database painter workspace. The new index is shown as a key connected to each column in the index.

Creating primary and foreign keys

There are several kinds of keys in relational theory, but only two are of practical importance—primary and foreign keys. The primary key of an entity identifies and distinguishes instances. The primary key must always be unique (i.e., two instances should never have the same value). It also must be known and available at all times. For example, SOCIAL_SECURITY_NUMBER might make a bad primary key of an EMPLOYEE table because it might be unavailable for foreign employees. Not always but most of the time the primary key and the clustering index are one and the same in content.

To make it simple, primary keys must always be unique and known. If possible, primary keys should have four additional characteristics. First, they should be stable. A changing primary key leads to confusion and errors. Second, they should not contain descriptive information like color or size. If the color changes, the primary key is unstable. Third, short and simple alphanumeric codes or integers are best, because they are easy to input and unambiguous. Finally, users should be familiar with the primary key so that they can enter it in database queries.

Names can change and are prone to data-entry errors, so they usually make bad primary keys. If you cannot find a good primary key, develop an artificial one, either an integer (e.g., a random number) or a short alphanumeric code. To discover the primary key of an entity, ask the user how the entity is identified. If you cannot determine a primary key, reconsider the entity. Perhaps it represents data, not a thing, is not important to your organization, or is poorly defined.

A key is not the same as an index. Keys are logical; they identify rows. Indexes are physical; they locate rows. Identifying a murder suspect is not the same as locating the suspect. A foreign key is a column (or group of columns) that matches the primary key of some table. For example, the SERIES_CDE in the EPISODE table is a foreign key to the SERIES table. Most joins compare a foreign key to its matching primary key. This is the case in our example join. This is called a primary/foreign key join. Because primary and foreign keys are frequently compared, they must be comparable. In other words, they must be defined over the same data type.

So far, we have discussed two rules for relational databases: primary keys must be unique and non-null, which sometimes is called *entity integrity*, and *referential integrity*, which governs foreign keys. Referential integrity requires that a foreign key must either be null or match some value of its primary key. It makes sense to allow a null foreign key.

Referential integrity (RI) is easy to state and important for error-free database management. It is hard to enforce, however, unless you are using a tool for generating triggers (e.g., ERwin) or the DBMS can enforce them with a declarative style of RI. Foreign key rules specify how to preserve referential integrity when foreign keys are inserted or updated and primary keys are updated or deleted. We'll examine alternative foreign key rules. First, we discuss deletion of a primary key value.

There are four options for primary key deletion. When the database administrator specifies the `Restrict` option, the primary key value cannot be deleted as long as there are any matching foreign key values. The data-entry user first must change or delete all matching foreign keys. The second option is `Cascade`. When a primary key is deleted, all rows that contain matching foreign keys also are automatically deleted. This is a dangerous option. Deletes automatically trigger deletes, which in turn trigger other deletes. If you specify this rule often, you might find that a single deletion can cause an entire database to disappear.

The third and fourth options are `Nullify` and `Set default`. These automatically set all matching foreign keys to null or default when a primary key value is deleted. A fifth option is to simply allow violations of referential integrity; that usually is not recommended. The fifth option will invariably lead to disaster when the orphans and broken links between database entities cause errors in the application components.

Even application enforced integrity is better than nothing. Rely on your DBA staff if you have a large database with lots of lineage (i.e., many relationships).

Similar options apply when a primary key is updated. For example, cascade automatically propagates the new primary key value to all matching foreign keys. However, updates to primary keys are strongly discouraged because primary keys should be stable. For this reason, the options for primary key updates are not as important as deletes. Similar options also apply when a foreign key is inserted or updated. Usually, the `Restrict` option is specified; new foreign key values cannot be entered unless a matching primary key value already exists.

If your DBMS supports primary and foreign keys, you can work with the keys in PowerBuilder. When you open a table with keys, PowerBuilder gets the information from the DBMS and displays it in the painter workspace. If your DBMS supports them, you should use primary and foreign keys to enforce the referential integrity of your database. If you use keys, you can rely on the DBMS to make sure that only valid values are entered for certain columns instead of having to write code to enforce valid values. For example, say you have two tables, SERIES and EPISODE. The EPISODE table contains the column series_code, which holds the name of the series. You want to make sure that only valid series are entered in this column; that is, the only valid values for series_code in the episode table are values for series_code in the series table. To enforce this kind of relationship, you define a foreign key for series_code that points to the series table. With this key in place, the DBMS disallows any value for series_code that does not match a series in the series table.

In the Database painter you can do the following:

- Look at existing primary and foreign keys.
- Open all tables that depend on a particular primary key.
- Open the table containing the primary key used by a particular foreign key.
- Create keys.
- Alter keys.
- Drop keys.

For the most part, you work with keys the same way for each DBMS that supports keys. However, there are some DBMS-specific issues. For complete information about using keys with your DBMS, see your DBMS documentation. When you open and expand a table that contains primary and/or foreign keys, PowerBuilder displays the keys in the workspace. The keys are shown as icons with lines connected to the table. When working with tables containing keys, you can easily open related tables.

To open the table that a particular foreign key references:

Step 1 Open and expand the table containing the foreign key.

Step 2 Click the right mouse button on the icon representing the foreign key.

Step 3 Select `Open Referenced Table` from the pop-up menu.

PowerBuilder opens and expands the table referenced by the foreign key.

To open all tables referencing a particular primary key:

Step 1 Open and expand the table that contains the primary key.

Step 2 Click the right mouse button on the icon representing the primary key.

Step 3 Select Open Dependent Table(s) from the pop-up menu.

PowerBuilder opens and expands all tables in the database that contain foreign keys that reference the selected primary key.

Defining primary keys using PowerBuilder. If your DBMS supports primary keys, you can define them in PowerBuilder. To define a primary key:

Step 1 Display the Create Table window for a table that you are creating, or display the Alter Table window for an existing table.

Step 2 Click the Primary Key button in the Table group. The Primary Key Definition window displays. (See Figure 19.11.) Some of the information in the window is DBMS-specific.

Step 3 Select each of the columns that comprise the primary key in the Table Columns box. PowerBuilder displays the selected columns in the Key Columns box.

Step 4 If you want, you can reorder the columns in the key by dragging them with the mouse.

Step 5 Specify any information required by your DBMS (such as a name for the primary key). For DBMS-specific information, see your DBMS documentation.

Step 6 Click OK. You return to either the Create Table or Alter Table window.

Step 7 Save your work by doing one of the following:

- Click the Create or Alter button. PowerBuilder submits the CREATE TABLE or ALTER TABLE statement to the DBMS. Some DBMSs automatically create a unique

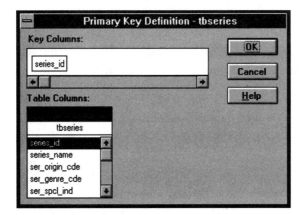

Figure 19.11 Defining a primary key.

index when you define a primary key so that you can immediately begin to add data to the table. Others require that you separately create a unique index to support the primary key before populating the table with data. To see what your DBMS does, see your DBMS documentation.

Defining foreign keys using PowerBuilder. If your DBMS supports foreign keys, you can define them in PowerBuilder. To define a foreign key:

Step 1 Display the Create Table window for a table that you are creating, or display the Alter Table window for an existing table.

Step 2 Click the Foreign Key button in the Table group. The Foreign Key Selection window displays. It lists all foreign keys defined for the current table.

Step 3 Click New to define a new foreign key. The Foreign Key Definition window displays. Some of the information in the window is DBMS-specific.

Step 4 Name the foreign key in the Foreign Key Name box. Check the naming standards.

Step 5 Select the columns for the foreign key in the Select Columns listbox. The selected columns display in the Foreign Key Columns box.

Step 6 You can reorder the columns by dragging them with the mouse.

Step 7 In the Primary Key Table listbox, select the table that contains the primary key referenced by the foreign key that you are defining. PowerBuilder displays the selected table's primary key in the Primary Key Columns box.

Step 8 Specify any information required by your DBMS (such as a delete rule). For DBMS-specific information, see your DBMS documentation.

Step 9 Click OK. You return to the Foreign Key Selection window.

Step 10 Click Done. You return to the Create Table or Alter Table window.

Step 11 Save your work by clicking the Create or Alter button. PowerBuilder submits the CREATE TABLE or ALTER TABLE statement to the DBMS.

General note about databases, keys, and indices. In most cases, it probably is easier to use a tool like ERwin or LBMS to build a complex database with many entities and relationships. The interaction can be planned, analyzed, and designed. These tools also have comprehensive schema generation to provide database triggers and DDL. We have mentioned index and key creation for completeness but warn against its casual use. Relationships and their update ramifications must be clearly thought out before definition.

Creating database views

A base table is stored on disk drives. So far in this chapter, we have discussed only base tables. A view table is not stored. It really is just a query; the rows of the view are derived by executing the query. When you construct a view with the CREATE VIEW statement, the definition is recorded in the catalog. When you run a query against the view, the system merges your query with this definition and executes the merged query. As you can see, views do not significantly affect performance; they are used primarily for convenience.

Views are quite useful. Sensitive information like salaries can be stored in a base table but excluded from a view. By giving users access to the view but not to the base table, you secure the salary data. Views also are used like macros, as a way of packaging complete queries in the guise of a table. Views can be used to present data in a format requested by the user, without affecting your database design.

Unfortunately, views have one major limitation. SELECT statements work well against views, but inserts, updates, and deletes might not. Suppose a view contains all of the table columns except the primary key. Insertions to this view might create a null primary key and will be rejected. If you have specified NOT NULL, updates and deletions can be ambiguous because the primary key is not available to positively identify rows.

You can define and manipulate views in PowerBuilder. Typically you use views for the following reasons:

- To give names to frequently executed SELECT statements.

- To limit access to data in a table. For example, you can create a view of all the columns in the Employee table except Salary. Users of the view can see and update all information except the employee's salary.

- To combine information from multiple tables for easy access.

A view is a set of columns that can be chosen from one or more tables. Views typically are not updateable but are used to provide a simple way to access natural database table joins or to provide for securing sensitive database data. In PowerBuilder, you can create single- or multiple-table views and can use a view to create a new view. You open and manipulate existing views in the Database painter. You define views in the View painter.

Exporting database objects

You can export the syntax for a table or view to the log. This feature is useful when you want to create a backup copy of the table or view before you alter it or when you want to create the same object in another DBMS. To export to another DBMS, you must have the PowerBuilder interface for that DBMS. To export the syntax of an existing table or view to a log:

Step 1 Select the table or view in the painter workspace.

Step 2 Select `Export Table/View Syntax To Log` from the Objects menu. If you selected a table, the DBMS window displays.

Step 3 Select the DBMS to which you want to export the syntax.

Step 4 Click OK. (See Figure 19.12.)

PowerBuilder exports the syntax to the log. The syntax is in the format required by the DBMS that you selected in the DBMS window. *Note*: the PowerBuilder cata-

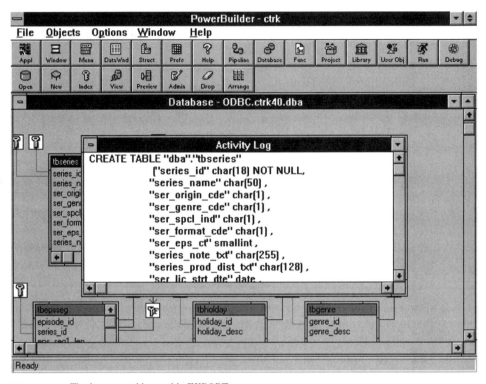

Figure 19.12 The log created by a table EXPORT.

log table rows that describe the object being exported also will be generated and added to the log. They can be quite extensive because the log generates all of the SQL Inserts required to populate.

Manipulating data

Now we turn to the second part of the relational model: the operators used to manipulate tables. The Codd father defined eight operators in his 1970 paper: *restrict, project, join, union, difference, intersect, product,* and *divide.* Of these eight, only five are necessary. *Join, difference,* and *divide* can be derived from the other five. Also, additional operators can be defined, such as *outer join.* Thus the original eight operators are a useful but somewhat arbitrary collection.

The operators act on tables, just as arithmetic operators act on numbers. When an operator is applied to one or two tables, the result is another table. Consequently we have an algebra of tables, just as we have an algebra of arithmetic. Codd called this *relational algebra.* In this section, we examine the three most important operators—*restrict, project,* and *join*—and learn how they are implemented in SQL and easily implemented using PowerBuilder.

Let's begin with *restrict.* The *restrict* operator eliminates rows from a single table. In the example query, we select comedy shows. The query result conforms to the definition of a table, although it does not physically exist. In SQL, the result of every query is another table; this principle is known as *closure.*

```
SELECT SERIES_CDE, SERIES_NAME
FROM SERIES
WHERE GENRE_CDE = "COMEDY"
```

The *project* operator eliminates columns from a single table. In the example, we select only SERIES_CDE and SERIES_NAME.

Most SQL queries combine *restrict* and *project*. The operator that best character-izes relational database management is *join*. The *join* operator combines two tables by comparing one column from each. The comparison here uses an equal sign and is called an *equijoin*. Joins involving ">" or "<" are possible but less common. An *equi-join* results in a table with two identical columns. To conform to the definition of a table, one of these columns must either be eliminated with a project or renamed. An equijoin that eliminates the duplicate column is called a *natural join*. The following example is a natural join, with additional columns eliminated for clarity:

```
SELECT         episod.series_cde,  pgmtrk.track_datetime,  episod.episode_cde,
episod.episode_name,
episod.eps_desc_txt,episod.eps_quest_star_txt
FROM pgmtrk, episod
WHERE ( episod.episode_cdc = pgmtrk.episode_cde )
  and ( episod.series_cde = pgmtrk.series_cde )
  and (pgmtrk.track_datetime between
      '1994-02-01 00:00' AND '1996-0401 23:59:00')
ORDER BY  episod.series_cde ASC,  pgmtrk.
    track_datetime ASC;
```

As you work on the database, you often will want to look at existing data or create some data for testing purposes. Also, you will want to test display formats, validation rules, and edit styles on real data. PowerBuilder provides the Objects menu and par-ticularly the Data Manipulation painter for such purposes. (See Figure 19.7.) In this painter, you can:

- Retrieve and manipulate database information.

- Save the contents of the database in a variety of formats (for example, Excel, dBASE, or Lotus 1-2-3).

Opening the Data Manipulation painter. To open the Data Manipulation painter, se-lect the table or view whose data you want to manipulate from the list of tables. (See Figure 19.13.)

Do one of the following:

- Click the Preview icon in the PainterBar. This will display the data in a grid format.

- Select `Data Manipulation` from the Objects menu and choose the format option from the cascading menu that displays:

  ~Grid, which uses a rigid spreadsheet format.

  ~Tabular, which uses rows and columns (i.e., multiple rows per page). You can arrange them as you like.

  ~Freeform, which resembles a freeform data-entry form (i.e., you can place se-lected columns anywhere, and you have one row per page displayed).

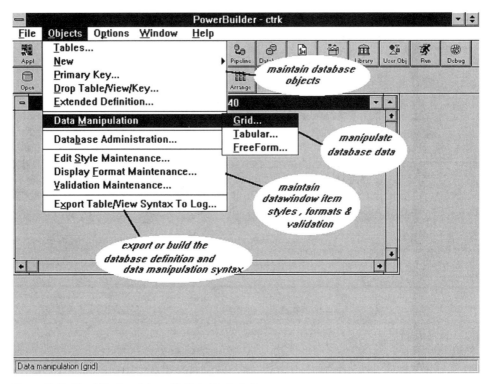

Figure 19.13 The Objects painter with Data Manipulation.

After you choose a form, the Data Manipulation painter opens and all rows are retrieved. (See Figure 19.14.) As the rows are being retrieved, the Retrieve icon changes to a Cancel icon. You can click the Cancel icon to stop the retrieval. This is a good idea if you will get back more rows than you could possibly review. The Data Manipulation painter actually is a DataWindow. The format style that you have chosen corresponds to a type of DataWindow object (i.e., grid, tabular, or freeform).

To retrieve rows from the database, click the Retrieve icon in the PainterBar, or select Retrieve from the Rows menu. PowerBuilder retrieves all of the rows in the current table or view. As the rows are being retrieved, the icon changes to Cancel. You can click it to stop the retrieval.

You can add, modify, or delete rows. When you are finished manipulating the data, you can apply the changes to the database. If you are using a view, you cannot update data in a view where it is comprised of columns from more than one table.

To modify existing data, tab to the field and enter a new value. The Data Manipulation painter uses validation rules, display formats, and edit styles that you have defined for the table in the Database painter. To save the changes to the database, you must apply them, as described later in this section.

To add a row, click the Insert Row icon. PowerBuilder creates an empty row. Enter data for a row. To save the changes to the database, you must apply them, as described later in this section.

To delete a row, click the Delete Row icon. PowerBuilder removes the row from the display. To save the changes to the database, you must apply them, as described in the following paragraph.

To apply changes to the database, click the Update Database icon. PowerBuilder updates the table with all the changes that you have made.

You can define and use sort criteria and filters for the rows. The sort criteria and filters that you define in the Data Manipulation painter are for testing only and are not saved with the table or passed to the DataWindow painter.

To sort the rows:

Step 1 Select Sort from the Rows menu. The Specify Sort Columns window displays.

Step 2 Select the columns that you want to sort the rows by and specify whether you want to sort in ascending or descending order. The order in which you select the columns determines the precedence of the sort.

Step 3 Click OK.

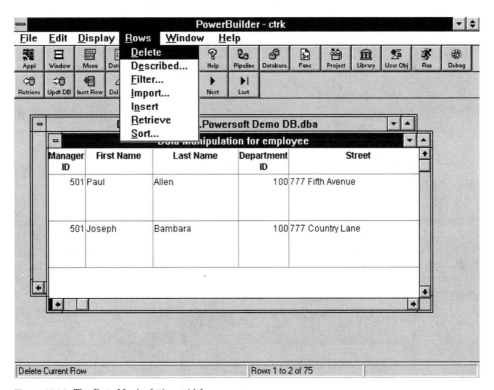

Figure 19.14 The Data Manipulation grid form.

You can limit which rows are displayed by defining a filter. To filter the rows:

Step 1 Select Filter from the Rows menu. The Specify Filter window displays.

Step 2 Enter a Boolean expression that PowerBuilder will test against each row. If the expression evaluates to TRUE, the row will be displayed. You can paste Power-Script functions, columns, and operators in the expression.

Step 3 Click OK.

PowerBuilder filters the data. Only rows meeting the filter criteria are displayed.

About filtered rows and database updates. When you update the database using PowerBuilder generated SQL, filtered rows are ignored:

- Filtered rows are not deleted when you update the database.
- Filtered rows whose values have changed since they were retrieved are not updated in the database.

You can display information about the data that you have retrieved. To display the row information, select Described from the Rows menu. The Describe Rows window displays. The Describe Rows window shows the number of:

- Rows that have been deleted in the painter but not yet deleted from the database
- Rows displayed in Preview
- Rows that have been filtered
- Rows that have been modified in the painter but not yet modified in the database

All row counts are zero until you retrieve the data from the database or add a new row. The count changes when you modify the displayed data or test filter criteria. (See Figure 19.15.)

Importing data. You can import data from an external source and display it in the Data Manipulation painter, then save the imported data in the database.
To import data:

Step 1 Select Import from the Rows menu. The Select Import File window displays.

Step 2 Specify the file from which you want to import the data. The types of files that you can import into the painter are shown in the List Files of Type dropdown listbox.

Step 3 Click OK.

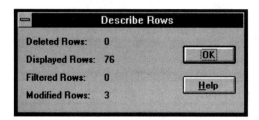

Figure 19.15 Describe Rows.

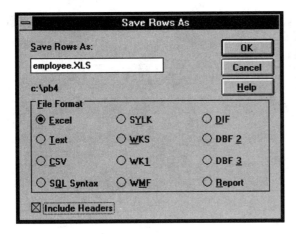

Figure 19.16 Save Rows As Excel spreadsheet.

PowerBuilder reads the data from the file into the painter. You then can click the Update Database icon in the PainterBar to add the new rows to the database. You can save the displayed data in an external file. The SaveAs function can be invoked programmatically using a script and the DataWindow SaveAs function. It is a powerful way to save database data to another form (e.g., an Excel spreadsheet). See Figure 19.16. To save the data in an external file:

Step 1 Select Save Rows As from the File menu. The Save Rows As window displays.

Step 2 Choose a format for the file. (See Figure 19.17.) Name the file.

Step 3 If you want the columns' headings saved in the file, select the Include Headers box.

Step 4 Click OK.

PowerBuilder saves all displayed rows in the file; all columns in the displayed rows are saved. Filtered rows are not saved. You can use the Database Administration painter to control access to the database and to create SQL for immediate execution.

Opening the Database Administration painter. To open the Database Administration painter, click the Database Administration icon or select Database Administration from the Objects menu in the Database painter. (See Figure 19.13.) The Database Administration painter displays.

The Database Administration painter is very much like the PowerScript painter; however, instead of building scripts in it, you build SQL statements to submit to the DBMS. The painter provides the same editing capabilities as the PowerScript painter. The Database Administration painter provides a series of windows that you can use to control access to the database. The windows are tailored to your DBMS. For information about PowerBuilder support for security options in your DBMS, see the PowerBuilder interface manual for your DBMS. You can use the Database Administration painter to build SQL statements and execute them immediately. The painter's workspace acts as a notepad in which you can enter SQL statements.

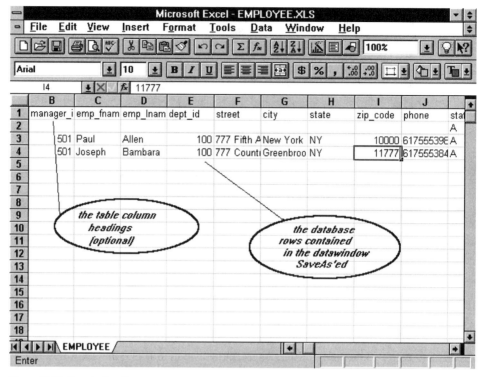

Figure 19.17 SaveAs function.

Figure 19.18 Paste SQL.

You can enter a SQL statement in three ways:

- Pasting the statement
- Keying the statements into the painter workspace
- Opening a text file containing the SQL

You can paste SELECT, INSERT, UPDATE, and DELETE statements to the workspace. (See Figure 19.18.)

To paste a SQL statement to the workspace:

Step 1 Click the Paste SQL icon in the PainterBar, or select `Paste SQL` from the Edit menu. The types of SQL statements that you can paint display in a window.

Step 2 Double-click the appropriate icon to select the statement type. The Select Table window displays.

Step 3 Select the tables that you will reference in the SQL statement. You go to the Select, Insert, Update, or Delete painter, depending on the type of SQL statement that you are painting.

Step 4 Follow the procedure described in Table 19.3 for the statement you are painting. In each case, you can select Show SQL Syntax from the painter's Options menu to see the SQL as you dynamically build it.

When you have completed painting the SQL statement (see Figure 19.19), click the Return icon in the PainterBar in the Select, Insert, Update, or Delete painter. You re-

TABLE 19.3 Procedures to Paint a Statement

Type of statement	Actions taken to gain desired result
SELECT	Define the statement exactly as in the Select painter when building a view. You choose the columns to select. If you want, you can define computed columns and specify sorting and joining criteria and WHERE, GROUP BY, and HAVING criteria.
INSERT	Type the values to insert into each column. You can insert as many rows as you want.
UPDATE	First, specify the new values for the columns in the Update Column Values window. Then, specify the WHERE criteria to indicate which rows to update.
DELETE	Specify the WHERE criteria to indicate which rows to delete.

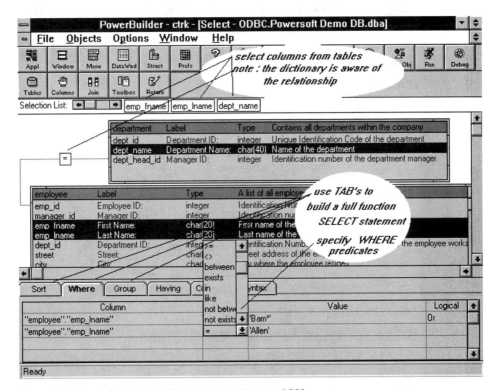

Figure 19.19 Developing a SELECT statement using pasted SQL.

turn to the Database Administration painter with the SQL statement pasted into the workspace. (See Figure 19.20.) If you want, you can simply type one or more SQL statements directly in the workspace. You can enter any statement supported by your DBMS. This includes statements that you can paint as well as statements that you cannot paint (for example, a database stored procedure or CREATE TRIGGER).

You can read SQL that has been saved in a text file into the Database Administration painter. To read SQL from a file:

Step 1 Select Paste from the Edit menu. The DOS File Open window displays.

Step 2 Select the file that contains the SQL, and click OK. PowerBuilder inserts the SQL at the current insertion point.

Sometimes there is more than one way to code SQL statements to obtain the desired results. When performance problems emerge, you can use Explain SQL on the Objects menu to help you select the most efficient method. Explain SQL displays information about the path that PowerBuilder will use to execute the statements in the SQL Statement Execution Plan window. This is most useful when you are retrieving or updating data in an indexed column or using multiple tables. The information displayed in the SQL Statement Execution Plan window depends on your DBMS. For more information about the SQL execution plan, see your DBMS documentation. When you have the SQL statement that you want in the workspace, you

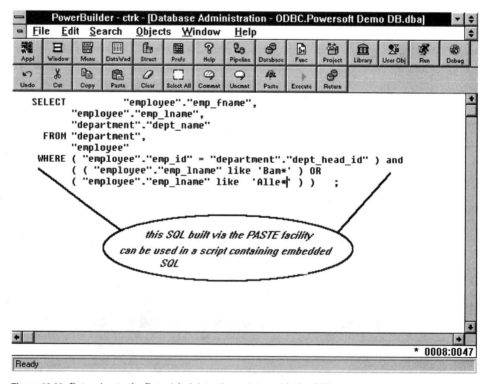

Figure 19.20 Returning to the Data Administration painter with the SQL.

can submit it to the DBMS. If the SQL retrieves data, the data appears in a window identical to a grid Data Manipulation painter. If there is a database error, you see a message box describing the problem.

Connecting to the other DBMSs

A LAN-based client/server application can use a growing number of DBMS platforms as a back-end to PowerBuilder. A PowerBuilder database interface is a native (direct) connection to a database or DBMS. If your site uses one or more of these databases and if you have the required database server and client software installed, you can access the data by installing the corresponding Powersoft database interface that comes with PowerBuilder or InfoMaker. For example, you can access an Oracle database by installing one of the Powersoft Oracle interfaces.

A Powersoft database interface does not go through ODBC to access a database (i.e., you go native). Therefore, you do not complete the ODBC Configuration dialog box to define the data source. Instead, you create a database profile in which you specify connection parameters for accessing the database.

The following Powersoft database interfaces are supported in PowerBuilder Enterprise and InfoMaker but not in PowerBuilder Team/ODBC or PowerBuilder Desktop:

- ALLBASE/SQL
- Oracle 7 (OR7 interface)
- IBM DRDA_DRDA
- SQL Server
- Informix 4 (IN4 interface)
- SQLBase
- Informix 5 (IN5 interface)
- Sybase Net-Gateway Interface for DB2
- Micro Decisionware Database Gateway (MDI) Interface for DB2
- Sybase SQL Server System 10
- Oracle 6 (OR6 interface)
- XDB

The list is a moving target that responds to developer demands. Check the availability of each interface at application deployment time to ensure that the DBMS and PowerBuilder are at the same release level. Otherwise you might have to stay at one release of a database or avoid new features until the two components are at the same release level set.

(*Note*: This list includes the database interfaces for DOS (Windows) PowerBuilder release 4 at the date of publication.)

We will spend a little time discussing some of the requirements for connecting to some of these databases as well as notes on some of their differences. We have worked with each one of the interfaces that we will discuss here using Windows, and each experience has been the same, only different. In each case, the client will require information like the name and location of the DBMS server, a logon ID and password, and specific database parameters to increase performance. Use the native DBMS catalog or the PowerBuilder extended attributes. The first developer to make each specific DBMS connection probably will encounter some small setup snafu. That is why it is so important to document the experience, especially the successful parts.

Connecting to Oracle 7

To connect to Oracle from PowerBuilder, you must install the PowerBuilder Interface for Oracle (PBORA040.DLL). It is included in the Enterprise version. It also copies the PBOR7040.DLL and PBOR6040.DLL to your PowerBuilder directory. It is a good idea to separate each DBMS interface into its own platform directory, especially in shops with multiple instances or versions of the particular DBMS. Your project might be forced to use a different version of the DBMS software. Making a connection to your Oracle 7 database assumes that you already have all of the proper Oracle client and server software, as well as the network layer software (e.g., TCP/IP). The PowerBuilder Oracle interface sits on top of the existing software and takes advantage of the existing connectivity. If you do not have the necessary software required to connect prior to installing PowerBuilder, you will get a series of PowerBuilder messages telling you what is missing at each invocation.

The prerequisites for connecting to Oracle 7 via PowerBuilder are the following:

- You might have used other tools to connect to Oracle; search to determine whether there are existing or multiple copies of ORA7WIN.DLL. If multiple copies exist, delete or rename all copies except the copy that you downloaded from the Powersoft BBS or obtained directly from Oracle; there should be only one copy of ORA7WIN.DLL on your PC. Check the operating system directory path.

- Install the Oracle database server following the instructions provided by Oracle. This typically will be done by the System Administrator or the Database Administration Group.

- Install the client SQL*NET software following the standard installation instructions. Installing SQL*NET ensures that the configuration files are available on your computer and that the SQL that you build will be translated properly before the request message block is sent to the Server. You must obtain the Oracle client/server and SQL*NET software from ORACLE.

- Place the directories that contain the Oracle Windows API DLLs (ORA7WIN.DLL and COREWIN.DLL) in your operating system path. You can obtain Oracle Windows API from Oracle or the Powersoft Bulletin Board (BBS) by downloading ORA7DLL.ZIP, then using PKUNZIP to uncompress it into the appropriate directory.

- Determine what network protocol that you are using (TCP/IP, Novell, etc.) and whether you are using SQL*NET for DOS or SQL*NET for Windows. The LAN system administrator (SA) should be involved to avoid ending up with each developer having a different connection setup.

- Edit a project sample PB.INI, and set up the database parameters for the Preferences and a Database Profile. Use the appropriate values for Oracle. See the

PowerBuilder "Database Interface" manual. Review material specific to Oracle. A profile that is set up correctly should be distributed to the development community to ensure uniform connections and reduce the time each developer takes to become connected.

- Make sure that the directories that contain these files are in your operating system path. If they are on a project file server and are logically mapped, put that device/drive information in your path as well.

Once you have identified your network protocol, determine from Table 19.4 which SQL*NET network driver you need. The driver should be loaded prior to entering the development environment (e.g., Windows). Your can load SQL*NET DOS from your AUTOEXEC.BAT file, from a file called at startup (e.g., AUTOEXEC.BAT file), or manually.

After you complete the standard Oracle client installation, there is an ORACLE directory on your computer. In this directory, there is a file named CONFIG.ORA (if you have SQL*NET for DOS) or ORACLE.INI (if you are using SQL*NET for Windows) that contains your Oracle configuration information. PowerBuilder also has .INI settings stored in PB.INI for each database profile. Each DBMS type used will have similar but specific values for accessing and optimizing access to each DBMS.

Set the values for Oracle database profiles to the values shown in Table 19.5.

The most difficult part of connecting to an Oracle database is determining the proper connect string. The connect string specifies the network protocol, the logical server name, and, optionally, the database name. This file is read by the Windows API.

TABLE 19.4 The SQLNet Network Drivers

Network connection	Driver
NamedPipes	SQLNMP
TCP/IP	SQLTCP (SQLNet for DOS: SQLNET.EXE; SQLNet for Windows: .DLL)
Novell	SQLSPX
NetBios	SQLNTB
Vines	SQLVIN

TABLE 19.5 Values for Oracle Database Profiles

Profile parameter	Value and description
Profile name	Meaningful name (e.g., Server/Database)
DBMS	OR7
Server name	The server connect string (discussed later in this section)
LogID	Your server logon ID
LogPassword	Your server logon password
DBPARM	See "Setting Oracle DBParm variables" later in this chapter.

You must set the `ServerName` variable in Database Preferences or Profiles (for PowerBuilder users) or Database Profile (for Infomaker users) into the appropriate connect string for Oracle. The format for the connect string is:

`@identifier:LogicalServerName`

for SQL*NET of DOS, and:

`@identifier:LogicalServerName:OracleInstanceName`

for SQL*NET for Windows.

Note: If you are accustomed to using another format for the connect string, use it. In most cases, you also can find the connect string in the CONFIG.ORA or ORACLE.INI file. Table 19.6 contains some ideas on how to set the `identifier` and `LogicalServerName`. `Logical/ServerName` is the name assigned to the server. (*Note*: The at sign and the colons are required.) `OracleInstanceName` is the name assigned to the Oracle instance that you are logging onto.

For example, to use SQL*NET for DOS TCP/IP to connect to an Oracle server named BUBBA, enter the connect string: `@T:BUBBA`.

To use SQL*NET for Windows TCP/IP to connect to an ORACLE server named BUBBA under the default oracle instance named OR7I01, enter the connect string: `@T:BUBBA:OR7I01`

The first time that a user uses PowerBuilder, PowerMaker, or PowerViewer to connect to an Oracle 7 Database, PowerBuilder automatically creates PowerBuilder extended attribute tables in the database. To ensure that these tables have the correct owner, the first user to connect to an Oracle database must set the Preference variables (i.e., LogID and LogPassword to the ID of the database owner).

Setting Oracle DBParm variables.   You can set variables in DBParm to:

- Set the blocking factor
- Disable binding of input variables
- Specify formats for Date, DateTime, and Time data
- Specify mixed case (make Oracle case sensitive)

TABLE 19.6 Setting the
Identifier* and *LogicalServerName

Identifier	The appropriate SQLNet communications identifier
P	Named Pipes SQLNMP
T	TCP/IP SQLTCP
X	Novell SQLSPX
B	NetBios SQLNTB
V	Vines SQLVIN
D	Decnet

TABLE 19.7 The System Tables and Extended Attributes

Attributes	Oracle table name	What is contained
Table level	SYSTEM.PBCATTBL	Default fonts for columns
Column level	SYSTEM.PBCATCOL	Formats, validation rules, headers, labels, case, and justification for database table columns
Display	SYSTEM.PBCATFMT	Column formatting (output)
Validation rules	SYSTEM.PBCATVLD	Column validation (input)
Edit style	SYSTEM.PBCATEDT	Column edit style information

When you paint a table or view in the Database painter, you can define extended table or column (catalog) information. This information is used in DataWindow controls when the table or view is referenced in the SELECT statement in the DataWindow definition.

PowerBuilder saves five types of extended catalog information. Each type of information is saved in its own system table within the database in which the table or view resides. As discussed, PowerBuilder creates these tables automatically the first time the system user uses PowerBuilder to connect to the database. These tables also can be created outside of PowerBuilder. You can have the DBA create the system tables outside the PowerBuilder environment. The DBA should grant privileges to Public. The system tables always have the one prefix (e.g., SYSTEM) so that all developers will share the same tables and extended attributes. (See Table 19.7.)

The PBOR7CAT.SQL script installs the PowerBuilder DBMS package on the Oracle 7 database server. The PowerBuilder DBMS package enables you to use Oracle 7 PBDBMS stored procedures as data sources for DataWindow objects and reports. (The PBOR7CAT.SQL script is stored on the Enterprise CD-ROM.)

To create an Oracle 7 stored procedure, you first create the Oracle 7 stored procedure as you normally do. The only difference is that you must code PBDBMS .Put_Line function calls to build the SQL SELECT statement. The PBDBMS.Put_Line function takes one parameter, a string. The SELECT statement is a concatenation of the parameters passed to the Put_Line function. You can call Put_Line repeatedly in the procedure (up to 100 times) until you have built the entire SELECT statement.

Here is a sample Oracle stored procedure:

```
CREATE PROCEDURE spmdw2 (dbname varchar2, dboth varchar2)
is_mystr varchar2(255);
BEGIN
PBDBMS.Put_Line('SELECT series_cde,episode_cde');
PBDBMS.Put_Line('FROM episode');
END;
```

The generated SELECT statement will be:

```
SELECT series_cde,episode_cde FROM episode
```

A DataWindow object or report using this procedure will have two retrieval arguments: dbname and dboth. After you set up the Oracle 7 database server and create a stored procedure, you create a DataWindow object or report using an Oracle 7 PB-

DBMS stored procedure as its data source. Set the PBDBMS DBParm parameter to 1 as follows to enable use of an Oracle 7. Using an Oracle PBDBMS stored procedure as a data source:

Step 1 Code DBParm = PBDBMS = 1.

Step 2 In the DataWindow or Report painter, click the New button in the Select dialog box. The New DataWindow or New Report dialog box appears. The Stored Procedure icon displays.

Step 3 Select the Stored Procedure data source, and define your DataWindow object or report.

To get the data, you call a DataWindow Retrieve function as you normally do. The appropriate SELECT statement is generated by the specified stored procedure and accessed internally by the DataWindow through the PBDBMS package on the database server. Using an Oracle 7 PBDBMS stored procedure as a data source for DataWindow objects and reports has the following limitations:

- The stored procedure must have no output parameters.
- The SELECT statement is limited to 25,500 (255 × 100) characters.

Closing the connection. PowerBuilder opens the database connection the first time that you need to connect to the database. The setting of the Database Preference variable StayConnected controls when PowerBuilder closes the connection. If StayConnected is 1 (the default), PowerBuilder closes the connection. If StayConnected is 0, PowerBuilder opens the connection each time you need it and closes it when you close the painter or the compile is complete.

Basic problem checklist for Oracle. If you have problems connecting to the Oracle database, check each of the following:

- The PowerBuilder or Infomaker directory is in your operating system path.
- The directory that contains the Oracle Windows API (ORA7WIN.DLL and CORE-WIN.DLL) is in your DOS Path, even if the files are in network directories that are mapped.
- You have an environment variable in your AUTOEXEC.BAT that reads SETCONFIG=C:\ORACLE\CONFIG.ORA (for SQL*NET for DOS) or SETCONFIG=C:\ORAWIN\ORACLE.INI (for SQL*NET for Windows), where C:\ORACLE is the directory that contains the CONFIG.ORA file for SQL*NET for DOS and C:\ORAWIN is the directory that contains the ORACLE.INI file.
- The directory that contains the Oracle client software is in your operating system path. (This directory typically is named something like C:\ORACLE\BIN.)
- The SQL*NET driver is running before Windows is started.
- The ServerName variable in Database Preferences is set to the appropriate connect string for Oracle.

If the connect string is correct and the network drivers are current and compatible with Oracle API, the connection should work. If you still cannot connect to Oracle, run the Oracle test connect program. This is WINSAM.EXE for SQL*NET for DOS and NETTEST.EXE for SQL*NET for Windows. The Oracle test program WINSAM.EXE can be found on the Powersoft BBS. Once you have one of these programs, run it from Windows. If you cannot connect using WINSAM or NETTEST, most likely the SQL*NET Driver that you are using is too old and is not compatible with Oracle Windows API. Call Oracle Support and ask whether there is a more recent version of the Oracle Windows API and the SQL*NET driver. Because Oracle does not notify Sybase or Powersoft when they update the ORAWIN.DLL, you need to call Oracle for this information.

Connecting to Sybase SQL Server

To begin the process of connecting to Sybase, install the database server software, per the instructions in your Sybase SQL Server System 10 documentation. You must obtain the database server software from Sybase Corporation. Make sure the appropriate network software is installed at your site and properly configured for your environment. Sybase SQL Server System 10 requires the use of a Windows Sockets compliant TCP/IP network protocol. You must obtain the network software from your network vendor. Install the following client software on your computer:

- Sybase Open Client Client-Library for Windows, Release 10.0.1 or higher
- Sybase Net-Library for Windows, Release 10.0.1 or higher, including the Windows Sockets Driver
- Windows Sockets compliant TCP/IP software

The Powersoft Sybase SQL Server System 10 database interface (PBSYC040.DLL) uses the Client Library (CTLIB) application programming interface (API) to access the database. When you connect to a Sybase System 10 database, PowerBuilder or InfoMaker makes the required calls to the API. Therefore, you do not need to know anything about CT-Lib to use the database interface. If you want to use the DB-Library (DBLIB) API to access an SQL Server database, you must install the Powersoft SQL Server database interface (PBSYB040.DLL).

Before connecting to Sybase SQL Server, a systems administrator must execute the PBSYC.SQL or the PBSYB.SQL script using ISQL on the server. This file must be run once per server. PBSYB.SQL is located on the PowerBuilder Enterprise CD-ROM kit. PBSYB.SQL contains a series of definitions for stored procedures used by PowerBuilder to carry out interface functionality. Here is an example of how to run this SQL using ISQL, which is the basic utility for executing SQL commands in all Sybase SQL Server environments:

```
ISQL /Usa /Sservername /Ia:/pbsyb.sql /P{password}
```

where /U gives the user name (always use SA), /S specifies the server name, /I provides the installation drive (A: if installing from disk), and /P is the password for the SA.

If you are using UNIX , substitute dashes for the slashes. Sybase from Sybase runs on a Unix platform. SQL Server from Microsoft runs on an OS/2 or NT platform. Both connections can use W3DBLIB.DLL and PBSYC040/PBSYB040.DLL. PBSYC040.DLL and PBSYB040.DLL reside in the PowerBuilder or Infomaker directory. W3DBLIB.DLL might be in many different directories (i.e., Excel, SQL/BIN, PowerBuilder, etc.). Find the latest copy and delete the others. This DLL comes from Sybase or Microsoft. If the client does not have a copy, they must purchase it directly from one of those companies. Please be aware of the version date of W3DBLIB.DLL that you are using. If connecting through TCP/IP, the WIN.INI file for DOS/Windows must have an [SQL SERVER] section.

For example:

```
[SQLSERVER]
servername=networkdll, network address, port #, e.g.
   dsquery=wdbnovtc, 192.82.003,4095, URGENT
```

Other common services include:

- WDBHPTCP.DLL—HP Arpa Services

- WDBNOVTC.DLL—Novell LAN Workplace

- WDBFTPTC.DLL—FTP Software Inc.

- WDBWOLTC.DLL—Wollongong Group

- WDBNOVSP.DLL—NetWare 3.11 NLM

- WDBCDCE.DLL—DecPathworks

Avoid having multiple copies of W3DBLIB.DLL. If more than one is found on your disk and path, use the latest possible and rename all duplicates. Attempt to attach to the server via another application. Try connecting through the connection utility that ships with Excel or another package.

For a Named Pipes connection look for the following files:

- DBNMP3.DLL

- NETAPI.DLL

The Open Client software includes the file WCTLIB.DLL, which contains the CT-Library programs. The Powersoft Sybase System 10 interface communicates with the database through WCTLIB.DLL. WCTLIB communicates with the Sybase Net-Library DLL (WNLWNSCK.DLL) installed on your computer. You must obtain the Open Client and Net-Library software from Sybase, and the TCP/IP client software from your network vendor.

Install the Powersoft Sybase SQL Server System 10 database interface (PB-SYC040.DLL) on your computer. Make sure the SQL.INI configuration file for the Sybase Open Client software is correctly configured for your environment. The SQL.INI file is installed by default in the \INI subdirectory of your Sybase System 10 product directory. It should contain an entry for each SQL Server database server that you want to access. Each entry should include the following information:

- Server name
- Sybase Net-Library for Windows driver (DLL) name
- Server Internet address or alias name
- TCP/IP port number

The basic format of an entry in the SQL.INI file is as follows:

```
[server_name]
WIN3_QUERY=driver,address,port_number
```

Here is a sample entry in the SQL.INI file for a database server named devsyb10:

```
[devsyb10]
devsyb10=wnlwnsck,192.1.200.27,5001
```

wnlwnsck is the Windows Sockets Net-Library driver, 192.1.200.27 is the server's Internet address, and 5001 is the server's port number.

When you connect to Sybase System 10, PowerBuilder or InfoMaker passes information from your database profile to WCTLIB.DLL. This information includes the database server name, which must match the server name specified in the SQL.INI file. WCTLIB then checks the SQL.INI file to find the corresponding entry for this server name to determine how to connect to it. When WCTLIB finds the appropriate entry, it loads the specified Net-Library driver and connects to the database. Make sure you can connect to the database server and to the SQL Server System 10 database that you want to access from outside PowerBuilder or InfoMaker.

To verify the connection, use the WSYBPING utility to check that you can reach the database server from your computer. WSYBPING is a network diagnostic utility included with the Sybase Net-Library for Windows software. The WSYBPING utility detects whether the process that you want to access is listening at the specified Internet address.

Table 19.8 lists the values that you should supply for each field in the Database Profile Setup dialog box when defining the Powersoft SQL Server System 10 database interface.

MDI Gateway for DB2

There are four tasks that must be accomplished to complete the configuration:

- Security access to CICS regions
- LAN protocol and transport
- SQL Server client
- PowerBuilder configuration

As you can see, there is no reference to DB2 because you are not a DB2 client. On the LAN, the gateway appears to be a Microsoft SQL Server, so you actually are configured as an MS SQL Server client. The gateways that we refer to generally are called *utility gateways*, which are theoretically available to the public. Most of the

TABLE 19.8 The Values that You Should Supply for Each Field in the Database Profile Setup Dialog Box When Defining the Powersoft SQL Server System 10 Database Interface

Profile field	Description
Profile name	The name of your database profile.
DBMS	SYC—Sybase System 10
User ID	Not applicable for use with PowerBuilder or InfoMaker.
Password	Not applicable for use with PowerBuilder or InfoMaker.
Database name	The name of the SQL Server System 10 database that you want to access.
Prompt for database information during Connect	Select this checkbox if you want to be prompted for connection information when creating or selecting a profile to connect to the database.
Server name	The name of the SQL Server System 10 database server. This name must match the server name specified in your SQL.INI configuration file.
Login ID	The login ID of your database server. To properly create the Powersoft repository tables, make sure the first person to connect to the database has sufficient authority to create tables and grant permissions to public.
Login password	The login password of your database server. The actual password does not display in this field.
DBParm	Specify DBMS-specific connection parameters in this field. Keep track of the information such as file names, version dates, and INI file contents.

current gateways are on OS/2, but UNIX and NT versions should be the most popular by the time of publication. To facilitate the distribution of files and documentation relating to the gateway, set up a SHARED directory called, for example, MDIGW. Do not perform clipboard operations (i.e., copy or cut) on any files in the MDIGW directory. Instead make a local copy, and use it for any clipboard operations.

The configuration process requires you to make changes to your AUTOEXEC.BAT and WIN.INI files, so it is a good idea to back them up first. Also, it will be necessary for you to shut down and reboot your system for the changes to take effect.

Secure access to CICS. The MDI Gateway uses IBM's SNA LU 6.2 protocol to communicate to the MVS environment. Because it does not use DRDA, it needs a Partner LU on the host side, preferably one capable of attaching to DB2. CICS fits that bill nicely. The utility gateways use CICS regions for access to DB2. The important thing is to determine if your ID has access to the regions. To accomplish this, do the actions described in the following paragraphs for each region.

From a 3270 screen, type in the region name and hit Enter. As with TSO, one or more pages of messages might be returned. Press Enter each time the page fills until the CICS login screen appears. Enter your logon ID and password, then press Enter. In the current configuration, clients communicate to the gateway using the Remote Named Pipes protocol. Both the DOS and Windows environments are affected by protocol selection; this section is limited to the DOS considerations.

To support Remote Named Pipes, you will have to modify your AUTOEXEC.BAT file. However, before you make any changes, back it up. There are three drivers—IPXODI, NETX, and DOSNP—that must be loaded for named pipes. Check your AU-

TOEXEC.BAT for these drivers and, if necessary, add them following the entry for the LANSUP driver. The sequence is significant, so add them in the following order:

C:\LAN\LANSUP

C:\LAN\IPXODI   <== Follows LANSUP

C:\LAN\NETX   <== Follows IPXODI

C:\LAN\DOSNP   <== Follows NETX

These modules already should exist in the same directory as LANSUP. The directory probably is called LAN, as illustrated. If you are using a memory manager, it is possible to load these in high memory, and you might be able to replace NETX with EMSNETX or XMSNETX, which use expanded and extended memory respectively. If you are unsure of your configuration options, consult your LAN Administrator.

There is a default number of Named Pipe Servers that DOSNP can recognize. To ensure that none are missed, a configuration file (e.g., SHELL.CFG) can be used to override the default value. Because it's a single line text file, you might find it quicker to use an editor to create it yourself. In either case, it should be in the root directory and read as follows:

```
NP MAX MACHINE NAMES = 50
```

Remember, you will have to reboot for these changes to take effect.

SQL Server client. As previously stated, gateway clients are configured as Microsoft SQL Server clients. This requires programs to provide database API services to applications like PowerBuilder and network services for Named Pipes transport.

SQL Server support for Windows 3.x clients is provided by two DLLs that already exist in our LAN's Windows directory. W3DBLIB.DLL provides the SQL Server API services interface for Windows 3.x clients, and DBNMP3.DLL provides the transport layer.

All that remains at this point is to supply the names of the servers (gateways actually) that we want to access. This is done by adding an [SQLSERVER] section to your Windows WIN.INI file. To make this easier and to ensure consistency throughout the department, create a file named SRVICENM.TXT, which contains the appropriate entries. Make a copy of this file, then copy, or cut, and paste the contents into your WIN.INI file. An example listing of the file follows:

```
[SQLSERVER]
UT01T=DBNMP3,\\MDIUT01\PIPE\TESTCICS
UT01P=DBNMP3,\\MDIUT01\PIPE\PRODCICS
UT02T=DBNMP3,\\MDIUT02\PIPE\TESTCICS
UT02P=DBNMP3,\\MDIUT02\PIPE\PRODCICS
UT03T=DBNMP3,\\MDIUT03\PIPE\TESTCICS
UT03P=DBNMP3,\\MDIUT03\PIPE\PRODCICS
```

Each entry represents a Named Pipe through which you communicate with a specific instance of the MDI Gateway. The format of the entry is as follows:

```
localname=DBNMP3,\\servername\PIPE\servicename
```

`localname` is a name (up to eight characters) by which you refer to the instance defined by the rest of the statement. This name is arbitrary, but we suggest that for consistency's sake you do not change them. DBNMP3 is the Named Pipes interface layer for MS Windows. *servername* is name that is defined as the Named Pipe Server name in the OS/2 CONFIG.SYS of the gateway machine. PIPE is a constant. *servicename* is the name by which a particular execution of the gateway is known and corresponds to the name specified when the gateway was configured. This is more commonly referred to as the *instance* of the gateway.

PowerBuilder setup and configuration (DBLIB). Before continuing, note that all prior configuration tasks must be complete and you should have:

- Rebooted after modifying AUTOEXEC.BAT
- Exited and reentered Windows if WIN.INI was modified from within Windows.

The PowerBuilder product uses either of two connectivity options: ODBC or DBLIB. The parameters and their values are listed in Table 19.9. We will discuss only DBLIB setup.

The Vendors item in the Variables listbox should be highlighted. Minimally, ODBC (case nonsensitive) should be listed in the Value window. The Vendors item is a comma-delimited list of vendor names for which PowerBuilder Interfaces are installed. Add MDIDB2 at any point in the list. Select DBMS from the Variables listbox and replace the current value, if any, with MDIDB2.

Click OK to exit the Preferences painter and return to the Power Panel. At this point, the configuration process is complete, and all that remains is to establish a connection to the gateway.

TABLE 19.9 The Parameters and Values for ODBC and DBLIB

Parameter	ODBC value	DBLIB value
Vendors	ODBC	MDIDB2
DBMS	ODBC	MDIDB2
Logid	Host MVS userid	Host MVS userid
LogPassword	Host MVS password	Host MVS password
Servername	ODBC datasource name	MDI service name (WIN.INI/SQLSERVER)
Database	Database name where the PowerBuilder catalog tables can be built (Optional)	Database name where the PowerBuilder catalog tables can be built (Optional)
Userid	Host MVS userid	Host MVS userid
Database Password	Host MVS password	Host MVS password
TableDir	1	1
StayConnected	1	1
AutoCommit	0	0
TerminatorCharacter	;	;
Columns	8	8
DBPARM	See discussion later in this section	See discussion later in this section

TABLE 19.10 The Values for MDI/DB2

Preference or Profile parameter	Description
Profile name	Text that describes the connection.
Vendor, DBMS	MDIDB2
Database	(Optional) The database used for creation of PowerBuilder catalog tables.
Tablespace	(Optional) The tablespace used to create PowerBuilder catalog tables.
Server name	The values specified as localname in the SQLSERVER section of WIN.INI (e.g., UT03T)
Logon ID	The ID used for this environment
Password	The password for your ID

TABLE 19.11 DBPARM Keyword Parameters

DBPARM keyword parameter	Enter to the right of the equal sign
GroupId	The owner name for the DB2 tables that you want to access.
SystemOwner	SYSIBM for IBM or whatever you have set up. This is the qualifier used for the catalog tables.
PBCatalogOwner	This is the qualifier for PowerBuilder's catalog extension tables.
TableCriteria	='Creator="SYSADMAD"' This will limit the tables brought back when the database is invoked. In this example, only tables qualified by SYSADMAD will be accessed.

TABLE 19.12 Preference Keyword Parameters

Preference keyword parameter	Enter to the right of the equal sign
ReadOnly	=1 will suppress PowerBuilder building the PowerBuilder catalog tables the first time a user accesses DB2.
NoCatalog	=1 will suppress storing information about edit styles and header information usually stored in the PBCatalog tables.

PowerBuilder uses a Login dialog box to define the connection parameters for the various DBMS it supports. The actual entries required vary from DBMS to DBMS, but the look and feel are consistent. Once entered, these parameters can be saved in profiles to simplify the connection process. Go to the PowerBuilder Database painter, and enter FILE, CONNECT, SETUP, and NEW.

The Profile setup window captures server and user information, as well as any DBMS-specific values. For MDI/DB2, supply values as shown in Table 19.10.

The DBPARM entries are of particular interest as they can help performance by causing the MDI gateway to focus on only those tables within the entire DB2 subsystem that are of interest to the user. (See Tables 19.11 and 19.12.)

It is a good idea to set up a profile for each database connection that you might have reason to use. This will make it easy for you to switch connections between different gateway instances or, for that matter, different DBMS connections that you have set up for your PowerBuilder interface.

Setup note: first connection. The first time that you use Micro Decisionware's Database Gateway to connect to DB2 from PowerBuilder, PowerBuilder displays message boxes asking you to enter a TableSpace. This tablespace name is the place where PowerBuilder will place the PowerBuilder catalog tables if they have not already been built. This prompt will occur if you set a database in the Preference painter or by editing the PB.INI database section and not specifying the TableSpace or if SystemOwner and PBCatalog Owner values in the DBParm database variable have not been set.

Setup note: extended column information. PowerBuilder saves four types of extended column information in the repository. Each type of information is saved in its own system table within the TableSpace or database selected by the DBA. You can create these tables through the database gateway by executing the script DB2SYSPB.SQL on the Micro Decisionware Database Gateway DB2 Interface diskette.

Note: Before you execute DB2SYSPB.SQL, change all occurrences of PBOwner to the name that will own the PowerBuilder system tables and change all occurrences of database.tablespace to the appropriate values.

Setup note: first user into the gateway. If you do not create the tables from the database gateway or use SPUFI or DSNTIAD, PowerBuilder creates them automatically the first time a user uses PowerBuilder to connect to the database. If PowerBuilder creates the tables, to ensure the proper access, the first user must:

- Sign on as DBA (i.e., with the CREATE Table authority).

- Have the appropriate TableSpace, database name, and PBCatalogOwner setup in the Preferences.

Connecting to Informix

Powersoft currently supports the following versions of Informix database products:

- InformixSe4.1
- InformixSe5.0
- InformixOL4.1
- InformixOL5.0

Software and hardware requirements. The software required on the client is INFOR-MIX-NET PC. INFORMIX-NET PC supports different TCP/IP drivers and Unix drivers:

- .PC-NFS from Sun Microsystem, Inc., version 4.0
- .PC.TCP from FTP Software, Inc., version 2.2

- .Pathway Access from Wollongong Group, Inc., version 2.0
- .StarGroup (not actually TCP/IP protocol) from AT&T, version 3.1

It also supports Novell's NetWare using IPX/SPX protocol of TCP/IP. INFORMIXDIR \BIN is the directory where the Informix software is located. The path should read: INFORMIXDIR\BIN.

Here again the setup involves the typical prerequisites and first time use implications. Purchase and install the PowerBuilder Interface for Informix (PBINF040.DLL) from Powersoft. Install the Informix database according to the vendor's instructions. Set the database variables in Prefaces to the appropriate values for Informix.

Making the connection. Except for the specification of the database, the connection essentially takes place outside of PowerBuilder and Windows. The connection occurs when you load INET.

At the command line, type:

```
RMSQL -hhostname -uusername -sservicename -ppassword
```

where *hostname* is the name of the host, *username* is your user ID or name, *servicename* is the service name of the client's Informix service, and *password* is your password.

Remember, setting the client's I-Net does not guarantee the ability to connect. The attributes set in the client I-Net only identify the preferences in the client's net layer that is used to communicate to the host. If the client has Informix-SQL, there is an executable named ISQL.EXE or PIQL.EXE that you can use to access the database from DOS. This is a quick check to determine the ability to connect. If you can access the database from DOS, you probably can use PowerBuilder to connect to the database. If the client does not have Informix-SQL, use the command PING *hostname* to ping the host; this tests access to the host.

Informix database preference variables. To connect to Informix, set these database variables in Preferences to the values shown in Table 19.13. This variable is used

TABLE 19.13 The Values for the Database Variables in Preferences

Preference variable	Set to
Vendor	Informix
DBMS	Informix
Database	The name of the desired database.
LockValues	Values:
	DIRTY READ
	COMMITTED READ
	CURSOR STABILITY
	REPEATABLE READ

only for Informix Online databases that were created with transaction support executes. SQLReturnData will cause the serial number of the row to be stored in this variable after an INSERT statement executes. If an error occurs during a connection, a message box displays the error message. After you click OK, a window displays so that you can change the database variables set in Preferences. PowerBuilder then uses the new values to connect to the database.

The data pipeline

The data pipeline is a feature that PowerBuilder provides to migrate data between tables on different databases and even different DBMSs. This feature makes it possible to copy rows from one or more source tables to a new or existing destination table either within a database, across databases, or even across DBMSs.

You can take advantage of data pipelines in different ways:

- As a utility service for developers
- To implement data migration capabilities in an application

They are described in the following two paragraphs.

While working in the PowerBuilder development environment, you occasionally might want to migrate data for logistical reasons (such as to create a small test table from a large production table). You can use the Data Pipeline painter interactively to do that migration right then and there. Another good development application is migrating the extended attribute tables. For example, we can develop the application in Watcom, then move to Sybase, Oracle, or DB2. If the application DataWindows uses the extended attributes for dynamic DataWindows, then the extended attributes will have to reside wherever the application executes.

If you're building an application whose requirements call for migrating data between tables, you can design an appropriate data pipeline in the Data Pipeline painter, save it, then enable users to execute it from within the application. This technique can be useful in many situations (e.g., when you want the application to download local copies of tables from a database server to a remote user or when you want it to roll up data from individual transaction tables to a master transaction table). It provides a basic replication server capability.

In general level, there are basic steps that you have to perform to pipe data in an application:

Step 1 Build the required objects.

Step 2 Perform some initial setup.

Step 3 Start the pipeline.

Step 4 Handle processing errors.

Step 5 Perform some final cleanup.

Implementing data piping in an application requires that you build a few different objects. These are illustrated in the PowerBuilder examples that come with version 4.0, and they include:

- Pipeline object
- Supporting user object
- Window

You must build a pipeline object to specify the data definition and access aspects of the pipeline that you want your application to execute. Use the Data Pipeline painter in PowerBuilder to create this object and specify characteristics. Among the characteristics that you can define in the Data Pipeline painter are:

- The source tables to access and the data columns to retrieve
- The destination table to which you want that data delivered
- The piping operation to perform: create, replace, refresh, append, or update
- The frequency of commits during the piping operation (either after every n rows are piped or only after all rows are piped; strike a balance here)
- The number of errors recorded before the piping operation is terminated
- Whether or not to pipe extended attributes to the destination database (from the PowerBuilder repository in the source database)

Your pipeline object defines the details of the data and access for a pipeline. However, a pipeline object doesn't include the object processing—attributes, events, and functions—that an application requires to handle the execution and control of the pipeline. To provide these logistical supports, you must build an appropriate user object inherited from the PowerBuilder pipeline system object. This system object contains various attributes, events, and functions that enable your application to manage a pipeline object at execution time. These include those listed in Table 19.14.

TABLE 19.14 The Attributes, Events, and Functions that Enable Your Application to Manage a Pipeline Object at Execution Time

Attributes	Events	Functions
DataObject	PipeStart	Start
RowsRead	PipeMeter	Repair
RowsWritten	PipeEnd	Cancel
RowsInError		
Syntax		

You also will require a window. This window provides a user interface to the pipeline. The user interface functionality should include:

- Starting the pipeline's execution
- Displaying and repairing any errors that occur
- Canceling the pipeline's execution if necessary

When you build your window, you must include a DataWindow control that the pipeline itself can use to display error rows (that is, rows that it can't pipe to the destination table for some reason). You don't have to associate a DataWindow object with this DataWindow control; the pipeline will provide one of its own at execution time.

Take care of some setup chores that will prepare the application to handle pipeline execution. To get the application ready for pipeline execution:

Step 1 Connect to the source and destination databases for the pipeline using two different transaction objects.

Step 2 Create an instance of your supporting user object (so that the application can use its attributes, events, and functions). First, declare a variable whose type is that user object. Then, in an appropriate script, code the CREATE statement to create an instance of the user object and assign it to that variable.

Step 3 Specify the particular pipeline object that you want to use (i.e., code an Assignment statement in an appropriate script); assign a string that contains the name of the desired pipeline object to the DataObject attribute of your user-object instance.

Because an application must always reference its pipeline objects dynamically at execution time (through string variables), you must package these objects in one or more PBD files when deploying the application. You cannot include pipeline objects in an executable (EXE) file.

Testing the Pipeline Start function's return value isn't the only way to monitor the status of pipeline execution. Another technique that you can use is to retrieve statistics that your supporting user object keeps concerning the number of rows processed. They provide a live count of the rows:

- Read by the pipeline from the source tables.
- Written by the pipeline to the destination table or to the error DataWindow control.
- In error that the pipeline has written to the error DataWindow control (but not to the destination table).

In many cases, you'll want to provide users (or your application itself) with the ability to stop execution of a pipeline while it is in progress. For instance, you might want to give users a way out if they start the pipeline by mistake or if execution is taking longer than desired (maybe because a large number of rows are involved).

To cancel pipeline execution:

Step 1 Code the pipeline Cancel function in an appropriate script.

Step 2 Make sure that either the user or your application can execute this function (if appropriate) once the pipeline has started. When Cancel is executed, it stops the piping of any more rows after that moment. Rows that already have been piped up to that moment might or might not be committed to the destination table, depending on the Commit attribute that you specified when building your pipeline object in the Data Pipeline painter. Test the result of the Cancel function.

When a pipeline object executes, it commits updates to the destination table according to your specifications in the Data Pipeline painter. You don't need to write any COMMIT statements in your application's scripts to do this.

When a pipeline executes, it might be unable to write particular rows to the destination table. For instance, this could happen with a row that has the same primary key as a row already in the destination table.

To help you handle such error rows, the pipeline places them in the DataWindow control that you painted in your window and specified in the Start function. It does this by automatically associating its own special DataWindow object (the Power-Builder pipeline-error DataWindow) with your DataWindow control.

When your application is all done processing pipelines, you need to make sure that it takes care of a few cleanup chores. These chores basically involve releasing the resources that you obtained at the beginning to support pipeline execution. To clean up when you're done using pipelines:

Step 1 Destroy the instance that you created of your supporting user object (i.e., code the DESTROY statement in an appropriate script and specify the name of the variable that contains that user-object instance).

Step 2 Disconnect from the pipeline's source and destination databases (i.e., code two DISCONNECT statements in an appropriate script). In one, specify the name of the variable that contains your source transaction-object instance. In the other, specify the name of the variable that contains your destination transaction-object instance. Then test the result of each DISCONNECT statement.

Step 3 Destroy your source transaction-object instance and your destination transaction-object instance (i.e., code two DESTROY statements in an appropriate script). In one, specify the name of the variable that contains your source transaction-object instance. In the other, specify the name of the variable that contains your destination transaction-object instance.

20

Related Tools, Libraries, and Publications

This chapter contains details for a number of product areas that combine with PowerBuilder to provide a feature-rich application development environment with connectivity to enterprise-wide server systems. Your demand for these products in a development project depends on a number of factors: the size and functionality of the application, time constraints, and budget constraints.

At the end of this chapter is a list of publications that are either dedicated to, or contain regular columns on, development techniques for PowerBuilder.

CODE, Client/Server Open Development Environment, is Powersoft's strategic framework for protecting existing technology investment and working with emerging client/server technology. It extends Powersoft's product capabilities and market scope by enriching the product functionality through links to other components of the client/server platform. This includes the development of vendor partnerships that cover the entire enterprise computing environment as well as the expansion of the company's training, consulting, and product-support services and alliances.

CASE Tools

Bachman/Generator for PowerBuilder

Bachman Information Systems, Inc.
8 New England Executive Park
Burlington, MA 01803
Phone: 800-BACHMAN or 617-273-9003
Fax: 617-229-9904

Bachman/Generator for PowerBuilder uses Bachman data models to create Power-Builder DataWindows, validation rules, PowerBuilder system table information, and PowerBuilder functions necessary to develop PowerBuilder applications.

EasyCASE System Designer

Evergreen CASE Tools, Inc.
8522 154th Avenue North East
Redmond, WA 98052
Phone: 206-881-5149
Fax: 206-883-7676

EasyCASE System Designer supports a wide range of methods for process event and data modelling. It can be used for logical and physical data modelling, which results in generation of SQL DDL scripts and supports forward and reverse engineering of xBASE databases. The professional edition also supports Watcom, SQL Base, SQL Server, XDB, Access, and Paradox.

ERwin/ERX for PowerBuilder

Logic Works, Inc.
1060 Route 206
Princeton, NJ 08540
Phone: 800-78ERWIN or 609-252-1177
Fax: 609-252-1175

ERwin/ERX for PowerBuilder is a entity-relationship logical data modeling tool. It facilitates the design of client/server database applications with a bidirectional link of the PowerBuilder user interface development environment to a database logical model in ERwin. The PowerBuilder catalog of extended attributes for each database column can be defined from within ERwin, or the existing definitions can be captured and synchronized, enabling both client- and server-side information to be defined and managed in one place, the model. These models then also can be stored in and retrieved from the DBMS. ERwin/ERX provides DBMS support for forward and reverse engineering. ERwin/ERX for PowerBuilder provides support for table-level and schema-level prescripts and postscripts, direct system catalog synchronization, multiple subject areas and stored displays, physical storage parameters, and stored procedures.

Excellerator

Intersolv, Inc.
3200 Tower Oaks Boulevard
Rockville, MD 20852
Phone: 800-547-4000 or 301-230-3200
Fax: 301-231-7813

Excellerator is an analysis and design tool that supports multiple approaches for distributed design of data, process, events, and user interfaces, as well as RAD and object-oriented methods. It includes a multiuser LAN repository that enables teams to share information and reuse design elements under multiple methodologies.

IE:Advantage

Information Engineering Systems Corp.
201 North Union Street, 5th Floor
Alexandria, VA 22314
Phone: 703-739-2242
Fax: 703-739-0074

IE:Advantage is a CASE product with a central repository that supports information systems' development life cycle. It develops logical data models, process models, and systems designs in implementation priority sequence. IE:Advantage includes goals and objectives of organization that can be linked to logical data/process models. It generates databases and application systems in various formats and languages and includes an IEW/ADW conversion utility, cross-reference reports, and IDEF1X data modeling capabilities. Implementation includes user-customizable SQL schema generation with an interface to PowerBuilder for application/code generation.

InfoModeler

Asymetrix Corp.
110 110th Avenue North East, Suite 700
Bellevue, WA 98004

InfoModeler uses conceptual modeling tools based in ORM (Object Role Modeling) that help to communicate and automate the process of building sound RDBMSs. Designers and end users use English language business rules and sample data to build the information model. InfoModeler then automatically generates a correctly normalized database and builds the PowerBuilder data dictionary.

SE/Open For PowerBuilder

LBMS, Inc.
1800 West Loop South, Suite 1800
Houston, TX 77027-3210
Phone: 800-231-7515 or 713-623-0414
Fax: 713-623-4955

SE/Open For PowerBuilder transfers CASE-based design data from Systems Engineer to PowerBuilder for development of applications. Systems Engineer is a multiuser, concurrent access CASE tool and integrated lifecycle development tool. SE/Open For PowerBuilder provides data-driven, process-driven, rapid application development (RAD), and joint applications development (JAD) capabilities.

LexiBridge Transformer

LexiBridge Corp.
605 Main Street
Monroe, CT 06468
Phone: 203-459-8228
Fax: 203-459-8220

LexiBridge provides a rule-driven interface that permits users to specify migration objectives at three levels: the Data Model, the Process Model, and the User Model. LexiBridge parses the COBOL/CICS source code modules, performs restructuring and code cleanup, then generates the appropriate PowerBuilder and SQL constructs.

MidPoint for IEF

MidCore Software, Inc.
49 Leavenworth Street, Suite 200
Waterbury, CT 06702
Phone: 203-759-0906
Fax: 203-759-2131

MidPoint for IEF provides a level of open access while allowing IEF applications to maintain complete integrity and security of business data and business rules. It provides access to data in IEF applications to GUI tools (including PowerBuilder, Visual Basic, and SQL Windows), to report writers (including ReportSmith and Crystal Reports), and to analytical tools such as Microsoft Excel.

PowerBuilder Companion

Chen & Associates, Inc.
4884 Constitution Avenue, Suite 1E
Baton Rouge, LA 70808
Phone: 504-928-5765
Fax: 504-928-9371

PowerBuilder Companion provides the capability to reverse-engineer existing database schemas into ER-Designer. It maintains PowerBuilder scripts for database design and implementation and adds the necessary link between modeling and implementing new systems developed with PowerBuilder. Also included is the Chen Normalizer, a tool for bringing the model to the third normal form (3NF).

S-Designer

SDP Technologies, Inc.
1 Westbrook Corporate Center, Suite 805
Westchester, IL 60154
Phone: 708-947-4250
Fax: 708-947-4251

S-Designer is a database design tool that allows users to construct entity-relationship data models and to describe entities and their attributes in dictionary. It produces analysis documentation, generates database creation scripts, and offers reverse engineering functions.

SA/PowerBuilder Link

Popkin Software & Systems, Inc.
11 Park Place
New York, NY 10007-2801
Phone: 800-REAL-CASE or 212-571-3434
Fax: 212-571-3436

SA/PowerBuilder Link is SQL smart, Windows rich, Object easy, MIS friendly, etc. It provides a two-way connection between System Architect's analysis and design capabilities and PowerBuilder's development environment. SA/PowerBuilder Link uses logical and/or physical model information in SA Repository to generate database tables for the target RDBMS. It creates extended attribute tables and allows screen and menu layouts created in System Architect to be used to generate menus and Response windows in PowerBuilder. Support for Sybase SQL Server, Microsoft SQL Server, Oracle 6 and 7, and Informix is provided.

Version-Control Tools

CCC/Manager

Softool Corp.
340 S. Kellogg Avenue
Goleta, CA 93117
Phone: 800-723-0696 or 805-683-5777
Fax: 805-683-4105

Using GUI and command-line interfaces, CCC/Manager provides change and version management for any type of software component, application management, change packaging, access control, and user hierarchy maintenance for a centralized or distributed database.

Endeavor Workstation (NDVR)

Legent Corp.
575 Herndon Parkway
Herndon, VA 22080-5226
Phone: 800-676-LGNT or 703-708-3000

Endeavor Workstation is a software management system that controls and manages changes to both workstation applications and to mainframe applications developed on the workstation.

LBMS Systems Engineer
See "SE/Open For PowerBuilder" in the previous section.

MKS Revision Control System (RCS)

Mortice Kern Systems, Inc.
185 Columbia Street West, Waterloo
Ontario, N2L 5Z5 Canada
Phone: 800-265-2797 or 519-884-2251
Fax: 519-884-8861

MKS Revision Control System (RCS) is a customizable revision control system that tracks changes to source code as it is created, tested, and revised by programmers. It includes configuration and document management, encryption, visual difference locking, branching, merging, locking, a menu-driven interface, and support for binary and text files.

PVCS Version Manager

Intersolv, Inc.
3200 Tower Oaks Boulevard
Rockville, MD 20852
Phone: 800-547-4000 or 301-230-3200
Fax: 301-231-7813

PVCS (Polytron Version Control System) Version Manager keeps track of revision, version, and release information of all development objects including source code, ASCII files, graphics, documentation, and binary files. Another of its services is the Configuration Builder. Its job is to record relationships between components and to re-create the specific sequence of steps to construct a software system reliably, completely, and accurately at any time.

Framework and Class Libraries

A framework library, ideally, should be able to provide central application functionality, taking care of issues such as security, intersheet communication, MDI frame and sheet management, and navigation.

A class library, ideally, is a set of ready-made intelligent PowerBuilder classes that are ready to use in an application, encouraging a consistent look and feel. The intelligence commonly is provided by encapsulating tried-and-tested data and methods.

The real trick is to find a framework and a class library that will work together.

aRenDeeco

aRenDeeco, Inc.
Phone: 403-295-6403
Fax: 403-295-6400

Advanced PowerBuilder Object Library

ScottSoftware, Inc.
Phone: 800-654-2734

The following classes are supplied by Advanced PowerBuilder Object Library: 3D tab folders, outliner, workbook, and MDI framework.

Astea Objects Library

Astea International, Inc.
55 Middlesex Turnpike
Bedford, MA 01730
Phone: 617-275-5440
Fax: 617-275-1910

The following classes are supplied by Astea Objects Library: DataWindows, functions, menus, user objects, and windows. Astea Objects Library provides a framework for development on large PowerBuilder applications. It contains a CASE tool with multilingual support, scheme generator, complete menu system with security, built-in microhelp, OLE interface, customized toolbars, and intelligent searching.

Component Toolbox

Gamesman, Inc.
1161 McMillan Avenue
Winnipeg, Manitoba, R3M 0T7 Canada
Phone: 800-670-8045 or 204-475-7903
Fax: 204-284-3307

Component Toolbox is a collection of VBX custom controls specifically designed to work with PowerBuilder. Each control has a property table that supports all of the properties, including font and picture attributes.

EnterpriseBuilder

Icon Solutions, Inc.
175 King of Prussia Road, Suite A
Radnor, PA 19087
Phone: 610-995-9000
Fax: 610-995-9005

EnterpriseBuilder is a suite of classes for designing, constructing, and maintaining large-scale client/server systems. It consists of a Base Class Library (BCL) of classes that provides common application functionality and a framework that provides the application architecture, low-level classes to support large-scale applications.

FirstClass

OSoft Development Corp.
6 Piedmont Center, Suite 303
Atlanta, GA 30305
Phone: 404-814-6030
Fax: 404-814-8401

The following classes are provided by FirstClass: DataWindows, functions, menus, structures, tab folder, user objects, and windows. FirstClass adheres to all recent Microsoft and PowerBuilder style conventions and supports automatic windows history, allowing rebuilding any windows from a history list.

First Impression

VisualTools, Inc.
15721 College Boulevard
Lenexa, KS 66219
Phone: 913-599-6500
Fax: 913-599-6597

First Impression is a business charting package built on top of a 3D modelling engine that allows graphic objects to be built in true 3D space. Its multiple light sources, true perspective, and unlimited customization options can render the most complex data sets.

ObjectStart

Greenbrier & Russel
1450 East American Lane, Suite 1640
Schaumburg, IL 60173
Phone: 800-453-0347 or 708-706-4000
Fax: 708-706-4020

The following classes are supplied by ObjectStart: controllers, DataWindow, edit, environment, exception, field string, filter, linked list, message, print, scroll, security managers, sort, and string utility objects. ObjectStart is a comprehensive toolkit that includes an object-oriented class library, MDI application framework, content-based DataWindow navigation objects, reusable graphical controls, and a flexible security management object. It also includes an application generator, security administrator, and a sample application. The professional edition also includes ObjectStart Professional Information Base, Developer's Tools, and object-oriented Enhanced Library. ObjectStart provides a roadmap for client/server project planning and implementation using PowerBuilder.

PB Architect

ANATEC
Phone: 800-ANATEC-3 or 810-540-4440

PB Architect is an application framework that comprises functions and objects with events that standardize and optimize the development of applications that connect to SYBASE SQL Server.

POWER-AID

CASE/MATE
3952 Spalding Hollow
Norcross, GA 30092
Phone: 404-448-0404

POWER-AID is a class library that offers a code class development environment for basic business applications. It includes a reusable graphical application interface, inherited relational database access controls, a dynamic context-sensitive help system, and an automatic query capability for any data window column.

PowerClass

ServerLogic Corp.
2800 Northup Way, Suite 205
Bellevue, WA 98004
Phone: 206-803-0378
Fax: 206-803-0349

The following classes are supplied by PowerClass: DataWindows, menus, structure, tab folder, and windows. PowerClass is an object-oriented add-on library that includes standard Windows elements and encapsulated language scripts for building applications. It maintains consistency to objects such as menus and windows in large application development projects. An additional product, PowerLock, is a security library that enables developers to control access to applications, windows, controls, and database columns. Security is layered at application, group, and user levels. An administration tool is included to manage the environment.

PowerBase

Millennium Corp.
22845 North East 8th Street, Suite 117
Redmond, WA 98053
Phone: 206-868-3029
Fax: 206-868-5093

PowerBase is a combination of base and template objects to maximize development productivity and application reliability. It offers dependability, reduced coding errors, reusability, functionality, accelerated development, and maintainability.

PowerFrame

MetaSolv Software, Inc.
14900 Landmark, Suite 240
Dallas, TX 75240
Phone: 214-239-0623
Fax: 214-239-0653

Application Framework Library. The following classes are supplied by Application Framework Library: DataWindows, functions, menus, structures, user objects, and centralized message management extension. Application Framework Library is a reusable application framework with inheritable windows classes, user objects, menus, and functions. It provides PowerBuilder extensions that can be integrated into the PowerBar. A sample application and tutorial are provided, in addition to a developer's guide in text and Microsoft Help format.

Application Security Library. The following classes are supplied by Application Security Library: DataWindows, functions, menus, structures, and user objects. Application Security Library is a comprehensive application security system to manage access to PowerBuilder applications, windows, window controls, and database columns. It defines users and groups called *profiles*. Authorization to application components can be granted at individual or profile level.

Project Administration Library. The following classes are supplied by Project Administration Library: DataWindows, functions, menus, structures, and user objects. Project Administration Library automates the tedious tasks of project monitoring and administration by directly extracting information your developers load into the PowerBuilder library files.

PowerGuide

Ajja Information Technology Consultants
457 Catherine Street
Ottawa, Ontario, K1R 5T7 Canada
Phone: 800-665-0823 or 613-563-2552
Fax: 613-563-3438

The following classes are supplied by PowerGuide: DataWindows, functions, menus, structures, user objects, and windows. PowerGuide is a comprehensive set of standards, guidelines, and object library templates designed to implement procedures needed for PowerBuilder development. It helps developers create their own object libraries.

PowerPlate

Paradigm Computer Solutions, Ltd.
91 Millpark Road South West
Calgary, Albany, T2Y 2N1 Canada
Phone: 800-593-5106 or 403-256-8398
Fax: 403-256-8398

The following classes are supplied by PowerPlate: Application, DataWindow, function, menu, and windows. PowerPlate is a foundation library set of development tools and guidelines that does not require expertise in PowerBuilder or object-orientation. It consists of an application development template, an integrated role-based security system, and an integrated application message management and display system.

PowerTOOL

PowerCerv
400 North Ashley Drive, Suite 1910
Tampa, FL 33602
Phone: 813-226-2378
Fax: 813-222-0886

The following classes are supplied by PowerTOOL: DataWindows, functions, menus, structures, user objects, and windows. PowerTOOL is a library of PowerBuilder objects that provide a methodology for developing applications. It is suited for all scales of client/server application development. An additional product, PowerFlow, allows developers to "workflow enable" their PowerBuilder applications by controlling the flow of work executed on client PCs and servers. It executes applications or waits for the conclusion of a task before another task is executed and also provides status information that can be used for decision branching in later steps of a task.

SearchBuilder

Fulcrum Technologies, Inc
785 Carling Avenue
Ottawa, Ontario, K1S-5H4 Canada
Phone: 613-238-1761
Fax: 613-238-7695

SearchBuilder provides visual objects for displaying result lists and viewing documents held in another Fulcrum product, SearchServer, which is a multiplatform fulltext indexing and retrieval server engine. Sample application code and a standalone development copy of SearchServer for Windows are provided.

Visual Developers Kit 1 and 2

Software Integration Consulting Group
10000 Richmond, Suite 660
Houston, TX 77042
Phone: 713-977-6421
Fax: 713-977-5048

The following controls are supplied by Visual Developers Kit: hierarchy list box, calendar/date, multimedia, and 3D effects painter. Visual Developers Kit provides new interface possibilities. Visual Interpak Extender (VIX) provides seamless integration to PowerBuilder for hierarchy, tab/folder, calendar, internationalization, and third-party controls. It customizes dialogs and controls.

Visual Developers Suite

VisualTools, Inc.
15721 College Boulevard
Lenexa, KS 66219
Phone: 913-599-6500
Fax: 913-599-6597

Formula One. Formula One is a fully functional spreadsheet tool, including 126 functions like patterns, borders, fonts, and colors. It provides Excel compatibility, database connectivity, flexibility, and royalty-free runtimes.

VT-Speller. VT-Speller allows a developer to integrate spell-checking functionality into any application. It comes with a 100,000-word dictionary and allows user-defined and custom dictionaries for simultaneous checking.

FirstImpression. FirstImpression provides presentation-quality output that creates understandable graphics from the most complex data. It includes 2D, 3D, 2.5D, and stacked permutations of bar, line, area, step, XY, XYZ, polar, radar, pie, and toroidal pie charts.

Imagestream VB. Imagestream VB is a Visual Basic custom control that allows developers to view, manipulate, and translate various vector and bitmap images.

Multimedia Tools

DocuData

LaserData
300 Vesper Park
Tyngsboro, MA 01879
Phone: 508-649-4600
Fax: 508-649-4436

DocuData offers three development approaches: a built-in viewer and browser that enables document management capabilities with little or no programming, document- or image-enabling of existing applications via a dynamic data exchange (DDE) interface, and creating new applications using its extensive application programming interface (API).

MediaDB

MediaWay, Inc.
3080 Olcott Street, Suite 220C
Santa Clara, CA 95054
Phone: 708-748-7407
Fax: 408-748-7402

MediaDB is a DBMS optimized for the storage and retrieval of multimedia information. Application Development Kit is a class library that provides custom controls necessary to develop multimedia applications.

OPEN/Image User Objects for PowerBuilder

Wang
1 Industrial Avenue
Lowell, MA 01851
Phone: 508-459-5000
Fax: 508-967-0828

OPEN/Image User Objects For PowerBuilder supplies user objects that integrate with standard PowerBuilder objects to add imaging functionality, including client/server image access, to new or existing applications.

Visual Voice

Stylus Innovation, Inc
1 Kendall Square, Bldg 1500
Cambridge, MA 02139
Phone: 617-621-9545
Fax: 617-621-7862

Visual Voice is a VBX user object that allows developers to build voice processing applications such as voice mail, fax-on-demand, interactive voice response, or outdialing. It includes sample applications.

Watermark Discovery Edition

Watermark Software
129 Middlesex Turnpike
Burlington, MA 01803
Phone: 617-229-2600
Fax: 617-229-2989

Watermark Discovery Edition uses Object Linking and Embedding (OLE) technology to enable images of incoming faxes and scanned documents to be stored, manipulated, copied, and distributed by applications.

WorkFlo

FileNet Corp.
3565 Harbor Boulevard
Costa Mesa, CA 92626
Phone: 714-966-3197
Fax: 714-966-3490

WorkFlo Application Libraries (WAL) enable applications to manage images and documents stored on the FileNet system. WAL is available for the following platforms: Windows 3.1, OS/2, Macintosh, SunOS, HP-UX, and IBM-AIX.

Host-Connectivity Tools

EDA/Extender for ODBC

Information Builders, Inc.
1250 Broadway
New York, NY 10001-3782
Phone: 212-736-4433
Fax: 212-967-6406

EDA/Extender for ODBC allows you to develop applications that can access EDA/SQL Servers on host machines. EDA/Extender for ODBC works in conjunction with EDA/Link to extend the PC's reach to major databases and files on host machines. PowerBuilder applications can join different relational and nonrelational file types and DBMSs in a single result set using normal SQL queries.

EXTRA! Tools for PowerBuilder

Attachmate Corp.
3617 131st Street Avenue South East
Bellevue, WA 98006
Phone: 800-426-6283 or 206-644-4010
Fax: 206-747-9924

EXTRA! Tools for PowerBuilder allows developers to create GUI front-end applications for 3270 host-based applications. Attachmate's Common Function Library provides a set of commands for capturing data, transferring files, and navigating mainframe databases and is combined with PowerBuilder Custom User Objects. This library is a Windows DLL that contains functions that automate mainframe activities through HLLAPI.

File' T/PC

Filet Software Corp.
P.O. Box 44518
Eden Prairie, MN 55344
Phone: 612-942-0826
Fax: 612-942-8091

File'T/PC provides fast access to remote data stored on IBM AS/400 Systems with no additional host code on the AS/400.

ODBC Integrator

Dharma Systems, Inc.
15 Trafalgar Square
Nashua, NH 03063
Phone: 603-886-1400
Fax: 603-883-6904

ODBC Integrator is a client-based product that moves data integration capabilities to desktop. It works on PCs and makes distributed ODBC data sources appear as one data source. ODBC Integrator lets developers join data transparently among multiple data sources. It works with all ODBC drivers and tools to provide data access, data synthesis, data synchronization, and data warehousing.

QuickApp for Windows

Digital Communications Associates, Inc. (DCA)
1000 Alderman Drive
Alpharetta, GA 30202-4199
Phone: 800-348-3221 or 404-475-8380
Fax: 404-442-4366

QuickApp is a communications middleware development tool that simplifies the creation of GUIs for host-based applications. QuickApp records your 3270 and 5270 host-based screens and keystrokes and assists in creating PowerBuilder windows using custom objects. Must be used in conjunction with DCA IRMA WorkStation for Windows or DCA IRMA/400 for Windows.

RUMBA Tools

Wall Data, Inc.
1303 Hightower Trail, Suite 350
Atlanta, GA 30350
Phone: 800-48-RUMBA or 404-552-9910
Fax: 404-552-9912

RUMBA Tools is a screen scraper for creating GUI front-ends for host-based applications. It requires RUMBA software for the host (IBM mainframe, AS/400, or DEC VAX).

ShowCase ODBC

ShowCase Corp.
4131 Highway 52 North, Suite G111
Rochester, MN 55901-3144
Phone: 800-829-3555 or 507-288-5922
Fax: 507-287-2803

ShowCase ODBC is a direct PC-to-AS/400 database driver. It provides direct access to AS/400 database for Windows tools and supports remote procedure calls and existing security and customizes catalog access security.

TransPortal PRO

The Frustum Group, Inc.
90 Park Avenue, Suite 1600
New York, NY 10016
Phone: 800-548-5660 or 212-984-0640
Fax: 212-984-0690

TransPortal PRO allows PowerBuilder applications to transfer data between PCs and mainframes, via a DLL, through a host emulation session running on existing PC terminal emulation hardware and software.

Windows Communications Library (WCL, WCL/ESO, WCL/DSO)

Multi Soft, Inc.
4262 US Route 1
Monmouth Junction, NJ 08852
Phone: 908-329-9200
Fax: 908-329-1386

WCL Windows Communication Library is a Windows Toolkit for creating client/ server applications against existing 3270 and 5250 mainframe host systems. It provides automatic generation of PowerBuilder windows and host navigation and processing code via DLL calls. It does not use HLLAPI.

WCL/ESO Enterprise Server Options provides middleware for processing between client PCs and one or more "open" WCL/ESO servers running under MVS/CICS. High-level functions at the PC Client are provided through DLL calls, and the same functionality is provided at the mainframe through API calls.

WCL/SDO Software Distribution Option provides a mechanism for controlling, auditing, and distributing applications, software, or data. It uses host-based master libraries to distribute applications and data to client and/or server locations.

Distributed-Computing Tools

Connection/DCE

Open Horizon, Inc.
1301 Shoreway Road, Suite #116
Belmont, CA 94002
Phone: 415-593-1509
Fax: 415-593-1669

Connection/DCE is a database connectivity product that offers full integration with DCE services, such as security, encryption, directory/name services, and transport-independent RPCs. The Connection DLL has the same name and is binary-compatible with the database vendors software products.

Distributed Computing Integrator (DCI)

Tangent International, Inc.
30 Broad Street
New York, NY 10004
Phone: 212-809-8200
Fax: 212-968-1398

DCI allows a PowerBuilder application to act as a client in a transaction processing environment. The integrator is composed of two parts: the transaction processing interface (TPI) and the transaction monitor connector (TMC). The TPI is a set of APIs that unite the different processing paradigms of PowerBuilder and the transaction processing systems. The TMC takes advantage of the connectivity and features of specific transaction monitors (currently Novell's Tuxedo and AT&T's TopEnd).

EncinaBuilder for Windows

Transarc Corporation (an IBM subsidiary)
707 Grant Street, Gulf Tower, 20th Floor
Pittsburgh, PA 15219
Phone: 412-338-4400
Fax: 412-338-4404

EncinaBuilder for Windows is an interface between PowerBuilder and Encina transaction monitor, based on OSF's Distributed Computing Environment (DCE). It allows developers to create applications using OLTP concept. EncinaBuilder for Windows is transaction processing software that will interface with Encina servers running on UNIX systems.

Encompass

Open Environment Corp.
25 Travis Street
Boston, MA 02134
Phone: 617-562-0900
Fax: 617-562-0038

Encompass is a suite of tools that enable client/server developers to build enterprise-wide distributed applications based on a three-tiered architecture. It includes RPC code generator, application management, security, distributed naming services, and application testing and debugging facilities. Encompass can be used in conjunction with RPCPainter from Greenbrier & Russel for connecting to existing legacy systems.

EZ-RPC

NobleNet
337 Turnpike Road
Southboro, MA 01772-1708
Phone: 508-460-8222
Fax: 508-460-3456

EZ-RPC is a suite of multiplatform tools that facilitate the distribution of applications across TCP/IP and/or SPX/IPX networks. EZ-RPC generates C language executables for Unix, WinRPC generates RPC DLLs, RPCWare generates RPC NLMs, and MacRPC generates C language executables for Macintosh.

Magna X

Magna Software Corp.
275 Seventh Avenue
New York, NY 10001-6708
Phone: 800-431-9006 or 212-727-6719
Fax: 212-691-1968

Magna X is an application generator for COBOL OLTP applications. It operates across distributed UNIX platforms and incorporates enterprise data on mainframes via generated COBOL programs. Magna X includes a GUI development environment and shared workgroup dictionary and produces applications for Novell Tuxedo and Transarc Encina.

RPCPainter

Greenbrier & Russel
1450 East American Lane, Suite 1640
Schaumburg, IL 60173
Phone: 800-453-0347 or 708-706-4000
Fax: 708-706-4020

RPCPainter allows developers to build enterprise-wide, client/server applications in distributed computing environments using the three-tiered architecture of Encompass from Open Environment Corporation. It includes a graphical tool for preparing and editing remote procedure interface definitions (IDL), automatic generation of Remote Procedure Call (RPC) stubs for server, automatic population of DataWindows with RPC results, and automatic upload of DataWindow changes through RPCs.

Help-Authoring Tools

Doc-To-Help

WexTech Systems, Inc.
310 Madison Avenue, Suite 905
New York, NY 10017
Phone: 800-939-8324 or 212-949-9595
Fax: 212-949-4007

Doc-To-Help is an add-on to Microsoft Word that lets users create tailored online help systems in the Windows environment by converting documents (.DOC) to help files (.HLP).

HyperHelp

Bristol Technology, Inc.
241 Ethan Allen Highway
Ridgefield, CT 06877
Phone: 203-438-6969
Fax: 203-438-5013

HyperHelp provides the same capability as the Help Compiler (HC.EXE) for Microsoft Windows. It uses the same Rich Text Format (.RTF), project (.HPJ), and bitmap (.BMP) files and compiles an online help file for use on UNIX platforms that run PowerBuilder for Motif applications. HyperHelp enables you to maintain a single source for your help system across Windows and UNIX platforms.

RoboHELP

Blue Sky Software Corp.
7486 La Jolla Boulevard., Suite 3
La Jolla, CA 92037-9583
Phone: 800-677-4946 or 619-459-6365
Fax: 619-459-6366

RoboHELP is a help-authoring tool, offering bidirectional Microsoft Word document (.DOC) to help file (.HLP) conversion. RoboHELP designs, tests, and generates context-sensitive help systems.

Testing Tools

ANSWER: Testpro for Windows

Sterling Software, Inc.
9340 Owensmouth Avenue, Box 2210
Chatsworth, CA 91311
Phone: 818-716-1616
Fax: 818-716-5705

ANSWER is designed to build a repeatable test script library for Windows and host-based applications. It features a capture/playback mechanism, script language, flexible image and text capture capabilities, and the ability to synchronize with host-based applications as well as the Windows environment.

Automated Test Facility (ATF)

Softbridge, Inc.
125 Cambridge Park Drive
Cambridge, MA 02140
Phone: 617-576-2257
Fax: 617-864-7747

ATF tests client/server or standalone OS/2, Windows, and NT applications. From a central point, it can perform simultaneous, unattended tests on up to 50 machines. It handles GUIs, distributed applications, and legacy systems testing.

Automator QA

Direct Technology Ltd.
551 London Road
Isleworth, TW7 4DS, England
Phone: +44-181-847-1666
Fax: +44-181-847-0003
US phone: 212-475-2747

Automator QA consists of four integrated modules: QA Plan, QA Run, QA Track, and QA Stress. It supports all aspects and stages of the software testing process.

AutoTester

AutoTester, Inc. (Software Recording Corp. subsidiary)
8150 N. Central Expressway, Suite 1300
Dallas, TX 75206
Phone: 800-326-1196 or 214-368-1196
Fax: 214-750-9668

AutoTester handles organization and execution of regression tests, including test synchronization, dynamic window placement and positioning, advanced control querying and manipulation, and actual text retrieval. It creates audit trails and conducts review and comparison of expected results to actual results.

EMPOWER/CS

Performix, Inc.
8200 Greensboro Drive, Suite 1475
McLean, VA 22102
Phone: 703-448-6606
Fax: 703-893-1939

EMPOWER/CS permits multiuser load testing without the need for a PC for each emulated user. For flexibility, it uses the C language for scripts and global variable and synchronization capability to emulate complex workloads. An interactive monitoring feature allows control and debugging of scripts during testing.

Microsoft Test

Microsoft Corp.
1 Microsoft Way
Redmond, WA 98052
Phone: 206-936-3468

Microsoft Test is a tool for automating software testing of windows-based applications.

ODBC Sniffer and SQL Sniffer

Blue Lagoon Software
6659 Hesperia Avenue
Reseda, CA 91335
Phone: 818-345-2200
Fax: 818-345-8905

ODBC (ODBC Sniffer) and DBLIB (SQL Sniffer) are trace and performance analysis tools for GUI programmers and database administrators. They allow users to see the amount of time in seconds or milliseconds spent in a call, which application made the call, the parameters passed to the call, and the return value from the call. Traces can be logged into text file in ASCII format.

PowerRunner

Mercury Interactive Corp.
470 Potrero Avenue
Sunnyvale, CA 94086
Phone: 800-TEST-911 or 408-523-9900
Fax: 408-523-9911

PowerRunner is an object-oriented testing tool that allows unattended testing. The results are analyzed with DataWindows verification and execution reports. Test scripts can be ported to run on Windows NT, OS/2, Open Look, and Motif platforms. LoadRunner/PC tests system functionality and response under stress load conditions by replicating heavy use of a system by distributing applications across the network. This allows you to find critical failures and unacceptable performance issues before going to production.

QA Partner

Segue Software, Inc.
1320 Centre Street
Newton Centre, MA 02159
Phone: 800-922-3771 or 617-969-3771
Fax: 617-969-4326

QA Partner creates superclasses of objects based on functions, which allows developers to create generic regression suites of tests using scripting language. QA Partner translates scripts using the appropriate GUI driver for each environment.

Rhobot/Client-Server

Promark, Inc.
8 Campus Drive
Parsippany, NJ 07054
Phone: 201-540-1980
Fax: 201-540-8377

Rhobot/Client-Server provides automated stress-testing to client-server architectures by emulating their online and batch functions via scripts representing transactions. It provides support for multiple scripts that are executed simultaneously. The results can be viewed or exported for further analysis by spreadsheet, statistical, and graphics packages.

SQA TeamTest

Software Quality Automation (SQA), Inc.
10 State Street
Woburn, MA 01801
Phone: 800-228-9922 or 617-932-0110
Fax: 617-932-3280

SQA TeamTest is an automated GUI-testing solution implemented on a team/work group model. It is based on network Test Repository, which is updated during all stages of testing process: test planning, test development, unattended test execution, test results analysis, and extensive incident/problem tracking and reporting.

Software-Distribution Tools

BrightWork Utilities

McAfee Associates, Inc.
2710 Walsh Avenue, Suite 200
Santa Clara, CA 95051-0963
Phone: 800-866-6585 or 408-988-3832
Fax: 408-970-9727

BrightWork Utilities is a suite of applications for small and medium-sized LANs. It tracks network software and hardware and allows users to support and troubleshoot Windows or DOS workstations on LAN. BrightWork Utilities monitors system performance, security, capacity, and configuration. It provides LAN users with access to printers attached to any PC on network.

Courier

Tivoli Systems, Inc.
9442 Capital Of Texas Highway North
Arboretum Plaza One, Suite 500
Austin, TX 78759
Phone: 800-2TIVOLI or 512-794-9070
Fax: 512-794-0623

Courier allows system managers to automatically distribute software updates. It identifies any applications package or collection of files, indicates machines that subscribe to software, and automatically distributes new module to these computers.

Doughboy Professional Install for Windows (V.2.0)

NeoPoint Technologies
PO Box 2281
Winnipeg, Manitoba, R3C 4A6 Canada
Phone: 800-665-9668 or 204-668-8180
Fax: 204-661-6904

Doughboy Professional Install is an installation program generator, allowing developers to specify where directory applications are located, modify customization options, and build master disks. It includes high-speed data compression, CRC-32 data integrity checking, automatic splitting of large files across multiple disks, and creation of program manager groups and items.

Enterprise Desktop Manager (EDM)

Novadigm
1 International Boulevard
Mahwah, NJ 07495
Phone: 708-527-0490
Fax: 708-527-0492

EDM manages the deployment of applications, including configuration management, distribution management, desktop installation, and version control of the Power-Builder execution environment. Direct links to version control system enable applications to automatically be distributed to clients upon the promotion of a new version.

LAN Management System for NetWare

Saber Software Corp.
5944 Luther Lane, Suite 1007
Dallas, TX 75225
Phone: 800-338-8754 or 214-361-8086
Fax: 214-361-1882

LAN Management System for NetWare is a combination of several Saber products that feature menuing, centralized file and software distribution, scripting languages, automatic software/hardware inventorying, remote control, disk/print management, real-time information viewing, and management and event manager to track, prioritize, and queue predefined activities.

NetWare Navigator

Novell, Inc.
122 East 1700 South
Provo, UT 84606
Phone: 800-NETWARE

NetWare Navigator is a management tool that enables managers to distribute files from a single workstation. The Administration Console allows managers to create distribution lists, create packages that contain files for distribution, schedule jobs, and receive network feedback. A distribution server holds utilities that are used by the Administration Console and staging servers' route files from the distribution server to their intended client destination in the distribution list.

Norton Administrator for Networks

Symantec Corp.
10201 Torre Avenue
Cupertino, CA 95014-2132
Phone: 800-441-7234 or 408-253-9600
Fax: 408-253-3968

Norton Administrator For Networks allows network managers to control software and hardware inventory, distribute software, and manage licensing system security and anti-virus protection from a central console. It automatically builds a database of information each time a user logs onto a machine, capturing information on system resources and configuration.

Q

Voyager Systems, Inc.
Pine Tree Place, 360 Route 101, Suite 1501
Bedford, NH 03110-5030
Phone: 603-472-5172
Fax: 603-472-8897

Q, which was developed using PowerBuilder 3.0a, is a batch scheduler and remote execution system for networks. It uses a reference database on the network to control scheduling and agent programs executing on the client PCs. A client agent "registers" with the database to see if there is work to be done and, if so, executes the instructions accordingly.

Software Update and Distribution System (SUDS)

Frye Computer Systems, Inc.
19 Temple Place
Boston, MA 02111-9779
Phone: 800-234-3793 or 617-451-5400
Fax: 617-451-6711

SUDS/LAN. Software Update and Distribution System is designed for remote distribution of shrink-wrapped packages as well as network drivers, tools, and utilities. It works across bridges and routers and includes distribution lists and user menu procedures, alarm options, master procedures, procedure retry, and per user log summary. A Macintosh version also is available.

SUDS/WAN. SUDS/WAN extends the range of Software Update and Distribution System by letting the network manager create a set of procedures at one server to be automatically copied to any or all installations of SUDS on the WAN. SUDS/WAN includes a package inspection security feature, the ability to define and save target lists, and report writing.

WinInstall

Aleph Takoma Systems
Distributed by: On Demand Software, Inc.
1100 Fifth Avenue South, Suite 208
Naples, FL 33940
Phone: 800-368-5207 or 813-261-6678
Fax: 813-261-6549

WinInstall automates installation, uninstallation, and upgrades of Windows and DOS applications on any network. It modifies all initialization files, copies necessary files (including OLE Registration Database), and installs icons and program groups. WinInstall supports environment application and global variables, displays custom messages, calls other programs, and keeps logs. It also allows you to record an installation and "discover" what has changed and build the necessary installation scripts for automated use.

Magazines and Journals

Data Based Advisor

Data Based Solutions, Inc.
4010 Morena Blvd., Suite 200
San Diego, CA 92117
Phone: 619-483-6400
Rate: $35 US per year (12 issues)

Data Based Advisor contains a monthly column for PowerBuilder developers.

PB Exponent

Advanced Communication Resources, Inc.
350 5th Avenue, Suite 7803
New York, NY 10118-7896
Phone: 212-629-3370
Rate: Free

Powersoft Applications Developer

Tetragrammaton Press
1015 Gayley #288
Los Angeles, CA 90024
Phone: 800-933-6977 or 310-281-7533
Rate: $179 US per year (6 issues)

PowerBuilder Electronic Magazine

Steve Benfield   (72727.1115@compuserve.com)
Michael MacDonald   (76517.2244@compuserve.com)
Andy Tauber   (71640.473@compuserve.com)
Terry Voth   (76605.3647@compuserve.com)
Rate: Charges for CompuServe connection and monthly download from Powersoft forum.

PowerBuilder Developers Journal

Sys-Con Publications, Inc.
46 Holly Street
Jersey City, NJ 07305
Phone: 800-825-0061 or 201-332-1515
Rate: $119 US per year (12 issues)

PowerLine

Powersoft Corp.
561 Virginia Road
Concord, MA 01742
Phone: 800-395-3525
Rate: Free (monthly)

PowerProgrammer

Sys-Con Publications, Inc.
46 Holly Street
Jersey City, NJ 07305
Phone: 800-825-0061 or 201-332-1515
Rate: $41 US per year (6 issues)

PowerSource

Pinnacle Publishing, Inc.
18000 72nd South, Suite 217
Kent, WA 98032
Phone: 800-788-1900 or 206-251-1900
Rate: $249 US per year (12 issues)

21

Standards and Guidelines

The purpose of this chapter is to provide model standards and guidelines for the development of client/server applications for the Windows environment using Power-Builder as the development tool. This chapter assumes that the developer has at least a base-level familiarity with the Windows environment (i.e., personal or professional use of Windows software at a minimum). This chapter assumes at least a reading knowledge of the PowerBuilder tool (i.e., you have read the first chapters of this book).

The kinds of standards and guidelines that should be in place at the start of the development include:

- User-interface guidelines

- Naming standards

- Programming guidelines

- Documentation standards

- Standard error and status routines

If you're working on a project team, it's common to have one or more team members who are responsible for maintaining and/or enforcing particular sets of standards and guidelines. For example, a Database Administrator (DBA) might handle standards related to database implementation, while someone in the role of object manager might oversee most of the application development standards.

If you're working solo, there still are plenty of reasons for coming up with standards and guidelines for yourself to follow. They promote consistency and order, especially on projects that involve many components and whose development life cycle extends over long periods of time. Enforced standards and guidelines are especially valuable later in the cycle as they make it easier for you to maintain or enhance an application in which the original development team is not directly available.

General Design Guidelines

The development team should presume that at least some users have no Windows expertise and should design the interface to be as foolproof as possible. A good design will allow for varying operating preferences and levels (i.e., provide menus with both keyboard- and mouse-access capabilities). A good design will provide for visual and functional consistency within the application, and to the extent possible, it should be consistent with other commercially available Windows-based applications. As we have mentioned, consistency will provide several advantages, including, but not limited to, the following development environment objectives. It will:

- Help in migrating from one application to another with ease and speed.
- Facilitate the learning process (i.e., what is expected of each developer).
- Minimize training requirements for additional applications that the team will develop.
- Increase overall productivity and harmony (i.e., give the workplace a good rhythm).
- Minimize user confusion and the time that it takes a new user to become confident.
- Provide users with a sense of stability, thereby increasing their confidence in the reliability of the applications that you provide.

Remember to design the application as a tool for those who want to use it. Try to make it self-explanatory and, if possible, intuitive. Prototype the Windows and Data-Windows in PowerBuilder through consultation with representatives of the user community early in the development process. This is sometimes referred to as JAD, or *joint application development.*

Try to keep any user messages polite and friendly, and avoid computer jargon. Get to know the users' business, and use labels for data that are familiar to the users. This will allow the user to be in control of the application and not the reverse. A good open design will provide the ability to get from any point in the application to any other appropriate point in the application directly (i.e., without having to return through levels of windows in a modal fashion). If the user must wait for processing to complete, it should be visually obvious (e.g., the pointer should change to the hourglass). The user should receive timely and tangible feedback for his or her actions. For example, if a user selects an object, visual feedback that the object has been selected should be provided; this can be in the form of graphical, textual and/or even auditory feedback. Accommodate user mistakes without pain or penalty. A good design will minimize opportunities for error, and when the inevitable occurs, it should handle errors consistently in a soft fail fashion. The application should provide error messages that state the problem objectively and, where possible, offer viable solutions.

Provide the appropriate tools or utilities within the application to aid the user. The application should provide functions rather than expect the user to remember or calculate information offline (i.e., the day of the week corresponding to a certain date). The application should present choices explicitly rather than expecting users to recall an involved set of options or commands.

Into the early phases of the development process, build iterations of design review with the users and, if required, a rework of the interface design. In designing and testing an interface, be certain to consider the larger context within which the application will be used initially and, to the extent known or predictable, eventually. For example:

- Will the distributed software be used standalone or on a network?
- Will the application be used alone or with other applications?
- Is this a custom application with different components for each user?
- Will the application be used with other commercially available applications or software?

Reflect and facilitate any required integration with other applications by providing data exchange techniques that are consistent across the applications. It is recommended that any common functions be identified and named during the design phase, thus allowing function development to be assigned as a separate project task. Other developers can avoid having to develop these function calls during script development. They need only mark a place in the application where the function call and arguments will be inserted later.

PowerBuilder provides a wide variety of components and options that you can use to construct the user interface of your application. While this gives you a great deal of flexibility, it also requires you to make choices about what is appropriate for your project. By making these choices early on and establishing them as conventions, you can make the application more consistent, attractive, and usable while also saving yourself from a lot of cleanup work later.

To gather intelligent user-interface conventions, you must either learn something about good graphical design or draw upon the expertise of someone who does. One suggestion for doing both of these is to find some good examples. You can find lots of good ideas for your user-interface conventions by looking at existing graphical applications, especially some of the more popular commercial products (for instance, Microsoft Word or Excel, Lotus 1-2-3, or PowerBuilder itself). You probably already use several of these applications and know which aspects of their user interfaces you like and which you don't. If the intended users of your application work frequently with a particular product (e.g., Microsoft Word), you might even consider adopting a similar user interface to take advantage of their experience and lower the learning curve.

Earlier, you learned that an application can employ different styles of user interface: SDI (Single Document Interface), MDI (Multiple Document Interface), or a combination. MDI is the most popular choice because of the flexibility it gives the user and all of the built-in services that it provides. You probably should think about using it by default.

SDI might be appropriate if your application is very simple, especially if it deals with only one kind of data and the user needs to perform only one operation at a time. A combination interface might be useful in an application that performs very diverse operations, but you must design it with great care to avoid confusing the user.

Window conventions that you might apply to the windows in your application include those shown in Table 21.1. Menu conventions that you might apply to the menus in your application include those shown in Table 21.2.

TABLE 21.1 Window Conventions that You Might Apply to the Windows in Your Application

Window area	Possible convention
Kinds of controls	To keep the interface intuitive, use an appropriate kind of control for each feature that you want to implement in a window. For instance, don't use a RadioButton to initiate a command. Use a CommandButton or PictureButton instead.
Number of controls	Limit the number of controls that you place in a window to avoid overwhelming the user. Use multiple windows instead of trying to cram too many controls into one.
Spacing of controls	Leave enough white space in a window. Don't crowd controls together.
Borders of controls	To make them stand out, display other controls (such as StaticText) without any borders.
Availability of controls	Gray out (disable) a control when it is not available to the user.
Length of list controls	Limit the number of items in a ListBox or DropDownListBox control to prevent it from becoming too long to scroll through. You usually will want to keep the number of items well under 50.
MDI sheets and buttons	Avoid placing CommandButton or PictureButton controls in MDI sheets. Use menu items instead.
Keyboard support	Provide keyboard access to every control in a window.
Colors	Use color judiciously. It is most effective for bringing out those portions of a window that you want the user to see most readily. Where possible, use color defaults so that the user's settings (from the windowing system) can take effect.
Fonts	Limit the number of fonts to one or two (and make sure that users will have those fonts installed on their computers). Keep font size large enough to be easily legible and use a very limited number of different font sizes.
Modality	Try to use nonmodal windows whenever possible to give the user maximum control over the interface. Use modal (response) windows only when the application must focus the user's attention.

If users might have small, low-resolution monitors, make sure you design your windows for them and not just for larger high-resolution monitors, such as those that developers might have.

The choice of some user-interface conventions will depend on the particular platform on which your application is to be deployed. For example, certain conventions that might be appropriate for Microsoft Windows users might not make sense for Apple Macintosh users. Make sure that you are familiar enough with your target platform to choose conventions that suit it. If you're planning to deploy an application on multiple platforms, your user-interface conventions should take any platform differences into account and specify how to handle them.

Development environment

A good development environment is a prerequisite to successful application development. The new developer should be able to hit the ground running when he or she receives their user ID. Standards, guidelines, and the like should be available and up-to-date. Global functions, etc. should be placed in a specific PBL file (such as FUN-CLIB.PBL), which should exist in all library lists. Virtual objects to be used throughout the application should be placed in a specific PBL file (such as xxxVIRTS.PBL, where xxx is an identifier of the application), which should exist in all library lists in the application.

A development environment should be established that consists of PowerBuilder libraries in directories for various levels of development/support activities including:

- "Development" directory for work in progress shared among developers.

- "Personal" libraries for each developer working on a new or existing version of an application component; existing versions should be "checked out."

- "Staging" directory for production ready code and rollout support.

- "Production" directory for released code (fully rolled out).

- "Backup" libraries that are copies of "production" libraries (optional).

TABLE 21.2 Menu Conventions that You Might Apply to the Menus in Your Application

Menu area	Possible convention
Number of menu items	Limit the number of menu items that you place in a menu to avoid overwhelming the user with choices.
Depth of menu items	If you use a cascading menu, go down only one level. Deeper menus confuse users.
Availability of menu items	Gray out (disable) a menu item when it is not available to the user.
Length of menu item	Try to make menu items just one or two words long names (and never more than four).
Wording of menu item	Make sure the name that you use is descriptive of what names that menu item does. To indicate a menu item that displays a dialog box, include ellipsis points at the end of its name (for example, Find... Be consistent in your use of either nouns or verbs for menu items.
Standard menu item names	Where possible, use standard names and positions for menu items (for instance, a typical menu bar should begin with File Edit)
Toggles	If a menu item serves as a toggle between one state and another (such as on or off), indicate the current state to the user either by displaying a checkmark or by switching the menu item name (such as from On to Off).
Help	Make sure that every menu bar provides menu items that display your application's Help system and information about the application.
Keyboard support	Provide keyboard access to every menu item.
MDI frame and sheet	In an MDI application, provide a menu for the frame menus (which display when no sheets are open) and a separate menu for each kind of sheet (which displays when a sheet of that kind is active).
MDI toolbars	In an MDI application, display toolbar buttons for a few of the most common menu items.
MDI MicroHelp	In an MDI application, provide MicroHelp text (which displays in the frame's status area) for every menu item.

Use of directories/libraries

The "development" libraries should be used for development of the application and any/all major enhancements to the application. It also should be used as the starting point for preparing any/all releases of the application, frozen at a point in time. It should be frozen only temporarily, long enough to capture/migrate to the "staging" directory of libraries. It probably always will be active until the entire application is complete (i.e., it will last forever). It should fully accessible to all developers.

The "staging" libraries are used for rollout preparation. They should be used for support during rollout (i.e., they will contain the source code corresponding to the application executable being rolled out). They will be emptied (by the administrator) after rollout is complete (i.e., at the conclusion of migrating to "production"). They should be accessible to all developers but would be used only on rare occasions.

Note: Care must be taken that any changes made in these libraries also be reflected in the "development" libraries for future releases of the application.

The "production" libraries should be used for reference. They will contain the source code that corresponds to application executable that has been fully released. They should be used as the starting point of source code for fixes after rollout is complete and new development has begun. They should be accessible to all developers on a read-only basis. They are only fully accessible by the administrator for capturing the source code that corresponds to application executable that has been fully rolled out by migrating from the "staging" directory of libraries.

Naming Standards

While using PowerBuilder to develop your application, you'll create lots of different components and have to specify names for them, too. These components include: database objects (such as tables and indices), PowerBuilder objects (such as windows and menus), controls that go into your windows, and variables for your event and function scripts.

To keep those names straight, you should devise a set of naming conventions and follow them faithfully throughout your project. This is critical when you're working on a team (to enforce consistency and enable others to understand your code), but it's even important if you work on your own (so that you can easily read your own code).

In general, all component names in PowerBuilder can be up to 40 characters long. Developers typically use the first few characters to specify a prefix that identifies the kind of component it is. Then they type an underscore character followed by a string of characters that uniquely describes this particular component.

Relational database object naming convention

The standards suggested in this section provide various naming standard formats. One format should be chosen for the application and followed for all objects. Any text marked in italics represents a variable and the application can substitute an appropriate value. The data definition language for database objects named throughout this section should be stored in the DDL subdirectory in the application file structure. Today, it is not uncommon to be migrating from mainframe DB2 to a server-based DBMS. If this is the case, then there are several reasons to use the DB2 naming standards for relational database objects:

- For a database that might be ported to DB2 from Sybase or Oracle, the DB2 naming standards should be followed so that names do not have to be changed for DB2.

- For a database that will be used in conjunction with a DB2 database, the DB2 standards are recommended for the relational database. This will provide a consistent standard for the cross-platform databases.

- For a database ported from DB2 where the DB2 database will not be retained, the DB2 standards are optional. However, use of these standards might ease the transition for developers familiar with the DB2 database.

If you are using the DB2 standard, then limit database and table names to eight characters and columns to 18 characters.

Table 21.3 contains a summary of the relational object name formats.

Database name. This object name describes an application database.

Format	db_aaa_databasename
Max length	21 characters
Where	db—Two-character constant (Required) _—Underscore (Optional) aaa—Three-character application ID (Optional) databasename—This name describes the objects contained within the database. The maximum length of this name can range from 14 to 18 characters, depending on the optional parts chosen. (Required)
Examples	db_abc_pgmtrk dbpgmtrk

TABLE 21.3 The Relational Object Name Formats

Object type	Format
Database	db_aaa_databasename
Table	tb_aaa_tablename
View	vw_aaa_viewname
Base View	vb_aaa_viewname
Index	xn_tablename
Stored Procedure (application)	pr_aaa_procedurename
Stored Procedure (system)	sp_procedurename
Trigger	t type_tablename

Table name. This object name describes a table contained within a database.

Format	tb_aaa_tablename
Max length	27 characters (limited length because of view, index, and trigger names)
Where	tb—Two-character constant (Required) _—Underscore (Optional) aaa—Three-character application ID (Optional) tablename—This name describes the contents of a table. The maximum length of this name can range from 20 to 24 characters, depending on the optional parts chosen. (Required)
Examples	tb_abc_series tbseries

Table column names. This object name will describe a column associated with a table. It is strongly recommended that the business names be used with some abbreviation list to construct the column names.

The column name should be created from an appropriate business name by applying an abbreviations list to each component word in the business name. Abbreviations for words and phrases should be maintained in the organization's central dictionary. If a word used in the business name is not found in the abbreviation list, it should be added to the list, or suggestions for an alternative from among available words or phrases should be sought. A maximum of 18 characters is permitted for each standard abbreviated name, including separators. This is to ensure compatibility with SQL requirements.

View name. This object name describes any view on a table. A view can be comprised of columns from one or more tables. There usually are two types of views:

- Views
- Base views

Format	vw_aaa_viewname
Max length	30 characters
Where	vw—Two-character constant (Required) _—Underscore (Optional) aaa—Three-character application ID (Optional) viewname—This name describes the contents of the view. The maximum length of this name can range from 24 to 28 characters, depending on the optional parts chosen. (Required)
Example	vw_abc_series vwseries

Base view name. This object name describes a view based on a single table. In addition, this view will always contain the same number, order, and name of the columns in the table from which the view is based.

Format	vb_*aaa_viewname*
Max length	30 characters
Where	vb—Two-character constant (Required) _—Underscore (Optional) *aaa*—Three-character application ID (Optional) *viewname*—This name should be the same as the table on which it is defined excluding the table prefix (tb) and applid if used. (Required)
Example	vb_abc_series vbseries

Index name. This object name describes an index defined on a table.

Format	x*n_tablename*
Max length	30 characters
Where	x—One-character constant (Required) *n*—A one-digit number from 0 to 9 that will be used to sequence multiple indexes defined on a table. Zero should be used for the clustering index, and 1 to 9 should be used for nonclustering indexes. (Required) *aaa*—Three-character application ID (Optional) *tablename*—This name should be the same as the table on which it is defined, excluding the table prefix (tb) and applid if used. (Required)
Example	*Clustering* x0_abc_series x0series *Nonclustering* x1_abc_series x1series

Stored procedure name (application). This object name describes a collection of SQL and program control language statements bound into an executable plan.

Format	pr_*aaa_procedurename*
Max length	30 characters
Where	pr—Two-character constant (Required) _—Underscore (Optional) *aaa*—Three-character application ID (Optional)

procedurename—This name describes the purpose of the stored procedure. The maximum length of this name can range from 23 to 27 characters, depending on the optional parts chosen. (Required)

Example `pr_abc_series`
`prseries`

Trigger name. This object name describes a stored procedure that will be executed when an insert, update, or delete is performed on a specified table.

Format `t` *type_tablename*

Max length 30 characters

Where `t`—One-character constant (Required)
type—One-character constant that indicates the SQL operation that will cause the trigger. The allowable values are `i`, `u`, and `d` (Insert, Update, and Delete). (Required)
`_`—Underscore (Optional)
tablename—This name should be the same as the table on which it is defined, excluding the table prefix (tb) and applid if used. (Required)

Example `tu_abc_series`
`tuseries`

Naming standards for menus, windows, and DataWindows

The naming of these objects is important both for recognition and for logically grouping the objects together. For these objects to be grouped together in the application libraries, the names must all begin with the same prefix. This grouping of objects will be helpful in the migration and library management activities.

The object name will begin with a one- or two-letter abbreviation indicating the object type (see Table 21.4), followed by an underscore and a descriptive name (the descriptive name might start with a one- to three-letter abbreviation that designates a portion of the application, such as a subsystem or conversation group). Short descriptive abbreviations are recommended. All letters should be lowercase.

**TABLE 21.4 Abbreviations
for Indicating the Object Type**

Object type	Abbreviation	Example
Menu	m_	m_main
Window	w_	w_mdi_sheet
Data Window Object	d_	d_series

TABLE 21.5 The Scope Abbreviations

Abbreviation	Scope
g	Global
s	Shared
i	Instance
l	Local (script-defined)

The naming of variables

When working with or using variables in PowerBuilder programs, please refer to this section for guidelines and standards for naming, declaration, and use. The concepts regarding scope of access can be loosely applied to structure and function declarations and use. Please keep this in mind while reading this section. PowerBuilder supports Global, Shared, Instance and Script-Declared or Local variables. Each type of variable has a different life expectancy, a different scope of access, and a different overhead.

Global, Shared, and Instance variables are all considered to be static because they are declared at design time, are loaded into memory once, and remain in memory even while no code is being executed. Local variables, on the other hand, are loaded into memory when their script is executed and disappear when the script completes.

Choosing the right scope of declaration for a variable is extremely important in good PowerBuilder development. The following sections describe the behavior of each variable type. As a general rule, when choosing the scope (type) of a variable, consider what code is going to have to access this variable. The whole application? A particular window? A specific script? The answer to this question will steer you toward the right choice of Global, Shared, or Instance variables.

The following naming convention should be used when declaring all types of variables in PowerBuilder for use in PowerScripts:

```
st_bbbb
```

where s is the scope abbreviation, $t\_$ is the data type abbreviation, and $bbbb$ is the business or application relevant name.

The scope information is critical because it gives developers an instant understanding of where the variable has been declared and, therefore, what its life expectancy is and what objects have access to it. The data type also is a very important part of the variable name because it indicates, without having to refer to the declaration of the variable, what the data type is.

The business or application name tells the developer what the significance of the variable is, thus giving it meaning outside of a particular code context.

The scope abbreviations are listed in Table 21.5. The data type abbreviations are listed in Table 21.6. (*Note:* These naming conventions are examples. The important thing is to have a standard.)

The business or application portion of the name should indicate the type of information that is contained in the variable and should comply with the application-specific abbreviation standards of your project. If the name is a conglomerate of a

TABLE 21.6 The Data Type Abbreviations

Abbreviation	Data type
bl	Blob
bo	Boolean
dt	Date
dtm	DateTime
de	Decimal
db	Double
do	DraggedObject
i	Integer
l	Long
o	Object
r	Real
s	String
t	Time
ui	UnsignedInteger
ul	UnsignedLong
w	window

TABLE 21.7 Variable Name Examples

Variable	Description
gs_version	A Global String that contains the application version number.
si_acctnum	A Shared Integer that represents an account number.
ibo_winmod	An Instance Boolean to keep track of whether a window has been modified.
li_counter	A Local Integer used for counting in a loop.

multiword description, the various words should have their first letters capitalized. If the name contains an abbreviation or word commonly displayed as all upper case, it should be named consistently.

Table 21.7 shows some variable name examples.

The naming of functions

A function can be global or window-specific in scope. A global function name should have a prefix of f_. It should have the first letter capitalized with the remainder in lowercase, and there should be no underscore separating words. If the name is a conglomerate of a multiword description, the various words should have their first letters capitalized. If the name contains an abbreviation or word commonly displayed as all uppercase, it should be named consistently. Use the firm's abbreviation list. Object-level functions should be named with the object type and the fact that it is a function. For example, a window function should begin with the prefix wf_. Likewise, a menu function should begin with the prefix mf_.

For example, f_ExcelPromptSave a global function to prompt for the name and save the data to an Excel spreadsheet as that name. wf_SetBaseWhere is a window function to set the base portion of the WHERE clause of a SQL SELECT statement to be executed to retrieve the data for this window.

The naming of constants

A constant should be in all uppercase with words separated by underscores. For example: OK and NOT_FOUND.

Internal naming standards

The following naming convention should be used when developing windows or user objects in PowerBuilder:

```
tt_ss_bbb
```

where $tt\_$ is the object type (see Table 21.8), $ss\_$ is the application or function to which the object is related, and $bbbb$ is the business or application relevant name.

The last portion of the name should be specific to the functionality of the window you are developing. Table 21.9 contains several window name examples.

TABLE 21.8 The Object Types and Their Abbreviations

Object type (tt)	Abbreviation
Window	w_
Virtual window class	wcls_
Standard visual user object	u_controlprefix
Custom visual	u_cv
External visual	u_ex
VBX visual	u_vbx
Standard class	u_sc
Custom class	u_cc
C++ class	u_cpp

TABLE 21.9 Window Name Examples

Window name	Description
w_series_sheet	The associate window for the Counterparty function.
w_ctrk_login	The login window for the Credit eXposure System application.
wcls_mdi_sheet	A class MDI window sheet to be inherited (e.g., by w_series_sheet).

Functions

The naming standards used for functions is described in the section "Naming Standards," which covers all PowerBuilder object types. A function can be global or object-specific in scope. It should have the first letter capitalized with the remainder in lowercase, and there should be no underscore separating words. If the name is a conglomerate of a multiword description, the various words should have their first letters capitalized. If the name contains an abbreviation or word commonly displayed as all uppercase, it should be named consistently. A window function should begin with the prefix wf followed by an underscore.

The function abbreviations are listed in Table 21.10, and examples are shown in Table 21.11.

Headers and Comments

The commenting of code acts as inline documentation for the benefit of other developers. The application specifications are essential to understand where the localized logic probably has been placed in an event-driven application component. There are two forms of comments that are a standard part of developing in PowerScript:

- Script headers
- Inline comments

Script headers

Figure 21.1 is an example of a script header comment block that should be placed at the beginning of all event scripts.

TABLE 21.10 The Function Abbreviations

Type	Prefix
Global Function Object	f_
Window Function	wf_
Menu Function	mf_
User Object Function	uf_

TABLE 21.11 Examples of Function Names

Function name	Description
f_ExcelPromptSave()	A global function to prompt for the name and save the data to an Excel spreadsheet as that name.
wf_SetBaseWhere()	A window function to set the base portion of the where clause of the select statement to be executed to retrieve the data for this window.
mf_GetFrame()	A menu function that returns the MDI frame window.

Figure 21.1 An example of a script header comment block.

```
/**************************************************************************
[SCRIPT]
        Put script name here.
        (EXAMPLE)
        clicked event for cb_ok

[DESCRIPTION]
        Write a description of the function that says only what the function
        does, not how it does it or in what order.

[INPUTS]
        Put a description of all inputs to the functions. This includes
        PARAMETERS, TABLES, EXTERNAL FUNCTIONS (DLLs), FILES, GLOBAL
        VARIABLES, etc.

        (EXAMPLE)
        PARAMETERS:
                AV_sINIFile - A string variable containing the name of an
                              INI file.
        EXTERNAL LIBRARY:
                XXXX.DLL - A custom written DLL that this function makes calls
                        to.

[ASSUMPTIONS]
        List here any assumptions that the program makes or dependancies that
        exist. For example, the function might require the existence of
        certain global variables or files. List these assumptions below.

[RETURNS]
        Describe all possible return values of the function in the following
        format.

        (EXAMPLE)
        POSSIBLE VALUES:
        0       =       Function completed successfully
        -1      =       INI file not found
        -2      =       INI section not defined
        -3      =       etc...

[CHANGE LOG]
        NAME        DATE        CHANGE DESCRIPTION
        PRA         9/20/94     original function
        JJB         10/25/94    added error checking code

**************************************************************************/
// VARIABLE DECLARATIONS
int     L_sMiscVar

//***************************** BEGIN SCRIPT *****************************

//
//
//          !!!!!! SCRIPT BODY GOES HERE !!!!!!
//
//
//

//***************************** END SCRIPT *****************************
```

Function headers

All functions (global, window, menu, or user object) should be formatted as shown in Figure 21.2.

Figure 21.2 An example function format.

```
/***************************************************************************
[FUNCTION]
        Put function name here in mixed case.
        (EXAMPLE)
        f_GetConnectInfo( )

[DESCRIPTION]
        Write a description of the function that says only what the function
        does not how it does it or in what order. This function description
        should be used for verification.

[ACCESS]
        Public, Private, Protected.

[INPUTS]
        Put a description of all inputs to the functions. This includes
        PARAMETERS, TABLES, EXTERNAL FUNCTIONS (DLLs), FILES, GLOBAL
        VARIABLES, etc.

        (EXAMPLE)
        PARAMETERS:
                AV_sINIFile - A string variable containing the name of an
                              INI file.
        EXTERNAL LIBRARY:
                XXXX.DLL - A custom written DLL that this function makes calls
                           to.

[ASSUMPTIONS]
        List here any assumptions that the program makes or dependancies that
        exist. For example, the function might require the existence of
        certain global variables or files. List these assumptions below.

[RETURNS]
        Describe all possible return values of the function in the following
        format.

        (EXAMPLE)
        POSSIBLE VALUES:
         0        =         Function completed successfully
        -1        =         INI file not found
        -2        =         INI section not defined
        -3        =         etc...

[CHANGE LOG]
        NAME        DATE        CHANGE DESCRIPTION
        PRA         9/20/94     original function
        JJB         10/25/94    added error checking code


***************************************************************************/
// VARIABLE DECLARATIONS
int     L_iRetVal

//*************************** BEGIN SCRIPT ****************************
//
//       !!!!!! FUNCTION BODY GOES HERE !!!!!!
//
Return L_iRetVal
//*************************** END SCRIPT ****************************
```

Inline comments

Inline comments should be used to explain particular lines or sections of code. Use double slashes (//) to comment out individual lines of code.

```
//Check to see if the file exists.
IF NOT FileExists(L_sINIFile) THEN
  MessageBox("Error", L_sINIFile + " does not exist.")
  Return -1
END IF
```

Use standard modification comment lines. This comment should consist of a description of the change and the reason for the change, followed by developer name and date:

```
//Description of change. Made by JSMITH 10/09/93.
```

Especially if you comment something out:

```
//This line was commented out because the logic is not needed. ALLENPA 10/25/93.
```

Put a standard modification comment line before any major addition to a piece of code or to explain why code has been commented out.

```
//Check to see if the file exists.
IF NOT FileExists(L_sINIFile) THEN
  MessageBox("Error", L_sINIFile + " does not exist.")
  Return -1
END IF
```

Use the block comment (/* ... */) for large, multiline comments. Comments are placed at the beginning of scripts that are complex or difficult to follow. Comments at the beginning of functions should describe the valid values for parameters and what the possible return codes are. Global, shared, and instance variable declarations also contain comments that identify their usage.

Spacing

Single spaces should be placed:

- Before and after all operators and the assignment verb.
- After the comma of each argument in function parameter lists.
- Before a close parenthesis if there are nested parentheses.
- Before the "THEN" clause of an IF...THEN...END statement.

Do not put spaces before the open parenthesis of a function call.

Capitalization

Use mixed case for the following:

- PowerBuilder function names (TriggerEvent, SetFocus)
- User-defined Functions (f_dbConnect, f_CheckSQL)

Use lowercase for the following:

- Graphic controls (w_main, cb_ok, sle_username)
- Object attributes (text, title, x, y, enabled, visible)

Use uppercase for the following:

- Script control words (IF, THEN, ELSE, WHILE, NEXT, etc.)
- Reserved words (THIS, PARENT, PARENTWINDOW, TRUE, FALSE)

Tabs and indenting

Tabs should be used to generally improve readability. Use tabs to align assignment statements for greater readability.

This is incorrect:

```
I_sFName = "Roseanne"
I_sLastName= "Silinonte"
I_sTelephoneNumber = "(718) 347-4703"
```

However, this is correct:

```
I_sFName           = " Roseanne "
I_sLastName        = " Silinonte "
I_sTelephoneNumber = "(718) 347-4703"
```

Tabbing is used for indenting. Statement blocks used with the following statements are indented one tab stop from the corresponding statement: CASE, DO UNTIL, DO WHILE, DO..LOOP, FOR..NEXT, and multiline IF..THEN.

Variable declaration

For static variables declared using the declaration dialog boxes (Global, Shared, and Instance variables), put the following comment header in the dialog box to indicate the object for which the variables are being defined.

For Global variables:

```
/* GLOBAL VARIABLES for Application "SAMPLE"
data type      variable name      */
string         Gs_UserName
boolean        Gb_LoggedOn
```

For Shared variables:

```
/* SHARED VARIABLES for Window "w_main"
data type      variable name      */
string         Is_UserName
boolean        Ibo_switch
```

For Instance variables:

```
/* INSTANCE VARIABLES for Window "w_main"
data type      variable name      */
integer        Ii_AcctNum
boolean        Ibo_WinModified
```

For Local variables:

```
// VARIABLE DECLARATIONS
data type        variable name        */
integer          Ii_AcctNum
boolean          Ibo_WinModified
```

Setting Up the Application

This section assumes that application development has not begun. If it has, simply review this section to ensure that your application PBL structure complies with this model.

Step 1 Create a PBL file in the common directory for the application. For example, if the project code is NEWAPP, create NEWAPP.PBL in N:\NEWAPP\ directory. This is accomplished by opening the PowerBuilder Library painter and selecting `Create...` from the Library menu. This will bring up the Create Library dialog box. Enter the name of the library in the entry field (e.g., NEWAPP.PBL), tab to the comments entry field, enter a comment about the library (e.g., "Main library for CounterParty Structure and Limits Application."), and click OK.

Note: Depending on how NetWare access privileges are defined in the development environment, rights to N:\NEWAPP\ might (and should) be restricted to users who are part of the NetWare Group for that application. If you are not able to create a library in that directory, check with your Development Coordinator or LAN Administrator.

Step 2 Create a new application object and place it into the PBL created in Step 1. This is accomplished by opening the PowerBuilder Application painter and selecting `New...` from the File menu. This will bring up the Save Application dialog box. Enter the application name (e.g., NEWAPP) in the entry field, select the library that the application object should be stored in by clicking on the appropriate entry in the Library listbox in the lower left corner of the window, and click OK. After creating the application object, view the Library Search Path by selecting `Library List...` from the Edit menu or clicking the toolbar icon in the Application painter. Library Search Path will look like this:

```
N:\NEWAPP\NEWAPP.PBL;
```

Note: If you click OK before selecting the destination library, PowerBuilder will create a PBL with the name of the application (e.g., NEWAPP.PBL). This method can be substituted for Steps 1 and 2.

Step 3 Using the Library painter, create a second PBL in the N:\NEWAPP\ directory that will be used to store standard PowerBuilder objects used by the application. The name of this PBL should be the application or project name, then an underscore and either a number or other meaningful suffix.

Step 4 Add this new code:

```
N:\NEWAPP\NEWAPP.PBL;
N:\NEWAPP\NEWAPP_1.PBL;
N:\NEWAPP\NEWAPP_2.PBL;
N:\NEWAPP\NEWAPP_3.PBL;
```

Step 5 Create additional PBLs as needed and add them to the Library Search Path:

```
N:\NEWAPP\NEWAPP.PBL;
N:\NEWAPP\NEWAPP_1.PBL;
N:\NEWAPP\NEWAPP_2.PBL;
N:\NEWAPP\NEWAPP_3.PBL;
```

Setting Up Each Developer

Have developers use the operating system to copy NEWAPP.PBL to their private directory (on the LAN or C: drive). Modify the search path to include their own work-in-progress (WIP) PBL in the Library Search Path such that their library is first in the list. For example, Library Search Path might look something like this:

```
M:\ALLENPA\NEWAPP.PBL;
M:\ALLENPA\PERSONAL.PBL;
N:\NEWAPP\NEWAPP_1.PBL;
N:\NEWAPP\NEWAPP_2.PBL;
N:\NEWAPP\NEWAPP_3.PBL;
```

This way the user will be using a copy of the application object that has the appropriate global declarations. The only thing that will have to be modified is the Library Search Path.

When a change to an object is required, have the developer check that object out (using regular CheckOut or PVCS CheckOut) into their WIP PBL. For example, checkout N:\NEWAPP\NEWAPP_1.PBL(d_report1) into N:\ALLENPA\ALLENPA.PBL. Because M:\ALLENPA\ALLENPA.PBL is before N:\NEWAPP\NEWAPP_1.PBL in the Library Search Path, when the developer executes the application, the revised object will be used and the developer will be able to test the new code.

Meanwhile, other developers are using their own application objects to run their code. For example, Library Search Path for their application objects might look something like this:

```
M:\BAMBAJO\NEWAPP.PBL;
M:\BAMBAJO\BAMBAJO.PBL;
N:\NEWAPP\NEWAPP_1.PBL;
N:\NEWAPP\NEWAPP_2.PBL;
N:\NEWAPP\NEWAPP_3.PBL;
```

Therefore, the changes made to d_report1 will not affect this developer because the object still is checked out into M:\ALLENPA\ALLENPA.PBL, which is not in the search path of this developer's application object.

If BAMBAJO attempts to modify N:\NEWAPP\NEWAPP_1.PBL(d_report1), Power-Builder will inform the developer that the object is checked out by ALLENPA and cannot be modified.

When the change to d_report1 is complete, the developer checks it back into N:\NEWAPP\NEWAPP_1.PBL. At this point, the changed code will be executed by other developers because N:\NEWAPP\NEWAPP_1.PBL is in their Library Search Path.

The advantage to this approach is that developers can make changes without worrying about overwriting others' work and to code without immediately impacting other developers.

Tips and Good Coding Practices

Do not use an evaluated expressing in the end portion of a FOR or WHILE loop. For example:

```
FOR L_iCounter = 1 TO Len(this.text)
        <statement block>
NEXT
```

In the previous code segment, the statement Len(this.text) will be evaluated (the Len() function will be invoked) during each iteration of the loop. A preferred coding method would be:

```
L_iStrLen = Len(this.text)
FOR L_iCounter = 1 TO L_iStrLen
        <statement block>
NEXT
```

Object Referencing

Implicit references to objects using the PARENT, THIS, and PARENTWINDOW reserved words should be used whenever possible instead of explicit references using object names. Using these generic references insulate code from particular object names and, therefore, make it more flexible and reusable.

Code should be placed in the application to take advantage of implicit or direct references. For example:

```
THIS.Title = "Details for Account" + String(Li_AcctNum)
```

instead of:

```
RemoteWin.Title = "Details for Account" + String(Li_AcctNum)
```

To accomplish this, you might need to send a message or TriggerEvent in the window to invoke the local code.

User Documentation and Error Handling

In addition to comments and online Help, you might want to address printed documentation in your standards as well. For instance, you might consider requiring one or more of the following:

- Developer reports—You can use the Library painter of PowerBuilder to print reports about the application components that you've developed. You should determine which reports you need to print and how often.
- Developer manuals—Would it be useful to have someone write one or more internal documents that developers then could reference for information on application components? If so, you need to specify what is to be described as well as how it is to be organized and formatted.
- End-user manuals—Do users need training or reference documents to assist them as they run your application? If so, you should indicate what these documents are to cover as well as how they are to be organized and formatted.

Standard Error and Status Routines

Housekeeping chores such as error and status checking often are good candidates for standardization. That's because you usually will want to handle them the same way across many applications and because you'll want to minimize the chance of accidentally omitting a particular test.

For example, you might consider standardizing the way you check for:

- Network connection errors
- Database access errors
- Data entry errors

Fortunately, the object-oriented features of PowerBuilder make it easy to standardize and implement common chores like these. You usually will want the DataWindow controls in your windows to check for various data entry and database access errors. The hard way to accomplish this is to write the appropriate event scripts in each individual DataWindow control. The easy, object-oriented way is to:

Step 1 Create your own version of a generic DataWindow control by defining a user object for it.

Step 2 Write your error-processing event scripts in this user-object DataWindow control.

Step 3 Inherit the DataWindow controls that you want to place in windows from your user-object DataWindow control. These inherited controls will automatically be able to perform your error processing.

Index

X

ABOUT THE AUTHORS

JOSEPH J. BAMBARA is the president of PowerTouch, Inc. (Greenvale, New York). He is a top PowerBuilder implementation consultant in the financial, entertainment, and manufacturing industries. He has over 20 years of experience with information technology, including three years with PowerBuilder. He holds both a B.S. and an M.S. degree in computer science, as well as a doctorate in Law. He has lectured on computing at the City College of New York as well as taught numerous courses on PowerBuilder and other client/server development tools.

PAUL R. ALLEN is the president of Allen International, Inc. (New York, New York). For more that a decade, he has developed and implemented applications all over the world. These applications span the gamut of the financial and manufacturing industries. He has extensive experience with several development platforms and network protocols. He custom develops and teaches introductory, intermediate, and advanced PowerBuilder courses.